D1175421

The American Mosaic

The American Mosaic

An In-Depth Report on
the Future of Diversity at Work

Anthony Patrick Carnevale

Susan Carol Stone

McGraw-Hill, Inc.

New York   San Francisco   Washington, D.C.   Auckland   Bogotá
Caracas   Lisbon   London   Madrid   Mexico City   Milan
Montreal   New Delhi   San Juan   Singapore
Sydney   Tokyo   Toronto

Library of Congress Cataloging-in-Publication Data

Carnevale, Anthony Patrick.
  The American mosaic : an in-depth report on the advantage of diversity in the U.S. work force / Anthony Patrick Carnevale, Susan Carol Stone.
      p.   cm.
  ISBN 0-07-011377-7 (hardcover)
  1. Diversity in the workplace—United States.   2. Affirmative action programs—United States.   3. Manpower policy—United States.
  4. Multiculturalism—United States.   I. Stone, Susan Carol.
  II. Title
  HF5549.5.M5C383   1995
  331.11'43—dc20   95-12618
                                                                   CIP

1 2 3 4 5 6 7 8 9 0   DOC/DOC   9 0 9 8 7 6 5 4

ISBN 0-07-011377-7

The sponsoring editor for this book was James H. Bessent, Jr., the editing supervisor was Caroline R. Levine, and the production supervisor was Donald F. Schmidt. This book was set in Palatino by Estelita F. Green of McGraw-Hill's Professional Book Group composition unit.

Printed and bound by R. R. Donnelley & Sons Company.

This book is printed on recycled, acid-free paper containing a minimum of 50% recycled de-inked fiber.

This project was conducted under Grant No. K-4031-3-00-80-60 from the Employment and Training Administration, U.S. Department of Labor. Grantees undertaking such projects under Government sponsorship are encouraged to express freely their professional judgment. Therefore, points of view or opinions stated in this document do not necessarily represent the official position or policy of the Department of Labor. Funding for this project was also generously provided by the Joyce Foundation; views expressed are those of the authors.

Contents

Acknowledgments

We are grateful to so many fine people and organizations that supported us as we were working through this book. Someone was always
available with valuable advice, challenging questions, and support for
the innumerable needs that arise in writing a book of this complexity.
Our first debt is to the Employment and Training Administration of
the U.S. Department of Labor and the Joyce Foundation who made the
book possible through their generous grants. Special thanks are due
the Department of Labor for patience as the project underwent trans-
formations that took it beyond its initial scope and time frame.

We are indebted too to many individuals. Janice Hamilton Outtz
provided copious material on demographic trends, reviewed early
drafts of the demographics chapter, and patiently responded to our
many questions. S. Kanu Kogod is an important contributor, for she
wrote the early draft chapter on valuing and managing diversity. She
also provided many useful insights and shared material on diversity.
Similarly, we are grateful to Lee Adair Lawrence for her excellent draft
chapters on gender and older workers and to Mary B. Dickson for hers
on workers with disabilities.

We have benefited from the conversations and research material that
many people kindly shared with us. For their insights into cultural
values of racial and ethnic minority groups, we thank Ilya Adler, Jeri
Brunoe, Andrew Carvely, Adrian Chan, Ann French, Thomas
Kochman, and Muhammad Samhan. They also kindly reviewed and
commented on specific sections on history and cultural values. Other

reviewers of sections on history and cultural values include Ken Goosens, Harold E. Hall, Deirdre Martinez, Sonia Perez, Billy Tidwell, and John Zogby. Without their comments and questions, this would have been a different and lesser publication.

Detailed comments by Nancy DiTomaso and Adrian Chan on the chapter on socioeconomic issues facing ethnic and racial minorities were very helpful as we worked through revisions. They also kindly provided research material that we consulted in our writing, as did Kathryn Neckerman, to whom we are grateful.

Others who reviewed various chapters and gave us valuable insights are Ann M. Morrision, on gender issues; Martin Sicker, on older workers, and Ann Tourigny, on workers with disabilities. We are grateful to each of them and to the anonymous reviewers who offered many thoughtful comments. Early in the writing process, Martin Sicker provided us with an interview and research data that helped us formulate our material on older workers. Averel Wilson and Penny Van Niel shared experiences with gender and older worker issues. Ken Sembly and John D. Ogden also provided helpful information.

Special thanks are due to Ed Mickens, who supplied research material, other resources, and advice that were invaluable in writing the chapter on gay and lesbian workplace issues, and who reviewed the chapter. Rick Dean, Erick Keller, and Tom Sachs also provided statistical information and other insights about gay and lesbian workers in the public and private sectors. Also, the detailed review comments of Bonnie J. Berger were helpful as we undertook revisions.

For material on labor union workers, several people from labor unions and related organizations offered help. We thank Tula Connell, who provided resource material; William R. Wilkinson for reviewing an early draft; Matthew Simon for patiently answering questions; and Ruth Needleman and Kate Bronfenbrenner for sharing their research with us. Jane Murphy, Lisa Oppenheim, and Tony Sarmiento kindly provided research leads. We want to express special appreciation to Ruth Needleman for taking time to read the chapter and providing so many helpful observations.

Several people gave us insights into international perspectives on diversity or put us in touch with others who did. We are grateful to Martine Besseteaux, Judee Blohm, Andre Cresson, Sandra M. Fowler, Junko Kondo, Baudouin Knaapen, and Eiji Takemae.

As time grew short, some people set aside other priorities to respond to our next-to-last-minute request for assistance: William U. Lawrence, Jude Setian-Marsten, Susan Swagler, and Lee Adair Lawrence all helped in important ways with the revision process. Additionally, William Lawrence lent his writing skills to draft chapters on gender and older workers, and Jude Setian-Marsten provided editorial assistance. We are very grateful to them. Thanks go too to Harold E. Hall who with his customary grace and expertise provided technical support that made the complex commute between computer systems much easier.

At ASTD, several people supported this project. Alice Grindstaff ably managed the project through many of its evolutions, and we thank her. Thanks are due, too, to Ron Ward Finnell, capably aided by Frances Richmann, who did the initial groundwork on the project. Much administrative support was provided by Lynne Allison. The lengthy research and writing process would have been much longer and more difficult without the assistance of Jim Johnston and Allison Kennett. They persistently tracked down many references and diligently responded to our other, assorted research needs. Edith Allen at the ASTD Information Center also went out of her way to assist with research. Our very special thanks go to Diane Peterson for her dedication and efficiency in handling administrative and technical aspects of the publication and for her advice, which helped us get the job done.

Finally, we are deeply grateful to Jane Gold and Marcia Kirkpatrick for their special contributions. Their support, encouragement, and sound practical advice were always available when we needed it. We thank them both.

While these many people provided support that enhanced this publication in numerous ways, the authors are responsible for its content and for any errors and distortions, which in a subject so sensitive and broad, are bound to have occurred.

Anthony Patrick Carnevale
Susan Carol Stone

Introduction

The American workforce has always been heterogeneous, but only recently have differences begun to be recognized and honored. There are two reasons for this. First, the American workforce has become much more diverse over the past three decades—a trend that will continue into the twenty-first century. Further, organization leaders are beginning to recognize that "honoring differences" is more than a pretty phrase: It is critical to the success of American organizations in the global marketplace as well as in Oshkosh, Eugene, and Lubbock.

It is practically axiomatic that organizations can be only as good as their workers. This means if American organizations are to be competitive at home and abroad, they need to develop their workforces. The process is challenging and frequently painful, for it often requires transforming organizational policies, practices, and cultures. Fundamental change is no easier for organizations than for individuals. But the stakes are high: Changes that enable organizations to value the diversity of their workforces can provide an advantage over less diverse competitors, for inherent in diversity is a tremendous potential for creativity. Diverse individuals bring a range of perspectives and problem-solving techniques to work issues that more homogeneous groups cannot muster. Our book is based on this theme.

Like most important issues, workforce diversity is controversial. There is no consensus on the terms of the subject—which are still being defined—much less on its policy implications. Analysis may be undertaken along more than one dimension, including those of organizations, individuals, or identity groups; and the focus can be on concepts, research, or application, including management issues, policy changes, training, and issues confronted by workers themselves. Discussion is made more difficult by the fact that the sensitivities of not just one identity group in our population are involved but of *every* identity group (with the possible exception of children). Their perceptions of themselves, their histories, values, socioeconomic issues, relations with each other and with their work organizations—all are the legitimate domain of workforce diversity.

Amid this range and complexity, our aim is to provide an overview of diversity issues and the identity groups comprising the new, diverse workforce. Addressing a general audience, we draw on data and research, which are often highly specialized, as well as on news media and other reports in an effort to put workforce diversity into perspective: defining it, examining forces shaping it, and surveying principal issues faced by the major identity groups in the workplace. We also focus on the dynamics of diversity in one institutional setting: labor unions.

Awareness of the need to value and manage diversity did not spring full-grown in the workplace like Athena from the head of Zeus. It evolved slowly, gaining momentum in the 1980s. Since the pioneering Hudson Institute study *Workforce 2000* announced in 1987 that demographic shifts are making diversity an enduring feature of the American workplace, some diversity initiatives have been driven mainly by the power of demographics. Growing workforce heterogeneity often is viewed as a stick prodding employers to adopt management practices to make the best of the inevitable. This is basically a negative incentive, similar to the punitive sanctions underlying affirmative action policies: organizations need to implement them—or else! Small wonder that some in the workplace view diversity initiatives skeptically as warmed-over affirmative action. In this book, we show that affirmative action is an important precursor but that valuing and managing diversity is much more. It is not driven by the threat of federal sanctions, which, beyond the moral imperative, is what ultimately prompts many organizations to implement affirmative action policies. Nor is it powered simply by jarring (to some) demographic realities. Diversity initiatives are based on a combination of moral, demographic, and economic forces and by a strongly positive impact they exert on an organization's bottom line. If valued and properly managed, diversity can be an American advantage.

Part 1 explores the context from which the need to value and manage diversity arises, and it discusses why diversity is an advantage. We update the demographic underpinning of diversity with new data based on the 1990 census and later surveys. In addition, Part 1 provides historical background against which to understand diversity. We analyze three models of American identity—the melting pot, cultural pluralism, and the civic culture models—and, within this context, we examine major historical developments that have shaped our current perceptions of diversity. The models also are considered more specifically, in the context of the American workplace.

Part 1 also examines new economic forces that make valuing diversity imperative. Our rationale maintains that changes in the structure of global and national economic competition are heightening the importance of satisfying diverse customer and client wants and needs. Further, economic and technological changes are increasing the competitive importance of effective human interaction on the job. These developments make compelling the need for both management and staff to understand and value human differences in the marketplace and workforce.

Beyond demographic and economic forces, affirmative action also has had a role in forging recognition of the need to value and properly manage diversity. We examine the framework of equal employment opportunity and affirmative action and the controversy surrounding the latter, its accomplishments, and, ultimately, its limits. Finally in Part 1, we explore the dynamics of diversity in organizations today. We examine a range of management issues, including tested strategies for managing diversity, the relationship of diversity to empowerment and total quality management (TQM), and other issues.

Part 1 concludes with a discussion of unions and the diverse workforce. The labor movement, whose mission has always been to represent workers, now represents women and racial and ethnic minorities in greater numbers than ever before. As the diversity of its constituents has increased, unions, like other organizations, are facing challenges in adapting. We examine how labor is coping and show how diversity means strength for the labor movement.

To promote understanding of workforce diversity, Part 2 surveys many of diversity's challenges, the work-related issues of concern to major new workforce identity groups. Going beyond the initial focus of diversity, which included only women and racial and ethnic groups, we give attention to workplace issues facing the full range of new identity groups in the workforce—women, racial and ethnic minorities, older workers, gay and lesbian workers, and workers with disabilities. The workplace roles of women and racial and ethnic minorities are the subject of numerous publications. But because these issues are continually evolving, they merit reexamination. Workplace issues of special interest to other identity groups—gay and lesbian and older workers—have received relatively little attention. They too are surveyed in this section. Also surveyed are workplace issues concerning workers with disabilities. With the implementation of the Americans with Disabilities Act in 1992, there is mounting interest in this subject.

Among ethnic and racial minorities, we focus on the largest groups: black Americans, Hispanics, Asian Americans including Pacific Islanders, and American Indians including Alaskan Natives. These are the groups about whom federal agencies gather data for statistical reporting purposes. We devote three chapters to racial and ethnic minorities, two to examining historical background and values, group by group, and one to examining current workplace issues. Another ethnic group also deserves attention: Arab Americans. Because, unlike the other groups, Arab Americans are not singled out for statistical reporting, little official data is regularly published about them. Nonetheless, they are one of the larger ethnic groups in our population and are a growing portion of the new workforce. We therefore include them in our presentation of historical background and cultural values.

Because our focus is on the new workforce, data about the white population is mainly used by way of comparison. However, white women are featured in the discussion on gender issues in the workplace, though there the focus is on gender, not race, and women from other racial groups are also included. This means that, by default, white men are the only major identity group in the population to whom we do not devote significant attention. (They, along with men from other racial groups, do receive secondary attention in the chapter on gender.)

In another sense, however, our discussion of white men is ubiquitous, even if often implied, because white men are the largest identity group in the workplace (except for all women as a group). Their values typically are reflected in the cultures of the organizations they created and where they still overwhelmingly are the power holders. Thus no examination of workforce diversity can occur without reference to white men: in important ways, they set the framework for discussion.

Still, omission of significant attention to issues facing white men per se risks implying that they are the only "nondiverse" group in the workplace. It can put them in an adversarial position with regard to everybody else. It also suggests that they are the only people who need to change to accommodate heterogeneity. This was pretty much the general understanding about workforce diversity until recently, and perhaps that was natural. Insight into any issue, be it on the individual or public level, usually evolves over time, with each new insight reflecting greater maturity. Discourse on workforce diversity is maturing. There is growing understanding that *all* workers are part of diversity, including white men. And all workers—not only white men—need to learn to adapt to the dynamics of diversity. In the near future, books such as ours on workforce diversity will probably routinely provide equal time for white men. Now, however, because recognition of diversity at work is still relatively new, we decided to focus our publication on the *new* workers, those groups who are entering the workforce in rising numbers. We hope this explanation obviates any impression that white men stand outside of or in opposition to diversity issues.

In our concluding comments, we look beyond our national boundaries to briefly view workforce diversity in an international context. This perspective enables us to see how American efforts to value and manage diversity are an advantage for U.S. organizations. It also points the way for future inquiry.

Our main focus however is on our national setting. Any publication exploring workforce diversity issues is incomplete without an acknowledgment of the national context in which these issues exist. Today, that context is acerbic. From our schools and universities to our streets, our national nerves are decidedly on edge. The news media daily report incidents involving controversy and often violence spawned by people's inability to value diversity. We all have been touched by this in some way.

In contrast, in the workplace, the leading edge of the debate has a unitive focus—that of valuing and sensitively managing differences. Of course, the debate is not without friction there, too. For example, some early diversity programs were too heavy-handed in efforts to identify stereotypes and created unnecessarily painful experiences for participants. Others seemed to single out the traditional, white-male organizational culture as the "enemy." In the process, they generated a backlash that undermines efforts to develop organizational cultures that value diversity. Diversity experts and managers now are learning to handle these issues more effectively.

Such friction is a natural part of the evolution of diversity initiatives on the job, and it is helping propel the process past its pioneering stages. It does not change the fact that the purpose of diversity initiatives is to promote understanding and respect for differences. It may well be that in the near term the workplace will more successfully address diversity issues than our institutions of higher education and other areas of national life. The workplace may serve as a premier forum in which we learn to value differences. To the extent that this publication helps promote valuing differences on the job, it may become a small force toward this end.

A Note on Terms

Words themselves can become a problem when discussing workforce diversity. Words can clarify or they can obscure, and when sensitivities are closely involved, as they are in diversity issues, they frequently perform the latter function. We therefore think it appropriate to comment on some terms used in this book, with the hope that this will help clarify our discussion.

"Employees should be defined by the skills they bring to the workplace, not by physical or cultural characteristics that are irrelevant to their jobs," says Catherine Petrini, managing editor of *Training & Development*.[1] No one wants to be identified solely by the racial, ethnic, or other identity groups to which they belong. We are all individuals with unique characteristics that cannot be summarized by a simple epithet. Yet in this book, we consistently refer to workers in terms of their racial or ethnic identities, their gender, age, sexual orientation, or physical disabilities. This is necessary because our focus is on groups rather than individuals. We are aware that these terms are unavoidably limiting.

We consider all of the people we discuss to be Americans, either legally because they are citizens or loosely because they live here and participate in one way or another in our national life. Because we need to refer to their racial and ethnic identities, we use terms currently acceptable to the groups involved. Even within identity groups, however, there is disagreement. Some black Americans prefer the term "African American"; others, "black" or "black American." "Black American" is more inclusive than "African American," because the former refers to blacks of all national origins while the latter technically refers to those of African heritage. These terms, however, are widely used synonymously, and we do so, too. Similarly, we use interchangeably both "American Indian" and "Native American," both being acceptable to at least some individuals from this group. Hispanics are divided in their preference for "Hispanic" and "Latino"—and for many, both terms are less appealing than references to their country of origin. "Hispanic" refers to European Hispanics as well as persons from Latin American cultures, and it is the term used in government publications. But many, especially younger people of Hispanic origin and persons on the West Coast, prefer "Latino." Again, we use both terms. Asian Americans, like Hispanics, much more readily refer to themselves by their country of origin ("Chinese American," "Filipino American") but since our focus is primarily on the group as a whole, we settle for "Asian American" or sometimes, when working with federal statistical categories, we use the term "Asians."

The term "multiculturalism," also causes confusion. To some, it refers only to interaction among different racial and ethnic groups. But, as we shall see, in the context of workforce diversity, it has a broader meaning. "Culture" refers to a set of shared ideas that guide members of a group in their interactions. By definition, members of any identity group—be they women, gay men and lesbians, black Americans, etc.—have a common culture; that is, they share certain ideas that make them identify with that group. (Of course, individuals internalize the values of more than one culture, depending on the identity groups to which they belong.)

The term "minority" is also controversial. First, it is time-linked. U.S. Census Bureau projections indicate that by the middle of the twenty-first century, 47 percent of the nation's population will be made up of those whom we consider "minority" today: African Americans, Hispanics, Asian Americans, and Native Americans. Even in this last decade in the twentieth century, there are places in the United States where a minority majority prevails. Further, many who belong to minority groups do not like the term, for it carries the implication of being lesser or inferior. Many prefer "people of color" instead. But, this term, too, has problems: Most Hispanics are caucasian, and technically they are excluded. Also "people of color" implies that "white" is not a color but that every other skin tone is. Recognizing there is no fully satisfactory term, we use both terms in this publication.

References

1. Catherine M. Petrini, "The Language of Diversity," *Training & Development*, vol. 47, no. 4, April 1993, p. 35.

PART 1

The New American Advantage

1
Diversity in America —in Hindsight

We need each other. And we must care for one another. Today, we do more than celebrate America; we rededicate ourselves to the very idea of America....An idea ennobled by the faith that our nation can summon from its myriad diversity the deepest measure of unity.
PRESIDENT WILLIAM JEFFERSON CLINTON
Inaugural address January 20, 1993

Any publication aspiring to survey the scope of workforce diversity issues needs to be set in a context that reaches beyond the workplace. This is especially true today when diversity, under the rubrics of cultural pluralism and multiculturalism, has become one of the most hotly debated issues of our time. That cultural diversity has added immeasurably to our creativity, energy, and strength as a nation is beyond dispute. Many add, however, that these days diversity and the debate surrounding it also are contributing to the weakening of national cohesiveness.

Cultural diversity is being discussed throughout the nation, in forums as varied as boardrooms, classrooms, government offices, and your dining room table. The intellectual establishment has weighed in on all sides. At some universities, diversity education sessions are offered to sensitize students to multiculturalism; standard courses, such as American history, are being taught in new ways in an effort to get beyond the traditional white-male focus. On the other side of the issue on campuses are voices, such as the National Association of Scholars, that oppose what they regard as the politicization of higher education.

In the media, columnists have expounded at length on the dangers and the strengths of multiculturalism. For example, George F. Will frequently waves the flag of danger. Even in a column on the Gettysburg address, he included a short jab at multicultural education:

> We are a polyglot nation of immigrants, a nation whose unity is based not on ethnicity but on an idea, a proposition. That is why clear-sighted Americans fight so fiercely for a certain educational canon, and against attempts, in the name of "multiculturalism," to locate civic identity not in shared convictions but in divisive ethnicities.[1]

At the other end of the opinion spectrum, Molefi Kete Asante, African-American Studies Chairman at Temple University, maintains that there is no common culture but rather a "hegemonic culture" that defenders of the status quo push as a common culture. He notes that "the real division on the question of multiculturalism is between those who truly seek to maintain a Eurocentric hegemony over the curriculum and those who truly believe in cultural pluralism without hierarchy."[2]

Several recently published books deal with a widely varying opinion on the issue. In *The Disuniting of America* (1992), eminent historian Arthur M. Schlesinger, Jr., calls for an appreciation of diversity while cautioning that the foundation of American culture is adapted Europeanism and repudiation of that heritage would "invite the fragmentation of the national community into a quarrelsome spatter of enclaves, ghettos, tribes."[3] In his book, *Culture Wars*, James Davison Hunter, of the University of Virginia, asserts that the culture wars derive from "different and opposing bases of moral authority and world views."[4] He defines the opposing views in terms of the "impulse toward orthodoxy" and the "impulse toward progressivism." Henry Louis Gates, Jr., of Harvard University, articulates the position of the more moderate liberal pluralist (as opposed to the "hard left" and "hard right") when he states, "it's only when we're free to explore the complexities of our hyphenated American culture that we can discover what a genuinely common American culture might actually look like. Common sense...reminds us that we're *all* ethnics, and the challenge of transcending ethnic chauvinism is one we all face."[5]

When one highlights the range of opinion about multicultural issues and then calls to mind the diversity-related suspicion and violence played out in our streets daily, the prospects for understanding seem bleak. But the multilayered process of accepting diversity is also occurring daily at all levels of society, and often it occurs so quietly that we may take it for granted: two saleswomen in a department store, one of Asian descent and one an Arab American, talking about family matters; an ethnic Christmas festival jointly sponsored by county conferences of African-American and European-American ministers; an auto body shop in which black American, Latino, and European-American mechanics work as a team.

How pluralism is manifesting in the workplace merits special attention. There, growing recognition of pluralism as a fact of life is leading to an affirmation of diversity. Many organizations are beginning to implement new approaches to diversity and are responding to a range of new issues—from removing structural barriers to the advancement of women and minorities (the glass ceiling) to providing their staffs with diversity training.

These issues are discussed in the remainder of this publication. What should be noted here is that the valuing of all peoples, which is one of America's most cherished ideals, may presently be more characteristic of our workplaces than it is of some other areas of our national life. Paradoxically, our workplaces may serve as educational forums in ways in which many of our schools currently are not. The daily dynamics of diversity in the workforce may serve as an agent that over time helps reduce our angst about multiculturalism in other areas of national life. When individual performance appraisal ratings as well as overall organizational success rely heavily on effective interaction among a diverse staff and managers—and, as this publication points out, this is increasingly the case—then people and organizations have compelling reasons, beyond the moral imperative, to learn to respect and understand each others' differences.

Three Models—The Melting Pot, Cultural Pluralism, and the Civic Culture

There can be no final verdict on the outcome of the "culture wars." In some respects, it is a debate that has raged since the founding of this nation, taking different expressions with each generation. Many have observed that during the conservative environment of the 1980s and early 1990s, cultural polarization progressively increased. And it is possible that in the current, more moderate political environment, multicultural tensions will decline—or at least not be aired so publicly. Whatever the case, the diversity issues have deep roots in this country's history.

The main issues gravitate around two models of the nature of American identity, which have long been part of our culture: the melting pot model and cultural pluralism. These models furnish a conceptual framework within which to explore the current controversy and thus gain insight into diversity in the workplace.

The melting pot principle holds that the experience of living in America serves as a "melting pot" that transforms peoples of different ethnic, racial, and religious backgrounds into a common culture. The concept dates back to the earliest days of the Republic. In 1782, J. Hector St. John de Crevecoeur, in *Letters from an American Farmer*, referred to the United States as a country in which "individuals of all nations are melted into a new race of men." Over time, others picked up the concept. The actual *term* "melting pot" was first used by Israel Zangwill, a Jewish Briton, in 1908 as the title and theme of a play. In *The Melting-Pot*, Zangwill invoked the "great Alchemist" who "melts and fuses" America's varied immigrant population "with his purging flames." The hero of his play, extolling the process, exclaims:

> There she lies, the great Melting-Pot—listen! Can't you hear the roaring and the bubbling? There gapes her mouth—the harbour where a thousand mammoth feeders come from the ends of the world to pour in their human freight.

Then he asserts apocalyptically, "Here shall they all unite to build the Republic of Man and the Kingdom of God."[6]

For subsequent generations of school children, the melting pot became part of their social studies catechism, along with the Declaration of Independence, the Constitution, and George Washington. Assimilation—or more accurately, acculturation—with mainstream culture was accepted as a virtual law of nature, though probably the only people who fully actualized it were white Protestants from Northern and Western Europe. (Assimilation and acculturation are different but overlapping processes. Acculturation involves adopting new cultural values. Assimilation entails integrating into the economic, social, and political life of the mainstream. Some degree of acculturation generally occurs before some degree of assimilation does. In this chapter, we generally use assimilation to refer to both processes.) In accepting the principle of the melting pot, many did not question its underlying assumption of Anglo-Saxonization, that is, the assertion that the American experience molds all into modern-day clones of the (mainly) white, Protestant Anglo-

Saxons who founded the Republic and established cultural hegemony here.

Horace Kallen was different. Kallen, an Hebraist (Kallen's term) who had immigrated to the United States from Germany, spent part of his academic career expounding an alternative model, cultural pluralism. According to this model, which Kallen first articulated in 1915, ethnic groups in America should retain their own identities while remaining loyal to the country and participating fully in national life. He believed that people should be respected for their contribution to the whole, not judged on the degree to which they are assimilable.[7] Variations of these principles are held by cultural pluralists down to the present day, though they have been broadened beyond Kallen's Eurocentric orientation.

If we disengage a bit and are willing to revisit the models with flexibility, we may find less of a conflict between them than the current culture wars seem to indicate. Neither model has a monopoly on applicability, but versions of both seem to have degrees of validity all of the time—sometimes more than others. The evolution of American history suggests that the cultural pluralist model or some variation of it is always applicable to a portion of our population. There are always people who identify strongly with their ethnic, racial, and religious groups. However, the cultural pluralist model appears more widely descriptive of reality during the first and maybe the second generation of a major wave of immigration, when newly transplanted peoples have just begun to cope with the dilemma of ethnic and, in some cases, religious preservation versus assimilation. The present is such a time.

With some revision, the melting pot model is also applicable: We need to drop the clearly fallacious notion that the American experience produces a uniform cultural broth. (Dropping Zangwill's assumption of proximity to godliness is also helpful.) When we do so, we may be in a position to accept the validity of a model in which we may remain diverse in our ethnic, racial, or religious backgrounds but simultaneously find a common identity as Americans and abide by the rules of our society. As Derrick Bell, an African-American activist and scholar, says about African Americans, "At some point, we have to hope for the best with regard to racial issues but recognize that we sink or swim with this society."[8] In fact, we *all* sink or swim together in the same pool.

In his excellent book, *The American Kaleidoscope: Race, Ethnicity, and the Civic Culture*, Lawrence Fuchs expounds on this concept. He holds that the civic culture is the unifying characteristic of American society and is that which protects individual rights, including the right to diversity. According to Fuchs:

> Since the Second World War the national unity of Americans has been tied increasingly to a strong civic culture that permits and protects expressions of ethnic and religious diversity based on individual rights and that also inhibits and ameliorates conflicts among religious, ethnic, and racial groups. It is the civic culture that unites Americans and protects their freedom—including their right to be ethnic.[9]

In other words, the American experience is one in which diversity is recognized and protected by the civic culture. And the civic culture is that which provides commonality. We designate this model the *civic culture model.*

While it is undeniable that the dominant civic culture established initially by this country's founders was essentially Anglo-Saxon, America's civic culture is not static. It evolves and is changed by each generation of Americans. It is probable that the culture wars we are witnessing do not augur the end of American unity, as some fear. They instead may be growing pains in the ongoing process of the defining of our civic culture. The civic culture and cultural pluralism models are similar in an important respect: Both describe systems in which diversity is protected. The major difference between them is a matter of focus. The cultural pluralist model is descriptive in the first instance of an individual's relationship with his or her chosen identity group or groups, asserting by implication that everyone has a right to be who they are. Secondarily, it concerns the nature of our relationship to the nation. Some cultural pluralists, like Kallen, deal with this relationship; others focus largely on asserting their right to group identity or denying the validity of a dominant culture. In contrast, the civic culture model first posits that there is a common culture which forms the cement of our national life and then defines the manner in which that culture functions to protect diversity.

Several developments have occurred over the past few decades that have combined to heighten national awareness of diversity in our society and in the workplace and to increase the diverse composition of our population. The remainder of this chapter deals with one of them: the civil rights and ethnic consciousness movements that gained momentum in the 1960s and 1970s. This development is discussed here in the context of the civic culture and cultural pluralist models. Two other major developments, changes resulting from domestic demographic shifts and new immigration as well as the growth of new economic forces, are explored in the following two chapters.

The Models in Society and the Workplace— The Civil Rights Movement Promotes Growing Awareness of Diversity

In the 1950s, cultural pluralism received scant attention from the general public. Those who did not buy into mainstream culture generally did not say so very loudly. We were in fact more homogeneous than in earlier decades in some important respects. Immigration percentages were spiraling downward. During the war, immigration had decreased, and by the mid-1960s more than 95 percent of Americans were native-born.[10]

These demographic trends enhanced the tendency to conform to mainstream values. Academic research in social psychology, such as the work by Solomon Asch, reflected this orientation and focused on the phenomenon of individual conformity to group norms rather than on the influence exerted by minorities on the groups. On a more popular level, the book *The Lonely Crowd* (1950) by David Riesman contrasted old-fashioned "inner-directed" people, who were self-motivating and uncompromising, with new "other-directed" conformists whose focus was materialistic and group-centered. The melting pot seemed to have done its work. Those who could not or chose not to conform were considered outsiders and were largely ignored.

The melting pot model seemed descriptive of workplace relationships, too. During the 1950s and 1960s, few questioned the near-monopoly white males had on positions of power in the workplace. Other workers were expected to conform to the traditional culture and were frequently subjected to blatant discrimination.

Then, in the 1960s, the civil rights revolution took the nation by surprise. There had been antecedents. Among them was a series of legislation aimed at integrating blacks into the military during World War II; the abolition of wage differentials by race in 1943; the breaking of the color line in major league baseball in 1947; the landmark Supreme Court decision, *Brown v. the Board of Education of Topeka*, which outlawed segregation in public education; and the quiet act of Rosa Parks, who one day in 1955 decided not to give up her seat to a white passenger on a bus in Montgomery, Alabama. In the 1960s and 1970s, the tide swept from the African-American community to the nation's other racial and ethnic minorities, women, as well as students, who lent support to various movements.

As these movements gained momentum, the popular perception of the melting pot model began to fray at the edges, and the cultural pluralist model gained sway. Stephen Steinberg, in *The Ethnic Myth*, observed:

> For decades the dominant tendency among the nation's ethnic and racial minorities had been toward integration into the economic, political, and cultural mainstream. Now the pendulum seemed to be swinging back, as these groups repudiated their assimilationist tendencies. Through art, literature, and politics, they sought to promote ethnic pride and solidarity, and to affirm their right to a separate identity within *the framework of a pluralist nation* [italics added].[11]

The impact of the movements was felt beyond the efforts of activists to communicate their assorted causes. Diversity began to be acknowledged in many spheres of our culture. For example, majority beliefs about sex were challenged, opening the way to a revolution in sexual values. Eastern religions began to attract a growing number of adherents. The new openness to diversity was seen in Congress too, which, among other legislation, passed the landmark Civil Rights Act of 1964. Title VII of this act banned employment decisions that discriminated on the basis of race, color, religion, or national origin. (A bar on discrimination based on sex was added later.) Thus, the principle of equal employment opportunity was born, and affirmative action soon followed. Cultural pluralism gradually began to be recognized in the workplace.

But it was just a beginning. Past workplace practices and attitudes about diversity were deeply entrenched. Even the well-intentioned did not readily perceive how far-reaching the changes needed to be. Although affirmative action was a necessary first step, it was negative in orientation, aimed at correcting past inequalities. This tended to lead to preferential treatment of minorities and women because it was often assumed that they had not been in the workforce long enough to perform on a par with white males. This deficiency premise could be self-fulfilling: Management hesitancy to counsel or reprimand female and minority employees tended to promote substandard performance. Managers, who had been trained to manage homogeneity, often had little understanding of why traditional management practices did not produce expected results. Management training had not sensitized them to the special concerns of minorities and women. Nor were employees trained to deal with growing diversity among their co-workers.

Thus, with the civil rights movement came the beginning of efforts to deal with diversity in the workforce. These efforts represented an epochal change in approach, and such changes do not happen quickly. The process has been one of slow evolution toward our current diversity strategies and beyond.

The Models and Today's Workforce

The heightening of our national awareness as a result of the civil rights movements, the new immigration, domestic population shifts, and the development of new economic forces have led to deepening understanding and application of the cultural pluralist model in the workplace. In the 1990s, the leading-edge focus in the workplace has moved beyond affirmative action. In his important book, *Beyond Race and Gender* (1991), R. Roosevelt Thomas, Jr., President of the American Institute for Managing Diversity at Morehouse College in Atlanta, noted that affirmative action was "never intended as a permanent tool." Its goal was to "fulfill a legal, moral, and social responsibility by initiating 'special' efforts to ensure the creation of a diverse work force and encourage upward mobility for minorities and women."[12] He asserted that it is time to go beyond the "specialness" of the affirmative action process and integrate women and minorities into the regular system.

Thomas and many others are calling for the adoption of the new strategies of valuing and managing diversity, while acknowledging that affirmative action still remains a necessary policy. According to Thomas, valuing diversity involves activities designed to "encourage awareness of and respect for diversity within the workplace."[13] Managing diversity involves empowering employees to reach their full potential. The process usually requires significant changes in an organization's root culture—which are seldom simple to accomplish. But the payoff is great. Empowered employees are more likely to put forth a 100 percent effort, giving full support to the organization and its goals. In turn, such commitment enables the organization to achieve higher levels of productivity. These issues are examined in this publication.

These developments bring us back to the models we have been discussing. The new approaches to diversity represent the cultural pluralist model operating at a deeper, more insightful level than is possible through the pursuit of affirmative action strategies alone. With the new strategies, diverse workers are empowered to participate fully in the organization's goals and practices; they are not expected to assimilate into the traditional white male culture in the workplace. Their differences are valued as a positive asset, and individuals are respected for their contributions to the whole. As a result of fully harnessing varied employee skills, abilities, and knowledge, the organization as a whole is strengthened.

The cultural pluralist model overlaps the workforce equivalent of the civic culture model through the mechanism of employee empowerment. Empowered employees, with their diversity respected and their talents unleashed, are likely to commit fully to the goals and norms governing life of the society (read "organization"). The civic (organizational) culture serves as a unifying factor in which the whole society (staff) finds commonality.

The Demographics of Diversity

Rapid change has always been a hallmark of the American experience. The post–World War II era, however, seems to contain more of it than many other periods in our history. One of the most profound ways in which we have been changing is demographically. In the past few decades, two major demographic developments have made us more diverse than ever before. These were the baby boom, which occurred between 1946 and 1964, and a new, great wave of immigration, which began after 1965. Although they occurred sequentially, these developments are having a compounding impact on the size and composition of the population that is projected to continue beyond the year 2000. To better understand these developments and their impact on the workforce, it is necessary first to examine the immigration patterns of our past.

The Pattern of American Immigration

When publicist Richard Hakluyt touted the advantages of settlement in the New World to a disinterested English nation in the sixteenth century, he could not have anticipated that the eventual flow of people to the shores of this continent would constitute the greatest mass movement in history. This immigration designed our racio-ethnic profile, and it has redrawn it in each successive generation.

Until the twentieth century, most immigrants came from Europe. They arrived slowly at first, drawn by prospects of greater political or religious freedom, economic opportunity, or adventure in a sparsely settled land. They came from England, but also from France, Sweden,

Holland, and other West European countries. By 1650, the colonial population totaled some 52,000. By 1700, it grew to 275,000. The first census in 1790 recorded the population of the infant United States at just 3.9 million.

At the same time, a much smaller but no less momentous development was occurring. In 1619, a group of Africans was forcibly brought to the English colony of Jamestown in Virginia. It is unclear whether these people were considered indentured servants or slaves, but those who followed were soon locked into slavery. Thus began the forced immigration of Africans to North America. The destination that millions of people in later centuries were to struggle to reach, some even willingly risking their lives, became for these Africans a hell. The slave population grew slowly. By 1650, there were only 300 blacks in Virginia, the most populous colony. Twenty years later they numbered some 2,000.

The concept of slavery stuck in the craw of the revolutionary generation, which had fought a war premised on the belief that all men were created equal. All states passed laws forbidding the importation of slaves, and the founding fathers, although many of them were slave owners themselves, wrote into the Constitution a prohibition against the importation of slaves. Slavery became a declining institution in post–Revolutionary War America, and forced immigration from Africa might have become a dead issue. Might have—but when the cotton gin revitalized the languishing Southern economy in the early 1790s, Southern planters suddenly discovered an overriding need for cheap slave labor. Some 25,000 slaves were smuggled into the country in the 1790s. Even after the Constitutional prohibition of slavery took effect in 1808, Africans continued to be clandestinely shipped into slavery. Between 1808 and the beginning of the Civil War in 1861, some 54,000 slaves were illegally imported into the country. This number was small, however, relative to the slave population, which grew mainly by natural increase and which totaled about 4 million by 1860.

White immigration also slowed to a trickle by the 1790s, although for different reasons. Wars in Europe and doubts about whether the new republic across the Atlantic would be viable kept many Europeans at home. That changed by the 1820s. Americans, wildly patriotic after their second victory over England in the War of 1812, looked like they were going to make it as a people after all. Moreover, the end of the Napoleonic wars in 1815 brought peace to Europe and increased opportunity for emigration. Between 1820 and 1860, some 6 million people crossed the Atlantic, each decade bringing immigrants in greater numbers. Many of these were Germans, who were driven by political upheaval and economic instability at home. And they were

Irish, mostly poor and uneducated, who were caught in the grip of potato crop failures and famine. Steamships facilitated the flow by midcentury, shortening the transatlantic voyage from an ordeal of perhaps three to four months to one of two weeks. The 1850 census estimated that 10 percent of the U.S. population was foreign born.[14]

From the beginning, Americans expressed hostility to new immigrants. There was a perennial suspicion that newcomers could not adapt to American ways. There were also fears that newcomers would take jobs, especially from poorer Americans. Others wondered if the economy could sustain the influx. Religious differences also stimulated animosity. Xenophobia was a factor as early as 1798 when the Alien Act invested the president with the power to expel aliens he thought dangerous to the well-being of the nation. The law was rooted in Federalist politics, but part of the target was French immigrants. Xenophobia was also the impetus behind the Know-Nothing Party in the 1850s, which initially represented "Nativist" sentiment against aliens and foreign-born Americans. At midcentury, anti-Catholic riots erupted in some urban centers, aimed mainly at new Irish immigrants. The China Exclusion Act of 1882 barred Chinese immigration after an influx of some 200,000 Chinese laborers. It was the first law prohibiting a specific *free* people from immigrating to this country. As such, it contradicted the notion that America was open to all.

Yet, also from the beginning, the "better angels of our nature" as President Lincoln might have termed it, often prevailed. The Alien and Sedition Acts were allowed to expire (as did the political circumstances from which they flowed). The Know-Nothing Party's meteoric rise to prominence ended in an equally meteoric plummet into oblivion. Anti-Catholic sentiment lost force as a national issue, though it did not disappear as a local one. The China Exclusion Act, however, remained on the books and was, in effect, expanded by the 1924 Immigration Act, which reduced to negligible Asian immigration.

Through it all, the flow of immigrants continued—and grew. After a downturn during the Civil War, immigration swelled to flood proportions in the 1880s and continued until the 1920s. Again, the immigrants were mainly from Europe. What was new was that by the second decade of the twentieth century most came for the first time from Southern and Eastern Europe. As political and economic conditions stabilized in Northern and Western Europe, they worsened elsewhere, driving a massive population outflow. Of the 23.5 million newcomers who arrived during the period, about 11 million were from Italy, Russia, and Austria-Hungary.

By 1920, over 13 percent of the nation's population, some 14 million people, were foreign-born. In the peak year of 1907, 1.3 million people arrived. Many of these newcomers were uneducated and poor. Cities, already overcrowded, expanded even further, while charitable organizations strained beyond their means to care for the poorest. Cultural differences often sparked clashes among immigrant groups as well as between the newcomers and native-born Americans. Many of the immigrants, especially those from Southern and Eastern Europe, were seen as hard to assimilate. Concerned by the proliferation of social problems, many native-born Americans began to think that some sort of restriction should be placed on immigration. Others, picking up on racist themes, called for the exclusion of Southern and Eastern Europeans on the grounds that they were racially inferior.

These varying issues led to the Immigration Act of 1924 and to an end of the great wave of immigration. The 1924 Act imposed for the first time a permanent quota system that excluded peoples considered hard to assimilate on the basis of race or religion. The intent of this blatantly racist legislation was to make immigration difficult for any except Northern Europeans. (The legislation was passed at a time when U.S.–Japanese tensions were at a high, and it explicitly prohibited Japanese immigration—a fact that triggered a further round of bilateral animosity.)

Immigration fell drastically, to a mere half a million people in the 1930s and only 1 million in the 1940s. This was fewer in an entire decade than during a single year at the height of great immigration influx. Between 1932 and 1935, more people left the United States than immigrated here. By the 1950s, immigration was on the rise, totaling 2.6 million, but was still only a fraction of the flow during the great wave earlier in the century. A large measure of the fall is attributable to international conditions—the Depression and World War II. But the new, restrictive immigration legislation was also an important factor. It linked the number of immigrants admitted from each country to a percent of the foreign-born people of that nationality in the United States according to the 1920 census. Because these numbers were very low for non-European nations, quota immigration remained at low levels. Nonquota immigration was also allowed for people born in the western hemisphere.

The New Immigration

Things changed in 1965. In a legislative about-face, Congress swung open the doors of the nation to people from all parts of the world. The growing momentum of the civil rights revolution plus the changing international situation and its domestic fallout helped effect this shift.

There were precursors. World War II produced ground tremors that began to shake Americans' calcified, racist views on immigration. To aid the war effort, in 1943 Congress established for the first time an annual quota on immigrants from China, our wartime ally. Although the quota was a mere 105, it ended the long-standing practice of barring Chinese immigration. Importantly, Chinese immigrants, including those already in the country, also became eligible for citizenship.*

This legislation was an opening wedge for other immigration laws. An important one was the McCarran-Walter Act in 1952. This act was passed partly in response to lobbying efforts by Japanese Americans, who were fortified in their efforts by the gross injustice dealt them and Japanese residents when they were interned during the war. The McCarran-Walter Act, also known as the Immigration and Nationality Act of 1952, assigned a quota to Japanese immigrants for the first time.

Although these laws broke new ground, they remained basically restrictive. The annual quotas were tiny: Japan's, which was the largest, was only 185. Further, American attitudes towards Asian immigrants remained less than welcoming, although not as hostile as before. Also, Asian spouses and minor children of U.S. citizens were also permitted entry, but this did not significantly raise the numbers of Asian immigrants.[16]

By the 1960s, the American public became more sensitive to the racist nature of the immigration admissions criteria. Both Democrats and Republicans began calling for a more equitable immigration system. A major factor in the sensitizing process was the civil rights revolution. But the domestic economic boom that resulted from the Vietnam-era buildup was also a factor. The economy was expanding, and there seemed no end to the number of additional workers we could absorb. Baby boomers were standing in the wings, but by the mid-1960s, they were only beginning to enter the workforce.

The timing was right for an amendment to the McCarran-Walter Act. The amendments passed in 1965 abolished the national-origins quota system and eliminated the strictures on Asian immigration imposed by the 1924 legislation. In its place, immigration was opened to people from both the western and the eastern hemispheres, and ceilings were placed on immigration from both. It was the first time that European immigration was so limited. The amendments established quotas of up to 20,000 annually from each eastern hemisphere country, and an overall ceiling of 120,000 was placed on the western hemisphere, with no individual country ceilings.

---

*The history of this legislation is traced in Fuchs, *The American Kaleidoscope: Race, Ethnicity, and the Civic Culture.*[15]

Knowledgeable observers expected that the new amendments would not significantly change the basically European composition of immigration. Although, technically, the legislation opened immigration to the entire world, visas were extended mainly to family members of U.S. citizens and residents, most of whom were European in origin. It was to be business as usual—or so they thought.

They were wrong. Third-world immigrants discovered numerous ways to enter legally—and sometimes illegally. Thereafter, they used provisions of the law to obtain citizenship or residency status. As Lawrence Fuchs observed, many Third Worlders enter the country under preference-system categories that permit entry to exceptional professionals and workers with needed skills. They later send for their families under family reunification provisions. Others come as tourists or students and later adjust their status to that of resident.

The newcomers fall into three broad categories: legal immigrants, refugees, and illegal immigrants.

Legal Immigrants

Over the next three and a half decades, the size of the annual flow of immigrants increased more than fivefold and its composition radically altered. For the first time in U.S. history, immigration became predominantly non-European. By 1990, immigrants from other than Europe and Canada constituted almost 92 percent of the total. This was a stunning change from 1960, when the figure was only about one third (36 percent). See Figure 1-1.

Figure 1-1. Immigrants Admitted by Region of Birth, Fiscal Years 1960, 1970, 1980, and 1990*
(Numbers in thousands)

Region	1960 No.	1960 % of total	1970 No.	1970 % of total	1980 No.	1980 % of total	1990 No.	1990 % of total
Total	265.4	100.0	373.3	100.0	530.6	100.0	1536.5	100.0
Europe	138.8	52.3	116.0	31.1	72.1	13.6	112.4	7.3
Asia	25.0	9.4	94.9	25.4	236.1	44.5	338.6	22.0
Africa	2.3	0.9	8.1	2.2	14.0	2.6	35.9	2.3
Canada	31.0	11.7	13.8	3.7	13.6	2.6	16.8	1.1
Latin America	67.1	25.3	137.3	36.8	190.9	36.0	1026.6	66.8
Mexico	32.7	12.3	44.5	11.9	56.7	10.7	679.1	44.2
Other	1.2	0.5	3.2	0.9	4.0	0.7	6.2	0.4
Oceania	1.2	0.4	3.2	0.9	4.0	0.7	6.2	0.4

*Percents may not add exactly because of rounding.
SOURCE: Statistics Division, Immigration and Naturalization Service.

The biggest shifts were in Asian and Latin American immigration. Asians accounted for only 9.4 percent of the total in 1960. By 1980, their share had leapt to 44.5 percent. In 1990, however, the Asian share of the whole dropped to 22 percent. This decline represented not a decrease in numbers. In fact, the numbers of Asian immigrants dramatically increased—from 236,000 in 1980 to 339,000 a decade later. What was new by 1990 was a prodigious growth in Latin American and especially Mexican immigration. While Latin American immigration rose from one quarter of the total in 1960 to 36 percent a decade later and held steady for another decade, by 1990 the figure reached two thirds of the total. Mexican immigration accounted for a sizable portion of the increase. Just 11 percent of the total in 1980, it jumped to over 44 percent by 1990.

Overall, Asian and Latin American legal immigration to the United States consisted of almost 90 percent of the whole in 1990. Undocumented immigration, which is mainly from Latin America, especially Mexico, raises this figure further.

The flip side of these developments is declining European and Canadian immigration, which dropped to a mere 8.4 percent of the total in 1990. In Figure 1-1 lies the story of how immigration trends are redefining America.

Refugees

Refugees form a second major group of the new immigrants. Before 1980, individuals were granted refugee status on an ad hoc basis, mainly to protect escapees from communist nations. The Refugee Act of 1980, designed to make U.S. refugee policy more consistent with international norms, broadened the definition of "refugee" to include persecuted individuals from any nation regardless of that nation's political orientation. In fact, however, during the 1980s, amid a conservative political climate, most people who were granted refugee status continued to come from communist-controlled nations. Figure 1-2 identifies countries of origin that were major contributors to the refugee population between 1961 and 1989. Of the thirteen nations listed, only two—Iran and Thailand—were not communist-controlled. During the 1980s, two other noncommunist nations not shown on the table—Iraq and Nicaragua—also contributed sizable refugee population (7,400 and nearly 4,000, respectively).

With the demise of Eastern-bloc communism, the communist-centered application of the law is changing. For what will undoubtedly remain a mix of political self-interest and humane considerations, the Refugee Act can be expected to be applied more in accordance with its

Figure 1-2. Immigrants Admitted as Permanent Residents Under Refugee Acts, by Country of Birth 1961 to 1989* (Numbers in thousands)

Total	1961–1970 No.	% of total	1971–1980 No.	% of total	1981–1989 No.	% of total	1961–1989 Total no.	% of total
Totals	212.84	100	539.44	100	916.24	100	1,668.52	100
Cuba	131.56	62	251.51	47	105.69	12	488.76	29
Vietnam	—	—	150.27	28	303.91	33	454.18	27
Laos	—	—	21.69	4	133.04	15	154.73	9
Cambodia	—	—	7.74	1	109.35	12	117.09	7
Soviet Union	.87	—	31.31	6	49.12	5	81.30	5
Romania	7.16	3	6.81	1	26.61	3	40.58	2
Poland	3.20	2	5.88	1	29.98	3	39.06	2
Iran	—	—	.36	—	38.13	4	38.49	2
Thailand	—	—	1.24	—	26.18	3	27.42	2
China*	5.31	2	13.76	3	7.59	1	26.66	2
Afghanistan	—	—	.54	—	20.81	2	21.35	1
Czechoslovakia	5.71	3	3.65	1	7.32	1	16.68	1
Hungary	4.04	2	4.36	1	4.08	—	12.48	1
Other	54.99	26	40.32	7	54.43	6	162.22	10

*Covers mainland China and Taiwan.

SOURCE: U.S. Immigration and Naturalization Service, Statistical Yearbook, annual; and releases; reprinted in Statistical Abstract 1991.

global intent. Thus, the law is likely to contribute increasingly to the growing pluralism among newcomers to our country and the continued predominance of the cultural pluralist model.

Illegal Migrants

Of special concern to many are a third group of newcomers, the undocumented immigrants. Illegal migration has long been a controversial issue in our country. Illegal aliens, mostly manual laborers, have come to the United States, especially over the border with Mexico, but also through other venues such as the long, virtually unguarded U.S.–Canadian border. Without recourse to the law, undocumented workers are an exploitable labor force, obliged to accept less-than-minimum wages and abysmal working conditions. They are the dream of many growers in the West and Southwest where farming needs are seasonal. Having no obligation to retain to them, employers release illegal immigrants when work dries up and readily replace them if they are unwilling to work the long hours that are frequently required. In such a buyer's market, not only are undocumented workers treated cheaply and laws broken with regularity, the presence of the illegals deprives legal workers of work.

Implementation in 1976 of a law placing a ceiling of 20,000 on immigration from each Western hemisphere nation heightened pressure on many to migrate illegally. It is estimated that after 1976, some 50 to 60 percent of the illegal aliens came from Mexico.[17] For most of the next decade, the number of unauthorized aliens captured annually near the Mexican border numbered more than a million. However, illegal immigrants came from other nations too, from as far away as Asia. Estimates of the size of the illegal alien population vary widely, but data regarded as reliable estimate it ranged from about 2 to 4 million in 1980.[18]

Such numbers spurred fears that we were losing control of our borders and were partly responsible for the adoption of the Immigration Reform and Control Act (IRCA) in 1986. This legislation was aimed at controlling illegal immigration sanctions against employers who hired undocumented workers. The legislation also established a program for special agricultural workers to meet growers' demands. However, to ensure that these workers did not get permanently stuck in an underclass, the legislation stipulated that special agricultural workers were free to work anywhere, even outside agriculture, as well as being eligible to become residents and citizens.[19] Further, it provided that aliens who had entered the U.S. illegally before January 1, 1982, had the right to choose permanent residency and citizenship. More than 3 million persons were eventually legalized under these two programs.[20]

Contrary to original expectations, however, IRCA did not substantially reduce the number of illegal aliens.[21] Bean, Edmonston and Passel cite as reliable an estimate of between 1.7 to 2.9 million persons by the beginning of 1989.[22] The Census Bureau estimates that net undocumented immigration totals about 200,000 persons each year.[23] Of course, such estimates are by their nature difficult to confirm and can be confusing. For instance, according to the Immigration and Naturalization Service, Asian gangs alone are responsible for smuggling into the country some 100,000 people annually. These people, who are mainly from mainland China, or their relatives pay a sizable fee, which they usually cannot afford, for the gangs' services, and often the illegals end up working as indentured servants in Asian communities here to pay for their passage.[24]

Concerns About the New Immigration

While the new immigration differs markedly from its predecessors in some ways, in one way it does not: Like earlier immigration flows, this one has touched off a growing storm of controversy. Many worry about the social fragmentation created by diversity. Some see their fears confirmed in areas such as northern New Jersey where a massive influx of Indian immigrants has generated racial strife and violence.[25] A new factor in this worry, which distinguishes it from concerns during previous large immigration inflows, is the melting of the melting pot model. Assimilation—or adherence to it as an ideal—is not what it used to be, and cultural pluralism is much more acceptable, as we have seen.

The economic impact of immigration also stirs controversy. Do immigrants take jobs from the poor and end up on welfare or do they create new jobs and enlarge the economy? The answer is all of the above. The question is: In what proportions? Opinions vary, depending on the authority cited. A 1993 study by the Carrying Capacity Network, concludes that immigrants cost U.S. taxpayers more than they contribute in taxes—$45 billion more a year.[26] On the other hand, a 1993 study by the Urban Institute reviewing data from Los Angeles County (where immigration is among the heaviest in the country) finds that the answer is not so simple. The study criticizes others who examine only recent immigrant data and finds that when long-term immigrants are also included, revenues from immigrants are greater than their share of the population.[27] An earlier study based on data from the November 1989 Current Population Survey (CPS), finds that the wages of recent immigrant groups (people who arrived between 1982 and 1989) are 42 percent less than those of native-born males and their unemployment rate greater than that of native-born Americans (7.5 percent for men and 8.4 percent for women compared to 5.2 percent for native-born men and women).[28] But the study also points to the importance of factoring in length of stay, noting that differences tend to even out as immigrants' length of stay in the United States increases and they become more assimilated into the workforce.

A further worry is that the United States will become too crowded. Observer Michael Kinsley notes, "Basic economic logic suggests that even when a new arrival 'takes' a job, the money he earns and spends will in turn create a job or so. The more the merrier is a tenet of capitalism dating back to Adam Smith." Acknowledging that there are limits to the the-more-the-merrier nostrum and that, at some point, the country will become too crowded, Kinsley observes that there is no reason to believe that we have reached the limit nor that we will in the foreseeable future as immigration increases.[29]

Amid the welter of opinion and data, people tend to listen to those arguments that support their predispositions. And it is clear that Americans are increasingly predisposed to take a negative view. A

Newsweek poll in 1993 finds that 59 percent of those polled think immigration was a good thing for the country in the past, but only 29 percent think it is a good thing today.[30] Support for immigration seems to be eroding less quickly among black Americans than others. Contrary to the popular impression that there is a high degree of resentment among blacks about immigration, a 1992 *Business Week*/Harris poll finds that 46 percent of black respondents think immigration is good for the country; only 26 percent of nonblack respondents feel the same way.[31] (The response by blacks was especially interesting because 73 percent think businesses prefer to hire immigrants over blacks; the figure for nonblacks was 49 percent.)

Immigration and the Future

More immigrants live in the United States today than ever before. According to the 1990 census, 19.7 million people are foreign-born. Their share of the total however was greater during the earlier wave of immigration. In 1990, immigrants accounted for just under 8 percent of the total population; in 1910, their share was approximately 15 percent.

The numbers of immigrants will increase, as will their fraction of the total population. In 1990, Congress further raised the numerical ceiling of the preference categories under which immigrants could enter the country. Under the preference system, 270,000 immigrants were admitted annually between 1965 to 1990. As a result of the raised numerical ceilings, 406,000 immigrants were permitted to enter annually between 1991 and 1994; thereafter, the number is projected to rise to 421,000 annually. But immigration under the preference system is only one avenue by which newcomers enter the country, such as family reunification. In its moderate-level projections of population trends, the Census Bureau assumes a future immigration flow of 880,000 yearly.[32] Most of the newcomers are expected to continue to come from non-European countries. As Alejandro Portes and Ruben Rumbaut pointed out in *Immigrant America*, "Never before has the United States received immigrants from so many countries, from such different social and economic backgrounds, and for so many reasons."

According to the Census Bureau, by the year 2000, about 60 percent of our population growth will be attributable to post-1991 net immigration. (Net immigration is documented as legal and illegal immigration minus outmigrants.) By 2050, post-1991 net immigration will account for 93 percent of the population increase. At that time, post-1991 immigrants and their descendants may number some 82 million people and may constitute 21 percent of the population.[33]

Domestic Demographic Changes

The baby boom hit America with a bang. The great surge in births between 1946 and 1964 added on average more than 4 million Americans annually to the census registers, a more than 50 percent annual increase in births over the 1940 figure. See Figure 1-3. Baby boomers made news wherever they went. School systems expanded to accommodate them. New industries were established to cater to them. Blue jeans, their generational trademark, became the leisure wear of choice for youngsters and their teenage brothers and sisters.* And the curvaceous Barbie doll began her successful career by appealing to sophisticated little baby boom girls who were increasingly being raised on the images of television. By the time boomers reached work-

Figure 1-3. Population by Race and Hispanic Origin: 1890 through 1990 (Numbers in millions)

Year	Total No.§	White* No.	White* %¶	African-American No.	African-American %	Other races† No.	Other races† %	Hispanic‡ No.	Hispanic‡ %
1990	248.71	199.69	80.3	29.99	12.1	19.04	7.6	22.35	9.0
1980	226.55	188.37	83.1	26.50	11.7	11.68	5.2	14.61	6.4
1970	203.24	177.75	87.5	22.58	11.1	2.88	1.4	NA	NA
1960	179.32	158.83	88.6	18.87	10.5	1.62	0.9	NA	NA
1950	150.70	134.92	89.6	15.04	10.0	.71	0.5	NA	NA
1940	131.67	118.22	89.8	12.87	9.8	.59	0.4	NA	NA
1930	122.78	110.29	89.8	11.89	9.7	.60	0.5	NA	NA
1920	105.71	94.82	89.7	10.46	9.9	.43	0.4	NA	NA
1910	91.97	81.73	88.9	9.83	10.7	.41	0.4	NA	NA
1900	76.0	66.81	87.9	8.83	11.6	.35	0.5	NA	NA
1890	62.95	55.10	87.5	7.49	11.9	.36	0.6	NA	NA

*Includes white persons of Hispanic origin.

†Persons of other races are mostly Asian and Pacific Islanders, American Indians, Eskimos, and Aleuts. In some instances, data are derived by subtracting African American and white from the total.

‡Persons of Hispanic origin may be of any race. Data on Hispanics are not available before 1980. All racial categories may contain persons of Hispanic origin.

§Numbers are in millions. Totals may not add exactly due to rounding.

¶Percent of total. Numbers may not add exactly due to rounding.

SOURCE: Compiled by Janice Hamilton Outtz from U.S. Census Bureau data.

---

*At present, baby boomers—no longer babies—still are having an impact on the jeans business. Lee and Levi Strauss have expanded their jeans line to include a new relaxed fit to accommodate less-than-trim boomer bodies. Other businesses are expected to adapt their products to the aging boomer population as well.

ing age, they were to profoundly rearrange the nature of the work-force.

Minority groups more than held their own during the baby boom. Because their numbers were small relative to the white population, in terms of percent of increase, their growth was spectacular. However, in terms of percent of the total population, it traced a slow, steady climb. As Figure 1-3 indicates, the African-American population, the largest minority group, rose 50 percent between 1950 and 1970, from 15 million to 22.6 million. In comparison, the white American population grew 32 percent. However, the African-American share of the total increased by only 1.1 percent during the period. Persons of other races also increased their share of the total. Numbering under three quarters of a million in 1950, they increased to 2.88 million by 1970—a 300 percent rise! This represented a 0.9 percent growth as a percent of the total.

It can be assumed that the Latino population similarly grew during the baby boom, but statistical evidence for this is fragmentary. Until 1980, persons of Hispanic origin were not considered a large enough group to warrant separate statistical attention. "Hispanic" and "Latino"—used interchangeably here—are ethnic, not racial, designations. Before 1980, censuses included a question about racial identity but none specifically inquiring about Hispanic identity.* (Hispanic persons may be of any race. About 95 percent identify themselves as white and are included in the white racial count.) The dual impact of baby boom growth and immigration made clear the need for separate statistical data about the group. The 1980 census added a question specifically about Hispanic origin, thus making available for the first time census data about the Hispanic population as a separate ethnic group.

These increases are especially significant when viewed in an historic context. During the preceding 20 years, from 1930 to 1950, the African-American population grew 26.5 percent, increasing by just over 3 million people. Other races as well as the white population grew 22 percent during the same period.

Because the 1930–1950 period included World War II and the Depression, which produced demographic anomalies, a more accurate perspective on the changes may be gained through a comparison with the 1890–1910 period, the most recent previous 20-year period in which there were no major dislocations (aside from the depression of 1893). Between 1890 and 1910, the African-American population increased 31 percent; other minorities grew 15 percent. In contrast, the

---

*Though questions about ancestry were included.

white population grew a significant 48 percent, an increase partly due to massive immigration from Europe.

The baby boom is only a small part of the story of the growth of the minority population in the United States. Before the boom, about 1 in every 10 Americans was a member of a minority group. At boom's end, that figure was more than 1 in 10. The dramatic climb however began after the boom. Despite a "baby bust" in the next two decades, by 1980 the minority population increased to 23.3 percent of the total. This meant that by 1980, about 2 in every 10 Americans were people of color. By 1990, the figure was almost 3 in 10.

These increases were due not only to natural increase but also to the new inclusion in the minority statistical counts of the Latino population as a separate group. The other important factor is immigration, which is discussed earlier in this chapter.

The growth in the diversity of the nation's population is projected to continue well into the next century. According to moderate estimates by the Census Bureau, the population is projected to grow almost 50 percent by midcentury, rising from 257 million in 1993 to almost 382 million. Please see Figure 1-4. At that time, racial and ethnic minorities will comprise almost half of the population (47 percent)—a development that will make our current use of the term "minority" obsolete.

Figure 1-4. Population by Race and Hispanic Origin: Projections 1993 to 2050 (Numbers in millions)

Year	Total No.‡	White, non-Hispanic No.	% of total	African-American, non-Hispanic No.	% of total	Hispanic No.	% of total	Asian & Pacific Islanders, non-Hispanic* No.	% of total	American Indian, & other, non-Hispanic† No.	% of total
1993	257.59	191.57	74	30.82	12	24.93	10	8.37	03	1.90	01
2000	274.82	196.70	72	33.83	12	30.60	11	11.58	04	2.10	01
2010	298.11	201.67	68	38.20	13	39.31	13	16.52	06	2.41	01
2020	322.60	206.16	64	42.91	13	48.95	15	21.82	07	2.76	01
2030	344.95	207.67	60	47.55	14	59.20	17	27.39	08	3.14	01
2040	364.35	205.59	56	52.29	14	69.83	19	33.07	09	3.58	01
2050	382.67	201.84	53	57.32	15	80.68	21	38.77	10	4.08	01

*Includes non-Hispanic Asians and Pacific Islanders.

†Includes non-Hispanic American Indian, Eskimo, and Aleut population.

‡Numbers may not add exactly due to rounding.

SOURCE: Jennifer Cheeseman Day, *Population Projections of the United States, by Age, Sex, Race, and Hispanic Origin: 1992 to 2050,* Current Population Reports, P25-1092, U.S. Department of Commerce, Economics, and Statistics Administration, Bureau of the Census, October 1992, Table 1.

At the same time, the non-Hispanic white share of the population is projected to decline from 74 percent of the total in 1993 to 53 percent by 2050. The *number* of non-Hispanic whites, however, will increase slowly, growing by 5 percent from 191.6 million in 1993 to 201.8 million. White Americans will remain the single largest racio-ethnic group in the country.

Most of the major minority groups are projected to increase their share of the total population. African Americans will grow from 12 to 15 percent of the total. Asians and Pacific Islanders will surge from 3 to 10 percent. Hispanics are projected to experience the largest growth of all, from 10 to 21 percent of the population. The only minority group that will remain steady in terms of share of the whole is the American Indian, Eskimo, and Aleut population. This group will continue to account for 1 percent of the total.

Implications for the Workforce

America is still coming to terms with the impact on the labor force of the demographic developments over the last four decades. They have been responsible for an enormous growth in labor force size. And they have also transformed the traditional, mainly white male labor force into a multicultural, bigenderal reality. These changes will continue to evolve in the future. The workforce of the future will continue to grow, but more slowly. It will also continue to become more diverse.

The More Slowly Growing Workforce

Since the 1950s, the American labor force has doubled in size. Numbering just over 62 million people in 1950, the labor force expanded to almost 125 million by 1990. See Figure 1-5. (The labor force is composed of people who are working or are looking for work.) This is a bigger growth over a shorter period than at any other time in the twentieth century.

A major reason for the increase was the coming of age of the baby boomers. Decade by decade, the baby boom presence rippled through the workforce, causing an accelerating growth rate. The first baby boomers reached working age (16 years) in 1962. While in the pre-boom decade of 1950 to 1960, the labor force grew 7.4 percent, between 1960 and 1970, it shot up 19 percent. By the 1970–1980 period, the growth rate was a prodigious 29.1 percent. The growth rate peaked in the mid-1980s, when boomers began passing peak levels of participa-

Figure 1-5. The Growing Labor Force, 1950 to 1990 with Projections to 2005

Year	Labor force (millions)
1950	62.2
1960	69.6
1970	82.8
1980	106.9
1990	124.8
2005	150.7

SOURCE: William B. Johnston and Arnold H. Packer, *Workforce 2000: Work and Workers for the 21st Century* (Indianapolis, Indiana: Hudson Institute, June 1987), p. 78; and Howard N. Fullerton, Jr., "Labor force projections: the baby boom moves on," U.S. Department of Labor, Bureau of Labor Statistics, *Outlook 1990–2005*. BLS Bulletin 2402 (U.S. Government Printing Office, Washington, D.C., May 1992), p. 31.

tion. Nonetheless, the workforce continued to grow. Between 1980 and 1990, the growth rate was a still-sizable 16.5 percent.

A second factor driving the increase was the influx of new immigrant workers. By 1989, immigrants who had arrived since 1965 added 8 percent—some 9 million people—to the number of employed persons in the country.[34] An additional half-million unemployed immigrants who were looking for work further augmented the workforce (which consists of both employed persons plus those seeking employment). New immigrant flows in the future will continue adding to the workforce. According to Hudson Institute estimates, two-thirds or more of immigrants of working age are likely to enter the workforce.[35]

While workers in other age groups were growing, entry-level young workers (ages 16 to 24) decreased. Between 1975 and 1990, the youth workforce dropped 0.4 yearly.[36] This was because, by the 1980s, the new workers were already being drawn from the baby bust generation, that is, the children of the baby boomers who were less numerous than their parents. The fall, however, was not enough to offset increases in other segments of the workforce.

A More Diverse Workforce

Bigness is not the only distinctive feature of the new workforce. Like the national population, the new workforce is also more diverse than ever before.

Non-Hispanic, White Workers—
A Declining but Still Dominant
Share of the Workforce

To understand the magnitude and nature of the new workforce diversity in perspective, it is important to bear in mind that white workers, and more specifically non-Hispanic white workers, continue to comprise a major share of the workforce. Further, despite their declining share in the workforce, non-Hispanic white males remain the single largest workforce group. A focus on the unparalleled growth in workforce diversity makes it easy to lose sight of these central facts. As Figure 1-6 indicates, non-Hispanic whites comprised 78.5 percent of the workforce in 1990. Non-Hispanic white males constituted 43.1 percent of the figure; non-Hispanic white women workers, 35.4 percent.

While they remain the dominant group, white workers' portion of the total is dropping. Because separate statistical data on Hispanic workers is unavailable before 1980, it is difficult to provide figures about the declining workforce share of non-Hispanic white workers over time. However, the drop in the share of white workers including Latinos can be documented. In 1975, white workers formed 88.3 percent of the total workforce. Although their numbers rose, their share of the total dropped to 85.9 percent in 1990.[37]

Figure 1-6. Share of U.S. Labor Force, Non-Hispanic and Hispanic Groups, 1990 and Projections for 2005
(Numbers in thousands)

Group	Labor force 1990		Labor force 2005	
	Number	Percent of total	Number	Percent of total
White, non-Hispanic	98,013	78.5	110,015	73.0
Men	53,784	43.1	57,545	38.2
Women	44,229	35.4	52,470	34.8
African American, non-Hispanic	13,340	10.7	17,447	11.6
Men	6,628	5.3	8,537	5.7
Women	6,712	5.4	8,910	5.9
Hispanic	9,577	7.7	16,789	11.1
Men	5,756	4.6	9,902	6.6
Women	3,822	3.1	6,888	4.6
Asian and other, non-Hispanic*	3,855	3.1	6,482	4.3
Men	2,064	1.6	3,356	2.2
Women	1,791	1.4	3,126	2.1

*Includes Asians, Pacific Islanders, American Indians, and Alaskan natives.

SOURCE: Compiled by Janice Hamilton Outtz, using *Outlook 1990–2005*, BLS Bulletin 2402, p. 39.

Women Workers' Increasing Role

The advertisement of the recent past that proclaimed "You've come a long way, baby" is more applicable to the growing women's presence in the workforce than to their cigarette habits. (That many women today would object to the appellation "baby" is also a sign of the long way they have come.) The most dramatic workforce change since the 1960s is the growing number of women who have entered the outside-of-home workplace.

Some were motivated by the heightened expectations created by the civil rights and women's movements. These movements broke old stereotypes that limited the roles women could readily assume in society and created new opportunities for them. Affirmative action legislation passed in the mid-1960s and amended periodically thereafter protected women and other classes of nontraditional workers. Women were armed with higher levels of education, too, because women's organizations and the civil rights movement worked to get more women into the educational system.

Other women were motivated by economic considerations: the decline in the real incomes of one-wage-earner families sent women into the workplace to bolster family finances. Also, more women became the heads of their households due to the rising divorce rate and to the growing number of children born out of wedlock. Once in the workforce, the advantages of economic independence and the challenges of work proved attractive, and many of those who had a financial choice chose to remain.

The growth in the female labor force coincided and interacted with other changes. One was a swing in social norms. Combining a career and having a family became socially acceptable, even commonplace. (In some circles, women who do *not* work have felt defensive, as illustrated by the bumper sticker that reads, "I'm a housewife—and proud of it!") Further, two major workplace changes especially benefited women: the proliferation of part-time jobs and the rise in the service occupations. Both of these areas traditionally have been strongholds of the female labor market and offer increasing work opportunities.

For all of these reasons, over the past four decades, the female participation in the labor force has risen a stunning 23.6 percent. Whereas in 1950 only one in three women were in the labor force, by 1990 the figure jumped to more than one in two.

The increased presence of women in the labor force was heightened by the fact that the population pool of working-age women mushroomed by the 1970s. At that time, a large number of baby boomers reached their mid-20s and early 30s, age levels characterized by high participation in the labor force. Thus the growing female participation rate was not based on a static population but on a vastly expanded one.

The greatest increase in workforce participation occurred among white women. Between 1975 and 1990, their participation in the labor force grew by 11.6 percent, from 45.9 percent to a total 57.5 percent of the white female population.[38] However, demographer Janice Hamilton Outtz noted that this dramatic rise was partly due to the fact that a significant portion of women of color already were working. Among African-American women, for example, almost 49 percent were in the labor count in 1975; by 1990, the figure rose to almost 58 percent. Hamilton Outtz commented that their participation rate was actually higher because many held jobs, such as maids, cooks, and babysitters, not counted by the Bureau of Labor Statistics (BLS).[39]

White women also registered the largest increase of *any* group, accounting for almost half of the new labor force growth. Between 1975 and 1990, 15 million white women (including white Hispanic women) entered the workforce, pushing the number of white women from 32.5 million to 47.9 million.[40] Please see Figure 1-7.

Minority Workers

Another way that the labor force is more diverse is in its racial and ethnic makeup. As a result of the baby boom and immigration, the number of minority workers has increased. By 1990, racial and ethnic minorities accounted for more than 20 percent of the workforce, shown in Figure 1-6. Although an accurate picture of the change over time is somewhat obscured by the lack of separate data for Latino workers before 1980, data for 1981 indicates that the Latino fraction of

Figure 1-7. The Civilian Labor Force by Sex, 1975 to 1990, with Projections to 2005

(Numbers in thousands)

		Women				Men	
		Total women		White*		Men	
Year	Total	Number	Percent of total workforce	Number	Percent of total workforce	Number	Percent of total workforce
1975	93,775	37,475	40.0	32,508	34.7	56,299	60.0
1990	124,787	56,554	45.3	47,879	38.4	68,234	54.7
2005	150,732	71,394	47.4	58,934	39.1	79,338	52.6

*Includes white Hispanic women.

SOURCE: *Outlook 1990–2005*, BLS Bulletin 2402, p. 34.

the total increased 2.2 percent for the 1981–1990 period, growing from 5.5 to 7.7 percent.* African Americans also accounted for a larger share of the total. As Figure 1-8 illustrates, African Americans constituted 10.7 percent of the total workforce in 1990, a 1.1 percent increase over the 1975 figure. During the same period, the Asian workforce increased to 3.3 percent of the total. (Numerical differences between Figures 1-6 and 1-8 are due to the inclusion in the latter table of Hispanic workers in racial group counts.)

While the view of minority growth as a share of the total may seem modest, it already has made significant differences in the racio-ethnic profile of the workforce. And it is a trend that will continue, creating even greater changes in the future workforce, as discussed subsequently.

In terms of percent of change within the minority populations, Figure 1-8 illustrates that the figures are more dramatic. The African-American labor force grew almost 46 percent. The growth in the "Asian and other" group was a whopping 145 percent.

Figure 1-8. Share of U.S. Labor Force by Race and Hispanic Origin, 1975, 1990, and Projections for 2005

(Numbers in thousands)

Group	Labor force 1975 Number	Labor force 1975 % of total	Labor force 1990 Number	Labor force 1990 % of total	Labor force 2005 Number	Labor force 2005 % of total	Percent change 1975–1990	Percent change 1990–2005
Total	93,775	100.0	124,787	100.0	150,732	100.0	33.1	20.8
White*	82,831	88.3	107,177	85.9	125,785	83.4	29.4	17.4
Men	50,324	53.7	59,298	47.5	66,851	44.3		
Women	32,508	34.7	47,879	38.4	58,934	39.1		
Black*	9,263	9.9	13,493	10.8	17,766	11.8	45.7	31.7
Men	5,016	5.3	6,708	5.4	8,704	5.8		
Women	4,247	4.5	6,785	5.4	9,062	6.0		
Hispanic	NA	NA	9,576	7.7	16,790	11.1	NA	75.3
Men	NA	NA	5,755	4.6	9,902	6.6		
Women	NA	NA	3,821	3.1	6,888	4.6		
Asian and other†	1,643	1.7	4,116	3.3	7,181	4.8	144.9	74.4
Men	931	1.0	2,226	1.8	3,783	2.5		
Women	712	0.8	1,890	1.5	3,398	2.2		

*Includes people of Hispanic origin.

†Includes Asians, Pacific Islanders, American Indians, and Alaskan natives.

SOURCE: Compiled by Janice Hamilton Outtz, using *Outlook 1990–2005*, BLS Bulletin 2402, pp. 31, 34.

---

*Figure for 1981 is from U.S. Department of Labor, Bureau of Labor Statistics.

Projections for 1990
to 2005

Old news is new news, and the new and future news in the labor force has a familiar ring. Together diversity and baby boomers will continue to shape workforce trends. They will do so, however, in opposite directions. Baby boomers are significant in that they will be a waning force in the workplace. Diversity will be a waxing force. Following are workforce projections developed by BLS for the period 1990 to 2005.*

1990–2005 Projection: A Fall in the Baby Boomers' Share of the Workforce

Although they will still be the dominant generation in the workforce, by 2005 baby boomers will begin to pass from the scene. Boomers are projected to be less than half the labor force by 2005. Their numbers will peak around the year 2000, but their share of the labor force peaked earlier, around 1985, when they accounted for about 55 percent of the total.

1990–2005 Projection: A Slowing Workforce Growth Rate— But No Workforce Shrinkage

The labor force will continue to grow between 1990 and 2005, but at a slower pace than it did in the preceding 15-year period, when baby boomers were entering in swelling numbers. Subsequent generations have not duplicated their magnitude. Contrary to some fears, however, the labor force of the future will not shrink.† The BLS projects a 21 percent increase in the labor force between 1990 and 2005—an increase

---

*Labor force projections rely heavily on BLS figures provided by Howard N. Fullerton, Jr., "Labor force projections: the baby boom moves on," Outlook 1990–2005, Bureau of Labor Statistics, U.S. Department of Labor, Bulletin 2402 (Washington D.C.: U.S. Government Printing Office, May 1992), pp. 29–42. The BLS figures do not reflect the 1990 Census. When the Census Bureau revises population projections to include 1990 data, higher levels of net immigration plus recent developments in undocumented immigration will impact the projections and consequently will alter workforce projections.

†A common misconception is that the workforce of the future will shrink. This is based on the influential studies by the Hudson Institute, Workforce 2000, and its follow-on, Opportunity 2000, published in 1987 and 1988, respectively. The position taken in these studies is that a slowdown in labor force growth will create an aggregate labor shortage as employers compete for qualified workers. The view itself is open to question, as discussed below. But the first point is that the concept of an "aggregate labor shortage" has been misinterpreted by many as workforce shrinkage in absolute terms. The misconception was reinforced by statements in Opportunity 2000 that erroneously indicated that one of the major trends of the workforce of the future would be a falling number of workers (p. 3).

of 26 million people (for an overall total of 150.7 million by 2005).* See
Figure 1-9. This increase represents a decline of 12 percentage points
over the preceding 15-year period (1975 to 1990), when the labor force
grew 33 percent. The slowdown actually began in the mid-1980s, when
baby boomers began moving past peak levels of participation. The
future workforce slowdown will result as the baby bust generation
(children of the baby boomers) enters the workforce in much smaller
numbers than did their parents.

Figure 1-9. Slowing Labor Force Growth by Group

Group	1975 to 1990 Growth (millions)	1975 to 1990 % increase	1990 to 2005 Growth (millions)	1990 to 2005 % increase	Growth slowdown (percentage points difference) 1975–1990/ 1990–2005
Total labor force	31.0	33.1	25.9	20.8	− 12.3
Men	11.9	21.2	11.1	16.3	− 4.9
Women	19.1	50.9	14.8	26.2	− 24.7
White	24.3	29.4	18.6	17.4	− 12.0
Black	4.2	45.7	4.3	31.7	− 14.0
Asian & others	2.4	144.9	3.1	74.4	− 70.5
Hispanic	unavailable	unavailable	7.2	75.3	unavailable

SOURCE: Compiled using U.S. Department of Labor, Bureau of Labor Statistics, *Outlook 1990 to 2005*, p. 31.

The reference should have been to a falling number of *young, entry-level* workers. (In a section dealing with this trend, *Opportunity 2000* made it clear that *overall* the labor force will grow slowly to the year 2000 but that the youth labor force will decline. [p. 5.]) Inattentive readers may have found reinforcement for the notion of a shrinking workforce in the fact, traced by both studies, that a growing number of males are leaving the workforce.

The view that a slowdown in the labor force growth rate will invariably create a tight labor market is contested by Lawrence Mishel and Ruy A. Teixeira of the Economic Policy Institute. They noted that industrial competitors such as Germany and Italy have experienced declining labor force growth rates and *increasing* unemployment rates. They further pointed out that productivity growth influences labor market status and needs to be factored into any analysis of labor market trends. (Lawrence Mishel and Ruy A. Teixeira, *The Myth of the Coming Labor Shortage: Jobs, Skills, and Incomes of America's Workforce 2000*, Washington, D.C.: Economic Policy Institute, 1991.)

New statistical data has appeared since *Workforce 2000* and *Opportunity 2000* were published. Data released by the BLS in 1992 reverses the assumption of a declining youth labor force between 1990 and 2005. This data assumes 0.8 percent growth in the youth labor force (*Outlook: 1990–2050*, pp. 3–4). This new information, plus the economic downturn of the early 1990s, further weaken the prospect of a tight labor market.

*The BLS releases projections based on assumptions of low growth, moderate growth, and high growth. The projections cited here are from the moderate-growth series.

1990–2005 Projection:
Non-Hispanic White Workers Still
Dominant but Their Share of the
Total Will Decrease

White non-Hispanic workers will continue to be the dominant group in the labor force, comprising 73 percent of the total by 2005. See Figure 1-6. This figure however will represent a decrease in overall workforce share. The BLS projects a drop in the non-Hispanic white workforce of 5.5 percentage points between 1990 and 2005. A major factor in the decline will be the falling number of non-Hispanic white male workers, some of whom will be moving toward retirement. With a drop in numbers of 3.8 million, their fraction of the workforce will fall almost 5 percent. The number of non-Hispanic white women will increase, but they, too, will suffer a decline—albeit a marginal decline—in workforce share.

1990–2005 Projection:
An Increase in the Youth Labor
Force (Ages 16 to 24)

The decline in the number of young, entry-level workers in the 1980s will be reversed in the mid-1990s. This group will register a 0.8 percent increase for the 1990–2005 period.

1990–2005 Projection: Half of
the New Workforce Entrants Will
Be Women but There Will Be a
Slowdown in the Increase of the
Female Labor Force

Between 1990 and 2005, half of the new entrants will be women. The number of women workers will rise a substantial 26 percent, as indicated in Figure 1-7. Nonetheless, this is less than the increase in the women's labor force during the 1975 to 1990 period, when the swelling number of baby boom entrants caused the figure to rise 51 percent. The projected increase represents a growth of 6 percentage points in the rate at which women will participate in the labor force. By 2005, more than 6 of every 10 working-age women will be in the labor force—close to the rate for men. The slowdown in the increase may signify that a saturation point is being reached and that the proportion of women in the labor force will not increase much more in the future. The rate of increase in the participation of younger women in particular is expected to decline.

1990–2005 Projection: Lowering of Numerical Growth of Male Workers

The number of male workers also will increase at a slower rate during the 1990–2005 period. Figure 1-7 shows the 16 percent projected increase in the number of male workers. This contrasts unfavorably with the 21 percent growth during the preceding 15 years. Again, the slowdown will be driven by the fact that baby boomers are passing through the years of peak participation when they supply workers in record numbers. In the near future, the growth in their participation will level off.

1990–2005 Projection: Minorities as a Larger Segment of the Workforce but the Minority Growth Rate Will Slow Down

Minorities will continue to increase their share in the workforce during the 1990–2005 period. As the largest minority group in the labor force, African-American workers are expected to represent 11.8 percent of the total, with 17.7 million workers. Please see Figure 1-8. Hispanic workers will number 16.8 million, just over 11 percent of the total. The "Asian and other" group will constitute almost 5 percent, with 7.2 million workers.

The rate of minority increase, however, will slow relative to the preceding 15 years. The number of blacks are projected to increase 32 percent between 1990 and 2005. This is 14 percent less than the increase during the 1975–1990 period. The growth in the "Asian and other" population is projected at 74 percent—a sizable rise but nonetheless a sharp fall of 60 percentage points from the growth in the earlier period. The Hispanic worker population also will increase, by 75.3 percent.

Despite the slowdown in the minority growth rate, the minority growth rate is expected to be greater than that of the total workforce. The overall workforce change between 1990 and 2005 is projected at 20.8 percent, with white workers (including Hispanics) increasing by only 17.4 percent. The higher minority growth rate is attributable partly to higher minority immigration rates and increases in minority female participation rates.

1990–2005 Projection: An Increase in the Number of Older Workers

The future workforce will be grayer. During the 1990–2005 period, baby boomers will begin to move into the older-worker age group,

Figure 1-10. The Older Workforce, Age 55 and Older
(Numbers in thousands)

Group	1975 Number*	1975 % of total workforce	1990 Number	1990 % of total workforce	2005 Number	2005 % of total workforce
Total workforce	93,775	100	124,787	100	150,732	100
Men, 55 and older	8,937	9.5	8,818	7.1	11,994	8.0
Women, 55 and older	5,365	5.7	6,577	5.3	10,128	6.7
Men & women, 55 and older	14,302	15.3	15,395	12.3	22,122	14.7

*Numbers may not add exactly due to rounding.
SOURCE: Compiled using U.S. Bureau of Labor Statistics, *Outlook 1990–2005*, p. 35.

that is, workers aged 55 years and over. (The first boomers will turn 55 in 2001.) By 2005, more than 22 million workers will be 55 years or older. This represents an increase of 6.7 million people, a leap of 43.7 percent between 1990 and 2005 and a stunning 54.7 percent increase over the 1975 level. See Figure 1-10. The number of older women workers will increase most dramatically, jumping from 5.36 million in 1975 to 10.13 million in 2005, an 89 percent increase. Older male workers will also increase—from 8.94 million to 12 million, representing a 34.2 percent increase.

Despite the dramatic surge in numbers, the older worker share of the total will grow only 2 percent over the 1990 level because boomers will still be concentrated in younger age groups. The 2005 figure for older workers will actually represent a marginal decrease over the 1975 share.

References

1. George Will, "272 Words," *Washington Post*, August 6, 1992, p. A25.

2. Patricia Aufderheide, ed., *Beyond PC: Toward A Politics of Understanding* (St. Paul, Minn.: Graywolf Press, 1992), p. 229.

3. Arthur M. Schlesinger, Jr., *The Disuniting of America: Reflections on a Multicultural Society* (New York: W.W. Norton, 1992), pp. 137–138.

4. James Davison Hunter, *Culture Wars: The Struggle to Define America* (New York: Basic Books/Harper Collins, 1991), p. 43.

5. Henry Louis Gates, Jr., *Loose Canons: Notes on the Culture Wars* (New York/Oxford: Oxford University Press, 1992), p. 176.

6. Israel Zangwill, *The Melting-Pot* (New York: Macmillan Co., 1909), pp. 198–199.

7. Arthur Mann, *The One and the Many: Reflections on the American Identity* (Chicago: University of Chicago Press, 1979), pp. 136–148.

8. Quoted by Henry Louis Gates, Jr., "A Pretty Good Society," *Time*, Nov. 16, 1992, p. 85. (Bell does not comment on any models.)

9. Lawrence Fuchs, *The American Kaleidoscope: Race, Ethnicity, and the Civic Culture* (Hanover and London: Wesleyan University Press, 1990), p. xv.

10. John A. Garraty and Robert A. McCaughey, *The American Nation: A History of the United States,* sixth ed. (New York: Harper & Row, 1987), p. 870.

11. Stephen Steinberg, *The Ethnic Myth: Race, Ethnicity, and Class in America* (New York: Atheneum, 1981), p. 3.

12. R. Roosevelt Thomas, Jr., *Beyond Race and Gender: Unleashing the Power of Your Total Work Force by Managing Diversity* (AMACOM/American Management Association, 1991), p. 23.

13. *Ibid.,* p. 24.

14. Garraty and McCaughey, *op. cit.,* p. 295.

15. Lawrence H. Fuchs, *The American Kaleidoscope: Race, Ethnicity, and the Civic Culture* (Hanover and London: Wesleyan University Press, 1990).

16. Fuchs, *op. cit.,* p. 233.

17. *Ibid.,* p. 126.

18. Frank D. Bean, Barry Edmonston, and Jeffrey S. Passel, eds., *Undocumented Migration to the United States: IRCA and the Experience of the 1980s* (Washington, D.C.: The Rand Corporation and The Urban Institute, 1990), p. 27. Chapter 1 provides a detailed discussion of methods of estimating undocumented aliens. *Ibid.,* pp. 11–31.

19. Fuchs, *op. cit.,* p. 253.

20. *Ibid.,* p. 254.

21. Jennifer Cheeseman Day, *Population Projections of the United States, by Age, Sex, Race, and Hispanic Origin: 1992 to 2050,* Current Population Reports, P25-1092, U.S. Department of Commerce, Economics and Statistics Administration, Bureau of the Census, November 1992, p. viii.

22. Bean, Edmonston, and Passel, *loc cit.*

23. Day, *op. cit.,* p. xxvii.

24. John Pomfret, "INS Criticized for Not Acting to Stem Smuggling of Asians by Gangs," *Washington Post,* February 9, 1993, p. A4.

25. Al Kamen, "When Hostility Follows Immigration," *Washington Post,* November 16, 1992, pp. A1, A6.

26. Barbara Vobejda, "Study of Immigration in L.A. County Challenges Government View of Costs," *Washington Post,* September 4, 1994, p. A9.

27. *Ibid.*

28. Joseph R. Meisenheimer II, "How do immigrants fare in the U.S. labor market?" *Monthly Labor Review,* December 1992, pp. 3–19.

29. Michael Kinsley, "What Makes America," *Washington Post*, December 12, 1992, p. A21.

30. Tom Morganthau, "America: Still a Melting Pot?" *Newsweek*, August 9, 1993, p. 19.

31. "America's Welcome Mat Is Wearing Thin," *Business Week*, July 13, 1992, p. 119.

32. Day, *op. cit.*, October 1992 draft, p. xxiii. Projections presented in this report are based on moderate (middle series) projections by the Census Bureau.

33. *Ibid.*

34. Meisenheimer II, *op. cit.*, p. 14, Table 9.

35. William B. Johnston and Arnold H. Packer, *Workforce 2000: Work and Workers for the 21st Century* (Indianapolis, Indiana: Hudson Institute, June 1987), p. xx.

36. Fullerton, *Outlook 1990–2005*, p. 31.

37. *Outlook 1990–2005*, BLS Bulletin 2402, p. 34.

38. *Ibid.*

39. Janice Hamilton Outtz, unpublished commentary, March 1993.

40. *Outlook 1990–2005, loc. cit.*

41. U.S. Department of Labor, Bureau of Labor Statistics, *Geographic Profile of Employment and Unemployment* (annual) (Washington, D.C.: Government Printing Office).

2
Diversity and the New Economy

Organizations are sensitive to the human diversity in their workplaces, communities, and markets in response to a complex mix of ethical, legal, and economic reasons. In most organizations, the representation of different individuals and groups in influential positions is highly skewed toward groups that dominate by virtue of their majority status or economic and cultural power. In the American culture, dominance and subordination in organizations based on individual or group identity is regarded as unfair. Consequently, in nations such as our own that value equal opportunity, organizations are attentive to diversity for ethical reasons. In addition, the translation of those same values into legal protections in American law encourages attention to diversity in organizations in order to comply with statutory requirements promoting equal access and opportunity.

In American organizations, the implications of diversity for economic performance have received less attention than the ethical and legal issues associated with fairness and opportunity. In recent years, however, a flammable mix of economic and demographic changes has focused attention on the impact of diversity on the economic performance of organizations and whole economies. As a result, recognizing and valuing diversity is increasingly regarded as important for economic as well as demographic reasons. The economic rationale for recognizing and valuing diversity derives from two interconnected but separable trends. First, changes in the basic structure of economic competition already in progress are increasing the overall competitive importance of satisfying diverse customer and client wants and needs. As a result, successful organizations are increasingly attentive and sensitive to their diverse customer and client base. A second trend is that economic and technological changes are increasing the competitive importance of successful human interaction at work. In general in the new global economy, the ability of a diverse workforce to work well together and to interact successfully with an equally diverse population of customers and clients has become critical to competitive success. The growing importance of human interactions at work presents an added challenge in a diverse workforce and customer population such as our own.

Valuing Diverse Customers and Clients

For more than two hundred years, the engine of material progress was the idea of mass production—the use of machine technology and highly rationalized production systems to produce increasing volumes of *standardized* goods and services at lower and lower costs per unit produced.* Standardized goods and services presumed an equally standardized customer. But customers no longer want standardized goods and services. In the emerging new economy, plain vanilla isn't good enough anymore. There are a variety of reasons why, including:

- Increasing wealth
- Economic globalism
- The increasing value of human time
- The commercialization of household labor
- Consumer involvement
- Technological advances

Consumers now can afford more and are willing to pay more to get what they want. Increasing economic wealth contributes to diversity in demand in three ways. First, increasing wealth changes what people want. As people get richer, they devote a declining share of their wealth to the basics like food, clothing, and shelter. As people get richer, they use their growing discretionary income to pay for goods and services tailored to their own tastes. Second, growing wealth gives economic

---

*For a more thorough review of changes in competitive requirements and their impact on organizational and human resource requirements, see Carnevale, *America and the New Economy*.[1]

voice to underlying differences in ethnicity, culture, gender, religion, values, and other variations on the human theme that were there all along. Third, as people earn more, they begin to demand more intangibles in the marketplace. Wealthier consumers can afford to let intangible differences in products and services influence their buying. As incomes increase, consumers often are more willing to buy products and services that cater to their identity and values. Consumers want to see themselves and their values in the products and services they buy and in the organizations from which they buy them.

Economic globalism has also increased the economic returns resulting from acknowledging and valuing diversity. Increasing American buying power has been more than matched by extraordinary growth in the buying power of the rest of the world. As the world gets richer, trade increases and forces employers to respond to the global diversity in tastes. Higher incomes also give rise to international markets for national specialties such as Italian textiles, Japanese consumer electronics, and Swiss watches.

In the global economy, standardized goods and services are no longer good enough. The one-size-fits-all goods and services characteristic of the mass production era have given way to a growing diversity of tastes. In the increasing share of goods and services that compete in global markets, the bottom line is that, if a domestic organization does not satisfy diverse tastes, a foreign competitor will.

The increasing value and scarcity of time also encourages diversity in products and services. As the processes of getting and spending take more time, busy people want goods and services tailored to their diverse tastes and needs. Successful organizations are those that are both responsive to the diversity in consumer wants and needs as well as to their timely and convenient delivery.

The commercialization of household labor increases sensitivity to diverse customers. Busy families earn more but have less time to care for each other. In a more mobile workforce, extended families are not only busier, they are also more out of reach. Personal services—from parenting to laundering—that used to be provided in the home, the community, or through voluntary agencies from churches to private charities are now provided commercially. For instance, a growing share of meals are purchased or eaten outside the home or brought into the home pre-prepared. Child care and elder care have long since become commercial enterprises. Consumer demand for personal services is highly sensitive to variations in tastes closely connected to ethnicity, religion, age, and other cultural distinctions.

Expanding consumer participation in the production and delivery of goods and services further increases the sensitivity of markets to customer and client diversity. Consumer involvement always has been the hallmark of service delivery. For instance, the patient needs to interact with the doctor to formulate a diagnosis. The doctor who cannot relate to or communicate with a diverse clientele will be less successful. Customer involvement is nothing new in manufacturing either. Manufacturers always have expanded consumer demand for goods by inventing hardware that used unpaid consumer labor to produce the final good or service. Tools for home workshops and washing machines are examples of consumer goods that combine with unpaid household labor to produce final goods and services. Standardized manufactured goods that ignore consumer differences are less successful in diverse markets.

Although consumer participation is not new, there is now much more of it. As services become more personal, consumer participation and the need for sensitivity to differences increases. User-friendly manufactured goods, from personal computers to home entertainment centers, increase consumer involvement as well. Ultimately, these new service formats and flexible technologies allow consumers to tailor goods and services to their own tastes and needs. The full array of offerings, from self-service salad bars to VCRs, gives full expression to the array of tastes in a diverse cultural market.

New flexible information-based technologies are at the heart of the growing ability of institutions to respond to a diverse market. Flexible technologies—our old friend the computer in its various disguises—allow tailored production in manufacturing and user-friendly interfaces with customers that allow tailoring of both goods and services as they are consumed. We can manufacture everything from magazines to soups for every taste and tailor services from automated teller machine banking to computer dating. Moreover, the inherent flexibility of new technologies allows variety and customization at mass production prices.

Valuing Diversity on the Job

Economic and technological changes characteristic of an emerging new economy are increasing both the value and the importance of successful human interaction in the workplace. In a diverse culture and workforce such as our own, successful interaction between employees and customers is predicated on our mutual ability to acknowledge and value the differences among us.

The growing economic importance of successful human interaction at work stems from dramatic changes in the way our economy functions. In the old mass production economy, organizations competed principally on the basis of their ability to produce high volumes of standardized goods at low prices. Mass production systems encourage the view of workers as interchangeable cogs in the organizational machine, ignoring diversity among workers. In mass production systems, products and services are broken into their smallest reproducible parts. Parts are matched to rigid machines that continuously reproduce the same part of the final product or service. Component parts of products and services and single-purpose machines are assigned to employees with equally narrow and rigid job responsibilities. The mass production process is organized into hierarchical institutions with white collar and technical elites assigned broader roles and authority to orchestrate the work of narrowly assigned workers down the line into final products and services.

Mass production organizations have their virtues and remain the most common form of work organization. They have produced high quantities of standardized goods and services at low prices, resulting in dramatic increases in wealth since their inception in the early 1700s. Broadly assigned roles at the top of mass production hierarchies have historically belonged to representatives of the majority culture with diversity increasing downward in the institutional hierarchy. Diversity issues in mass production institutions center around two concerns that have more to do with the distribution of organizational status and earnings than the way diverse workers interact on the job. The distribution of earnings between managerial elites dominated by the majority culture and more diverse nonsupervisory workers has been a consistent concern. A second source of conflict centers on access to elite jobs at the top of the hierarchy and the broadly assigned roles, organizational power, and earnings they confer. But these persistent conflicts reflect economic much more than cultural differences.

Mass production institutions are fundamentally incapable of benefiting from more successful interaction among diverse workers. There are relatively few broadly assigned roles that rely on successful human interaction. These more general roles are concentrated at the top of the organization where employees are least diverse while the vast majority of employees have narrow and rigid task assignments down the line where diversity is greatest. Moreover, the core competitive advantage in mass production organizations lies in their ability to produce high volumes of standardized goods and services at least cost. Their central organizing principle is a corollary standardization of organizational practices and human interactions. Highly rationalized and bureaucratized structures promote uniformity and regimentation in human factors. Even diverse workers who climb the organizational hierarchy to take on more general roles do so only after they have successfully internalized the culture of impersonal uniformity essential to maintaining the core competency of the mass production organization.

Mass production organizations make diversity irrelevant by attempting to minimize or specify in advance every human interaction on the job. Functionaries who run the organization are guided by performance standards that emphasize impersonality at work and deny the importance of norms of behavior critical to effective social interaction on the job. In the end, the organization is driven by rules, procedures, and authority rather than trust and successful relationships among diverse workers. Workers in mass production organizations use only part of their skills on the job. They comply with narrowly assigned roles rather than bringing all their capabilities and experience to work.

A growing accumulation of evidence suggests that the historical dominance of mass production institutions is giving way to new organizational formats that rely on successful interaction among diverse employees for their success. These new organizational formats are driven by profound changes in performance requirements. In the new competitive environment, the ability to produce high volumes of standardized goods at low prices is not enough. Price is still a primary competitive advantage, but it has been joined by quality, variety, customization, convenience, speed, and social responsibility. These new competitive requirements increase the importance of human interactions on the job. Moreover, in a diverse workforce such as our own, the success of human interactions depends at least in part on the ability of organizations to acknowledge, value, and manage diversity.

Quality is the emblematic standard for the new competition. Organizations that provide quality need employees willing to take responsibility for more than their work effort or narrow job assignment. Organizations that provide quality need employees willing to take responsibility for the final product or service. Quality requires workers willing to make personal commitments to organizations, co-workers, and customers that are hard to imagine in impersonal mass production bureaucracies that either ignore or devalue differences in their workforce. Acknowledging, valuing, and managing differences are keystones to building the commitment necessary to produce quality products and services.

Quality, variety, customization, and convenience are performance standards that presume an ability within organizations to give customers what they want. In diverse global and domestic markets, the ability of organizations to give customers what they want requires a workforce with the capacity to empathize and communicate with a diverse customer base as they design, produce, and deliver goods and services. Organizations that compete on the basis of speed require flexible interactions among diverse workers that can be greatly enhanced in organizations that acknowledge, value, and manage diversity successfully. Organizations that are socially responsible are sensitive to diversity in their hiring and promotion, as well as in the design and delivery of product and service.

In order to meet new performance requirements, organizations are installing flexible information-based technologies. Flexible information-based technologies allow organizations to provide quality, variety, customization, convenience, and speed at mass production prices. At the same time, however, new flexible technologies require more successful interactions among diverse workers. New information technologies organize workforces into interactive networks that increase the volume of interaction and interdependence among diverse workers. Moreover, as new technologies perform a growing share of the repetitive physical and mental work, employees spend more of their time interacting with diverse co-workers and customers. As a result, acknowledging, valuing, and managing diversity are critical to successful exploitation of the unique capabilities of new information-based technologies.

In order to meet new standards and exploit new technologies, organizations are installing new organizational formats that cannot work without successful interactions among diverse workers. More flexible organizational formats are required in order to exploit flexible technologies. Flexible organizational formats empower diverse workers who are concentrated down the line in most organizations for two interrelated reasons. First, a substantial share of any organization's ability to provide quality, variety, customization, convenience, speed, and social responsibility comes at the point of production or service delivery and at the interface with the customer where diverse workers are concentrated. Second, new flexible technologies are widely distributed in organizations and available to diverse workers up and down the line.

As a result of both these realities, a growing share of organizations are flattening and pushing autonomy down the line where products are made and customers served. Mass production hierarchies used top-down authority to coordinate and integrate work while the new organizational structures allow workers up and down the line broad discretion to work together in order to meet consensus goals. Empowered workers need to be enabled with the ability to acknowledge, value, and manage the diversity among them if new organizational formats are to succeed.

New competitive standards and the flexible technologies and organizational formats they inspire have made work more dependent on social processes and successful interactions among diverse workers. As employees become more interdependent, social skills become more important. The technical knowledge necessary to perform a task must be accompanied by the more complex capability for assuming roles in the context of a diverse group.*

The fundamental social skill is the ability to manage oneself. Self-esteem is the taproot to effective self-management and successful interaction with others. People with low self-esteem tend to find it difficult to set goals and meet them. Low self-esteem can be encouraged by a failure of others to value diverse or individual group identities in the workplace. Self-awareness is also critical to self-management. Self-aware employees understand their impact on others and appreciate the differences in their own work, problem-solving, and communication styles and the styles of others.

As the frequency of personal interaction with co-workers and customers increases, the ability to communicate in a multicultural context becomes crucial. Employees must be able to listen and express themselves verbally and in writing. If individuals are to be effective in diverse groups, they need good interpersonal, negotiation, and teamwork skills. Interpersonal skills in a diverse workplace include the ability to judge the appropriateness of behavior and cope with undesirable behavior, stress, and ambiguity. Negotiation skills include the ability to manage and to defuse potentially harmful disagreements. Teamwork skills include the ability to cope with and understand the value of diverse team members' different work styles, cultures, and personalities and to provide and accept feedback constructively.

As work becomes more of a social process, the ability to influence diverse co-workers also becomes more important. Influencing skills include both organizational and leadership skills. Explicit power structures usually ignore diversity. Networks of diverse workers are after a part of the implicit power structure. Each organization is a bastion of implicit and explicit power structures and, to be effective inside the organization, every employee needs to understand both. At its most elementary level, leadership is the ability to influence diverse others. As group processes increase in importance, leadership skills become critical for every employee.

---

*For a review of skill requirements associated with new economic requirements, flexible technologies, and flexible work formats, see Carnevale, Gainer, and Meltzer, *Workplace Basics: The Skills Employers Want.*[2]

Greater autonomy and higher levels of human interaction at work challenge the competencies of even the most homogeneous workforces and present special challenges and opportunities in a diverse workforce and culture such as our own. Moreover, the challenge is greater because the greatest increases in autonomy and social interaction are occurring at the point of production, service delivery, and at the interface with the customer where diversity is greatest in the American economy. In the American case, this reality presents a dual challenge to recognize and value diversity down the line and to encourage a mutual trust and respect for diversity in organizations that are still predominately white, male, and homogeneous up the line.

Diversity and the Service Economy

The rapid growth in services of both employment and overall economic activity further increases the volume and importance of successful interactions among diverse workers and customers. The ability to empathize and interact with diverse others is at the core of services and the skill set required of service workers. The most noticeable trend in the shift toward the new economy is an acceleration in the shift toward service work and the increasing volume of human interactions inherent in service functions. During the 1990s manufacturing employment will actually decline by an estimated 300,000 jobs, and extractive jobs in agriculture and industry will decline by an equal number. In contrast, service jobs will increase by at least 17 million.

There are many reasons for the increasing share of service jobs. One is that people buy more services as incomes grow, satisfying their need for manufactured and agricultural goods early as they climb the income ladder. People can eat only so much and sleep under only one roof. As a result, services always absorb a rising share of increasing incomes. The share of jobs going to service workers is also increasing because we are able to make more and more agricultural and manufactured goods with fewer workers. Our agricultural output has increased astronomically over the century while agriculture workers have gone from almost half to less than 3 percent of the total workforce. The real value of manufacturing output per production worker has increased threefold since 1930, while production workers have declined from 27 percent of the workforce to 15 percent over the same period.

The competitive requirements of the new economy increase the importance of service functions and the diverse human interactions they bring in every job and every industry. As machines do more of the repetitive work, people spend more of their time interacting with others to deploy machine capabilities and meet new requirements for quality, variety, customization, convenience, and speed. In the new economy, every worker spends more time serving diverse internal and external customers. In addition, new competitive requirements increase the proportion of service jobs in every industry. For example, while manufacturing jobs are expected to decline in the aggregate, there will be almost a million new jobs in manufacturing companies for managers, sales, professional, and other service personnel over the decade.

Front-line workers are supported by an increasing number of service workers in more elongated value-added chains necessary to meet new competitive requirements. In 1930, every production worker was supported by 12 nonproduction workers. Today, every production worker is supported by a value-added chain of 21 nonproduction workers. The success of these value-added chains depends on the quality of human interactions among diverse individuals and groups both within and among institutions.

Diversity and High-Performance Workplaces

Studies of effective organizations, dating back to the experiments at the Western Electric Hawthorne Plant in the 1920s, tend to agree on the motivational underpinnings that encourage employees to elicit "discretionary effort" and support high levels of organizational performance. Those studies discovered a consistent hierarchy of four organizational characteristics.* The hierarchy of characteristics associated with effective organizations, according to almost 75 years of empirical study, consistently begins with the notion of voice—a sense among workers in high-performing organizations that they are allowed to speak on organizational issues and that they will be heard.

But the available evidence from various disciplines agrees that voice is not enough to guarantee high performance. The second step on the hierarchy of high-performance attributes is *involvement*—the belief among employees that they are not only heard but actually participating in organizational decisions. Voice and involvement encourage a sense of *procedural justice*—the belief that the processes for making decisions are fair.

---

*For an historical review of studies on organizational performance, see References 3, 4, and 5.

The third step on the hierarchy of high-performance organizational attributes is *distributive justice*—the belief by employees that not only are they heard and included in decisions but that the impact of decisions is generally fair.

The pinnacle of the hierarchy of organizational attributes is *trust*—an expression of faith in an institution to be fair, reliable, ethical, competent, and nonthreatening. Trust is an integral energy in organizations that makes all else possible. It encourages risk taking, learning, and positive views toward change. In low-trust organizations, behaviors are cautious and protective, learning is repressed and rarely shared, and change is feared and resisted.

Diversity adds another dimension to the classic hierarchy of attributes associated with successful organizations. In modern workplaces and markets, voices are diverse. Employees and customers do not feel they are being heard unless they are allowed to speak authentically rather than emulate the characteristic voice and communications style of the dominant group. Similar involvement loses its legitimacy unless it is grounded in a context that allows the expression of authentic differences in influencing styles. A sense of distributive justice is all the more difficult to achieve in organizations where rewards and power are concentrated in a single group.

Voice, involvement, justice, and, ultimately, trust are more difficult to achieve in diverse settings. There are ample findings in studies of organizations and group behavior to suggest that homogeneous groups with high levels of congruence in values can achieve a common sense of voice, involvement, distributive justice, and trust more easily than diverse groups.[6,7] But there are two important caveats that accompany these findings: First, while studies find less friction and more cohesion in homogeneous groups, they do not find that cohesion necessarily results in higher levels of motivation or superior performance. Homogeneous groups are more comfortable but not necessarily more effective. Homogeneous groups fall prey to an unhealthy conformity and groupthink. Second, an apparent conformity and the accompanying "don't rock the boat" ethic it tends to encourage can cloak important differences in interests, functions, and expertise that need to surface in the interest of improved performance.

Diversity and the Bottom Line

As organizations and customers become more diverse, the cost of a poor job in responding to diversity increases. In addition, the costs of failing to successfully manage diversity mount as organizations attempt to integrate more homogeneous elites with more diverse employees and customers down the line. In a world where diversity is inevitable, institutions that respond effectively will enjoy a measure of competitive advantage, and those that do not will suffer inevitable costs.

A growing body of research documents the more direct and obvious costs of not responding effectively to a diverse workforce. Evidence suggests that diverse workers are less psychologically committed to their employers and their jobs.[8] Other studies show that commitment predicts motivation and turnover rates. Empirical studies consistently show higher turnover rates for females, minorities, and people of color compared with white males without disabilities. Recent studies also show that blacks are significantly less satisfied with their careers compared to whites. Other studies show that female managers leave their jobs at much higher rates than men because of dissatisfaction with opportunity and slow career growth.[9] Although hard data on the benefits of responsiveness to diversity are rare, studies of flexible benefits, child care, and flexible work schedules show consistent cost savings in reduced absenteeism and in turnover.[10]

Taylor Cox and Stacey Blake provide a concrete example of potential cost savings from reduced turnover that might result from more effective responses to diverse workers:

> [L]et us assume an organization has 10,000 employees in which 35 percent of personnel are either women or racioethnic minorities. Let us also assume a white male turnover rate of ten percent. Using the previous data on differential turnover rates for women and racioethnic minorities of roughly double the rate for white males, we can assume a loss of 350 additional employees from the former groups. If we further assume that half of the turnover rate difference can be eliminated with better management and that total cost averages $20,000 per employee, the potential cost saving is $3.5 million.[11]

The Benefits of Diversity

Much of the initial thinking on the economic impact of diversity posed diverse workers and customers as a challenge to traditional organizations. Diversity was often viewed as a barrier to high performance that needed to be overcome. The general view has been that diverse employees were inevitable, given the demographics of the American workforce. In addition, competitive requirements in the new economy and the installation of new flexible technologies made the empowerment of diverse workers, concentrated down the line in most organizations, equally inevitable. Similarly, the emerging diversity of demand in both domestic and global markets challenged organizations to be responsive to diverse customers.

More recent findings on the impact of diversity suggest that diversity is not only a challenge and a barrier to high performance to be overcome but an asset to be cultivated.[12-15] An increasing volume of research literature and experience suggests that a sensitivity to diversity can enhance organizational performance. The findings on the benefits of diversity tend to fall into three broad categories: workforce quality, market sensitivity, and organizational agility.

The inevitability of a diverse workforce in American organizations suggests that organizations sensitive to diversity will be best able to attract and retain the best available human resources. As women, minorities, and people of color become an increased share of available workers, it becomes more important for organizations to be successful in hiring and retaining workers from these groups. A variety of publications and informal networks inform prospective female and minority workers on which organizations are most receptive. Companies, such as Merck and Xerox, that are in competitive labor markets actively promote and advertise their receptivity to women and minorities as an asset in recruitment. The ability to attract the best available talent in host countries is especially important for multinational organizations. Organizations that are insensitive to diversity at home are unlikely to be successful in recruitment and retention in host countries.[16]

Organizations sensitive to diverse employees are more likely to be attuned to diverse markets characteristic of both modern domestic and global competition. In the United States, for instance, Asians, blacks, and Latinos now represent more than half a trillion dollars in market power. People who like to work for organizations that are attentive to diversity are just as likely to want to buy from organizations that demonstrate a sensitivity to differences. In addition, there is compelling evidence that cultural differences do affect buying behaviors both in global and domestic markets.* Sensitivity to diversity inside organizations translates into greater sophistication in diverse markets. If it can be effectively mobilized, America's unique cultural heterogeneity and tolerance for differences gives us a natural advantage over less diverse and less tolerant nations.

USA Today deliberately hired diverse workers to better understand diverse markets and attributes much of the newspaper's success to its diversity strategy. Avon turned its sales around in once unprofitable

---

*For example, see Redding, "Cultural Effects on Marketing in Southeast Asia."[17]

inner-city markets by giving black and Latino managers authority over product development and marketing in downtown areas.

Research in a variety of disciplines demonstrates that diverse work groups are more agile. Work by Rosabeth Moss Kanter shows that organizations that employ diverse work groups by design tend to be more innovative.[18] An extensive body of research by Charlan Nemeth testifies to the flexible capabilities of diverse work teams. Nemeth's research builds on a long-standing body of work on group behaviors demonstrating the overpowering effect of majority views on diverse groups. This and other research shows that, in groups that encourage minority views, creativity and the ability to solve problems improve markedly. Nemeth's work finds that the mere presence of a minority viewpoint, even when the minority view is proven suboptimal, stimulates creativity among other group members. The presence of a minority viewpoint forces reexamination of basic assumptions. In addition, the presence of a minority viewpoint teaches the larger group the habits of mind and behaviors necessary for an open dialogue and frank discussion of alternatives and new ideas.[19,20] Work by Nemeth and others also suggests that diverse groups make better decisions because they have a broader base of experience from which to draw. Early studies at the University of Michigan showed that diverse groups provided higher-quality outcomes at three times the rate of homogeneous groups. Subsequent research confirming the Michigan studies traces the poor performance of homogeneous groups to the conformity of groupthink—an absence of critical thinking in homogeneous groups due to a preoccupation with maintaining group cohesion and solidarity. Other case studies, including those of the Kennedy Administration's decision to invade Cuba and the *Challenger* disaster, portrayed decision processes driven by groupthink. Nemeth and others have also found that the level of critical analysis is higher in diverse groups. In diverse groups, the problem-solving process consistently examined a larger number of alternative solutions and made a more thorough examination of assumptions and the impact of alternative decisions.[21]

Studies also show that diverse workgroups tend to be more agile, increasing organizational flexibility. Enhanced flexibility from diverse workgroups stems from a variety of factors. First, diverse workgroups learn flexibility in their interpersonal dealings that carries over into organizational processes. Second, there is some evidence that the life experiences of females and minorities result in flexible problem-solving styles that allow them to move more easily than majority males between dominant and subordinate roles as leaders and followers. In addition, a series of studies on bilingual and monolingual groups shows that bilingual groups have a higher level of cognitive flexibility.

The higher concentration of bilingualism among ethnically diverse groups provides indirect support for the notion that differences increase flexibility.[22]

In sum, diverse groups do have an ability to enhance agility in organizations because of the variety of perspectives brought to bear, a higher level of critical thinking because they are less likely to fall prey to groupthink. But the benefits of diversity do not occur automatically. Conscious steps must be taken to create environments that can realize the potential benefits of diversity in workplaces. Diverse workers are inevitable, but the benefits of diversity are not. As already discussed, homogeneous groups are naturally more cohesive, and cohesive groups have higher morale and fewer communications problems. People seek out homogeneous groups with clear status distinctions. The introduction of a female or minority boss, for instance, confuses status distinctions and creates dissonance. While homogeneous groups create comfort and cohesion, they do not necessarily result in higher performance. The inevitability of diversity in American work environments creates starkly different possibilities. Diversity left untended can be a barrier to high performance. At the same time, a sensitivity to diversity can result in performance improvements beyond those possible in more homogeneous groups.

References

1. Anthony P. Carnevale, *America and the New Economy* (San Francisco, Jossey-Bass, 1991).

2. Anthony P. Carnevale, Leila Gainer, and Ann Meltzer, *Workplace Basics: The Skills Employers Want* (San Francisco, Jossey-Bass, 1990).

3. David G. Carnevale, *Trust: Creating High Performing Public Organizations* (San Francisco, Jossey-Bass, 1994).

4. Eileen Applebaum and Rose Batt, *Transforming Production Systems in U.S. Firms, A Report to the Sloan Foundation,* January 1993.

5. Thomas Bailey and Donna Merritt, *Discretionary Effort and the Organization of Work, A Report to the Sloan Foundation,* August 1992.

6. Charlan Nemeth, "Dissent, Group Process, and Creativity: The Contribution of Minority Influence," in Edward L. Lawler, ed., *Advances in Group Process,* vol. 2 (Greenwich, Conn., JAI Press, 1985).

7. Taylor Cox, Jr., *Cultural Diversity in Organizations: Theory, Research and Practices* (San Francisco, Berrett-Koehler, 1993).

8. Taylor Cox and Stacey Blake, "Managing Cultural Diversity: Implications for Organizational Competitiveness," *Academy of Management Executive,* vol. 9, no. 3, 1991.

9. Felice Schwartz, "Management Women and the New Facts of Life," *Harvard Business Review,* January/February 1989.

10. Stewart A. Youngblood and Kimberly Chambers-Cook, "Childcare Assistance Can Improve Employee Attitudes," Personnel Administrator, February 1989; Jay S. Kim and Anthony Compagna, "Effects of Flextime on Employee Attendance," *Academy of Management Journal,* December 1981.

11. Cox and Blake, *op. cit.*

12. R. Roosevelt Thomas, Jr., "From Affirmative Action to Affirming Diversity," *Harvard Business Review,* March/April 1990.

13. Lennie Copeland, "Learning to Manage a Diverse Workforce," *Training,* April 1988.

14. Barbara Mandrell and Susan Kohler Gray, "Management Development That Values Diversity," *Personnel,* March 1990.

15. Katherine Etsy, "Diversity Is Good for Business," *Executive Excellence,* November 1988.

16. Nancy Adler, *International Dimensions of Organizational Behavior* (Boston, Kent Publishing, 1986).

17. S. G. Redding, "Cultural Effects on Marketing in Southeast Asia," *Journal of Market Research,* vol. 24, June 1990.

18. Rosabeth Moss Kanter, *The Change Masters* (New York, Simon and Schuster, 1983).

19. Charlan Nemeth, "Differential Contributions of Majority and Minority Influence," *Psychological Review,* vol. 3, April 1984.

20. H. C. Triandis, E. R. Hall, and R. B. Ewen, "Member Homogeneity and Dyadic Creativity," *Human Relations,* vol. 18, February 1965.

21. J. Simpson, S. Warchel, and W. Wood (eds.), *Group Process and Productivity* (Beverly Hills, Sage, 1989).

22. Naomi G. Rotter and Agnes N. O'Connell, "The Relationship Among Sex Role Orientation, Cognitive Complexity and Tolerance for Ambiguity," *Sex Roles,* vol. 8, May 1982.

3

Dealing with Difference in the Workplace: Equal Employment Opportunity and Affirmative Action

The preceding chapters trace how demographic factors have created a profile of diversity in our nation's workforce and why economic forces are making it imperative to deal with diversity in new ways. Workplace diversity has been a challenge for decades. The first stage was merely to recognize its existence. Since the 1960s when this challenge was first widely accepted, people have devised various means of dealing with difference in the work setting. Two sets of approaches have evolved: equal employment opportunity (EEO) and its offspring, affirmative action, which were born in the moral fervor of the 1960s; and what looks to be approaches of the future, valuing and managing diversity.

Each set has a different origin and responds to different levels of concern. Complementary in nature, they represent incremental responses to the changing facets of workforce diversity. EEO and affirmative action are government-mandated approaches. Valuing and managing diversity, which gained momentum in the 1980s, involve voluntary initiatives in both the business and the government sectors to deal with workplace diversity. The first set is a response to the moral imperative to right the old wrong of discrimination against certain workers. It outlaws discrimination and, through affirmative action, provides a legally mandated process to effect change in strictly prescribed ways, especially with regard to women and racial and ethnic minorities. Valuing and managing diversity represent a natural progression from EEO and affirmative action, and, in contrast to them, they take a positive approach to difference by focusing on the strengths of a diverse workforce. This second set of approaches is also more inclusive than affirmative action, broadening the concern to *all* identity groups in the workplace. Thus, affirmative action is driven by a push to comply with legal requirements; valuing and managing involves a pull to fulfill organizational potential.

Any initiatives dealing with a major issue such as workplace diversity are bound to spark controversy. And they have. While there is general agreement on the principle of EEO, opinion divides sharply as to whether affirmative action policies are justifiable and whether they have served their purpose and should be discontinued.

Unlike EEO and affirmative action, valuing and managing diversity are new frontiers. They are wide open territory, with people exploring new ways to cope. Public debate about them is still in the early stages, but some trends are clear. There seems to be consensus that valuing and managing diversity need to be permanent features of organizational policy, practices, and structures. Public discussion tends to be dynamic, focusing on improving techniques and expanding the definition of just who constitutes the diverse workforce. Unlike the acrimony surrounding affirmative action, sharing lessons learned is a major feature of discussions about valuing and managing diversity. Such discussions are providing insights that enable institutions to become progressively more effective in responding to the challenges of their diverse workforces.

Because discussion of the two sets of approaches ranges from acerbic, especially in the affirmative action debate, to brightly optimistic, it is often difficult to obtain a balanced view. To help provide such a balance, this chapter examines EEO and affirmative action issues and summarizes the main features of the debate. The next chapter explores the new issues involved in valuing and managing diversity.

By way of moving toward balance, it is important to recognize that few nations have attempted to deal with workforce discrimination to the extent that the United States has. We have officially banned discrimination, devised ways, however flawed, to ensure compliance, and a growing portion of both the private and public sectors are voluntarily trying to respond creatively to the challenges it presents. Amid the rancor of public scrutiny, we need to give ourselves credit.

Equal Employment Opportunity and Affirmative Action—The Legal Framework

From the turmoil of the 1960s rose the legal framework that officially banned discrimination in the workplace. Until the 1960s, the law largely, though not entirely, ignored racial and gender issues in the work setting. Theoretically it applied to everyone impartially. While this orientation was consistent with the cherished principle of equal treatment for all under law, reality did not work that way. Discrimination on the job was systemic. People of color and women routinely faced barriers to equal employment opportunity, such as discriminatory hiring practices and race- and sex-segregated lines of progression.

The legal edifice gradually erected against workplace discrimination, known collectively as EEO law, consists of federal laws, executive orders, state and local laws, federal regulations and guidelines, constitutional provisions, collective bargaining agreements, and court-made law.*

The most important of these was passed in 1964. The 1964 Civil Rights Act bans discrimination in voting, public places, federal programs, federally supported public education, and employment. Title VII of the act provides for equal employment opportunity for specified classes of workers. Title VII forbids employers, employment agencies, and unions to discriminate in employment and membership on the basis of race, color, religion, sex, or national origin. Title VII also creates its own administering agent, by establishing the Equal Employment Opportunity Commission (EEOC).

Banning discriminatory employment practices was just a first step. On the proposition that merely abandoning such practices would not ensure justice for groups that had long suffered discrimination, Title VII states that a court may order "affirmative action" as appropriate to

---

*An outline of EEO laws, orders, and agencies is found in Sedmak and Levin-Epstein, *Primer on Equal Employment Opportunity.*[1]

redress discrimination. (It did not, however, require affirmative action as a matter of policy—that was to happen later.) The precedent for affirmative action is found in labor relations law.[2] According to that law, employers discriminating against union members or people trying to organize a union may be required not only to stop discriminating but also to restore the individuals to the situation they would have held if there had been no discrimination.*

Because opponents of Title VII feared that racial disparity always would be construed as discrimination, agreement was reached to provide protection against reverse discrimination. Thus, Title VII states that employers are not required to give preferential treatment to any individual or group. Like the term "affirmative action," the exact meaning of "preferential treatment" was left unclear, and the meaning of the two concepts has been debated ever since.[3]

Although many areas of affirmative action are still being defined, it is clear that the concept covers not only hiring but also other employment practices such as promotions, transfers, and training and membership opportunities for protected classes of people. Its aims are clear: to compensate for past discrimination, overcome ongoing discrimination, and provide equal employment opportunities without regard to race, color, religion, sex, or national origin. (The prohibition of bias based on sex was not included until 1967.)

Just how these goals should be attained, however, is not spelled out in Title VII. That law merely states that following the determination of intentional discrimination, a court may order "such affirmative action as may be appropriate." The amended version of Executive Order 11246 is a little more explicit, requiring federal contractors and subcontractors to adopt "result-oriented" affirmative action programs that include identifying areas where minorities and women are underutilized (not represented in fair numbers) and establishing numerical hiring and promotion goals to correct the situation. The order also requires federal contractors to report periodically on their compliance efforts. Executive Order 11246 established the Office of Federal Contract Compliance Programs (OFCCP) to monitor federal contractors and subcontractors. The requirements of both Title VII and Executive Order 11246 were defined further by the EEOC and OFCCP.

---

*There were other precedents. In 1959, Vice President Richard Nixon, heading a special Committee on Contracts, recommended that federal contractors provide limited "preferential" treatment for qualified blacks who were seeking jobs. In the first official use of the term, an executive order issued in 1961 by President John F. Kennedy called upon federal contractors to take "affirmative action" to hire racial minorities to foster equal opportunity.

Other key elements in the antidiscrimination edifice include:

- *National Labor Relations Act of 1935 and related laws.* Employees covered by collective bargaining contracts were afforded protection under the law before unorganized workers. The National Labor Relations Act of 1935 and related laws make it unlawful for employers to participate with unions in discriminatory practices based on race, religion, or national origin, and forbid unions from discriminating in membership or other opportunities. Currently, organized workers with employment discrimination claims have an advantage over unorganized workers in that a grievance-arbitration procedure can frequently provide an additional means for seeking redress. According to a 1974 Supreme Court ruling (*Alexander v. Gardner-Denver Co.*), a union-represented employee who does not like the outcome of the grievance-arbitration procedure may pursue the claim in the courts under Title VII.

- *The 1968 Civil Rights Act.* Establishes criminal penalties for interference with a person's employment rights based on race, color, religion, or national origin.

- *EEO Act of 1972.* Extends Title VII coverage to include almost all private employers and labor unions with 15 or more persons; all educational institutions, employment agencies, and state and local governments; and labor-management apprenticeship and training committees. The Act also expands the powers of the EEOC.

- *The Rehabilitation Act of 1973.* OFCCP enforces Section 503 of this Act, which was the predecessor of the ADA's provisions on employment discrimination.

- *Age Discrimination in Employment Act (ADEA) of 1967.* Protects older workers (40 years and over) from job bias. In addition, the 1975 Age Discrimination Act and Executive Order 11141 specifically prohibit recipients of federal funds and federal contractors from engaging in discriminatory practices against older workers.

- *The Equal Pay Act of 1963, as amended.* Obliges employers to give equal pay for men and women performing similar work.

- *Vietnam Era Veteran's Readjustment Assistance Act of 1974.* Obliges federal contractors to take affirmative action on behalf of disabled veterans and qualified veterans of the Vietnam era.

- *Immigration Reform and Control Act (IRCA) of 1986.* Provides criminal penalties for employers who discriminate against legal aliens because they are aliens or look foreign. The 1986 IRCA was amended by the

Immigration Act of 1990, which, in effect, protects U.S. citizens by making it harder for foreign nationals to obtain employment.

- *Americans with Disabilities Act (ADA) of 1990.* Protects persons with disabilities by banning discriminatory employment practices against qualified people with disabilities, including requiring employers to provide such employees with reasonable accommodation in physical facilities; provides the same remedies as are available to other minorities under Title VII of the 1964 Civil Rights Act. The ADA also prohibits discrimination against persons with disabilities in other areas of public life. The Rehabilitation Act of 1973 forbids federal contractors to discriminate based on disabilities.

- *Civil Rights Act of 1991.* Extends the ban against racial discrimination, including extending the statutes of limitations and simplifying filing procedures. It offers for the first time substantial protection, including monetary awards, to members of protected groups subjected to intentional job discrimination, and it overrules key Supreme Court decisions including requiring employers to prove that challenged practices do not involve disparate impact and providing protection from job discrimination to U.S. citizens working overseas.

- *The Civil Rights Acts of 1866 and 1871 and Amendments to the Constitution.* These laws ban discrimination in employment. They have been used to redress discrimination cases based on race, alienage, and national origin; and cases in which, under state law, individuals have been deprived of federally ensured workplace rights. The 1866 law covers hiring but not posthiring practices, such as discharge and demotion. Certain Constitutional Amendments also bear on EEO law. These are the First Amendment (guarantees freedom of religion); Fifth Amendment (ensures due process of law); and the Thirteenth Amendment (prohibits slavery); and Fourteenth Amendment (forbids states to abridge federally conferred privileges).

- *State and local statutes.* State and local laws frequently provide greater on-the-job protection than federal law. In such cases, employers are subject to the more comprehensive laws in the jurisdictions in which they operate.

In addition to legislative and executive law, an evolving body of court-made law defines affirmative action.* These laws are not always consistent, and there is dynamic tension between court-made law and

---

*A synopsis of major Supreme Court decisions on affirmative action is found in Sedmak.[4]

the legislative process. In an era in which the Court has tended toward greater conservatism on affirmative action, Congress has occasionally overturned court-made affirmative action rulings. For example, in cases involving disparate impact, the 1991 Civil Rights Act reverses an earlier Supreme Court ruling (*Wards Cove Packing Co. v. Atonio*, 1989) by placing on the employer, rather than on the employee, the burden of showing that the challenged practice is job-related and a business necessity. This issue has come full circle under the law because the *Wards Cove* ruling placed the burden of proof on the employee/plaintiff; however, the pre–*Wards Cove* position under legislative law had placed it on the employer/defendant. Thus the 1991 Civil Rights Act reestablished the pre–*Wards Cove* position.*

At present, organizations with federal contracts exceeding $50,000 must go beyond adopting an affirmative action strategy to developing an annual, written affirmative action program (plan). Such plans involve establishing goals (percentages) and timetables by which members of protected classes are to be represented at each level in the institution. The distinction is fine between affirmative action goals, which are mandated, and quotas, which are not. Technically, a quota is a rigid number that must be met or penalties are imposed. One problem with a quota, as the 1978 Supreme Court ruling in *Regents of the University of California v. Bakke* illustrated, is that fixed quotas provide the basis for reverse discrimination charges. Goals, on the other hand, are targets that an organization works toward but will not be punished for if they are not achieved, if there are valid reasons for the shortfall. Organizations required to develop a written affirmative action plan must show that they are making good-faith efforts toward achieving their affirmative action goals. (Good-faith efforts are voluntary and range from college recruiting efforts that focus on people of color and women to sponsoring functions of minority and women's professional associations.) Affirmative action plans involve meticulous statistics-gathering efforts and documentation and are subject to periodic OFCCP audits.

Several federal agencies, involving thousands of people, deal with EEO law. In addition to those already named, they include the National Labor Relations Board, the Office of Management and Budget, and local Fair Employment Practices agencies. The EEOC and OFCCP, however, are the major players, and there are significant dif-

---

*An analysis of other Supreme Court rulings that were overturned by the 1991 Civil Rights Act is found in Mickey and Oliner, "The Impact of the New Civil Rights Act of 1991 on Employers."[5]

ferences between them. The EEOC, an independent federal agency, administers Title VII of the 1964 Civil Rights Act, the ADEA, the Equal Pay Act, and the ADA. The EEOC is reactive in the sense that it investigates and conciliates charges of discrimination that are brought before it. It does not actively seek out instances of discrimination.

In contrast, the OFCCP, part of the Department of Labor, functions more proactively. Tasked with administering and enforcing Executive Order 11246, the OFCCP monitors federal contractors through periodic audits to ensure compliance. (On occasion, the OFCCP also investigates charges of discrimination.) Currently, the OFCCP monitors some 117,000 federal contractors, employing more than 28 million people, who are required to develop affirmative action plans. Contractors found to be in noncompliance may have federal contracts terminated or denied.

The Affirmative Action Debate

When it comes to affirmative action, maybe there is one thing everybody can agree on: it is confusing. It involves legal subtleties that are hard to understand. Its moral issues are arguable from multiple points of view. What's more, though it has many committed supporters, affirmative action is under attack from all sides—its beneficiaries as well as those who consider themselves its victims, and sometimes these are the same individuals. There is even disagreement on just what constitutes the central issue. Observing that it is hard to hold an honest conversation about affirmative action, black scholar and lawyer Stephen Carter noted, "It may be harder still to hold an honest conversation about the reasons why it is hard to hold an honest conversation about affirmative action."[6]

Like Carter in his book, we in ours try to do so, though using a very different approach. While much thinking on affirmative action occurs in law review articles, we focus here mainly on the public debate, the debate that has come to most of us through the press and other popular media. To place in context the welter of public opinion and emotion over affirmative action, we provide a brief historic background to the debate. We then identify basic attitudes that seem to underlie views on affirmative action and from there examine the shape of the debate. Any review of an issue so complex risks running headlong into further controversy. That is not the aim of this discussion. The aim is to provide a framework for understanding the major issues being addressed by the public without distorting the range and complexity of opinions held. The aim is to hold an honest conversation.

The original EEO policies addressed individual rights. Based on the principles of democracy and egalitarianism, they focused on, among other things, equality of opportunity for individuals through the elimination of Jim Crow laws and the passage of legislation banning employment discrimination, such as Title VII. Not surprisingly, there was little initial understanding of just what institutions needed to do to comply. Organizational responses were haphazard and job discrimination charges ballooned. Court findings of violations of Title VII resulted in a proliferation of law suits.

At the same time, it became clear that while EEO laws aimed at eliminating current discrimination, they did little to alter the impact of long-standing discrimination. Many people of color, especially the poor and uneducated, were so victimized by the cumulative effects of historic discrimination that they were incapable of taking advantage of the new opportunities available to them under law.*

This combination of circumstances galvanized business, government, and civil rights organizations in a search for a different tack. Limited arrangements were tried first. In 1969–1970, the government implemented the Hometown approach. Aimed mainly at the construction industry, Hometown plans called for antidiscrimination agreements between local contractors and the unions that usually controlled access to jobs. The plans were not highly successful for varying reasons including periodic downturns in the construction industry.

By the early 1970s, a more systemic means of resolving the issues was introduced. This was affirmative action. Based on principles established in Executive Order 11246 and other mandates, officials began establishing specific ways to measure affirmative action and requiring compliance by government contractors. As we have seen, affirmative action addressed several issues. It aimed at redressing past discrimination by focusing on protecting group rights. By ensuring adequate minority representation in organizations, affirmative action moved beyond merely banning discrimination to actively expanding the numbers of minority persons in the workforce, including presumably a greater portion of the poor and uneducated. Affirmative action consists of positive, nondiscriminatory measures to ensure fair treatment in the workforce for qualified employees or applicants who face employment barriers because of such factors as their race, sex, and national origin. Affirmative action does not require the selection of the unqualified, nor does it require the relaxation of employment selection standards.

---

*For an elaboration of this argument, see Wilson, *The Truly Disadvantaged: The Inner City, the Underclass, and Public Policy.*[7]

By providing for preferential treatment for individuals based on their membership in protected groups, affirmative action is color- and gender-conscious. (In contrast, the EEO focus is color- and gender-blind. Forbidding discrimination based on race, gender, and other specified characteristics, the original EEO laws aimed at impartial treatment for all.) In effect, affirmative action policies stated that to the extent an institution is not remedying past discrimination, it is engaged in unlawful discrimination. Affirmative action was meant to be temporary, a remedy for a gross injustice threaded throughout American history. Once adequate amends were made, preferences were to quietly disappear into the sunset like the cowboy hero in Hollywood westerns.

Affirmative action policies also offered surer protection for companies against expensive lawsuits. Federal guidelines and regulations required that organizations observe specific reporting and monitoring procedures. Affirmative action also represented a means of trying to break barriers to EEO administratively so that disputes could short-circuit the legal process. Existence of affirmative action plans tends to cut the number of lawsuits and strengthens an employer's ability to successfully argue that it did not discriminate.

Since the 1970s much of the public discussion about affirmative action has polarized into well-entrenched camps. Critics were bolstered by support from two administrations and an increasingly conservative federal judiciary as well as by the resentment of whites impatient about the temporary policies that showed no sign of fading. Some used the term "quotas" as a scare word to whip up further opposition and to flog affirmative action supporters.* Hunkered down under these blows, proponents meanwhile were engaged in a kind of internecine warfare. Moderates were on guard against charges from more extremist proponents to the effect that any reevaluation of preferential treatment indicated a lack of political correctness. Amidst it all, what suffered most, perhaps, was free public debate. Many concluded that fresh thinking about affirmative action was not worth the cost, that the best they could do was try to preserve the gains made in the 1960s and 1970s.

---

*The suspicion many blacks harbored about the affirmative action views of the conservative political establishment was uttered by Randall Kennedy when he said, during the 1980s, that even if decisive evidence pointed toward the elimination of affirmative action policies, many supporters would probably reject it based on "their fears of their opponents." He maintained that "a tenacious and covert resistance to further erosion of racial hierarchy" explained much of the conservative establishment's racial policy, "including its attacks on affirmative action."[8]

Recently, however, the logjam in the debate has been breaking up. New ideas are beginning to flow. Driven by a recognition that standing in the same spot can only be self-defeating, some have begun searching for alternative approaches, while others are finding fresh ways of reaffirming their support for or opposition to preferences.

The discussion that follows provides a summary of recent thinking about affirmative action. Three basic attitudes seem to shape the current debate. Although congruent in some respects, they tend to lead to very different formulations of the central issue. One is grounded in the predicament of minority groups in society. The second hinges on the issue of perceived fairness. The third seems to be rooted in pragmatic considerations. The three perspectives are not exclusive, and they— especially the third—may be held in conjunction with either of the other two.

Another view is what we term "the business perspective." This perspective may be held in combination with others, but it differs from them in an important way. The attitudes previously identified impact how one forms the central affirmative action issue, but they do not predetermine support or opposition. The business perspective, in contrast, is predetermining: Most companies seem to support preferences.

From the Minority Plight

The first attitude is rooted in the minority experience in our society and is the natural vantage point from which many minority spokespersons view the issue. (Blacks have been the most outspoken minority group on affirmative action, and comments by black spokespersons form the core of the data used in this chapter. But, of course, affirmative action protects Hispanics, Asians, and Native Americans too. It also covers women regardless of race and ethnicity. As the number of Hispanics and other people of color in the workforce increases, their views on affirmative action will undoubtedly receive wider attention.) This attitude focuses on the issue of responsibility. The basic problem is determined by where one places *primary* responsibility for remedying the predicament. There seem to be two options: The first focuses on the racism that has been and continues to be inherent in society and carries the logical implication that society has an obligation to redress the situation. The second turns on the need for minorities to take stock of their shortcomings and advance under their own steam instead of relying on preferential treatment with its demoralizing psychological effects.

There is division in the black community over the nature of the central issue. Some, like Thomas Sowell, of the Hoover Institution, assert that the focus needs to be on efforts at self-development. The road ahead, maintains Sowell, needs to be a "struggle between the inherent requirements of quality education and the habits, attitudes, and beliefs of people who have not had to deal with such requirements before."[9] For others, the main focus is on the legacy of oppression that has victimized blacks. Scholar and civil rights activist Roger Wilkins of George Mason University exemplified this focus when he said, "our fundamental problem is not in our fears or uncertainties or defensiveness. Our fundamental problem is that we live in a racist society that's tilted against us."[10] Of course, an individual's views may evolve over time, and he or she may swing between the two. Proponents of each often acknowledge validity in the other. Wilkins, for example, recognizes the need for blacks to do more for themselves, referring to "a lot of effort required on our part to move us out of our predicaments." At the same time, Sowell refers to "the unique historic suffering of blacks" in the United States.[11] The difference remains one of emphasis.

Those who place primacy on past and ongoing oppression (what we call here, for the sake of brevity, "the minority plight") seem likely to support affirmative action as an important means of leveling the playing field. The prevailing sentiment here is that preferential treatment is just, because it helps offset the legacy of racism. Randall Kennedy, of the Harvard Law School, expresses this view when he states, "affirmative action should generally be retained as a tool of public policy because, on balance, it is useful in overcoming entrenched racial hierarchy."[12] Because we have already examined aspects of the argument favoring affirmative action, we will not cite statements by proponents here. There does, however, seem to be a sense that most people of color as well as civil rights organizations support some form of affirmative action.[13]

Where support decreases among minorities is over just what is involved in affirmative action. "Quota" seems to be a scare word, among both blacks and whites. A 1991 Harris nationwide poll found that 71 percent of white respondents and 93 percent of black respondents favored federal laws requiring affirmative action programs, "provided there are no rigid quotas." In contrast, a 1991 Gallup poll asking if quotas "are necessary to accomplish fairness in education, hiring and promotion" found much less support. White backing dropped to only 29 percent of respondents; black support also dropped, but by less: 61 percent of blacks felt quotas were necessary.[14] While these polls reflect nothing about the attitudes underlying these reactions, it is clear that backing among black Americans is greater than among whites and that it drops among both groups when quotas are invoked.

There seems to be a second attitudinal framework among individuals whose primary focus is on the plight of people of color. These are people who advocate individual effort and are critical of affirmative action. Their numbers may be relatively small, but they are highly vocal. Sometimes described as "neoconservatives," advocates such as Sowell and Shelby Steele, of San Jose State University, are among the most articulate and sometimes vehement opponents of affirmative action.* An essential problem in Steele's view is that "racial representation is not the same thing as racial development, yet affirmative action fosters a confusion of these very different needs. Representation can be manufactured; development is always hard-earned."[16] Sowell maintains that preferential treatment and improvement programs are incompatible and affirmative action needs to be dropped because assurance of preferential treatment erodes incentives to improve.[17]

Some of those who have benefited from affirmative action consider themselves among its greatest victims. They decry its undermining psychological effects. They maintain that affirmative action tends to reinforce the view held by some whites that blacks are inferior, incapable of competing without the extra boost from preferential policies. And they add that when black Americans do prove their merit, whites are sometimes surprised. H. Naylor Fitzhugh, retired vice president of PepsiCo, recounted instances in which business associates, after congratulating him on an idea, added, "'It's hard to remember you're black.' Now that's hardly a compliment," Fitzhugh observed dryly.[18]

Maybe an even more important effect of affirmative action is that blacks themselves may suffer a sense of victimization. Stephen Carter has a lot to say about that. As one of the youngest professors to receive tenure at Yale Law School and himself a middle-class graduate from an Ivy League school, Carter has no doubts about his brilliance or about his ability to make it on his own. Yet, in his book *Reflections of an Affirmative Action Baby,* Carter relates how he benefited from affirmative action each step of the way, and he finds it a mixed blessing.[19] He resents affirmative action for denying him the chance to prove he could have done it on his own.

Although Carter may be exempt from self-doubt about his abilities as a result of preferential treatment, many blacks and other minority group members are not. And there is another, perhaps steeper, price

---

*The terms "conservative" as well as "neoconservative" are considered pejorative among black people, not because they are hostile but, as Stephen Carter explains, "it is far better at explaining what is wrong with civil rights than what is right with them; because it seems far more comfortable standing against black people when it thinks they are wrong than standing with black people when it thinks they are right."[15]

for preferential treatment. Steele maintains that affirmative action encourages many blacks to blame their failures on white racism rather than on their own shortcomings.[20] In such cases, he argues, "they [use] their race to evade individual responsibility."[21] For these reasons, he believes that blacks "now stand to lose more from it than they gain."[22]

Other critics argue that affirmative action policies do not benefit all blacks. Although not a conservative, William Julius Wilson, of the University of Chicago, adopts this position. In his seminal work *The Truly Disadvantaged*, Wilson argues that affirmative action programs help working- and middle-class blacks, but they do little for the ghetto underclass who are socially isolated and have a high rate of joblessness. "The crucial point is not that the deteriorating plight of the ghetto underclass is associated with the greater success enjoyed by advantaged blacks as a result of race-specific programs, but rather that these programs are mistakenly presumed to be the most appropriate solution to the problems of all blacks regardless of economic class."[23]

From the Fairness Axis

While from the perspective of the first attitude about affirmative action minority groups are the referent, from the perspective of the second attitude perceived fairness is. Here, the degree of fairness is the main measure of affirmative action, and opinion ranges along an axis from fair to unfair.

We need to make clear that evaluating preferences necessarily involves making a judgment about fairness, whatever the underlying attitude. We are not implying that whites judge only along the fairness axis and people of color only on the basis of the minority plight without considering fairness—for, in fact, the latter is centered in the unfairness of the historic and present circumstances faced by people of color. We are saying that those who judge on the basis of the minority plight (and they seem to be mainly people of color) come at the issue from a different angle than those (people of color and whites) whose main hinge is the fairness criterion.

Susan D. Clayton and Faye J. Crosby comment on the attitude in *Justice, Gender, and Affirmative Action*. Clayton, of Wooster College, and Crosby, of Smith College, write,

> Probably the greatest determination of one's attitude toward affirmative action is one's conception of fairness: whether one thinks it is fair for women and men to be largely restricted to separate spheres or for extraeconomic factors to be taken into account in allocating economic resources.[24]

Their comment can be generalized beyond gender. Clayton and Crosby clearly believe it is fair to weigh extraeconomic factors into the balance. They "do not sanction the sacrifice of individual rights but feel that affirmative action surpasses other systems, including equal opportunity, in ensuring that justice obtains at both the societal and the individual level."[25]

Paul R. Spickard, of the Cultural Development Institute in Aromas, California, speaks on the fairness theme from a Christian perspective. Himself twice a victim of reverse discrimination, Spickard states:

Affirmative action may not always be fair. But I am willing to take second best if overall fairness is achieved. After all, for Christians, fairness—often translated in our Bibles as "justice" or "righteousness"—is a fundamental principle by which God calls us to live. And affirmative action is an appropriate part of a larger program aimed at achieving the godly goal of putting other's welfare before our own.[26]

Political commentator Charles Krauthammer also uses the fairness criterion, though from a different perspective. He maintains that affirmative action is a "breach of justice" because it asserts that the rights of the disadvantaged override those of individuals (aggrieved whites); group entitlements supersede individual rights. But he observes that this breach of justice is not unique; public policy frequently discriminates against groups for the sake of society as a whole. Krauthammer states that the issue finally cannot be adjudicated on the grounds of justice. In effect, he invokes a higher justice, namely the "overriding goal" of rapidly integrating blacks into American life.[27] If affirmative action were eliminated, he maintains, "justice would perhaps score a narrow, ambiguous victory. American society would suffer a wide and deepening loss."

One of the reasons most frequently cited for opposition to preferences is that they are unfair. Opposition is just as heated, maybe more so, among those responding based on the unfairness premise as it is among those whose attitudinal underpinning is grounded in the minority plight. In one respect, the arguments of the two groups are analogous. Grappling with the individual-versus-group dilemma, some in the latter group come down hard in favor of the individual. So do those in the former group.

People opposing preferential treatment on the fairness principle do so on the grounds that the policy is inequitable. By favoring some, they argue, it discriminates against others. By protecting groups, it discriminates against the individual. As Nathan Glazer puts it, preferential treatment "offends against what many have believed to be the main thrust of liberalism in America, the primacy of individual rights. The outrage an American feels when he (or she) is deprived of a job or a promotion because of his race or ethnic background is no less when that person is white than when he (or she) is black, or yellow, or brown.[28] *Business Week* phrases the "painful contradiction" more succinctly: "Compensating for past discrimination against some people can create fresh discrimination against others."[29]

And the "others" being penalized are usually white workers. It boils down to reverse discrimination, some claim. Jared Taylor, for example, asserts, "Our crusade to undo the mischief of the past has done mischief of its own, and by formally discriminating against whites, it has stood both justice and the law on their heads."[30] Taylor adds that the terms "affirmative action" and "equal opportunity" are, in effect, exact opposites because affirmative action means giving preferential treatment to some, and this can only be accomplished at the expense of others (whites), thereby denying them equal opportunity.

Only a limited number of people consider themselves to have been victims of reverse discrimination. According to a survey undertaken by Gordon Black Associates in 1984, one in ten white males polled felt they had experienced some form of reverse discrimination.[31] Of course, such a figure can only be suggestive of reality, but whatever the actual percentage, victims of reverse discrimination can be vehement opponents of preferences. (Though some transcend self-interest and support preferences, as, for example, does Paul Spickard, quoted elsewhere in this chapter.) In his book *Invisible Victims*, Frederick Lynch examines the impact of affirmative action on intellectual discourse and characterizes the ideological taboos it has spawned as "the new McCarthyism."[32]

The economic recession of the 1990s seems to have acted as a catalyst for anti–affirmative action sentiment. As many organizations downsize, a growing number of white workers feel their jobs are on the line when minorities receive hiring preferences.[33] These fears are heightened by technological changes that have cut out low-end jobs.

There is also resentment at the longevity of a policy designed to be temporary. Affirmative action was to end when the disadvantaged achieved equality. Some 30 years into affirmative action, neither has there been such an achievement nor is an end to the policy in sight. Some whites feel they have been patient long enough. Nathan Glazer points out that the protected groups are as unlikely to give up preferences as government agencies are to give up the oversight powers they have attained.[34] Opponents are not the only ones who think that affirmative action is an idea whose time has gone. Some supporters express that opinion, too, although for different reasons. One reason is the mounting weight of political opposition. Another is the departure of buoyant economic conditions under which affirmative action thrived.*

Some who hold the unfairness view assert that Americans agreed to a preference policy in the first place due to a sense of guilt. Terry Eastland and William Bennett maintain that the reason the majority voluntarily agreed to subordinate their rights to those of the minority was "white Americans were adjudged guilty of imposing the condition of slavery, and were held responsible for its manifestations....to redeem itself, the majority was called upon not only to ensure freedom and opportunity for blacks but to furnish `reparations' as well."[36]

We have been discussing the unfairness argument in terms of ideological belief and a sense of victimization. The argument also may be influenced by three other factors: racism, the "just world" assumption, and political advantage. Racism is an accusation readily used against opponents of affirmative action. This is unfair. Some opponents undoubtedly are animated by racist sentiment. But many are not. Such accusations only heighten tension and further polarize debate.

Another factor is the "just world" assumption. Dear to many, this assumption holds that the world is basically a fair place. Psychologists Clayton, Crosby, Max Lerner, and others label this a "fundamental delusion."[37] At core, the assumption concerns a passion for justice and fair play. But psychologists have found that many Americans are willing to rationalize extensively in order to convince themselves that they and others have received fair treatment. "People get what they deserve" is the refuge when evidence fails to support the fair treatment premise. In its application to affirmative action, logic suggests that the assumption may work in subtle ways to reinforce opposition. It may translate into a devaluing of the injustices experienced by blacks and thus undermine the justification for preferential policies.†

Political advantage is a final factor that may motivate opponents. In recent years, opposition to affirmative action has been a device effectively used to garner white support. Political commentator Ronald Brownstein maintains that as white resentment of affirmative action has deepened, preferences have "joined busing, welfare, and crime on the list of issues the GOP has used to insinuate to whites that Democrats favor minorities."[38] Some have accused conservative politicians of using opposition to preferences to drive blue-collar Democrats into the Republican camp.[39] As a strategy, opposing affirmative action

---

*For the economic argument, see Browne, "The Road to Rectification."[35]

†In their discussion of the just world assumption, Clayton and Crosby draw other interpretations but do not explicitly draw this one.

as a means of gaining political advantage works covertly in a sense; that is, it works behind some form of the unfairness argument.

From the Pragmatic Attitude

"Where from here?" is the question common to the pragmatic attitude regarding affirmative action. More than a decade of a political environment unfriendly to preferential policies, reinforced by recognition of the limits of such policies, plus growing public resistance to their continuation, has caused many to search for fresh options. The pragmatic attitude, a third attitudinal perspective, may involve a critique of affirmative action, acceptance, or both. Its focus is primarily on finding new ways to meet the challenges of diversity, in the workplace and in society as a whole. The attitude is a reflection of a new candidness in the ongoing debate over affirmative action.

Among the most influential voices is that of William Julius Wilson. Wilson maintains that neither affirmative action nor equal opportunity programs addresses the problems of the ghetto underclass, the "truly disadvantaged." He asserts that by 1970 equal opportunity programs, with their focus on individual opportunity, revealed their inability to provide opportunity for all segments of minority groups. Group entitlements provided by affirmative action are no more effective. What is needed, he maintains, are policies that are universal rather than race-specific. According to Wilson, the general public has become wary of affirmative action programs targeted to poor minorities but would be willing to support an economic and social reform program that applies to all of society. Such a comprehensive program (comprising employment polices and labor-market strategies, including training) could then contain specific programs targeted to the needs of the underclass regardless of race and ethnicity.[40]

A growing number of people agree with the direction of Wilson's thinking. Paul Starr certainly does. In the first of a series of recent articles exploring alternatives in *The American Prospect*, Starr, of Princeton University, states that he personally favors affirmative action but finds that, in a conservative political and judicial environment, its costs outweigh its benefits.[41] Believing that even if preferential policies were curtailed, their import would be upheld under antidiscrimination law, Starr recommends adopting policies benefiting middle- and low-income Americans, regardless of race, plus reconstructing society in minority and especially black communities through strengthening "intermediate" institutions. He maintains that "reparations" should be paid to black institutions in particular because "the obligations of the United States to black Americans are historically singular."[42] He also notes that the conservative shift in the Supreme Court may be "a blessing in disguise" because it may force liberals and progressives to devise alternatives that address racial inequality more effectively.

Responses to Starr's article were varied, as might be expected. About affirmative action, Theda Skocpol maintains, "If the medicine works for a while, it is worth it." Skocpol, a sociologist at Harvard University, believes that affirmative action will persist both as outreach and as tacit targets but cites the urgent need to expand socioeconomic opportunity:

> Quite simply, most of the minority children who will provide the future pool of applicants for middle-class jobs are now being raised in impoverished circumstances. Unless such children and their parents become more secure, healthy, and well-educated..., the most rigorous forms of affirmative action will not pull them into universities and middle class jobs.[43]

Acknowledging the depth of public resistance to race-specific policies, like Wilson, she urges adoption of race-neutral social programs.

Cornel West, a professor of religion at Princeton University, argues for both the continuation of affirmative action and attention to issues of black identity. West stresses the need to confront black identity issues but criticizes black conservatives who focus on self-respect "as if it is the one key that opens all doors to black progress."[44] Another key he maintains is the reduction of black poverty. And that is where affirmative action plays a role. West acknowledges that affirmative action is not a major solution to poverty nor a sufficient means to ensure equality, but it does ensure the reduction of discriminatory practices against people of color and women. As such, it is " part of a redistributive chain that must be strengthened if we are to confront and eliminate black poverty."

Clayton and Crosby provide new justification for affirmative action based on psychological processes. They examine the theory of relative deprivation in terms of sexism. As applied to gender discrimination, the theory involves the phenomenon that women who recognize sexual discrimination when it happens to other women deny such discrimination when they themselves are its victims, even imagining that they have somehow luckily escaped. Clayton and Crosby examine the processes that make it difficult for people to perceive they have suffered discrimination and assert that in the face of such mechanisms "affirmative action was [is] necessary to maintain progress toward gender equality."[45]

R. Roosevelt Thomas, Jr., of the American Institute for Managing Diversity, Inc., at Morehouse College in Atlanta, has a different angle on the issue. Basically critical of affirmative action, though he recognizes it still has a role to play in some places, Thomas views affirmative action from an organizational perspective. He asserts:

> affirmative action is an artificial, transitional intervention intended to give managers a chance to correct an imbalance, an injustice, a mistake. Once the numbers mistake has been corrected, I don't think affirmative action alone can cope with the remaining long-term task of creating a work setting geared to the upward mobility of *all* kinds of people, including white males.[46]

Thomas is more concerned with developing new strategies for valuing and managing diversity, and in this regard, he is in the vanguard of those carving out a new niche in the workforce diversity debate. His views and those of others are explored in the next chapter.

The Business Perspective

The business sector holds a position on preferential policies that does not fit neatly into our schema of underlying attitudes. Although in the thick of the fray over affirmative action, the business community seldom mans the ramparts. It quietly supports affirmative action—not because it is fair nor because individual business leaders personally identify with the minority plight, though in fact they may hold either attitude. Business supports affirmative action mainly because it is the law of the land and because it prevents lawsuits.

While others judge the policies, business implements them. Since preferential policies were instituted, many organizations, large and small, have adopted written policies to recruit and promote minorities and women. Some who are not required by law have adopted affirmative action programs voluntarily. Organizations have found that affirmative action can produce several benefits, such as more rational hiring practices, improved community relations, and heightened creativity. Wayne Garber, corporate vice president of Mantech International, a Virginia-based professional services company, maintains that affirmative action is a source of strength and competitive advantage. "We've gotten past the mindset that affirmative action is just numbers and demographics. For our company the payoff has been a more dynamic and creative culture that helps us deal better with the changing marketplace."*

The punitive side of preferences provides bottom-line incentive to support the policies. No institution lightly risks the possibility of ter-

---

*Interview, May 18, 1993.

mination of federal contracts and expensive law suits. In 1993, discrimination charges investigated by the EEOC led to settlements amounting to $161 million recovered through lawsuits and out-of-court efforts.[47]

Further, many firms support affirmative action simply because the mechanisms are in place to do so—affirmative action managers, lawyers, and the annual development of affirmative action plans. One critic sourly characterized this annual effort as "a great thrashing about and accumulation of paper signifying nothing."[48] Nonetheless, shifting gears or—worse—coping with conflicting guidelines would be more inconvenient for many organizations than continuing in the same mode.

For this combination of reasons, when the federal government released a draft order abolishing racial quotas and set-asides in hiring by the federal government and federal contractors in November 1991, business rushed to protest. The order was not signed, partly on the strength of this opposition.[49]

But many organizations go beyond mere compliance and undertake proactive efforts to enhance their affirmative action status. The logic of the demographic shifts and new economic forces discussed elsewhere in this publication is becoming clear to many in the business sector. They are recognizing that it is in their interest to bolster their diversity profile. And beyond a concern with affirmative action, many in business are in the forefront of those working on developing new approaches to value and manage diversity. In this respect, business joins the forces with those animated by the pragmatic attitude toward affirmative action.

Concluding Comments

There can be no definitive evaluation of affirmative action. Each argument, pro and con, has validity, as do the varied underlying attitudes that shape one's definition of the core issues. It is clear that preferential policies carry steep costs *and* confer important benefits. Judgment about which is weightier is an individual matter.

In concluding this chapter, we think it is appropriate to state our position on affirmative action and the underlying attitudes from which it flows. They are the fairness principle combined with pragmatism.

Affirmative action is one current expression of the defining American principle that "all men are created equal." Throughout U.S. history, this principle has found expression in different ways. It has never been easy to live with. Some Americans have died for it. More often, society seems anxious to ignore it in practice. Today, few would disagree that there is a moral imperative to ensure equal rights for all. But the conflicting demands of reality, the prickly side of diversity, tend to obscure the principle and cause seemingly irreconcilable differences about how to implement it in the workplace.

We believe that if our society is to head in the right direction—the direction that affirms the equality of all—Americans need to deal with diversity through every means possible including, for the foreseeable future, some form of preferential policies. We need every tool in the toolbox, and new ones, too. Though there may be surer ways of ensuring fair representation of minorities and women in the workplace, they have not yet been devised. Until they are, the current preferential system serves an important function.

Like all policies, and maybe more than some, affirmative action is flawed. It paints with a broad brush and its application is imperfect. It has created a backlash that promotes the very racism it intends to diminish. Self-defeating, too, is the fact that a company may lose interest in minority and female advancement when hiring goals are met.* This may stem from a feeling that the mission has been accomplished. Also, a factor is wariness about possible reverse discrimination charges from unsuccessful white applicants if hiring goals are exceeded. However, we believe that the short-term cost of heightened tensions, however risky, is outweighed by the long-term gains generated by ensuring added opportunity for people of color and women.

It is important to understand the proper scope of affirmative action. It does more than just promote the presence of fair numbers of members of protected groups within organizations through hiring practices. By requiring monitoring of the numbers of minorities and women at all organizational levels, it also provides momentum toward getting them up the organizational ladder. But affirmative action alone cannot be expected to break the glass ceiling, and it has not done so.

Nor can affirmative action eliminate poverty. It has been criticized for not helping to alleviate the financial plight of the poorest members of minority groups, especially blacks. And surely policies are needed to do just that. Affirmative action, however, has helped improve the financial position of a growing portion of the minority population by expanding opportunities available to them. This is suggested by the surge in the number of minority households that have achieved mid-

---

*This issue has hit Asians hard, especially in admissions to universities. Asians tend to be high achievers and if they were admitted based solely on achievement, their share of the university population would far exceed their share of the general population. As a result, some universities have placed ceiling quotas on admission of Asian students. See Neili.[50]

dle-class status in recent years. Between 1979 and 1989, the number of minority households with an inflation-adjusted income of $50,000 or more rose from 1.7 million to 3.1 million.[51] The growth of the black middle class, specifically, is reflected in the fact that the number of households in the top fifth of the aggregate income distribution range for the black population rose from almost 2.7 million in 1967 to almost 5.6 million in 1992.[52] The mean income of this group rose as well—from about $48,700 in 1967 to nearly $63,000 in 1992 (in 1992 dollars).

Without some form of affirmative action, there is no guarantee that the effort to achieve fair levels of minority and female representation within organizations would be as widely maintained. Progress was inadequate in the late 1960s before affirmative action went into effect. Organizational cultures are changing, but change is a protracted process. Big gains have been made in some industries, but there is still a long way to go, as discussed elsewhere in this publication. Furthermore, the elimination of preferences would very likely result in a certain amount of backsliding, even if largely unintentional.

From another perspective, it may be moot to argue whether affirmative action should stay in place. As long as antidiscrimination laws remain on the books—and they will remain—a rational means of implementing them is needed. Organizations clearly favor affirmative action over the alternative, an uncertain environment where the absence of clear guidelines would expand the potential for lawsuits. Thus, even if current affirmative action policies were curtailed, they are likely to be resurrected in another form.

This is not to dismiss the pain of those black and white, who feel victimized by preferential policies. We disagree, however, with an assessment in the *Chicago Tribune* that seems to sum up a portion of the debate. According to Paul Greenberg, blacks are faced with a choice between alternative models represented by W. E. B. DuBois (who focused on political solutions, which in terms of the current debate might translate into support for preferential policies) or Booker T. Washington (whose emphasis was on economic competence and self-development efforts).[53] We believe blacks and other people of color should be empowered to take advantage of both models—W. E. B. DuBois *and* Booker T. Washington—as well as any others they find useful. Of course, these words are more readily written than they are realized. Encounters with bias, however subtle, are not likely to engender a sense of empowerment. Quite the opposite. But in response to the rationale that the DuBois and Washington models are incompatible, we maintain that for every individual whose efforts at self-development are undermined by preferential treatment, there are many more who can and do benefit from both.

For whites who have been subject to reverse discrimination, perhaps no argument favoring continued preferences is convincing. It requires an act of faith and a sacrificial bent for victims of reverse discrimination to assert that group entitlements are more important than individual rights. Their personal pain is heightened by a tight job market that makes it even harder to replace a lost job or obtain a promotion after having been bypassed in favor of a minority or female applicant perceived as less qualified.

Open debate among policy makers, scholars, and other professionals on policies and approaches to diversity needs to proceed. The issue is far too critical to the welfare of our society to be straitjacketed. Ultimately, we need to look beyond preferences, in whatever form they may take, to policies and approaches that deal with workplace differences in more positive, creative ways. New approaches emerging in the workplace focus on valuing and managing diversity. These issues are examined in the next chapter. It is important to point out here that they are a complement to, not a substitute for, EEO and affirmative action policies.

References

1. Nancy J. Sedmak and Michael D. Levin-Epstein, *Primer on Equal Employment Opportunity*, 5th ed. (Washington, D.C.: Bureau of National Affairs, 1991) pp. 3–11.

2. Nathan Glazer, *Ethnic Dilemmas, 1964–1982* (Cambridge: Harvard University Press, 1983), p. 162, citing Thomas Sowell, "'Affirmative Action' Reconsidered," *The Public Interest,* no. 42, 1976, p. 48.

3. Susan D. Clayton and Faye J. Crosby, *Justice, Gender, and Affirmative Action* (Ann Arbor: University of Michigan Press, 1992), p. 13.

4. Sedmak, *op. cit.,* pp. 14–18.

5. Paul F. Mickey, Jr., and Joyce L. Oliner, "The Impact of the New Civil Rights Act of 1991 on Employers," unpublished presentation, March 5, 1992, Shaw, Pittman, Potts & Trowbridge, Washington, D.C.

6. Stephen L. Carter, *Reflections of an Affirmative Action Baby* (New York: Harper Collins/Basic Books, 1991), p. 2.

7. William Julius Wilson, *The Truly Disadvantaged: The Inner City, The Underclass, and Public Policy* (Chicago: University of Chicago Press, 1987), pp. 112–114.

8. Randall Kennedy, "Persuasion and Distrust: A Comment on the Affirmative Action Debate," *Harvard Law Review,* reprinted by Russell Nieli, ed., *Racial Preference and Racial Justice: The Affirmative Action Controversy* (Washington, D.C.: Ethics and Public Policy Center, 1990), p. 48.

9. Mona Charen, "Affirmative Action Marked by Fault Lines," *Newsday*, December 13, 1989, p. 58.

10. Gene Seymour, "The Great Debate," *Newsday*, October 10, 1990, p. 8.

11. Thomas Sowell, " `Affirmative Action': A Worldwide Disaster," vol. 88, no. 6, December 1989, p. 22.

12. Randall Kennedy, "Persuasion and Distrust," *op. cit.*

13. Sylvester Monroe, "Does Affirmative Action Help or Hurt?" *Time*, May 27, 1991, p. 22.

14. John Brennan, "Polls Find Whittle Favors Remedial Programs Until `Quota' or `Preferences' Are Mentioned," *Los Angeles Times*, August 21, 1991.

15. Carter, *op. cit.*, p. 168.

16. Shelby Steele, *The Content of Our Character: A New Vision of Race in America* (New York: St. Martin's Press, 1990), p. 116.

17. Thomas Sowell, *op. cit.*, p. 41.

18. Colin Leinster, "Black Executives: How They're Doing," *Fortune*, January 18, 1988.

19. Stephen L. Carter, *op. cit.*

20. Monroe, *op. cit.*

21. Shelby Steele, *The Content of Our Character: A New Vision of Race in America*, cited by Charles Johnson, "A Challenge for Black Americans," *Los Angeles Times*, September 30, 1990, p. 1.

22. Steele, *op. cit.*, p. 113.

23. Wilson, *op. cit.*, p. 111.

24. Susan D. Clayton and Faye J. Crosby, *op. cit.*, p. 25.

25. *Ibid.*, p. 26.

26. Paul R. Spickard, "Why I Believe in Affirmative Action," *Christianity Today*, October 3, 1986; reprinted in Nieli, *op. cit.*, p. 109.

27. Charles Krauthammer, "Why We Need Race Consciousness," *New Republic*, reprinted in Nieli, *op. cit.*, p. 148.

28. Nathan Glazer, *op. cit.*, p. 177.

29. Howard Gleckman, Tim Smart, Paula Dwyer, Troy Segal, Joseph Weber, "Race in the Workplace," *Business Week*, July 8, 1991, p. 52.

30. Jared Taylor, *Paved with Good Intentions: The Failure of Race Relations in Contemporary America* (New York: Carroll & Graf, 1992), p. 17.

31. Cited by Frederick R. Lynch, *Invisible Victims: White Males and the Crisis of Affirmative Action* (New York: Praeger, 1991), p. 51.

32. *Ibid.*, pp. 109–118.

33. Howard Gleckman, *et al.*, *op. cit.*, p. 52.

34. Glazer, *op. cit.*, p. 176.

35. Robert S. Browne, "The Road to Rectification," *The American Prospect*, no. 10, Summer 1992, pp. 93–96.

36. Terry Eastland and William J. Bennett, *Counting by Race*, p. 128 ff., Quoted in Clint Bolick, *Changing Course* (New Brunswick, N.J.: Transaction Books, 1988), p. 56 ff. and Jared Taylor, *op. cit.*, p. 128.

37. Clayton and Crosby, *op. cit.*, pp. 26–29.

38. Ronald Brownstein, "Racial Politics," *The American Perspective*, no. 9, Spring 1992, p. 122.

39. Gleckman, *et al.*, *op. cit.*, p. 52.

40. Wilson, *op. cit.*

41. Paul Starr, "Civil Reconstruction: What to Do Without Affirmative Action," *The American Prospect*, no. 9, Winter 1992, pp. 7–14.

42. *Ibid.*, p. 14.

43. Theda Skocpol, "Race, Liberalism, and Affirmative Action (II)," *The American Prospect*, no. 10, Summer 1992, p. 90.

44. Cornel West, "Race, Liberalism, and Affirmative Action (I); Equality and Identity," *The American Prospect*, no. 9, Spring 1992, p. 121.

45. Clayton and Crosby, *op. cit.*, p. 6.

46. R. Roosevelt Thomas, "From Affirmative Action to Affirming Diversity," *Harvard Business Review*, vol. 68, no. 2, March-April 1990, p. 108.

47. Phone interview with Michael Widomski, EEOC, March 9, 1994.

48. Glazer, *op. cit.*, p. 167.

49. Starr, *op. cit.*, p. 10.

50. Neili, *op. cit.*, pp. 455–473.

51. William P. O'Hare, "American Minorities and the Demographics of Diversity," *Population Bulletin* (a publication of the Population Reference Bureau, Washington, D.C.), vol. 47, no. 4, December 1992.

52. U.S. Department of Commerce, Bureau of the Census, *Money Income of Households, Families, and Persons in the United States: 1992*, Current Population Reports, Consumer Income, Series P60-184 (Washington, D.C., US GPO, 1993), p. B-7.

53. Paul Greenberg, "A Trio of Sensible Thinkers on the Subject of Affirmative Action," *Chicago Tribune*, September 7, 1990, p. 21C.

4

Valuing and Managing Diversity*

"Diversity," as it is understood in the workplace today, implies differences in people based on their various identifications with group memberships. But it is also more. Diversity is a process of acknowledging differences through action. In organizations, this involves welcoming heterogeneity by developing a variety of initiatives at the management and organizational levels as well as at the interpersonal—that is, individual and intergroup—levels.

Why do organizations bother? In one respect, they are galvanized by what organizational expert Taylor Cox, Jr., of the University of Michigan, calls the "moral imperative."[1] The moral imperative—doing it because it is right—has driven EEO and affirmative action initiatives, and now it also underlies the diversity agenda. But there are other compelling, more pragmatic reasons. As we have seen, demographic changes have created a more diverse society. In the workforce, too, these shifts and the impact of the civil rights and follow-on movements have generated changes. Further, we have shown how new economic forces are creating conditions in which the most productive organizations, organizations with a competitive advantage, are those that welcome the diversity resident among their workers. Workers in an environment receptive to diversity are empowered to use their full capacities and, as a result, they, their work, and the organization as a whole benefit. Welcoming diversity is directly connected to the bottom line.

---

*S. Kanu Kogod provided an early draft of this chapter. The authors are grateful for her work.

Further, the penalty for not welcoming diversity can be serious. If not managed properly, the advantages of diversity unravel. As people with differing value systems and backgrounds interact increasingly in dynamic team situations, in organizational networks, and with an increasingly diverse customer base, diversity has a growing potential to create friction. Like a pebble tossed into a pond, such tensions can reverberate, causing reduced productivity, increased costs, and lower quality of products and services. The downside of diversity is itself a powerful negative incentive for organizations to adopt diversity initiatives.

Finally, experience with EEO and affirmative action policies has shown that, while they are important steps in opening the workplace to diversity, they alone do not create conditions that capitalize on the full potential of heterogeneity. EEO and affirmative action policies are limited and basically punitive in nature. To respond effectively to the dynamics of diversity at work, another, more open-ended and positive impetus is needed. This approach, the action-oriented aspect of diversity, is known as *valuing and managing diversity*.

"Valuing diversity" means responsiveness to a wide range of people unlike oneself, according to any number of distinctions—race, gender, class, native language, national origin, physical ability, age, sexual orientation, religion, professional experience, personal preferences, and work style. Valuing diversity involves going beyond the golden rule of treating others as you wish to be treated yourself. It invokes a higher behavior, one that is receiver-centered rather than self-centered.[2] Sometimes called the "platinum rule," valuing diversity involves treating others as *they* wish to be treated.

The implications for this shift in perspective are profound. It requires setting aside one's own perspectives or personal filter to see others for who they are. This means recognizing that other people's standards and values are as valid as one's own. Simple as this may sound, in a culture that has long been accustomed to being relatively monolithic—which is to say, dominated by white, male values—the shift is often difficult and painful. Even well-intentioned organizations (and individuals) may fail to recognize the self-centered judgments they make about others, simply because they have been doing it for so long.

"Managing diversity" expands the notion of valuing by implementing initiatives at all levels in an organization in order to develop an environment that works for all employees, as leading spokesman on diversity, R. Roosevelt Thomas, Jr., observes.[3] Or, as Cox suggests, it means managing in such a way that maximizes the potential benefits of diversity and minimizes the potential disadvantages.[4]

In this chapter, we look at some of the major management-level issues involved in diversity. We explore theory and the practice of diversity to better understand why diversity is an important leadership issue and how it affects organizations today.

Diversity in Theory

Part of the challenge of managing diversity lies in the fact that it is a new field of endeavor. Its meaning and parameters are still being defined, and there is only a relatively small, though growing, body of experience for organizational leaders to consult for precedents. In the last few years, a number of books have been published that seek to define the issues and provide practical approaches. As yet, however, this new paradigm continues to evolve in its definitions and strategies. It can mean anything from valuing differences in people to the politically acceptable, multicultural integration of people. No matter how it is defined, "diversity" is the buzzword (next to "quality") for organizational issues that need to be addressed in the 1990s.

Management consultants who have published on this topic, such as Cox, Jamieson, O'Mara, and Thomas, as well as Marilyn Loden, Judith B. Rosener, Ann M. Morrison, John Fernandez, and others, emphasize the need to change organizational culture rather than trying to change people to fit the culture. For the most part, they offer steps similar to those found in organizational change models: defining current reality; creating a vision of the desired future state; and from the disparity between the real and the ideal, creating systems to bring the organization closer to the goal.

In *Managing Workforce 2000*, Jamieson and O'Mara define "portraits of diversity" from five perspectives: age, gender, education, disabilities, and values.[5] These two professionals were among the first to provide practical management strategies for responding more flexibly to heterogeneity. They identify four strategies: matching people and jobs, managing and rewarding performance, informing and involving people, and supporting lifestyle and life needs. Designating their approach "flex-management," they assert that by changing an organization's policies and systems, organizational values will also change. The new values are "a new corporate mindset" based on "individualizing, providing choices, seeing people as assets, valuing differences, encouraging greater self-management, and creating flexibility."[6]

Another definitive work of the early 1990s was *Workforce America!* by Marilyn Loden and Judith Rosener. This book emphasizes creating organizations that "capitalize on differences" as a way to tap into the potential contributions of individuals from diverse backgrounds.[7] "Managing diversity" is a way to recognize the need for respecting an individual's culture while valuing performance. These now classic books propose sensible management strategies with an appreciation for the mix of culture and values in organizations today.

An appealing response to supervising people from different cultures is to have managers study those cultures and adjust their management practices accordingly. This is what Sondra Thiederman recommends in *Profiting in America's Multicultural Marketplace*.[8] The drawback to this approach is that effective multicultural management would require studying each culture and then implementing appropriate adaptations. With the increasing mix of cultures and the resources required to make adjustments, the approach, while necessary for global operations, is unrealistic in the American setting in view of the many demands on today's managers.

What was missing from earlier approaches to diversity was a clear focus on understanding and changing the organizational culture to support the strategies. Along came R. Roosevelt Thomas's contribution, *Beyond Race and Gender*. In this book, Thomas focuses on describing the substantial problems organizations face in trying to change—as opposed to "create"—a corporate culture to support diversity.[9] Thomas provides a helpful framework that contrasts differences in goals, motives, benefits, and challenges among three paradigms that define approaches to difference on the job. These are (in the order in which they were developed) affirmative action, valuing differences, and managing diversity.[10] He maintains that today organizations tend to respond to the paradigms according to how they perceive the issues, how willing they are to address them, and what resources they have available to commit to change.

The earliest paradigm was equal employment opportunity (EEO) and affirmative action. These programs are a "right-the-wrongs" approach that essentially deny differences by promoting assimilation into the larger culture. Recognizing that specific groups in the organization have been systematically disadvantaged by the dominant culture, EEO and affirmative action focus on women and the four major racial and ethnic minority groups, African Americans, Hispanics, Asian Americans, and Native Americans. Programs and efforts to reduce prejudice and overcome barriers faced by the disadvantaged groups center on creating upward mobility for them. From this normative position, to acknowledge differences means to risk making judgments of right and wrong, superiority and inferiority, normality and oddity.

The second paradigm Thomas describes, valuing differences, means respecting people for their differentness. People are encouraged to be conscious of and responsive to a wide range of people who are different from themselves. More emphasis is placed on interpersonal relations, less on systems and culture.

Thomas defines the newest paradigm by stating, "Managing diversity is a comprehensive managerial process for developing an environment that works for all employees."[11] Managing diversity operates in an environment in which diversity is viewed "not as an us/them kind of problem to be solved but as a resource to be managed." He views managing diversity as a process to tap the potential of all employees—including white males.

Thus, Thomas's view of managing diversity is not about helping people assimilate into already existing organizational cultures. Nor are acceptance, tolerance, and an understanding of differences enough by themselves to create an empowered workforce. According to Thomas, managing diversity is needed. Supplementary efforts to change people do not get at the real need. The real need is to change the system by modifying the core culture. Such change requires time, in-depth analysis, effort, knowledge, and a clear understanding of the implications of change.

Transforming Organizational Cultures

In most organizations, valuing and managing diversity requires nothing less than cultural transformation. This is a prodigious task, for it requires people—especially those of the dominant culture—to let go of their assumptions about the universal rightness of their own values and customary ways of doing things and to become receptive to other cultures.

Anthropologists have long recognized that culture is not suddenly created, nor is it easily changed. Defined as "a shared design for living," culture is based on the values and practices of a society, that is, a group of people who interact together over time. People imbibe culture through the early process of socialization in the family and then this process carries over to the ways people perceive themselves and the world. We all develop a world view—a simplified model of the world that helps us make sense out of all we see, hear, and do. Values are the standards we use to determine if something is right or wrong. They are often the unexamined assumptions, never fully articulated, that guide our actions.

People naturally bring their culture to the workplace. The dominant culture of most American organizations reflects the values of the

American-born, white (Anglo) males who established them. Even organizations established by women or people of color often display values of the dominant culture. As our workforce grows more diverse, tensions over cultural issues are rising. The values of nontraditional workers often differ from those of the Anglo-dominated organizational cultures in which they work. These culture clashes can be a significant drain on the energy of the people involved, especially minority workers, who are more likely to feel oppressed by the differences. Work relationships and output can suffer as people struggle through misunderstandings. Some strive to repress their own values and behaviors in order to fit into the organizational mold, and they may become angry and resentful in the process. Others express their anger openly or seesaw between repression and anger. Whatever the case, people, productivity, and the organization suffer. In later chapters, we examine types of culture clashes that are likely to arise in Anglo-dominated organizations based on the values of each of the main "new" racial and ethnic groups in the workplace.

Transforming an organization's culture into one that welcomes diversity challenges the tendency of most people to want to surround themselves with (i.e., hire and promote) others like themselves. It calls for a realization that people from different backgrounds may be just as competent, although in different ways, as those who look, talk, and behave similarly. It also means letting go of "the way we do things here at organization X." Certainty and control are often institutionalized by rigid rules and by the tendency to rely on "proven," usually top-down, control methods for doing things. From this perspective, creative problem solving and tolerance to allow different values to guide decision making may seem too risky. The need to be certain that error does not occur can be seen to offset the advantages of multiple perspectives.

Managing diversity implies a measure of uncertainty. Far from relying on fixed rules, it requires a relativistic approach. This orientation begins with an attempt to understand varying beliefs and behaviors and works to adapt organizational culture accordingly. In contrast, the traditional orientation assumes that people fit the culture, an assumption that was truer of the workforce in the past than today.

There are no step-by-step rules for cultural transformation. Each organization needs to examine the issue within its own context. Nevertheless, it seems clear that two processes need to occur: There needs to be flexibility and open-mindedness in the views of upper management regarding the characteristics of a good manager or leader. Further, employees from different backgrounds need to acquire and assimilate the necessary knowledge and ways of acting that will permit them to enter power circles. In essence, managing diversity obliges people and organizations to examine and modify their responses in order to accommodate each other.

Organizational Obstacles

Cultural differences are at the core of the obstacles to opportunity in the workplace. They may be expressed as interpersonal culture clashes, as we have seen. Or they may be translated into the variety of organizational formal and informal roadblocks that nontraditional workers encounter on the job. Some of these practices may work well for the dominant culture—or at least for dominant members of the dominant culture—but they present problems when nontraditional workers are brought into the fold. Then, they are often applied in discriminatory ways, reflecting a tendency to circle the wagons around one's "own kind" in the face of a perceived threat from "outsiders."

In a later chapter, we analyze the nature of prejudice and examine how it is reflected in discriminatory behavior in organizations. We also examine other organizational and background barriers to the advancement of nontraditional workers. Here it is necessary merely to point out that while discrimination in the workplace has been outlawed for years, subtle—and some unsubtle—forms remain. Indeed, prejudice (biased attitudes) and discrimination (biased behaviors) are major obstacles to the advancement of women and people of color.

Research by Morrison and others supports this observation. Surveying managers from 16 corporations, Morrison and her colleagues found that prejudice is the *biggest* barrier for nontraditional managers. Defining prejudice as "equating a difference with a deficiency," they state, "Negative stereotypes about blacks, women, and members of other groups shape that perception. Prejudice, in its many subtle forms, continues to pervade decisions made in organizations, even in the 1990s."[12]

Because prejudice and discrimination are often subtle, impediments may be left unaddressed. People may even believe they are fair and just; in today's climate, expressing any other belief—or even admitting it to oneself—is unacceptable. But until they are willing to accept in other people values and behaviors that are dissimilar from their own, they will continue to carry a judgmental perspective that can, in spite of themselves, be prejudicial.

Here is where learning, communication, and dialogues can be most effective in changing old mental models. Whether in training workshops or in dialogue groups sanctioned by an organization, increasing understanding and changing attitudes can make a difference. By expanded understanding, prejudice can be killed and workplace relationships enhanced.

Other major organizational barriers to developing diversity, as documented in Morrison's research, include (in order of importance):

- Poor career planning, resulting in the failure to give to many nontraditional employees the breadth of experience and credentials required to compete for senior management posts

- A lonely, unsupportive, and even hostile working environment for many nontraditional managers, especially in upper management

- Lack of corporate savvy or political skills on the part of nontraditional managers, which makes them seem awkward and feel vulnerable

- The fact that people are more comfortable dealing with other people similar to themselves

- Difficulty in balancing career and family needs, especially for women[13]

Obstacles to opportunity can be viewed from another analytical perspective—namely, in terms of the level at which they occur. According to Cox, barriers occur at three levels: the individual, the group, and the organizational. These interact with each other to create the climate that thwarts diversity efforts. Cox's interactional model demonstrates the impact of diversity issues on individual career outcomes and organizational effectiveness.[14] His model suggests that individual level factors (personal identity, prejudice, stereotyping, and personality type), along with intergroup factors (cultural differences, ethnocentrism, and intergroup conflict) and organizational factors (organizational culture and acculturation processes, structural integration, informal integration, institutional bias, and human resource systems), all define the diversity climate of an organization.

Building Diversity

Building diversity in organizations is not simple. Organizational leaders are moving through uncharted territory. Not only are they dealing with issues that are new in terms of content, they need to develop new ways of thinking about and implementing them, and that is the bigger challenge. Enumerating dimensions of the diversity challenges organizations face, prominent management consultants David Jamieson and Julie O'Mara observe that managers need to "unlearn practices rooted in an old mindset, change the way organizations operate, shift organizational culture, revamp policies, create new structures, and redesign human resource systems."[15] No small task!

Not surprisingly, it is a multiphased process. In her book *The New Leaders*, Morrison outlines five major steps (and several guidelines) involved in the process of putting diversity into action.[16] According to Morrison, the first step is to identify the diversity problems in one's organization. Because diversity issues are not static, this is a recursive process, requiring an ongoing effort to reidentify or rediscover problem areas. A second step is strengthening management commitment. Selecting solutions that fit the organization's needs and culture and comprise a balanced diversity strategy is next. The final steps are demanding results by establishing meaningful numerical goals (and revisiting goals to ensure their continued relevance) and maintaining momentum.

Lawrence M. Baytos offers a different perspective. He identifies six steps that are needed to initiate successful diversity activities.[17] The first is to establish a clear business rationale for the initiatives. Important for any human resources program, this is especially critical with respect to diversity initiatives because the culture change that they involve is likely to meet organizational and personal resistance. Other goals include seeking employee input; converting employee input into action steps; setting the timing, focus, and breadth of training; and preparing to sustain the momentum from the initiatives.

These formulations are sufficient to show that the process of building diversity requires careful attention and a methodical approach. Our focus in this section is on two elements that are important to the building process: leadership commitment and diversity strategies.

Obtaining Leadership Commitment

Before diversity can be valued and properly managed in any organization, the leadership must be committed to it. At present, enormous resources are being expended on interventions for managing diversity, but a substantial share of such efforts are doomed because leaders are not "on board."

The terms "managers" and "leaders" can create confusion. Although we use the terms interchangeably in this book, a distinction can be drawn between them. "Managers" are those charged with the control of tasks and direction of people to carry them out. Within their frame of responsibilities, managers always have discretionary power. This is the range of actions they may but do not have to take. It is in the realm of discretionary power that leaders are born. "Leaders" are people in an organization who have the power of position and who use their discretionary power to carry out a vision that moves the organization to meet its goals.

Because the responsibility for managing diversity falls heavily on managers, it is important to understand how this distinction operates with respect to diversity issues. Leaders are managers who model what is expected so that those subordinate can follow. They treat people with respect, value the contributions of each person, and support and develop their people to be successful and make temporary sacrifices for long-term gains. In a diverse workplace, leaders have no fixed recipes for accomplishing these gains. On the other hand, managers (in the specialized sense) avoid the leadership role and become anxious when faced with questions for which there are no easy answers. Innovative ideas often get squelched by the tendency to fall back on traditional practices. "We've never done it that way before. What if everyone wanted to do that?"

Thus, within their organizations, managers can be either powerful change agents (in their role as leaders) or the greatest barriers to diversity, as Thomas observes.[18] They may be change agents in that they are carriers of culture as well as models for the qualities and values necessary to get ahead in the culture. They also are expected to lead and anticipate the future. On the other hand, in many organizations, managers traditionally are selected based on their ability to supervise tasks and projects, not on their ability to manage people. These traditionally directive managers (or "doer managers," as Thomas calls them) tend to be a barrier to diversity. They carry the culture of the status quo and exert leadership in a narrowly prescribed manner.

Three factors contribute to the tendency to act as a barrier. First, directive managers are likely to discourage the acceptance of multiple perspectives and diverse work styles because listening and evaluating varying points of view take more time and effort, and it may be unclear that this is value added. It often is not easy to determine at the outset how diversity aids an organization's delivery of services or adds to customer or client satisfaction. Second, by definition, directive managers are more interested in tasks than people. They are rewarded for getting the job done, not for dealing with people. As a result, people management is often viewed as a roadblock that gets in the way of job completion. Finally, there is the related perception that employees are tools to control for getting the job done, not resources to achieve business objectives.

This examination of the roles and functions of leaders and managers brings us to the challenge of obtaining leadership commitment to diversity. Diversity specialist Kay Iwata describes three critical lessons she learned from her experience in implementing and managing diversity change processes.[19] First, distinguish between buy-in and leadership commitment. "Buy-in" is expressed by managers who are carrying out directives to implement diversity without the commitment to actually making it happen. They may espouse the rhetoric of diversity (such as articles in the company newsletter) and appoint task forces or steering committees to study the problem, but they allocate little, if any, resources (monetary or personnel) to it. And they tend to expect others to get things done. In contrast, "commitment" is action-oriented. Leaders get personally involved in making things happen. They may personally chair an executive action committee to facilitate a culture change process. They lead by example and hold others accountable.

Iwata's second lesson is to not proceed without leadership commitment. Too often, organizations roll out education and awareness programs with little, if any, leadership commitment (though there may be buy-in). Expectations are raised and frustration, skepticism, and distrust increase as employees see no follow-through and observe management behavior that is contrary to the principles of managing diversity.

Third, Iwata warns people engaged in diversity work that, when leadership commitment is lacking, it is important to stop and design a strategy to get it. Commitment requires time to develop. Leaders need to understand exactly what the managing diversity process involves in order to make a personal commitment to support actions necessary for success.

To obtain leadership commitment, Iwata has developed a strategy that she admits is not steeped in research, nor does it have a long, successful track record. Rather, it is a strategy born of frustration over a lack of progress with current managing diversity interventions. A few of her clients have agreed to stop "playing at the game," backtrack, and do the critical leadership development work required to get the commitment necessary for success. The key ingredients are simple but powerful: honesty, patience, and accountability. To implement them, Iwata has designed two tactics. First is the creation of an executive action council with its membership comprising key decision makers, women, and people of color. Their overall task is to champion a managing diversity strategy. The word "action" is important, because they are to lead by example. The second tactic is one-on-one coaching for key decision makers. It is a critical element in the eventual construction of a personal leadership development plan which they are to design and execute. The concern, then, is with commitment rather than rhetoric, with "walking the talk," rather than "talking the talk."

Creative Associates International, Inc., a Washington-based international development firm, already walks the talk. Established by minority women, CAII has, from its inception, had an organizational culture that explicitly celebrates individual differences. Because transformation of culture, practices, and policies to welcome diversity is not an issue, the focus is on responsibility over accountability: flexibility is a watchword and there is recognition of multiple individual styles. CAII believes that successful organizations of the future will be shaped by cultures not unlike its own, according to president Charito Kruvant.*

Most organizations, however, need to work at transformation. For them, accountability is a key component in ensuring commitment of line managers. They are having line managers devise their own diversity aims as well as specific means to achieve them. Others adopt organizationwide tools designed to ensure accountability. For example, they link achieving hiring and other diversity goals with performance appraisal ratings or to annual bonuses.

Another well-known principle for securing commitment is management participation in the planning process. This provides a sense of ownership, hence commitment to diversity goals. In the planning process, coaching managers is often an important strategy to help them plan areas of concentration. Through identifying areas of greatest concern or greatest impact in the organization and focusing on them, managers can keep their momentum going. Seeing positive results is often the catalyst for continuing improvement.

So whether a manager is held accountable for processes put in place (hence, the manager is being pushed into diversity activities) or a leader is pursuing a vision (the leader is pulling others toward diversity goals), the effect may be the same: valuing people and relationships in organizations.

Because progress is often uneven at best and resistance may be formidable, leaders engaged in diversity work find that personal discouragement can be a familiar companion. Barbara Walker, the first diversity manager and pioneer of diversity work at Digital, says that she stays charged by keeping connected with people she regards as allies. These are "the colleagues in the organization who share the vision, give me straightforward and honest feedback, help me build strategies, help me do my own personal development, sign up to help lead the work, and celebrate with me our little accomplishments."[20]

---

*Interview with Charito Kruvant, April 5, 1994.

Diversity Initiatives—One Swallow or a Summer?

The range of diversity initiatives being used by organizations is broad. Any one activity may provide a starting point for organizations to begin moving closer to welcoming multiple perspectives and tapping the talents of their people. But no single activity, used in isolation, is likely to constitute an adequate strategy for managing diversity: one swallow does not make a summer, nor does one fine day (though one swallow may be better than none!). In contrast, a careful selection of initiatives adapted to organizational needs, tied to business aims, and used strategically in an ongoing manner become mutually reinforcing. Then diversity goals are likely to be met.

Diversity strategies need not be complex to be successful. Simple, informal activities may form an effective strategy, depending on the organization. The activities may be simple but achieving an effective strategy is not. In any organization, the people interested in valuing and managing diversity are themselves diverse, and they are likely to have varying interests and motives as they design a strategy. All may be seeking responses that value diversity but basing their decisions on different assumptions.

Sometimes diversity activities are initiated not in support of goals to value and manage diversity but as part of an effort to comply with affirmative action requirements. For example, a diversity statement by top management may be a response to the mandate to devise and distribute throughout the organization a written equal employment opportunity statement. Diversity training programs may likewise be viewed as part of an organization's affirmative action efforts. The Hudson Institute study, *Opportunity 2000,* which surveys a range of diversity initiatives, casts them in the framework of "creative affirmative action goals."[21]

To be effective, a diversity strategy—that is, a strategy aimed at valuing and managing diversity, not merely at meeting affirmative action requirements—should not be fixed. The mix of activities will probably need to change over time as organizational requirements change. This means that the activities and organizational needs must be monitored and remonitored to ensure a good match on a sustained basis.

The Conference Board developed an inventory of diversity initiatives, grouped in several topic areas, based on its survey of leading corporations in 1992.[22] We consider them on a category-by-category basis, though in fact some activities within and across topic areas are overlapping and could readily be placed in more than one area.

The topic areas include, first, communications activities such as senior management communications on diversity, diversity vision and mission statements, a disseminated diversity policy in the employee handbook and elsewhere, and articles in organizational newsletters. Diversity communications are a beginning, but, as we have seen, effectively valuing and managing diversity is an action agenda. Rhetoric alone, no matter how well-intentioned, may be less than a nod in the right direction: Although they indicate a concern for diversity on the part of management, unless they are backed by action, they can create unfulfilled expectations that generate frustration and backlash.

Another area of activities is education and training classes. These include skills and awareness training for management and employees, sexual harassment training, orientation for the board of trustees, and mainstreaming diversity training into other training programs. We discuss diversity training in greater detail subsequently. Here, however, it should be stressed that training programs, which are widely used, are a good way to raise awareness and impart diversity management skills. Long-term improvement cannot be sustained, however, without also changing organizational policies and practices to support diversity.

Diversity-related employee involvement initiatives is a further key category. These include establishing task forces, focus groups, networking groups, diversity councils, corporate and business unit advisory committees, and others. Career development and planning activities related to diversity are important if diversity is to be valued and properly managed within an organization. Poor career planning opportunities is one of the main reasons minority and women employees fail to get ahead in many organizations. Such activities entail mentoring programs, including multitrack mentoring; career pathing; developmental programs for nontraditional employees; educational programs ranging from executive M.B.A. programs to remedial education; and English as a second language classes, among others.

Performance and accountability initiatives are especially important. Specific tools establishing accountability and rewards for performance provide managers with concrete incentive to implement and maintain momentum behind programs. Without such incentive, many diversity goals are likely to remain unfulfilled. Among performance and accountability initiatives are developing quantitative and qualitative diversity performance measures, linking diversity performance to other corporate objectives, evaluating managers' and employees' performance based on diversity measures, and rewarding behaviors that reinforce diversity.

A final area of diversity activities is culture change initiatives. As we have seen, managing diversity requires cultural transformation in organizations that have traditional Anglo cultures. Tools for effecting such change include internal diagnostic studies, benchmarking other companies, developing a corporate diversity strategy, integrating diversity into a total quality strategy, emphasizing line ownership, and revising policies and benefits to support diverse needs. The growing momentum created by the use of diversity initiatives in other topic areas also contributes to cultural transformation.

Revising policies and benefits so that they support diverse needs is one of the most critical areas of initiatives. The range of possibilities is broad, and we deal with some of them elsewhere in this book. Here, however, a survey of the range is useful. *Opportunity 2000* examines many (but not all) of the areas of change in terms of what specific organizations are doing to implement them.[23] Among them is changing recruiting policies to focus on recruiting women, people of color, older workers, and people with disabilities. Recruitment policies can be broadened to include recruiting women into traditionally male occupations, and recruiting returning and second-career women. Other areas in which policies and benefits may be changed to support diversity are implementing flexible work schedules, part-time scheduling, and flexible vacation and sick-leave policies; providing for child and elder care; ensuring pay equity for all workers; establishing equal benefits for partners of gay and lesbian workers; making employment more attractive than retirement for older workers; and many others. Accommodations for persons with physical and mental disabilities is no longer optional; it is mandated by law.

From this menu of activities, organizations are adopting those most suited to their needs. They are also developing additional ones. The process involves trial and error as managers work to identify components of an appropriate diversity strategy and effectively implement them. Many organizations are seeking help in developing diversity strategies. Others are moving ahead full throttle.

Among the many organizations who have developed diversity strategies are Motorola, Hughes Aircraft, and Northern States Power Company (NSPC). At NSPC (which is located in Minnesota—not exactly the demographic mix of Los Angeles or New York), the diversity issue is called "Capitalizing on Diversity." They have six stated goals with multiple action strategies for each goal. These include communicating shared values, creating a company culture that supports diversity, linking diversity to every business strategy, investing in training so diversity flourishes, delivering diversity-focused community programs, and linking diversity to rewards. Strategies around each goal have been further clarified by action plans.

While full-fledged diversity programs, like that at NSPC, are often desirable and effective, even small businesses can adopt strategies.

Stacia Cooper of Cambridge Savings Bank suggests several simple initiatives that organizations and individuals can use to create an inclusive environment, regardless of the level of formal programming. Their program, called "Managing for Inclusion" is divided into three parts: managing assumptions, managing language, and managing policy.[24] The first two areas can be undertaken by individuals; organizations can implement all three, in any sequence the culture will tolerate.

Diversity Training—One Arrow in the Diversity Quiver

As we have seen, organizations are using a broad range of initiatives in their efforts to value and manage diversity. One of the most widely used activities is diversity training. Training workshops are a good way to enable organizations to begin raising awareness about diversity issues. Through in-house trainers, as well as outside diversity experts contracted to present workshops and seminars, managers and employees alike are being sensitized to diversity and are learning skills to deal with it.

Two main diversity training approaches are being used: awareness-based training and skill-based diversity training. While the two are interrelated and reinforcing, skill-based training represents a progression in intent. Awareness training aims at heightening awareness of diversity issues and revealing workers' unexamined assumptions and tendencies to stereotype. Skill-based training goes beyond consciousness-raising to an effort at providing workers with a set of skills to enable them to deal effectively with workplace diversity, be it in the role of manager or employee.

Awareness-Based Diversity Training

When people from diverse cultures interact, they tend to respond according to their cultural conditioning about acceptable behavior. Such responses are reflexive and are usually based on the assumption of the universality of one's own belief system. Culturally-based "thought processing" causes people to judge according to their own standards the behavior of others who are acting from a differing cultural context. People may experience discomfort, even anxiety, in such interactions. To alleviate these feelings, they unintentionally may oversimplify—that is, stereotype—and even dehumanize their images of the other people. When this happens, behavior is directed at images, not actual people. The result of such responses is misunderstandings, which in a workplace setting can seriously impact performance, impair employee and customer relations, or diminish safety.

Awareness-based training is designed to increase employee knowledge, awareness, and sensitivity to diversity issues. It is the starting point for the development of diversity programs. The immediate objectives are to provide information about diversity, heighten awareness and sensitivity through uncovering hidden assumptions and biases, assess attitudes and values, correct myths and stereotypes, and foster individual and group sharing. Figure 4-1 depicts an awareness-based training model which we have developed.

In the organizational context, the longer-range goals of awareness-based training are, through promoting effective intercultural communication, to improve morale, productivity, and creativity, thereby contributing to the organization's overall competitive position.

Awareness-based training focuses mainly on the cognitive features of diversity training. It provides information about diversity, ranging from statistical presentations, illustrating the business necessity for diversity training, to anecdotes. Programs differ in emphases, some focusing on heightening awareness by providing substantive information about the cultures of the various identity groups in the American workplace. Others are more process-oriented, aiming at uncovering the participants' unconscious cultural assumptions and biases. A stan-

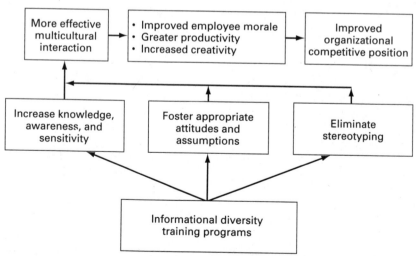

Figure 4-1. Awareness-Based Diversity Training Model.

dard feature of this latter type of training is experiential exercises aimed at helping put participants more in touch with themselves and their feelings about diversity. Exercises encourage participants to view others as individuals rather than as representatives of a group and thus to avoid stereotyping.

Important as these goals are, awareness-based training is not without its detractors. Beverly Geber, associate editor of *Training*, notes that for behaviorists, awareness training is "far too squishy, psychological, and unmeasurable."[25] Further, awareness-based training is open to criticism for its limitations. It seeks to heighten awareness but does not provide skills to enable participants to act more effectively. Commenting on awareness training's impact on managers, Geber states that some organizations assume that "managers will emerge from those (awareness training) sessions thunderstruck—amazed by the revelation that they might be making unconscious, erroneous assumptions about people" and hoping that these revelations will be a first step toward changing attitudes. Many are finding, however, that, without skills training instructing people how to deal with cultural differences, people may be at a loss as to what to do with their new understanding.

Skill-Based Diversity Training

While awareness-based training is primarily cognitive, skill-based training is behavioral. The two approaches are closely interrelated because the latter is based on increased self-awareness of diversity-related issues. Providing tools to promote effective interaction in a heterogeneous work setting, skill-based training has three important objectives: to build new diversity-interaction skills, to reinforce existing skills, and to inventory skill-building methodologies.

As with the awareness training, skill-based training has longer-range, organizationwide goals. These include improving morale, productivity, and creativity through effective intercultural communication and, consequently, helping increase an organization's competitive edge. These relationships are illustrated in our skill-based training model (please see Figure 4-2).

Skill-based training is still relatively new, and authorities differ as to the specific skill mix required. Diversity consultant Beverly A. Battaglia cites four diversity skills that are critical for creating a collaborative environment:

- *Cross-cultural understanding.* Knowledge about how and why culturally different team members act the way they do and respect for another's cultural operating styles

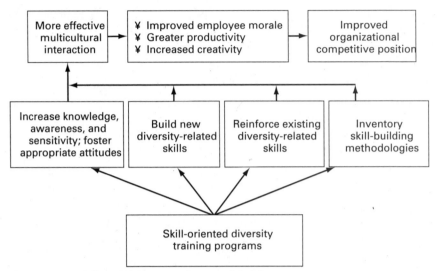

Figure 4-2. Skill-Based Diversity Training Model.

- *Intercultural communication.* The ability to eliminate communication barriers such as insufficient exchange of information, semantic difficulties, receivers hearing only what they want to hear, senders and receivers having different perceptions, nonverbal cues being ignored or misinterpreted, and lack of language fluency. This skill requires patience, awareness, and constant checking of the interaction process to detect barriers.

- *Facilitation skills.* The ability to mediate differences and assist others in negotiating misunderstandings. The growing use of teamwork and the concomitant heightened potential for conflict and misunderstanding makes facilitation skills increasingly important.

- *Flexibility/adaptability.* The ability to modify expectations, readjust operating norms, utilize new approaches, and be patient. Diverse employees need to learn to adapt to their work environment while maintaining their individuality.[26]

A skill-based diversity training program involves a specific range of skills. According to James B. Williams, these include:

- *Self-awareness.* The ability to recognize the assumptions one has harbored about those who are "different."

- *Clear-headedness.* A refusal to rely on stereotypes and instead to use valid individual character and skills assessments when allocating job assignments, promotions, or rendering other key decisions.

- *Openness.* A readiness to share with "outsiders" the information and knowledge of the "rules of the game," and to provide access to mentors necessary to penetrate invisible barriers and to move up in the organization.

- *Candor.* The ability to engage in constructive dialogue about differences, whether they are individual, ethnic, cultural, or organizational. (This is a challenging task, because many organizational policies and practices are designed to minimize differences. Yet, the fact remains that people should not be treated as identical.)

- *Adaptability.* The willingness to change old rules that discourage or thwart the full realization of the benefits of diversity to the organization.

- *Egalitarianism.* The commitment to encourage employees to grow professionally and participate fully in the success of the organization.[27]

Regardless of the specific skill mix, many believe that diversity training needs to move beyond consciousness-raising to provide workers with the tools to build more effective interaction among diverse individuals.*

Additional Considerations

The benefits of diversity training have been amply and repeatedly demonstrated. As trainers and organizations compile a record of experience, they gain new insights into what is effective and what is not. Naturally, mistakes have been made along the way. Some early training efforts conveyed the impression that white males were oppressors who stood outside of and in opposition to the diversity process. People are learning now that diversity training programs are more effective when they are inclusive and when they focus primarily on interacting in the present rather than on accusations about injustices of the past. Maintaining that diversity training should be more pragmatic and less attitude-driven, diversity experts H. B. Karp and Nancy Sutton think an environment needs to be created where all participants feel free to express their attitudes, where the trainer is sensitive to the views of the trainees (including groups of white male managers and employees), and where present realities are more the focus than past injustices.

---

*Not everyone agrees. See Morrison and von Glinow, "Women and Minorities in Management."[28]

This shift makes sense from a practical as well as a training standpoint. White men are a major segment of the workforce, and they are still overwhelmingly the power holders in most organizations. Training programs that cast them primarily as adversaries alienate a large part of the workforce and can undercut efforts to obtain their commitment as leaders to diversity strategies.

Several additional considerations have become clear. First, training is unlikely to be effective when it is a one-time approach. Like other diversity activities, it needs to be used on a sustained basis; that is, training programs should be provided at appropriate intervals. Also, follow-up is needed to evaluate training programs. This means not merely requesting participants to provide written or verbal evaluation sheets about the quality of training sessions, but devising tools to monitor changes in behaviors as a result of the training.

Taking the Pulse: Organizational Responses to Diversity

Organizational responses to diversity are as varied as the organizations themselves. In general, however, there is growing appreciation of the importance of diversity initiatives. At the same time, many continue to be skeptical of diversity's benefits. In some organizations, unsuccessful initiatives have soured opinion. In others, resistance to diversity has prevented initiatives supporting diversity from being implemented in the first place.

Growing Acceptance...

The ubiquity of diversity material in management literature and the frequency of diversity seminars, workshops, and conferences across the country indicate just how topical the issue has become among human resource practitioners. What's more, a growing number of top-level, corporate executives are recognizing its significance. In Fall 1991, as part of this diversity project, the American Society for Training and Development (ASTD) conducted a national HRD executive survey of *Fortune* 1000 companies regarding diversity issues. In this survey, led by Ron Ward Finnell, responses were received from 213 executives (48 percent of those surveyed) representing 10 industry groups including manufacturing, financial services, electronics, retail, agriculture and food products, chemical and allied products, consumer products, energy products, communications, and diversified services. When asked to assess their company's level of attention to diversity issues, 73 percent indicated that the issues were receiving attention, ranging from high priority (11 percent) to moderate attention (29 percent) and just beginning to look (33 percent). Please see Figure 4-3. This response, especially the sizable number initially focusing on diversity in a recession year, suggests senior managers see a connection between the bottom line and diversity.

An abundance of research supports these findings. In a 1991 survey, Towers Perrin found a growing concern for the diversity issues raised in the landmark Husdon Institute study, *Workforce 2000*. Over half (55 percent) of the corporate respondents to the Towers-Perrin survey said that management support for programs aimed at managing the changing workforce had increased over the past two years. Forty-one percent said the level of management support was the same as it was two years ago, and only 4 percent said it declined over the 2-year period.[29]

A full 91 percent of the Towers-Perrin respondents agreed that their senior management believes people are the "make-or-break corporate resource of the 1990s."[30] Moreover, 61 percent acknowledged that workforce programs were implemented in large part because senior management believed such programs would enhance the organization's competitive position. Phrased another way, the survey found the most important factor contributing to increased management support for workforce-related programs is greater senior management awareness of the significance of such programs. Other factors include the

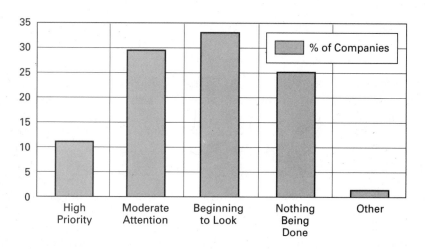

213 respondents out of possible 444

Figure 4-3. Current Attention to Managing a Culturally Diverse Workforce.

need to attract and retain a skilled workforce; impact of workforce trends currently affecting the company; similar action being taken by other companies in the area or in the industry; employee demands; retention and turnover problems; and government mandate or social pressure. Please see Figure 4-4.

Similarly, a survey by The Conference Board found that top management most commonly views diversity as a competitive opportunity. According to a 1992 survey of 131 leading organizations in human resource practices, 42 percent of executives surveyed thought that "learning to capitalize on diversity will increase productivity and competitiveness."[31] Other views cited were that diversity is a part of good management (24 percent); it is a major challenge (22 percent); it is an affirmative action issue (8 percent); and it has no serious impact (4 percent). These numbers show that diversity initiatives have gained legitimacy and that the connection between valuing and managing diversity and the bottom line is clear to many. What the numbers do not reflect is the level of commitment to change.

Some diversity activities are more widely used than others. A survey conducted in 1993 by the Society for Human Resource Management

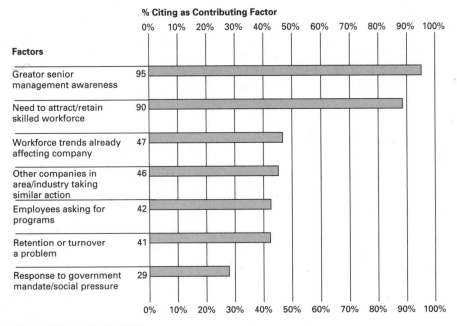

(Source: Towers Perrin, 1991)

Figure 4-4. Factors Supporting Increased Management Support of Workforce-Related Programs.

and the Commerce Clearing House (SHRM/CCH) finds that, among respondents, the most prevalent diversity activities are sexual harassment policies (93 percent of organizations surveyed) and physical access for employees with disabilities (76 percent)—two activities linked to legal concerns.[32] Other widely used activities supportive of diversity are flexible work schedules (almost 66 percent); greater flexibility for days off for religious holidays, beyond legal requirements (almost 58 percent); and parental leave policy (nearly 57 percent).

Although not included in the SHRM/CCH ranking of policies and programs, diversity training is widely used as an element in many diversity strategies. Almost two-thirds of the 406 companies participating in a Harris survey in 1991 indicated that they conducted diversity training for managers.[33] Almost 40 percent conducted such training for all employees. What's more, most organizations in the Harris survey indicated that they have future plans to train managers (80 percent) as well as their entire workforce (65 percent). The same survey found that 50 percent of organizations used a communications statement from senior management; an additional 16 percent intend to do so in the future. Twenty-eight percent have mentoring programs for women and minorities; about half again as many intend to put such programs in place in the future. Those who used diversity task forces totaled 31 percent, with another 22 percent intending to establish them in the future.

It appears that a smaller portion of organizations use tools to measure diversity performance or link such performance with individual accountability. The SHRM/CCH survey found that only 30 percent of its respondents who conduct diversity training measure resulting behavior at work; less than 20 percent reward managers for increasing the diversity of their work groups.[34]

...And Some Resistance

While acceptance of a diversity agenda in the workplace is growing, the story of its progress is not simply that of a snowball effect, picking up adherents as it rolls along. In some organizations, resistance to diversity initiatives is formidable. One way this is visible is through the absence of diversity programs and policies. Another indicator is found in the way questions about diversity are formulated.

Ellen J. Solomon, an organization consultant, notes that valid questions that are typically raised to explore diversity initiatives are sometimes reformulated to resist it. For example, "what is the business case for diversity?" may be expressed as procrastination: "we need more (and more and more) data."[35] The open-ended question, "why are we doing this work now?" can become the negative judgment, "this just isn't practical when we have so many competing business and financial priorities." Or "what does a managing diversity effort involve?" may be rephrased to include its own answer: "doesn't managing diversity just mean diversity of thought and perspective?"

Discrimination underlies some of the backlash. The American workplace cannot be separated from society as a whole. Resistance to diversity initiatives in the work environment undoubtedly is partly traceable to the racism and sexism that taint many areas of our national life. Solomon maintains that failure to recognize resistance to diversity initiatives "prevents the organization from addressing discrimination on other levels as well."[36] But discrimination is not the only factor involved in resistance to diversity. Fear and prior experience with ineffective diversity programs are others. To understand these factors, we also need to explore who is being resistant.

Change is seldom easy for individuals or organizations. And diversity initiatives spell change, for they challenge entrenched practices. Diversity specialist Judith Katz points out that resistance is part of the process of change. She says change "moves us out of our comfort zone. We knew how to interact and be successful in the old culture. But it is very scary when the rules change. At the same time that we say we want change, we will also resist."[37]

Among those (but by no means the only ones) who resist diversity activities are some white males. Part of the reason for this is the perception that white men are not only excluded from diversity concerns but they are the *cause* of the concerns. Because theirs is the dominant culture in most organizations and because they are typically the power holders, the nontraditional workers in the organization—namely, everybody else—are relatively disempowered and many are resentful. Small wonder that some white males see diversity issues as threatening!

Katz maintains that fear is an important factor in the resistance to diversity activities offered by white men. The change process creates ambiguity about the future, and many white men are uncertain where they will fit in organizations where valuing and managing diversity is a priority. Katz observes that such backlash is "a clue that something else needs to happen."[38] Inclusion is the key. White males—and others, too—need to be given a "vision of the future" and their role in it. "As part of the change process, we have to create an atmosphere where people feel safe."

While white men, fearing exclusion, resist diversity programs, some organizations are finding that some minorities and women also are resistant because they fear *inclusion* in diversity programs. They hesitate to participate in diversity support networks, for example, because they do not want to be seen as outside the mainstream. The chief personnel officer at a leading professional service firm, says that some women professionals in his organization are "concerned about being branded as a woman."* They feel they can make it on their own credentials. Such a mindset establishes its own barriers by keeping people from taking full advantage of resources available to them. "We need to break through that mindset," he observes.

Among managers, groups seem to differ in terms of degree of support for diversity initiatives. Questioning human resource professionals, line managers, and top management across a range of diversity-related issues, the SHRM/CCH survey finds that HR professionals tend to view diversity programs more positively than line managers. The latter, skeptical about its benefits, are more likely to think that diversity makes their jobs harder. Between these two groups are senior managers.[39] For example, while 60 percent of HR professionals surveyed think a more diverse workforce will enable their organizations to better serve their clients and customers, the figure for line managers is 21 percent; for senior managers, about 41 percent. Over 50 percent of HR professionals think diversity programs are "socially desirable" and almost 41 percent believe they would lose some of their best employees without diversity programs. Opinion among line managers presents a striking contrast: only 18 percent think such programs "socially desirable," and only 12 percent think top employees would be lost without them. Among top management, the figures are 35 percent and 26 percent, respectively. One area where line managers and senior management hold similar beliefs is with regard to diversity's cost-benefit ratio: about 15 percent of both groups think the costs outweigh the benefits. (Among HR professionals, the figure is 11 percent.)[40] The other side of the coin is the presumably overwhelming majority of all groups who think diversity's benefits are greater than its costs.

Ineffective diversity initiatives also can sour people on diversity. Many of these activities now have been in place long enough to be assessed, and while the link between ineffectiveness and skepticism is not spelled out in the surveys we examined, it is probably reasonable to assume a correlation (not necessarily one-to-one).

The ASTD study finds that 52 percent of respondents judged their in-place diversity programs to be effective or moderately effective, but almost half either did not know (30 percent) or considered their programs ineffective (18 percent). The SHRM/CCH survey is more exhaustive, querying respondents across a range of diversity policies and programs. Those with the highest ratings for effectiveness were

---

*In a telephone interview, March 24, 1994.

sexual harassment policy (of organizations with a sexual harassment policy, 91 percent judged them to be effective); physical access for employees with disabilities (85 percent); parental leave policy (73 percent); and flexible work schedules (72 percent).[41] Programs and policies with the lowest effectiveness ratings are health insurance coverage for partners of gay and lesbian employees (among organizations with such a policy, only 15 percent thought them effective); plan to reduce geographic relocation to accommodate dual-career families (24 percent); fast-track program for minorities (27 percent); and translation of corporate materials into other languages for employees with language problems (37 percent).

An index of perceptions about the effectiveness of diversity training programs is presented by the SHRM/CCH survey: Only about 3 percent of respondents whose companies used such programs found them to be extremely successful; almost 30 percent found them to be quite successful. Significantly, most respondents thought diversity training programs at their companies were neutral (50 percent), largely unsuccessful (about 13 percent), or extremely unsuccessful (5 percent).

All of these factors suggest that resistance to diversity activities is significant. Diversity professionals Michael Mobley and Tamara Payne maintain that handling backlash is the "biggest challenge facing diversity trainers."[42] The Conference Board provides evidence that backlash is a challenge to the full range of diversity activities. The Conference Board survey finds 61 percent of respondents feel that fear of backlash from white males is among the three most serious barriers to implementing diversity initiatives.[43]

The jury is not in with regard to the effectiveness of diversity programs nor on how to cope with resistance to them. The diversity learning process is still partly terra incognita. Managers, trainers, and others involved in valuing and managing diversity are searching for answers, and, naturally, they make mistakes. Diversity expert R. Roosevelt Thomas, Jr., observes that "mistakes at the cutting edge are different—and potentially more valuable—than mistakes elsewhere." Citing an example of an effort to value diversity that went wrong, Thomas adds that these people "need to be told that they were pioneers, that conflicts and failures came with the territory, and that they would be judged accordingly."[44]

Diversity and Other Business Issues

Our focus on diversity should not prevent us from remembering that it is only one of a number of important business issues. And it is not generally viewed as the most important one. The ASTD survey asked executives to rank management issues in order of importance. Only 2 percent cited diversity as the most important issue. Customer service received the highest rating (33 percent), with productivity ranked at 29 percent, total quality management at 21 percent, and performance management at 7 percent.

With a different perspective, the SHRM/CCH compared diversity with other human resource issues. The survey found half or more of the respondents rated diversity management as a lower priority than nine other issues. These include profitability, market share, capital investment, health care, total quality management, revising compensation, restructuring, downsizing, and education and training.[45]

Out of Isolation—Close Connections of Four Kinds

We have explored at some length the theory and practice of valuing and managing diversity. Now we need to recognize that these functions are not isolated from other business practices. Human resources experts John Fernandez and Elizabeth Shaw point to crucial—and often overlooked—connections between managing diversity and team building, total quality management (TQM), and reengineering. They state, "Well-managed diversity leads to high-performance quality teams, which in turn lead to quality products and services."[46]

Connections between diversity and TQM have been noted by others. TQM is a process of continuous evaluation and adjustment to ensure that the customer receives the highest quality service or product at the lowest cost. Although its efficacy is a hotly debated subject in the business world today, many organizations have found that it is a key long-term business strategy.[47] The process involves several concepts that parallel those relating to managing diversity. As identified by The Conference Board, these include, first, customer satisfaction and the concept of the internal customer.[48] The common theme in this concept is the need to meet internal requirements (those of a diverse workforce or various departments) before the focus on quality for external customers can be successful. A second key concept is alignment. This means that organizations can more effectively unite diverse employees and groups behind a common goal when they feel that their differences are valued. Third is the concept of employee empowerment. When employees as team members are empowered to make decisions affecting their work, they are likely to communicate most effectively in an environment of openness, respect, and trust, that is, an environment in which diversity is valued. A fourth common concept is the changing role of managers. In the TQM process, the role of managers has changed from a directive to a facilitative, team-building role. Effectively managing a diverse workforce is part of enabling workers to perform up to their potential.

Other links between diversity and TQM have been identified. Both feed into organizational learning—one from a people orientation, the other from a processes orientation. In diversity, there is awareness of cultural diversity issues; in quality, the focus is an awareness of TQM and benchmarking other organizations. Further, diversity carries an intention of valuing diversity; quality bears the intention of providing continuous quality improvements.[49]

Additional parallelisms include the fact that both diversity and TQM activities are driven by top management. In both, critical tasks for assuring success include identifying appropriate champions, implementing systemic changes, breaking down barriers, and clarifying roles. And both share a vision of an organizational culture change to support new ways of doing high-performance work and to support the people doing it. There is also linkage in the role of quality facilitators at the unit level. These people act formally as team leaders in team-building meetings and activities. They also act informally as culture brokers to enable information to flow among cultural groups in the unit. As culture brokers, quality facilitators interpret behaviors of diverse groups. They link teams with each other, departments to units, or clients (especially multicultural clients) to services. In short, in their informal role, quality facilitators promote understanding and appreciation of the richness of cultural diversity.

Our discussion leads us to a further set of connections in the chain: the connection among diversity, TQM, and team building. Team building is an integral part of the TQM process. High-performance teams are needed to create quality products and services. Fernandez and Shaw observe that developing effective quality teams is becoming more difficult for several reasons.[50] Among them are the fact that customers are becoming more diverse. So, too, are employees. Quality teams are likely to consist of people who differ in race, ethnic background, gender, age, sexual orientation, and other dimension. Fernandez and Shaw maintain that these difficulties are surmountable if organizations train their people to (among other things) understand and respect their diversity as well as to understand team work and other tools for innovation.[51]

The final connection in this set of four is reengineering. Reengineering is a new, customer-centered strategy that focuses on processes. It is designed to give companies a competitive advantage by determining the most effective processes to best serve customers in the most cost-effective, quality way. The link with diversity lies in the fact that decisions about what should be reengineered, and how, are made by people. In most organizations, this means that decisions are made by diverse people working in teams who need to know how to subordinate some measure of their individuality to the group without denying the existence of differences or regimenting them into a uniform approach that would squelch creativity. According to Fernandez and Shaw, the effect of these four connections in combination will "improve the success ratio" of companies as they move into the global marketplace.[52]

And Empowerment and Learning Organizations, Too

These four connections are not the whole story. There are also key linkages with two other important processes: employee empowerment and learning organizations.

Employee empowerment involves pushing problem solving and decision making to the lowest appropriate level. The process gives employees a greater sense of ownership, and it calls on them to work in new, more flexible ways, ways that the traditional control model (where employees were told what to do) did not require. Use of the empowerment approach has been given impetus by organizations that have or are restructuring in response to economic pressures. Because restructuring involves eliminating layers of middle management, decisions previously made by middle managers become the responsibility of employees at lower levels who are directly involved in the tasks.

To transition successfully to the empowerment model, employees need to gain confidence and competence to take actions not covered by the organization's rules. A successful transition entails four ingredients, according to management specialists David E. Bowen and Edward E. Lawler: providing employees with information about the organization, knowledge to enable them to contribute to organizational performance, power to make decisions that influence organizational performance, skills, and rewards based on the organization's performance.[53]

There is a close connection between empowerment and diversity. Employees will be most creative and make the best decisions when they work in a setting of trust, openness, and respect—in other words, a setting in which diversity is valued. Management and quality specialist Mary-jo Hall points out that the aim of diversity work is "to create an environment where every person is valued as a contributor—and therefore empowered to maximize their contributions."[54]

For R. Roosevelt Thomas, Jr., empowerment is a defining ingredient in the managing diversity paradigm—and vice versa. He points out that "empowerment" is "another word for the process of tapping employees' full potential" and he also observes that managing diversity is a "critical determinant" of the success of efforts to empower employees.[55]

Because much decision making by empowered employees occurs in team situations, their ability to communicate effectively with team members becomes a critical component of an organization's success. Since team members are likely to be as heterogeneous as the workforces of which they are part, each person becomes a culture broker who contributes to transforming organizational culture to one that values diversity.

Empowerment requires that managers act in ways that value diversity. Empowered managers need to adopt a facilitating management style rather than a directive or control style. Their role includes facilitating employee risk taking and ownership, openly sharing information with employees (thus eliminating unwritten rules characteristic of the "old boy" network in traditional, homogeneous organizations), coaching and counseling subordinates, and recognizing and using subordinates' expertise.

What all of these processes—diversity, empowerment, team building, TQM, and reengineering—have in common is a commitment to continuous learning. Learning organizations integrate such commitment into their practices and culture. They design processes, products, services, and their approaches to their clients, customers, and own employees to be open-ended in order to respond to rapid change. They develop too an openness to learning how to learn.* David Garvin of the Harvard Business School comments "Continuous improvement requires a commitment to learning."[57]

According to Fred Kofman and Peter Senge, learning communities are based on three factors: a culture rooted in transcendent human values of love, wonder, humility, and compassion; a set of practices for generative conversation and coordinated action (primarily dialogue in

---

*Innovation and openness to learning have many precedents in the history of American enterprise. Americans were not known for their "Yankee ingenuity" for nothing. In addition to often-cited examples in which Americans put aside the standard mindset to explore new options (development of the telephone, electric lighting, etc.), there are countless less-publicized instances. An example is corporate education initiatives practiced by organizations such as the Bell System (AT&T) and Arthur D. Little, Inc. Such initiatives can range from remediation to postgraduate learning. See Gold, ed., *Business and Higher Education: Toward New Alliances.*[56]

which language functions as the medium for connecting, inventing, and coordinating action); and, finally, a capacity to see and work with the flow of life as a system, rather than dissecting and trying to fix the problematic parts.[58] Because of their commitment, openness, and ability to deal with complexity, the participants in a learning community influence others in an organization. A shift in perspective occurs—a shift in which security resides not in stability (the old model) but in a dynamic equilibrium between holding on and letting go of beliefs, assumptions, and certainties. What people know takes second place to what they can learn, and simplistic answers are less important than penetrating questions.[59]

To some, these ideas are too far removed from daily life to seem practicable. Garvin observes about similar recommendations that they sound desirable but do not provide a framework for action. He does so. Garvin establishes four management building blocks that provide guidelines for practice: systematic problem solving, experimentation with new approaches, learning from past experience and best practices of others, and transferring knowledge quickly and efficiently throughout the organization.[60] He notes that many organizations practice such activities but do not do so in a systematic manner. Creating systems and processes supporting these guidelines will enable organizations to manage learning more effectively, Garvin maintains.

Many organizations are finding that commitment to continuous learning is idyllic rhetoric but a strategic business. Arie P. De Geus, former head of strategic planning at Royal Dutch Shell, says, "We understand that the only competitive advantage the company of the future will have is its managers' ability to learn faster than their competitors."[61] Expanding on this statement, management specialist William Fulmer adds that a competitive edge is dependent on the ability of all of its people—not just its managers—to learn. In view of the uncertainty with which most organizations must deal, "all levels of the organization must be given opportunities to learn how to anticipate and adapt to change," says Fulmer.[62]

The connections with diversity—and the other factors we have discussed—are clear. Learning organizations value their workforces. Managers in such organizations encourage multiple perspectives while honoring and pursuing the fundamental financial needs of the organization. Recognizing that today's immediate needs may be unimportant tomorrow, managers recognize that they do not have all the ready answers about the best way to manage. They are learners as well as facilitators of learning and, in doing so, they respect differences in their people and encourage them to perform to their potential. These are the components of valuing and managing diversity.

References

1. Taylor Cox, Jr., *Cultural Diversity in Organizations: Theory, Research & Practice* (San Francisco: Berrett-Koehler, 1993), p. 11.

2. Kochman Communication Consultants, *Seminar on Culturally Based Patterns of Difference,* March 31, 1994, Washington, D.C.

3. R. Roosevelt Thomas, Jr., *Beyond Race and Gender: Unleashing the Power of Your Total Work Force by Managing Diversity* (New York: Amacon, 1991), p. xv.

4. Cox, *op. cit.,* p. 11.

5. *Ibid.,* pp. 13–31.

6. *Ibid.,* p. 182.

7. Marilyn Loden and Judith B. Rosener, *Workforce America! Managing Employee Diversity as a Vital Resource* (Homewood, Ill.: Business One Irwin, 1991).

8. Sondra Thiederman, *Profiting in America's Multicultural Marketplace: How to Do Business Across Cultural Line* (Lexington, Mass.: Lexington Books, 1991).

9. Thomas, *op. cit.*

10. *Ibid.,* p. 28.

11. *Ibid.,* p. 10.

12. Ann M. Morrison, Marian N. Ruderman, and Martha Hughes-James, *Making Diversity Happen: Controversies and Solutions* (Greensboro, N.C., Center for Creative Leadership), 1993, p. 10.

13. Ann M. Morrison, *The New Leaders: Guidelines on Leadership Diversity in America* (San Francisco: Jossey-Bass, 1992), pp. 34–52.

14. Cox, *op. cit.*

15. David Jamieson and Julie O'Mara, *Managing Workforce 2000: Gaining the Diversity Advantage* (San Francisco: Jossey-Bass, 1991), p. 7.

16. Ann M. Morrison, *The New Leaders, op. cit.,* pp. 159–266.

17. Lawrence M. Baytos, "Launching Successful Diversity Initiatives," *HR Magazine,* March 1992, pp. 91–97.

18. Thomas, *op. cit.,* pp. 35–49.

19. Anthony P. Carnevale and S. Kanu Kogod, *The American Advantage: Tools for a Diverse Workforce* (Washington, D.C.: U.S. Department of Labor/ASTD, forthcoming).

20. Cited by Sybil Evans, "Barbara Walker: Diversity Pioneer," *Cultural Diversity at Work,* vol. 6, no. 3, January 1994, p. 3.

21. Kevin R. Hopkins and William B. Johnston, *Opportunity 2000: Creative Affirmative Action Strategies for a Changing Workforce* (Washington, D.C.: Hudson Institute for U.S. Department of Labor, 1988).

22. Mary J. Winterle, *Work Force Diversity: Corporate Challenges, Corporate Responses,* Report Number 1013 (New York: The Conference Board, 1992), p. 22.

23. Hopkins and Johnston, *op, cit.* The study does not deal with gay and lesbian workers.

24. Carnevale and Kogod, *op. cit.*

25. Beverly Geber, "Managing Diversity," *Training,* July 1990.

26. Beverly A. Battaglia, "Skills for Managing Multicultural Teams," *Cultural Diversity at Work,* vol. 4, 1992, p. 4.

27. James B. Williams, "The New Workforce," *Healthcare Forum Journal,* January-February 1992, p. 22.

28. Ann M. Morrison and Mary Ann von Glinow, "Women and Minorities in Management," *American Psychologist,* vol. 45, no. 2, February 1990, p. 204.

29. *Workforce 2000 Today: A Bottom-Line Concern; Preliminary Results from the 1991 Towers Perrin Survey on Corporate Responses to Workforce Change* (New York: Towers Perrin, 1992), p. 5.

30. *Ibid.,* p. 1.

31. Winterle, *op. cit.,* p. 13.

32. Human Resources Management, "SHRM/CCH Survey," Part II, May 26, 1993, p. 5.

33. Winterle, *op. cit.,* p. 21.

34. SHRM/CCH, *op. cit.,* p. 1.

35. Ellen J. Solomon, "Recognizing Resistance: Creating Readiness of Organization Change," *The Diversity Factor,* vol. 1, no. 2, Winter 1993, p. 18.

36. *Ibid.*

37. "Resistance *Is* Part of the Change Process," *Cultural Diversity at Work,* vol. 5, no. 1, September 1992, p. 1.

38. *Ibid.,* p. 10.

39. *Ibid.*

40. *Ibid.*

41. "SHRM/CCH Survey, " *op. cit.,* p. 5.

42. Michael Mobley and Tamara Payne, "Backlash! The Challenge to Diversity Training," *Training & Development,* vol. 46, no. 12, December 1992, p. 46.

43. Winterle, *op. cit.,* p. 15m.

44. R. Roosevelt Thomas, Jr., "From Affirmative Action to Affirming Diversity," *Harvard Business Review,* March-April 1990, vol. 68, no. 2, p. 116.

45. "SHRM/CCH Survey, *op. cit.,* p. 3.

46. John Fernandez and Elizabeth Shaw, "Engineering, TQM, Team Building and Managing Diversity: The Crucial Linkage," unpublished paper.

47. "TQM: Dead Or Alive?," *Training,* July 1993, p. 63.

48. Winterle, *op. cit.,* p. 19.

49. University Associates Consulting and Training, Inc., handout.

50. Fernandez and Shaw, *op. cit.*, p. 4.

51. *Ibid*, p. 5.

52. *Ibid.*, p. 10.

53. David E. Bowen and Edward E. Lawler, III, "The Empowerment of Service Workers: What, Why, How, and When," *Sloan Management Review*, Spring 1992, reprint 3333, p. 32.

54. Mary-jo Hall, "Diversity Work: Empowering the Workforce," unpublished paper, 1993, p. 7.

55. Thomas, *op. cit.*, p. 10.

56. Gerard G. Gold, ed., *Business and Higher Education: Toward New Alliances* (San Francisco: Jossey-Bass, 1981), p. 15.

57. David A. Garvin, "Building a Learning Organization," *Harvard Business Review*, vol. 71, no. 4, July-August 1993, p. 78.

58. Fred Kofman and Peter M. Senge, "Communities of Commitment: The Heart of Learning Organizations," *Organizational Dynamics*, Autumn 1993, p. 17.

59. *Ibid.*

60. Garvin, *op. cit.*, pp. 81–89.

61. Quoted by William E. Fulmer, "Anticipatory Learning: The Seventh Strategic Imperative for the Twenty-first Century," *Journal of Management Development*, vol. 12, no. 6, 1993, p. 65.

62. *Ibid.*

5

Unions: Workers' Voice in a New Era

The American labor movement, which is as old as the American colonies, is reinventing itself. Ever since the Massachusetts Bay Company allowed the "shoomakers" and coopers of Boston to assemble in 1648, American workers have organized to safeguard their rights. By 1955, the labor movement consisted of 14.3 million people, some 35 percent of the workforce. The numbers had grown and the movement had become vastly more complex, but two things had not changed: labor's central mission as the worker's advocate and the fact that most union members were white males. Today, the second factor, too, is changing. Women now make up almost 40 percent of the labor movement. Persons from racial and ethnic minorities, including new immigrants, account for over 22 percent of membership. And their numbers are growing. These developments mean more than a demographic shift. They are creating a new era for unions with important implications for union strategies and union culture.

Women and minorities tend to be the most exploited groups in the workforce, groups that have much to gain from organizing. Labor, too, has much to gain from the inclusion of nontraditional workers in terms of enlarging its membership and broadening its base, enabling it to speak with a more powerful voice in advocating worker interests and rights. Unions, like the workplace itself, will continue to benefit from diversity. In this section, we shift our focus to view the new workforce through the lens of the institution that has long been the workers' voice.

The labor movement is often described as though it were a monolith. In fact, trends within unions are typically as varied as the unions themselves. The labor movement is the sum of these divergent factors. Despite exceptions to any characterization of labor as a whole, an eagle's eye view is valid—and important. From that perspective, few would deny that organized labor needs to be revitalized. With its membership shifting and its labor force numbers and share in a long-term decline, the labor movement is exploring new approaches. Many union leaders recognize that the growing presence of women and minorities, while creating a myriad of new challenges, also offers one of labor's best hopes for a revitalized future.

Background and Demographic Trends

Many unions brought in minorities before they began to gain acceptance in society as a whole, but this is not to say that their record was either consistent or impeccable. Black scholar–activist W. E. B. DuBois characterized the trade unions' lack of effort to organize freed slaves after the Civil War as labor's "lost opportunity," and, until well into the twentieth century, most crafts unions excluded women, blacks, and other minorities. (Management capitalized on this racial barrier, often making a show of using black workers to break strikes.) People of color who wanted union representation had few options other than to organize independently. The National Colored Labor Union was one such effort, and to its credit, it was one of the first unions—if not the first—to promote women into leadership positions. Hispanics and Asians fared no better. Hispanic miners participated in the Industrial Workers of the World (IWW) in the early part of this century, but efforts by Hispanic migrant workers to organize agriculture in the southwest, beginning in the 1920s, were often greeted with hostility by the unions. Asian workers found the unions even more opposed to their participation. Asians were explicitly banned from membership in most American Federation of Labor (AFL) unions and were segregated into "blood unions" or limited, guild-type associations.

These exclusionary practices typified labor's general response to minority workers as well as women during this era, although labor scholar Ruth Needleman of Indiana University points out that some early unions such as the Knights of Labor and the IWW were more inclusive.[1] In general, from the earliest years of the modern labor movement, two trends coexisted: one toward inclusion and the involvement of unskilled workers, another that was more exclusionary and oriented toward the crafts. The latter view, associated with the American

Federation of Labor (AFL), predominated, in part because employers generally considered the unionizing of a smaller, select group of skilled workers more or less tolerable if it meant that the majority of workers in mass production industries would not be organized.[2] In this, the employers miscalculated; however, it illustrates the point that while union policies and actions are often considered in isolation, they were not and are not made entirely independently—to a greater or lesser degree they reflect current employer attitudes and practices.

For minorities, the situation began to change when the Congress for Industrial Organizations (CIO) accepted black workers into its industrial unions in the 1930s. (Many later played an important role in CIO organizing.) But it was not easy. It required a 12-year struggle with the railroads, beginning in 1925, before the legendary A. Philip Randolph could organize the Brotherhood of Sleeping Car Porters and give black workers a rare opportunity to enjoy a measure of job security. It was the first labor contract ever signed by a white employer and a black labor leader. The union became part of the AFL, and Randolph went on to serve in executive positions in the AFL-CIO. Some have suggested that the first steps to include blacks may have been motivated in part by a desire to end their use as strikebreakers by giving them a stake in the unions. Needleman avers that "the strongest arguments for opposing racism and sexism tended to be practical rather than moral; and still are."[3]

Whatever motivations were operating, in the end, black workers began to join "mainstream" unions and enjoy the greater protections and benefits that these organizations could provide. And, even though many may have resisted the trend, the effort of minorities to make unions even more inclusive produced benefits for all workers. During World War II, for example, blacks in the labor movement worked for fair employment practices that benefited labor generally. Needleman cites the example of African-American steelworkers who fought to move out of the segregated workplaces to which they were consigned in coke plants and open hearths, in the process helping to establish the principles of seniority enjoyed today by all union workers. Similarly, efforts to open up skilled crafts to minorities worked to everyone's advantage by helping to limit arbitrary practices and favoritism, and encouraging the practice of hiring from within.[4]

Women fared a little better than minority groups, but not much. By the 1880s, the American Federation of Labor began to formally espouse unionization of women, but it did not soon overcome its fundamental opposition. Working women labored under a double burden of inferior pay and working conditions and the Victorian notion that work in the trades was inappropriate activity for "ladies." According to this view, women's place was in the home,[5] and men professed to believe it fervently. There was also a general perception that women constituted a threat to men in the workplace. Taken together, these attitudes meant that the needs of women workers could be generally ignored, and when accepted into the AFL at all, they typically were segregated into separate unions. And there was little effort to negotiate an equal pay scale for women.

The influx of women into industry during World War II forced AFL and CIO unions to open their membership further, but they remained very much an overlooked minority. Minorities within that minority had their own special set of burdens, and still do. Women of color have always been forced to cope with racism—from white women as well as from men—in addition to sexism. They worked in race-segregated labor markets and did not compete with white women, let alone men, until needed for wartime jobs during World War II. Even then, the going was tough. When African-American women were first hired at a Detroit plant in the 1940s, white women co-workers protested. The local United Auto Worker Union (UAW) leader—a male—intervened, threatening to recommend that protesters be fired. (Today, the president of the AFL-CIOs Coalition of Labor Union Women [CLUW] is Gloria Johnson, an African-American woman who rose from a clerical support position to become a union leader.)

Despite losing their jobs in large numbers following World War II, working women were permanent fixtures in the U.S. labor force and in the unions. And momentum was building. In the 1960s, many states passed public sector bargaining laws that allowed state and local employees to become union members for the first time. A substantial portion of these new members were women. African Americans, too, were active, forming coalitions that forced changes in union agendas and worked to put minority members on union staffs and executive boards. George Meany's AFL-CIO threw its support behind the passage of the new civil rights legislation, which, along with the new immigration legislation, created a growing pool of nontraditional workers whose rights were now legally protected. When legislation was passed, different unions responded in different ways: Some tried to hold on to old practices and beliefs; others took the initiative to champion the cause of their women and minority members. Eventually, these internal and external pressures, including litigation, led unions to recognize that civil rights was a workplace and a union issue and that labor's marching orders had to include the fight against discrimination against its members, regardless of their gender or racioethnic background.

Today, minority representation in trade unions is almost equal to the minority share in the general population. (Racial and ethnic minorities represent over a quarter of the total population and over 22 percent of union membership.) Although there is increasing interest in the subject, empirical research on minorities in unions is scant. Part of this is because there is little statistical information available on both workers' union coverage *and* their ethnic background. The 1990 census is the first decennial census to include questions about unions. The only regularly published figures linking gender, race, and union coverage are annual averages from the Current Population Survey (CPS). Compiled since the 1980s and published by the Bureau of Labor Statistics (BLS) in *Employment and Earnings*, CPS racial and ethnic data focus on black and Hispanic coverage. Averages for Asian and Native-American workers are not included.

CPS statistics for 1983 and 1991, shown in Figure 5-1, record an overall decline in union membership as well as a decline in almost every racial, ethnic, and gender category. Based on BLS data,[6] the percentage of people represented by unions fell 5 points between 1983 and 1991, from 23 percent of the total workforce to 18 percent. ("People represented by unions" is a more inclusive category than "union members."

Figure 5-1. Union Members, by Selected Characteristics: 1983 and 1991

Characteristic	Total workforce (millions)		Represented by unions*—no.		Represented by unions—% of total workforce	
	1983	1991	1983	1991	1983	1991
Total	88.3	102.8	20.5	18.7	23.3	18.2
Men	47.9	53.9	13.3	11.5	27.7	21.3
Women	40.4	48.9	7.3	7.2	18.0	14.8
White	77.0	88.0	17.2	15.3	22.3	17.4
Men	42.2	46.6	11.4	9.6	26.9	20.6
Women	34.9	41.4	5.8	5.7	16.7	13.8
Black	9.0	11.3	2.9	2.8	31.7	24.4
Men	4.5	5.5	1.6	1.5	36.1	27.7
Women	4.5	5.8	1.2	1.2	27.4	21.2
Hispanic†	NA	8.2	NA	1.4	NA	17.7
Men	NA	4.9	NA	0.9	NA	18.6
Women	NA	3.3	NA	0.5	NA	16.2

*Members of a labor union or an employee association similar to a union as well as workers who report no union affiliation but whose jobs are covered by a union or an employee association contract.

†Persons of Hispanic origin may be of any race.

SOURCE: U.S. Bureau of Labor Statistics, *Employment and Earnings*, January issues, 1992. (Based on Current Population Survey.)

It includes members of unions and employee associations, and workers with no union affiliation but whose jobs are covered by a union or an employee association contract.)* During the same period, union members—that is, people who were members of unions and employee associations—dropped from 20 to 16 percent of the total. The numbers dropped as well. People represented by unions declined by almost 2 million, a 9 percent drop. In contrast, the labor force (employed wage and salary workers) grew 16 percent, to 14.5 million.

Several factors are involved in the decline. One is the erosion of American manufacturing. Manufacturing accounted for almost 50 percent of union membership in 1956, but by 1991, it had dwindled to a mere 20 percent, as plants closed or moved operations to take advantage of cheaper conditions abroad. The shift away from goods production, which was mainly blue-collar, was accompanied by the growth of the service sector with its predominantly white-collar workforce. Here, except for transportation, unions were relatively inexperienced. It was partly this inexperience, combined with pressures from their constituents, that led many unions to emphasize actions designed to save manufacturing jobs even as they were developing strategies to organize this new and expanding workforce, many of whom were in service industries. (Illustrative of the possibilities in the service sector is the success in recent years of the Service Employees International Union [SEIU] in growing its membership.)

Other reasons for unionism's decline include the growing complexity of union functions, which tended to cause some union leaders to lose touch with members; a lingering public image of union corruption, despite thorough union housecleaning efforts; and a political climate unfriendly to unions, especially in the 1980s, which lent support to anti-union strategies by employers. Although unions are relatively free to organize in the public sector, especially at the state and local government levels, it is another matter in the private sector. Increasingly, many employers have taken the offensive, hiring union-busting private consultants to thwart, sometimes illegally, labor's efforts to organize at nonunionized sites. This has coincided with an upsurge in recent years in the number of workers dismissed for union activity. Others have taken a more proactive stance, establishing employee participation programs responsive to the kinds of work practices that are typically the unions' bailiwick.

---

*Although the numerical difference between the two categories is not great, the broader category was selected for presentation here. With a few exceptions, which are discussed in the text, the trends are generally the same for both categories.

Finally, labor's slide has also been due to the slowness of unions to face the multicultural realities of the new workforce. Until recently, organizing new members was not a big item on labor's agenda. Organizing women and minority members had even lower priority. Some male union leaders viewed women and immigrant workers as less organizable than male workers. Although exclusion has not been practiced for decades, its imprint probably impeded the development of widescale efforts to organize minority workers. When unions did begin to focus on organizing minorities and women, they understandably went about it in ways that had been successful in the past. But they were not dealing with the traditional white male culture, and their assumptions about organizing women and minorities were often off the mark. Their relative lack of success tended to confirm an existing presumption that these groups were not readily organizable.[7]

As a result of these factors, even in areas where union membership has increased recently, growth generally has been feeble, and positive trends must be measured more often in terms of the smallness of the decline rather than growth. In this context, women have fared better than men. Figure 5-1 shows that the number of women represented by unions fell by about 100,000 between 1983 and 1991, a 3 percent fall. Males represented by unions decreased 1.8 million, a 7 percent drop.

Minority workers represented by unions dropped, too. The number of black workers represented by unions fell by over 7 percent between 1983 and 1991. Data is not available for Hispanic workers for 1983, but according to Gregory DeFreitas of Hofstra University, the numbers declined.[8] CPS statistics do not include data on the union coverage of Asian or Native-American workers.

Among minorities, women again fared better than men. The number of black women represented by unions rose marginally by about 1,000 over the period, and their share of union membership also rose marginally (by less than 1 percent). Black male union representation, however, dropped by almost 1 million, a more than 7 percent fall.

Among the racial and ethnic groups shown in Figure 5-1, black workers enjoyed the highest proportional union representation. Over 24 percent of the black workforce (which totaled 11.3 million) was represented by unions in 1991. For white workers, the figure was slightly less at about 22 percent; for Hispanics, almost 18 percent.

An analysis by DeFreitas produced findings broadly similar in the pattern of racial and ethnic group membership to the CPS statistics, though the point spread among groups is greater.[9] Based on a workforce population aged 23 to 30, the DeFreitas analysis found African-American workers have a higher rate of collective bargaining coverage than any other group, including white Americans.* Almost 30 percent of the African Americans in the study were covered in 1988. Please see Figure 5-2. Coverage of African Americans in this age group was almost 9 percentage points higher than Hispanic coverage and almost 13 points higher than white coverage. The DeFreitas data also include Asian Americans, 12.5 percent of whom were covered. This group has the lowest rate of coverage, some 17 points lower than that of black Americans.

In every racial and ethnic group, women have a lower rate of unionization than men. Overall, 30 percent more men than women are union members, according to Figure 5-1. Among white workers, the disparity is 33 percent; and for black workers, it is 23 percent. Hispanics come closest to parity, with only a 13 percent difference. Among younger workers (shown in Figure 5-2), the gap is even bigger overall—almost 35 percent. Among Asian workers, a stunning 90 percent more men than women are union members! Figure 5-2 also suggests that, among younger workers, organizing efforts among black women are effective, because the gap between male and female coverage is only about 9 percent. The same reasoning suggests, however, that much work needs to be done among younger female Hispanic workers, for the difference in collective bargaining coverage is about 35 percent.

An examination of patterns of collective bargaining coverage by occupation shows that black workers have the highest rate of coverage in

Figure 5-2. Collective Bargaining Coverage of Whites, Blacks, Hispanics, and Asians, 1988

Characteristics	Percentages with collective bargaining coverage				
	Total	White	Black	Hispanic	Asian
Total	19.2	16.7	29.4	20.5	12.5
Men	22.6	20.8	31.2	24.3	23.2
Women	15.8	13.6	28.4	15.8	2.4
Native-born	19.3	17.4	29.2	20.2	11.9
Foreign-born	20.3	18.4	33.8	20.9	13.8
1975-1979 migrant	16.4	22.0	0.0	14.2	5.2
Pre-1975 migrant	19.5	17.6	40.2	23.2	18.8
NB, parents FB	23.4	25.1	37.3	21.4	11.9

SOURCE: Gregory DeFreitas, "Unionization Among Racial and Ethnic Minorities," *Industrial and Labor Relations Review*, vol. 46, no. 2, January 1993, p. 292.

---

*The study is based on the 1977–1988 National Longitudinal Survey of Youth (NLSY). The main sample for his study consisted of 5,222 men and women aged 23 through 30 in the 1988 wave of the NLSY.

Figure 5-3. Collective Bargaining Coverage of Whites, Blacks, Hispanics, and Asians, by Occupation, 1988

Characteristics	Percentages with collective bargaining coverage				
	Total	White	Black	Hispanic	Asian
Total	19.2	16.7	29.4	20.5	12.5
Occupation					
Professional & technical	15.2	14.2	23.1	17.1	2.2
Clerical & admin.	16.0	13.0	32.2	17.5	6.7
Service	17.6	14.8	25.8	19.0	23.1
Blue collar	24.0	22.7	31.6	24.1	20.1

SOURCE: Gregory DeFreitas, "Unionization Among Racial and Ethnic Minorities," *Industrial and Labor Relations Review*, vol. 46, no. 2, January 1993, p. 292.

each occupational category. Please see Figure 5-3. Asian-American workers generally have the lowest rate, except in service occupations. Union underrepresentation of Asian workers is most striking in the professional and technical occupations. Almost a quarter of the total Asian-American workforce holds professional and technical jobs according to the 1990 census, but just over 2 percent of younger Asian workers held union jobs (that is, were covered by collective bargaining agreements). On the other hand, in some occupational categories, union coverage exceeds the share of jobs held by these groups. For example, some 12 percent of the black workforce was employed in professional and technical jobs according to the 1990 census, but 23 percent of younger black workers in these occupations held union jobs. For black workers employed in clerical and administrative jobs, the figures were 18 percent (total black workforce) and 32 percent (younger workers with union jobs).

The Union Advantage

The nontraditional worker–union link is not a marriage made in heaven, but it is pretty close to it. Despite the many, weighty problems (what marriage does not have problems?), unions and nontraditional workers have much to gain from each other. Unions need to increase the presence of minorities and women at all organizational levels and adapt their culture to them if they are to survive. But union workers, too, benefit from membership in important ways. And nontraditional workers, who are frequently subjected to discrimination in the workplace, perhaps have even more to gain.

First is the empowerment that may be gained from union membership. Members have an increased voice in the workplace, allowing them an important role in determining employment conditions. And because unions at the local levels are democratic, workers run their own organizations. All this translates into an increased sense of worth. Characterizing the labor movement as "one of the greatest civil rights workers," black union activist and vice president of the CLUW, Clara Day, observed, "Even before King's time, they were there with the union contract, which caused a systematic integration of jobs. It brought people together to understand each other, and to realize that they lived, they died, they hurt, they bled, they were just human."[10] Unions, once integrated in the 1940s, stayed that way even during periods when communities, schools, and even churches became more segregated with the suburbanization of America.

A more tangible union advantage is higher wages. Comparative union-nonunion wage data vary by source. Here we use data based on the CPS.* Please see Figure 5-4. The data clearly show that, like white males, union-

Figure 5-4. Median Usual Weekly Earnings in Dollars:* 1983 and 1991

Characteristic	Total		Represented by unions[†]		Not represented by unions	
	1983	1991	1983	1991	1983	1991
Total	313	430	383	522	288	404
Men	378	497	416	567	349	473
Women	252	368	307	462	237	348
White	319	446	391	539	295	415
Men	387	509	421	581	362	488
Women	254	374	313	473	240	355
Black	261	348	324	452	222	314
Men	293	374	360	485	244	330
Women	231	323	287	414	209	302
Hispanic[‡]	NA	315	NA	438	NA	295
Men	NA	328	NA	482	NA	305
Women	NA	239	NA	376	NA	278

*For full-time employed wage and salary workers; 1983 revised since originally published.

†Members of a labor union or an employee association similar to a union as well as workers who report no union affiliation but whose jobs are covered by a union or an employee association contract.

‡Persons of Hispanic origin may be of any race.

SOURCE: U.S. Bureau of Labor Statistics, *Employment and Earnings*, January issues, 1992. (Based on Current Population Survey.)

---

*A more detailed analysis, which uses three data sources, is found in Anderson, Doyle, and Schwenk, "Measuring union-nonunion earnings differences," *Monthly Labor Review*.[11] Also see Lewis, *Union Relative Wage Effects: A Survey*.[12]

represented women and minorities earn higher wages than their nonunion counterparts. Further, wage differentials, which are found within both unionized and nonunionized sectors, are less in union settings.

In 1991, the median usual weekly earnings of workers represented by unions was $118 more than those received by nonunion workers. For union-represented women, median weekly wages in 1991 were $114 higher than those of nonunion female workers. However, like female workers in most circumstances, union-represented women earned less than their unionized male counterparts. In 1991, the difference was $105. This represents an improvement of only $4 over the 1983 female-male wage differential. But even this marginal improvement contrasts favorably with the nonunionized female-male wage differential. Between 1983 and 1991, the wage gain of nonunion women was $13 less than that of nonunion men.

The largest wage gap between union-represented and nonunion workers occurred among Hispanic men. Their median weekly earnings in 1991 were $177 more than those of their nonunion counterparts. Black male union-represented workers earned $155 more per week than nonunion black males, while white male union-represented workers earned $93 more than their nonunion counterparts. Among women, the largest union-nonunion wage differentials occurred among white women and black women. White women made $118 more and black women made $112 more than their nonunion counterparts. For Hispanic women, the difference was $98. The relatively low figure for Hispanic women is especially striking because union-represented Hispanic males showed the greatest wage gap over their nonunion counterparts.

Another way that unionized workers have an advantage is diminished discrimination in the union setting. CPS data show that ethnoracial-correlated wage differences are larger in the nonunion sector than among union-represented groups. In 1991, the black-white wage gap for union-represented workers was $87; for nonunion workers, it was $101. The Hispanic-white differential was $101 for union-represented workers; for nonunion, $120. And the Hispanic-black gap was $14 in the union setting and $19 in the nonunion setting (favoring black workers in both). CPS data show, however, that over time the wage differential between black and white workers has *increased* in both the union and nonunion sectors. In 1983, the black-white wage gap for union-represented workers was $20 less than in 1991. The wage gap for nonunionized black and white workers was even larger: $28.*

---

*Annual median weekly earnings data by union affiliation were first published in 1983. Data for Hispanic workers is not available for that year.

Union workers also have the advantage of due process, the guarantor of individual rights and a concept of critical importance to minorities. Workers cannot be fired without cause, and they are protected by explicit grievance procedures through which they can voice complaints about workplace discrimination. Ironically, empowering workers through the grievance procedure may also *promote* worker perceptions of discrimination and complaints about it. According to John S. Heywood of the University of Wisconsin–Milwaukee, white union members—both men and women—are much more likely to claim discrimination than their nonunion counterparts.[13] Black women union members are somewhat more likely to see themselves as victims of discrimination than nonunionized black women, while unionized black males are no more likely to make such claims than black male nonmembers. (Data about Hispanic and Asian workers were not included in the study.)

The Tasks Ahead

The labor movement is engaged in a soul-searching mission. There is wide acknowledgment that new directions must be taken, and many are pointing to the need to organize more women and minority workers. The tasks facing labor, however, go beyond recruiting greater numbers of women and minorities. Voices within labor insist that women and minorities can contribute to unions in other ways too. Needleman observed about women—and her observation can be extended to minorities—that increasing their numbers in the union rank-and-file and leadership can have a qualitative effect on the character of American unions.[14] The discussion that follows summarizes issues that have special relevance for labor and its new workforce.

Women's Issues in the Labor Movement

Women are a vital sector of the labor movement's membership. Overall, their numbers are growing, while those of men are declining, as previously discussed. Women led one of the most dramatic and highly publicized recent union victories. The successful strike against American Airlines in 1993 by flight attendants (a female-dominated industry) heightened public support for labor and helped invigorate the labor movement. (One commentator observed about the effects of the strike, "As more and more Americans find themselves at economic risk, millions of travelers, TV viewers, and newspaper readers must have concluded from the energetic flight attendants that a union might not be a bad thing to have around."[15])

Despite their importance for the labor movement, union women still struggle for equality on several fronts. Big changes take time, and while organized labor has made progress, the legacy of sexism has not been eliminated. Labor faces two overlapping types of challenges on gender equality—in the union setting and on the job. In the first category, labor's responsibility is direct; in the second, it is more complex. Employers, not unions, are prime determiners of most hiring practices, wages, and working conditions for their workforce. Labor's job, however, is to bargain for greater equality for women, and it has been doing so for years—with mixed results. New strategies are needed.

The percentage of women workers is great in certain occupations such as health and personal service, professional, and administrative support jobs, but they are woefully underrepresented in many blue-collar occupations with long histories of unionization. According to the 1990 census, women hold only 1 percent of the jobs in transportation and material-moving occupations.[16] In construction trades, they have made little progress since 1980, their job share representing less than 3 percent of the total. In mechanics and repair jobs, their share is a mere 4 percent. Labor has long used affirmative action programs as a bargaining strategy to prod employers to hire more women. As these statistics indicate, success has been limited, particularly in traditionally male areas of employment (including administrative and executive positions) that are the focus of affirmative action strategies. Margaret Hallock of the University of Oregon explains that affirmative action policies apply to a relatively small segment of employers. Their impact also has been limited because they do not apply to women as a class. Success is attained one woman at a time.[17]

The gender wage gap, discussed elsewhere in this publication, is a further area of union concern. Women still get less income for equal work, though some progress is being made. Many jobs still are segregated by sex, and women's jobs are often undervalued. At the same time, the wage gap among women is getting bigger, with greater percentages of women moving into the higher and lower ends of the wage scale.

Hallock describes two main strategies unions have used during the past three decades to combat the gender wage gap: equal employment policies and pay equity strategies.[18] The former focuses on negotiating affirmative action programs to get women into female-dominated jobs. But these positions are typically undervalued, so they do little to remove the gender wage gap. Some unions have established career development programs to help train women to move into traditionally male jobs, where presumably they will receive higher pay. But Hallock cites evidence showing that once a traditionally male job is dominated by women, wages decline.[19] She also points out that most women do not switch; they remain in relatively low-paying female-dominated jobs.

The second type of labor strategy is pay equity, which aims at improving pay in traditionally female-dominated jobs to levels comparable to those associated with equivalent male jobs. As a result largely of union bargaining, these strategies have produced some successes, including raising wages, stimulating women as a class to question the wage gap, and providing an issue around which many women have organized and developed strong union ties. But pay equity strategies, too, have been limited in their success. According to Hallock, the reduction in the wage gap has been only slight and mainly has been confined to the public sector. Moreover, they have often caused divisiveness, even between men and women in unions, as they debate the relative value of duties associated with traditionally male and female jobs.

Hallock argues that it is time for new union strategies to reduce the gender wage gap. She calls for gender-blind initiatives to promote wage equality, suggesting, for example, that unions advocate a family wage for *all* workers, not just men.[20] She also calls for expanding training opportunities beyond the traditional male trades to semiprofessional and technical jobs, including those in female-dominated industries. Hallock and others, such as Elizabeth Engberg of SEIU, support labor's adoption of strategies to represent the (mainly female) contingent workforce.[21]

Debate surrounds the use of job evaluations as a means of attaining pay equity. Some pro-union analysts hold that reform efforts in this area are likely to meet with limited success. They maintain that job evaluation processes are inherently political and gender-biased, and they promote management control of wage determination.[22,23] However, Marlene Kim of Rutgers University argues that, because job evaluation is an important tool, unions cannot afford to ignore it.[24]

Another task facing the unions is to continue to bargain for employer policies to ensure a discrimination-free environment for all workers, including women. Despite EEO laws and union efforts in this direction, women often face gender bias. There are special problems with blue-collar jobs. Being the only woman at a blue-collar worksite or one of a small minority is not easy. For a member of Cleveland's Hard Hatted Women, being the only woman meant "having no one to relate to at my job; not having restroom facilities; having to speak up for myself on issues that I feel are unfair practices at work and not having any support."[25]

In the traditionally male blue-collar domain, women tend to be viewed as outsiders. And practically speaking, they *are* outsiders, or were until recently. Because schedules and facilities were built around the needs of men, the early women working in the trades did not have adequate washroom or locker facilities, and their workshifts often kept them from fulfilling their parenting responsibilities. (Women are typically expected to be home for their children; men are not.) Further, many male co-workers were hostile.

Some of these conditions still prevail. Women's skills and knowledge are often ignored; they may be stereotyped as emotional and incompetent. There is also fear. Women may be perceived as threatening male positions and taking the place of men who support families— a notion that overlooks the fact that a large percentage of working women are family breadwinners, too.

In such a setting, women feel pressed to work harder than men and to prove themselves repeatedly. The experience of Verlett Allen is not exceptional. Initially the only woman on a 14-person crew with the Washington-area Metro, Allen, a radio technician, described her first seven years as "virtual hell."[26] Sexism can range from outright sexual harassment to subtle nonverbal cues to assignments of tasks well below the worker's proven abilities.

Some unions have been fighting sexual harassment for decades, with varying levels of commitment. Linda Housch Kwanza Collins reports on responses of the UAW in an industry where sexual favors were "routinely demanded" of women.[27] Citing historian Nancy Gabin, Collins notes that the UAW appeared more responsive to women's demands for protection from sexual harassment than any other "women's issue," including that of pay equity.[28] The UAW Women's Bureau helped provide resources for the civil rights and feminist movements of the 1960s and 1970s, including participating in drafting the first law in the United States (in 1978) that made sexual harassment in the workplace illegal. Assurance of such protection was the factor that prompted some women to join the UAW.

It is easier for a union to deal with sexual harassment when management, rather than a male co-worker, is at fault. A film developed by Dottie Jones and Linda Ross of the UAW, often shown at UAW educational seminars, addresses this issue. The film stresses the illegal nature of sexual harassment rather than its immorality. According to Jones, "Men may be more willing to point out unacceptable behavior to other male workers if they can focus on the illegality and repercussions of sexually harassing female co-workers."[29]

It is significant that the blue-collar jobs in which women have made considerable progress tend to be those where people work alone and thus encounter minimal discrimination. As more women seek out such blue-collar situations, however, the job categories themselves may undergo a transition from "male" jobs to "female" jobs. The 1990 census shows, for instance, that women now account for almost 50 percent of the bus drivers and 80 percent of the public transportation attendants—both examples of occupations in transition. It remains to be seen at what point an equilibrium will be established.

When women are successful on the job, the price is often conformity to the male culture. Studies have shown that women in male-dominated groups in organizational settings tend to behave like the men or to fade into the background. Sociolinguist Deborah Tannen characterized male-female conversation as "cross-cultural communication." She noted that when women are in a group of men, especially in the workplace, they tend to defer to and adopt the male, information-oriented conversation style rather than maintaining the typically female relational style.[30]

Often, the result of these combined pressures is burnout. Tradeswomen appear especially vulnerable. According to two experienced tradeswomen, "Unless you can afford good therapy or have the psychological stamina to withstand constant emotional battery, staying on in the trades is a chancy thing."[31]

Another, interrelated task the labor movement faces is to clear the way for more women to move into leadership positions at all union levels. Many women are stewards and union representatives, and a growing number hold local and state leadership roles. But in a number of unions, national-level positions are still largely out of reach—the "glass ceiling" operates in unions as well as in corporations.

Dorothy Sue Cobble of Rutgers University compiled leadership information for selected labor organizations and found that, in each organization, women were substantially underrepresented in officer and board member positions *in relation to their membership share.* Women's leadership position was strongest in the National Education Association (NEA). Representing 72 percent of NEA membership in 1990, they constituted 45 percent of the officers and board members.[32] However, this figure was a 10 percent decline in status over their position 12 years earlier (when they were 75 percent of the total membership). The International Brotherhood of Teamsters and the International Brotherhood of Electrical Workers had no women officers or board members in 1990 (or in 1978), though in each of these organizations, women constituted a quarter or more of the membership. (The Teamsters have subsequently elected at least one woman to a leadership position.) In the United Food and Commercial Workers, Communications Workers of America, and Hotel and Restaurant Employees unions, in which about half the members were women, they held less than 10 percent of leadership positions.

Some progress is being made. The women's leadership position strengthened in several of Cobble's selected organizations between 1978 and 1990. These included the American Federation of State, County, and Municipal Employees (AFSCME), SEIU, American Federation of Teachers, Amalgamated Clothing and Textile Workers (ACTWU), and International Ladies' Garment Workers' Union (ILGWU). The most significant increase occurred in SEIU, where female leadership jumped 19 percentage points, from 15 to 34 percent of the total. (Women constituted a declining share of SEIU members during the period: 50 percent of the total in 1978 and 45 percent in 1990.)[33] Women steelworkers pushed through a resolution at their most recent convention calling for women in leadership roles and have launched a national education campaign—"Women of Steel"—aimed at developing leadership.

It would seem that part of the leadership problem lies in the persistence of male-dominated union cultures. Because union leadership consists primarily of males, women are at a disadvantage in establishing the ties that would give them access to the "inner circles." Family responsibilities may further hinder them from spending extra time to cultivate ties, while their male counterparts are often freer to do so. When stereotypes about women and their inability to lead are added to these obstacles, the route to leadership positions becomes difficult indeed.

Even women who have made it into union leadership positions, however, are not immune from discrimination. Diana Kilmury, who was elected as first vice president of the International Brotherhood of Teamsters, observed about her assignment to the outer fringes of the union power structure, "It's just interesting that they do not see Kilmury, one of the leaders of the democratic fight, or Kilmury, the original proponent of the ethical practices, or Kilmury, the construction driver, or Kilmury, the film industry driver. All they see is Kilmury the woman."[34] As Needleman points out, however, it may be easier for the next wave of Kilmurys. "It is always the `first' ones who are regarded as representatives of `their own' only," she says. Others will be looked at more on the basis of their records.[35]

Union women are actively working toward change. To promote women's issues in the labor movement at the national level, they established the Coalition of Labor Union Women (CLUW) in 1974. In addition to its organizing activities, the CLUW deals with issues such as child care, flextime, a shorter work week, and greater attention to the language of union contracts as they bear on women's concerns. The organization also advocates increased women's participation in organized labor.

Women are also combating sexism on a more personal level through the formation of support groups. Groups such as the Boston Tradeswomen's Network, Oregon Women in the Trades, and Florida Tradeswomen's Network sponsor educational events for tradeswomen as well as help place them in construction jobs. They also provide a forum for women to get together informally to trade stories about stresses on the job and to relax. While the groups include both union and nonunion women, the national organization, the National Tradeswomen's Network (NTN), which was organized in 1990, has strong union ties. The NTN encourages building bridges between union and nonunion women.

New Modes of Interaction Within Labor

In this new era, unions are searching for means to increase their memberships and to interact more effectively with their rank and file. The need is particularly urgent with regard to women and people from racial and ethnic minorities, the fastest-growing groups in the workforce. Certain established modes of operation, developed when organized labor consisted predominantly of white males, are not responsive to the needs and cultures of women and minority members. This situation resulted in the formation of groups within—yet, in a sense, outside—the union. Black caucuses and coalitions have been formed within AFSCME, the United Food and Commercial Workers' Union (UFCW), and numerous others. Women formed the Post Office Women for Equal Rights (POWER), now the official women's department of the Postal Workers' Union, and are active in other unions. The AFL-CIO has also attempted to build bridges to minorities by organizing groups that address race and gender issues: the CLUW, the A. Philip Randolph Institute (APRI), the Labor Council for Latin American Advancement (LACLAA), and the Asian Pacific American Labor Alliance (APALA). These informal networks and coalitions have all made their contributions, although there is often a creative tension between such groups and the parent unions.

Two overlapping issues coming under scrutiny within the labor movement are internal organizing and union culture. An important issue underpinning both is the empowerment and commitment of the membership. By the 1950s, the labor movement had evolved into a group of organizations that depended increasingly on local leaders and specialists to supply the needs of the rank and file: representing them in Washington, recruiting new members, and bargaining with increasingly large and powerful corporations. Known as the servicing model of unionism, this approach seemed to make good sense.* Lobbying for legislation and negotiating contracts were ever more complex processes, ones that specialists were better trained to handle than the local rank and file. Increasing government regulation and disclosure and reporting requirements further intensified the trend toward larger, more centralized union bureaucracies.

The problem was that the development of the servicing model and the increased use of arbitration tended to remove the locus of power from the shop floor, generating apathy among the rank and file. ACTWU in Miami was a case in point. Monica Russo, district manager, notes that before ACTWU switched to the organizing model, "most of our Florida members only thought of the union as a means for free insurance, low cost insurance for their spouses, a retirement plan, and the place to get their claims form."[37] Like spectators at a baseball game, many in the rank and file became accustomed to watching the pros rather than playing themselves.

New Organizing Strategies

Today, many within organized labor are calling for change. They advocate an organizing model of unionism reminiscent of strategies used by the CIO in the 1930s and 1940s. The subject of a landmark AFL-CIO teleconference in 1988, the organizing model aims to get members involved in solving their own problems. The underlying premise is that the best union members are deeply committed union members, and it recognizes that people will not be committed unless they are empowered to handle their own problems and feel their unions reflect their own cultures.

Until relatively recently, organizing new workers was not a high priority for many unions. Organizing campaigns that were undertaken generally focused on mass techniques, such as distribution of leaflets, rather than personalized one-on-one approaches. Today, things are changing. One dimension of the organizing model of unionism is a shift in perceptions about organizing campaigns. Jose La Luz, former Education Director of ACTWU, notes that "it [organizing] is still conceived in some quarters of the labor movement as a selling and marketing activity—thus, the emphasis on the adoption of technology and manipulation techniques."[38] He stresses that "most workers won't `commit' unless they develop a sense of ownership." La Luz states that

---

*For a discussion of the servicing model and its limitations, see *LRR 17, An Organizing Model of Unionism.*[36]

organizing is basically educational in nature. Workers must understand how their ability to meet their own needs "by developing their own vehicle" outweighs the risks inherent in joining a union.

Workers are more likely to realize this if the union organizers speak their own language, figuratively and literally. A study by Kate Bronfenbrenner of Pennsylvania State University and the AFL-CIO Organizing Department showed that organizing campaigns conducted by foreign-born immigrants, people of color, and women were more successful than those conducted by white males. Undertaken between 1986 and 1988, the study examined the tactics and results of 261 union certification elections and found that women organizers won 60 percent of their elections, minority organizers won 58 percent, and white males won 38 percent.[39] These results are more striking because only 12 percent of the organizers were women and 15 percent were people of color.

This is consistent with another finding: That unions do best in organizing units with a majority of women or minority workers.[40] Both of these groups are expressing more interest in joining unions, and it is generally easier to organize homogeneous groups than heterogeneous ones. The results were even stronger for minorities than for women. Units with a more than 75 percent minority population registered a 66 percent win rate (compared to 37 percent rate for all white units). Those with a substantial majority of women registered a 59 percent win rate, compared to 47 percent with no women, and 33 percent where women were less than half of the unit. In an organizational model that depends on effective communication to educate workers in an attempt to develop a "sense of ownership" that will bring them on board, Bronfenbrenner's conclusion that "unions need to do a much better job recruiting more minority and women staff"[41] would seem to make good sense.

Bronfenbrenner's voice is one of a growing chorus, and labor leaders are listening. About a dozen unions have established the Organizing Institute in Washington, D.C., where a focus is initiating organizing drives among the new workforce and training women and persons from minority racial and ethnic groups to be organizers. Bob Lawson, a union recruiter at the Institute, observes that the new focus in organizing is on "the changing nature of the workforce," referring to "women, people of color, new immigrants...that are being most exploited."[42] Lawson believes that women and minority organizers will be "the backbone of rebuilding the labor movement in this country" because they can best relate to the people being organized.

Women and minority organizers do not merely represent a different gender or racio-ethnic background. They also provide alternative styles to the traditional model of organizing. (It is tempting to label it as a generic "white male" model, but it seems younger male workers do not seem to relate to it any better than women.) Insight into what might be called the "feminine model" of organizing was provided by Kris Rondeau and Gladys McKenzie, organizers from the American Federation of State, County, and Municipal Employees (AFSCME). In successful campaigns at Harvard, the University of Minnesota, and elsewhere, their focus was on relationships.[43] Rather than impersonal newsletters and leaflets, they used intensive one-on-one approaches ("Each person deserves our respect and to be treated as an individual—not as an amorphous blob to hit with one big sales pitch."). They allowed people to talk about themselves, noting that once they feel comfortable and tell their stories, people begin to form a "heart connection." Rondeau and McKenzie did not organize around narrow issues or conduct "anti-boss" campaigns; rather they conducted positive campaigns focused on values and taking responsibility for one's own life.

While a focus on the organizing model of unionism is increasingly being moved to the front burner, there is recognition among many union leaders that it should not be used to the exclusion of the servicing model. An AFL-CIO spokesperson observes that to be effective, a union needs to embrace both.* There are times when expertise and resources beyond those which reside at the local level are needed. Issues involving pensions, employee buyouts, and workers' compensation are examples. At such times, locals affiliated with a national union need to bring in outside services. Simultaneously, the need to give local rank and file a sense of ownership in their own union is also manifest. Problems arise only when unions become rigidly attached to either the service or the organizing model rather than flexibly using both to their advantage.

Changing Union Culture

The implications of the organizing model for women and minority workers go beyond union strategies and organizing campaigns. Union culture is at stake. Many assert that this culture, which was created by earlier generations of white males who long made up the overwhelming majority of members, needs to be changed, to be made more democratic and inclusive. At a labor conference on pay equity in January 1993, Needleman observed that adopting an organizing model will

---

*Telephone interview, March 22, 1994.

mean that unions need to review all of their practices—down to the meals they serve at functions, types of recreation, and meeting styles—to determine whether they reflect the real rank-and-file membership.[44] For example, evening meetings over a round of beer are apt to discourage the participation of women. Because working women are more likely to be single parents than are men, they may not have the liberty that men do of leaving their children to attend such meetings. And an evening setting in which beer is a feature may be unappealing to many in any case. Although this may seem relatively minor, taken together with other aspects of a union's culture—from its leadership style, customs, and traditions to the language it relies on for communications—conditions are created in which the working majority of the union may not feel at home in the organization.[45] Such a lack of connection can be a serious matter.

Training for Diversity

Another way unions are responding to the growing numbers of nontraditional workers in their ranks is through training. Today, training for diversity in the trade unions has three separate but mutually reinforcing dimensions: training that enhances workers' on-the-job skills, leadership training, and training that enables employees and managers effectively to interact with individuals who are different from them.

The first dimension is not new, although new features are being added. Since the beginning of the union movement, training programs have given union members an important advantage over nonunion workers. In 1937, Congress passed the National Apprenticeship Act, known as the Fitzgerald Act, a law that required the Department of Labor to support registered apprenticeship programs. Under the terms of the act, apprentices are registered with the Department of Labor. Today, 80 percent of those registered are union apprentices.[46] Programs such as those provided by the Brotherhood of Electrical Workers, which involves some 40,000 apprentices each year, and the training branch of the Laborers' International Union enable workers to become skilled with tools and machinery in manufacturing and construction industries. Interestingly, some training programs offer physical strengthening training for women to enable them to handle more physically demanding jobs. There is still a real question about the extent to which women are being offered apprenticeship opportunities in high wage, skilled craft jobs in some of the construction industries. Here again, there may be a relationship between employer practices and policies and union actions that is not always apparent. It is clear that a start has been made and that the situation is changing.

Also new is a social component to many skills training programs, such as programs in workplace literacy. These are geared to non-English-speaking immigrants and other workers who need training in fundamental job-related skills, such as reading.

Unions are expanding into innovative partnerships with community organizations. For example, in response to the failure of New York's adult education services to provide adequate access to workers, especially immigrants, New York–based unions joined in 1985 to form the Consortium for Worker Education (CWE) and established a Worker-Family Education Program. With funding from the state, CWE member unions developed training programs and expanded existing ones. Originally consisting of seven unions, including the ILGWU and ACTWU, consortium membership has grown to more than 20.

Other unions are also addressing the needs of foreign-born workers. For instance, as part of a leadership development task force, the Bakery, Confectionery, and Tobacco Workers International Union has developed a set of guidelines for its member locals. These include guidelines for communicating and working with non-English-speaking members, as part of and beyond formal ESL training. SEIU is broadening strategies undertaken in its Justice for Janitors campaign, providing more language-related assistance and added bilingual and bicultural staff to develop community-based coalitions.[47]

Leadership training is a second component that involves diversity. The AFL-CIO's George Meany Center for Labor Studies in the Washington, D.C., area offers training in practical union skills based on the aggregate experience of trade unionists over the decades. Ranging from such traditional topics as arbitration to organizing, courses offered also include union issues for working women and training strategies for AIDS in the workplace. Practical training in organizing, with a focus on women and minorities, is also offered by the Organizing Institute in Washington, D.C.

A third component of training for diversity is thoroughly new. Knowing how to effectively interact with co-workers who are different from them is a skill that union workers—like workers in other sectors—need to learn. A growing number of unions at all levels, as well as union-affiliated and educational institutions, have developed workshops, seminars, and discussion programs on multicultural differences. Designed to increase knowledge, awareness, and sensitivity, such programs provide the starting point for the development of a comprehensive multicultural program.

The International Brotherhood of Electrical Workers is developing multicultural programs to incorporate into already existing leadership programs. Other unions such as the American Federation of Teachers, the Newspaper Guild, and SEIU have already integrated multicultural awareness in ongoing education and training programs.

Union partnerships with university centers also have resulted in the development of awareness-based programs. In one instance, the United Auto Workers cosponsored a four-day Summer School for Women Workers with the Labor Studies Centers at the University of Michigan and Eastern Michigan University. The program included a seminar on cultural diversity in the workplace. Summer schools for women, initiated in the 1970s as an update of Bryn Mawr's Summer School for Women in the 1920s and 1930s, are held on university campuses throughout the country. The courses provide union women with training in union-based issues in order to empower them as stewards and organizers in their local unions. There are also four regional summer schools for union women sponsored by the University and College Labor Education Association and the AFL-CIO and cosponsored by CLUW. In addition, many states have schools for union women, thanks to strong cooperation between university labor education programs and state AFL-CIO organizations.

At the organizational level, AFSCME recently conducted a cultural diversity seminar, a voluntary training session which brought together all levels of staff members for a day-long program designed to foster awareness.

One of the most comprehensive awareness-based models was commissioned by the Communications Workers of America (CWA) and is being developed by Cornell's School of Industrial and Labor Relations. Expanding on the CWA's ongoing "Combating Racism and Sexism" seminar initiated in 1987, the ambitious Cornell project is evaluating existing training programs employed by management and unions nationwide. The project is also incorporating into lesson plans archival materials, such as oral histories and worker interviews, as well as focus group discussions among unionists.

The Newspaper Guild has been developing and conducting programs since 1983 that address sexual harassment, gender awareness, and multicultural diversity. As part of an effort to make the full participation of women and minorities at all leadership levels a top priority, the Guild expanded its diversity workshop in 1991 "to help all of us address our own biases." The Guild works with individual locals to determine if sexual harassment exists at specific worksites and follows up with surveys and additional work with local leaders where necessary.

While sketchy, this survey of union activities in diversity training suggests the importance that labor attaches to this effort. It is an important component of the overall education mission that unions are undertaking. The comment by La Luz regarding ACTWU's education mission can be broadened to the entire labor movement. Although there is still a long way to go on diversity training, there is a growing realization that the benefits are great. Education is "central to the life of the union," according to La Luz. "It is an ongoing uninterrupted process of building the union itself."[48]

New Immigrants—New Union Members?

More than 1.5 million immigrants arrive in the United States annually, and most belong to what in America are minority racial and ethnic groups: about 85 percent are Hispanics and Asians. These people form an important source of new union membership, and some unions are recognizing this. Jack Sheinkman, president of ACTWU, characterizes his union as a "mini United Nations" which is "built on the dreams and aspirations of immigrants."[49] The AFL-CIO has developed associate membership programs to reach out to immigrant workers, helping them, among other things, to meet the new citizenship requirements. The union supports the California Immigrant Workers Association, whose program includes such things as credit counseling and legal assistance, and the Rio Grande Workers Alliance in El Paso, Texas, which concentrates on English language training.

Participants in these AFL-CIO programs are not yet full union members, but associates. Unions generally have found that the recruitment of new immigrant workers raises special issues that have caused some unions to balk at launching organizing efforts. Most new immigrants are unfamiliar with American ways; many do not speak English well or at all, and they may have inadequate job skills. Their training needs can be formidable. Further impeding recruitment is the traditional union perception—which still lingers, according to DeFreitas—that immigrants are transient and too difficult to organize.[50]

Immigrants are often seen as a threat to low-skilled, native-born workers—a view that has held sway at least since poor Irish immigrants flocked to urban areas in the 1830s and accepted whatever wages employers offered. An alternative view is that the newcomers are willing to work hard at low-end jobs that native-born workers avoid. In either case, DeFreitas points out they are often perceived as being overly pliant in the face of employer demands—which implies to union recruiters that, in general, immigrants will be unwilling to take the sometimes difficult steps necessary to unionize.

Reinforcing these views is the tendency for urban immigrants to work in small, independent, ethnic businesses that provide them with a comprehensive network of support.[51] These businesses are owned by employers—often relatives—who are in a position to sponsor immigration of workers' family members and who assist with housing, social contacts, and other needs. Workers do not easily risk breaking such ties by advocating unionization of their shop—if they are aware of the possibility in the first place, which many are not.

There is little comprehensive quantitative research on the organizability of immigrants, but a first effort shows surprising results. A study by DeFreitas found that foreign-born workers were more likely to have union jobs than native-born workers.[52] (Please see Figure 5-2.) In each racial and ethnic group as well as in the total figures, more foreign-born workers held union jobs (jobs covered by a collective bargaining agreement) than native-born workers. Total foreign-born coverage, based on a sample population of 5,222, was 20 percent; native-born coverage was 19 percent. Among the racial and ethnic groups, blacks had the highest rate of union coverage: Immigrant black workers had 34 percent coverage, while the native-born rate was 29 percent. In all groups, immigrants led native-born workers. Further, in all cases except that of Asians, native-born persons with foreign-born parents registered higher rates of coverage than native-born people with native-born parents.

Successful organizing campaigns among immigrant workers need to be carefully planned. New immigrants are unlikely to respond to the massive leaflet-type campaigns that were the hallmark of many organizing efforts in the past. Identifying some of the special features of successful organizing among immigrants, organizer Katie Quan notes that Chinese immigrant workers usually ("99 percent of the time") identify first with their ethnic heritage and only secondarily with their role as workers.[53] This means that immigrant community issues, such as fighting for social services, are often of vital interest to them. To reach these people, unions need to draw organizers and other leaders from communities being organized, according to Quan.

Ho Nhu Lai agrees. An organizer and board member of the AFL-CIO's APALU, Ho states that a prerequisite for successful organizing "is the ability to communicate with the workers in their own language and also to work with their community in every level—to understand culture and custom."[54] Ho points out that new Asian immigrants do not understand labor unions and need to be educated. Because family ties are important among them, it is crucial to educate not only workers, whom he talks with individually, but also their family members. Ho explains that in addition to fighting for fair wages, unions are a community service. And he demonstrates the point on occasion by providing needed services, such as helping with income taxes.

Another challenge some unions face is developing policies responsive to undocumented immigrants. This is the case in the apparel industry, where 39 percent of the workforce are illegal aliens. ACTWU, therefore, focuses on issues of concern to them. And "as a matter of civil and human rights," ACTWU supports the repeal of employer sanctions embodied in U.S. immigration laws.[55] Most unions have not taken this position (the ILGWU and SEIU are the only other AFL-CIO unions to do so). But it is an example of the kind of reevaluation unions are undertaking in response to issues raised by the new workforce.

References

1. Ruth Needleman, unpublished letter, February 24, 1993, p. 4.
2. *Ibid.*
3. *Ibid.*
4. *Ibid.*, p. 3.
5. James J. Kenneally, *Women and American Trade Unions* (Montreal: Eden Press Women's Publications, 1981), pp. 19, 47.
6. BLS, *Employment and Earnings, Statistical Abstract, 1992* (Washington, D.C.: U.S. GPO, 1993), p. 422.
7. Ruth Needleman, "Women Workers: A Force for Rebuilding Unionism," *Feminizing Unions, Labor Research Review* (hereafter *LRR*), vol. VII, no. 1, Spring 1988, p. 4. Professor Needleman refers only to confirmed assumptions about the unorganizability of women.
8. Gregory DeFreitas, "Unionization among Racial and Ethnic Minorities," *Industrial and Labor Relations Review*, vol. 46, no. 2, January 1993, p. 285. The decline in Hispanic participation rate in unions is probably due to immigration status, duration of U.S. residence, English-language skills, and nationality.
9. *Ibid.*, pp. 284–301.
10. "Black Women in the Labor Movement: Interviews with Clara Day and Johnnie Jackson," *LRR 11*, vol. VII, no. 1, Spring 1988, pp. 82–83.
11. Kay E. Anderson, Philip M. Doyle, and Albert E. Schwenk, "Measuring union-nonunion earnings differences," *Monthly Labor Review*, June 1990, pp. 26–38.
12. Gregg H. Lewis, *Union Relative Wage Effects: A Survey* (Chicago: University of Chicago Press, 1986).
13. John S. Heywood, "Race Discrimination and Union Voice," *Industrial Relations*, vol. 31, no. 3 (Fall 1992), p. 501.

14. Needleman, *op. cit.*, pp. 1–2.

15. Robert Kuttner, "So You Thought Unions Were Obsolete?," *The Washington Post*, November 28, 1993, p. C7.

16. U.S. Department of Commerce, Bureau of the Census, *1990 Census of Population, Supplementary Reports: Detailed Occupation and Other Characteristics from the EEO File for the United States*, 1990 CP-S-1-1 (Washington, D.C.: U.S. Government Printing Office, October 1992), Table 1.

17. Margaret Hallock, "Unions and the Gender Wage Gap," Dorothy Sue Cobble, ed., *Women and Unions: Forging a Partnership* (Ithaca, N.Y.: ILR Press, 1993), p. 31.

18. *Ibid.*, pp. 27–42.

19. *Ibid.*, p. 30.

20. *Ibid.*, pp. 40–41.

21. Elizabeth Engberg, "Unions Responses to the Contingent Workforce," *ibid.*, pp. 163–175.

22. Hallock, *op. cit.*, pp. 36–37.

23. Carrie Donald, "Comments," Dorothy Sue Cobble, ed., *Women and Unions: Forging a Partnership* (Ithaca, N.Y., ILR Press, 1993), p. 100.

24. Marlene Kim, "Comments," Dorothy Sue Cobble, ed., *Women and Unions: Forging a Partnership* (Ithaca, N.Y., ILR Press, 1993), pp. 90–92.

25. Anne Abend-Brophy and Lynn Dabney, "Tradeswomen's Support Group: Helping Women Make It in the Skilled Trades Jobs," *Labor Notes*, September 1992, p. 6.

26. *Ibid.*

27. Linda Housch Kwanza Collins, "To Hell with You, Charlie," *LRR 20, Building on Diversity*, vol. XII, no. 1, Spring/Summer 1993, pp. 71–77.

28. Nancy Gabin, *Feminism in the Labor Movement: Women and the United Auto Workers, 1935–1975* (Ithaca, N.Y.: Cornell University Press, 1990).

29. Collins, *op. cit.*, p. 76.

30. Deborah Tannen, *You Just Don't Understand: Women and Men in Conversation* (New York: William Morrow, 1990).

31. Abend-Brophy and Dabney, *op. cit.*, p. 6.

32. Cobble, ed., *Women and Unions: Forging a Partnership* (Ithaca, N.Y.: ILR Press, 1993), p. 11.

33. *Ibid.*

34. "Who Shall Lead," *New York Newsday*, Sept. 6, 1992, p. 75.

35. Ruth Needleman, unpublished letter, February 24, 1993, p. 10.

36. *LRR 17, An Organizing Model of Unionism*, vol. X, no.1, Spring 1991.

37. Monica Russo, "This World Called Miami," *LRR 20, op. cit.*, p. 44.

38. Jose La Luz, "Creating a Culture of Organizing: ACTWU's Education for Empowerment," *LRR 17, op. cit.,* p. 62.

39. Kate Bronfenbrenner, *Successful Union Strategies for Winning Certification Elections and First Contracts: Report to Union Participants, Part I: Organizing Survey Results,* unpublished paper, Penn State University, New Kensington Campus, n.d., p. 7.

40. *Ibid.,* p. 4.

41. *Ibid.,* p. 8.

42. Nat Hentoff, "Don't Mourn: Organize," *Washington Post,* January 29, 1994, p. A19.

43. "Women's Ways of Organizing: A Conversation with AFSCME Organizers Kris Rondeau and Gladys McKenzie," *LRR 18, Let's Get Moving! Organizing for the '90s,* vol. X, no. 2, Fall/Winter 1991/92, pp. 45–59.

44. Bureau of National Affairs, Inc., "Organized Labor's Fight for Pay Equity Must Focus on Re-Valuing Low-Wage Jobs," *Labor Relations Week,* vol. 7, January 1, 1993, p. 46.

45. Ruth Needleman, "Building an Organizing Culture of Unionism," paper presented at the *Annual Conference of the Industrial Relations Research Association,* Gary, Indiana, January 6, 1993, p. 2.

46. "Apprenticeship," *Occupational Outlook Quarterly* (DOL), Winter 1991–1992, p. 29.

47. Tula Connell, "Multicultural Leadership Development at the Service Employees International Union (SEIU)," 1992, unpublished paper.

48. Jose La Luz, "A multicultural framework for workers' education," International Labor Organization, Worker Education Division, *Labor Education,* no. 53, February 1991, p. 18.

49. Jack Sheinkman, "Multiculturalism in Building the Union," *LRR 20, op. cit.,* p. 1.

50. DeFreitas, *op. cit.,* p. 288.

51. Roger Waldinger, "Immigration and Industrial Change in the New York City Apparel Industry," *Hispanics in the U.S. Economy,* ed. by George Borjas and Marta Tienda (New York: Academic Press, 1985), p. 344.

52. DeFreitas, *op. cit.,* p. 292.

53. Katie Quan, "Organizing Immigrant Workers in the Global Economy," *Labor in a Global Economy: The Perspective From the U.S. and Canada,* Steven Hecker and Margaret Hallock, eds. (Seattle: University of Oregon Books, 1991), p. 227.

54. Ho Nhu Lai, "Organizing Immigrant Asian Workers," *LLR 20, op. cit.,* p. 50.

55. Sheinkman, *LRR 20, op. cit.,* p. 2.

PART 2

Our Diverse Workforce

Identity Groups in the New Workforce and Their Issues

As we saw in the preceding section, workforce diversity can provide American organizations and the economy as a whole with a competitive advantage. But this can happen only when organizations are responsive to diversity's many challenges. In this section, we discuss some of these challenges. Many publications identify management strategies for the new workforce. And we have discussed some of them previously. Here, we investigate from the workers' perspectives major issues of special concern to member groups in the new workforce. We expand on the definition of diversity found in early publications on the subject, a definition based on EEO categories including women and major racial and ethnic minority groups. Our focus includes other identity groups as well: older workers, workers with disabilities, and gay and lesbian workers. Each of these groups has distinguishable workplace concerns that need to be understood before they can be successfully addressed.

The one important group in the workplace that receives less attention here than others is white men. While their workplace concerns are as legitimate as those of any other group, we deal with them mainly in a secondary way in our chapter on gender. Also, their concerns provide the backdrop against which issues of many other groups are played out. This relative omission makes sense because our focus is on the "new" workforce. But it risks implying that white men are the only "nondiverse" group in the workplace and suggests they are in an adversarial position with regard to the others. This is not our intent.

For the sake of clarity, we discuss identity groups in relative isolation from each other. But drawing such distinctions caricaturizes reality. Life is not neatly delineated. Real people hold multiple group identities, and they are pushed and pulled by often-conflicting workplace issues stemming from their various identities. Real-life identities are further complicated by the unique characteristics of every person. These characteristics add immeasurably to the richness of our natures, and they tend to influence our responses in the workplace. A person who is an introvert (that is, one who takes his or her energy from being alone or with few people in quiet situations), for example, is unlikely to respond well to a high-pressure work environment requiring continual team work.

So we need to be clear that our focus on group identities is an effort to provide a general map of workplace issues. It is not an attempt to define any person along a single dimension nor to deny the individuality that is such an important part of our nature. Ed Mickens, editor of a gay and lesbian newsletter on workplace issues, while pointing out that gay and lesbian workers belong to more identity groups than most people, notes that all workplace issues are finally human issues. He says that the ultimate effort is to "build bridges" among human beings. This is what we hope to do here.

6

Racial and Ethnic Groups in the New Workforce: History and Cultural Issues—1

We start with a riddle: Who is a minority American? There is no answer to this riddle. Rather, there is no *single* answer. There are not even a few answers. The only way to solve the riddle is to provide millions of answers, one for each American, for we all belong to minorities of some sort. Clearly, such an elaborate response is impractical, and we must settle here for some level of generalization. Our discussion in this and the following two chapters focuses on people of color, that is, the ethnic and racial groups that comprise the "new workforce." We use the same categories used by federal agencies for statistical reporting. They are also the groups that are explicitly protected under affirmative action guidelines: black Americans (also referred to here as "African Americans"); Hispanics (whom we also refer to as "Latinos"); Asians and Pacific Islanders (also referred to as "Asian Americans"); and American Indians, Eskimos, and Aleuts (referred to as "Native Americans, " "American Indians, " or "Indians").

The focus on identity groups in the new American workforce limits the scope of our examination. And this is just as well. On the 1990 census, Americans answered the question about racial identity by citing more than 250,000 different categories. What constitutes a minority group is a matter of the categories selected!

The definition of "minority" is also a function of time. By the year 2050, groups now considered minorities (blacks, Latinos, Asians, Native Americans, and others) will collectively comprise some 47 percent of the population. Whites still will be the dominant racial group— 72 percent of the total, when white Hispanics are included in the count. Nonetheless, the old picture of a "typical" American being a white person of European derivation will no longer hold true. By the year 2050, Latinos are projected to increase from 10 percent of the population (in 1990) to 21 percent. Blacks will increase from 12 to 15 percent of the total; Asians, from 3 to 10 percent; Native Americans are expected to hold steady at 1 percent.

The terms "race" and "ethnicity" also need defining. According to scholars Taylor Cox, Jr., of the University of Michigan, and Stella M. Nkomo, of the University of North Carolina, "race" refers to "major divisions of humankind with distinctive heredity and transmissible physical characteristics." An "ethnic group" is "one that shares a common cultural tradition and sense of identity."[1]

While the definitions appear simple, reality is not. Nkomo, surveying recent literature on race within organizations observed that race has a variety of formulations. It is variously understood as, for example, a sociohistorical concept, a matter of individuality as well as collectivity, a discrete demographic variable that can be objectively observed and measured, and a basically unstable variable that cannot be readily quantified.[2] Anthropologist Kanu Kogod observes that "race" often is used as a political term. She adds that within racial groups, physical characteristics, such as skin color, may vary so widely that individuals may bear more resemblance to members of other racial groups than to their own.[3] A further complication is raised by Cox and Nkomo who note that many people confuse "race" and "ethnicity, " using "the former to refer to blacks and whites and the latter to refer to Hispanics and Asians.[4] This confusion leads to the false conclusion that blacks and whites have distinct physical traits but only Hispanics and Asians have distinct cultural traits. In fact, each of these groups has distinctive cultural traits, some of which are examined in our discussion to follow.

Our discussion of racial and ethnic minorities (whom we also refer to as "people of color") is divided into three parts. In this chapter and the following, we examine two types of dimensions affecting people of color in the workplace: politico-historical and cultural. In a third chapter, we focus on the current socioeconomic status of people of color, analyzing background issues that hinder them in the workplace as well as practical issues they currently face on the job. While the first two chapters engage mainly in a group-by-group analysis, the third is an issue-based examination with references to the various groups interwoven.

Since the earliest European immigrants came to this continent, people have been arriving on our shores seeking religious or political freedom and, more frequently, economic opportunity. Understanding of other peoples begins with a knowledge of "where they are coming from," literally. Therefore, we briefly survey the social and political histories of each major group in the new workforce. Our focus is on their evolving roles in the United States, especially in regard to U.S. government policy and their historical status in the workplace.

Our historical and cultural survey includes Arab Americans—that is, persons from Arabic-speaking countries of North Africa and Southwest Asia. An important group in the new workforce, Arab Americans are not usually highlighted separately in literature dealing with workforce issues. This is because they are, by official count, the smallest of the major minority groups and not explicitly covered by affirmative action guidelines. Many, however, believe their numbers are considerably larger than the official count. And, like some other groups in the new workforce, their numbers have been significantly increased by post-1965 immigration.

Each of the racial and ethnic groups in the new workforce is characterized by enough common patterns to permit meaningful generalization. Yet each is also exceedingly diverse, comprising major subgroups with different histories and sometimes different languages. The terms "Hispanic" and "Asian" are, in fact, umbrella categories devised by the U.S. government for statistic-gathering purposes. "Arab American" might likewise be seen as such a category. Because Latinos and Asians comprise a significant part of the new workforce, we briefly examine the American histories of important subgroups within each, rather than trying to provide a composite group history.

In our discussion of cultural values in this and the following chapter, we venture beyond the relative safety of quantifiable data onto much more slippery ground. We then turn to key values of the cultures that major groups in America's new workforce claim as their heritage. Our focus is on how these values are likely to be expressed on the job. Difficult to discuss in quantitative terms, these values influence perceptions, attitudes, and behaviors. They are important factors shaping the experiences of minority and nonminority individuals on the job.

"Culture" is a set of shared ideas that guide members of a group in their interactions as they perform the tasks of everyday life. Cultural traits are learned from our social environment; they are not inherited. While cultural traits occur with frequency within a group and are characteristic of it, not every single group member necessarily displays every trait that forms the group's culture. As Hofstede points out, "Statements about culture are not statements about individuals."[5] The tendency to confuse the individual and the group is called the *ecological fallacy,* and it leads one mistakenly to assume that a discussion about culture automatically is a discussion about every individual within that culture. Such an assumption leads to stereotyping. This point is worth emphasizing here because we devote considerable attention to cultural values and the workforce.

Values are the standards a group uses to determine which attitudes and behaviors are acceptable and which are not. The core of any culture, values shape perceptions and behavior. Each of the major identity groups discussed in this and the following chapters, whether a racial or an ethnic group, has its own distinctive set of cultural values, and these influence, to varying degrees, their perceptions and behaviors at work.

Sociologist Geert Hofstede of the University of Limburg (Maastricht, The Netherlands) has pointed out that culture is generally overlooked in American management literature. The tendency is to attribute cultural differences to individual interactions.[6] He notes that this is not too surprising because the United States is the world's most individualistic culture.

And there is another reason the role of culture may be overlooked in management theory. It is the same reason it has been overlooked on the job: Until relatively recently, the overwhelming majority of workers shared the same broad cultural values, which in this chapter we identify as "Anglo" or "mainstream" values.* So it usually *was* accurate to ascribe differences to interpersonal differences.[7] But this is no longer the case. Not only are the numbers of minority and women workers growing, but, as multicultural expert Thomas Kochman has pointed out, they no longer are willing simply to accommodate to the dominant male Anglo culture; they want reciprocal accommodation to their cultures.[8] Any attempt to understand today's workforce issues needs to include an understanding of the different cultural perspectives of the people who are in the workforce.

---

*It is a common psychological phenomenon for people to assume that others behave and think as they do. In psychology, this is called the *false consensus effect.* White Americans may find it especially easy to assume consensus simply because they *are* the majority. (One doesn't have to probe far, however, to find a multitude of differences within the white population, as within any other.) But the false consensus effect is not limited to white people. It may exist among people regardless of racial or ethnic identity.

And the issue goes further: Lack of insight into the values of people from other groups commonly leads to misunderstandings on the job that can damage working relationships and impede productivity. Ignoring cultural differences and considering groups collectively as "minorities" or merely as statistical entities overlooks the unique contributions each can make in the workplace. Intercultural understanding is crucial to high performance standards. Hofstede's observation about cross-cultural cooperation is applicable: "One of the reasons why so many solutions do not work or cannot be implemented is because differences in thinking among the partners have been ignored. Understanding such differences is at least as essential as understanding the technical factors."[9]

There is a prodigious range of cultural difference within each group surveyed. In most cases, group members derive from a large region consisting of several countries or even a continent. Native Americans too, who within recorded history derive from North America, have a wide range of tribal differences. Further, individuals within each group represent the full range of class backgrounds, education, and degrees of acculturation and assimilation. Despite the many intra-group differences, each is characterized by certain common values that make possible discussion, however broad, of each group as an entity. Such discussion is especially relevant in the context of the American workplace where workers continually come into contact with the dominant Anglo culture. We believe that the contrasts *between* minority and Anglo cultural values supersede the many cultural differences *within* each group.

Our examination attempts to identify ways in which cultural values are expressed on the job and the cultural misunderstandings that can occur when people holding different values work together. We contrast minority-group values and Anglo values or, more specifically, values associated with white males. Although among white Americans (commonly called "Anglos" though they derive from many ethnic groups) only half are males, these are the values that dominate American culture. They also characterize the culture of most organizations, which were established and still are dominated by white males. Organizational values reflect an organization's history, discourse, and leadership over time. Even employees who are not white men may be bearers of their organization's culture. Minority- or female-owned organizations also may have a male Anglo culture because people, regardless of race and gender, tend to buy in to the dominant way of doing things in order to be competitive in the marketplace.

Organizational cultures in America are in transition. They are slowly beginning to evolve away from the Anglo standard into pluralistic cultures more reflective of the demographics of their workforces. But this change will take time. In our discussions on cultural values in the workplace, we assume for the sake of simplicity that organizational cultures are characterized by Anglo values. Our aim is to provide insights to help counter the common assumption that people of color need to accommodate the dominant culture without reciprocity.*

An examination of cultural values is wide open to criticism. Cultures are highly complex, and generalizations about them are always risky. Generalizations almost certainly are incomplete, and they readily slip into stereotyping (as we will see). No person is simply a compilation of the learned values of his or her culture. Individuals have unique inherited and learned characteristics as well, and we all share a universal human nature.

What's more, cultural generalizations are bound to be only partly applicable. Invariably, some group members do not hold them or they hold them to lesser degrees. Immigrants are usually the most distinctive cultural group. Second- and third-generation Americans almost certainly are more acculturated and probably somewhat more assimilated than the immigrant population.† That is, they are more likely to have adopted Anglo cultural values to some degree and to be at least somewhat integrated into economic, social, and/or political life of the mainstream.

Still, values have staying power. The search for ethnic identification is a natural human tendency that spans generations. Many have observed that, in America, this search seems to involve a process by which first-generation immigrants identify more with their old cultural heritage rather than with their new nationality; the second generation tends to reject their cultural heritage and identify more with their American nationality and mainstream culture; and the third generation, while acculturated into the mainstream values, often seeks to rediscover cultural roots.[11] Even when this pattern holds—and it is not invariable—some traditional values are likely to be retained to varying degrees while others are lost. Acculturation is a multidimensional process.

Nor is there necessarily a progressive decline in traditional values over generations, no simple continuum in which a group or individual

---

*Thomas Kochman discusses the unidirectional, nonreciprocal nature of the accommodation process in "Black and White Cultural Styles in Pluralistic Perspective," Bernard R. Gifford, *Test Policy and Test Performance: Education, Language, and Culture*.[10]

†These are two different processes. Acculturation involves the adoption of new cultural values. Assimilation entails integrating into the economic, social, and political life of the mainstream. Some degree of acculturation generally occurs before some degree of assimilation does.

sheds a traditional identity and adopts an Anglo-American identity. Observers have found that life in the open, fast-moving, democratic society of the United States often produces a new ethnicity, one that is not simply a replica of traditional patterns, Anglo patterns, or some straight-line blend of both but has characteristics of its own. Author Michael Novak of the American Enterprise Institute comments, "The old ethnicity tended to be parochial; the new ethnicity is...cosmopolitan. Those who persist in seeing ethnicity as atavistic confidently predict its doom. Misunderstanding its subtlety, overlooking its spiritual habits, they miss its enduring power and capacities for self-transformation."[12]

A significant segment of three of the minority groups discussed subsequently are first-generation Americans. Because immigrants are likely to most strongly maintain traditional values and later generations to maintain them in varying degrees, our discussions focus primarily on values of the traditional cultures and how they are likely to influence behavior and perception in the workplace. In some instances, we also identify areas in which traditional values are being transformed into new patterns in the American context. With regard to black Americans, we discuss values characteristic of "community" blacks, which by no means encompasses the entire black population. Native American values examined are traditional tribal values.

Although each culture has its own distinctive ways of dealing with key values, the values that influence workplace behaviors and perceptions are largely the same across cultures. They include relation to authority, the individualism-collectivism spectrum, attitudes about aggressiveness and the control of emotions.* Attitudes about gender are also relevant and are discussed in this section as well as in the chapter on gender in the workplace.

Examination of differing cultural values is only one step. To interact effectively with persons holding different cultural values, one must also be aware of his or her own values. Our own values provide a framework that shapes our actions and judgments of others. To the extent that we are unaware of them, we let them color our understanding of others' behaviors and evaluate others by the degree to which they do or do not measure up to our standards and values. When we become aware of our own values, we are in a better position to suspend judgment of others and understand them within their own frame

---

*In his classic work *Culture's Consequences,* Geert Hofstede identified these values in somewhat different and broader terms of spectrums dealing with power distance, individualism-collectivism, uncertainty avoidance, and masculinity-femininity.[13]

of reference. It is beyond the scope of this publication to deal with this critical area of awareness.

A Short History of African Americans

To designate a person a "black American" in fact says little about him or her. Is he an African-American descendant of slaves or is he African-born? Is she an immigrant from the West Indies or Haiti? Did she travel here from Cuba, Brazil, or Guyana? Depending on the answer, the history and culture of the person in question will vary tremendously. Indeed, in 1920, West Indian blacks made up 25 percent of the population in Harlem, but, although they faced the same racial discrimination from the white majority as indigenous blacks, they mixed little with them.[14]

In this publication, we use the terms "African American," "black American," and "black." (According to a recent survey, the term "African American" is rapidly gaining popularity among black people, although the designation "black" is still preferred.[15]) Although we use the three terms interchangeably, we do not mean to obscure the many differences that exist among American blacks. Our focus, however, is on the experience of the African-American community, which represents the largest group of American blacks and thus provides a useful outline of the heritage of today's black Americans.

More than any other group, oppression has marked and marred black experience in America. While most immigrants to this country came for greater economic opportunity and some to escape religious or political oppression, for over 200 years most black immigrants were forced to migrate. Once they arrived, their lives and those of their children were usurped by their involuntary occupation of slavery. In the later half of the nineteenth century, emancipation and the protection of the 13th, 14th, and 15th Amendments put the days of slavery behind black Americans, but they by no means ended oppression on the job or elsewhere in American society.

During and after Reconstruction, many Southern whites, impoverished by the war, blamed their troubles on the new independence of former slaves and were determined to destroy it. Southern state governments established Black Codes to define blacks' new status by denying them many basic economic and legal rights. Occupations open to them were strictly limited, as were educational opportunities. As a result, most blacks lacked the education to pursue many types of careers, even if they had been open to them. Individuals and groups like the Ku Klux Klan resorted to violence against them. Nor was the discrimination limited to the South: Northern states, too, put Jim Crow laws and practices into place.

Because blacks were deprived of formal education during the centuries of slavery—when it was illegal to teach a black even to read—black communities did not have a strong intellectual tradition on which to draw.* Black people were also hindered by stereotypes fostered by the images of slavery. For many white people, images of field hands and domestic laborers lingered, but the fact that many free blacks in the North as well as slaves in the South had been highly skilled artisans was not part of their mental store.[16] Such stereotypes seemed to legitimatize the concentration of blacks in low-wage occupations.

The stereotypes also reflected present reality. The 1890 census, the first census to ask about employment, found that the great majority of blacks *did* work either in agriculture or domestic service.[17] And their living standards *were* low. In the absence of systematic studies, opinions vary about the degree of improvement, if any, in black living standards in the decades following the Civil War. Some writers suggest that living standards among blacks at the turn of the century were no better than they had been under slavery.[18] Data on black life expectancy seems to support this view. Extrapolations from census data suggest little improvement in health conditions among blacks. Investigators variously estimate that the average life expectancy of black women by 1900 ranged from between 27 to 35 years, and some suggest that the mortality rate actually dropped in the late nineteenth century.[19] In comparison with Sweden (which has the oldest systematic demographic records), the black female mortality rate in the United States in 1900 was lower than the average life expectancy in Sweden in 1700.[20]

Despite the constraints of Jim Crow laws, the proportion of black men working in occupations other than agriculture and domestic service grew steadily after the turn of the century. According to census data, between 1890 and 1910, the share of black men working in manufacturing, trade, transportation, and the professions rose from 17 to 27 percent.[21] The black mortality rate also slowly declined, though it was still greater than the mortality rate among whites. Based on incomplete data compiled by states, the age-standardized death rate of blacks in

---

*Unlike, for example, Jewish communities in European ghettos, which were strengthened by a scholarly tradition, although they were barred from full participation in society. (The authors are indebted to Dr. Morton Leeds for this point.)

1910 was 24 percent; of whites, 15 percent. By 1940, the black death rate fell some 7 points to 16.7 percent; the white rate dropped some 6 points to 9.3 percent.*

Since the end of the Civil War, blacks individually and collectively fought job segregation and discrimination elsewhere. One of the most prominent organizations waging this battle was—and is—the National Association for the Advancement of Colored People (NAACP), established in 1909. Historian Cynthia Greggs Fleming of the University of Tennessee, Knoxville, observes that the NAACP put segregation on trial through the court system.[23]

For the most part, though, it was a losing battle. The regime of segregation required systematic separation of blacks and whites in every public area and in some important private areas, too. All Southern states, and some others as well, banned interracial marriage. Invariably, the facilities and services available to blacks were inferior; in the workplace, jobs were strictly segregated, and the quality of life of black people was lower than that of whites by just about every quantifiable measure. For example, during the 1939–1940 school year, the average per-pupil expenditure and value of school property in selected Southern schools was $18.82 for black students, $58.69 for white students.[†] The average educational level of black men in 1940 was 4.7 years; for white men, it was 9.38 years. During the same year, the mean income of black men in 1940 was $4,531; the white male mean income was more than twice that: $10,459.[25]

A large portion of the white population thought this was the way things should be. The National Research Council (NRC) cites a 1944 survey by the National Opinion Research Center that found 80 percent of white Southerners and 47 percent of white Northerners surveyed sanctioned labor market discrimination, agreed that "whites should have first chance at any kind of job," and thought inequality between blacks and whites was basically fair and was mainly the fault of blacks.[26] The NRC study observes, "Segregation was more than simple black-white separation. With its potential violence and basic inequality, segregation was a potent system of white control over the black population."[27]

Entrenched as they were, the barriers of segregation began to shake during the 1940s and 1950s. Several factors were responsible. Among

---

*Based on the Death Registration Area of 1910.[22]

†According to unpublished data from the U.S. Department of Education, cited by Jaynes and Williams, Jr., eds., *A Common Destiny: Blacks and American Society, Committee on the Status of Black Americans.*[24]

them was the great migration of blacks from the rural South to cities in the North and elsewhere. Black Americans had been emigrating from the rural South in growing numbers throughout the early part of the twentieth century.[28] Economic opportunities created by World War II brought even more up out of the South, as the war created a demand for black labor to replace white workers who went off to combat. This military- and industrial-based move fostered contact with many whites for the first time. The impact was profound. The social and political views of many blacks broadened, and whites began to realize that segregation was incompatible with democratic ideals. Just as importantly, as Nell Irvin Painter observes, "Only when large numbers of blacks were voters—which meant only when large numbers of blacks had left the South—did the Federal Government begin to support black civil rights."[29]

The publication of Gunnar Myrdal's *An American Dilemma* in 1944 marked a major turning point in the study of race relations in the United States. A monumental work documented with qualitative data, objective analysis, and descriptive statistics, it provided a well-organized means of assessing U.S. race relations. In the book, Myrdal gave all Americans—not just blacks—ideas to consider when he wrote:

> The American Negro problem is a problem in the heart of the American. It is there that the interracial tension has its focus. It is there that the decisive struggle goes on....Though our study includes economic, social, and political race relations, at bottom our problem is the moral dilemma of the American—the conflict between his moral valuations on various levels of consciousness and generality.

The pressure of external events helped weaken the walls of segregation, too. Embracing its role as an international leader after the second World War, the United States became more sensitive to criticism from abroad. One of the areas where it was especially vulnerable was race relations.

These forces made possible the passage of new civil rights laws and judicial decisions in the 1950s. One such was the momentous 1954 Supreme Court decision in *Brown v. the Board of Education of Topeka,* a case brought by the NAACP, that ended school segregation by ruling that the practice of "separate but equal" public school facilities was unconstitutional. The civil rights initiatives fostered hope among blacks and were supported by many whites, but there was also active white resistance, which spilled over into violence. In some ways, the federal government displayed a pattern of ambivalence to these events. It was reluctant to rigorously enforce civil rights laws and judicial decisions even as it took new initiatives to expand black rights.[30] When the Arkansas governor opposed desegregation in Little Rock in 1957, the federal government was forced to take action. President Eisenhower felt that black equality could not be gained by government edict. He had commented that the attempt to do so was "nuts" and felt the *Brown* decision had set back the desegregation process in Southern schools by 15 years.[31] But he nonetheless sent National Guard troops to Little Rock to ensure that federal authority prevailed. And it did. Tensions rose, and a black protest movement was spawned. By the day in 1955 in Montgomery, Alabama, when the quietly courageous Rosa Parks decided she would never again give up her seat on a bus to a white person, a growing number of black Americans were prepared to rally to the black rights cause. Led by Dr. Martin Luther King, Jr., a year-long boycott of buses in Montgomery resulted in bus desegregation. By 1960, black students, later joined by whites, initiated sit-ins at segregated facilities and succeeded in desegregating them. A variety of nonviolent protest efforts followed, with persons of various backgrounds joining in. The nation watched on television, horrified as whites responded to some of these efforts with violence—bombings, beatings, and the use of cattle prods.

Even while the black nonviolent protest continued, a new violent dimension developed. Urban uprisings exploded first in Rochester, New York, in 1964, then over the next few years in other cities. Over a hundred cities burned during the next few years: most of the damage and injuries occurred in black communities. Following the assassination of Martin Luther King, Jr., in 1968, Washington, D.C., also erupted into violence.

The National Advisory Commission on Civil Disorders (the Kerner Commission) was established by presidential order in 1967 to learn what had happened in the cities, what had caused the riots, and what could be done to prevent similar occurrences in the future. In the final report, issued in February 1968, the Commission concluded that "our nation is moving toward two societies, one black, one white—separate and unequal."[32] The study listed causes for the riots and suggested many changes in local, state, and federal responses to civil disorder. The Commission also made several policy recommendations to improve conditions in the ghettos. Changes in the welfare system were suggested along with ideas on increasing employment, and, perhaps most importantly, improving education. The Commission suggested the use of federal money and power to improve both the physical and social conditions of ghetto schools. Segregation was to end, teaching improvements were to be made, and steps were to be taken to make the schools integral parts of the communities they served.

On the legislative front, the movement also was proceeding. The 1964 Civil Rights Act was a landmark piece of legislation which banned formal racial segregation and dismantled barriers to black voting in Southern states. Title VII of that act banned discrimination in the workplace based on race and other characteristics. A year later, the voting rights act authorized federal officials to ensure the end of discriminatory practices at the ballot box, especially in the South, where they were routine since the days of Reconstruction. By 1968, the number of registered black voters in the South tripled.

By the 1970s, the protest movement and its violent offspring fragmented and it began to lose momentum. Also an important component in the movement's decline was the loss of white support. The growing violence and anti-white sentiments expressed by more militant black leaders caused a strong negative reaction among many. And like the other great civil rights reform era in America, Reconstruction, the movement lost white adherents after legislative milestones were attained. Harvard Sitkoff points out that even by the mid-1960s white political figures were elected to office partly on the strength of their opposition to the civil rights movement.*

The protest and the black pride movement have enormous significance in the history of our country. Among other things, their impact rippled throughout ethnic America, inspiring Americans of other ethnic and racial origins to take increased pride in their own backgrounds. Among black Americans, there are widely differing views about what the movement meant. Civil rights legislation clearly opened opportunities for many, enabling them to progress economically and socially. Black male income rose from about $4,500 (in 1984 dollars) in 1940 to almost $19,000 by 1980.[34] And black male wages increased 52 percent faster than white wages, rising from only 43 percent as much as their white counterparts in 1940 to 73 percent by 1980. In their study on black economic progress, undertaken in the mid-1980s, Smith and Welch conclude that "the real story of the last forty years has been the emergence of the black middle class."[35]

Evidence of growth of the black middle class can be seen in the increase of the mean household income of black Americans. In figures broken down for each fifth of the black population and expressed in 1992 dollars, the mean income of black households in 1967 was about $25,400 for the fourth fifth of the population and about $48,700 for the

---

*Sitkoff cites several reasons for the white backlash: the riots that rationalized white hostility toward blacks; the linking of many of the civil rights leaders with the counterculture student rebellion; anti-white statements by black power proponents; and white working-class fears that racial equality would come at their expense.[33]

highest fifth. In 1992, those figures rose to over $31,400 for the fourth fifth of the population and about $63,200 for the highest fifth.[36]

The civil rights movement also caused some blacks to acquire a new perception of themselves. George Davis of Rutgers University and journalist Glegg Watson, commenting on the dominant black perspective before the civil rights movement, wrote:

> Before the sixties, only a few among us actively questioned the rightness of whiteness. The march of civilization was toward the white way of being. The idea behind the long battle to integrate public schools was to give black children an opportunity to mix with children of the ruling caste, and thereby join the march.[37]

They believe that part of the significance of the civil rights movement was "we blacks...overthrew the rule of white men in our minds." Although white male dominance still remained, "we underwent a psychological revolution." The marching song "black is beautiful" signaled the psychological emancipation those events meant for many blacks.

For others, the events of the 1960s signaled a time of renewed questioning about black identity, a questioning that still has not been resolved. Fleming states that, as a result of the civil rights movement, "many began to recognize that the integration they had so desperately desired demanded a very high price: conformity to Anglo-American values and cultural norms."[38] But the alternative is still at issue. She concludes:

> African-Americans still feel their twoness: They remain marginal, negative Americans. They have strong emotional and cultural ties to both Africa and America. Sometimes they identify with one or the other. Sometimes they identify with both, sometimes they feel alienated from both. Du Bois's question remains unanswered: Will it ever be possible to be both black and American?[39]

For blacks of the ghetto underclass, the civil rights movement had yet another meaning. For them, it meant that middle- and working-class blacks now had new opportunities from which they (the underclass) were largely excluded. In his influential work, *The Truly Disadvantaged*, sociologist William Julius Wilson points out that the discontent demonstrated in the riots of the period transcended the civil rights movement.[40] Legislation could do little to remove the historic effects of discrimination that prevented ghetto blacks from developing the skills needed to compete in society, including in the workplace. Even at the height of the movement, when many were focusing on achieving gains, there were those who understood its impact on the underclass. Wilson quotes Kenneth Clark, who said in 1967, "The masses of Negroes are now starkly aware of the fact that recent civil rights victories benefited a very small percentage of middle-class Negroes while their predicament remained the same or worsened."[41]

In fact, the predicament of the underclass worsened dramatically during the 1970s. Incomes among most black families had been growing with respect to their white counterparts in the 1960s, and those making the greatest gains had been low-income blacks.[42] During the 1970s, however, while gains made by upper-income blacks accelerated, low-income blacks lost ground. This was due to several interrelated events. Wilson explains that until the 1960s, black urban families of all classes resided in ghetto areas, albeit on different streets. Middle-class professionals serviced the communities they lived in because they "provided stability to the inner-city neighborhoods and perpetuated and reinforced societal norms and values. In short, their very presence enhanced the social organization of the ghetto communities."[43] Once housing restrictions began to be lifted and middle- and working-class blacks began leaving the ghettos for higher-income neighborhoods, it became "more difficult to sustain the basic institutions in the inner city (including churches, stores, schools, recreational facilities, etc.) in the face of prolonged joblessness. And as the basic institutions declined, the social organization of the inner-city neighborhoods...likewise declined."[44]

As a result of these events, the number of black families below the poverty level increased from about 1.5 million in 1967 to almost 2 million in 1982. Jaynes and Williams state that, while in 1969, 25 percent of black men earned less than $10,000 (in 1984 dollars), in 1984, 40 percent made less than $10,000.[45] As the economy stagnated in the 1970s, the poorest quarter of the black male population, men who had not finished high school, found they could not compete and a growing number dropped out of the labor force. The labor force participation rate among black men, ages 36 to 45, fell 5.6 percent between 1970 and 1980 (the decline in white male participation by the same age group was only 1.3 percent).[46] Among older black men, ages 46 to 54, the decline was even steeper: 9.8 percent (for white males of the same age, the decline was 3.5 percent). As joblessness rose, so did the poverty level and family instability. Female-headed households below the poverty level increased in number by almost 50 percent from 1967 to 1981.*[47] Ghettos became increasingly isolated from the mainstream, and crime and despair spread.

Discussing the increasing polarization among black Americans, Wilson refers to a "growing economic schism" between low-income

---

*We examine current numbers in the next chapter.

and upper-income blacks. In fact, it is more than an economic schism. There is also a psychological schism. Black social commentary as well as everyday conversation reveal a deep emotional divide between lower- and upper-income blacks. The tension between a common racial identity and history and divergent life styles, and frequently attitudes, seems to be producing a conflicted mix of anger, compassion, aversion, and solidarity. And maybe most of all, profound pain. Though responses vary from person to person and change from situation to situation, it appears all blacks are being forced to address the issue, not merely intellectually but at a visceral level. Across the schism and within each group, too, blacks sit in harsh, pained judgment of each other's behavior and attitudes.

Thus, it appears that black Americans today are grappling with a triple identity crisis—not just the double identity that W. E. B. Du Bois discussed early in this century. Today black Americans may have to cope simultaneously with expressing their individual sense of self (as does everyone else), maintaining balance in the face of the degrading stereotypes with which some white people perceive them, *and* dealing with the judgment of other blacks. There is also a fourth dimension to the crisis: gender tensions, which are reflected in part in a drastic decline in the institution of marriage. Coping with any one of these challenges is a major task. Dealing with all simultaneously has got to be immensely draining. And the task is made harder because each challenge interacts with and conditions the others.

In his influential book, *Race Matters,* Cornel West, professor of religion and head of the black studies program at Princeton University, discusses the "profound sense of psychological depression, personal worthlessness, and social despair so widespread in black America."[48] He believes that this "nihilistic threat to its very existence" is the most basic issue now facing black America. He maintains:

> Nihilism is not overcome by arguments or analyses, it is tamed by love and care. Any disease of the soul must be conquered by a turning of one's soul. This turning is done through one's own affirmation of one's worth—an affirmation fueled by the concern of others. A love ethic must be at the center of the politics of conversion.[49]

African-American Cultural Values and the Workplace

African Americans have a rich cultural heritage. Although the complex aspects of this heritage cannot be discussed in full here, it is worth remarking this fact because it is so often overlooked in public discourse, which usually is framed in terms of economic, political, and social issues concerning black Americans. Black American cultural patterns, forged in the interaction between their African and other heritages and their experiences in North America, developed in closer interaction with Anglo culture over a longer period than those of any other minority. (Native Americans on the whole have been more insulated from Anglo cultural influences than blacks, having been shunted into isolated reservations in the latter part of the nineteenth century, where a third of the American-Indian population still lives.)

Black Americans are a diverse community. Today the overwhelming majority are native-born, with roots in this country that date back farther than those of many other groups. Some are recent immigrants from Africa, the Caribbean (where there has been increased emigration in recent decades), Latin America, and elsewhere, and they speak a variety of languages. In his influential book, *The American Kaleidoscope*, ethnologist Lawrence Fuchs, referring to the complexity of the situation of black immigrants, notes that before the 1970s immigrant blacks had little incentive to identify with native-born African Americans; however, the end of the most blatant discrimination against native-born black Americans and the emergence of the black pride and power movements in the 1970s caused many to begin to readily identify with other blacks.[50]

In his ground-breaking work, *Black and White Styles in Conflict*, Thomas Kochman, of Kochman Communication in Chicago, examines the black "style" or culture. He states that these are the ethnic patterns and perspectives especially characteristic of black "community" people or ghetto blacks.*[51] Acknowledging that these characteristics are less frequently displayed among blacks at middle- or upper-income levels where individuals tend to be more Anglicized, Kochman points out that, in any ethnic or racial minority, cultural distinctiveness is frequently greatest among poorer group members. In fact, the expression of black cultural values is probably growing more intense rather than less because ghetto communities have grown increasingly isolated from the mainstream during the past few decades.

But blacks living outside ghetto communities are also likely to maintain black cultural values in varying circumstances. While blue-collar workers (whether in or outside the ghetto) may more often display these values than middle-class blacks, they have not disappeared among the latter. Many middle-class blacks are likely to be bicultural,

---

*This section draws heavily on material provided by Dr. Kochman in interviews May 17 and September 8, 1993.

holding both black and white cultural values. Many compartmentalize their lives by displaying white values more frequently in a predominately white context such as the work environment and black values more at home and in other predominately black contexts.*

One obvious example of this is through speech. Psychologist Adelbert H. Jenkins writes that a dialectal pluralism (of black English vernacular and standard Anglo English) allows a black person to "come home" culturally. "Maintaining black communicative styles side by side with using standard forms permits them to commute psychologically from a personal-cultural home to the common world of work and culture shared with other ethnic groups in America."[53]

The effort to compartmentalize is stressful, however. Black white-collar workers in a predominately white organizational culture often feel they need to leave their identities at the door. An example of a black worker who felt the price too high and quit her job is former *Washington Post* correspondent Jill Nelson. In her book *Volunteer Slavery*, Nelson said that at the *Post*, she did "the standard Negro balancing act when it comes to dealing with white folks, which involves sufficiently blurring the edges of my being so that they don't feel intimidated, while simultaneously holding on to my integrity."[54] She observed, "There's a thin line between Uncle Tomming and Mau-Mauing."

While many other blacks may not have as hard a time as Nelson did adapting to a white organizational culture, all are likely to experience stress as they do it. They pay a price in terms of inner conflict, sapped energy, and in forfeiture of respect among some other blacks, who count their behavior as cultural betrayal.

There is considerable controversy among black intellectuals on the subject. Many naturally resist efforts characterizing them as a racial or ethnic group as stereotyping. And, in fact, too often such efforts have been simplistic, hence inaccurate or downright malicious. Also some feel that they have already fought this battle and do not want to defend themselves again. Author Shelby Steele writes compellingly of the "double bind" middle-class blacks such as himself experience: being caught between middle-class values, which he considers raceless and assimilationist, and racial identification, which he views as adversarial toward the mainstream and urges separatism. His conclusion is that "there is no forward movement on either plane that does not constitute backward movement on the other."[55]

---

*Researchers are investigating the process of compartmentalization. See, for example, Bell, "The bicultural life experience of career-oriented black women," *Journal of Organizational Behavior.*[52]

A growing number of middle-class black workers, however, are betting that he is wrong. They are exploring another alternative: bringing their blackness into the workplace and other predominantly white environments with the conviction that their black and white cultural values can—or at least should—coexist with some semblance of harmony. These people, many of them relatively young, object to what Kochman characterizes as "detribalization." Justifiably proud of their racial and ethnic heritage, they want to hold on to their identification with their blackness while simultaneously not diminishing their middle-class values. They do not oppose assimilation—indeed, for many who were raised with these values, dropping their middle-class values is not a realistic possibility—but they also resist dissimilation from their black identity, according Kochman.

Perhaps because middle-class blacks have been especially conflicted by these issues as they advance in the workplace, they have been more vocal than poor groups in demanding reciprocity in the workplace for cultural differences. Kochman notes that these individuals are consciously aware that they have been hiding a part of their cultural identity on the job and find that behavior no longer acceptable. They are demanding that organizations recognize them for who they are culturally and value them for what they have to contribute.

As expressed in the workplace, black cultural values differ from those of the dominant Anglo culture in many important ways, but here, of course, we must limit discussion to a few salient points. One of these is differing values attached to individualism and collectivism. Anglo culture ranks high in its stress on individualism. In his study of 50 nations and three regions, Hofstede finds that the United States is first in the individualism index. West Africa—from where most African Americans derive—ranks thirty-ninth and forty-first.[56] Considerable research confirms that African Americans tend toward a collectivistic orientation. W. Nobels observes that in the African American world view, the self comes into being only in the context of the group: "I and we cannot be meaningfully separated."[57] Taylor Cox, Jr., an expert on organizational behavior at the University of Michigan, comments on the implication of these contrasting values in the workplace: "Organizations are increasingly extolling the values of teamwork, but organizational reward systems often are not aligned with this goal and continue to foster individualism."[58]

Another difference occurs with regard to expressive intensity. The black culture is people-oriented, and, in terms of an aggressiveness spectrum, it ranks high. Yet "aggressiveness" is a misleading term, one often understood by white people as synonymous with "hostility." In the context of black culture, "expressive intensity" more accurately describes the high-energy, passionate confrontation that characterizes discourse, according to Kochman. In the black culture, high-energy confrontation is an expression of being "for real," an expression of sincerity, not hostility. Conversation is frank and forceful, and criticism is freely given and taken.

The proportions of such an effort for many blacks are suggested by the wide gap in black and white modes of debate. Kochman observes that the black mode is animated, involved, and generates affect; the white mode is relatively low-keyed, detached, and without affect. He notes, "when blacks are working hard to keep cool, it signals that the chasm between them is getting wider, not smaller."[59] Blacks tend to assume that whites are not listening when they are not responsive; whites are likely to view black's animated responses as interruptions.[60] Whites focus on goal achievement; blacks also consider the *style* with which one achieves the goal.*

The reserve that characterizes much conversation among whites, especially in the workplace, appears insincere to blacks, according to Kochman. Among blacks who value expressive intensity, reserve can create suspicion that whites are not saying what is really on their minds, that they are "fronting" and possibly may even be hostile.

Donald Cheek, in his book *Assertive Black...Puzzled White,* which he calls "a black prospective on assertive behavior," advocates assertiveness training to help blacks learn to switch language codes and behavioral styles in shifting from a black-black to a black-white interpersonal situation. What comes through as assertive in one setting—for instance, an all-black setting—may be seen as hostile in an interracial setting by a white person.[61]

In the context of engaging in sincere disagreement and dispute, black and white cultures are nearly at opposite poles of the conflict-avoidance spectrum. Black culture is low in conflict avoidance. It places value on being candid, on "truth before peace." In contrast, white culture values "peace before truth" and is relatively high in conflict avoidance. Kochman notes that the white culture tends to value an insincere peace to a sincere quarrel in order to preserve civility. Black culture has much less regard for civility if it is at the expense of honesty and personal integrity.

In the workplace, these contrasting values can be lethal to organizations. Exposed to the dominant value system daily, black workers are likely to accommodate to the prevailing culture and stifle their natural,

---

*Kochman examines this area of cultural difference in the context of sports, but it also applies to the workplace.

candid style. But feeling forced to place such constraints on one's behavior is likely to create resentment, and this resentment, in turn, can fuel suspicion that white managers are racists. Kochman points out that when, out of frustration, black workers express their suspicions openly, white managers are likely to be caught off guard. Unaware of the degree to which black workers feel forced to change their behavior, managers are shocked. The lack of earlier signs of resentment led them to believe that there were no problems. Such developments can seriously damage working relations and harm productivity.

It is paradoxical that, if other factors were equal—and typically they are not—the high-energy style of blacks could be parlayed into advantage in the workplace.* The black style involves an assertiveness, even aggressiveness, that is among the characteristics the Anglo tradition values in its leaders. But in an Anglo organizational culture, black workers, like other workers of color, are typically expected to learn to be assertive or aggressive in a manner acceptable to the dominant culture.

Closely interlinked are the contrasting black and white leadership styles. Black culture values high "power distance," to use Hofstede's term. Top-down leadership with clear lines of authority is respected, and leadership is expected to take a strong role. Anglo culture values low power distance. In the workplace, the movement increasingly is toward more participatory forms of leadership. Further, Kochman notes that for blacks, commitment tends to be personal, based on principle. For white management, commitment is pragmatic, subject to change as situations change.

Values differ with regard to time as well. Summarizing research on the subject, Cox notes that Anglo organizational culture favors a linear orientation, stressing promptness, deadlines, and long-range planning. Black American culture—like that of many other minority groups in America—tends to be circular or procedural in orientation. Research traces this orientation among black Americans to West African cultures, from which much black American culture derives. Cox observes that, among American blacks, this heritage is reflected in the "frequent absence of specific ending times for social events planned in the Black

---

*A highly publicized successful example was a Senate debate in summer 1993 over renewal of a design patent for the insignia of the United Daughters of the Confederacy. Senator Carol Moseley-Braun, the first black woman to serve as a senator, vigorously opposed the proposal and succeeded in reversing the course of the debate. The proposal failed. In another incident, five black women representatives in the House extracted an apology from a congressman whom they accused of using racially offensive language. The congressman later commented that the experience was "intimidating," "like lighting a firecracker."[62]

community and the existence of `CP (colored people) time,' a colloquialism meaning that scheduled starting times for events and appointments are treated with a great deal of flexibility."[63] In the workplace, black Americans adapt to mainstream values regarding time, but to the extent that their orientation is circular, this is accomplished with some stress.

The black value on stylistic self-expression is another area of potential misunderstanding on the job. Anglo-American organizational culture is task-oriented. Accomplishing a task is viewed as an end in itself, and there is little tolerance for anything that might distract from getting the job done. Kochman points out that for blacks, task accomplishment is valued but so too is the style with which a task is accomplished: "The functional rule for Blacks is `so long as the moves that are made do not interfere with getting the job done, they should be allowed.'"[64] Thus, blacks are likely to resent micromanagement. Their culture does not accept the (typical Anglo) premise that the procedures by which a plan is implemented should rest with the plan designer. Black workers who are implementing someone else's plan generally want to have the leeway to determine how to carry out a plan; in other words, self-expression in carrying out a plan is important. Kochman observes that this approach can get black workers into trouble: They may be accused of assuming a level of authority beyond their rank, or they may be accused of insubordination.[65] The new focus on participatory leadership should fit nicely with this black cultural value.

A further source of cultural clash on the job stems from the fact that black culture, like Hispanic culture, tends to focus on personal relations. In the work environment, this translates into an orientation toward socializing as an integral part of work life. Unlike the Anglo approach, which stresses some level of socialization in order to build effective working relationships, black culture values relationships for their own sake. Such relationships are with a whole person, not just with one role an individual assumes, such as truck driver, computer specialist, student, mother, etc. At work, this conflicts with the standard task orientation of Anglo organization. A manager who is strongly task-oriented is likely to view such socializing among black subordinates as simply a waste of time.

A Short History of Hispanic Americans

"Hispanic" is a term of convenience. Selected by the U.S. federal government in the 1970s, it—like the other new identity, "Asian

American"—is deceptive. It implies a homogeneity that does not exist. While "Hispanic" is gaining currency, especially among more acculturated second- and third-generation Hispanics, many Americans of Hispanic origin do not readily identify with it, nor with the alternative "Latino." They prefer instead to characterize themselves according to their country of origin. The countries from which persons of Hispanic-origin derive are diverse in economies and histories. Many have legacies of animosity with neighbors that have heightened people's senses of national rather than regional identity. Immigrants find it especially jarring to be lumped with other Hispanic-origin groups.

But, for the purpose of our discussion, we need to do so here. As we do, we should bear in mind that our use of generalizations, while helpful and necessary in a general discussion, is not an attempt to characterize all Hispanics.

Because we repeatedly focus on the Hispanic population as a whole, it is appropriate to look a little more closely at our terms. "Hispanic" refers to people of Spanish culture or origin, from Latin American countries and the Caribbean, as well as from Europe and elsewhere. It refers to an ethnic and cultural group, not a racial group, for persons of Hispanic origin may be of any race. According to the Census Bureau's system of self-identification, respondents are considered Hispanic if they identify themselves as such. Following the preferences of a significant segment of the Hispanic population, we also use the designation "Latino." Technically, it applies only to people from Latin America, but it is commonly used more broadly in the United States as a synonym for "Hispanic."*

As the second largest minority group in the country, Hispanics number more than 22 million, or 9 percent of the total population.[66] They are also the fastest-growing group, their population having swelled 53 percent between 1970 and 1990. And by 2010, Hispanics will be the largest minority in the country, with an estimated 39 million people.[67] They all speak Spanish, and their shared Latin culture gives them some common ground; however, each group has its own story, including the circumstances under which each came to this country. Perhaps what most sets Latinos apart from other minorities is their ability—in most cases—to return to their native countries. For Mexicans and

---

*Another term that perhaps needs comment is "American." To avoid awkward circumlocutions, we use it, as do most other people in the United States, to denote a U.S. citizen. Of course, all those living in the Americas—from Latin America in the south to Canada in the north—are Americans, and there is understandable sensitivity to the fact that we in the United States often expropriate the label when referring to ourselves and to the United States.

Puerto Ricans, this proximity to the *tierra madre* proved a mixed blessing: While it gave individuals greater flexibility, it also made them vulnerable to forced repatriation and deportation. At times, it has also silenced them, for white Americans have often responded to Hispanics' complaints by suggesting—or insisting—they go home. Cubans are exceptions, however. As long as Castro is in power, they cannot return to their homeland. As a result, their community is polarized between a strong group of highly educated, upper-class immigrants and a group of poorer, less educated workers.

In this section, we take a closer look at the three principal Latino groups in the United States: Mexican Americans (over 60 percent of the Latino population in 1990), Puerto Ricans (about 12 percent), and Cubans (about 5 percent).[68]

Mexican Americans

As the largest Hispanic group, Mexican Americans numbered some 13.5 million people in 1990.[69] Mexican Americans are also the oldest Hispanic group in the country, and they are especially heavily concentrated in the southwest. By the year 2000, they are expected to make up close to 50 percent of the population of California.

Well before Anglos were in the southwest, Mexicans were. (And, before Mexicans were there, Indians were.) The Spanish, who held the area from the sixteenth through the eighteenth centuries, tried to consolidate their hold on their empire by enticing settlers to the area. The policy was mildly successful.* When Mexico gained independence from Spain in the early nineteenth century and the southwest became Mexican territory, there were about 3,000 Mexicans there.[70] But not for long. An initial group of a few hundred Americans was invited by the Mexican government to settle in the Texas area in the early 1820s. Others soon began to trek westward unbidden, and they illegally entered sparsely populated Mexican territory in Texas. For a short time, in the 1820s and 1830s, the Mexicans who were there and Americans who were arriving lived in relative harmony. The Mexicans were landowners, and Americans were land-hungry. There was plenty to go around. The interests of both groups coincided in a desire for greater autonomy from outside authority.[71] When the Mexican government sought to impose stricter controls in response to the growing ille-

---

*Successful from the Spanish point of view, but not from the Indian. Indians fought a long, unsuccessful battle to defend their territory from foreign incursion. For some 250 years, they periodically conducted guerrilla warfare against the Spaniards. This was continued against Mexicans and, later, against Americans.

gal influx of Americans, both groups resisted. The 187 men surrounded by Mexican government troops at the Alamo in 1836 included some Mexican settlers as well as Texans.[72] And when Texas declared itself an independent republic, Mexican settlers played a role in the new government.

Borne on a self-serving belief in manifest destiny, a swelling number of American settlers fanned out across the West into Mexican territory in Texas and the California area. By the mid-1830s, Americans in Texas already outnumbered Mexicans four to one.[73] As their numbers increased, so, too, did the prejudice they displayed toward the Mexican inhabitants. In the wake of the American victory in the Mexican-American war in 1848, Mexico ceded territory to the Pacific, and the slide in the status of Mexicans in the newly acquired territory accelerated. Americans extracted their property by more or less legal, as well as extralegal, means.[74]

After the Civil War, the United States again turned its attention to the west. The flow of settlers grew. New farm land and newly opened mines required much menial labor. Mexican immigrants increasingly supplied it. And because California was now there to be reached and railroad technology was at hand to facilitate it, Mexicans also came to be viewed as a source of cheap labor to build railways westward. Mexican labor in railway construction became even more desirable after Chinese immigration was barred in 1882. Yet, the more Mexicans flowed in to build the railways, the more they contributed to the deterioration of their status: The railroads opened territory to the ever-growing numbers of Americans who dispossessed Mexican landowners and who had a burgeoning need for cheap Mexican labor.[75]

Immigrants as well as Mexican Americans encountered not only exploitation on the job but hostility, even brutality, in other areas of daily life. Racism, reinforced by theories of biological superiority promulgated by social Darwinism, flourished in the United States after the Civil War, and Mexicans were especial targets. More Mexicans were lynched in the southwest than blacks were in the south.[76] By the end of the century, many lived in barrios (areas largely Mexican in residence) for protection. But the barrios segregated Mexicans even further from mainstream society.[77] The cycle was perpetuated as widespread discrimination and proximity to the Mexican border caused many to retain strong ties to Mexico and to their traditional culture, factors that contributed to further discrimination against them.

Thus developed a system that Lawrence Fuchs characterizes as *sojourner pluralism*.[78] Mexicans, like Asian immigrants, were subjected to a degree of exploitation more extreme than European immigrants faced. For most Mexicans, citizenship was not an option. Work in the

United States represented a way to support families back home in Mexico. American employers, police, and local, state, and federal government cooperated in a system that promoted circular migration: They ensured the availability of Mexican labor when it was needed and dismissed it when it was not. Authorities often looked the other way at harvest time, allowing an influx of illegal labor, and periodically rounded up "illegal aliens" when there was a labor surplus. Because most moved back and forth over the border regularly and sometimes were forcibly deported, most Mexicans remained unwelcome strangers in the strange American land. (Even those born in the United States were made to feel "un-American" if they desired to preserve something of their cultural heritage.) The hostility Mexicans encountered and the probability that they would be returning soon to Mexico provided little incentive to learn English, get additional schooling or training, participate in the political system, or put down roots in the United States.

The industrial revolution and opening of new land in the southwest greatly increased the need for Mexican labor. To ensure the continued flow of unskilled workers, the American government signed an agreement with the Mexican government for contract labor during the second decade of the twentieth century. The flow became a flood. It is estimated that between 1910 and 1930 about 10 percent of the Mexican population emigrated to the United States.[79] Overland immigration grew from 6,000 in 1906, the first year such a count was made, to some 500,000 between 1925 and 1929.[80] The increase was driven partly by the disruption caused by the Mexican Revolution from 1910 to 1917 but probably even more by the demands of the growing American economy and by the labor shortage caused by the mobilization of Americans during World War I. Although most Mexican immigrants remained in the southwest and California, a growing number were attracted to industries in cities elsewhere. And many of them returned home periodically, crossing and recrossing the border again and again.

Economist Gregory DeFreitas points out that, at this time, the distinction between legal and illegal immigration first began to be made. Immigration legislation began to try to control a flow that previously had been unregulated. Until this time, the illiterate peasants who migrated viewed the border as "little more than an imaginary line through a unified Mexican-American economy in which...[they] had become incorporated as a vital component."[81] It was an attitude shared by employers when labor was in short supply, and repudiated when the need evaporated.

Still the immigrants came, both legally and illegally, lured by the prospects of wages that were many times as high as in Mexico. In an age of exploitation, their illegal status made Mexicans especially vulnerable. Employers were free to pay them lower wages than they paid American workers, demand long hours, force them to work under abysmal conditions, and lay them off at will. Even legal immigrants were victims. This system especially suited growers in the southwest, whose need for labor varied widely from year to year depending on the weather. This pattern was to become entrenched.

Despite systematic exploitation of the Mexican workforce and, for many, a circular pattern of migration, many new Mexican communities developed in the United States. While isolated from the mainstream and poor by American standards, they were vibrant enclaves.[82] Many workers earned regular wages. And some Mexicans and Mexican Americans succeeded in breaking out of menial labor into jobs offering wider opportunities. In each generation, some broke sojourner patterns and developed roots and allegiances in the United States. Such changes were to enable them and their children to develop more stable, secure lives.

But not right away. The Depression that began in 1929 brought widespread changes that were anything but secure. More than one-third of the Mexicans laborers were quickly laid off. Companies closed, jobs were eliminated, and many remaining positions were given to Americans. A massive, government-sponsored repatriation program in the early 1930s forced many to return to Mexico. Although Mexicans had been forcibly, if erratically, repatriated for decades, during the early years of the 1930s, over 400,000 people were deported, including U.S. citizens whose deportation was illegal.[83]

The same themes played out yet again with the onset of World War II. The wartime economy again created a labor shortage. Another contract labor agreement was concluded between the Mexican and American governments. Some 250,000 workers came to America during the war under the Bracero program, initiated in 1942. Many more came illegally, and they were exploited like workers before them. Neither the undocumented workers nor braceros had the right to join labor unions to protect themselves. Nor were they protected off the job. In 1943, violent anti-Mexican riots erupted in Los Angeles, and many Mexicans were beaten.

Additional bracero contracts were negotiated after the war. The ebb and flow of hundreds of thousands of legal and undocumented workers at the border continued as did, in the 1950s, government-sponsored deportations. Under such conditions, smugglers did a booming business, for the need for cheap, temporary labor was ongoing. Some 4 million were apprehended at the border between 1947 and 1955, but a sufficient flow of illegal workers was allowed to enter to meet growers' and other employers' needs.[84]

The bracero contracts ended in 1964 when the labor movement and liberals successfully joined forces, animated by a concern that braceros were taking jobs from American workers and appalled at the braceros' abysmal working conditions. One result of the termination was increased employer demand for illegal immigrants. Employing undocumented workers meant big savings for employers: They did not have to be paid a minimum wage, benefits were not an issue, and they could readily be turned over to authorities and deported if they proved to be a problem.

By the 1960s, large numbers of Mexicans were living in the United States, and most were American-born. Perhaps more than any other minority in the United States, those of Mexican origin faced a special challenge in developing a sense of identification with the United States—and they still do. The never-ending flow of illegal migrants was and is a constant reminder of the closeness of Mexico. Mexican Americans are, as Alejandro Portes wrote, "simultaneously the oldest Latin-origin group and the most recent." He notes, "American-born and -raised Mexican Americans never dream of rejoining Mexico. For them, the problem is that Mexico never ceases coming to them."[85] For Mexican Americans, the influx of the illegal aliens can create feelings of social marginality, and this in turn may be a factor that prompts them to distance themselves, if possible, from the undocumented. Mexican Americans who are able to leave the barrio to reside in higher-income areas may choose to have little contact thereafter with illegal immigrants or, for that matter, with legal residents of the barrio, according to Jose Limon.[86] Connected with this dynamic is the identification of the Spanish language with low socioeconomic status, an issue discussed in the next chapter.

Although the struggle for identity was ongoing, many were sure enough of their American roots in the 1960s to take up the banner of civil rights that was being unfurled by many minority groups in the country. Mexican-American rights groups sprang up. Most important of these was the farm workers' movement, led by Cesar Chavez. The strength of the early farm workers' movement in the southwest and California had ranged from extremely feeble to nonexistent. Earlier efforts at strikes had resulted in the importation of strike-breaking illegal aliens and braceros, with the help of law enforcement authorities. The decade of civil rights protest in the 1960s raised national consciousness about ethnic and racial issues, and Chavez's group contributed importantly to the effort. After a five-year campaign to secure some protections, the farm workers succeeded in 1970 in winning concessions from growers—a significant victory for farm workers and Mexican Americans. Much, however, remains to be done. The 900,000 farm workers in California in 1993 had less spending power in 1993 than farm workers 15 years previously, according to correspondent Jeffrey Kaye.[87] Kaye reported that some earn as little as $2.50 an hour and children as young as two years old are working in the fields. Further, while in the 1970s, some 100,000 workers were under contract, today there are fewer than 10,000.

Simultaneously, the landmark 1965 immigration legislation opened the door to a new surge of immigration. Placing no country quota on western hemisphere nations (an overall annual ceiling of 120,000 was placed on persons from the western hemisphere), many Mexicans and others from Latin America and Canada could now immigrate legally to the United States. As adjustments were made to the law, the annual flow of Mexican immigrants swelled from 33,000 in 1960 to 680,000 in 1990.[88]

But the illegal flow of immigrants rose too, with an estimated 50 to 60 percent of the undocumented newcomers coming from Mexico.[89] This growing illegal population (by 1980, their number was estimated at between 2 to 4 million)[90] caused increasing concern. To control the flow, the Immigration Reform and Control Act (IRCA) of 1986 offered amnesty to illegal aliens who had been in the country since 1982. The IRCA also tried to cut employer demand by levying sanctions on those who hired undocumented workers.* Until this time, a legal contortion had prevailed: It was illegal for undocumented workers to find employment in the United States but not illegal for employers to hire them. The IRCA also prohibited discrimination against U.S. citizens based on national origin, a provision aimed at preventing discriminatory practices resulting from the requirement that employers check the documents of all new hires.

Mexican-American groups and others objected to the IRCA, protesting that the sanctions and the antidiscrimination provisions fostered employment discrimination because employers did not adequately understand the law or, ignoring it, they discriminated against legalized Mexican Americans and others.[91] Others supported the law, maintaining that it achieved its aim of sustaining a liberal immigration policy by threatening penalties on employers but not intending to enforce them.[92]

Ultimately, the IRCA has not succeeded in curbing illegal immigration. While many who had been classified as illegal aliens were given amnesty and the sanctions temporarily reduced employer demand for illegal workers, the flow of illegal immigrants has again accelerated. According to Fuchs, commenting in 1993, as many as 500,000 illegal

---

*This was the law that doomed two of President Clinton's candidates for the office of Attorney General at the beginning of his administration. Both had hired undocumented aliens as nannies.

immigrants may be entering the country each year.[93] It is estimated
that there were 2 to 4 million in the country in 1993.[94] While not all of
the illegal immigrants are Mexicans, a significant portion is. Some supporters of the North American Free Trade Agreement (NAFTA) argue
that the agreement may prove to be the most effective way in the long
run to staunch the flow of illegal Mexican immigrants. They argue that
it will promote improvement in Mexican wages, thus eventually
reducing incentive to illegally seek jobs in the United States. Jorge
Castaneda, however, points out that *in the short run*, migratory flows
will be stimulated "as displaced peasants and laid-off employees take
advantage of large wage differentials and head north."[95]

The pattern of sojourner pluralism is changing. Among people of
Mexican origin legally residing in the United States, almost a third is
foreign-born.[96] And a growing portion of them are establishing roots
here. (As Alejandro Portes pointed out, American-born people of
Mexican heritage already *are* rooted.) Of the foreign-born Mexicans surveyed in 1989 to 1990 by the Latino National Political Survey (LNPS),
76 percent indicated that they intended to remain permanently in the
United States.* Moreover, the overwhelming majority of foreign-born
Mexicans surveyed either wished to be naturalized (65 percent) or
already were United States citizens (15 percent). Only 15 percent had
no plans to apply, and 5 percent were undecided.[98] These numbers do
not reflect the status and intentions of those living in the United States
illegally, but they clearly indicate the existence of a trend among
Mexicans in the United States toward discarding sojourner status.

Mexicans in the United States have changed in another way, too.
They are no longer primarily engaged in agricultural work. In fact, in
1992, less than 7 percent of the Mexican-origin labor force (documented immigrants and Mexican-American workers) held agricultural jobs,
according to the 1993 Current Population Survey (CPS) of the Bureau
of Labor Statistics.[99] If the number of undocumented workers in this
sector were known, this figure would almost certainly have to be
revised upward; however, it is clear that a high percentage of persons
of Mexican origin are participating in other sectors of the economy.
They are still concentrated near the bottom of the occupational ladder,
however, due in part to low levels of education and limited skills. Of
6.3 million workers, some 22 percent were in low-skilled blue-collar
jobs; 20 percent were technical sales and administrative support per-

sonnel; almost 17 percent were in the service industry; almost 13 percent were in skilled blue-collar jobs.[100] The smallest portion, under 10 percent, were managers or professionals. Full-time workers accounted for four-fifths of the total. Almost 12 percent were unemployed.

Like other Latino groups, many Mexican Americans seem stuck at the level of the working poor. Hispanic males generally have a higher labor force participation rate than non-Hispanics; however, Hispanic families with *a working member* are more likely to be poor, with lower median earnings than either white or black Americans.[101]

Puerto Ricans

Puerto Ricans have come to the mainland United States mainly to seek economic advantage, like most other migrants to this country. They are, however, distinct in several ways. Sociologist Clara Rodriguez points out that they have the distinction of being "the only colonial group to arrive en masse and the first racially heterogeneous group to migrate to the United States on a large scale."[102] Also, unlike other Latino groups, Puerto Ricans were granted U.S. citizenship in 1917; thus, they have freedom of entry, which some exercise frequently in the circular, sojourner pattern of migration. They are also one of the poorest minority groups in the country.

The island population, which has commonwealth status, is 3.5 million, according to the 1990 census.[103] On the U.S. mainland, Puerto Ricans are the second-largest Hispanic-origin group in the country, numbering some 2.7 million.[104] By almost every economic indicator, Puerto Ricans are among the worst off. Puerto Rican infant mortality is about 50 percent higher than that of Mexican-Americans and nearly three times as high as that among Cubans.[105] The Puerto Rican unemployment rate is higher than those of Mexicans and Cubans. According to the LNPS undertaken in 1989–1990, 38 percent of Puerto Ricans were not in the labor force and another 12 percent were temporarily unemployed. In comparison, the LNPS found that 28 percent of Mexicans were not in the labor force and 12 percent were temporarily unemployed; for Cubans the figures were 25 percent and 6 percent; the Anglo figures were 31 percent and 5 percent.[106]

In New York City, where one-third of the Puerto Rican population lives, they are worse off than the black population. Their median family income is lower than the median black family income and is rising less quickly. The home ownership rate of Puerto Ricans is less than half that of black Americans in New York City, and almost two times as many Puerto Ricans are on welfare.[107]

Although Puerto Ricans began moving to the mainland United States in large numbers only in the late 1940s, their historical and economic relationship with the United States goes back far earlier. Formerly a Spanish colony, Puerto Rico became a possession of the United States in 1898 after the Spanish-American war. Giant American sugar companies moved to the island and established large plantations, transforming the island economy. Thousands of independent subsistence farmers sold their land to the sugar interests and were drawn into the plantation economy. Living in company-owned shanty towns, they became dependent on the sugar companies. In the words of U.S. Secretary of the Interior Harold Ickes several decades later, they were "reduced to virtual economic serfdom."[108] Opportunities to acquire an education and learn English were limited: No one saw any pressing need to educate agricultural workers.

The Puerto Rican economy, too, became dependent on the United States. In 1897 (before the United States gained control of the island), about one-fifth of the island's trade was with the United States; by 1930, the figure had risen to 96 percent of Puerto Rico's exports and 87 percent of its imports.[109]

Since the early nineteenth century, rural, low-skilled Puerto Ricans had migrated to the mainland, where they took jobs mainly as farm laborers. Their numbers were small—only 1,500, according to the 1910 census.[110] Their status as American citizens made Puerto Ricans eligible for service in the U.S. military during World War I, and some 18,000 were drafted. Labor shortages created by the war provided opportunities on the U.S. mainland for a growing number of Puerto Ricans attracted by the availability of work. By 1920, there were almost 12,000 Puerto Ricans on the mainland, some two-thirds of them in New York City.[111] Like Mexicans in the American southwest, most Puerto Ricans were discriminated against and had few opportunities to learn English or get more than a rudimentary education. Many regarded their stay in the United States as temporary, further reducing their motivation.[112]

By the 1940s, depressed sugar prices hit the Puerto Rican plantations hard. No longer able to eke out a living, massive numbers of plantation workers crowded into urban slums in Puerto Rico, desperate for any economic opportunity that might come their way. For some, that opportunity arose in the form of labor shortages created by World War II. U.S. growers especially sought low-skill, low-wage Puerto Rican agricultural workers for seasonal work, and although many subsequently returned to the island, others remained on the U.S. mainland and formed nuclei around which later arrivals clustered.[113] In the late 1940s, the Puerto Rican and U.S. governments made it even easier to emigrate by helping to establish competing airline companies offering inexpensive passage to the United States, payable in installments.[114] Many went, mostly to New York City, where the Puerto Rican government established an office to help newcomers find jobs.

In the early 1950s, more labor shortages, this time produced by the Korean war and a booming economy, further increased the flow to the mainland. Between 1940 and 1960, the Puerto Rican population of New York City jumped from about 70,000 to 613,000.[115] By 1970, the Puerto Rican population there was greater than the population of San Juan. One study of the early postwar immigrants (Mills, Senior, and Goldsen) found that, although many had higher levels of educational attainment and higher job skills than the average Puerto Rican, their illiteracy rate still was double that of the New York City population.[116] And most Puerto Ricans, even white-collar workers, had to take work at lower skill levels than they had had in Puerto Rico.[117]

Despite their depressed conditions, during the 1960s, the Puerto Rican position in New York improved modestly. But in the 1970s, these gains were reversed, and the economic fortunes of Puerto Ricans dropped precipitously. This was partly due to the decline of the manufacturing industry and of northeastern cities generally. New York City alone lost almost a half a million jobs between 1971 and 1976, almost half of them in manufacturing.[118] Because Puerto Ricans were heavily concentrated in that sector, a large number lost their jobs, a slide that continued into the 1980s. Largely confined to inner cities, Puerto Ricans were doubly bereft of opportunities to advance themselves. Sociologists Marta Tienda and Frank Bean found that Puerto Ricans were the only minority group whose family income fell during both the 1970s and 1980s.[119] Furthermore, the South Bronx, where the largest group of Puerto Ricans lived, was reduced to a virtual wasteland in the 1970s. Due to a combination of economic and other factors, including arson, the area disintegrated into the worst slum in the country, likened to the bombed-out cities of Europe after World War II.

The fall-off in job opportunities is one of many complex, interrelated factors operating to keep Puerto Ricans one of the most depressed minorities in the United States. Historically, low levels of educational attainment and a lack of opportunity to develop marketable skills have also played a role in keeping many Puerto Ricans from participating in the labor force. More than 50 percent of Puerto Rican respondents to the LNPS have no high school degree, and 30 percent of those have eight or less years of schooling.[120] (On the brighter side, 11 percent have education beyond high school.) Related to this is a lack of English-language skills, a deficiency that is markedly higher in the Puerto Rican than in either Mexican- or Cuban-origin communi-

ties. It is, therefore, not surprising to learn that Puerto Rican participation in the labor force is low relative to the Mexican and Cuban
rates. According to the BLS, in 1992, only 57 percent of the Puerto
Rican population was in the labor force, compared with 61 percent of
the Cuban-origin population and almost 68 percent of the Mexican-
origin population.[121] Moreover, the unemployment rate (those who
are in the labor force but not employed) was higher for Puerto Ricans
than for the other two groups: Puerto Rican unemployment was over
14 percent in 1992; for Mexicans the rate was almost 12 percent; for
Cubans, almost 8 percent.

In a seeming paradox, the distribution of Puerto Ricans by industry
differs from that of the total Hispanic population in that a larger portion of Puerto Ricans are at the upper end of the occupational ladder.
BLS data shows that, in 1992, about 16 percent of Puerto Ricans were
in managerial and professional occupations, compared to 12 percent
for the overall Latino population.[122] Also, a smaller portion of Puerto
Ricans work in low-skilled occupations than the overall Latino population—16 percent and almost 20 percent, respectively, in 1992. The
largest portion of Puerto Ricans, some 28 percent, are in technical,
sales, and administrative support occupations. The remaining distribution by occupation is 15 percent service and 9 percent skilled blue
collar. Less than 1 percent of Puerto Ricans on the mainland are in
agriculture.

Citing Bureau of the Census statistics, the National Council of La
Raza states that, in 1991, the median earnings of Puerto Rican men
were four-fifths of the earnings of non-Hispanic men and slightly less
than the median for men in other Hispanic subgroups.[123] Taken together with statistics on occupational distribution, this points to something
of a socioeconomic polarization within the mainland Puerto Rican
community itself. Puerto Rican poverty seems to be more a matter of
unemployment than kinds of work or wages earned by those with
jobs. According to the LNPS, some 44 percent of the adult population
is simply not in the labor force or is temporarily unemployed. The per-
capita household income of almost 50 percent of the Puerto Rican population is less than $5,000.[124] (In comparison, less than 20 percent of
Anglo households have a per-capita income of less than $5,000.)

There are other elements in this story. Puerto Ricans in the United
States have one of the highest birth rates in the nation: Puerto Rican
women give birth early and have more children than many others.
They also tend to have large households: 50 percent have four or more
persons. This becomes more problematic because the marriage rate of
Puerto Ricans is low—less than 40 percent, according to the LNPS—
and many urban Puerto Rican households are headed by single moth-

ers who are rarely able to work outside the home in the absence of the kind of extended family support, especially child care, that is more the norm in Puerto Rico. Tienda asserts that an important reason the Puerto Rican poverty rates in New York have soared while the rates for black families have declined is the greater success of black women in the labor market.[125] Caught in a cycle of poverty, many Puerto Ricans are forced to rely on welfare support. This state of affairs is reflected by statistics indicating that three-fifths of all Puerto Rican children under 18—57.9 percent—were poor in 1991 compared to two-fifths of all Hispanic children and almost half of all African-American children. The poverty rate for white children was 16.8 percent.[126]

The overwhelming poverty of the Puerto Rican population in New York—where the vast majority of Puerto Rican–origin people live—obscures the fact that outside of New York, Puerto Ricans are substantially better off. The New York statistics depress the statistical profile for the overall group. The Puerto Rican population in California, for example, was better off in 1980 than the Mexican and black population, based on important measures.[127]

Although harder to quantify, the effects of discrimination must also be taken into account. Although Puerto Ricans are multiracial and range from fair to dark-skinned, a significant number are dark enough to be considered nonwhite by many Anglos. For these, race joins with language, class, and cultural differences to confirm an "otherness" that leads to forms of discrimination at least somewhat akin to that suffered by black Americans, thus limiting their chances to better themselves. Those with lighter skins appear to fare better and are frequently found to be higher on the socioeconomic scale. Puerto Rican newcomers tend to have a particularly hard time adjusting when they first face discrimination on the mainland because in the more integrated Puerto Rican society, distinctions are commonly based on a complex mix that emphasizes class over race.

Although the concept has sparked controversy, some point to a sojourner mentality allegedly evidenced by many Puerto Ricans as another obstacle to progress. The argument holds that such a mindset can produce negative effects, undercutting the motivation to learn English, establish roots, and develop a long-term commitment to advancement in the workplace on the U.S. mainland. As U.S. citizens, Puerto Ricans travel unimpeded—and often—from the mainland to the island, with potentially disruptive effects. Even relatively short-term visits may mean giving up employment, whether temporary or permanent. Children taken out of school for weeks and even months at a time are seriously disadvantaged; the stresses accompanying the changes of location affect both adults and children. And for some Puerto Ricans, the return is permanent. For some, the dream is to make enough money in the United States to be able to retire back home. (While most do not achieve this goal, low-skilled workers in particular find that employment experience gained on the mainland provides them with an extra opportunity to move up the skill ladder if they return to Puerto Rico.)[128]

The 1989–1990 LNPS found that 24 percent of the Puerto Ricans surveyed intended to return to live in Puerto Rico, and 19 percent were undecided (56 percent intended to remain permanently on the U.S. mainland).[129] The survey questioned only island-born Puerto Ricans; the percentage of those intending to remain on the mainland would undoubtedly be greater if U.S.-born people had been included. Nonetheless, of the three Hispanic groups surveyed (Puerto Ricans, Mexicans, and Cubans), Puerto Ricans ranked highest in their intent to return to their place of birth. (Cubans ranked lowest.) Critics point to the difficulty in quantifying the effect of such an attitude on those who hold it and others around them, let alone the extent to which it contributes to Puerto Rican poverty. The National Council for La Raza, an advocacy group, believes the evidence is unclear, citing, among others, an analysis by Edwin Meléndez that suggests that circular migration is not a significant factor.[130] Multicultural expert Ilya Adler agrees, pointing to discrimination and other factors as the real culprits.

Cuban Americans

Cuban Americans, the third major Hispanic-origin group in the United States, are the most well-educated and the best off financially of the Hispanic-origin groups in the United States. About 70 percent live in the Miami area.

A small flow of Cubans came to the United States before World War II, drawn mainly by the cigar industry. Settling mostly in Key West and Tampa, Florida, they numbered an estimated 18,000 to 19,000 people in 1930.[131] The pattern of Cuban migration to the states changed dramatically with the Cuban revolution in 1958. Large numbers of Cuba's best-educated, wealthiest citizens left the island. During the 1960s, some one million Cubans, about 10 percent of the population, migrated from Cuba, creating the largest shift in population in Latin American history.[132] This wave of exiles went to several countries, almost 257,000 of them coming to the United States.[133] Most of them settled in the Miami area, a location close to Cuba and with a similar climate. Like the early Puritan settlers in America, most of these early Cuban émigrés believed they would return home when conditions there changed. The LNPS found that as late as 1973, 60 percent of the Cubans surveyed said they intended to return to Cuba if Castro fell.[134]

Despite the temporary nature of their plans, the newcomers began investing in commercial ventures, especially in the Miami area. Many were professionals and entrepreneurs and, soon, they also included disaffected members of the revolutionary government. This "golden wave" of generally well-educated and well-to-do émigrés followed the pattern of European immigrants before them, investing in businesses, banks, and other institutions. Their community flourished.

By the 1970s, as economic restrictions and political repression in Cuba increased, people of more humble means began fleeing. Some 276,000 Cuban refugees, many of them relatively young, skilled, blue-collar workers, entered the United States during the decade.[135] By 1980, the population of skilled Cuban laborers in the United States exceeded that in Cuba. The arrival of this second wave of émigrés worked to the benefit of the established Miami Cuban community as well as the new émigrés. The newcomers encountered a ready-made market for their skills, because Cuban-owned businesses established in the 1960s were growing and expanding their labor force. About half of the new immigrants found employment there, and they tended to earn better wages than Cuban blue-collar workers employed outside the enclave.[136]

Miami became not only the Cuban economic center in the United States but also its social and cultural heart, with charitable and other institutions established to assist new émigrés. Called the "Cuban capital of the United States" with its "little Havana" quarter, Miami became (and still is) home to the second-largest concentration of Cubans after Havana. As with any group of immigrants, some individuals suffered exceptional hardships adapting to their new environment. There were dramas of personal failure and tragedy. Joblessness was a problem for many. In 1976, Cuban unemployment in Florida was more than 1.5 times that of non-Hispanic whites.[137] Also, some émigrés from families well established in Cuba found that their social and political networks, while re-created in the new setting, were insufficient to guarantee success. A number found themselves outstripped by other Cuban immigrants from less well-to-do backgrounds, who were better able to learn the skills (and, perhaps, hustle) needed for success in their new environment. Overall, however, the Cuban community flourished. Cuban-owned businesses in Dade County, Florida (where Miami is located) grew from 3,447 in 1969 to 24,898 in 1982.[138] By 1980, over 70 percent of the Cubans in the city owned their own homes.[139] Lawrence Fuchs points out that in Miami, Cuban Americans achieved political, economic, and cultural success more quickly than any immigrant group in any other city in U.S. history.[140] The importance of Miami was enhanced because many Cubans, thinking of their stay in the United States as temporary, were initially reluctant to move to other locations in the United States.

A third wave of immigration began in 1980 when the Cuban government suddenly opened the port of Mariel to people who wished to leave. About 125,000 people (known as *Marielitos*) took advantage of the opportunity, and many more probably would have done so had the operation not proven so embarrassing for Cuba that it closed the window of opportunity. These people were, on average, much younger and poorer than earlier Cuban immigrants, and a smaller portion was white. (About 95 percent of the first wave, 80 percent of the second wave, and 60 percent of the *Marielistas* were white.[141]) They encountered a more hostile reception than had their predecessors: Earlier Cuban immigrants had been received with much sympathy because, unlike most migrants to this country, they were political, not economic refugees, fleeing from an oppressive Communist regime. By 1980, however, Americans were becoming wary of the swelling number of immigrants worldwide. Also there were more focused concerns about alleged Cuban involvement in organized crime in Miami and New York.[142] Fears as old as the United States surfaced about the immigrants depriving other minorities of work opportunities. There had been incidents of violence between Cubans and blacks, and the new émigrés, being mainly low-skilled workers, now threatened to cut into the low end of the job market even more. A sharp edge was added to the concerns about the *Marielistas* because Fidel Castro included among them people considered socially undesirable. About 26,000 had prison records (mostly for minor or political offenses), and, of those, some 5,000 were hard-core criminals.[143] The federal government subsequently asked the Cuban government to take back some 4,000 people.

Over the years, Cubans' plans to return to their native land have dissipated. By 1979, only 22.6 percent said they intended to return, down 40 percent from only six years earlier.[144] The LNPS found in 1989–1990 that 86 percent of the foreign-born Cubans surveyed intended to remain permanently in the United States.[145] The share of those intending to remain would have been higher if American-born Cubans had been surveyed. As Cubans settled into the United States, some moved outside the Miami enclave. They are currently represented in all regions of the United States, with an especially high concentration in New Jersey. Most remain in Miami, however, and, in fact, there has been a return flow to the enclave. Still, those living outside Miami tend to be better educated and have a higher income than those remaining.[146] Regardless of where they live in the United States, they have evolved, as Alejandro Portes observed, from "political exiles to ethnic minority."[147]

Of the three major Hispanic-origin groups in the United States, Cubans have enjoyed the highest median income. In 1978, it was $15,326, compared with median income for all U.S. families of $17,640. The median income of those of Mexican origin was $12,835, with Puerto Ricans trailing at $8,282.[148] In 1989–1990, Cubans still ranked ahead of the other two groups. According to the LNPS, 16 percent of Cuban households had an annual income of $50,000 or more. The figures were 9 percent and under 5 percent for Mexican and Puerto Rican households, respectively.[149]

In 1992, the Cuban unemployment rate of almost 8 percent was less than that for the total Latino population, which was over 11 percent.[150] Moreover, a greater percentage of Cubans are employed in managerial and professional positions than is the overall Latino population. According to the CPS for 1992, the Cuban rate was 23 percent.[151] In contrast, the rate for the total Hispanic workforce was about 16 percent. Further, Cubans have a smaller percentage of workers at low skill levels than other Hispanic-origin groups. The 1992 CPS showed 14 percent of Cubans were employed as operators, fabricators, and laborers. The figure for Hispanics in general was almost 20 percent.

Hispanic Cultural Values and the Workplace

Despite their many differences, Latinos acknowledge that they share some common cultural values. The LNPS found that 75 percent of the Mexicans, Puerto Ricans, and Cubans surveyed believe that Latinos are either "very similar" or "somewhat similar" culturally.[152] When contrasted with Anglo cultural values, as they frequently are in the workplace, these similarities appear even greater.

Among the most important cultural considerations affecting Hispanic workers, one that cuts across classes, is that Hispanic culture is a "being" culture, according to multicultural expert Ilya Adler.* Latinos tend to place high priority on human relationships, placing particular value on warm, easy-going, attractive people who are fun to be with. These qualities are summed up in the word *simpatia*, which has its equivalent in many southern or Mediterranean cultures. Hispanics are holistic in their relationships, interacting on a multidi-

---

*This section draws heavily on material from an interview with Ilya Adler, July 8, 1993. Director of Hispanic-Anglo Research at Kochman Communication Consultants and formerly of the University of Illinois–Chicago, Adler is currently writing a book examining Hispanic-Latino/Anglo cultural differences.

mensional basis rather than focusing on primarily one role. Their concern is with the whole person, and this is expressed in all environments, including the workplace. Hispanic co-workers frequently engage in personal conversation, considering the workplace as appropriate a setting as elsewhere.

Because of their people focus, Latino managers tend to take a sincere interest in the employees they supervise, according to Adler. They are genuinely solicitous about all aspects of an employee's welfare and are likely to offer advice on a range of personal issues. The fact that a happy employee is apt to be a more productive employee is not lost on an Hispanic manager; nonetheless, the focus tends to be a concern for the employee as a person first, and as a productive team member second.

Given these values, it is not surprising that Latinos generally prefer to work with people, not in isolation. When they take a break, they are more likely to go to the coffee station and talk with co-workers. In contrast, Anglos are more likely to remain at their desks, daydreaming or thinking about personal matters, perhaps consciously giving the appearance of productivity. Adler observers that no one checks to see if a worker sitting at his or her desk is actually working.

Another example of the importance of the personal touch to Latinos is revealed in the seemingly small matter of greeting someone in passing. Many Latinos would find it appalling and rude if a co-worker or supervisor walked by without saying "hi." Many, perhaps most, Anglos would also find it impolite, but they are more likely to excuse the person for focusing on work to the exclusion of "mere" sociability, considering this behavior somehow more professional. Using professionalism or "press of work" as an excuse to avoid acknowledging someone one encounters is difficult for many Hispanics to understand. This kind of behavior, according to Adler, "is one reason why Hispanics often see Anglos as people who `live to work' and see themselves as people who `work to live.'"[153]

In contrast, the Anglo culture can be characterized as a "doing" culture. Anglos are more likely than Latinos to judge people largely in terms of what they do. They are also more likely to keep their work and leisure activities separate. On the job, they tend to talk about work, and in a play environment, about play, while an Hispanic is more likely to mix the two. Although Anglo co-workers do engage in some personal conversation on the job, at least some of it falls into the category of "schmoozing"—casual conversation, often for strategic purposes to strengthen working relations. Findings by psychologists Susan Keefe and Amado Padilla illustrate these contrasting Anglo and Hispanic behaviors toward mixing work and leisure. In a study of Mexican-American and Anglo-American behavior patterns, Keefe and Padilla found that Anglos are less likely than Mexican Americans to visit co-worker friends outside of work.[154] The tendency to differentiate between a "work friend" and a friend in one's personal life is telling.

These contrasting value systems can make for cultural misunderstandings in the workplace. Hispanics may assume that the Anglo mode of behavior is artificial, insincere, and cold. Anglos are likely to view the Hispanic approach as unprofessional and "unserious."

Contrasting attitudes about self-promotion can provide fertile ground for cultural misunderstandings as well. In the Hispanic value system, self-promotion is considered selfish behavior. While it is acceptable, even desirable, for friends, a boss, or co-workers to praise and promote a person, it is extremely bad taste to tout one's own accomplishments. In Mexico, for instance, to be described as "ambitious" is not a compliment; it is a criticism. The reluctance to promote oneself may be played out in several workplace behaviors—resumés that do not adequately reflect abilities and accomplishments, the failure to negotiate a salary when first offered a position, quietness at meetings when one's past accomplishments are germane to the discussion.*

In the Anglo value system, a worker is expected to be forthcoming—though not boastful—about his or her accomplishments. Underlying this expectation is the assumption that if one does not look out for oneself, no one else will. In the workplace, self-promotion, done in the right way, is considered a sign of confidence, even leadership ability. The key here is the phrase "done in the right way," which translates into doing it the Anglo way. If a person operating on the basis of an Hispanic value system gradually accommodates to the Anglo culture that sets the rules in the workplace, it is relatively easy to miss the behavioral nuance that spells the difference between acceptable and unacceptable. If, for instance, a person guided by Hispanic values decides he (or she) needs to be more aggressive in calling attention to his strong points (as he sees others doing), it is easy to cross the barely discernible line and undo the effect. Adler points out that some have been led to adopt exaggerated versions of self-promoting behavior. For example, Cubans in Miami and Puerto Ricans in New York have gained reputations for boastfulness. Such behavior is not well received in a workplace dominated by an Anglo value system.

---

*Ilya Adler speculates that one reason Hispanics consistently make less than their white counterparts in the public sector may be that it simply does not occur to Hispanics that they can bargain for their salary. In Hispanic cultures, government salaries are strictly fixed. Hispanic workers may not be aware that American managers have a salary range within which they are willing to negotiate.

By the same token, many Hispanics cringe when they encounter instances of Anglo self-promotion. A Latino manager encountering it in a subordinate will often react negatively, leaving the Anglo worker wondering what went wrong. An Anglo manager witnessing a Latino employee's reluctance to speak up for him- or herself is likely to conclude that that person lacks assertiveness and self-confidence. To an Anglo manager, such behavior is likely to cast doubts on the employee's leadership potential and overall effectiveness. To further complicate matters, if in such a case the Hispanic does not get the job or the promotion, he or she is likely to attribute the failure to discrimination, unaware that the issue is actually more cultural misunderstanding rather than active prejudice on the part of the manager. Such failures of cultural communication are likely to occur most often when there are few Latinos in the workplace, and they could ultimately have a negative effect in other areas, such as in hiring practices. Thus, at some point, cultural miscues can and often do lead to full-blown discrimination.

A further cultural difference is the hierarchical Hispanic versus the more egalitarian Anglo value system. Hispanic culture is strongly hierarchical and patriarchal. The gap between superiors and subordinates is more marked in the Hispanic culture than in Anglo culture. One way of describing this (using Hofstede's term) is that Hispanic culture displays "high power distance"; the Anglo American culture displays "low power distance." This concept would hold, for example, that those most steeped in Hispanic culture are most likely to have a hard time freely exchanging ideas if a superior is present if they did not agree with his or her ideas. Adler cites the example of the general manager of a large multinational company operating in Puerto Rico who discovered that if he left his Hispanic employees alone to brainstorm, their meetings could produce "incredible creativity." If he were present, however, the participants would fall silent, waiting for his opinion and then speaking only to affirm it.[155] Open disagreement or confrontation with one's superior is unthinkable for a person motivated by Hispanic values. If this is understood and the boss does not insist on sitting in on the brainstorming session, he or she will be amply rewarded for this sensitivity.

The implications of high power distance do not seem to square with the image of the concerned Latino manager conjured earlier in this discussion. Where has the *símpatía* gone? In some Hispanic behaviors on the job, high power distance may indeed take precedence over the human relations focus. A study conducted by psychologists Harry Triandis and others found that while many behaviors fall into the *símpatía* pattern, certain work relationships do not. These latter relationships are linked to high status (power distance). Triandis and his colleagues found that

Hispanics view relationships between supervisor and worker and naval officer and seaman as less intimate and more characterized by discipline than do non-Hispanics.[156] But while Latino managers may not feel it necessary to be *simpático*, the value system in which they are operating implies that the ideal authority figure is one who is concerned about subordinates on a personal level.

If given an option, Latino workers are likely to prefer working under a more egalitarian Anglo boss, though the Hispanic-personal-interest-versus-Anglo-cool-professionalism tradeoff would also be a consideration, according to Adler. Also, while the comfort level in working for an Anglo boss would be greater, an Hispanic worker would tend to have difficulty believing that such an approach was sincere. So deeply ingrained is the hierarchical tradition that an egalitarian approach is almost instinctively greeted with skepticism.

These and other cultural differences need to be understood and even maximized in the effort to capitalize on the diversity that increasingly characterizes the workplace. In discussing them—which is a first step toward achieving understanding—it is necessary to make rather sweeping generalizations based on the most obvious aspects of the differences between Anglo and Latino attitudes and values. Obviously, these generalizations break down at the individual level. A large segment of the Hispanic population are U.S. citizens who were born and raised in this country. Others may have arrived as adults and are having their first experience in a U.S. work setting. An individual Hispanic, therefore, may fall anywhere along a continuum that stretches from a person steeped in a particular Hispanic culture to one who fully understands and shares Anglo attitudes and values—all in all, a good argument for sensitivity and for dealing with people as they are rather than on the basis of assumptions or stereotypes.

References

1. Taylor Cox, Jr., and Stella M. Nkomo, "Invisible Men and Women: A Status Report on Race as a Variable in Organization Behavior Research," *Journal of Organizational Behavior,* vol. 11 (1990), p. 429.

2. Stella M. Nkomo, "The Emperor Has No Clothes: Rewriting `Race' In Organizations," *Academy of Management Review,* vol. 17, no. 3, 1992, pp. 487–513.

3. Comment by S. Kanu Kogod in a telephone conversation, January 14, 1994.

4. Cox and Nkomo, *loc. cit.*

5. *Ibid.,* p. 253.

6. Geert Hofstede, "Cultural Constraints in Management Theories," Distinguished International Scholar Lecture, *1992 Annual Meeting of the Academy of Management*, Las Vegas, Nevada, August 11, 1992, unpublished paper, p. 24.

7. Taylor H. Cox, Sharon A. Lobel, and Poppy Lauretta McLeod, "Effects of Ethnic Group Cultural Differences on Cooperative and Competitive Behavior on a Group Task," *Academy of Management Journal*, vol. 34, no. 4, 1991, p. 828.

8. Thomas Kochman of Kochman Communications Consultants (Chicago) in an interview, May 17, 1993.

9. Geert Hofstede, *Cultures and Organizations: Software of the Mind* (London: McGraw-Hill, 1991), p. 4.

10. Bernard R. Gifford, "Black and White Cultural Styles in Pluralistic Perspective," *Test Policy and Test Performance: Education, Language, and Culture* (Boston: Kluwer, 1989), pp. 264–265.

11. John D. Buenker and Lorman A. Ratner, *Multiculturalism in the United States: A Comparative Guide to Acculturation and Ethnicity* (New York: Greenwood Press, 1992), p. 4.

12. Michael Novak, "Making It in America—and in the World: The Cultural Factor," in M. Mark Stolarik and Murray Friedman, *Making It in America: The Role of Ethnicity in Business Enterprise, Education, and Work Choices* (Lewisburg, Pa.: Bucknell University Press, 1986), p. 131.

13. Geert Hofstede, *Culture's Consequences: International Differences in Work-Related Values*, vol. 5, Cross-Cultural Research and Methodology Series (Beverly Hills: Sage Publications, 1980).

14. Teresa L. Amott and Julie A. Matthaei, *Race, Gender & Work* (Boston: South End Press, 1991), p. 169.

15. Richard Morin, "From Colored to African American: What's in a Name," *Washington Post*, January 23, 1994, p. C5.

16. Herbert Hill, *Black Labor and the American Legal System: Race, Work, and the Law* (Washington, D.C.: Bureau of National Affairs, 1977), p. 6.

17. Reynolds Farley and Walter R. Allen, *The Color Line and the Quality of Life in America* (New York: Oxford University Press, 1989), p. 29.

18. *Ibid.*

19. *Ibid.*

20. *Ibid.*

21. Census data cited by *ibid.*

22. *Ibid.*, p. 27.

23. Cynthia Greggs Fleming, "African Americans," John D. Buenker and Lorman A. Ratner (eds.), *Multiculturalism in the United States: A Comparative Guide to Acculturation and Ethnicity* (New York: Greenwood Press, 1992), p. 10.

24. Gerald David Jaynes and Robin M. Williams, Jr., eds., *A Common Destiny: Blacks and American Society, Committee on the Status of Black Americans,* Commission on Behavioral and Social Sciences and Education, National Research Council (National Academy Press, 1989), p. 59.

25. *Ibid.,* p. 5.

26. *Ibid.,* p. 60.

27. *Ibid.,* p. 59.

28. Joe William Trotter, Jr., ed., *The Great Migration in Historical Perspective: New Dimensions of Race, Class, and Gender* (Bloomington: Indiana University Press, 1991).

29. *Ibid.*

30. Fleming, *op. cit.,* p. 11.

31. John A. Garraty and Robert A. McCaughey, *The American Nation: A History of the United States,* 6th ed. (New York: Harper & Row, 1987), p. 853.

32. The National Advisory Commission of Civil Disorders, *The 1968 Report of the National Advisory Commission on Civil Disorders (The Kerner Report)* (New York: Pantheon Books, 1988), p. 1.

33. Harvard Sitkoff, *The Struggle for Black Equality, 1954–1992* (New York: Hill and Wang, 1993), p. 211.

34. Jaynes and Williams, *op. cit.,* p. 275.

35. Smith and Welch, p. ix.

36. Bureau of the Census, *Money Income of Households, Families, Persons in the United States: 1992,* Current Population Reports, Consumer Income Series P60-184 (Washington, D.C.: U.S. GPO, 1993), p. B-7.

37. George Davis and Glegg Watson, *Black Life in Corporate America: Swimming in the Mainstream* (New York: Doubleday, Anchor Books, 1982), p. 33.

38. Fleming, *op. cit.,* p. 12.

39. *Ibid.,* p. 23.

40. William Julius Wilson, *The Truly Disadvantaged: The Inner City, the Underclass, and Public Policy* (Chicago: University of Chicago Press, 1987), p. 125.

41. *Ibid.*

42. Jaynes and Williams, *op. cit.,* pp. 274–275.

43. Wilson, *op. cit.,* p. 143.

44. *Ibid.,* p. 144.

45. *Ibid.*

46. Smith and Welch, *op. cit.,* p. 81.

47. Bureau of the Census, *The Black Population in the United States: March 1991, op. cit.*

48. Cornel West, *Race Matters* (Boston: Beacon Press, 1993), pp. 12–13.

49. *Ibid.,* p. 19.

50. Lawrence Fuchs, *The American Kaleidoscope: Race, Ethnicity, and the Civic Culture* (Hanover: Wesleyan University Press, 1990), p. 333.

51. Thomas Kochman, *Black and White Styles in Conflict* (Chicago and London: University of Chicago Press, 1981), pp. 13–14.

52. Ella Louise Bell, "The bicultural life experience of career-oriented black women," *Journal of Organizational Behavior,* vol. 11, 1990, pp. 459–477.

53. Adelbert H. Jenkins, *The Psychology of the Afro-American: A Humanistic Approach* (New York: Pergamon Press Inc., 1982), p. 114.

54. Jill Nelson, *Volunteer Slavery, My Authentic Negro Experience* (Chicago: Noble Press, 1993), p. 10.

55. Shelby Steele, *The Content of Our Character: A New Vision of Race in America* (New York: St. Martin's Press, 1990), p. 96.

56. Hofstede, *Cultures and Organizations, op. cit.,* p. 53.

57. Quoted by Taylor Cox, Jr., *Cultural Diversity in Organizations: Theory, Research & Practice* (San Francisco: Berrett-Koehler Publishers, 1993), p. 114.

58. *Ibid.,* p. 115.

59. Kochman, *Black and White Styles in Conflict, op. cit.,* pp. 18, 20.

60. *Ibid.,* pp. 112–113.

61. Quoted by Adelbert H. Jenkins, *op. cit.,* p. 185.

62. Kevin Merida," 'Sisterhood' of the Hill 'Shaking Up the Place'," *Washington Post,* August 2, 1993, p. A1.

63. Cox, *op. cit.,* pp. 110–111.

64. Kochman, "Black and White Cultural Styles in Pluralistic Perspective," p. 269.

65. *Ibid.,* p. 270.

66. Bureau of the Census, *Hispanic Americans Today,* Current Population Reports, P23-183, p. 1.

67. Jennifer Cheeseman Day, *Population Projections of the United States, by Age, Sex, Race, and Hispanic Origin: 1992 to 2050,* Current Population Reports, P25-1092, U.S. Department of Commerce, Economics and Statistics Administration, Bureau of the Census, November 1992, p. 41.

68. *Hispanic Americans Today, op. cit.,* p. 4.

69. *Ibid.*

70. Ronald Takaki, *A Different Mirror: A History of Multicultural America* (Boston: Little, Brown, 1993), p. 168.

71. Kerr, p. 217.

72. *Ibid.*

73. Samuel Eliot Morison, *The Oxford History of the American People* (New York: Oxford University Press, 1965), p. 551.

74. Fuchs, *op. cit.*, pp. 110–111.

75. Kerr, *op. cit.*, p. 219.

76. *Ibid.*, p. 220.

77. *Ibid.*, p. 219.

78. Fuchs, *op. cit.*, pp. 110–127.

79. *Ibid.*, p. 118.

80. Gregory DeFreitas, *Inequality at Work: Hispanics in the U.S. Labor Force* (New York: Oxford University Press, 1991), pp. 15–16.

81. *Ibid.*, p. 16.

82. Kerr, *op. cit.*, p. 221.

83. Fuchs, *op. cit.*, p. 121.

84. *Ibid.*, p. 123.

85. Alejandro Portes, "Latinos: A Biography of the People: Book Reviews," *The New Republic*, April 26, 1993.

86. Jose E. Limon, "Language, Mexican Immigration, and the `Human Connection': A Perspective from the Ethnography of Communication," Harley L. Browning and Rodolfo O. de la Garza, eds., *Mexican Immigrants and Mexican Americans: An Evolving Relation* (Austin: CMAS Publications, 1986), pp. 195–196.

87. Jeffrey Kaye, reporting on the *MacNeil-Lehrer Newshour,* September 2, 1993.

88. Statistics Division, Immigration and Naturalization Service.

89. Fuchs, *op. cit.*, p. 126.

90. Frank D. Bean, Barry Edmonston, and Jeffrey S. Passel, eds., *Undocumented Migration to the United States: IRCA and the Experience of the 1980s* (Washington, D.C.: The Rand Corporation and The Urban Institute, 1990), p. 27.

91. Mexican American Legal Defense and Educational Fund and American Liberties Union, "The Human Costs of Employer Sanctions," November 1989.

92. Jeffrey Rosen, "Good Help: Race, Immigration and Nannies: Zoe Baird," *New Republic*, February 15, 1993, p. 13.

93. Tom Morganthau, "America: Still a Melting Pot?," *Newsweek*, August 9, 1993, p. 20.

94. *Ibid.*

95. Jorge G. Castaneda, "Can NAFTA Change Mexico?" *Foreign Affairs*, vol. 72, no. 4, Sept/Oct 1993, p. 74.

96. *Hispanic Americans Today, op. cit.*, pp. 4, 14.

97. Rodolfo de la Garza, Louis DeSipio, F. Chris Garcia, Johan A. Garcia, and Angelo Falcon, *Latino Voices: Mexican, Puerto Rican, and Cuban Perspectives on American Politics* (Boulder, Colorado: Westview Press, 1992), p. 44.

98. *Ibid.*, p. 45.

99. Bureau of Labor Statistics, U.S. Department of Labor, *Employment and Earnings,* January 1993 (Washington, D.C.: U.S. GPO., 1993), p. 219.

100. *Ibid.*, pp. 219, 221.

101. Sonia M. Pérez and Dierdre Martínez, *State of Hispanic America 1993: Toward a Latino Anti-Poverty Agenda* (Washington, D.C.: National Council of La Raza, July 1993), p. 7.

102. Clara E. Rodriguez, *Puerto Ricans Born in the U.S.A.* (Boston: Unwin Hyman, 1989), p. xiv.

103. *Hispanic Americans Today, op. cit.*, p. 4.

104. *Ibid.*

105. Nicholas Lemann, "The Other Underclass: Puerto Ricans in the U.S.," *The Atlantic*, vol. 268, no. 6, December 1991, p. 96.

106. de la Garza, et al., *op. cit.*, p. 55.

107. Lemann, *op. cit.*

108. DeFreitas, *op. cit.*, p. 29.

109. *Ibid.*, p. 28.

110. *Ibid.*, p. 34.

111. *Ibid.*

112. Fuchs, *op. cit.*, p. 119.

113. Amott and Matthaei, *op. cit.*, pp. 274–275.

114. Lemann, *op. cit.*, p. 119.

115. *Ibid.*

116. DeFreitas, *op. cit.*, p. 35.

117. Rodriguez, *op. cit.*, p. 2.

118. Joan Moore and Harry Pachon, *Hispanics in the United States* (Englewood Cliffs, N.J.: Prentice-Hall, 1985), p. 47.

119. Frank D. Bean and Marta Tienda, *The Hispanic Population of the United States*, The Population of the United States in the 1980s, A Census Monograph Series, for the National Committee for Research on the 1980 Census (New York: Russell Sage Foundation, 1987), pp. 346–347 and Lehman, *op cit.*

120. de la Garza, et al., *op. cit.*, p. 29.

121. BLS, *Employment and Earnings, op. cit.*, p. 219.

122. *Ibid.*, pp. 219, 221.

123. The National Council of La Raza, *Mainland Puerto Rican Population Fact Sheet,* Washington, D.C., November 1993, p. 2.

124. L. H. Gann and Peter J. Duignan, *The Hispanics in the United States: A History* (Boulder: Westview Press and Hoover Institution on War, Revolution and Peace, 1986), p. 31.

125. Cited by Lemann, *op. cit.*

126. National Council of La Raza, *op. cit.*, p. 3.

127. Fuchs, *op. cit.*, pp. 490–491.

128. de la Garza, et. al., *op cit.*, p. 83.

129. *Ibid.*, p. 44.

130. Pérez and Martínez, *op cit.*, p. 18.

131. Moore and Pachon, *op. cit.*, p. 36.

132. Gann and Duignan, *op. cit.*, p. 101.

133. U.S. Department of Commerce, *Statistical Abstracts of the United States 1986* (Washington, D.C.: U.S. Government Printing Office, 1985), p. 86.

134. Fuchs, *op. cit.*, p. 350.

135. U.S. Department of Commerce, *Statistical Abstracts of the United States 1986, loc. cit.*

136. Gann and Duignan, *op. cit.*, p. 102.

137. George J. Borjas and Marta Tienda, *Hispanics in the U.S. Economy* (Orlando: Academic Press, 1985), pp. 137, 138.

138. Fuchs, *op. cit.*, p. 349.

139. Gann and Duignan, *op. cit.*, p. 108.

140. Fuchs, *op. cit.*, p. 454.

141. Moore and Pachon, *op. cit.*, p. 36.

142. *Ibid.*, p. 84.

143. Thomas D. Boswell and James R. Curtis, *The Cuban-American Experience: Culture, Images, and Perspectives* (Totowa, N.J.: Rowman & Allanheld, 1984), p. 53.

144. Fuchs, *op. cit.*, p. 350.

145. de la Garza, et al., *op. cit.*, p. 44.

146. *Ibid.*, p. 104.

147. A. Portes quoted by Fuchs, *op. cit.*, p. 350.

148. Gann and Duignan, *op. cit.*, p. 107.

149. de la Garza, et al., *op. cit.*, p. 33.

150. BLS, *Employment and Earnings, 1992, op. cit.*, p. 219.

151. *Ibid.*, pp. 219, 221.

152. de la Garza, et al., *op. cit.*, p. 143, 194.

153. Ilya Adler, unpublished letter, March 6, 1994.

154. Susan E. Keefe and Amado M. Padilla, *Chicano Ethnicity* (Albuquerque, University of New Mexico Press, 1987), p. 1643.

155. Adler, *loc. cit.*

156. Harry C. Triandis, Judith Lisansky, Gerardo Marín, and Hector Betancourt, "*Simpatía* as a Cultural Script of Hispanics," *Journal of Personality and Social Psychology*, vol. 47, no. 6, 1984, p. 1371.

7

Racial and Ethnic Groups in the New Workforce: History and Cultural Issues—2

A Short History of Asian Americans

There are some 6.9 million persons of Asian descent in this country, according to the 1990 Census.* Like Hispanics, Asian Americans are of several races. But while Hispanics share a common cultural tradition, Asian Americans come from widely differing cultures. They have no more in common than the fact that they or their ancestors came from the same land mass, the world's largest continent, stretching some 6,000 miles, or from the island nations off the Asian coast, which span several thousand miles of ocean. A tenuous link indeed.

Historically, Americans' national focus has been eastward. European culture was first planted on our Eastern shores, and from there it

---

*The Census Bureau groups Asians and Pacific Islanders in one category, but it also provides separate statistics on Asians. In this chapter, we refer to Asians only. The combined category of Asians and Pacific Islanders numbers 7.2 million people.[1]

evolved a distinctive American character and slowly expanded across the continent. Thus, Asian immigrants to the United States were long understood to be an exception to our immigration pattern, an anomaly, for they came across the Pacific "through the back door." That the first migrants to these shores, the ancestors of Native Americans, also came from Asia has often been held in a special parenthesis as an aside to our "real" history. Asian Americans were an exception in another way, too: They were racially different. Until the post–World War II period, the process of becoming American was commonly understood as the assimilation of ethnically diverse but racially homogeneous white Europeans, preferably from Northwestern Europe. Asian immigrants, like black immigrants, clearly did not fit the stereotype. Many white Americans doubted their ability to assimilate and, maybe more to the point, opposed such assimilation and took actions that effectively prevented it.

Today, our views have changed radically for several reasons. Our national focus has gradually become bicoastal.* The immigration flow from Asia is larger than that from Europe. Asians, like blacks, have demonstrated their ability to assimilate at the same time that they have asserted the right to maintain their own cultural identity. And many white Americans welcome the diversity that constitutes the rich pattern of our immigration history.

We are thus now in a better position to view the Asian-American experience as an integral part of that history. The Asian-American experience has often been expressed as a "negative history," as historian Roger Daniels points out. "Asians have been more celebrated for what has happened to them than for what they have accomplished," he observes.[2] In this section, we briefly examine the history of the three largest groups of Asian Americans: Chinese, Filipino, and Japanese Americans.† While we survey the outlines of what has happened to them in the past, now, in the last decade of the twentieth century, their accomplishments, too, are becoming abundantly clear. We give attention to these as well.

Chinese Americans

Chinese were the first Asians to come to America, and today they are the largest Asian group in the country, with a population in 1990 of

---

*Of course, the imprint of our East Coast beginnings remain. It is found, for example, in the phrase "back East," used nationwide to designate the East Coast.

†The seven largest Asian American groups and their populations (1990 Census data) are as follows: Chinese (1.65 million); Filipino (1.42 million); Japanese (.87 million); Korean (.80 million); Asian Indian (.79 million); Vietnamese (.59 million); Cambodians (.15 million).

1,649,000.[3] Chinese records indicate that as early as the fifth century A.D. a few explorers traveled to "Fusang," which is believed to have been North America and Mexico. In more recent times, there are records of Chinese in America in 1781 and possibly before, earlier than many white ethnic groups, as anthropologist Bernard Wong of San Francisco State University points out.[4] But migration in substantial numbers did not begin until the 1850s.

Chinese experience in the United States has broad significance. As multicultural expert Ronald Takaki of the University of California notes, the Chinese experience influenced the reception of other Asians here.[5] From the beginning, the cards were stacked against them. A naturalization law passed in 1790 made it illegal for Asians to become naturalized citizens. This meant that those who did venture to these shores were condemned to be "sojourners," to use Lawrence Fuchs's term. They were not allowed full participation in the civic culture, and that restriction plus other, massive cultural and racial prejudice consigned them to second-class status, if not lower. The naturalization restriction was not a deterrent to the early arrivals, however, who probably did not know about the law anyway. Most Chinese émigrés did not intend to become citizens. They initially planned to remain in America only temporarily, just long enough to earn money to support their families back home, and then they expected to return.

Some of the earliest Chinese arrivals experienced a brief period in which they were welcomed,[6] but it did not last long. White Americans quickly came to resent the economic competition that the Chinese represented. Further, in a highly racist era, they viewed Chinese as racially alien. Assuming they were unassailable, Americans went about establishing conditions, both legislative and informal, that made it impossible for Chinese migrants to acculturate and assimilate. Over the long run, by the time the permanence of their stay in this country became clear, they had evolved into an isolated community. Wong suggests that assimilation would have come early had discrimination not been present.[7]

The early Chinese émigrés were lured by the prospect of riches in America. From a few returnees and from labor brokers, they heard stories of the California gold rush and of the seemingly wide-open opportunities in the land that they wishfully called "Gold Mountain." These people were also pushed by the desperate situation in China. The Qing dynasty was in decay. The deterioration was evident after the Chinese humiliation at the hands of the British in the Opium war. Ending in 1842, the Opium war began the process of opening an unwilling China to Western incursion. To help offset its economic decline, the government levied heavy taxes on peasants who were barely subsisting anyway. Further, in the 1850s and 1860s, the Taiping rebellion, a peasant uprising, convulsed much of China and caused an estimated 20 million deaths. And the Guangdong and Fujian regions from which most of the early émigrés came were plagued by a series of natural disasters that made life even more precarious. In desperation, some fled. These people, mostly peasants, risked their lives to seek opportunity in America, for by law the penalty for leaving China was death. Some of them migrated as free laborers. Others sold themselves into contract labor. And still others were illegally coerced by a variety of shenanigans into becoming "coolies," forced to work in America for a specified time before they were freed from their contractual obligation.

Those who survived the crossing—reminiscent in its horror of the "Middle Passage" that had carried Africans into slavery—found work mainly in California. The need for labor to open the west was burgeoning. Once California achieved statehood in 1850, the imperative was to link it to the rest of the nation, to tap its mineral resources and develop its agricultural potential. Because the supply of white workers was insufficient to do these jobs, recruiting Chinese labor seemed to be one answer. Chinese were willing to work more cheaply than white people and they took jobs most whites disdained. By 1860, there were almost 35,000 Chinese in the United States, according to U.S. Census figures.[8] That number tripled by 1880.

Everywhere, they encountered discrimination and abuse. Chinese laborers who opened mines were obliged to pay special California taxes, which were often extracted by violence. Chinese miners frequently encountered vigilante groups and were robbed, beaten, and sometimes killed. Others worked as laborers on agricultural land and did not fare much better.

Despite the hardships, Chinese contributions were many. They were hardworking and provided relatively cheap labor. The special taxes to which many were subjected in California accounted for between a quarter to a half of all state revenue by 1870.[9] Their contribution to the construction of the first transcontinental railway was especially important. The Central Pacific Railway Company began hiring Chinese laborers in 1864 to assist with its rush job of linking up with track being laid by a competing railway company. The hiring process was facilitated by treaty between the United States and China in 1868, which legalized the emigration of contract labor. Eventually, an estimated 12,000 Chinese worked on the railway, the core of the Central Pacific work crew.[10] Conditions were hard—long hours of work in the high Sierras during the winter under a thick blanket of snow. (They lived and worked in tunnels under the snow.) Many died at their tasks.* When the Chinese organized a protest in 1867, the company cut off food supplies and starved them into submission.

When the railway was completed in 1869, Chinese railroad laborers went to urban areas in California where they were thrown into competition with white workers. Economic depression in California in the 1870s intensified white resentment over the Chinese economic threat. Race riots broke out. Anti-Chinese protests continued as Chinese immigration increased to almost 40,000 in 1882 (though the amount was only a fraction of the immigration total from some European countries).[12] Responding to these pressures, Congress passed the China Exclusion Act in 1882. Banning Chinese immigration for 10 years, the China Exclusion Act was the first piece of legislation to ban immigration on the basis of nationality (aside from an 1808 law, sanctioned by the Constitution, that banned importation of slaves from Africa). The China Exclusion Act was renewed and, in 1902, it was extended indefinitely. As a result, the Chinese population in the United States plummeted, from a high of 107,000 in 1890 to 61,600 in 1920, as many chose to leave the hostile American environment and return to their homeland.

With new immigration brought to a virtual halt, those who remained in the United States beat a retreat. Under the stress of rampant discrimination, they grouped into ethnic enclaves in urban centers—Chinatowns—where they did not have to compete in the general economy. Some left California and went to urban centers elsewhere and established Chinatowns there. Largely isolated from the rest of the population, many opened their own small businesses, especially laundries, restaurants, and grocery stores. About one-quarter of the Chinese male population worked in laundries by 1900.[13] Thus arose the stereotyped image of Chinese laundries, though, in fact, it was an occupation into which the Chinese were pressed by circumstances. Takaki points out that, in China, laundry was considered women's work.[14] In the United States, however, it had the advantages of requiring little skill and capital outlay, and it provided no competition with white establishments.

Under such circumstances, it is not surprising that the Chinese did not assimilate. Various states passed laws that further prohibited Chinese from working in specified occupations. In New York state, 27 occupations were banned.[15] California passed legislation forbidding

---

*For a powerful, partly fictionalized account of life building the railways from the perspective of Chinese laborers, see Kingston, *China Men*.[11]

Asians (along with blacks and mulattos) to intermarry with whites. Nor were they allowed to own property, except in Chinatowns.

In Hawaii, conditions were less restrictive. There, Chinese were allowed to buy property and to intermarry with Hawaiians, who welcomed them as they welcomed whites to their islands. Many prospered and entered the ranks of the middle class. But in Hawaii, too, anti-Asian sentiment on the part of whites was a way of life. For example, Asians were generally relegated to unskilled positions on the sugar plantations, the skilled positions being largely reserved for American citizens and those eligible for citizenship.[16] After passage of the China Exclusion Act, the Hawaii government implemented similarly restrictive measures, although over time these were modified.

Isolated from the broader culture, the Chinatowns became bustling enclaves reflecting many aspects of traditional Chinese life. Relations were close and well organized. The Chinese established a variety of associations that provided mutual aid, helped immigrants, and served as social centers. Because the inhabitants had little contact with non-Chinese, most did not have the chance to learn English (or to practice what little English they did learn), and this situation reinforced traditional culture in the enclaves.

However, in some important ways, the Chinatowns were anything but traditional. Their inhabitants were overwhelmingly male. The pioneer Chinese immigrants were mostly males, and, although many had wives and families in China, they were reluctant to bring them to join them in the hostile environment of the United States. In 1860, only about 5 percent of the population were women.[17] By 1890, the share fell to under 4 percent. This meant that family life was not possible for most Chinese, and American-born, second-generation Chinese Americans were few in number. The passage of the Immigration Act of 1924 further restricted the Chinese by banning the entry of Chinese wives.

The Chinese bachelor society created its own special needs. One of these was for prostitution. The 1870 census recorded that 61 percent of the Chinese women in California were prostitutes.[18] Many of them had been brought to this country by force; some were sold into prostitution when they were children. Gambling, drunkenness, and opium were also common, providing temporary outlets for peoples' misery. Further, Chinese workers lived in intensely crowded, squalid conditions. Too poor to afford better accommodations, they often crowded 15 to 20 men in a small room. Reacting to the unsanitary conditions of such living arrangements, the California legislature passed a cubic air law in 1870, which required that a lodging provide 500 feet of clear air for each adult tenant.[19]

Unsurprisingly, the general public image of the Chinese communities was unfavorable. There was little sympathy for their degraded circumstances, nor was there understanding of the role played by the broader society in shaping them.

World War II brought drastic change to peoples throughout the world. For Chinese Americans, it was nothing short of a blessing, for it provided the first real opening toward acceptance by the larger society. Because China was a U.S. ally and was valiantly fighting against the invading Japanese, Americans began to view more favorably Chinese here at home. Also, Americans were goaded into shifting their position by a Japanese propaganda assault touting the degraded conditions of Chinese Americans, which rang only too true.

Chinese Americans were drafted into the armed forces. Some 35 percent of the Chinese population served, a larger portion of the population than from any other minority group.[20] One reason for the large enlistment rate was the lopsidedly male composition of the Chinese population. But many welcomed the opportunity.

Legislative changes were also made. The China Exclusion Act, on the books for 60 years, was finally repealed in 1943. The right of naturalized citizenship was extended in 1952 to the Chinese and other non-white immigrants after the McCarran-Walter Act nullified the 1790 naturalization law. A small number of immigrants was now allowed to enter the country (150 a year), and Chinese were permitted to bring wives from China. The postwar period thus marked the beginning of Chinese family life in the United States. Much other anti-Chinese legislation also was removed from the books, including the lifting of the prohibition against buying property outside of Chinatowns.

The war provided an opportunity in another way: Labor shortages caused by the war meant new opportunities for Chinese Americans to work in the broader economy. Many got positions in the expanding defense industries, some being trained by employers and taking skilled positions. Wong suggests that the contemporary Chinese prominence as engineers and in technical professions may have gotten its start in World War II.[21] After the war, the GI bill enabled many Chinese-American veterans to attend college and attain skills needed to move into professional positions.

The 1965 Immigration Act, which opened the doors to peoples from all over the world, brought a new influx of Chinese immigrants. The Chinese population, already on an ascending curve, almost doubled between 1960 and 1970, jumping from 237,000 to 431,000.[22] According to the 1990 Census, the figure rose in 1990 to 1.6 million, 1.1 million of whom were foreign-born.[23] The population's predominately male composition also changed. Many of the new immigrants were women accompanying their husbands. By 1980, approximate parity between men and women was achieved; by 1990, there were slightly more women than men.

Chinese Americans face the paradox of being both a very old and a very new group. They were the first Asian immigrants, but because of the lopsided male-female ratio, there were few American-born offspring. Their numbers were replenished mainly by new immigration rather than natural increase. It was thus an ever-new population, one which was continually adjusting to the American environment. Today, the Chinese community is still a new population, although the American-born component is sizable and growing: In 1990, 30 percent—506,000 people—were American-born.[24] An increasing influx of immigrants, mostly from mainland China, keeps the community new, however. Since 1980, almost 650,000 newcomers entered the country; some 490,000 entered before 1980.

Thus, within the Chinese-American community, there are strongly contrasting demographic features. Roger Daniels points out that Chinese Americans themselves draw a distinction between the ABCs (American-born Chinese) and the FOBs (fresh off the boat).[25] The former tend to have college educations and middle-class occupations, and they are not likely to live in Chinatowns. The new immigrants are largely poorly educated with poor English-language skills, and they are likely to work in low-skill, low-wage jobs and to live in Chinatowns. (Daniels notes that there are, of course, exceptions among the newcomers, that is, well-educated, middle-class people with considerable capital.)

The low English-language skill level is reflected in 1990 Census findings. According to the Census, 50 percent of persons five years and older do not speak English very well and 35 percent of persons five years and older live in households that are linguistically isolated.[26] While this is a sizable segment of the population, it is a stunning departure from the situation earlier in this century when most Chinese Americans did not speak English well.

The rate of naturalization is also increasing. Less than 1,000 people a year became naturalized citizens between 1944 and 1951; in 1960, almost 2,000 persons became naturalized.[27] Between 1980 and 1990, the rate of naturalization jumped to an average of 11,600 persons a year, as Chinese responded to the new, more open American immigration standards and were spurred by instability and change in China.[28] In 1990, a total 76 percent of the foreign-born Chinese Americans were naturalized citizens.

While these trends suggest a growing degree of acculturation and assimilation among Chinese Americans, they do not necessarily reflect a falling away of Chinese cultural characteristics. Many Chinese Americans, including many second-generation persons, are involved in both their ethnic culture and in the mainstream world. They have a strong sense of Chinese identity as well as a sense of identification with the larger society.*

Chinese Americans have reached some relatively high levels of attainment. Their education level is higher than that of the total population. While 2.4 percent of the total population has some college or an associate degree, the figure for the Chinese population is 14 percent, according to the 1990 Census.[31] For a bachelor's degree or higher, both the total population and the Chinese population register almost 5 percent. Chinese higher-education figures, however, are lower than those of the overall Asian population. Twenty-two percent of the Asian population has some college or an associate degree (compared to 14 percent for the Chinese); almost 9 percent of the total Asian population has a bachelor's degree or higher.[32]

The per-capita income of Chinese Americans in 1989 was about comparable to that of the total population and of the Asian population: $14,877, $14,420, and $13,806, respectively.[33] It is interesting to note the substantial jump in the per-capita income of naturalized Chinese citizens, which was $24,216. With regard to family income, the median Chinese and Asian family incomes were greater than that of total population ($41,316, $41,583, and $35,225, respectively). Part of the Chinese (and Asian) advantage over the total population can be explained by the extended family system. Chinese and Asian families tend to be larger than those of the general population, and they also tend to have more wage earners per family. Forty-eight percent of Chinese families had two income earners; another 20 percent had three income earners.[34] In contrast, in the total population, almost 46 percent had two income earners, but only 13 percent had three or more income earners.

At the low end of the economic scale, 11 percent of Chinese families were below the poverty level in 1989, which is about the same as the Asian families and one percent more than the figure for the total population. Among Chinese families, the poverty level of those who are not citizens was greater than those who were naturalized—just over 6 percent of families in the former group were below poverty level in 1989, and almost 12 percent of the latter.

By occupation, more Chinese had managerial and professional specialty occupations (almost 36 percent) than any other single category.[35] A greater portion of Chinese are in this category than are Asians as a whole (31 percent) or the total population (26 percent). Thirty-one per-

---

*Insightful literary accounts of Chinese-American life include Amy Tan's best selling novel and movie, *The Joy Luck Club*,[29] and Maxine Hong Kingston's bio-novel, *The Woman Warrior*.[30]

cent of Chinese workers were in technical, sales, and administrative support occupations, the next-highest category.

Filipino Americans

There have been two waves of Filipino immigration to the United States: from 1906 to 1934 and from 1965 to the present. While Filipinos first began coming to this country in significant numbers later than Chinese and Japanese, since the change in immigration laws in 1965, they have become the second largest Asian group in the country. In 1990, Filipino Americans totaled 1,420,000 people.[36]

The history of Filipino-American relations has been complex and painful, and Filipinos in the United States have been an integral part of that history. The first Filipinos arrived in the Americas unwillingly. As early as the 1560s, Filipino seamen who had been pressed into naval duty by their Spanish conquerors jumped ship in Mexico. Most of them settled in Mexico, but one party of a few hundred eventually went to Louisiana and settled on the outskirts of New Orleans. Other Filipinos came individually, but the first real wave of Filipino migration to this country did not occur until the first decade of the twentieth century, under very different circumstances.

Following the Spanish defeat in the Spanish-American war in 1898, the United States annexed the Philippines. Filipinos had long opposed Spanish rule. During the war, they had joined with the United States against Spain with (what they understood was a mutual) understanding that the United States would support Filipino independence thereafter. However, unable to withstand the lure of empire, the United States decided that Filipinos were unready for independence and required America (in the words of President McKinley) to "uplift and civilize and Christianize them."[37] Filipinos were outraged but powerless. The Philippines became a U.S. possession.

Plagued by depressed economic conditions at home, especially in rural areas, Filipinos emigrated to Hawaii (which was a U.S. territory) and to a lesser extent to the U.S. mainland in search of economic opportunity. The first major wave did not begin until 1906. At that time, Hawaiian sugar growers began to recruit Filipinos as contract laborers for their plantations. The supply of Chinese laborers had dried up due to the China Exclusion Act of 1882.* Japanese workers, however, were plentiful—too plentiful, according to the growers, for in numbers there was strength, and the growers understood that their own interests

---

*The influx of Japanese workers, too, was soon to be drastically cut as a result of the Gentlemen's Agreement between the United States and Japan in 1908.

would best be served by diversifying their workers, thereby keeping them weak. Thus, once the Korean government stopped Korean emigration to the islands in protest of working conditions there, the importation of Filipinos became an important part of the divide-and-rule strategy. In 1906, only 15 Filipinos were recruited, but their numbers grew. Between 1909 and 1931, about 113,000 Filipinos emigrated to Hawaii to work on the sugar and pineapple plantations. Of these, some 39,000 returned home, 55,000 stayed in Hawaii, and 18,600 eventually migrated to the west coast on the mainland.[38]

The Filipinos came to Hawaii because work on the plantations offered them an option in an otherwise dire economic situation. Because they were citizens of a U.S. possession, they were able to travel freely to and from the United States and its possessions. Mainly poor people from depressed rural areas, these immigrants found the wages being offered attractive, though in fact they were low by American standards. (In 1915, male Filipino plantation laborers received, on average, $1 a day; by 1925, their wages averaged between $2.22 and $2.50 a day. Women got less—about $.70 a day in 1915.[39]) Soon, Filipino peasants were also enticed by examples of others from their region who had worked on the plantations and returned with enough money to buy land. By 1925, so many Filipinos were emigrating to the Hawaiian plantations that the sugar growers stopped recruiting.[40]

Like other Asian immigrants, Filipinos were sojourners in the United States. A law passed in 1790 made all nonwhite persons ineligible to become naturalized citizens. (American-born Filipinos, however, like all persons born on American soil, were automatically U.S. citizens, but that factor had little immediate relevance for the pioneering immigrants.) The Filipino pioneers intended to remain in Hawaii or the United States only long enough to make money to return home with financial security. Life did not always work out like that. Many became stuck in America and never returned. Some did not have enough money to return. Others had spent so long away from home they no longer felt comfortable returning. And many did not want to return, having put down roots in their newly adopted country.

Plantation life was hard. The plantations were thoroughly hierarchical organizations, based on race, with white men securely ensconced at the top. All others were arrayed in descending order below them. (Even housing was arranged hierarchically.) Filipinos, being the latest arrivals and nonwhite in addition, were on the lowest rung. They received less pay for equal work and were given the dirtiest jobs. But plantation work was thoroughly regimented and hard for all Asian workers: 10 hours a day, six days a week, in intense heat, working under the supervision of whip-carrying supervisors (usually Portuguese) who addressed people by their assigned number not by name and who tolerated no relaxation. Takaki cites an incident, not atypical, in which a luna, to brandish his authority, took a hoe from a worker, worked "like hell" for two minutes, and turned to the workers and asked why they did not work like that. One worker commented, "He knows and we know he couldn't work for 10 minutes at that pace."[41] Filipinos found few opportunities for work elsewhere on the islands. By 1930, only 5 percent worked off the plantations.[42]

By the time they began recruiting Filipinos, the growers knew that they wanted to avoid problems caused by the bachelor lifestyle of most Chinese and Japanese laborers (though there were some Japanese women on the plantations). Many contracts with Filipino laborers required a small contingent of women. And because Filipino culture was not as prohibitive of women traveling as were the Chinese and Japanese cultures, a larger share of the Filipino plantation population were women. Still, the population was overwhelmingly male. To compensate for a lack of home life, single Filipino men from the same village (barrio) or region tended to group together in a makeshift family, sharing the same living quarters and home chores.

Fewer Filipinos emigrated to the mainland. Between 1909 and 1931, the number was about 50,000.[43] They came mainly to the west coast, especially California, because travel beyond the coast to the interior was expensive and did not hold any special employment prospects. For all of its difficulties, plantation life in Hawaii was easier than life on the mainland for Filipinos. Plantations offered security. There was none on the mainland. Rather than arriving under labor contracts, they were obliged to find work after arrival. Most occupations were closed to Filipinos, even had they had the training and credentials to perform them, which they did not. Most of the Filipinos who came to the mainland, like those who went to Hawaii, were illiterate, with little or no English-language skills and no money. Nor did unions allow Filipinos to join; so few held jobs in construction or the trades. The occupations that were open to them were seasonal agricultural and low-wage, low-skill service jobs in hotels and restaurants. Some went to Alaska and other areas in the Pacific Northwest to work in salmon canneries for a season. Most traveled from job to job during the growing season and took service jobs in cities, if they could find them, during the winter months.

Like members of other immigrant groups, Filipinos tended to group together in their living arrangements in the urban centers. The Filipino population on the mainland was predominately male—in 1920, the male-female ratio was 14 to 1.[44] They established Little Manilas in poor sections of west coast cities (they could afford no better). Men lived several to a room and engaged in all the features of bachelor life—frequenting prostitutes, gambling, some exposure to petty crime, and some that were particularly Filipino, such as cockfighting.

While Filipino laborers were struggling at their work, a relatively small but very different kind of Filipino immigration was also occurring. These were young people, mainly men, who came to the United States to study. Plans were implemented in 1903, during the administration of the first American civilian governor in the Philippines, to send bright young Filipinos to top universities in the United States to study in specialized areas. The program was well meant but patronizing (Howard Brett Melendy, author of *Asians in America*, characterizes it as a manifestation of the "white man's burden."[45]) Selected students, called *pensionados*, had their expenses paid by the government and housing provided with American families. Stern estimates that about 500 eventually participated in the *pensionado* program, some 200 of whom graduated.[46] The students returned to the Philippines to become leaders in their respective areas. Inspired by the example of the *pensionados*, an estimated 14,000 other Filipinos came to this country independently to study through the 1930s.[47] Many were successful, but many were not, finding their English-language skills inadequate for the challenge or being otherwise distracted from the discipline of higher-level academic work. The latter group tended to drift into temporary jobs as laborers.

In America, Filipinos faced the same circular, race-based pattern of discrimination as other Asians. Because of their race, they were ineligible for naturalized citizenship, and because they were not citizens, they were discriminated against. Even second-generation, American-born Filipinos, who were citizens by birth, endured continual harassment—less pay for equal work, exclusion from many occupations and from union membership (although the CIO did admit Filipinos), prohibition of intermarriage with whites, and countless subtle and not-so-subtle daily instances of harassment. White Americans simply were not prepared to accept people of other races as Americans. Opinion about nonwhite immigrants could be virulent. Melendy cites a statement made before the House Committee on Immigration and Naturalization in 1930 by a man who claimed that Filipinos were a "social menace" who would "not leave our white girls alone."[48] San Francisco authorities claimed in 1931 that "the Filipino is our greatest menace. They are all criminally minded."[49] (Melendy notes that, in fact, the Filipino arrest rate was no higher than that for black and white Americans.[50])

Filipinos were not merely passive bystanders to the discrimination. On the plantations they, like the Japanese before them, learned to organize into ethnic unions to protest working conditions. The first of their labor strikes on the plantations occurred in 1909, when Japanese workers protested differential wages based on ethnicity. At that time, Filipinos were only 1 percent of the plantation labor force, and growers used them as scabs to break the Japanese strike. By 1919, they constituted about 30 percent of the labor force, and like the Japanese, the Filipinos had organized into a workers union. In 1919, the Filipino Federation of Labor and the Japanese Federation of Labor initially struck separately for better conditions. What was especially significant about this strike was that both unions came to realize that their case would be strengthened by cooperation. For the first time, the two ethnic labor groups coordinated efforts to obtain improved conditions for all. The growers responded with their standard divide-and-rule strategy: They brought in scabs of other nationalities, and they also offered the leader of the Filipino union a bribe.* The strike was broken, but Filipinos and Japanese learned a valuable lesson about cooperation and protest. Over the ensuing decades, as Japanese immigration was virtually halted, Filipinos became the largest ethnic group on the plantations. By 1929, Filipinos were about 70 percent of the male workers on the sugar plantations.[52] As their numbers grew, so did their determination to fight for improved working conditions. By 1950, as a result of the struggle of Filipino and other labor groups on the islands, the wages of Hawaiian agricultural workers were the highest in the world.

By the 1930s, prejudice against Filipino workers escalated into violence. There are several reasons for this. First, Filipinos were the only Asian group still permitted to immigrate to America by the 1930s. Chinese and Japanese immigration had been largely halted, as discussed elsewhere, but Filipinos were exempt from such restrictions because they were American nationals, not aliens. This angered some white Americans, and a movement grew to stop this "third wave" of immigration. Some even called for evacuation of those who were already in the States and Hawaii. The mounting intensity of the Filipino labor movement in Hawaii added to the resentment. Filipinos were seen as troublemakers. Finally, as the Great Depression deprived many Americans of jobs, those Filipinos (and other immigrants) who retained theirs—and many were among the first to lose jobs—were viewed with bitterness; they were seen as aliens who were depriving white Americans of employment.

The situation was inflammable and several instances of violence resulted. Fistfights broke out in agricultural areas in California and

---

*See Takaki for a detailed account of the strike.[51]

Washington state—incidents which the press widely covered. As tensions mounted, riots broke out in the California farming towns of Exeter, in 1929, and Watsonville, in 1930. Filipino deaths resulted, and Filipinos were banned from some towns.[53]

On the legislative front, the anti-Filipino sentiment culminated in the passage of the Tydings-McDuffie Act in 1934. This piece of legislation granted the Philippines commonwealth status for 10 years, a period that was to serve as a transition to independence. The Philippines hailed the act with enthusiasm. However, the act also limited Filipino immigration to only 50 persons a year. Thus, it effectively brought immigration from the Philippines to an end.* As for those who were already in the States, they, too, were subject to new, restrictive legislation. For example, the U.S. Merchant Marine had been an employer of Filipinos, hiring as many as 8,000 in 1930 (at lower pay than that for whites).[54] Legislation in 1936, in effect, banned Filipinos from serving on American vessels.

The Filipino population in Hawaii dropped after 1931, as more people returned home than emigrated. By 1940, the Filipino population on the island fell to less than 53,000, a 16 percent decrease over the 1930 figure.[55] Some exclusionists, feeling that the Tydings-McDuffie Act had not gone far enough, supported Filipino repatriation, and in 1935, the Repatriation Act was passed. This piece of legislation provided free transportation back to the Philippines for immigrants who wished to return. Few accepted. As of 1937, only 7,400 returned and the outmigration slowed as the U.S. economy began to recover from the Depression.[56]

During World War II, with the Philippines under siege by Japanese forces, Filipino Americans petitioned for the right to fight in the American forces. In 1942, an all-Filipino-American unit was established. Melendy points out that this group fought with much valor but less recognition than the much-decorated 442 Japanese Combat Team.[57]

Others served in the U.S. Navy. Such service was not new: They had been allowed to serve since the 1920s, but only as mess stewards. The same strictures held during World War II. While they were dissatisfied with these limitations, many were happy to serve. Military service offered greater security than the jobs most held in the mainland economy. The pay was far better than what they could hope to get either in the Philippines or in jobs in American civilian life, and it provided

---

*Also, under the Tydings-McDuffie Act, progressive tariffs were levied on Filipino products in the United States (previously they had been duty-free). American products in the Philippines were to continue without import duties.

them with a means of circumventing naturalization restrictions and becoming naturalized citizens.

Legally, Filipinos had always been in a somewhat ambiguous position with regard to the United States. They were American nationals but were ineligible to become naturalized citizens. Traveling on U.S. passports, they could freely enter and depart from the United States and were not subject to immigration laws as were aliens. But they did not have the same rights in court as American citizens. As Melendy points out, unlike aliens, Filipinos did not have recourse to an independent foreign office to present their grievances to the U.S. government.[58] Nor were they entitled to the benefits conferred by citizenship but rather to a pared-down version, the limits of which were the subject of ongoing debate in the United States. There was confusion during the Great Depression as to whether Filipinos were eligible to receive federal relief. They did not. And during World War II, when Filipino Americans first tried to volunteer for military service, they were denied because American law did not specify that American nationals could fight. Nor were they initially allowed to work in defense industries.[59]

On July 4, 1946, the Philippines finally received independence from the United States. Along with it came clarifying change in the legal status of Filipino Americans. Filipino immigrants in the United States became aliens. Under law, the number of Filipinos allowed to enter annually was expanded from 50 to 100. While this was a very small change, those who did immigrate during this period were mainly wives and other female family members of Filipino immigrants. This meant that more Filipinos were able to live normal family lives in this country, and more Filipino children were born in America, and hence, were American citizens. Furthermore, two days before Filipino independence, Congress enacted legislation proclaiming that Filipinos who had come to the United States before 1934 were eligible for naturalization. In 1952, with the abolition of the 1790 naturalization law, all Filipino immigrants and other nonwhite immigrants became eligible for naturalized citizenship.

With the enactment of the 1965 immigration law, a second major wave of Filipino immigration began. Fleeing instability and corruption in the Philippines, these new immigrants were the elite of their nation. Their departure constituted a "brain drain" that deprived the Philippines of some of its best talent but was a gain of highly skilled people for the United States. In just 10 years, from 1965 to 1975, more Filipinos entered the United States than resided here in 1960. During that period, over 250,000 Filipino immigrants arrived.[60] Filipinos became third, after Asian Indians and Chinese, in their rate of naturalization. Fuchs observes that "those who had been excluded longest from membership in the American civic culture had rushed to embrace it once the barriers were lifted."[61]

The Filipino immigration rate remains high. Of a population of 1.4 million in 1990, 31 percent entered the country since 1980.[62] The naturalization rate also remains high: 26 percent of 1980-to-1990 immigrants were naturalized citizens by 1990. The high rate of recent immigration is seen in the sizable portion of the population—24 percent of those over 5 years old—who do not speak English very well.[63]

In contrast to their degraded economic status when subjected to massive discrimination earlier in this century, Filipino Americans as a group are doing relatively well today. According to 1990 Census data, their median family income was $46,698 in 1989.[64] This is more than $16,000 higher than the figure for the total population and is just about the same as the figure for the total Asian population. Only 5.2 percent of Filipino families lived below the poverty level in 1989.[65] As with other Asian groups, part of the explanation for the high family income level lies in the extended family structure. Extended families tend to have more workers per unit than a nuclear family structure. Almost 30 percent of Filipino families in 1989 had three or more workers.[66] The comparative figure for the total American population was 13 percent. The relative economic position of Filipino Americans is perhaps better seen in the per-capita income figures, which for Filipino Americans was $13,616 in 1989.[67] This is almost $1,000 less than the figure for the total population ($14,420).

A further stunning contrast between present and past is seen in Filipino-American occupational categories. While most had been agricultural and service workers in the past, today 1990 Census data shows that the largest single group of the Filipino American workforce—almost 37 percent—have jobs in technical, sales, and administrative support occupations.[68] Almost 27 percent are in managerial and professional specialty occupations. Less than 2 percent are in farming, forestry, and fishing occupations, and about 17 percent are in service occupations.

Japanese Americans

Japanese Americans are the third-largest group of Asians in this country, with a population of 866,160 (in 1990). Japanese first began emigrating to the United States in the 1880s. Some of the earliest immigrants were students from the Japanese elite and businessmen. Many more came as a result of economic dislocations caused by policies of the new Meiji government in Japan. This first modern government in Japanese history undertook extensive economic measures to establish a modern economic infrastructure. In the process, it created widespread disruption in many sectors, including the traditional agricultural sector. Enduring extreme hardship, even starvation, some farmers felt forced to leave Japan in search of economic security. The shores of their Pacific neighbor, the United States, was an obvious destination, and Hawaii was a staging point for many. (Others were to emigrate across the Pacific to Canada and Latin American nations.)

This was not the first contact between the United States and Japan. Each had hosted a handful of shipwrecked seamen from the other's shores. Just beginning to expand its reach across the Pacific, the United States had looked longingly at the prospects of using Japanese ports as coaling stations in the early nineteenth century. The interest had not been reciprocated, for Japan had lived in self-imposed exile from the rest of the world. In 1854, however, after decades of futile attempts to establish contact with the island nation, the United States forced Japan to open its doors, and in the process touched off internal forces that led to the establishment of the Meiji government and, eventually, to the emigration of Japanese farmers.

Initially, most Japanese immigrants were men, but women soon joined them. This was partly a result of some early contract labor agreements, especially in Hawaii, which stipulated that a percentage of laborers should be women. But it was also government policy. The new Meiji government, acutely conscious of its international image, wished to avoid the kinds of problems faced by the mainly male Chinese immigrant population in the United States. Prompted by the negative example of the Chinese, the Meiji government instituted a human quality-control effort, establishing a board to review prospective Japanese emigrants to ensure that they were healthy, literate, and would maintain Japan's national honor.[69] After their arrival in the United States, Japanese emissaries continued, at least in the beginning, to periodically monitor activities of the émigrés and to report on those whose presence might prove embarrassing to Japan.[70]

From the beginning, many Japanese immigrants had an advantage that many newcomers from other Asian groups did not: They planned to stay. Unlike Asian sojourners, they had a level of commitment and a long-range focus that facilitated success in their efforts. Yet, even had these early arrivals been superpeople, they would have faced an uphill battle gaining acceptance in America. An initial and enduring issue was race. Most Americans were unprepared to accept nonwhites; those on the west coast, where the immigrants landed, were no exception. Japanese immigrants, like Chinese, were barred from citizenship by the 1790 law that permitted only white people to become naturalized citizens. And that was just the beginning. The Japanese faced harassment and discrimination at every turn, and it intensified with time. In the first decade of the twentieth century, the California press mounted a campaign against Japanese immigrants (Chinese immigration had already been "taken care of" by the China Exclusion Act of 1882.) The press whipped up anti-Japanese sentiment with headlines such as "Japanese A Menace to American Women," "The Yellow Peril—How Japanese Crowd Out the White Race," and "Crime and Poverty Go Hand In Hand With Asiatic Labor."* Jobs in many occupations were denied to Japanese immigrants. On the level of everyday experience, there were countless incidents of harassment. Takaki cites the story of a Japanese visitor from Hawaii who went into a barber shop in California, was asked his nationality, and, when he responded "Japanese," was driven out of the shop like "a cat or a dog."[72]

A further, if indirect, factor in white American hostility toward Japanese immigrants was growing Pacific rivalry with Japan. Since the end of the nineteenth century when the Meiji government began to reach into the Pacific and encountered American aspirations there, bilateral relations have been characterized by fluctuating levels of tension. Japanese Americans were victims of these tensions. The California anti-Japanese press campaign got a boost in 1905 during the Russo-Japanese war, the first modern war in which an Asian nation defeated a Western (white) nation. The treatment of Japanese Americans during World War II is the most egregious example of bilateral relations impacting the Japanese-American minority.

Paradoxically, it was the obstacles and harassment that caused many Japanese immigrants to remain permanently in the United States. Robert Wilson and Bill Hosokawa point out that many had originally come as sojourners, intending to make enough money to return home to live with a measure of economic security. A nest egg of a thousand dollars was thought to be sufficient. But harassment made even a thousand dollars hard to accumulate, and changing economic conditions in Japan meant that it would not be enough anyway.[73] And so, frustrated in their attempts to save money, many stayed on and became permanent residents. These people, the first generation—the *issei*—were the beginnings of the Japanese-American community in the United States.

After the early labor contracts, the United States refused to permit contracts made before an immigrant arrived here. Therefore, immigrants had to look for jobs upon arrival. A network of laborer contrac-

---

*Headlines from San Francisco's leading paper, *The Chronicle*, in 1905, quoted by Daniels.[71]

tors sprang up on the west coast, especially in California. Denied employment in industry, many found employment as railway construction labor or as seasonal laborers in California's agriculture sector.

Working in construction or on someone else's land was unpredictable and unappealing. As soon as they could scrape the money together, many became entrepreneurs, setting up businesses for themselves. Some became shopkeepers. Many, who had come from farming families at home, began to lease land or, where possible, buy it outright. Takaki points out that, in entering California farming, the Japanese were in the right place at the right time: Industrialization and urbanization created a growing nationwide demand for agricultural produce. The development of irrigation in California enabled that state to transform its desert land into rich fruit and vegetable farms. And the transcontinental railway and development of refrigerated cars made it possible to distribute the produce throughout the United States.[74] The Japanese had a further advantage in group solidarity. They formed revolving credit systems where each member contributed to and could draw from the pool. Japanese labor helped convert the California desert into rich farmland and orchard, and in the process, some Japanese flourished. In 1900, Japanese farmers owned or leased some 4,600 acres of land; by 1920 the figure increased to 458,000 acres. Crops grown on their farms accounted for about 10 percent of the total value of California crops by 1920.[75] Their very success heightened anti-Japanese sentiment. The Japanese farmers were considered an economic threat (although they were only 2 percent of the California population in 1920).

In Hawaii, the situation was different. First imported to Hawaii by white Americans who wanted to offset and weaken the presence of Chinese laborers on the islands' sugar plantations, Japanese came to be the largest single ethnic group on the islands. By 1920, Japanese formed about 40 percent of the Hawaiian population.[76] The first sizable group of Japanese contract laborers arrived in Hawaii in 1884. Between 1885 and 1924 some 200,000 Japanese entered Hawaii where they worked mainly on the sugar plantations.[77] About 55 percent of them found conditions too hard and returned to Japan. Those who stayed were relegated (by race) to unskilled field labor. Thoroughly regimented in their labor, from the moment they awoke to the end of their work day, they were supervised by Europeans whose main job qualification seemed to be meanness. They were incited to conflict with Asian plantation laborers of other nationalities—Chinese, Filipinos, and Koreans—as a means of maintaining supervisory control.

Despite the harshness of conditions in Hawaii, the level of anti-Japanese sentiment was nowhere near that of the mainland (read west coast). In 1906, tensions spilled over into an international incident. The San Francisco school board ordered Japanese school children to be segregated from white children. The outraged Japanese government pointed out that this action breached an 1894 treaty between the United States and Japan which extended most favored nation rights of residence to nationals of both countries. In 1908, the United States negotiated a "gentlemen's agreement" with the Japanese government whereby the Japanese agreed to stop sending laborers to the United States. In exchange, the school board segregation order was rescinded. While the agreement was hailed as a diplomatic victory, in the long run it heightened tension between the two nations, as Daniels points out.[78] It also effectively brought a halt to the entry of new Japanese laborers to the United States.

But Japanese women continued to arrive. The agreement permitted entry to women who were family members of Japanese in the United States. Over 60,000 women came to the United States as a result. Many came as "picture brides," that is, brides whose marriages were arranged by go-betweens who used photographs of prospective brides and grooms to cement the deal.* By 1920, the Japanese-American population on the mainland numbered 110,000—only 0.1 percent of the total U.S. population. They became the largest Asian group in the country. Eighty-five percent of the Japanese population was on the Pacific coast, mainly in California.[80]

The gentlemen's agreement by no means brought anti-Japanese sentiment to a halt. In its wake, California and other states enacted restrictive legislation that excluded Japanese immigrants from owning and leasing land, based in theory on their ineligibility for naturalized citizenship. But the real drive was to exclude Japanese the way Chinese had been excluded in the 1880s. This was accomplished with the 1924 Immigration Act, also known as the National Origins Act. Among other things, this legislation banned entry of "aliens ineligible to citizenship," meaning Japanese.

Although fresh immigration was banned, the Japanese-American population was growing, from 110,000 in 1920 to 127,000 in 1940. Over a quarter of the population in 1920 consisted of second-generation Japanese Americans; by 1940 they were 40 percent of the Japanese-American population. These people, called *nisei*, were American citizens, and they took their citizenship seriously. Taught American

---

*The compelling story of one picture bride, with some variation from the standard tale, is told by Etsu Inagaki Sugimoto about her own experiences in *A Daughter of the Samurai: How a Daughter of Feudal Japan, Living Hundreds of Years in One Generation Became a Modern American*.[79]

democratic values in school, many *nisei* fervently took the values to heart, holding to them all the more strongly perhaps because society neglected to apply them to Japanese Americans. Their patriotism was expressed, for example, in the Japanese American Citizens League (JACL), a patriotic organization with a tiny membership established by *nisei* in the 1930s. Citizenship did not, however, open doors to equality for the *nisei*. Although their education level was above the national average, many were denied jobs. The same suspicions were directed toward them as were directed to their parents' generation.

The bombing of Pearl Harbor in December 1941 was the beginning of a nightmare for Japanese Americans, *issei* and *nisei* alike. Many had anticipated trouble as they followed with horror Japan's growing militarism during the 1930s. Contemplating the possibility of war with Japan, a University of California *nisei* student wrote in a campus magazine in 1937, "Even if the *Nisei* wanted to fight for America, what chances? Not a chance!...our properties would be confiscated and most likely [we would be] herded into prison camps—perhaps we would be slaughtered on the spot."[81] The student was right in two respects: Japanese properties were confiscated, and they were interned in prison camps.*

Pearl Harbor shocked and terrified Japanese Americans. Many *nisei* rushed to join the JACL, and that organization quickly sent a telegram to the president pledging support and loyalty to the United States. It was not enough. American outrage poured over the heads of the vulnerable Japanese-American community on the west coast. Elements of the west coast press, patriotic organizations, politicians, military, the government, and, significantly, some farming interests combined to whip up panic over the supposed threat posed by Japanese Americans.† Calls grew to evacuate them from the west. Many knew better, however. For example, one naval intelligence officer who specialized in Japanese Americans wrote, "there was never a shred of evidence found of sabotage, subversive acts, spying, or fifth column activity on the part of the *Nisei* or long-time local residents."[83] He estimated that most Japanese Americans were loyal, at least passively so, and only about 3,500 were potentially dangerous, and he stated that there was no need to relocate most of the population. The Attorney General likewise saw no need to relocate the Japanese-American population.

---

*Some referred to them as "concentration camps." The term became controversial once the magnitude of German atrocities in concentration camps became known.

†Details of this American tragedy are found in Bill Hosokawa's *Nisei: The Quiet Americans*.[82]

War hysteria prevailed. In February 1942 an executive order was issued indicating that most Japanese Americans on the west coast were to be evacuated by the army. The order affected 110,000 Japanese Americans, more than 60 percent of whom were native-born American citizens. Beginning in March 1942, these people were evacuated from their homes, and relocated in one of 10 different internment camps.

The irrational nature of the internment is highlighted by the fact that only about 1,400 of the 150,000 Japanese in Hawaii were interned. Their actions throughout the course of the war showed that all of the other 148,600 Japanese Americans were loyal citizens. In fact, Washington ordered the evacuation of all Japanese Americans from Hawaii, but the military governor of Hawaii refused. He, the Hawaiian press, and influential individuals and organizations on the islands responded rationally to the voices of hysteria from the mainland. They knew that Japanese Americans posed no threat. The position of the Japanese American community in Hawaii differed sharply from that on the west coast. As Takaki notes, in Hawaii they were a sizable segment of the population, and they held jobs throughout the Hawaiian economy.[84] Internment would have meant disruption in the Hawaiian economy, as the military governor in Hawaii pointed out. In contrast, on the west coast, Japanese Americans were more vulnerable, for they formed only a small percent of the population, and few held jobs in the mainstream economy.

Although there was some dissent among Japanese Americans, the JACL became the mouthpiece for the community. The JACL dictated a policy of accommodation and cooperation with government policies— which was probably the policy most Japanese Americans would have adopted even without JACL leadership. Families packed up a few belongings, quickly sold items at whatever price they could get, and quietly allowed themselves to be shipped off to detention centers and from there to 10 internment camps. Most of them lost the rest of their property.

Most of the camps were located in isolated desert areas in California and elsewhere, mainly in the west.* The Japanese Americans did not know where they were. Each family was assigned a room in barracks, the size of the living space varying according to the number of family members. All, however, were crowded and, at the beginning, many rooms were partitioned only by curtains. Accommodations were spartan at best: one electric light bulb (at the beginning some had no electricity), no running water, army cots for each person. This was to be

---

*There were two camps in California, two in Arizona, and one each in Utah, Idaho, Wyoming, and Colorado. There were also two camps in Arkansas.

home for the next three years. Mess halls provided community meals. Food was nutritious but cheap. (Japanese food was not on the menu.) Schools were established in each of the camps, and teachers were usually dedicated, competent white Americans. With the support of authorities, the internees established libraries, community organizations, temples, churches, and hospitals, and they generally did their best to make the camps livable areas.

After considerable debate in government and military circles, a decision was made in 1943 to allow some *nisei* to serve in the armed forces. A special Japanese-American unit was formed: the 442 Regimental Combat Team. This decision was recognized as a step toward the relaxation of restrictions against Japanese Americans. The JACL, which had petitioned the government to allow *nisei* to serve, rightly saw the decision as a victory, although they knew they faced opposition, possibly violence, from some Japanese Americans.[85] For most *nisei*, the decision offered an opportunity to demonstrate their loyalty and, hence, to redeem their honor. They jumped at the chance. Some 23,000 *nisei* eventually served during World War II, in both the Pacific and European theaters.[86] They served with great distinction. General Charles Willoughby estimated their military contributions shortened the war by two years.[87] The record of the 442 Regimental Combat Team was especially outstanding; it became possibly the most decorated unit in the history of the U.S. military. Welcoming the 442 home, President Harry Truman remarked, "You fought for the free nations of the world...you fought not only the enemy, you fought prejudice—and you won."[88]

Prejudice did not vanish after the war, but as Takaki observed, it was becoming "un-American."[89] A series of measures after the war through 1965, discussed elsewhere in this publication, barred discrimination in employment and elsewhere, nullified the 1790 naturalization law, and opened immigration to peoples from all nations.

Japanese Americans reestablished roots in their communities as best they could, and as a community they flourished. Most quietly bore their sense of shame at having been interned. By the 1970s, some third-generation Japanese Americans, the *sansei,* began to realize that nothing short of a formal apology from the government would redress their shame. They reasoned that, if the issue were left unattended, a stigma would attach to the lives of all Japanese Americans; all would continue to live under a cloud of suspicion. Inspired by the black rights and other movements, they began a campaign for redress. In 1988, they were successful: A bill passed Congress that provided for an official apology for internment and awarded $20,000 to each survivor who had been interned. The money was not meant as compensation for years of suffering and shame—no amount of money could do that—but it was a gesture that concretely underscored the official apology.

From 1920 to 1970, Japanese Americans were the largest Asian group in the country. Today they are the third largest. The change is due, on the one hand, to the relatively low fertility rate among Japanese Americans: 1,651 children born per 1,000 Japanese-American women ever married. In comparison, the fertility rate for all Asian Americans in 1990 was 2,056 children born per 1,000 women ever married, and for the total population it was 2,100.[90] The slippage is also due to low immigration figures in the post-1965 period. Asians from other nations have emigrated in growing numbers, spurred by the variety of dislocations faced by their nations. In contrast, Japan has grown into an economic superpower, and its emigration flow has been moderate. For example, Japanese immigrants entering the country between 1980 to 1990 account for only 17 percent of the total Japanese-American population. In comparison, 1980–1990 immigration accounts for almost 40 percent of the Chinese-American population and almost 32 percent of the Filipino-American population.[91]

The median family income among persons of Japanese origin is $51,550, far above the figure for the total population ($35,225) or for the total Asian population ($37,007). Only 3.4 percent of Japanese-American families are below the poverty level. The figure for the total population is 10 percent and for the Asian population, 11.4 percent. The largest single occupational category for persons of Japanese origin is managerial and professional specialty occupations. Some 37 percent of the employed persons over 16 years are engaged in these occupations. The next-largest category is technical, sales, and administrative support occupations, with 34 percent of Japanese-American workers involved.[92]

The relatively high income of the Japanese Americans stands in interesting contrast to educational achievement figures, which are lower for the Japanese population than for the Asian population as a whole. Five percent of persons of Japanese origin have some college or an associate degree and only 1 percent have a bachelor degree or higher, according to the 1990 Census.[93] In comparison, the figures for the Asian population are 22 percent and 9 percent, respectively. (The total population figures are 2.4 and 5 percent.)

The number of workers per family may be taken as an index to extended-family living arrangements. It is also an important factor in raising family income. Asians are more likely to have extended families (hence, more likely to have higher incomes) than the rest of the population. This is seen in the figures representing numbers of workers per family: In 1990, 20 percent of all Asian-American families had three or more workers; only 13 percent of families in the total population had three or more workers. Statistics for Japanese Americans fall between these two numbers, with just over 15 percent of Japanese-American families having three or more workers.[94] Without stretching the point too much, this statistic may point to an important characteristic of the Japanese-American community: their ability to live in two social contexts simultaneously, in their ethnic community *and* in the mainstream society.

Many Japanese Americans are both highly assimilated yet retain a strong sense of being a distinguishable community. Ethnologists Stephen Fugita and David O'Brien observe the paradox of Japanese Americans who "possess a greater sense of peoplehood and homogeneity than many other groups, yet their cultural traditions permit considerable latitude with respect to adapting the attitudes and behavioral characteristics of other peoples."[95] They maintain that Japanese Americans "do not experience intense psychic cross pressure as a byproduct of living in two different social worlds..."[96] Ethnic cultural identity may be even stronger among *sansei* than among *nisei* Japanese Americans. A study undertaken by Fugita and O'Brien found that over 90 percent of the *sansei* respondents and 84 percent of the *nisei* respondents saw themselves as belonging to a distinguishable community.[97]

Asian Cultural Values and the Workplace

The cultures of Asia, from East and Southeast Asia and the Indian subcontinent to Western Asia (such as ancient Mesopotamia, currently Iran) are among the richest and oldest in the world. In this study, we limit our discussion of cultural values to those of the East Asian countries, China, Korea, and Japan. Persons of East Asian origin constitute the largest segment, over 45 percent, of the Asian population in the United States. Of the 7.2 million total Asian population in 1990, 1.6 million identified their ancestry as Chinese, the largest single Asian ancestry group; 0.85 million are Japanese; and 0.82 million are Korean.

Japan, China, and Korea differ widely in culture. Underlying all three is the Confucian tradition, stemming from the sixth century B.C. Chinese philosopher-scholar Confucius. For many centuries, their histories have intertwined in diverse ways—from wars, conquests, rivalries, and hatreds to adulation and the purposeful borrowing of cultural institutions. For example, part of the Japanese written language uses Chinese characters.

The most important borrowed institution was the Chinese Confucian value system, an ethical system based on patriarchy, discipline, and a respect for learning and order born of harmonious relations. These values provided the underpinning for much of daily behavior in society. Traditional Chinese society eventually evolved a network of institutions, such as the civil service examination system, that were later characterized as a "Confucian" system. Although most Confucian institutions no longer exist, the Confucian value system has not disappeared in China or elsewhere in East Asia, despite modern revolutions and determined efforts on the part of the Chinese communists to eradicate it.

One of the key values in the East Asian tradition is a collectivist orientation. Unlike the Anglo cultural tradition, which values individualism, the East Asian tradition stresses subordination of the individual to group needs.* In the workplace, the collectivist orientation translates into a high comfort level with teamwork and a strong inhibition against drawing attention to one's individual accomplishments. The Japanese maxim "the nail that stands out gets hammered down" reflects this attitude. Thus, although praise from others is valued, self-promotion is abhorrent. On the job, an Asian American is likely to be modest and reserved about his or her own work and possibly in other areas, too.

As a result, accomplishments may go unnoticed and unrewarded by American managers accustomed to more assertive behavior by employees. As with Latino workers—perhaps even more so—East Asian workers may be viewed as lacking in confidence and assertiveness, that is, deficient in the traits that are requisite to managerial responsibilities. Their modesty is likely an important reason why Americans of East Asian descent are underrepresented in managerial positions, though they are highly represented in the technical and professional ranks that typically lead to such positions (discussed in the next chapter).

East Asian culture is patriarchal. The family or clan unit is primary, and the focus is unidirectional: The male authority figure dominates. This contrasts with the Anglo culture, where the focus is multidirectional: attention is scattered among individuals within groups. Reinforcing the monodirectional East Asian focus is the traditional master-learner paradigm. Typical of East Asian cultures, this is the model by which learners are apprenticed to masters in many disciplines, from smithies and other trades to Zen training and the art of being a geisha. The learner spends long years in training, seldom questioning the master's guidance.

---

*This section was developed in close consultation with Dr. Adrian Chan, Assistant Vice Chancellor for Academic Affairs, the University of Wisconsin-Milwaukee. Telephone interview July 9, 1993.

In the workplace, East Asian Americans reflect this value in respect for authority. They are unlikely to challenge the boss. They assume the boss knows best. Even when it is clear that the boss does not know best, respect will prevent an East Asian worker from openly disagreeing. When co-workers speak up in disagreement with authority, an East Asian American is apt to cringe silently at the display of what he or she considers bad manners.

When East Asian workers really buy in to an organization, they tend to go beyond mere respect for authority to intense loyalty. In the American context, this loyalty is more likely to be focused on a person (the boss) than on the institution. For them, links are personal between superior and subordinate. East Asian workers can experience severe stress when their boss is transferred to another position or department within the organization or leaves the organization altogether.

Because of their respect for authority, East Asian-American workers also are less likely to complain about inadequacies with regard to salary, promotions, or other forms of recognition. They may even be reluctant to indicate their accomplishments at the annual performance review. Their assumption is that the boss is aware of the accomplishments and will provide appropriate rewards in time. This may not be the case, however, since the Anglo manager may rely on input from the employee. The result, then, is that the manager has an inadequate appreciation of the employee's work, and, over time, the employee gets discouraged because due recognition is not forthcoming.

Furthermore, like Latino workers, East Asian Americans are not likely to be good at brainstorming if someone in a position of greater authority is present. East Asian workers have additional constraints on their behavior in such situations: Their cultural heritage values rote memorization and repetition rather than originality. Children are typically taught to "stay within the lines." As a result, first-generation workers, in particular, are unlikely to be adept at the free-wheeling coupling and uncoupling of ideas that is the heart of successful brainstorming. These factors plus a possible lack of facility with the English language (which is a social, not a cultural, issue) prevent them from substantively participating in brainstorming sessions. The Anglo perception of such behavior is likely to be that the individual is not interested, not "up to speed" in his or her field, and has low social skills.

There are also major cultural differences in decision-making and management styles. Whereas the Anglo style tends to be publicly visible, verbal, and assertive, the East Asian style is indirect and behind the scenes. The East Asian system values cooperative behavior. This value on harmony means that open disagreement in public is avoided. At the very least, such disagreement is considered bad manners. Even in private, East Asians usually couch criticism discreetly amid many words of praise. The target of the criticism emerges from such a conversation with the knowledge that he or she has the support of the critic and that the critic is aware of one's positive accomplishments as well. This approach enhances the worker's motivation to improve.

Underlying the East Asian aversion to open argument is a concern for "face," that is, for safeguarding one's own and others' dignity in public situations. In professional matters, East Asian values translate into a preference for working out details of an issue privately in one-on-one conversations rather than in group discussions. In that way, differences can be aired without anyone losing face in public. The occasion at which the decision is formally reached becomes a formality, a public acknowledgment of that which was previously decided in private. All parties concerned have preserved face.

In the American workplace, however, a different process occurs. Private discussions and other behind-the-scenes preparation do occur. But group meetings are also typical of the Anglo decision-making process. As options are aired in meetings, give and take flows freely and disagreement is common. Typically among Anglos, no offense is taken; workers who differ around a table over a business issue can walk away amicably. From the East Asian viewpoint, however, this is a highly stressful procedure. Because they do not readily criticize others in public, when they themselves are criticized, they tend to acquiesce and back away from the situation, unsure how to handle it. By not making a stand for their point, they are apt to be viewed from the Anglo perspective as weak and lacking in confidence. It is a small jump in reasoning to further assume that the individual, if placed in a managerial position would not be likely to stand up for his or her people and programs.

What's more, criticism that is aired in front of others is seen in the East Asian perspective as a personal, verbal assault. An East Asian worker who is the target of such criticism is likely to be deeply hurt. If the criticism originated from someone in a position of higher authority, the worker is likely to feel disgraced. The critic would be unaware of the storm of emotion the criticism aroused because the worker is apt to brood over it quietly, trying to determine what actions merited such disgrace. In extreme cases, the worker might even resign.

A Short History of Native Americans

Native Americans are the only indigenous group in the country. They are also the most economically deprived. For many Indians, higher education, responsible jobs, material comfort, and even good health are not a realistic option. They have the highest suicide, alcoholism, and infant mortality rates in the nation. About a third of the population of some 2 million lives on reservations in sometimes deplorable material circumstances.* Off the reservations too, Indians tend to cluster at the bottom of the socioeconomic ladder, although they are making important economic gains. Overall, only 46 percent of adult Indians over age 25 have completed high school or the equivalent, compared with 85 percent for the country.[98]

In this section, we survey politico-historical events that brought much of the Indian population to its present situation. In doing so, we should not lose sight of the fact that, for many Indians, the tragic course of their external history is an important part of their story, but it is only one part. In the next section, we hope to throw some light on the other part, the cultural values sacred to many Indians.

Every American knows that the encounter between Indians and European settlers and their American descendants was a catastrophe for the Indians. Some claim it was no less than genocide, as defined under the United Nations Convention on Genocide.[99] From the beginning, most European settlers had little regard for Indian rights, though some had moral and legal qualms. Even the early Pilgrims of Plymouth Plantation, notwithstanding their gratitude to the Indians who taught them how to survive that first desperate year, were convinced God meant the land for them: Indian deaths from an epidemic in the Plymouth area just before their arrival were viewed as a Divine sign, for it provided the Pilgrims with cleared land in their time of need. Nor did later generations of Americans doubt that they possessed a divinely ordained right—or at least a higher right than the original inhabitants—to the land.

In a 100-year span dating from 1778, the federal government concluded about 1,000 treaties with Indians (though less than half were ratified by Congress). The treaties were not indicators of respect for the sovereignty of the native people. In fact, breaches of the treaties by the U.S. government and its citizens were legion. Treaties were often ignored, and disputes were frequently settled by force. Author and Indian activist Vine Deloria, Jr., of the University of Colorado, maintains that the young federal government formed the early treaties with Indians because it was "fearful that its own claim to national political independence would be

---

*The U.S. Census Bureau defines Native Americans as American Indians, Aleuts, and Eskimos. The latter two groups comprise about 4 percent of the Native-American population. It is possible that the total of 2 million is too high. Claiming Indian ancestry has become popular, and there has been a surge of people who are doing so on census forms.

challenged by the established nations of Europe." It, therefore, went to "extravagant lengths" to assert independence and its right to do what European nations did—make treaties with other sovereign states.[100] The Indian nations were handy for that purpose.

Sovereign or not, the presence of Indians in their midst became more inconvenient as the population of the United States expanded. Thomas Jefferson believed the most humane response was to "remove" eastern Indians from the path of settlement and relocate them westward. Most Americans agreed. From their point of view, because Indians did not wish to adopt "civilized" ways, the alternatives were either extinction or removal; remaining on their ancestral lands in the east was becoming an increasingly nonviable option.

Removals began during James Monroe's administration, but it was during the administration of Andrew Jackson (whom the Indians called "Sharp Knife") that large-scale removals went into effect. As a westerner (from the frontier state of Tennessee), Jackson had no love and little tolerance for Indians, whom he saw as a threat to settlers. The Indian Removal Act of 1830 authorized signing treaties with Indian tribes, by which the government purchased aboriginal Indian territory and agreed to relocate tribes at government expense in sparsely settled territory west of the Mississippi. And in 1831, the Supreme Court made serious inroads into the concept of Indian sovereignty by declaring the tribes "domestic dependent nations." Though later Court rulings seemed to contradict the validity of this incursion, government actions upheld it by ignoring Indian rights.

Contrary to Jefferson's views, the Indian removals had little about them that was humane. Thousands of Indians were moved westward. Those who did not go willingly were forced to relinquish their lands through a variety of forms of persuasion (such as bribery and getting recalcitrant tribal leaders so drunk that they signed treaties forfeiting their lands for Western territory). Corrupt federal officials often pocketed payment due to Indians, and many Indians, having exhausted their own funds in the move, arrived at the end of the "trail of tears" impoverished, exhausted, and unable to plant crops in their new locations. Many never arrived. Large numbers died on the way from disease; others, from heartbreak. In theory, the government maintained that Indians who became "civilized" and were willing to assimilate into American society could remain on their lands. But practice did not work like that. The Cherokee of Georgia took up farming, adopted a written language, and a constitution—all to no avail. Georgia did not want them, and despite Supreme Court decisions explicitly granting them sovereignty on their land, the Cherokee were removed to Oklahoma in 1838.

By the time of the removals, there had been considerable intermarriage between Europeans and Indians. Since colonial times, the French had intermarried with Indians and moved in with them to facilitate the French fur trade in the north and west. In the south, Scots and Irish also intermarried with Indians. Their offspring formed a separate class, the "respectable" Indians, as opposed to "real" Indians, Deloria notes.[101] He observes that by the 1830s, "the leading families of the tribes and the Southern states were often cousins and could at least trace themselves back to a common ancestor not far removed from their own generation." Common ancestry did not forestall the harsh treatment of removal.

Policy makers had assumed that removal would solve the "Indian problem" for a long time to come. They were wrong. Settlers poured westward at a far faster rate than anyone had anticipated, and they poured into land now designated as permanent Indian Territory. Partly to justify the disregarding of the Indian treaties, but also borne on a growing wave of confidence about America and its future, Americans marched westward under the banner of Manifest Destiny. A concept first articulated in the 1840s, Manifest Destiny—the belief in the God-given right to expand across this continent from coast to coast—seemed to excuse all forms of infringement on Indian rights.

After the conclusion of the Civil War and the completion of the first transcontinental railway in the 1860s, the American conquest of Western territory began in earnest. And with it, began what Dee Brown characterizes as the "doom period of their [Indian] civilization."[102] As new priorities developed, government policy toward Indians changed. Treaty-making days came to an end when it became clear that settlers coveted land in Indian Territory and elsewhere and that Indians had no intention of assimilating (in the opinion of many white people, they had no ability to do so). The last treaty with an Indian tribe was concluded in 1871. The new policy aimed at subduing the Indians and forcing them onto reservations. This aim was fulfilled in what amounted to a government policy of "ethnic cleansing" between 1860 and 1890.* Research scholar A. J. Jaffee observes with irony that Indians were dispensed with for the same reason as the buffalo herds that freely roamed the prairie.[103] It is possible that the buffalo were killed for another reason too: Buffalo were critical to the plains Indians' way of life, and their slaughter doomed that way of life as surely as the bullets of the U.S. Army.

Indians who did not die fighting for their territory and way of life were shunted onto reservations in isolated areas. Now that Indians no

---

*It is not possible to discuss the history of the period here. Many sources are available; among them is Dee Brown's classic work *Bury My Heart At Wounded Knee*, which provides an account of the struggle from the Indian viewpoint.

longer impeded westward progress, government policy mellowed. Having reduced them to desired proportions, the government enunciated a sincere, paternalistic concern to protect them. Another word describing the government relationship with Indians is "colonialist." Policy makers readily assumed they knew what was best for the Indians. They made Indians who remained on reservations wards of the government. Simultaneously, they encouraged assimilation by setting aside portions of reservation land for individual farms. Undertaken partly out of a misguided humanitarianism as well as underlying arrogance, the General Allotment Act of 1887 gave tribal members the choice of remaining on their reservation, retaining tribal identity, and becoming government wards or obtaining a land allotment carved from their reservations and eventually acquiring U.S. citizenship. A not-so-well-intentioned provision of the Act authorized the government to sell Indian land perceived to be "surplus." Remaining in effect for some 40 years, the policy was a disaster.

Garraty and McGaughey point out that Americans did not understand that Indians could not be "transformed into small agricultural capitalists by an act of Congress."[104] Because a large part of the allotted land was barren and unproductive, it could not be readily farmed in any case. Also, unscrupulous settlers as well as government officials took advantage of the Indians in all manner of ways. By 1920, the overwhelming majority of the some 300,000 Indians still lived on reservations.[105] They could do little about the steady hemorrhaging of their lands into the hands of white people, for which they received little compensation. By the mid-1930s they had lost almost two-thirds of the 167 million acres of land they had possessed before 1887.[106]

What the land policy did not do to reduce them to destitution, the Depression did. Many reservation people routinely required food, medical, and other supplies from the government. Their life expectancy was more than 10 years less than that of the total U.S. population.[107] Most had meager income if any. In 1930, about half of the labor force (which does not include those who dropped out due to discouragement) were unskilled workers; another almost 30 percent were farmers; only about 2 percent were professional workers.[108] Perhaps the only thing Indians had to hold on to was their culture, many aspects of which endured despite—and maybe partly because of—the relentless attempts to assimilate them. Paradoxically, their special legal status as sovereign nations granted by the government has kept many Indians from assimilating into American society, according to Deloria.[109]

The assimilationist policy of the Allotment Act reaped disaster, but it staked out one of the poles between which U.S. policy has swung in this century as it has groped to deal with the "Indian problem." Since the Allotment Act, assimilation or, as one scholar put it, to "place Indians on the same plane of citizenship as other individuals"[110] has been one of the government's stated long-term aims. Each major Indian policy initiative in the twentieth century, up until the 1970s, embodied different methods for reaching this aim. Because the melting-pot process worked for most European immigrants, they and their descendants assumed it to be practically a law of nature. The problem was that many Indians wanted no part of it, and some are skeptical that they would ever be accepted on the "same plane" as whites in any case. This puzzling situation left policy makers searching for answers. It was difficult for many Americans, so long bred on the superiority of Western culture, to recognize the validity of cultural pluralism. Theorizing about the day when Indians would take their places as equals within established structures was one thing. Such liberalism made Americans feel good about themselves (even though they did not grant all Indians citizenship until the 1920s, and many states did not allow them to vote thereafter). But respecting Indians' right to be different and formulating policies that effectively promoted that right was not so easy. The Indian Reorganization Act, adopted in 1934, came closer to that recognition than any prior policy.

In the Indian Reorganization Act was embedded the other policy pole toward and from which federal policy oscillated. This was a focus on reservations. As previously discussed, a reservation policy was by no means a new concept. But as policy moved along the assimilationist-reservationist spectrum—there have been three major policy shifts in the twentieth century—it became less coercive. Throughout the shifts, even as policy focused more on one element than the other, both have been present to some degree.

In 1934, government swung back to a reservation policy—but with a difference. Dropping the allotment policy, the Indian Reorganization Act encouraged Indians who held land individually to return the land to their reservation. It promoted establishment on reservations of tribal governments that could represent Indian interests in dealings with the federal government. (These groups could negotiate as citizens because 10 years earlier citizenship had been extended for the first time to all Indians, including those born on reservations.) The policy also reaffirmed federal trust responsibility for Indian lands. In response to a sentiment among policy makers that the 1934 policy coddled the Indians too much, policy shifted in 1953 toward the other end of the spectrum, and an active assimilationist goal was adopted. The federal government funded relocation of Indians who chose to move from reservations to urban areas and provided assistance to them during the transition period. Simultaneously, the government terminated support for many tribes in the areas of health, education, welfare, and tribal responsibility for resources. It fell to states and the tribes themselves to move in and provide alternate forms of assistance to these reservations. Working itself out of the "Indian business," as one official termed it, had long been a government objective. Thoughtful officials, like John Collier, commissioner of the Bureau of Indian Affairs, believed this needed to be done gradually as Indian and state organizations developed a capability to handle these functions.[111] In the 1950s, many tribal governments did not have the sophistication and experience to do so.

The policy succeeded in prompting some Indians to move to cities, but many of these people found themselves unable to adapt to an urban environment and subsequently returned to the reservations. The termination policy created such opposition among Indian and non-Indian groups that, by the end of the 1950s, the government de-emphasized it in favor of improving Indian conditions to prepare Indians for eventual termination.

Years of wrestling with Indian issues produced no notable success. Despite rich timber, mineral, and other natural resources, many reservations remained impoverished. Government management of reservations' natural resources contributed significantly to the situation. Debate on this issue continues at present, as does (many charge) government mismanagement of Indian resources. The debate centers partly on the conflict of interest inherent in the Department of the Interior's dual roles as the trustee of Indian lands and real estate agent and developer for national industry. Some have charged the government with a pattern of using cheap Indian resources to stimulate the national economy. According to lawyer and researcher Russel Lawrence Barsh of the University of Washington, the government's outright confiscation of Indian land and resources during an earlier era, in many cases simply evolved into "confiscation through administration" in order to bolster the overall economy.[112] The impact on reservation entrepreneurs of such administrative hijacking has been to promote low-cost, "fugitive" retail enterprises, like fireworks, liquor, and tobacco products. These do little to develop tribal economies, but they have the advantage of being subject to only minimal federal control, according to Barsh. He maintains that such enterprise is less risky, hence more rational, than investment in natural resources and structures where the government has the power to force liquidation as well as conservation of resources.[113]

Government-sponsored education programs also contributed, though inadvertently, to the dismal picture in the 1950s. Deloria points out that because American policy makers believed Indians incapable of mastering academic subjects and assumed they preferred to work with their hands, Indians were provided with vocational training. For their part, most Indians did not object because they wished to learn skills that would enable them to work on or near their reservation. Most reservations being far from urban centers where professional skills are useful, they saw little need to acquire such skills.[114]

It is not surprising, therefore, that Indians were ill-prepared to compete in the American job market. According to census information cited by Jaffee, 54 percent of Indian workers (on and off the reservations) in 1960 held semiskilled or unskilled jobs, and less than 10 percent held professional or managerial positions.[115] These figures compare with 37 percent and almost 20 percent, respectively, for the total U. S. population. Indians were suffering from marginalization in American society and devastating ills on their reservations.

In the 1960s, past policy failures, international contact with third-world nations, and, here at home, the civil rights and the Indian rights movements raised American consciousness about cultural pluralism. This resulted in the adoption of a new Indian policy: a move toward self-determination. This broadly meant including Indians in policy formulation and providing them with greater authority to administer Indian programs. This orientation was embodied in legislation passed in the 1970s. The new policy focused specifically on assisting Indians on or near reservations to achieve economic self-sufficiency. While maintaining its trust commitment, the federal government did not actively promote assimilation.

As government policy changed in the 1960s and 1970s, so, too, did the ways in which Indians perceived themselves. This was evident in, and fostered by, the Indian rights movement that developed at that time. A growing number of Indians now lived off of reservations, and many had received higher education in mainstream institutions. These people gained a broader view of American society and their role in it than had the preceding generation. Many were also sensitive to the developing momentum of the black civil rights movement.

The Indian rights movement came to wide public notice in 1969 when a group of Indians took control of Alcatraz prison. Deloria, who participated prominently in the movement, states that the activist agenda was a switch from past Indian strategies of promoting tribal eligibility for social welfare assistance. The new activist strategy was to demand government accountability for past crimes toward the Indian people.[116] Writing at the time, he commented, "tribes are reordering their priorities to account for the obvious discrepancies between their goals and the goals whites have defined for them."[117] Among the activist groups that emerged were the National Indian Youth Council and the American Indian Movement (AIM). At the height of the movement from 1973 to 1976, AIM and other groups occupied Wounded Knee, South Dakota, where one of the greatest atrocities against Indians had occurred.

Among the general public, support for Indian rights waned with the recognition that yielding to Indian demands would be at public expense. But not before legislation was passed reflecting the new government policy toward Indians. (The first such law was the Indian Self-Determination and Education Assistance Act of 1975.)

Among Indians, too, the rights movement has had a lasting effect. New pan-Indian organizations were established, such as the North American Indian Women's Association, which continues to work on issues of concern to all Indians. The call of the Indian rights movement to safeguard treaty rights is carried on today. There is growing recognition of the need to establish an effective pan-Indian political network to protect tribal rights from threatened erosion through legislation and other government actions.*

The Indian rights movement also helped instill in individuals a deepened sense of pride and determination to carry on their cultural traditions. Many of the younger generation of leaders, most of them not yet in top tribal positions, are "new traditionals," according to Deloria. These are people who are trying to "derive principles of action and understanding from the (Indian) traditions and apply them to modern circumstances..."[119] Still, Indians overall are divided on what direction their future in relation to American society should take, their views and actions ranging all along the tradition-assimilation axis.

Whatever their views on the tradition-assimilation dilemma, Indians clearly need to take into consideration the dire socioeconomic conditions on many reservations. The BIA estimated that in 1991 unemployment on reservations was 45 percent.[120] Up to half of reservation employment (and a third of off-reservation employment) is funded by the federal government.[121] And only about a quarter of those employed on or near reservations earn more than $7,000 annually.[122] That means a large portion of the Indian population remains dependent on the government for welfare support. Sar Levitan points out, "Most reservation economies are more dependent on welfare than on employment as a source of income."[123]

At the same time, however, gambling is providing a substantial income for several tribes. Based on the 1988 Indian Gaming Regulatory

---

*In his speech to the Tribal Leaders Forum in 1990, Senator Daniel Inouye, Chairman of the Select Committee on Indian Affairs, warned, "It is a sad but true reality that tribal rights are continually under assault....If tribes are to protect their own rights and those of other tribes from such assaults, you must form strong political alliances."[118]

Act, Indians have constructed gaming facilities on reservations that are drawing in huge profits and providing jobs for many who would otherwise be unemployed. This year alone, gambling is expected to gross some $6 billion for 58 tribes.[124]

Self-determination remains federal government policy. This policy operates under certain constraints. Sar Levitan and Elizabeth Miller of George Washington University point out that control over policy formulation and funding for Indian assistance programs is located in Washington. Further, because of their prolonged dependence on Washington, many tribal governments are not sophisticated or united enough to break their reliance on government supervision and assistance.[125] Some tribes do not want self-determination; others are divided internally on how to administer tribal affairs. Levitan and Miller conclude, "While tribes cling to the federal government for support, they also strive for greater control over the policies and programs affecting their lives. Given the inherent clash of goals, it is not surprising that consensus for accepting self-determination remains elusive."[126]

Native-American Cultural Values and the Workplace

To say that Native Americans are the only indigenous ethnic group in the country—and they are—is to ignore the fact that some do not consider themselves primarily an ethnic group in the first place. Deloria states that "Indians do not see themselves as an ethnic group within a larger society but as a small but faithful remnant of a people called to a larger vocation."[127] "Their ethnicity," he points out, "is a product of historical process [i.e., interaction with European Americans] and [white] political ideology rather than racial and cultural homogeneity," though he acknowledges that recently tribal intermarriages have created a "national sense of pan-Indianism."[128]

Whether their self-perception is one of an ethnic group or of a people bound by a larger, spiritual mission or neither, most North American Indian tribes share certain common cultural values. These values transcend the vast array of tribal differences, and they remain strong among many Native Americans today.

About one-third of Native Americans live on or near reservations, where Anglo values tend to be less integral to the pattern of daily life than elsewhere. Like other people of color, many Indians grapple daily with the tensions created in the interaction between their native values and the process of acculturation to mainstream values. There is growing recognition that they do not have to abandon traditional values along the way, that they can adapt to mainstream life *and* maintain their distinctive cultural values. A comment by Scott Bear Don't Walk, a University of Montana student and member of the Crow and Satish-Kootenai tribes, is illustrative. Upon learning that he had been selected as a Rhodes scholar, he said of the honor, "It's not just a personal, individual way for me to get ahead. Being Native American today means being able, through your culture, to adopt to your tribe's advantage the best the world has to offer."[129] There is a movement among Native-American tribes to reteach native values and acquire mainstream survival skills.*

Central to the traditional Indian value system, as Deloria's comment suggests, is a spiritual orientation.† This orientation defines and gives coherence to their value system as well as to their behavior in the workplace and elsewhere.‡ The core belief is in a world animated by the Spirit that expresses through human beings and all living things. Most tribes believe that humans are composed of three dimensions: body, mind, and spirit. The focus is on maintaining harmony among all three. Plants and animals are also part of the spirit world, as they are of the physical world, which intermingles with the spiritual. Most Native Americans value living harmoniously with nature, not dominating or conquering it. The earth is cherished, with a knowledge that it will provide for them as does a mother.

Harmony also is reflected in tribal life, and collectivity is honored. Each person has a valued role within the tribe, regardless of status or function. Associated with this perspective is the belief among most Indians that each spirit chooses not only the physical body but also the roles through which it will accomplish its purposes in life.[131] High-status and low-status positions are part of a greater scheme.

These values may transfer to Indian behavior in the workplace. Native Americans who buy in to their organizations are likely to place the needs of the group ahead of those of the individual. In contrast to the Anglo value system where competition and "getting ahead" typically are emphasized, Native-American workers are likely to be

---

*Reflective of this movement is the agenda of the 1993 annual conference of the North American Indian Women's Association, held in the Washington, D.C., area in June. The focus was on the role of Indian women in improving the Indian educational system to attain the same educational standards found elsewhere in the country. The agenda also stressed the importance of finding a balance between the Indian value system and the values taught in schools.

†This section was developed in close coordination with Ann French, president of the North American Indian Women's Association, and Jeri Brunoe of Jeri Brunoe Consulting, Arlington, Texas.

‡Carol Locust observes that most Indian cultures have a high degree of integration among their religious beliefs, their beliefs about health, and their social behavior.[130]

uncomfortable with competitive behavior. To the extent that they are motivated by traditional values, competition is more likely to be with their own past performance than with co-workers. Moreover, advancement at work may be viewed as relatively meaningless. They are not defined by the job they do, and the accumulation of titles may have as little significance as the accumulation of other material possessions. The focus is more on finding contentment and meaning in the job at hand than on strategizing about advancement.

Because of their value on collectivism, many Native Americans are sensitive to being singled out in a group. Even if they have contributed a major share to a work effort, Native Americans are likely in a group situation to attribute the work to the entire team.

Modesty and a preference for anonymity in groups make many Indians reluctant to speak up for themselves even when they have been misunderstood. Nor are they apt to negotiate salary increases or identify their accomplishments on annual performance appraisal forms. Native-American workers tend to be self-reliant. Once begun on a task, they work well alone without expecting much give and take with their supervisor until it is completed. They tend to expect the supervisor to be aware of the work they are doing and to ensure that they receive the proper rewards. These patterns present special challenges to supervisors. Accustomed to more verbal interaction, an Anglo manager may not fully appreciate the accomplishments of a Native-American worker. From the Anglo perspective, such Indian behaviors may be seen to demonstrate diffidence and unassertiveness, qualities that are considered weaknesses on the job.

Cooperation with co-workers is another implication of the traditional emphasis on harmony. When a Native-American worker buys in to a system, he or she can be expected to work within groups without regard to personal advantage. Always a strength in the workplace, this orientation may become even more highly prized as organizational practices shift toward increased teamwork. The focus on cooperation is an advantage in managerial positions, too. Native-American managers are likely to be strongly people-oriented, concerned for the welfare of each employee as well as for the smooth running of the group. Their traditional leadership style is an asset when applied to the workplace. Focusing on expressing the shared views of the group, this approach is consensus-based and democratic in nature, and it lends itself naturally to the participatory style of management.

But there is a disadvantage to the focus on harmony, too. Because Native Americans tend to have strong concern for others and are careful not to make others lose face, they may be hesitant to provide constructive criticism in a group situation. The result could be withholding valuable input to a group effort. Also, the Indian worker would have failed to accurately demonstrate his or her knowledge and analytical skills.

Because most Indians consider public criticism rude and disrespectful and are reluctant to engage in it themselves, they are likely to be offended when criticized by others in public. Co-workers and managers probably would not be aware of this reaction because most Indians are reticent about personal matters. They value privacy and do not readily talk about issues of personal concern, even when such a discussion would be helpful to them.

On the job, the strong Indian focus on people and respectful behavior toward them may be expressed in traditional gestures that are likely to be misunderstood by non–Native Americans. As a sign of respect, Native Americans may avoid eye contact when talking with another person. In fact, among the Navajo tribe, prolonged eye contact is viewed as a sign of anger. Many Indian tribes consider a strong handshake to be aggressive. All of these traditional behaviors contrast sharply with Anglo behavior patterns, and they may be misinterpreted as signs of weaknesses, uneasiness, or lack of confidence.

In further contrast with Anglo values is the Indian focus on inner and outer quietness. Most Indians are comfortable with silence. They do not readily display anger or other strong emotions. Believing that words have power, they also tend to avoid small talk. Many tribes traditionally do not say "hello" or "good-bye" as part of daily conversation. In the workplace, where casual friendliness is practiced, the placid demeanor valued by many Native Americans may be viewed as aloofness or sulking. From the Indian perspective, the easy flow of light conversation that occurs in most workplaces is considered insincere. They are likely to shrink from boisterous conversation, loud voices, and displays of strong emotion by co-workers.

The traditional Indian view of time also has implications for behavior on the job. In contrast to the Anglo view that time is fixed and linear, the traditional Native-American assumption is that it is flowing. Many Indian languages do not contain a word for "time" nor words expressing the future tense. The focus is on the present. In traditional Indian culture, key activities were performed in harmony with the cycles of nature. People were not controlled by time but in attunement with it. In the workplace, Native Americans conform to work schedules and deadlines like everyone else, but their traditional view can arm them with an advantage. The traditional perspective can enable them to navigate among competing deadlines and schedules with some sense of detachment and, thus, with less stress.

The importance attached to the present moment is frequently displayed in the patience with which many Native Americans work.

Whatever their task, they are likely to undertake it steadily and thoroughly, for each moment is valued in itself, not merely as a means to an end. If the importance of a long-term task is clear, then they are apt to readily persevere until it is completed. To the extent that they are motivated by traditional values, they may view their work, not as a personal accomplishment, but as a product of the Spirit that animates the world.

A Short History of Arab Americans

Like other non-Anglo minorities, Arab Americans are a growing presence in the workplace. Arab Americans are a "new" identity group in another way, too: Arab Americans have only recently begun to view themselves as a unified ethnic group. The aggregate term "Arab American" was inaugurated in the late 1960s. It began to be widely used among group members in the 1980s.[132] But there is still disagreement on its definition. Political scientist John Zogby of the John Zogby Group International in Utica, New York, defines "Arab American" as "all immigrants from the Arabic-speaking world."[133] This definition includes Christians as well as Moslems.* Historian Alixa Naff points out that lack of consensus about who is an Arab and what is Arabness has "inhibited the development of a common Arab identity in the United States."[134] For some, the group identification still has little resonance.

Among the more politically active, there is a somewhat embattled sense that their claim to a separate ethnicity has not yet received adequate public recognition. Part of the problem stems from the fact that "Arab American" is not one of the standard groups profiled in government EEO statistics. The 1980 census provided the first official demographic data about people from Arabic-speaking nations and their descendants. The information was not, however, reported separately because of their small numbers.

It is unclear just how many Arab Americans there are. According to the 1990 census, just over 920,000 persons identified their place of

---

*Zogby points out that there is a gray area with regard to the inclusion of Jews from Arabic-speaking countries. Technically, a Jewish immigrant from Algeria, say, is an immigrant from the Arab world, just as a Palestinian immigrant from Israel is an Israeli. But the Palestinian is generally considered an "Arab American" and the Jew from Algeria is not. Zogby notes that, in any case, the numbers are small and they tend to balance each other out. (Telephone conversation with John Zogby, October 21, 1993.)

ancestry as the Arabic-speaking world.* Some analysts, however, suggest that the actual number is far larger: between 2 and 2.5 million people.[135] Zogby, commenting on the too-low population in the 1980 census (where the number was reported as just over 600,000), explained that third- and fourth-generation Arab Americans are highly acculturated and assimilated, and often they have intermarried with other ethnic groups. Thus, many chose not to identify their ancestry as Arab American. Further, many new immigrants bring with them a deep distrust of government and, therefore, simply ignore census forms. Zogby also notes that some immigrants tend to identify with religious groups, not with national boundaries. Finally, because the census is in English, many people in non-English-speaking households are likely to ignore it.[136]

Persons of Arab origin were in North America before the republic was established.[137] But mainly, Arabs have come to the United States in two waves: the first, dating from the end of the nineteenth century to the end of World War II, and the second, after World War II to the present. About half of the Arab-American population consists of people who arrived between the 1890s and 1940s and their descendants; the other half are people who came since World War II and their descendants.[138]

The first wave of Arab Americans began coming to this country late in the nineteenth century. They came mainly to improve their economic condition. They had little sense of ethnic identity. Their cultural and religious background rather than national boundaries was the locus of their identity. Being part of the Ottoman empire, the Syrian region from which they hailed, like much of the rest of the Arabic-speaking world, was not independent and had little sense of a separate national identity. Nor did the immigrants identify with pan-Arabism, which was barely extant at the end of the nineteenth century. (The sense of a pan-Arab identity was given impetus by the Arab revolt during World War I, which was romanticized outside the Arab world by T. E. Lawrence's participation.) In fact, it was U.S. immigration authorities who, in 1899, designated the immigrants "Syrians."[139] The immigrants themselves did not readily identify with the term.

---

*From unpublished data from the Bureau of the Census. These ancestry groups included 13 major and several other categories (designated as "other North African and Southwest Asian") which can be aggregated into the generic category "Arab American." Included among the major categories are Syrian, Assyrian, Arab, Middle Eastern, Palestine, and several Arab countries. Because we are including persons only from Arabic-speaking countries, persons identifying themselves as being of Iranian, Turkish, and Israeli descent are not included in the total.

Most of the new immigrants did not intend to remain in the United States permanently. They hoped to make enough money in America to enable them to return home to enjoy the fruit of their labors. And some did return. Between 1908 and 1910, for example, the return rate was about 25 percent.[140] These were mainly single males, who presumably returned to marry without having made their fortunes first.

But, despite their intentions, most stayed and acculturated and assimilated over time relatively easily. There are several reasons for this. First, acculturation was facilitated by the fact that about 90 percent of the immigrants were Christians.* Another major factor was the occupation of pack peddling that most adopted. Naff points out that peddling offered several advantages: Most of the immigrants were illiterate or only barely literate in Arabic, and they had to learn English from scratch. They had been artisans or farmers in Syria and had little capital to invest in business ventures in the new country. Pack peddling enabled them to earn money immediately, and it did not require advanced training, capital, or language skills. It suited their individualistic and ambitious nature, allowing them to operate on their own terms, without being subject to job lines or layoffs. According to Naff, they found peddling preferable to the "drudgery of factory and to the isolation of farm life."[143] Through peddling, they were exposed to a wider range of American life and ideas than they would have had they stayed in one place. Further, the sense of impermanence fostered by peddling fortified them to deal with their new life in America.

World War I was a watershed in the history of Arab Americans. By 1914, there were about 100,000 Syrians in the United States.[144] The war interrupted immigration and, although the influx revived afterwards and continued until World War II, it did so in greatly diminished volume. The Immigration Act of 1924 placed very limited fixed quotas on immigration from all countries other than West European nations. (In the wake of the collapse of the Ottoman empire during World War I, independent nation-states had been established in the Arabic-speaking world.) Quotas were limited to a mere 100 persons annually from each Mediterranean country. Thus, for the next two decades, the Syrian communities in the United States were relatively fixed in size.

The war was important in another way too: The development of mass production and mass consumption were making obsolete the door-to-door occupation of the peddler. But by the war, many mem-

---

*The low ratio of Moslems to Christians was due to a fear by Moslem Arabs that they would not be able to maintain their Moslem traditions in Christian America.[141] Also see, Elkholy, *The Arab Moslems in the United States, Religion and Assimilation.*[142]

bers of the pioneering generation were ready to move on to other occupations. Peddling had hastened their assimilation, and it brought a measure of financial success that provided them with capital to make the move. While most American miners, factory workers, and farm laborers earned about $600 per year before the war, the pack peddlers earned about $1,000 a year.[145] By the 1920s, many began to acquire small businesses and they bought homes—signs of their new status in the ranks of the middle class.

Their allegiance, too, was shifting. Imperceptibly, over time, the initial goal of returning to their homeland faded, and identification with the United States evolved naturally. Financial success in the United States brought a sense of attachment rather than signaling a time for departure. The Syrians had a deep-felt need for rootedness. After having lived in the United States for several years, the pioneers found increasingly intolerable the in-between state of being at home neither in Syria nor America. Syria was far away and, like much of the rest of the Middle East, underwent profound political changes after World War I. Among them was the political transformation of the Syrian region from which the immigrants came into the country of Lebanon under French control. The immigrants' sense of disconnectedness from their area of origin was further heightened by the drastic drop in the flow of new immigrants.

The forces that heightened their psychic distance from their homeland reinforced ties to America. The decrease in the immigrant flow meant a lack of cultural reinforcement that enabled them to more readily acculturate to American patterns. The use of the Arabic language declined in many homes, and a half-hearted effort by leaders of the Syrian community to revive an interest in their Syrian heritage proved futile.[146] Naff points out, "If political and economic events [after World War II] had not reactivated Arab immigration and interest in Arab culture, Syrian Americans might have assimilated themselves out of existence."[147]

The second wave of Arab Americans began coming after World War II. The wide range of political events and profound economic changes in the Middle East after the war created an outflow of people. Palestinians, Egyptians, North Africans, and people from many other Arabic-speaking countries flowed to the United States. The establishment of the state of Israel in the late 1940s created an outflow of Palestinians. Another major surge in emigration from the Middle East occurred after the 1967 Six Day War. Increased demand to come to the United States coincided with the passage of the 1965 U.S. immigration laws that allowed more immigration from the region and elsewhere. Between 1945 and 1990, an estimated 420,000 Arab immigrants migrated to the United States.[148]

For some of these new immigrants, adjustment in America was eased by the presence of the Syrian communities. The newcomers had an easier time settling in their new home than did the pioneers. For, example, the long-established, mainly Moslem, Arab community in South Dearborn, Michigan, housed and instructed the steady stream of newcomers to their midst.[149]

Overall, however, differences between the two waves of immigrants were the outstanding feature of their relationship. Not only did the new influx come from all over the Middle East, rather than from just one area, they came from independent nation-states. In strong contrast to their predecessors, they had a strong sense of nationalism and ethnic identity. Also unlike the earlier wave, most were Moslems, and their level of education was higher than that of their predecessors. Many had college degrees or came with the expectation of obtaining them.

From amidst these people and the reaction to them by the pioneers' American-born descendants arose the sense of community and Arab American identity. Naff notes that the 1967 Six Day War and, thereafter, the deprecation of the Arab image in the United States created a strong nationalistic reaction among new immigrants.[150] American-born descendants of the pioneers reacted by trying to bridge the gap between their own upbringing with its low political-awareness quotient and the high political consciousness of the newcomers. Furthermore, Zogby notes that past divisiveness in Syrian-Lebanese organizations in the United States had left the American-born descendants with a feeling that it was time to transcend internal feuds.[151] Finally, the growing ethnic awareness among other American ethnic groups also had an impact among Arab Americans. These factors coincided after 1967 and mobilized Arab Americans to redirect their attention to political and social issues of special interest to themselves.[152] They also sparked a new interest in the Arab cultural heritage. Arab Americans began to establish organizations to respond to these issues. Among them are the Association of Arab American University Graduates, the National Association of Arab Americans, the American-Arab Anti-Discrimination Committee, the Arab American Institute, and several professional organizations. Through their varied organizational missions, these groups and others promote Arab-American ethnic awareness. They also are channels through which Arab Americans are gaining influence as a group. This is a new goal, for as Naff notes, prior to this, focus had been placed on individual achievement.[153]

Despite the new sense of community, tensions remain between the two immigrant groups. Many of the first generation and some of their descendants look down on the generally less wealthy recent immigrants and their distinct ethnic patterns. For their part, the later immigrants tend to view the earlier generation as people who have lost their identity. Many of the American-born, caught in the middle, are questioning the nature of Arabness and their own identity. Naff states that such questions "for which no common answers have been agreed on, have inhibited the development of a common Arab identity in the United States."[154]

Economist Muhammad Samhan of the University of the District of Columbia, observes that there is another difference between the two groups: The older generation has an institutional infrastructure with which the newcomers felt unconnected until recently. Many of the newcomers still remain unconnected with political parties in the United States, while the earlier generations have become politically active.[155]

The demographic profile of the Arab-American community is primarily urban. Based on Zogby's analysis of unpublished 1980 census data, Arab Americans were concentrated primarily in urban centers in the northeast and midwest. (Data from the 1990 census are not yet available.) They tended to be younger than the U.S. population, with a median age of 26.1 years, compared with the total U.S. median age of 30 years.[156]

Many Arab Americans are bilingual, but in 1980, English was the predominant language. About 70 percent of Arab Americans from 5 to 17 years of age spoke only English at home; for persons 18 years or older, almost 54 percent spoke only English at home. Among those of all ages who spoke a language other than English at home, Arabic was the predominant language. And, even among the Arabic language speakers, only about 10 percent of the older category of Arab Americans indicated that they did not speak English well or did not speak it at all.[157]

Educational attainment levels of Arab Americans in 1980 were high. Over 70 percent of Arab-born and almost 82 percent of U.S.-born people were high school graduates. Almost 49 percent of Arab-born and over 55 percent of U.S.-born had some college education, and almost 32 percent of the Arab-born and over 26 percent of the U.S.-born Arab Americans were college graduates, plus.[158]

Household incomes for Arab Americans in 1980 were higher than they were for the total U.S. population. For Arab Americans, the median household income was $18,133, while the figure for the total U.S. population was $16,841. Among the Arab American population, the median household was significantly higher for the U.S.-born—$23,522, compared with $18,146 for Arab-born Americans.[159]

In the workplace, the Arab-American labor force was 93.5 percent employed and 6.5 percent unemployed in 1980. A higher percentage of

Arab Americans were in management and professional positions than in the U.S. population as a whole—over 31 percent of Arab Americans compared with almost 23 percent of the U.S. total. Almost 51 percent of Arab Americans were in technical fields or administrative support and clerical positions, compared with almost 48 percent for the total U.S. population. In the rest of the occupational distribution, fewer Arab Americans were in unskilled jobs than the total population—less than 13 percent of Arab Americans, compared with over 18 percent of the total. More than 11 percent of Arab Americans were in service occupations; 1 percent in farming, forestry, and fishing; and less than 9 percent in skilled blue-collar jobs.[160] By industry, about one in four were occupied in retail trade.[161]

Traditional Arab Cultural Values and the Workplace

As with the other identity groups, Arab Americans are culturally diverse. Their countries of origin number more than 20 and span two continents. There are several dialects of Arabic as well as other indigenous languages (such as Berber), not to mention languages imported by their former English, French, and Italian colonial occupiers. While most Arabs are Moslem, some are Druze and others are Christian. Arab cultural traditions are ancient and they vary widely. There is also some variation in values. In his authoritative intercultural research, Hofstede resolves the issue of value differences by devising an index representative of the several Arabic-speaking countries he studied.* Yet, despite the differences, a common core of values exists across the Arab world. Arab observers, such as Naff, readily refer to these common values.† In this section, we discuss common values and point out areas where differences seem to exist.‡

---

*The research, undertaken in 1968 and 1972 in more than 40 countries, surveyed IBM employees on values and other issues. First reported in his classic work *Culture's Consequences*, the research also forms the basis of *Cultures and Organizations*. In this latter work appears the indexes for the Arab countries surveyed. The Arab countries are Egypt, Iraq, Kuwait, Lebanon, Libya, Saudi Arabia, and United Arab Emirates. Results were further verified by populations outside IBM.[162]

†In a discussion of Syrian values, Naff makes frequent reference to their identity with Arab values.[163]

‡This section is based in part on information supplied by Middle East expert Mr. Andrew Carvely of NTW Publications in Sumerduck, Virginia (in a telephone interview July 30, 1993) and by economist Dr. Muhammad Samhan of the University of District of Columbia (in a telephone interview August 17, 1993).

The values discussed in this section are those of traditional Arab culture. Our concern is how these values influence the perceptions and behavior of Arab Americans on the job. Clearly, not all group members in the workplace hold the values to the same extent, if at all. In fact, as our historical survey indicates, a large portion of the Arab-American population is highly acculturated and assimilated. The values are most likely to be reflected by first-generation and perhaps second-generation Arab Americans, especially the self-employed and blue-collar workers. Highly educated, highly skilled professionals, including first-generation immigrants, tend to be sophisticated and are likely to adapt more readily to the Anglo-dominated value system on the job, though they do not necessarily abandon their own cultural heritage in doing so. Like individuals from many other minority groups, Arab Americans may compartmentalize their values and switch between those of the dominant Anglo culture and their heritage, depending on the situation.

Much of the Arab cultural heritage can be traced to the desert. Though their behavior patterns have changed with their changing environments over the centuries, the imprint on their values of the tribal system operating in the desert persists.[164] Naff points out that contemporary Arabs disdain the bedouin's way of life while simultaneously revering their social ideals. These "noble virtues" include "manliness and sense of honor, individualism and group loyalty, magnanimity and munificence, as well as heroism..."[165] A further important attribute, if not a value, is a remarkable ability to combine contrasting, sometimes seemingly contradictory, attitudes in the same situation.[166] This ability, plus a high level of emotional intensity, can lead to attitude swings. These values and attributes are expressed, in varying degrees, today in the behavior and perceptions of some Arab-American workers.

Traditional Arab culture is both collectivistic *and* individualistic. Hofstede points out that Arab nations vary with regard to these values (noting for example, that Saudi Arabia seems to be more collectivistic than Lebanon), and he found them to rank about in the middle of the individualism-collectivism index.[167] The implication is that Arab culture is neither strongly collectivistic nor strongly individualistic. In fact, it is both, though individualism has a somewhat different meaning in traditional Arab culture than in the Anglo context. Collectivism is expressed through an honor-shame centered system in which traditional tribal allegiances have been transformed into family loyalty. Naff's comment about Syrian immigrants in America can be generalized: "Implicitly, the honor of one's ancestry and his Arab heritage were inextricably intertwined and became indistinguishable from his own. An existence apart from kin or primary group was almost inconceivable for an individual."[168]

In the contemporary American context, identification with family and a determination to maintain its honor remains important to many Arab Americans. Equally prominent, and interlinked with the family factor, is identification with Islam.* In the American workplace, an Arab worker is likely to be highly motivated to do well not simply as a matter of personal fulfillment but also, even more significantly, to uphold family honor and status. Financial success enables one's family to live with social graciousness, which traditionally has been considered an important feature in maintaining family honor. As a result, Arab-American workers are likely to be strongly success-oriented, and this can be an important asset on the job. Negligence on the job could mean a loss of face and would be shameful for oneself and family.

The concern for honor can breed an extreme sensitivity to the opinion of others. Naff points out that the inner concern with honor is paralleled with an outer concern with public image—that is, a concern for others' assessments of how one has projected honor.[170] On the job, such honor consciousness can have both negative and positive implications. It can generate responsiveness to coworkers' needs or, if one is a manager, to subordinates' needs. Thus, it enhances job performance.

At the same time, however, such sensitivity can foster difficulties in working relationships. Naff points out that it can lead to a preoccupation with redressing affronts, real or imagined.[171] Criticism, even justified criticism, may be difficult to accept and perceived as an insult. In the traditional culture, an elaborate social interplay is mandated among those "in the know" to ensure that appropriate perceptions are maintained. To the extent that such value-based behavior is carried into the American workplace, it is likely to baffle non–Arab-American coworkers. When behaviors considered neutral or even supportive in the Anglo context are perceived as insulting, non–Arab Americans are likely be at a loss as to how to respond appropriately.

Also valued in traditional Arab culture are certain forms of individualism. In the American workplace, this may be expressed in certain specific ways. According to Andrew Carvely of NTW Publications of Sumerduck, Virginia, those who work in large organizations are likely to have a strong sense of their goals within the organization. This can provide a clear sense of self in the work environment. Further, Muhammad Samhan explains that in many areas individualism is not expressed as self-reliance as it is in the Anglo culture, but in the eco-

---

*For values associated with Islam, see Haddad and Lummis, *Islamic Values in the United States: A Comparative Study*.[169]

nomic area it is. There, it is seen in the Arab-American preference for self-employment. The pioneer Arab Americans strongly preferred self-employment, as discussed elsewhere. That preference is still visible in the one-quarter of the Arab-American population who were in retail trade in 1980. (Higher than the national average of 16 percent.)

Another factor in the preference for self-employment is an engrained distrust of institutions. Samhan and Carvely explain that Arabs have long experience with repressive governments imposed especially by foreign conquerors but by indigenous leaders as well. In many Arab countries, the police, the military, and other forms of authority traditionally have been feared. This experience has instilled in many Arab newcomers to the United States a desire to avoid involvement with large institutions where possible. The preference for self-employment may in part be traced to this source.

In the workplace, distrust for organizations also tends to be expressed in a preference for personal rather than functional relationships. Dealings with people based on the workforce function they perform involves relying on an institution. A personal relationship with the person behind the title becomes irrelevant, and that is perceived as unsafe.

For a similar reason, first-generation Arab Americans with low skill and sophistication levels, are especially likely to view a task force or group project as something of a waste of time, according to Carvely. Such groups are functional and relations are impersonal. There may be the assumption that much of the work would be better done by individuals and that task-force meetings provide a break from the real work, time off rather than an integral part of the work schedule.

Authoritarianism is a value strongly reflected across the Arab world. Hofstede found that the combined score of the Arab nations he sampled placed them seventh on the power index out of 50 countries and three regions. As high power distance nations (Hofstede's term), they expect and accept the unequal distribution of power within institutions. In contrast, American organizations tend to be flatter (on Hofstede's power index, the United States ranked 38). In the American workplace, the expectation is for relatively democratic working relationships.

This contrast in values has several implications. First, Arab-American workers who hold traditional values are likely to respect a strong manager and likely to perceive state-of-the-art participatory management as weakness. Moreover, when in supervisory roles themselves, they tend to prefer an authoritarian style, unless they have been educated differently. The observation of fourteenth-century historian Ibn Khaldun is relevant: "Every Arab is eager to be a leader.

Scarcely one of them would cede his power to even his father, his brother or the eldest (most important) member of his family."[172] While this is an overstatement, the direction still holds true.

Authoritarianism may also be linked with honor consciousness. Naff points out "So much depends on the individual's performance that the inevitable undercurrent of anxiety must be veiled by haughtiness and contempt for the ability of others, even one's betters."[173]

Paradoxically, while they respect and perhaps fear authoritarianism, Arab Americans tend to appreciate looser working relationships, according to Carvely. It offers them more room to take initiative on the job (another way in which Arab individualism asserts itself). Samhan notes that there is a tendency among Arab-American workers to idealize the democratic aspects of the American workplace. When they experience some of its authoritarian aspects, they are likely to swing to the opposite extreme, saying "we are back in the Arab world."

Hofstede found that Arab nations ranked about in the middle on the uncertainty avoidance index (27th out of 50 countries and three regions). The Arab-American experience, however, has shown a rather high tolerance for uncertainty, at least in the economic area. In their preference for self-employment, they have invited into their lives high levels of uncertainty—far higher than those opting for employment in established organizations. Coupled with honor consciousness, it has produced a competitive, entrepreneurial spirit that helps enable many Arab Americans attain financial success in the workplace.

Traditional Arab culture places a high value on masculinity. As Naff points out, manliness is considered one of the "noble virtues," and it is extolled throughout the Arabic-speaking world.* This value carries implications for gender relations in the workplace.

Diversity Amid Diversity

The word "diversity" is rapidly attaining the status of sanctity in some circles. In others, it is a red flag symbolizing what people would rather

---

*Paradoxically, the Arab countries involved in Hofstede's study ranked only moderately on the masculinity index (23rd)—even lower than the United States, which ranked 15th. The contrast between the Arab self-perception of a high value on masculinity and Hofstede's findings is a result of differing definitions. Hofstede found among the questions he asked about job goals several on which men and women surveyed consistently scored differently, and he associated these with masculine and feminine poles. At the masculine pole, importance was attached to high earnings, recognition on the job, advancement opportunities, and challenge. At the feminine pole, value was placed on a good working relationship with the superior, cooperation with co-workers, desirable living area for oneself and family, and employment security.[174]

ignore. In both, it has come in an odd way to imply a kind of unity that, in fact, discords with reality.

Discussion of workplace diversity, minorities, and a dichotomy of interests between minorities and power holders can lead us into a "them-us" mentality. We tend to limit our thinking about differences to those characterizing the dominant group, which wants to maintain power, and the others, who want to get it. Such thinking suggests that both sides are relatively monolithic, but reality is not so simple. There is no more unity among minority groups than there is among the Anglo majority. Nor are there two sides engaged in some sort of entrenched warfare, though repeated references to the dichotomy seem to suggest it.

The illusion of unity among minority groups is reinforced in many ways these days. For instance, the term "people of color" promotes a one-big-happy-family notion. By focusing on minority issues, publications such as this one can do the same inadvertently. For this reason, it is important to remind ourselves of the diversity that exists amid diversity, the deep tensions within and among the racial and ethnic groups of the new workforce on the job and elsewhere in society.

While broadly shared workplace interests may enable people from diverse racial and ethnic backgrounds to keep a lid on differences temporarily, they do not prevent potentially disruptive tensions from arising in the first place. Values, attitudes, and behaviors vary, and clashes occur among as well as within groups. Very often they damage interpersonal relations. In the workplace, they may harm productivity. These clashes can be examined under two broad categories: social and cultural.

Social clashes, which include differences over the broad range of social, economic, and political issues that arise in social interaction, take several forms. Some are gender-based. For example, black males in managerial and professional positions sometimes have felt threatened by the growing number of black women professionals. Some Native-American women, hesitant to risk breaching tribal sovereignty, have been constrained to take separate, active roles on Native-American social issues. Black rappers routinely refer to women, including black women, as "bitches."*

Others are generational. Arab Americans are sharply divided in outlook between those who arrived earlier in this century and their children; further sharp differences in outlook exist between these two

---

*Many blacks are objecting to this practice. See, for example, William Raspberry, "Foulmouthed Trash."[175]

groups and more recent Arab arrivals. Generational tensions between recent immigrants and longer-term residents came to violence in the American Sikh community in Northern Virginia in 1993 when a scuffle broke out in a Sikh temple.

Discrimination within a minority group, called *internalized oppression*, is also based on skin color. Despite the tendency to associate racism based on skin color with the prejudice of white people, individuals from other racial groups, including black Americans, often regard lighter skin among their group members more favorably than darker skin. Such an attitude does not simply reflect the influence of the white-American bias. Many of the cultures that racial and ethnic minorities claim as their heritage traditionally include this bias. In Japanese culture, for example, the preference dates back at least 1,000 years. In Mexico, too, there is a preference for light-skinned and preferably light-haired children. (The birth of a blond-haired child is cause for special celebration in Mexican communities.)

Country or region of origin is further source of bias among groups. Among East Asians, Japanese Americans may regard Korean Americans as having lesser status. Hispanics tend to have diminished regard for people from certain Central American countries. Even within countries, Indians whose origins are in northern India may regard as socially inferior those American citizens of Indian origin whose native region was southern India or the northeastern Bihar area, for example. Often, individuals from groups belonging to the same broad ethnoracial category do not get along well—Puerto Ricans and Dominicans, Koreans and Japanese, Pakistanis and Indians, to cite a few.

Across minority groups, too, clashes are numerous. Minority groups frequently hold negative stereotypes of each other. In his book, *Managing a Diverse Work Force*, diversity specialist John P. Fernandez examines many of these.[176] Such stereotypes have fed other tensions. For example, Koreans may be perceived as standoffish by many black Americans. When tensions between the two groups erupted into violence in the Los Angeles riots in 1992, this perceived attitude was mentioned by some black observers. The violence was also sparked by black resentment over the prevalence of Korean-owned small businesses, including liquor stores, in black neighborhoods.

Latino and black American leaders managed to suppress their differences in recent decades as they fought for equality, but now rifts are growing. Tensions have expanded as Latino numbers rise, putting them more into contention with black leadership in minority affairs. At issue are jobs, immigration, and political cooperation. Both groups are increasingly suspicious that one's gain means the other's loss. Tensions are likely to increase as Latinos overtake blacks early in the next century as the nation's largest racio-ethnic minority. These tensions have spilled over into violence. Cubans and blacks periodically have come to blows in Miami, where the Cuban population predominates. The wounding of an Hispanic man by a black police officer touched off black-Hispanic violence in Washington, D.C., in 1991, where the black population is dominant.

Violence between individuals from other minority groups has dotted American history—for example, between blacks and Chinese workers in the west in the last century. Recently, new Asian-Indian immigrants have been harassed by black, Hispanic, and white people in New Jersey. On college campuses throughout the nation, many students of color are not only separated from white students but from each other. A series of *Doonesbury* cartoons in 1993 portrayed a fictive college president who met resistance from all segments of the multicultural student body when he tried to promote the "revolutionary" strategy of integration.

Another important kind of clash is cultural. Cultural clashes may be less frequently recognized, for they are intangible, manifesting over behavioral differences. But they are important just the same. They can intensify social conflicts. In the workplace, they produce the same kinds of disruptions among minority workers from different cultures as they do between minority and Anglo workers.

A few examples illustrate the point: In terms of assertiveness, the black and East Asian cultures are close to polar opposites. The black culture is highly assertive; East Asian culture strongly emphasizes modesty. On the job, this value divergence readily translates into misunderstanding. A black-American worker may see a Japanese-American worker as weak and indecisive, while a Japanese-American worker may view black expressiveness as bad manners and intimidating. Hispanic and Arab cultures value the expression of warmth and caring between people, including at work. A task-oriented approach expressed by an East Asian, for example, may be misunderstood as cold and uncaring.

Of course, not all people of color are party to the rifts cited here or the many others not mentioned. But as these few examples indicate, the notion of unity among minority groups is a fiction. The American advantage in the workplace—workforce diversity—can readily become an American weakness unless mutual understanding prevails. Frequent contact can help promote understanding, but it can also can widen divergences: It can make workers, especially those from ethnic enclaves with minimal previous intercultural contact, more aware of their own ethnic identity. Diversity training is often essential to help people deal with such differences.

References

1. U.S. Department of Commerce, Economics and Statistics Administration, Bureau of the Census, *Census '90, 1990 Census of Population, Asians and Pacific Islanders in the United States*, 1990, CP-3-5 (Washington, D.C.: U.S. GPO, August 1993), p. 5.

2. Roger Daniels, *Asian America: Chinese and Japanese in the United States Since 1850* (Seattle: University of Washington Press, 1988), p. 4.

3. Bureau of the Census, *1990 Census of Population, Asians and Pacific Islanders in the United States, op. cit.,* p. 6.

4. Bernard Wong, "Chinese Americans," Buenker and Ratner, *op. cit.,* p. 193.

5. Ronald Takaki, *A Different Mirror: A History of Multicultural America* (Boston: Little, Brown, 1993), p. 7.

6. *Ibid.,* p. 195.

7. Wong, *op. cit.,* pp. 194–195.

8. *Ibid.,* Table 1, p. 194.

9. Takaki, *op. cit.,* p. 195.

10. *Ibid.,* p. 197.

11. Maxine Hong Kingston, *China Men* (New York: Knopf, 1980).

12. Garraty and McCaughey, *The American Nation: A History of the United States*, 6th ed. (New York: Harper & Row, 1987), p. 499.

13. Takaki, *op. cit.,* p. 202.

14. *Ibid.,* p. 201.

15. Wong, *op. cit.,* p. 198.

16. Takaki, *op. cit.,* p. 253.

17. *Ibid.,* Table 1, p. 194.

18. *Ibid.,* p. 211.

19. Shih-Shan Henry Tsai, *The Chinese Experience in America* (Bloomington: Indiana University Press, 1986), p. 38.

20. Wong, *op. cit.,* p. 199.

21. *Ibid.*

22. *Ibid.,* p. 194.

23. Bureau of the Census, *Census '90, 1990 Census of Population, Asians and Pacific Islanders in the United States, op. cit.* p. 6.

24. *Ibid.*

25. Roger Daniels, *op. cit.,* p. 324.

26. Bureau of the Census, *Census '90, 1990 Census of Population, Asians and Pacific Islanders in the United States, op. cit.,* p. 76.

27. Wong, *op. cit.,* p. 203.

28. Bureau of the Census, *Census '90, 1990 Census of Population, Asians and Pacific Islanders in the United States, op. cit.* p. 7.

29. Amy Tan, *The Joy Luck Club* (New York: Vintage Books, 1991).

30. Maxine Hong Kingston, *The Woman Warrior* (New York: Knopf, 1977).

31. Bureau of the Census, *Census '90, 1990 Census of Population, Asians and Pacific Islanders in the United States, op. cit.,* pp. 71, 74.

32. *Ibid.,* p. 75.

33. *Ibid.,* pp. 41, 45, 147.

34. *Ibid.,* p. 111.

35. *Ibid.*

36. *Ibid.,* p. 10.

37. Jenifer Stern, *The Filipino Americans* (New York: Chelsea House, 1989), p. 29.

38. Lawrence Fuchs, *The American Kaleidoscope: Race, Ethnicity, and the Civic Culture* (Hanover: Wesleyan University Press, 1990), p. 117.

39. Stern, *op. cit.,* p. 44.

40. Howard Brett Melendy, *Asians in America: Filipinos, Koreans, and East Indians* (Boston: Twayne, 1977), p. 37.

41. Takaki, *op. cit.,* p. 256.

42. Fuchs, *op. cit.,* p. 147.

43. Stern, *op. cit.,* p. 14.

44. Melendy, *op. cit.,* p. 42.

45. *Ibid.,* p. 31.

46. Stern, *op. cit.,* p. 40.

47. *Ibid.*

48. Melendy, *op. cit.,* p. 67.

49. *Ibid.,* p. 66.

50. *Ibid.*

51. Takaki, *op. cit.,* pp. 259–261.

52. Stern, *op. cit.,* p. 45.

53. *Ibid.,* pp. 62–65.

54. Melendy, *op. cit.,* p. 83.

55. *Ibid.,* p. 40.

56. *Ibid.,* p. 65.

57. *Ibid.,* p. 52.

58. *Ibid.,* p. 49.

59. *Ibid.,* p. 50.

60. Stern, *op. cit.,* p. 13.

61. Fuchs, *op. cit.*, p. 238.

62. Bureau of the Census, *Census '90, 1990 Census of Population, Asians and Pacific Islanders in the United States, op. cit.*, p. 10.

63. *Ibid.*, p. 80.

64. *Ibid.*, p. 150.

65. *Ibid.*

66. *Ibid.*, p. 115.

67. *Ibid.*, p. 150.

68. *Ibid.*, p. 115.

69. Takaki, *op. cit.*, p. 248.

70. Daniels, *op. cit.*, pp. 104–106.

71. *Ibid.*, p. 116.

72. Takaki, *op. cit.*, p. 266.

73. Robert A. Wilson and Bill Hosokawa, *East to America: A History of the Japanese in the United States* (New York: William Morrow, 1980), p. 44.

74. *Ibid.*, p. 268.

75. *Ibid.*, pp. 269, 270.

76. Takaki, *op, cit.*, pp. 266–267.

77. *Ibid.*, p. 264.

78. Daniels, *op. cit.*, p. 126.

79. Etsu Inagaki Sugimoto, *A Daughter of the Samurai: How a Daughter of Feudal Japan, Living Hundreds of Years in One Generation Became a Modern American* (Garden City, N.Y.: Doubleday, Doran, 1934).

80. U.S. Census figures cited by Daniels, *op. cit.*, p. 115.

81. UC Berkeley *Campanile Review,* quoted by Daniels, *op. cit.*, p. 183.

82. Bill Hosokawa, *Nisei: The Quiet Americans* (New York: William Morrow, 1969).

83. From the papers of Lt. Commander Kenneth D. Ringle; quoted by Daniels, *op. cit.*, p. 210.

84. Takaki, *op. cit.*, p. 379.

85. Hosokawa, *op. cit.*, pp. 360–364.

86. Daniels, *op. cit.*, p. 253.

87. Takaki, *op. cit.*, p. 383.

88. *Ibid.*, p. 384.

89. *Ibid.*, p. 4.

90. Bureau of the Census, *Census '90, 1990 Census of Population, Asians and Pacific Islanders in the United States, op. cit.*, pp. 1, 11, 15.

91. *Ibid.*, pp. 10, 11, 12.

92. *Ibid.*, p. 116.

93. *Ibid.*, p. 81.

94. *Ibid.*, pp. 106, 110, 116.

95. *Ibid.*, p. 165.

96. Stephen S. Fugita and David J. O'Brien, *Japanese American Ethnicity: The Persistence of Community* (Seattle: University of Washington Press, 1991), p. 168.

97. *Ibid.*, pp. 167–168.

98. Sar A. Levitan and Elizabeth I. Miller, *The Equivocal Prospects for Indian Reservations,* Occasional Paper 1993-2, Center for Social Policy Studies (Washington, D.C.: George Washington University, May 1993), p. 2.

99. Lyman H. Legters, "The American Genocide," Fremont J. Lyden and Lyman H. Legters, eds., *Native Americans and Public Policy* (Pittsburgh: University of Pittsburgh Press for the William O. Douglas Institute, 1992), pp. 101–112.

100. Vine Deloria, Jr., "American Indians," John D. Buenker and Lorman A. Ratner (eds.), *Multiculturalism in the United States: A Comparative Guide to Acculturation and Ethnicity* (New York: Greenwood Press, 1992), p. 33.

101. *Ibid.*, p. 37.

102. Dee Brown, *Bury My Heart At Wounded Knee: An Indian History of the American West,* (New York: New American Library/Bantam, 1972), p. xii.

103. A. J. Jaffee, *The First Immigrants from Asia: A Population History of the North American Indians* (New York: Plenum Press, 1992), p. 113.

104. Garraty and McCaughey, *op. cit.*, p. 496.

105. Jaffee, *op. cit.*, p. 114.

106. Levitan and Miller, *op. cit.*, p. 12.

107. Jaffee, *op. cit.*, p. 164.

108. *Ibid.*, p. 299.

109. Deloria, *op. cit.*, p. 34.

110. Theodore W. Taylor, *The States and Their Indian Citizens,* U.S. Department of the Interior, Bureau of Indian Affairs (Washington, D.C.: U.S. GPO., 1972), p. 28.

111. Cited by S. Lyman Tyler, *A History of Indian Policy,* U.S. Department of the Interior, Bureau of Indian Affairs (Washington, D.C.: U.S. GPO., 1973), p. 161.

112. Russel Lawrence Barsh, "Indian Resources and the National Economy: Business Cycles and Policy Cycles," Lyden and Legters, *op. cit.*, p. 198.

113. *Ibid.*, p. 215.

114. Deloria, *op. cit.*, p. 41.

115. Jaffee, *op. cit.*, p. 215.

116. Deloria, *op. cit.*, pp. 44–45.

117. Vine Deloria, Jr., *Custer Died for Your Sins: An Indian Manifesto* (New York: Avon, 1971), p. 10.

118. Daniel K. Inouye, "Indian Tribes in the 21st Century," address to the Tribal Leaders Forum on Framing a National Indian Agenda for the 1990s, American Indian Resources Institute, "Forum Report," February 9–10, 1990, unpublished report, p. 6.

119. Deloria, "American Indians," *op. cit.*, p. 47.

120. Levitan and Miller, *op. cit.*, p. 2.

121. *Ibid.*

122. *Ibid.*, p. 16.

123. *Ibid.*, p. 17.

124. Coleman McCarthy, "Odd Reservations About Indian Gaming," *Washington Post*, September 21, 1993, p. D20.

125. Levitan and Miller, *op. cit.*, p. 14.

126. *Ibid.*

127. Deloria, "American Indians," *op. cit.*, p. 32.

128. *Ibid.*, pp. 31, 38.

129. *News of the People, Monthly Newsletter for the Virginia Native American Cultural Center,* February 1993, p. 3.

130. Carol Locust, *American Indian Beliefs Concerning Health and Unwellness,* unpublished monograph, Native American Research and Training Center, University of Arizona, Tucson, Arizona, n.d., p.1.

131. Carol Locust, *Learning Difference—Handicapped American Indians: Beliefs and Behaviors,* unpublished monograph, Native American Research and Training Center, University of Arizona, Tucson, Arizona, n.d., p. 6.

132. John Zogby, *Arab America Today: A Demographic Profile of Arab Americans* (Washington, D.C.: Arab American Institute, 1990), p. vii.

133. *Ibid.*

134. Alixa Naff, *Becoming American: The Early Arab Immigrant* (Carbondale: Southern Illinois University Press, 1985), pp. 3–4.

135. Zogby, *op. cit.*, p. 19.

136. *Ibid.*, p. 39.

137. Naff, *op. cit.*, p. 2.

138. Zogby, *op. cit.*, p. vii.

139. Naff, *op. cit.*, p. 14.

140. Alixa Naff, "Arabs in America: A Historical Overview," Sameer Y. Abraham and Nabeel Abraham, eds., *Arabs in the New World: Studies on Arab-American Communities* (Detroit: Wayne State University, 1983), p. 14.

141. Naff, "Arabs in America," *op. cit.*, p. 13.

142. Abdo A. Elkholy, The Arab Moslems in the United States, Religion and Assimilation (New Haven, Conn.: College & University Press, 1966), p. 22.

143. Naff, *Becoming American, op. cit.,* p. 129.

144. *Ibid.,* p. 2.

145. Zogby, *op. cit.,* p. viii.

146. Naff, *Becoming American,* p. 268.

147. *Ibid.,* p. 330.

148. Zogby, in a telephone conversation, October 21, 1993.

149. Naff, "Arabs in America," *op. cit.,* pp. 24–25.

150. Naff, *Becoming American,* p. 330.

151. Zogby, in a telephone conversation, October 21, 1993.

152. Zogby, *Arab America Today, op. cit.,* p. viii.

153. Naff, "Arabs in America," *op. cit.,* p. 26.

154. Naff, *Becoming American, op. cit.,* pp. 3–4.

155. Dr. Muhammad Samhan, telephone interview, August 17, 1993.

156. Zogby, *Arab America Today,* p. 4.

157. *Ibid.,* p. 8.

158. *Ibid.,* p. 9.

159. *Ibid.*

160. *Ibid.,* pp. 13, 14.

161. *Ibid.,* p. 15.

162. Hofstede, *Cultures and Organizations, op. cit.,* p. 26 *et passim.*

163. Naff, *Becoming American, op. cit.,* pp. 55–63.

164. *Ibid.,* p. 55.

165. *Ibid.,* p. 56.

166. *Ibid.,* citing A. Kh. Kinany.

167. Hofstede, *Cultures and Organizations, op. cit.* p. 26.

168. Naff, *op. cit.,* p. 57.

169. Yvonne Yazbeck Haddad and Adair T. Lummis, *Islamic Values in the United States: A Comparative Study* (New York: Oxford University Press, 1987).

170. *Ibid.,* p. 60.

171. *Ibid.*

172. Quoted by Naff, *ibid.,* p. 61.

173. *Ibid.,* p. 61.

174. Hofstede, *Cultures and Organizations, op. cit.,* pp. 81–82.

175. William Raspberry, "Foulmouthed Trash," *Washington Post,* July 30, 1993, p. A21.

176. John P. Fernandez, *Managing a Diverse Work Force: Regaining the Competitive Edge* (Lexington, Mass.: D. C. Heath, 1991).

8

The New Workforce—Socioeconomic Issues on the Job

All workers face career-related issues that require strenuous intellectual and emotional effort and often a lot of luck, such as obtaining a desirable job (or sometimes just any job!); juggling demands of work and family; developing career goals and managing daily in ways that enhance one's goals; dealing with difficult bosses, peers, and subordinates; and a host of others. Minority workers face the same issues, squared. When they arrive at the workplace door, many are, by virtue of simply being a member of a minority group, burdened with a heavy load of hindrances that their white counterparts do not bear. And most encounter further hindrances on the job. These make ordinary, daily experiences at work harder to deal with, and they often keep minorities from progressing as rapidly as their white peers.

Ethnic and racial minorities of the new workforce are typically underrepresented in the workplace in relation to their share of the overall population. Exceptions may occur at lower rungs of organizational ladders, where minority workers tend to cluster. At the upper reaches, however, minorities are generally scarce, significantly fewer than their portion of the population.

While much has been written about the special issues facing racial and ethnic minority groups comprising the new workforce, most publications examine only one minority group, or one gender within a group, rather than surveying and comparing issues faced by all. Others focus on a specific issue. In the preceding chapters, we explored some of the cultural issues minority workers are likely to encounter in an Anglo-dominated workplace. Here we survey the range of special socioeconomic issues confronting minorities in workplaces where they are not adequately valued. These issues are not static. Because they and perceptions about them evolve, it is important to revisit them periodically. We do so here. We have the advantage of access to 1990 census data and other recently released statistical information that enable us to update some of the fine material that already has been published.

There is sharp divergence in views about factors most responsible for the relative lack of minority progress. Minority workers are likely to place priority on discrimination, both systemic and individual. White organizational management, on the other hand, is more likely to give top billing to insufficient education and inadequate minority skills traceable to a background of deprivation. In their excellent study, *Ensuring Minority Success in Corporate Management*, Nancy DiTomaso and Donna E. Thompson, both of Rutgers University, surveyed managers at top American companies about hindrances to minority advancement. Responses from black and white managers reflected this divergence.[1] Other literature on minorities in the workplace as well as anecdotal information suggest that this divergence exists across organizational levels and that the views expressed by black managers in the DiTomaso-Thompson survey are broadly representative of those of many other minority groups.

Within the two views, there naturally is variation. Some minority spokespersons assert that organizational power structures are in "deep denial" about the existence of discrimination in the workplace, to use the phrase of *USA Today* journalist Barbara Reynolds.* This is true, but not equally true for all organizations. Organizations vary in the extent to which they recognize the problem, ranging from deep denial to degrees of recognition and proactive commitment to providing opportunities to enable minorities to expand their contributions and

---

*The term "deep denial" was used by journalist Barbara Reynolds at the workforce diversity conference entitled "Breaking Down Racial Barriers in the Workplace: Successful Models for Diversity," sponsored by the School of Public Affairs, University of Maryland, College Park, Maryland, December 3, 1993.

advance. There is a long way to go and progress is inadequate, but some progress is being made.*

There is wide variation, too, in the views of minority workers on the source responsible for minority difficulties. In their caring, comprehensive handbook on career strategies for black women, *Work, Sister, Work,* Sydney and Leslie Shields identify "old school thinkers" and "new school thinkers," noting that the difference between them is "like the parting of the Red Sea."[3] Although referring specifically to black women, their categorization can probably be generalized. According to the authors, the old-school thinkers are people who ascribe their workplace difficulties to ways whites treat blacks. A lawyer made an illustrative comment: "When I think about being black in the workplace, I just don't think about being equal. I think invisible. Sometimes you see us, more often than not you don't....I'm a member of a race that nobody wants to know." A bank manager said, "It's hard to explain that you feel your color is preventing you from making it, especially when a company has Equal Opportunity signs posted everywhere.... No one seems to understand what I go through at work. If the organization emphasizes equality, I may work for the one person who makes me feel different. Mine becomes a private struggle, because I work for an institution that doesn't recognize that it has individuals who discriminate." And a marketing director: "I wish that nonminorities would understand that most of what bothers black people is our pride. We just want to be recognized. It hurts to be treated like an outsider."[4]

According to the Shields sisters, new-school thinkers (like conservative black thinkers) take the view that some of the barriers to success lie with blacks' attitudes and problems with black-black relations, and they advocate self-help. For example, a data processor commented, "It's not just whites that need the diversity training. We need it, too....I think whites need to learn how to understand blacks, but blacks also have to change their mindset. No one can question, there's racism. It's built into our society....However, our problems aren't all about laws, but miseducated individuals and our attitudes....We have to learn to create our own opportunities." And a bus driver observed, "I've seen a lot of discrimination in my time, but I can't blame all my failures on being black. Some things stemmed from my own attitudes. My point is that everything's not always a `them versus us' issue....Some of us are

---

*Telephone survey of organizations that value minorities undertaken by lawyer and minority rights activist Lawrence Otis Graham, entitled *The Best Companies for Minorities.*[2]

so hostile that people are afraid to approach us. Let's do each other a favor and unload some of our hostilities."[5]

In this chapter, we examine background issues that affect daily life on the job for many minority workers. We turn to practical workplace issues facing them.

Background Hindrances— It's Not a Level Playing Field

We believe no single factor accounts for the relative lack of minority success in the workplace. Discrimination is a major barrier. So are educationally and financially deprived backgrounds. And a fourth factor can also make minority entry and advancement difficult: attitudes. All of these factors are, to varying degrees, sources of minority underrepresentation in the workplace and reasons why their progress is inadequate. We discuss these hindrances here but do not try to assess the relative weight of each, which in any case varies from instance to instance.

Discrimination

Discrimination, one of the biggest barriers minorities face in the workplace, is not what it used to be. Workplace discrimination in any form is outlawed. Discrimination legislation is continually evolving, refining the circumstances under which legal protection is available.* As a result, certain forms of overt discrimination are much less common than they used to be. But, reality has not caught up with the law. Many forms of discrimination still disadvantage minority workers. Some forms are subtle and cannot be readily legislated in any case.

Two sources of discrimination impact minorities in organizations: individual and systemic or institutional. We examine these subsequently. We should stress that our focus is necessarily on white individual and institutional discrimination toward racial and ethnic minorities, but discrimination does not discriminate. Individuals from racial and ethnic minorities may also be practitioners. And some are.

---

*The course of antidiscrimination legislation fluctuates, both extending and cutting back legal protection available to job applicants and workers. A case in point is a June 1993 Supreme Court decision that made it harder to prove cases of subtle job discrimination. In a split decision, the high court ruled that a person claiming employment discrimination must not just prove an employee lied about a hiring or firing decision; an individual must prove that an employer intentionally discriminated.

Some minority people discriminate against each other, which is a subject discussed in the preceding chapter. Some also discriminate against white people. To be sure, these instances are few when compared with the magnitude of historic and contemporary white discrimination against minorities in the United States.* We need to remember that discrimination is not a one-way street, flowing only from power holders to the disenfranchised. It is even probable that if minorities widely held power, they too would discriminate to some extent against the outgroup. This is not meant to excuse any discrimination but rather to place our discussion in a realistic framework.

Discrimination and Us.   Discrimination by individuals is one reason for minority underrepresentation and lack of advancement in the workplace. It is also often a factor in interpersonal friction on the job. Supervisors sometimes cannot get past their own biases to hire, develop, or promote minority staff. Employees sometimes cannot readily work with peers from different racial and ethnic groups. Often, practitioners are unaware that they are discriminating. In all of its forms, discrimination involves negative behavior towards an individual or group. Harmful as discrimination is, some of it is rooted in normal psychological processes.

Discriminatory behavior is based on biases, that is, the attitudes that shape individual and organizational behaviors and policies. Biases or prejudices come in many forms. Like other attitudes, they can go so deep that we fail to recognize how they impact our behavior. A Washington-area banker recently acknowledged this when explaining why the Washington-area home loan process evolved into a system that regularly discriminates against minorities: "We all carry thousands of pieces of baggage or bias that we've built up over a lifetime— whether it's been taught or whether it's just been assimilated, whether it's about people with bow ties or people with bows and arrows."[6]

---

*However, racist acts committed by minorities have a high public profile these days. One reason is the presence of the electronic media. Network news was not around to televise the evils of slavery or the lynchings of blacks in the south and Mexicans in the southwest in the nineteenth and early part of the twentieth centuries. Nor was television on the spot to record beatings of Asians in the streets of San Francisco and elsewhere earlier in this century. Thus America's (white) collective memory tends to be truncated. (Americans are a notoriously ahistoric people anyway.) Most of us do remember, though, the highly publicized beating of black American Rodney King by Los Angeles police and, equally, the beating of white trucker Reginald Denny by angry blacks, as well as the killing in 1993 of passengers on a New York commuter train by a man inflamed by racial hatred and frustration. In 1993, the Southern Poverty Law Center, a civil rights group, reported a new trend toward black hate crimes; this reverses an historic pattern of the overwhelming prevalence of white-on-black crimes.

Among the most common sources of bias are stereotyping and the tendency to ascribe homogeneity to members of the outgroup. These are normal cognitive processes. We are less familiar with people who do not belong to our own group (ingroup), so we are less likely to recognize differences among them. What's more, by identifying traits we believe are common to a group, we create a framework in which to place our experience, thus enhancing our ability to make sense of the social world around us. This is stereotyping.

These normal processes can lead to bias. Bias occurs when we maintain false notions about other groups and when we apply notions, either accurate or false, to individuals without regard to their many unique characteristics. When we do so, we often fall unconsciously into bias. When we stereotype, we include new information consistent with our stereotype and exclude inconsistent information. For example, Doberman pinschers have a reputation for being mean dogs. We stereotype when we allow a story about a Doberman pinscher attacking a person to reinforce this impression while discounting a story about a Doberman pinscher who is a loyal pet ("yes, but their *real* nature is different").

Stereotypes applied to specific groups may change with historical circumstances, and they are perpetuated to justify exploitation. (The *content* of stereotypes, however, tends to be similar across groups. That is, certain characteristics repeatedly occur in stereotypes.) Shifting white stereotypes about American Indians is a case in point. During the revolutionary generation, American Indians were seen as symbols of freedom; hence, the rebels at the Boston Tea Party in 1773 wore Indian garb.* Later, as people began expanding across the continent and Indians became more active competitors for territory, whites viewed them as cruel and barbaric. "Removal" policies were implemented to eliminate Indians from the path of expansion. Once Indians were forced into life on reservations that crushed much of their traditional culture and robbed many of their self-esteem, the white stereotypic belief was that Indians were drunken and lazy.

Over history, white stereotypes about most American minority groups have been a mix of both positive and negative views. Black Americans are probably the exception. Organizational and diversity specialist John Fernandez notes that white stereotypes about blacks have rarely been positive. Observing that black Americans are the least-accepted minority and have suffered the most severe racism,

---

*The costumes were not primarily disguises—they did a poor job at that—they were a statement about liberty.

Fernandez attributes the consistently negative stereotypes to the legacy of slavery, their darker skin color, larger numbers than other minority groups, and the fact that black Americans are located throughout the country.[7] The continued perception of black Americans as a cheap labor pool contributes to stereotypic thinking in the workplace today.

In addition to the obvious damage inflicted by specific discriminatory circumstances, stereotyping can cause enduring psychological damage to its victims. Eminent black scholar and activist W. E. B. Du Bois discussed the burden blacks carry in terms of "double consciousness," always looking at themselves though the racially prejudiced eyes of others. Nonblacks cannot know firsthand a black person's experience as a target of stereotyping, but almost everyone these days, including white males, has been a target at some point.

We are all familiar with the pain of being judged on the basis of a few, often erroneous characteristics.* For some, that kind of experience and pain is ongoing. It creates anger and can stifle natural behavior. In the workplace, it erodes energy that could otherwise be channeled into productive work. Former *Washington Post* correspondent Jill Nelson knows what that feels like. Her perception is that she was a target of ongoing stereotyping. In her book about her four and a half years at the *Post*, she writes, "At work I'm treated like a great, big, intimidating Negress, so I spend half of my time trying to make myself nonthreatening, even though I'm not *really* threatening, so the Caucasians can deal with me—even though it's not *really* me they feel threatened by, it's their *image* of me."[8]

More subtle but just as serious is the harm people who stereotype do to themselves. Stereotyping limits one's understanding of reality. By stereotyping and engaging in other forms of discrimination, we allow only a filtered version of reality to penetrate our consciousness. Refusing to seeing others for who they are as individuals, we impoverish our lives, limit our experience, and deny ourselves information needed to make sound decisions. In effect, we discriminate against the quality of our own lives. To get by *richly*, we need to constantly work at understanding people on their own terms, not according to who we *think* they are. That means a willingness to stop imposing our own views and desires for control and to let things be.

---

*One instance (not the only one) experienced by one of the authors of this publication occurred when her car broke down on an interstate and she was picked up by another motorist who drove her to a service station. While grateful to the motorist, a marine on his way to base, for his concern and helpfulness, she experienced conflicting emotions over the way he clearly stereotyped her as "lady in distress"—weak, lacking in knowledge, and in some sort of imminent danger when he left her at the service station in the middle of the day to call AAA.

Just how prevalent are negative racial stereotypes is uncertain. The answer depends on which study is cited. According to one recent University of Chicago survey of racial attitudes, they are quite widespread: The survey found that three out of four white respondents believe black and Hispanic people are more likely than whites to be lazy, less intelligent, less patriotic, and more prone to violence.[9] Stereotypical views are reinforced by television, says George Gerbner of the University of Pennsylvania in a report for the American Federation of Television and Radio Artists and the Screen Actors Guild. Analyzing almost 20,000 screen parts for over 1,300 television shows, Gerbner found that parts for white males predominate, while blacks, Latinos, and immigrants are usually portrayed as victims.[10] Gender stereotypes are also common. Mature women are frequently shown as crazy or witches. In an action that speaks to Gerbner's findings, the internationally acclaimed children's program *Sesame Street*, after 25 years of a mostly male cast of characters, introduced its first major female character in 1993.

John Dovidio, psychologist and authority on racism, maintains that racial attitudes are improving. He cites a 1990 survey that shows only 4 percent of the white population describes blacks as lazy, but he also notes that most surveys and polls find 10 to 20 percent of whites still express overt bigotry.[11] A survey by the B'nai Brith Anti-Defamation League (ADL) adds mixed support for this view. A 1992 survey by the ADL found a drop of 9 percentage points in the size of the "most antisemitic" segment of the American population between 1964 and 1992, from 29 percent to 20 percent.[12] Moreover, a 1992 ADL audit reported an 8 percent drop in antisemitic incidents in 1992 over 1991 figures (1991 figures, however, represented an all-time high).[13] The ADL finding of a strong link between antisemitism and racism suggests that racism also may be declining.

On the other hand, people may just be learning to say the right thing and may even be unaware of their own racism. Dovidio maintains that a new, subtle form of bias, aversive racism, is prevalent. Unlike old-fashioned bigotry, aversive racism is unconscious. It is manifested by many white people who hold egalitarian convictions and truly believe they are not prejudiced but who simultaneously possess unconscious negative racial feelings from which they try to disassociate themselves. Because they do not wish to discriminate, aversive racists will not do so when their discrimination would be clear to themselves and others. This form of racism is expressed in ambivalent attitudes, sometimes biased and sometimes not. Dovidio explains, for instance, that, while negative attitudes against blacks are typically suppressed, aversive racists consistently value whites more highly than blacks. They express bias especially strongly toward higher status African Americans.[14] In organizations, aversive racism is most strongly reflected at higher status levels and probably helps account for minority underrepresentation in executive positions.

Different Perceptions of Racism.   If the subtlety of aversive racism makes it hard to deal with, so does the fact that different groups and individuals view discrimination differently. What is discrimination to one may not be so viewed by another. Different perceptions about what constitutes discrimination are predicated on varying assumptions about racism. Focusing on assumptions of black and white Americans, sociologist Robert Blauner of the University of California at Berkeley points out that blacks tend to view racism as central to the way American society is organized; white people do not.[15,16] Adding support to this view, philosopher Judith Lichtenberg of the University of Maryland observes that, while black Americans see race as a pervasive condition of American life, white people tend to be specific, believing that it refers to an "explicit, conscious belief in racial superiority."[17]

How these different assumptions play out in daily life might be seen in the 1993 Independence Day parade in Annapolis, Maryland. The two all-black, private groups of paraders were placed at the end of the parade, after several all-white, private groups and just before a final group of fire trucks. (The public groups of paraders, mainly military contingents, were racially integrated.) A white bystander holding the view described by Lichtenberg is likely to have assumed there was reasonable justification for placing the two all-black groups at the parade's end (luck of the draw, they registered last). He or she might also dismiss the racially segregated composition of many of the private groups as being simply "the way things are." Black bystanders, on the other hand, are more likely to have come away with painful reinforcement of their experience that blacks come last, that access to social groups is limited by race, and that social reality is asymmetrical, falling more heavily on blacks than whites.*

In the business environment, there has been another kind of divergence in views between groups, and the character of this divergence has not been static. Comparing his research findings over time, Fernandez points out that 1977 data showed that 46 percent of black males surveyed and 45 percent of white males perceived their *own* race

---

*It is tempting to speculate what a Fourth of July parade might be 50 years from now when almost half the population will consist of people from groups now considered minorities. A Fifth of July (1993) parade in Takoma Park, Maryland, celebrating diversity and the freedom to be different, may provide a clue.

to be a handicap to their career advancement. By the mid-1980s, perceptions had changed sharply: Data from his 1984–1985 research found that, among black males, perceptions of their race as a handicap rose to 65 percent, but only 27 percent of white males believed themselves handicapped by their own race. Fernandez comments that these findings parallel a decrease of racism in the 1970s and an upsurge in the 1980s.[18]

Organizational Factors.   The biases people bring to organizations, or that they brought in the past, tend to be institutionalized as policies, practices, and organizational culture. These have a life of their own and are the basis for systemic discrimination. Within such a system, even individuals who consider themselves unbiased may fall into discriminatory behavior. Fernandez remarks that organizational rules and procedures prestructure choice for people. Individuals do not have to make a choice, they just have to conform.[19] As sensitivity to the need to value workforce heterogeneity grows, many institutions are beginning to scrutinize their policies, practices, and culture for hidden bias. But change is hard and organizational inertia is powerful.

Despite the critical need for organizations to reduce discriminatory barriers, there is a paradoxical scantiness of research on the subject. Surveying published research on race in organizations between 1964 and 1989, scholars Taylor Cox, Jr., of the University of Michigan and Stella Nkomo of the University of North Carolina at Charlotte found relatively little research on the effects of racial diversity on organizational behavior in leading academic journals.[20] Most of the existing research focuses on black Americans; other minorities have been almost ignored. They also found that existing research is generally narrowly designed so that many gaps are left in our knowledge. Results of studies Cox and Nkomo surveyed showed very high percentages of race effects in many key areas. All of the studies addressing issues of compensation, labor relations, leadership, and power and influence found that race significantly impacted organizational behavior in some manner. (Note: these findings do not necessarily translate into racism but rather into "race effects"—a subtle but important difference.) Other topics in which 70 percent or more of the studies found race to be significant were job attitudes and satisfaction, hiring and promotion practices, and EEO/affirmative action. Career planning development, communication, motivation and needs values, perception, performance evaluation, and test evaluation were also identified as areas of significant race effects.

The DiTomaso-Thompson study took a different angle on the impact of race in organizations. Their study surveyed black and white managers at 218 top corporations. Respondents evaluated problems of minority managers in three areas: organizational issues, interpersonal relations, and preparation of minority managers. The study found that white and male managers were more optimistic about the lack of racial problems than minority and female managers. Overall, the 10 areas judged to be the greatest problems (in descending order) were insufficient number of qualified candidates, lack of other minorities to provide support, lack of role models, lack of promotion opportunities, lack of mentors, lack of company career planning, writing skills, educational preparation, lack of connections, and problems with ability to fit in.[21]

In the following sections, we examine these various issues, although we organize them differently.

Background Disadvantages. A background of deprivation is another roadblock to success for many minority workers. Segments of each minority group—but by no means all group members—come from an economically deprived background. Many interrelated factors contribute to this deprivation. Among them are historical and present-day discrimination and lack of job opportunities. Further, Hispanics and Asian Americans, whose combined numbers comprise about half of America's minority population, have large immigrant populations. Some 36 percent of Asian Americans and more than 12 percent of Hispanics immigrated legally to this country since 1980. More came illegally. Many of these immigrants are urban and rural poor searching for economic opportunity. With little money, low levels of education, and poor or nonexistent English-language skills, many newcomers arrive to face a future of struggle and deprivation.

Yet American history is sprinkled with examples of "Horatio Algers" who hurdled poverty to become financially successful. America's new Horatio Algers have names like Shanthi Jayasundera, Phoung Nguyen, and Ana De Avila. Many come from close, supportive families that help them surmount poverty and attain their goals. One refugee of Cambodian origin, who escaped the killing fields of Kampuchea with his family, observed that he has no hope of attaining financial success, but he is working hard (as a taxi driver) so his children will. Asian Americans have been particularly successful. In 1990, one-quarter of Asian-American households had incomes above $50,000 a year. Almost 10 percent had incomes over $75,000.[22]

But for all of those who escape their impoverished backgrounds, many do not. Despite the epithet "model minority" (decried by Asian analysts), 11 percent of Asian-American families live below the poverty line,[23] and they live in deplorable circumstances, according to Peter

Kwong of Hunter College.[24] The poverty rate for other minority groups is even greater. Twenty-one percent of black American households made less than $15,000 in 1992; only about 13 percent made more than $50,000 a year.[25] Figures for Hispanics fall between those of black Americans and Asian Americans: 15.5 percent with incomes of more than $50,000 in 1992; 16.5 percent under $15,000.[26] Comparable data is not available for Native Americans, but Bureau of Indian Affairs statistics suggest even higher levels of poverty.[27]

The situation is especially dire for black Americans whose representation in the underclass outstrips that of any other group, except possibly Native Americans. Many blacks are caught in a net of conditions that keep them in the underclass. These include fractured families, low education levels, inadequate job opportunities, a system that fosters dependence on welfare, black-on-black violence, extensive low self-esteem and hopelessness, inadequate government intervention, and, until very recently, a reluctance by black leaders to openly address the issues.

Family fragmentation is a central concern. Characterized as the "greatest impediment to black economic and social progress,"[28] black family fragmentation now results in four out of five black children being raised in single-parent families. Typically, these are families headed by a single mother. (The proportion of families headed by a single woman has more than doubled since 1950, rising to a total of 46 percent of all black families in 1991.[29]) Sixty-five percent of them are poor.[30] Extended families, which are traditional in black culture, help buffer the impact of the decaying marriage institution, but today even extended-family arrangements are breaking down.

William Julius Wilson points to a strong correlation between the declining rate of black marriages and the high rate of unemployment, incarceration, and mortality among black males.[31] *Newsweek* recently observed, "Fatherless homes boost the crime rate, lower educational attainment, and add dramatically to the welfare roles."[32] Fatherless homes also produce children who are being ill-prepared to compete in the workplace of the future. Wilson explains that in inner-city neighborhoods, "the chances are overwhelming that children will seldom interact on a sustained basis with people who are employed or with families that have a steady breadwinner."[33] Many young people grow up knowing only joblessness. They are isolated from the mainstream, lacking in job skills, and harboring a sense of alienation and hopelessness. Many are lured by glittering prospects of profits from illegal activities.

For poor, single mothers, many of them teenagers, holding a job may not be a reasonable option. Most receive greater benefits from welfare assistance than they could from a job. They do not have the skills required for higher-paying jobs that would enable them to support their families and pay for child day care. They are thus locked into welfare dependency, a widely debated dilemma that is the subject of a presidential reform initiative.

A related aspect of this multifaceted tragedy is the insufficient number of jobs in inner cities. As the national economy began to switch in the 1970s to a service base from a manufacturing base, central-city blacks lost jobs in large numbers. Newly created jobs were largely low-paying, white-collar jobs traditionally filled by women. Many black Americans, especially black males, were unqualified to obtain them. Between 1967 and 1990, the segment of black families with no earners nearly doubled, growing from about 10 percent to about 19 percent.[34] The number of earners per family fell as well: two-earner families declined from 42 to 36 percent, and families with three or more earners fell from 16 to 11 percent.[35]

Sociologist Kathryn Neckerman of Columbia University observes that entry-level clerical positions are "a critical avenue of opportunity for inner-city workers."[36] Neckerman states that even those who finish high school and go on to community college are hindered in the workplace by their blue-collar backgrounds. Entering a white-collar environment, they continue to hold working-class expectations about job strategies and advancement that are inimical to success. For example, blue-collar and low-level service positions tend to provide on-the-job training and relatively high starting pay. White-collar positions, on the other hand, typically involve training both on the job and in school. Initial pay is relatively low, and advancement is slower and typically requires learning the unwritten rules of organizational culture. Success in white-collar jobs involves acquiring higher-order language skills, too. This means compromising the racial and ethnic speech styles that workers grew up with and that are appropriate in blue-collar jobs. To advance, inner-city workers face the personal dilemma of forsaking an aspect of their identity. This dilemma is much less likely to occur with middle-class minority workers whose backgrounds foster expectations and skills consistent with white-collar employment.

Education. Insufficient education and workplace skills are a third critical factor that blocks advancement for many people belonging to minority racial and ethnic groups. Disadvantaged and outside the economic mainstream, many have not attained the education and skills needed to get ahead in the workplace. While the problem is not specific to people of color—many white Americans are similarly deprived—a greater portion of minority groups are educationally disadvantaged than are white Americans.

As we examine the comparative educational statistics, we need to remember that low minority achievement levels relative to white achievement provide a somewhat biased perspective: Based on averages, they do not take into account the many minority individuals with above-average attainment. Because the relatively poor minority showing is often cited as justification for minority underrepresentation at professional and management levels, it needs to be stressed that while the relative averages tend to be low, the numbers of highly qualified individuals belonging to minority groups are increasing.

Further, references to the low minority–white education ratio obscure the divergence that is occurring at advanced levels. Asian Americans are compiling a stunning record of achievement at higher educational levels. At many advanced levels, they are not just matching but also outdistancing white Americans in terms of percentages of degrees obtained. At the lower end of the educational ladder, however, the Asian-American profile resembles that of other minority groups: a greater percentage of Asian Americans are educationally disadvantaged than are white Americans.

Many minority individuals do not possess even basic literacy skills, and this has direct bearing on the workplace. Poor literacy skills not only block advancement at work, they also cause unacceptably high business losses. American businesses are reported to lose an estimated $25 to $30 billion a year as a result of errors traceable to workers' limited literacy.[37]

A recent study of adult literacy for the Department of Education shows that about half of all American adults (16 years and older) do not know English well enough to summarize information they have read in a newspaper article, nor can they locate and compute numbers to complete a catalogue order form for supplies.[38] The National Adult Literacy Survey (NALS) tested for literacy skills needed in the workplace, including reading comprehension, filling out documents, and performing simple arithmetic problems. It found that adults belonging to racial and ethnic minority groups—black Americans, Hispanics, Asian Americans, and American Indians—are more likely than white adults to perform at low literacy levels.

Based on the NALS scales, the national average proficiency in prose literacy is 272; in document literacy, the figure is 267; average quantitative proficiency is 271. Minority groups fell below this average in every category while white adults scored above the average, as shown in Figure 8-1. American Indians scored highest overall among the minority groups in the first two categories; Asians and Pacific Islanders scored highest among minority groups in the quantitative category. Hispanic adults had the lowest overall average proficiency

Figure 8-1. Average Literacy Proficiencies by Race and Ethnicity

Literacy category	National	Black	Hispanic	Asian/ Pacific Islander	American Indian	White
Prose	272	237	220	242	254	286
Document	267	230	218	245	254	280
Quantitative	271	234	217	256	250	287

SOURCE: Irwin S. Kirsch, Ann Jungeblut, Lynn Jenkins, and Andrew Kolstad, *Adult Literacy in America: A First Look at the Results of the National Adult Literacy Survey*, National Center for Education Statistics, Department of Education (Washington, D.C.: U.S. GPO, September 1993), pp. 17, 33.

levels, followed by black adults. Breaking down each literacy category into five levels of proficiency, the NALS found that a larger percentage of adults belonging to minority groups are at the bottom and a smaller percentage are at the top of literacy proficiency levels than white adults.

One reason for high limited literacy rates among people of color is the large number of immigrant adults whose first language is not English. The NALS found that for almost every racial and ethnic minority group, American-born persons had higher English-language literacy proficiency rates than foreign-born persons. This is not surprising. But what is disturbing is that black adults are an exception: American-born black adults performed about equally with foreign-born black adults.

There is a strong correlation between literacy and education levels. The NALS found that adults performing at low literacy levels were likely to have relatively few years of formal education. Like the literacy figures, educational attainment statistics show that minority groups generally have lower attainment records than white persons. In 1990, almost 20 percent of the total workforce did not have a high school diploma (see Figure 8-2), and a portion of this group did not complete primary school. Of workers with less than a high school education, almost 40 percent are minority persons, although people of color form only about 20 percent of the labor force. Hispanics, who represent about 8 percent of the labor force, constitute almost 20 percent of the workers who did not complete a high school education. The high school noncompletion rate for black workers was also greater than their representation in the workforce: black workers form over 10 percent of the workforce, but black workers without a high school degree form almost 15 percent of the total who did not complete high school. Similarly, the high school noncompletion rate for American Indians is half again their share of the total: American Indians form 0.6 percent of

Figure 8-2. Educational Attainment of the Civilian Labor Force, by Percentage of Educational Category, 1990
(In thousands)

Educational category	All Groups Number	%	Hispanic* %	White %	Black %	Amer. Indian %	Asian or Pacific Is. %
All categories	123388	100	8.1	78.0	10.4	0.6	2.8
Not high school graduate	22611	18.3	19.7	61.9	14.8	0.9	2.6
High school graduate	36700	29.7	6.5	80.2	11.0	0.7	1.7
Some college or associate degree	36350	29.5	6.2	80.2	10.4	0.7	2.6
Bachelor's degree	18144	14.7	3.4	85.4	6.3	0.3	4.6
Graduate or professional degree	9579	7.7	3.3	85.4	5.6	0.3	5.3

*Hispanic may include persons of any race.

SOURCE: U.S. Department of Commerce, Economics and Statistics Administration, Bureau of the Census, *1990 Census of Population, Supplementary Reports, Detailed Occupation and Other Characteristics from the EEO File for the United States,* 1990 CP-S-1-1 (Washington, D.C.: U.S. GPO, 1992), p. 20, Table 3.

all workers, but their high school noncompletion rate is 0.9 percent. Asians and Pacific Islanders are the only minority group whose high school noncompletion rate is just about equal to (actually slightly less than) their representation in the labor force.

The magnitude of the high school noncompletion rate for Hispanics is partly due to the large number of adult immigrants who had not completed their high school, and sometimes primary school, education when they emigrated to this country. Such people are not necessarily dropouts from the American system.[39] The Asian-American population, too, has a high portion of adult immigrants who arrived in this country with inadequate education and little or no English language skills. Yet, at the upper levels of literacy proficiency and educational attainment, Asian Americans are distinguished by remarkable gains, as discussed subsequently.

Black Americans face a different situation. For generations, they had no access to educational opportunities. Under slavery, it was illegal for slaves to receive an education, even to learn to read and write. Although slavery was abolished over five generations ago, its consequences and the denial of *equal* educational opportunity in subsequent generations continue to take a devastating toll.* Since the days of slavery, black Americans have made significant gains in education: In 1860, only 2 percent of black children were enrolled in school; by 1930,

---

*The authors are grateful to Dr. Elizabeth Lambert Johns and Dr. Morton Leeds for their insights on this subject.

60 percent were enrolled. In 1940, the median years of schooling for blacks was 5.7 years; in 1991, it was 12.7 years—close to the figure for whites (12.9).[40,41] Yet de facto if not de jure inequality in education remains. Also remaining are psychological and cultural barriers created by a history of societal neglect and abuse.*

Native Americans faced still a different set of circumstances. An inferior educational system was imposed upon them, which ensured that they could not participate as equals in the broader society—though, to be sure, for years a large portion of the Indian population did not wish to participate. The educational system also attempted to eliminate tribal culture, thus depriving them of their heritage. In the nineteenth century, the federal government began establishing boarding schools for Indian children on reservations, taking them away from their parents (abducting them on occasion) on the grounds that they could be better controlled that way.[43] The schools forbade the use of native languages or the practice of any native traditions. The curriculum was generally inferior to that in public primary schools in urban areas, where education was geared to readying students for high school. Because high schools were located mainly in urban areas, not on reservations, and attendance meant moving from reservations, and because most students were not prepared academically for a secondary school education, only a small portion went on to high school during much of this century. At present, a growing number of high schools have been established on rural reservations, as have a small number of tribal colleges. Also growing are the numbers of Indians enrolled in public and private four-year colleges off the reservations. About 7 percent of the population had bachelor's degrees in 1990 and over 3 percent had graduate or professional degrees (see Figure 8-3). Despite these gains, American Indians confront the barrier of a legacy of inferior education, a legacy that hinders their ability to respond readily to the rising requirements of the workplace.

At higher educational levels, too, most minority groups are underrepresented in terms of their share of the workforce, while white Americans are marginally to significantly overrepresented. At every educational level above high school, Hispanic and black workers are underrepresented. American Indian workers are marginally overrepresented at the associate and bachelor's degree level and underrepresented for higher degrees. Asian Americans are a stunning exception. They are overrepresented at all advanced levels, except the associate level.

---

*For an analysis of historical and current factors, see Farley and Allen.[42]

Figure 8-3. Educational Attainment of the Civilian Labor Force, by Percentage of Racial/Ethnic Group, 1990*

				Not of Hispanic origin	
Educational category	Hispanic†	White	Black	Amer. Indian	Asian or Pacific Is.
Not high school graduate	44.5%	14.5%	26.1%	26.4%	16.8%
High school graduate	23.7	30.6	31.3	32.1	18.1
Some college or associate degree	22.5	30.3	29.4	31.1	26.5
Bachelor's degree	6.1	16.1	8.9	6.8	23.9
Graduate or professional degree	3.2	8.5	4.2	3.4	14.6

*Civilian labor force is 16 years and over.
†Hispanic may include persons of any race.
SOURCE: U.S. Department of Commerce, Economics and Statistics Administration, Bureau of the Census, *1990 Census of Population, Supplementary Reports, Detailed Occupation and Other Characteristics from the EEO File for the United States*, 1990 CP-S-1-1 (Washington, D.C.: U.S. GPO, 1992), p. 20, Table 3.

At the level of graduate or professional degree, which are generally prerequisite to professional and managerial positions, 1990 figures show that Hispanics have an attainment rate of 3.3 percent; blacks, 5.6 percent; and American Indians, 0.3 percent—well below their labor force representation. White attainment of 85 percent and Asian attainment of over 5 percent at these level are well above their representation levels.

Because the quality of education differs widely from institution to institution, the reality may be worse than the numbers indicate. Groups with low *quantities* of education also tend to receive lower *quality* educations.[44] This varies, but it is clearly seen in secondary schools, where a two-tier system provides unequal education to our nation's youngsters. Middle-class parents—those from racial and ethnic minorities as well as white parents—are increasingly sending their children to private schools. Public school enrollment is shrinking along with budgets and often, though not invariably, educational standards. At the same time, the portion of minority students in public schools is increasing. According to a recent survey of the 47 largest American cities, three-quarters of the students in public schools are members of minority groups.[45] A 1993 study conducted by Harvard University for the Department of Education found that, for the first time since the 1954 Supreme Court decision on school desegregation, progress toward integration is reversing. Nationwide, some 70 percent of black and Hispanic students are now in schools with a predominantly minority enrollment.[46]

What's more, for many students, a public high school diploma does not mean that a student is college-ready. In Virginia alone, a quarter of all 1992 high school graduates who went on to state colleges had to enroll in remedial courses in reading, English, and mathematics.[47] A Virginia Department of Education spokesman commented, "A standard [high school] diploma in Virginia means you have warmed a seat for a requisite number of years....It doesn't show that you can do very much of anything."[48] The implications for the workforce are devastating.

A gloomy picture for most minority groups also emerges from an examination of educational attainment within each group. As Figure 8-3 shows, the scale is bottom-heavy for most minorities. Forty-five percent of Hispanic workers are not high school graduates; 26 percent of blacks and American Indians are in the same category. At the upper reaches of the scale, only 9 percent of Hispanic workers have bachelor, graduate, or professional degrees. Ten percent of American-Indian workers hold these degrees, and 13 percent of black workers do.

These figures contrast sharply with the Asian-American record. Asian Americans are the only group to outstrip white workers in any educational category. A whopping 38 percent of Asian-American workers have bachelor, graduate, or professional degrees—13 points higher than the figure for white workers. At the lower end of the scale (noncompletion of high school), the Asian-American record is only 2 points worse than that for white workers.

The stunning educational achievements of Asian Americans have helped fuel the myth that Asians are smarter than others. A more realistic explanation may be rooted partly in cultural factors. Though it is hard to generalize about cultures, three of the largest Asian-American groups—Chinese, Japanese, and Korean Americans—derive from a Confucian cultural tradition, which reveres learning, sanctions strong family and group support for scholars, and instills strict discipline.* To the extent that Asian Americans, whether from a Confucian or any other cultural tradition, hold such values, they are strongly motivated to excel in education.

The educational picture for other minorities has a brighter side too. A comparison of higher degrees awarded in 1980–1981 and 1990–1991 in the entire population shows that the number of minority advanced degree holders increased by almost 55,000, and their share increased a significant 21 points over the same period. Please see Figure 8-4.

---

*Chinese culture is an example. Learning has always been prized in China. An elaborate, government-sponsored examination system was an important avenue for advancement into positions of prestige and power in China for more than 1,000 years, and in later dynasties the mandarin class consisted of individuals known as "scholar gentry." Although the traditional system has disappeared, many of its values are still deeply ingrained. And even today Chinese children learn strict discipline from the moment they are born.[49]

Figure 8-4. Distribution of Bachelor's, Master's, Doctorate, First Professional Degrees, 1980–1981 and 1990–1991*
(In thousands)

| Period | Total no. | Hispanic† | | White | | Black | | Amer. Indian | | Asian or Pacific Is. | |
		No.	%	No.	%	No.	%	No.	%	No.	%
1980–1981	1333.2	29.8	2.2	1139.0	85.4	82.0	6.2	4.6	0.3	27.6	2.1
1990–1991	1519.9	48.2	3.2	1245.0	81.9	86.2	5.7	6.0	0.4	58.1	3.8

*Percentages do not total 100 percent because nonresident aliens are not included as a separate category but degrees awarded to them are counted in the total.
†Hispanic may include persons of any race.
SOURCE: National Center for Education Statistics, Office of Educational Research and Improvement, U.S. Department of Education, *Race/Ethnicity Trends in Degrees Conferred by Institutions of Higher Education: 1980–81 through 1989–90*, E.D. Tabs, NCES 92-039 (Washington, D.C.: U.S. GPO, May 1992), p. 8; and *Race/Ethnicity Trends in Degrees Conferred by Institutions of Higher Education: 1984–85 through 1990–91*, E.D. Tabs, NCES 93-356 (Washington, D.C.: U.S. GPO, August 1992), pp. 8–9.

(Degrees include bachelor's, master's, doctoral, and first professional.) White Americans still account for the lion's share of advanced degrees—almost 82 percent in 1990–1991, although their share is falling. Asian Americans made the most impressive gains. The number of degree recipients rose by more than 30,000, and their share of the total grew 3.8 percentage points. The percentage of Asian-American advanced degree holders exceeds their share of the total population. (They represent about 3 percent of the total.) The Hispanic percentage increased by 1 point, and the American Indian share rose marginally; both groups increased their number of degree recipients.

The trends for black Americans are more complex. About 4,000 more black Americans received advanced degrees in 1990–1991 than a decade earlier. As a percentage of the total, however, there was a marginal decline (less than one percentage point). But the 1990–1991 figures do not tell the full story. During the 1980s, black Americans lost both in numbers of advanced degrees awarded and in share of the whole. (In 1989–1990, they received about 81,000 advanced degrees, representing 5.5 percent of the whole.) The 1990–1991 figures thus represent a reversal of the decline. While more blacks are getting degrees, it appears that the proportion of black men who are attending college is dropping. A recent study by the American Council on Education finds that between 1990 and 1992 there was a 5 percentage point drop in the number of black men who have graduated from high school and are attending college.[50]

Because candidates for management and professional positions typically are recruited from the pool of individuals with scientific and technical fields of specialization, especially at the master's level, an examination of the racial and ethnic composition of degree recipients provides insight into how many minority group members are in the pipeline for managerial jobs. Comparing master's degree recipients over a nine-year period, Figure 8-5 indicates that people of color made some significant gains. Asian Americans increased their share of degree holdings in every category. In computer and information sciences their share rose over 4 points! Hispanics and Native Americans increased their share in all but one category. And although black Americans received fewer advanced degrees overall, at the master's level, they increased their share in all but two of the categories. In business and management, black Americans increased their share almost a full percentage point, and their increase in computer and information sciences was 1 point.

The minority educational lag affects far more than the personal lives of unskilled and underskilled minority group members. It is also a critical national concern. New, global economic forces are creating new requirements in the American workplace. If the United States is to

Figure 8-5. Percent Distribution of Master's Degrees in Selected Fields of Study, 1980–1981 and 1989–1990*

Period	Total no., thousands	Hispanic[†] %	Not of Hispanic origin			
			White %	Black %	Amer. Indian %	Asian or Pacific Is. %
1980–1981						
Business & management	57.5	1.5	82.6	4.1	0.2	2.8
Computer & information sciences	4.1	1.5	68.7	1.7	0.3	6.8
Engineering & related technologies	16.4	1.7	61.9	1.6	0.2	6.6
Life sciences	6.0	1.1	86.8	2.9	0.3	2.4
Mathematics	2.6	1.5	72.7	2.6	0.3	3.7
Physical sciences	5.2	1.0	79.1	2.0	0.2	2.9
1989–1990						
Business & management	77.2	2.1	79.0	4.3	1.0	3.9
Computer & information sciences	9.6	1.9	56.6	2.7	0[‡]	10.9
Engineering & related technologies	24.8	1.8	57.8	1.8	0.2	8.1
Life sciences	4.9	1.9	74.9	2.3	0.3	4.8
Mathematics	3.7	1.3	62.0	2.0	0.2	5.2
Physical sciences	5.5	1.5	66.2	1.7	0.2	4.5

*Percentages do not total 100 percent because nonresident aliens are not included as a separate category but degrees awarded to them are counted in the total.
†Hispanics may be of any race.
‡Numbers less than 0.05 are rounded to 0.

SOURCE: National Center for Education Statistics, Office of Educational Research and Improvement, U.S. Department of Education, *Race/Ethnicity Trends in Degrees Conferred by Institutions of Higher Education: 1980–81 through 1989–90*, E.D. Tabs, NCES 92-039 (Washington, D.C.: U.S. GPO, May 1992), pp. 19–21, Table 6.

remain competitive internationally, the workforce must acquire a higher-level mix of skills—more conceptual, personal management, and interpersonal skills.* At the lower end of the skill ladder, there is a growing need for workers to adapt to a changing variety of products and situations, instead of focusing solely on narrow, repetitive tasks. This requires at minimum a solid foundation in reading, writing, and computational skills, as well as the capacity to learn, solve problems, and be creative. Even most unskilled jobs nowadays require functional literacy and other basic skills. At higher-level jobs, advanced educational attainment is required. For management and professional positions, a college degree is almost invariably prerequisite.

Discussing another dimension in the upskilling of the labor force, Lawrence Mishel and Ruy A. Teixeira of the Economic Policy Institute in Washington, D.C., point to the "abysmal inferiority" of the cognitive skills that American workers possess relative to their counterparts among America's economic competitors. Mishel and Teixeira assert that, to remain competitive, American workers need to sharpen skills they already possess. This needs to be done through improving the content of American educational and training programs.[52]

No one is certain just what the need will be for advanced education in the years ahead. According to some studies, no more than 30 percent of the labor force will require college degrees by the year 2000.[53] But whatever the portion, no one disputes that the overall skill level required on the job is shifting upwards and that America is not keeping pace.

Attitudes.   No one wants to be told they have an "attitude" or a "'tude," to use current lingo—least of all someone who, in fact, has a 'tude. Yet it is true that some minority workers impede their own progress by expressing negativism toward the white organizational power structure, supervisors, and peers. It is also true that white workers and organizations have 'tudes, too. "Having an attitude" is partly a matter of definition—and of who is doing the defining. Because our focus is on issues facing minority workers, our discussion centers mainly on attitudes in relation to them. But we do not mean to imply that minority workers are the only ones who need to accommodate to the work environment. The premise of this book is that valuing diversity is a reciprocal process. Organizations and workers, be they people of color or white, need to learn to value each other. That means that all must become more aware of their attitudes toward difference through self-exploration of their assumptions. When this does not occur, all parties pay a price, but

---

*For a survey of the new skills, see Carnevale, Gainer, Meltzer, and Holland, "Skills Employers Want," *Training and Development*.[51]

minority workers may pay the highest price. For they are typically the disempowered (as are, in varying degrees, women and members of other "new" identity groups), theirs are the options that are truncated, and they are the ones who are likely to feel most keenly the stress of culture clashes within organizations.

How one responds to discrimination at work and elsewhere may depend largely on the identity development process. Views of self, members of one's identity group, other minority groups, and the dominant culture vary according to where one is in the process. Cross-cultural experts and others have proposed identity development models that define the process in regard to specific racial and ethnic groups, including white people. And some have developed generalized models, applicable to all people of color in the United States.

According to Donald R. Atkinson, George Morten, and Derald Wing Sue, their Minority Identity Development (MID) model can be applied to all minority individuals based on their common experience with oppression.[54] The MID is a five-stage paradigm of minority attitudes and behavior with regard to self, fellow group members, other minorities, and the dominant group. In stage one, the conformity stage, an individual's reactions are characterized by a preference for dominant cultural values over one's own culture. The individual tends to be depreciative of himself or herself and fellow group members, discriminatory toward other minority groups, and appreciative of the dominant group. In the second stage, dissonance, there is confusion, conflict, and questioning of the conformity stage. Appreciation for self and one's group vies with attitudes of depreciation. Similar conflict exists in attitudes toward other people of color and the dominant group, the latter of which is regarded with new suspicion. The third stage, resistance and immersion, is characterized by complete endorsement of self and others in one's group, a growing sense of solidarity with other minorities, and a depreciating attitude toward the dominant culture. In the introspection stage, there is greater individual autonomy and the growing evaluation of the rigid attitudes in the previous stage. The fifth stage, synergetic articulation and awareness, is defined by a sense of self-fulfillment concerning cultural identity. With conflicts resolved, the individual has a sense of self and group worth and an appreciating attitude toward other minority groups. The attitude toward the dominant group is one of selective appreciation. The authors observe that all of the stages are not experienced by all minority individuals.

Derald Wing Sue and David Sue caution that because the identification development process is dynamic, the various stages are a framework for understanding, not fixed entities. Moreover, the stages are not linear: while one characteristic may dominate, there may also be a mixture of characteristics from different stages.[55]

The identity formation process functions with regard to white people, too. Though less research has been done on this subject, some models of white identity development have been constructed. These models define stages similar to the MID and share some of the same assumptions. All of the models of white identity development assume that racism is basic to American life and that whites acquire certain biases through the standard socialization process. These models also assume that there is an identifiable series of sequential stages that whites pass through to achieve their racial identity.

As with the MID, the stage of a white individual's identity development affects any interracial relationship. And the stage most likely to result in a successful relationship is one where the white person accepts his or her whiteness and defines it in a nondefensive, nonracist way.[56]

Floyd Dickens, Jr., and Jacqueline B. Dickens present a more specific model focusing on attitude changes successful black managers experience when working in predominantly white institutions. Acknowledging that all managers undergo challenges competing for top jobs, they state that black managers have a special set. Dickens and Dickens maintain that special behavioral processes, occurring in four stages, are experienced by successful minority managers.[57] The entry phase is characterized by uncertainty about one's direction. Anger at racial inequities is repressed and discomfort with the job is ignored. Second, in the adjusting phase, anger and frustration grow and are more often expressed in reaction to favored treatment received by white peers. This phase is a crossroads where successful managers, realizing the futility of continuing their debilitating behavior, decide to move on to more productive modes. In the third phase, planned growth, rage is largely controlled and career goals are established. Finally, in the success stage, the manager has learned to use the system skillfully and produces high-quality work. Basic career goals are met and confidence grows, and new, harder goals are established. While the authors focus on black managers, they maintain that their schema is applicable to other minorities, too.

Another, interrelated way to understand minority attitudes at work is in terms of the response to an Anglo-dominated organizational culture. There appear to be four options: separation, assimilation, compartmentalization, and integration. Separation means insistence on one's own values and rejection of organizational values. Assimilation involves adopting organizational values and forfeiting one's own. Employees who compartmentalize draw a rigid line between behaviors at work, where they practice organizational values, and elsewhere, where they maintain their own. The fourth option is integration, which means learning to use the organizational style and values while maintaining one's own identity.

The first approach is a recipe for disaster on the job, though it may bring a measure of personal satisfaction. The second may bring success, but at a heavy personal price. The third, biculturality, may also bring success but requires fragmenting one's behavior.* A more unitive option is the fourth: integration. Employees who learn to integrate into the organization fit their own style into that of the organization. This allows them to be successful as well as enables them to live peacefully with themselves without switching regularly between value systems.

From this brief discussion, it should be clear that attitudes at work— whether appreciating or depreciating—are deeply rooted in the personality and that, over time, a minority individual may evolve in his or her reactions to other workers, groups, and the organization. This process is long term. It cannot be forced. Workers, however, need to succeed in the short term first. And their efforts to do so can be undermined by a negative attitude.

Negativity on the job is dangerous. Authors Sydney and Leslie Shields count it among "fatal actions" at work. Addressing black women workers, they observe, "Some of us let our lips hang so low you could almost step on them, or give you looks that say, `I dare you to speak to me.' Other women walk around the office as if they're mad at the world."[59] In fact, some are. Many minority workers—not just black women—bring hostility with them when they walk through the door. This may be particularly true of working-class and underclass employees from the inner cities, who have been isolated from the mainstream. The workplace cannot be separated from the rest of life, and, as one black working-class employee we interviewed observed, many people from the inner cities live with "an ocean of anger in their communities and homes." Attitudes bred during a lifetime of isolation and exposure to degradation, fear, or violence cannot be shed on weekdays from 9 to 5, even in the most supportive workplace.

For some people, possibly the best that can be achieved in the short term is to repress anger and other negative attitudes at work while becoming aware that other, more positive emotional reactions are possible. The Shields sisters advise black women workers to not wear their feelings on their sleeves. "Choose the time and place to air your grievances. While you're at it, treat your black and white coworkers with the same respect. No one wants to work with someone who's unapproachable. So, learn how to control your emotions."[60]

On a day-to-day basis, experienced minority workers adopt a range of

---

*For a study of compartmentalization among black women, see Bell, "Bicultural Life Experience of Career-Oriented Black Women," *Journal of Organizational Behavior.*[58]

attitudes, but they seem to agree that positive behaviors are critical. In their well-regarded book, *Black Life in Corporate America,* George Davis and Glegg Watson interview a black manager who says that although she is very conscious of her race, she tries hard "never to say that anything that happens to me occurs because I am a woman or because I am black."[61] A black male manager cautions, "Race does not enter the picture during day-to-day interactions with people on matters that are basically colorless. When promotion time comes, when assignment time comes, when evaluation time comes, that is when you have to be aware."[62]

Ernest Chu, vice president of finance at an east coast firm, maintains that "every minority person must come to terms with who he or she is." He asserts that one must not use "one's minority status as a crutch or to focus constantly on discrimination...[but] concentrate on what is positive in your minority culture and to try to use these differences to your advantage, at the same time finding out what you need to do to get ahead despite potentially closed doors."[63]

A sense of humor is also important. Yolanda T. Moses, anthropologist and vice president for academic affairs at California State University–Dominguez Hills, stresses that in view of the special pressures minorities face, they "must develop a sense of humor because it helps them maintain confidence in their own expertise."[64]

Hector Juan Montes, vice president at an investment firm, asserts that, in maintaining their own identities within an organization, minority managers need to respect themselves and their heritage. He provides a few personal examples: On appropriate occasions, he speaks Spanish at work because "it helps me remember my roots, and it provides a symbol to those around me that I have a heritage that may be distinct from theirs."[65] He also occasionally wears cowboy boots in his New York firm, acknowledging that this deviates from the norm but is within the bounds of appropriate behavior because he travels often to the southwest.

Issues on the Job

Minority Representation— and the Lack of It

Members of racial and ethnic minority groups accounted for about 20 percent of the labor force in 1990 and their share is growing. By 2005, they will be almost 30 percent of the total. Among minority workers, black Americans accounted for the largest share in 1990: 10.4 percent of the workforce. Hispanics were next with 8.1 percent; Asians and Pacific Islanders, 2.8 percent; and American Indians, 0.6 percent.[66]

Hiring. The legal ban on workplace discrimination has greatly reduced access discrimination. A large portion of new jobs is going to minority workers. In the Washington, D.C., area alone, three-quarters of the almost 600,000 new jobs went to women and minority group members between 1980 to 1990. According to a recent report, gains made by women in high-skill jobs in the Washington area were greater than minority gains. Minorities, especially black Americans and Hispanics, are overrepresented in service and lower-paying jobs.[67] This pattern prevails in many urban areas.

There is evidence, however, that minority candidates sometimes still have trouble getting through the workplace door. A 1991 study by the Urban Institute showed that in 20 percent of the tries, a white applicant advanced further in the effort to get an entry-level job than an equally qualified black applicant.[68] Similar results were found in an earlier Urban Institute study. Reporting in 1990 on pairs of white and minority (black and Hispanic) applicants who were sent to job sites, the Urban Institute found that blacks in Washington faced a 23 percent chance of being denied employment opportunities; in Chicago, they faced a 17 percent chance of denial.[69]

There are other indicators, too, that barriers to minority hiring still exist. For example, a recent *Wall Street Journal* report indicates that black employees gained a disproportionately low share of jobs during the 1990–1991 recession. Surveying the more than 35,000 companies reporting to the Equal Employment Opportunity Commission (EEOC), the *Journal* found that black Americans gained only 11.4 percent of the jobs at organizations that were adding jobs during the recession, but they lost an even greater share.[70]

These studies are by no means comprehensive, but they do suggest that optimism about the elimination of access discrimination is unwarranted.

Firing. Once they are hired, minorities may not hold onto their jobs as long as white workers. That is what happened during the economic recession of the early 1990s. In an analysis of data from the more than 35,000 EEOC companies, the *Wall Street Journal* produced dramatic findings. Black Americans were the *only* racial and ethnic group to suffer a net job loss. After having maintained their share of corporate jobs for nine years, blacks lost more than 59,400 jobs during 1990–1991. Asians, Latinos, and whites, on the other hand, each *gained* more than 40,000 jobs during the same period, with whites gaining most.[71] African Americans suffered net losses in six of nine industry categories, with deepest cuts in blue-collar jobs where they lost almost one-third of their jobs. (Blacks gained, as did all other groups, in the high-end occupations of managers, professionals, and technicians, but the *Journal* notes that, because their share in these occupations was so small, their gains were meager.)

Black losses occurred in companies that were downsizing as well as in those adding jobs, where black net gains were much lower than those of other groups. At Dial Corporation, blacks represented 26.3 percent of the workforce, but they lost 43.6 percent of the jobs eliminated. At Coca Cola Enterprises, 42.6 percent of jobs cut were held by blacks, though they formed only 17.9 percent of the workforce. And Sears Roebuck initially reported the black job loss at 54.3 percent of the total, but later, claiming statistical error, they reduced the figure to 20 percent. (African Americans constituted 15.9 percent of the Sears workforce.)

Many companies claim the disproportionate black job loss was a fluke, the result of corporate downsizing during the recessionary period. However, civil rights advocates conclude that racism was a factor. Other factors include the ongoing decline in blue-collar jobs, where African Americans are heavily concentrated, and the seniority rule of "last hired, first fired," which unions enforce.

A disparity in discharge rates also exists between minority and white dismissals in the federal government. According to data recently released by the Office of Personnel Management (OPM), minority workers were fired at almost three times the rate of white workers in fiscal 1992.[72] The OPM found that minority workers were fired at the rate of 10.2 per 1,000 employees; the white rate was 3.7 per 1,000 employees. Differences in the firing rate occurred across all pay grades, with the greatest disparities being at lower levels, including clerical workers. Although minorities comprised 28 percent of the federal civilian workforce of about 2.2 million people, they accounted for 52 percent of dismissals.

Concentration Patterns.   Minority workers tend to be concentrated at the lower organizational levels. This pattern gives rise to the skeptical view that diversity is an issue concerning the bottom rungs of organizational ladders. We show elsewhere that diversity in fact affects the *entire* organization in important ways. Nonetheless, it is true that minorities are acutely underrepresented in many higher-level positions.

Census data for 1990 shows that minority representation is lower in higher-level occupations and greater in lower-level occupations. In 1990, white representation (percentage of the white workforce) in executive, administrative, and management (EAM) positions was half again as great as overall minority representation. Whites were over one-and-a-third times more likely to have professional occupations than people of color. (See Figure 8-6.) While overall minority and

Figure 8-6. Patterns of Racial Concentration in Selected Occupations, 1990
(Percentage of each group's workforce)

Occupation	White	Black	Hispanic	Amer. Indian	Asian or Pacific Is.
Executive, administrative, & managerial	13.1	7.0	6.5	7.9	12.3
Administrators & officials, public administration	0.4	0.5	0.2	0.6	0.3
Financial managers	0.6	0.2	2.0	0.2	0.6
Managers, marketing, advertising, & public relations	0.6	0.1	0.2	0.2	0.3
Professional specialty occupations	14.6	9.5	6.6	9.0	17.7
Engineers, architects, & surveyors	1.7	0.5	0.6	0.7	3.7
Mathematical & computer scientists	0.7	0.4	0.3	0.3	1.4
Teachers, except postsecondary	4.0	3.4	2.0	2.9	1.9
Social, recreation, & religious workers	0.9	1.3	0.6	1.2	0.6
Technicians & related support occupations	3.7	3.0	3.2	2.9	6.0
Sales occupations	12.5	7.9	8.9	8.5	11.7
Supervisors & proprietors, sales occupations	2.7	1.2	1.6	1.4	2.3
Administrative support occupations, including clerical	16.0	17.6	13.8	13.9	15.1
Supervisors, administrative support occupations	0.8	0.9	0.6	0.3	0.6
Secretaries, stenographers & typists	4.1	3.3	2.7	3.3	2.4
Service—private household occupations	0.3	1.1	1.3	0.5	0.4
Cleaners & servants	0.1	0.9	0.9	0.3	0.2
Service occupations, except protective and private household	9.7	18.3	16.0	15.7	13.5
Precision production, craft, and repair occupations	11.8	8.0	12.9	13.7	7.9
Supervisors, mechanics, and repairers	0.2	0.2	0.1	0.2	0.1
Supervisors, construction occupations	0.8	0.3	0.5	0.7	0.2
Machine operators, assemblers, & inspectors	6.1	9.6	11.7	8.2	7.9
Handlers, equipment cleaners, helper's, & laborers	3.8	6.0	7.0	6.4	2.7

SOURCE: U.S. Department of Commerce, Bureau of the Census, 1990 Census of Population, Supplementary Reports, *Detailed Occupation and Other Characteristics from the EEO File for the United States,* 1990 CP-S-1-1 (Washington, D.C.: U.S. GPO, 1992), Table 1.

white representation in technician and related support occupations were equal, in sales occupations the figure for whites was more than one-and-a-third times greater than the minority average. At the lower end of the skill level, people of color were three-and-a-half times more likely than whites to be employed in overall private household occupations, and one-and-a-half times more likely to be employed in unskilled occupations such as handlers and laborers. In housemaid and domestic-cleaning occupations, minority representation was almost six times that of whites.

A more detailed view of representation figures shows that minority groups differ widely in their representation profiles. Overall, black, Hispanic, and American-Indian workers are much more likely to have lower representation rates in prestigious occupations and higher rates in less skilled, low-paying occupations than are Asian-American workers.

In EAM occupations, whites have twice the representation of blacks and Hispanics. American-Indian representation is over one-and-a-half times less. Minorities who do attain managerial positions are typically in jobs with no line responsibilities, such as public relations and affirmative action officer. Yet even in many of these positions, minority concentration is significantly lower than that of whites. In the occupation of financial manager, the representation rate for black, Hispanic, and Native-American workers is 0.2 percent—three times lower than the rate for whites. Black Americans are six times less likely than whites to be managers in marketing, advertising, and public relations. Hispanics and American Indians are three times less likely, and Asian Americans, only half as likely.

There are exceptions. For example, the concentration of blacks in public administration (0.5 percent) and American Indians (0.6 percent) is higher than that of whites (0.4 percent). Black and American-Indian representation in this occupation is also greater than Hispanic and Asian representation, which are 0.2 percent and 0.3 percent, respectively.

In the professional specialties category, black, Hispanic, and American-Indian groups lag behind both whites and Asian Americans. While 15 percent of the white workforce is in these occupations, black representation is 9.5 percent; Hispanic, 6.6 percent; and American-Indian, 9 percent. It is significant that Asians are even more highly represented than whites in this category, with almost 18 percent representation.

Among the selected professional specialty occupations, black representation is highest in social, recreational, and religious occupations, where 3.4 percent of the black workforce is employed—a significantly larger share than any of the other minority groups as well as the white workforce. Blacks also lead minority groups in representation in teaching occupations, exclusive of the postsecondary level.

Sociologist Seymour Spilerman of Columbia University observes that part of the reason for the underrepresentation of black Americans and Hispanics in EAM occupations is because they are more likely to obtain degrees in education and social services than in the technical and business fields that usually lead to management.[73] Recent educational attainment figures (examined previously), plus the weight of discriminatory practices, suggest the disparity in representation in EAM and professional occupations between whites and people of color is likely to continue in the near future, though some narrowing of differences will occur.

In administrative support positions, including supervisory positions, black Americans are more likely than whites to be represented. Asian-American and white rates differ by 1 percentage point, while Hispanic and American-Indian rates are about 2 percentage points lower than the white rate.

At lower-end occupations, the tables are reversed: minority representation tends to be greater than that of whites. Especially striking disparities appear in the household services occupations, where the black and Hispanic rate is nine times greater than that of whites. The American-Indian rate is three times greater; and the Asian rate, twice as large. Minority representation rates were also significantly higher in other service occupations, such as food preparation and cleaning and building service occupations. The black representation of 18.3 percent in service occupations was almost twice the white rate. The rates for the other minority groups were also substantially greater than the white rate.

Hispanics and American Indians have greater representation in production occupations than whites, but their representation in selected supervisory positions is generally less (the exception is the identical rate for American Indians and white supervisors in the mechanics and repair occupations). Black Americans are less likely to work in these occupations, but they are as likely or more likely than white workers to hold supervisory positions.

In the unskilled occupations, Hispanics are more highly represented than any group. They are 1.8 times as likely to work in these occupations as whites. American Indians are 1.6 times as likely; blacks 1.5 times; Asians are least likely to work in these jobs.

Unemployment. In their unemployment profile as well as in employment, minorities are disadvantaged relative to whites. According to the

Department of Labor's *Employment and Earnings,* white unemployment rose between 1991 and 1992 from 6.0 to 6.5 percent. Black unemployment, however, which was already more than twice the white rate in 1991, rose even more in 1992, from 12.4 percent to 14.1 percent. The black unemployment rate has been about twice that of whites for the past 20 years.[74] It was also greater than the unemployment rate for other minorities. But Hispanics, too, had a rising unemployment rate that exceeded the white rate: 9.9 percent in 1991, rising to 11.4 percent in 1992.[75] Data for Asian Americans and Native Americans were not provided. Reynolds Farley and Walter R. Allen observe that, beginning with the first census gathering data about work activity in 1890, a continuing trend has been the growth in numbers of black Americans who are out of the labor force and not looking for employment.[76]

It is easy to assume that the unemployment differential is mainly an underclass issue, but this is not true. The differential between white and minority unemployment rates exists at other levels, too. Research by Franklin Wilson and Lawrence Wu of the University of Wisconsin and Marta Tienda of the University of Chicago found that the biggest gap in black and white unemployment occurred among college-educated, experienced men. The unemployment rate of black men with one or more years of college was almost two-and-a-half times greater than the rate for their white counterparts: 8.1 percent compared to 3.4 percent.[77]

Income—The Continuing Gap.   With regard to minority income, there are both positive and negative trends. On the positive side, minority income has increased over time. Between 1940 and 1980, mean income for black men grew more than fourfold, rising from $4,531 to $18,723.* This was an even bigger increase than that experienced by white males, whose mean income rose two-and-one-half times over the 1940 level. (The mean income for whites was significantly higher however: $25,791 in 1980.) On the negative side, more recently the differential between minority and white income levels persists in many categories, including among some requiring high educational levels.

Income information for all major minority groups is not readily available from a single source. (For Native Americans, it is scarce from any source.) The *Current Population Survey (CPS),* which has long tracked black earnings, has included Hispanic earnings since 1985. *CPS* figures show that between 1985 and 1992, both groups have progressed, with blacks improving their position more. Overall black median weekly earnings increased 26.5 percent; Hispanic earnings

---

*In constant 1984 dollars.[78]

Figure 8-7. Median Weekly Earnings of Families, 1985, 1991, and 1992*

Type of family, number of earners, race & Hispanic origin	Median Weekly Earnings			Percent change	
	1985	1991	1992	1991–1992	1985–1992
White					
Total families with earners	543	695	716	3.0	31.9
Married-couple families	589	767	791	3.1	34.3
One earner	395	474	483	1.9	22.3
Husband	452	549	561	2.2	24.1
Wife	218	280	296	5.7	35.8
Two or more earners	723	922	954	3.5	32.0
Husband and wife	735	940	975	3.6	32.7
Families maintained by women	311	399	409	2.5	31.5
Families maintained by men	476	529	545	2.9	14.5
Black					
Total families with earners	378	484	478	−1.2	26.5
Married-couple families	467	−625	646	0.3	38.3
One earner	257	313	309	−1.3	20.2
Husband	292	366	359	−1.9	22.9
Wife	206	272	279	2.6	35.4
Two or more earners	622	776	806	3.9	29.6
Husband and wife	646	796	834	4.8	29.1
Families maintained by women	259	339	328	−3.2	26.6
Families maintained by men	360	401	412	2.7	14.4
Hispanic					
Total families with earners	404	495	496	0.2	22.8
Married-couple families	444	546	552	1.1	24.3
One earner	285	322	333	3.4	16.8
Husband	304	355	365	2.8	20.1
Wife	185	235	264	12.3	42.7
Two or more earners	595	732	743	1.5	24.9
Husband and wife	612	757	778	2.8	27.1
Families maintained by women	270	343	341	−0.6	26.3
Families maintained by men	366	462	476	3.0	30.1

*Data exclude families with no wage or salary earner or where husband, wife, or other persons maintaining the family is self-employed or in the armed forces.

SOURCE: Department of Labor, Bureau of Labor Statistics, *Employment and Earnings* (Washington, D.C.: U.S. GPO, 1986 and 1993), Table 52.

rose 22.8 percent (please see Figure 8-7).[†] Married-couple families in both groups also progressed. Weekly earnings of black married couples rose 38.3 percent; the increase for Hispanics was 24.3 percent. For families with two or more earners, the percent increase for blacks was 29.6 and for Hispanics, 24.9.

[†]"Earnings" is money earned from wages, salary, self-employment, and farm income. "Income" includes earnings as well as income from other sources such as public assistance or welfare, investments, pensions, alimony, etc.

There is a flip side to this progress, however. Relative to white families, black and Hispanic families earned significantly less in all categories, and the gap between them has grown over time. In 1992, black families earned $240 less per week than whites; Hispanics, $220 less. For married-couple families, the disparity with whites was $145 per week for blacks and $239 for Hispanics. For families with two or more earners, there was a $148 disparity for blacks; $211 for Hispanics.

The earnings gap increased in almost every other category too. The overall disparity between black and white weekly earnings in 1985 was $165; in 1992 it was $238. For Hispanics and whites, it was $139 in 1985 and $220 in 1992. Where husbands and wives were both earners, the gap between black and white families grew 88 percent! It rose 65 percent between married-couple Hispanic and white families with two or more earners. There was only one category where people of color made a substantial gain relative to whites: The weekly earnings gap between Hispanic and families maintained by men fell $41 per week. (There was a hint of improvement—one dollar—in the Hispanic-white ratio for families where the wife was the sole earner.)

White families, who started from higher earnings levels, progressed even more than blacks and Hispanics in most categories. For example, total white family earnings increased 31.9 percent, 5.4 points more than the black increase in the same category and 9.1 points more than the Hispanic figure.

Minority gains did outstrip white gains in three categories. Significant among them is the 38.3 percent gain of married-couple black families, which is 4 points greater than the white increase. Weekly earnings of wives in Hispanic single-earner families also rose impressively: 42.7 percent, or about 7 points above white and black increases. Also, the more than 30 percent earnings increase among Hispanic families maintained by men was over 15 points greater than the changes for blacks and whites.

The economic recession of the early 1990s meant bad news for minority earnings, especially for blacks. *CPS* figures for the 1991–1992 period show that median weekly earnings of black families decreased in four of nine categories and barely held steady in a fifth (please see Figure 8-7). The greatest decrease occurred among black single women heading families, whose weekly earnings fell 3.2 percent during the recession.

This points to the critical problem created by the growing number of single black women who are heading families—46 percent in 1991 compared with 18 percent in 1950.[79] Most of these women have inadequate means of supporting their families and have barely raised their income over time. In 1967, the median income of single women heading families was $11,800; in 1990, it increased to only $12,130.[80] Thus, the recession meant a setback for a group who, along with their children, already lived in poverty.

Overall, this data indicates a reversal of the trend toward a narrowing wage gap between black and white workers, analyzed by Smith and Welch. Tracing black and white wages between 1940 and 1980, they found rising black income levels relative to those of whites. While some black groups benefited more than others—younger blacks gained more than older workers, for example—the trend prevailed across income, age, and educational levels.[81] (However, gender was not factored into their study, which dealt only with male income.)

Overall, these data indicate a reversal of the trend toward a narrowing wage gap between black and white workers, analyzed by Smith and Welch. Tracing black and white wages between 1940 and 1980, they found rising black income levels relative to those of whites. While some black groups benefited more than others—younger blacks gained more than older workers, for example—the trend prevailed across income, age, and educational levels.[82] (However, gender was not factored into their study, which dealt only with male income.)

The current data mask the economic fissure within the black population. There is a growing economic gap between the black middle class on the one hand and, on the other, working-class, lower-class, and underclass blacks (using William Julius Wilson's categories).* The middle class has the lion's share of the aggregate income of the black population, and its portion is growing, while that of the poorest segments of the population is decreasing. In 1967, the upper two-fifths of the black population earned 71 percent of the aggregate income of that population; the top fifth earned 46.7 percent of the total.[84] By 1992, the share for the upper two-fifths increased to 74.5 percent of the total with the upper fifth earning almost 50 percent. In contrast, the lowest two-fifths of the black population had only 10 percent of the aggregate income in 1992. This was less than its share in 1967, when it was 13.1 percent of the total.

The economic cleavage in the black population is greater than that among whites and Hispanics: In 1992, the share of aggregate black income of the top two-fifths of the black American population was 4.2 points greater than the share of white aggregate income held by the top two-fifths of the white population. The disparity between blacks and Hispanics at the upper two-fifths of their respective populations was 3.5 percentage points. At the lower end, the share of the lowest

---

*James Smith and Finis Welch analyze black economic gains over a 40-year period.[83]

two-fifths of the black population in 1992 was 3.8 points less than that of the comparable segment of the white population and 3.3 points less than the Hispanic figure.

The comparative economic picture for Hispanics during the recession was somewhat brighter than that for blacks. Hispanic families experienced an earnings loss in only one category shown in Figure 8-7. They gained in most of the others, and, in a few categories, Hispanic gains were greater than those of whites. The most significant improvement in the Hispanic–white ratio occurred in married-couple families where the wife was the sole earner. There, the Hispanic increase was 6.6 points greater than that of whites.

Of all the minority groups, Asians and Pacific Islanders have the highest annual income levels. By comparing different data sources, we find that the median annual income for Asian-American families in 1989 was about $35,200.[85] For blacks, it was about $21,300; and for Hispanics, about $25,800.[86,87]

On a per-capita basis, the median annual Asian-American income is lower than that of whites: about $13,400 in 1990 compared to about $15,200 for whites.[88] But their median family income was higher. In 1990, the median income of Asian married-couple families was $6,200 more than that of white families ($46,500 compared to about 40,300).[89] In other family and household categories, too, Asians outstripped whites. For example, the median income for Asian single women householders was about $22,600; for whites, about $19,500.[90] The median income of about $41,700 for single Asian male householders was a stunning $10,100 higher than for the comparable white group. Part of the reason for the high Asian family and household income is that they tend to have more earners per family than whites. Sixty-three percent of Asian-American families had at least two or more earners in 1990 compared with less than 60 percent of white families.[91]

Despite their high per-capita income figures, a larger percentage of Asians and Pacific Islanders live below the poverty level than whites. The poverty level of Asians is also higher than that of the total population. This combination of high average income and high poverty levels among Asian Americans can be attributed to the bimodal character of the working Asian-American population: jobs are clustered at the very high and low ends of the income range. In 1990, 12.2 percent of the Asian population was below the poverty level.[92] In comparison, 10.7 percent of the white population was. This points to the fact that contrary to the popular image of Asian Americans as a "model minority," a significant number are struggling to make ends meet.

Among Asians, an economic divide revolves, not surprisingly, around the year of entry and naturalization status. Median income of foreign-born Asian Americans who entered before 1980 was almost $47,000, about $15,000 higher than those who entered between 1980 to 1990.[93] Among naturalized Asian Americans, there is also divergence according to year of entry, with those who entered before 1980 earning about $51,800, compared with $36,600 for those who were naturalized later.

Comparable data is not readily available for Native Americans. But a study published in 1991 by the Bureau of Indian Affairs (BIA) is suggestive. The BIA estimates that only about 25 percent of Indian tribal members who lived on or near reservations between 1989 and 1991 earned more than $7,000 annually.[94] The figure is based on some rough estimates and covers only about half of the total Native-American population (the other half lives off the reservations). A survey of the total Native-American population presumably would have produced a higher figure because Indians living off reservations are more likely to have earnings comparable to those of the general population. Income for American Indians on reservations is dismally low—far below that of the total U. S. population—where in 1991 the median per-capita income was about $15,000.[95] The BIA study further estimated that 45 percent of the American-Indian population surveyed was not employed. Of those who were unemployed, a full 35 percent were not seeking work either because opportunities were not available in the immediate area or because they had no means of transportation to seek work elsewhere.

Income is tied to education levels, and people with lower levels of education—which includes a disproportionately large share of minority populations—are experiencing declining income over time. In contrast, income levels are increasing for people with more education. Over the past 15 years or so, earnings for people with high school diplomas have declined by 9 percent, while college-educated males aged 24 to 34 have increased their earnings by 10 percent.[96] Similarly, the earnings differential between professional and clerical workers has increased from 47 to 86 percent, and the differential between white-collar workers and skilled tradespeople has risen from 2 to 37 percent.

Despite rising income at higher educational levels, a wage differential for some highly educated minority and white workers continues to exist for men. Earlier data has shown a disappearing wage gap for black and white male workers.[97] Comparative median earnings data for 1990 in two occupational categories requiring four or more years of education indicate a substantial gap still exists in relative male earnings. Between black and white women, however, the gap is much narrower. Among executive, administrative, and managerial (EAM) workers, black men earned about $40,400 in 1990. This represented a disparity of 19 percent with regard to white male earnings—a substantial difference.[98] Among male professional specialty workers, the earnings differential was almost as high: black men earned $37,100, representing a 16 percent wage differential with the white male earnings. The earnings of black and white women executives, administrators, and managers, on the other hand, were almost equivalent, with the figure for black women ($32,450) being about $100 higher. Median earnings of black women in professional specialty occupations in 1990 were $28,900—about 5 percent less than that of white women. It should be noted, however, that the comparisons between the incomes of black and white women may be misleading because minority women are somewhat more likely to be full-time year-round workers than white women.

We also compared the Asian–white earnings ratio for workers with four or more years of college. Presumably, most of these people are employed in upper-level occupations such as the EAM occupations and professional specialties. (Our sources did not provide comparative earnings data by occupation.) Census Bureau data shows that in 1989, median earnings of Asian and Pacific Islanders with four or more years of education totaled about $37,800. This was $2,300 less than white male earnings, a 6 percent differential. During the same period, female Asian and Pacific Islanders earned $29,400—$2,000 *more* than white women.[99]

Based on these data, there appears to be an analogous trend in the earnings ratio with whites among highly educated black and Asian workers. Although the categories, drawn from different sources, are not identical, it is interesting to note that, in the selected areas, where workers have four or more years of education, Asian and black men earned less than white men, while the earnings of Asian and black women were almost equal to or greater than those of white women. In all cases, the disparity in the female earnings ratio was less than that in the male ratio. Thus, an earnings gap still exists for minority men in these cases, and it is substantial. But it is narrower for minority women. The smaller income gap between black and white women may be somewhat misleading. Factoring in full-time versus part-time employment might increase the disparity.

Minority Advancement and the Cement Ceiling. In their efforts to advance in the workplace, minorities and women are often blocked by a glass ceiling or, the term many minority observers feel is more accurate, a "cement ceiling." For many minorities, the invisible barrier to advancement is not so invisible. A disproportionate number of qualified minority employees find upper-management and even middle-management positions out of their reach.

The 1990 census found that non-Hispanic whites, who were 77.9 percent of the labor force in 1990, represented 85.9 percent of the EAM positions.[100] Blacks, 10.4 percent of the labor force, held 6.2 percent of the EAM jobs. Hispanics, 8.1 percent of the labor force, represented only 4.5 percent of these positions, and Native Americans, 0.6 percent of the labor force, held 0.4 percent of them.

Asian Americans were the only minority group to be adequately represented in EAM positions, although, because many Asian Americans are self-employed, this statistic can be somewhat misleading. Representing 2.7 percent of the labor force in 1990, they held 2.9 percent of the EAM jobs. Dr. Adrian Chan of the University of Wisconsin, Milwaukee, points out that multiple factors may affect the career choices of Asian Americans: English-language proficiency, family pressures, verbal and social skills, salary levels, perceived potential advancements, and status of the occupation. These influential factors, particularly job status and prestige, may explain the higher percentage of Asian Americans in EAM positions.[101]

Other minorities are slowly improving their positions, however. Based on 1980 census data, blacks held 1.5 percent fewer EAM jobs in 1980 than a decade later.[102] Hispanics held about 1.7 percent fewer. (Figures for Asian and Native Americans were not reported separately in 1980.)

Minority managers are more concentrated in the public and non-profit sectors than in corporations, but even in the public sector they are underrepresented. In the federal government, people of color account for 28 percent of all federal positions but occupy only some 8 percent of the top jobs.[103] Percentages vary from department to department, ranging from less than 6 percent of top posts in the Defense and State Departments to as much as 20 percent in Housing and Urban Development. Of black federal workers, 4 percent occupy top posts although they account for 17 percent of the federal workforce. Hispanics, who are 5 percent of the federal workforce, hold 2 percent of the top positions; Asians, 4 percent of federal workers, hold only 1 percent of the top positions; and American Indians, accounting for 2 percent of the federal workforce, hold 1 percent of the top jobs.

These figures suggest that the cement ceiling is becoming more permeable. But the numbers do not tell the whole story. Because they include public sector jobs where minorities are highly concentrated, they do not provide an accurate view of the minority position in management in corporate America. What's more, the aggregate EAM category does not reflect the fact that people of color in the private sector tend to be excluded from line positions where the real responsibility and power reside. According to a study by Korn/Ferry International, whites control 95 percent of the real power positions in American corporations.[104] *Business Week* puts the number of white senior executives at 97 percent.[105]

Minorities are making gains in management positions. During the 1990–1991 recession, management was one of the few areas in which all minorities, including African Americans, improved their positions. (Blacks experienced a net loss in most other job categories.) Nonetheless, there is not much optimism about significant minority gains in senior executive ranks in the near future. Earl S. Washington, president of the Executive Leadership Council, a group of black executives, comments that despite gains, "we have the same problem we've always had. Once you look back over the shoulders of our most senior ranking members, there are not a lot of folks moving up to take their place. And last year, that pipeline was thinned out even more."[106]

No one denies that minorities hold a disproportionately small share of senior positions. What is debated are reasons why. Minorities are more likely to cite discrimination. White executives tend to emphasize lack of qualified minority candidates. They also cite economic conditions, organizational restructuring, and other external factors.[107] The divide comes with regard to responsibility, with each group tending to place it elsewhere, though there are many exceptions.

Theories about discrimination as the prime factor blocking minority advancement have been fairly widely researched. They fall into three groups, according to Ann Morrison and Mary Ann von Glinow of the Center for Creative Leadership. One group of theories assumes that differences among minorities (and women) are deficiencies and handicaps that lead to differential treatment. A second set posits biases and stereotypes held by white male powerholders as the main cause of differential treatment. The final set assumes that lack of adequate minority advancement is due to structural and systemic discrimination.[108] In this publication we do not exclude any of these assumptions.

Historical Perspective.   George Davis and Glegg Watson provide an historical view of the advancement of black Americans in managerial positions. They characterize the 1950s as a decade of tokenism, a time when, as described by one long-time black manager, "you could go for days in one of these places without seeing anyone black, except the messengers and the janitors."[109] Those blacks who were in management positions were mainly from the middle class.

The civil rights movement of the 1960s brought a growing number of blacks from all backgrounds into the organizational mainstream. This passage created a sense of "anomie" among many, according to Davis and Watson. While attempting to adjust to corporate culture, many found "some persistent blackness of their spirits that kept them from wanting to assimilate."[110] The conflict between the erosion of their traditional values and the new, generally inhospitable corporate culture tended to create a sense of isolation. There was also guilt at their own financial success, which stood in stark contrast to the financial struggles faced by most blacks as well as with their own past. The emotional distance that developed between blacks in corporations and the rest of the black community often was profoundly disturbing. Black managers also faced the daunting challenge of discerning between prejudiced behavior on the part of white colleagues and behavior that had no racial overtones. One black manager commented, "You have to look at how white people treat each other; then you'll feel better about the disrespect and insubordination shown toward you."[111]

By the 1970s and 1980s, a growing number of affluent young black professionals were in the workforce. Like their white peers, many were self-centered and ambitious. As part of the "me" generation that placed priority on personal advancement and material success, they typically had little concern for less fortunate members of the black community.[112] Such attitudes occurred in the context of a larger social movement. Davis and Watson, citing Gerald R. Gill, refer to the "meanness mania" that swept the country.[113] One manifestation was a white backlash against gains made by minority groups and women. White accusations of reverse discrimination increased, and some white males felt their own positions threatened.

In a later work, published in 1988, Davis describes the present as an "open future" for minority managers.[114] The problems of earlier decades have not disappeared, and blacks feel a greater responsibility to find their own way within their organizations. Many have progressed to substantial positions and have the potential to advance even further, while others, frustrated by invisible barriers, actively contemplate resigning and starting their own entrepreneurial ventures.

Promotion Practices. One factor directly affecting minority mobility is organizational promotion practices. People of color often feel that the deck is stacked against them in the job performance appraisal process. And there is some evidence that these perceptions are accurate. A study by Kurt Kraiger and J. Kevin Ford found that black employees received lower evaluations than white employees on performance appraisals.[115] These results may be partly attributable to poorer performance by blacks. But they may also stem from bias on the part of the rater or discriminatory practices within the organization, that is, systemic discrimination that prevents minority employees from receiving the same on-the-job opportunities as whites.[116] In another study, Jeffrey Greenhaus, Saroj Parasuraman, and Wayne Wormley found that black managers perceive themselves as having less job discretion and lower acceptance levels than whites. Their performance appraisal ratings were lower than whites; their promotability assessments were lower; their careers likely to plateau earlier; and their dissatisfaction with their jobs greater.[117] Greenhaus and his colleagues caution that organizations need to examine managers' performance appraisals, experience, and attitudes for bias.

Minority promotion opportunities are also often restricted by lack of access to certain positions. Some key posts within organizations may be "hard-wired"—filled by favored protégés before they are posted.

Mentoring.   Finding a mentor is an important part of career planning. Mentors offer experienced guidance, constructive criticism, and support in a one-on-one development process over time. They provide networking opportunities and may serve as role models. A growing awareness of the importance of mentoring programs on the part of many organizations—particularly for women and minority groups—is reflected in the results of a recent Louis Harris poll. A 1991 survey of 406 U.S. corporations indicates that 28 percent are currently offering mentoring programs for women and minority groups and another 27 percent plan to implement such programs.[118]

Mentors may be from outside the organization, but having a mentor within is especially important, for only a person who knows the internal ropes of an organization can supply guidance about the organization's unwritten rules and politics.

Some organizations have a formalized mentoring process. Others, like Federal Express Corporation, use "facilitated mentoring," a less formalized matching of mentor and protégé. Still others are establishing multiple tracking mentoring to help coach and counsel employees through a multiple career path system.[119] But in many organizations, where there is no established mentoring process, employees—all employees, whites as well as people of color—have to make their own connections. This may not be easy. There is no guarantee a person will agree to become a mentor. Moreover, because many people have not acquired coaching skills, they may not be effective at mentoring, even if they do agree. For minority groups, the task is even harder. Should they select a white mentor or minority mentor from the same racial or ethnic group? In many organizations, where there are few or no minority persons in senior positions, the option does not exist. But where there is a choice, there is a dilemma. A minority mentor has the advantage of being able to identify with a minority employee's experience.

Having already been there, he or she can provide the kind of advice and support that helps a less experienced worker overcome culture shock and operate effectively in a predominantly white environment. On the other hand, a white worker may be more experienced within an organization and is likely to have a stronger network among the organization's movers and shakers.

An added complication for a minority employee may be the gender issue. Mentoring across genders may present problems under any circumstances. It is sometimes more difficult to establish a comfortable close professional relationship with someone of the opposite sex. Kathy E. Kram, in her book, *Mentoring at Work*, discusses the complexities of cross-gender mentoring. Such problems as the limitations of role modeling across genders, sexual concerns, and excessive scrutiny (and sometimes resentment) of the relationship by peers of both parties to the relationship, make successful cross-gender mentoring difficult.[120] When differing racial and ethnic identities are part of the equation, the likelihood of a close relationship declines even further. This may be a special issue for minority women employees.

Old Boy Network.   Another expression of institutional racism (and sexism) is the "old boy network." John Fernandez describes the old boy network as "a system that works for its members in ways that include finding candidates for the higher-level jobs in public and private institutions."[121] Because the network's composition is almost exclusively white male, "by using the network as the primary-selection agent, chances are the candidates will be white men." Or, as RJR Nabisco vice president Jason Wright put it, "The reality of life in America is that if you're white, most of the people you know are white. If someone says to you, `do you know anyone for this job?,' the people you recommend will probably be white."[122] Thus the old boy network tends to be a self-perpetuating, white male institution.

Networks are natural. People of like interests and values tend to group together. The old boy network in American organizations is no exception. What is insidious, however, is the systematic exclusion of people based on race, ethnicity, and gender. By its nature, the old boy network contradicts the equality in the workplace that organizations officially endorse.

Lawrence Otis Graham has a lot to say about that. A graduate of Princeton University and Harvard Law School, Graham, a black American, went undercover to work as a busboy at a prestigious New Jersey country club. Graham experienced firsthand the condescending way club members, who support equal opportunity in the workplace, behave toward minorities when not on the job. He recalls the incredulity of one club member who remarked that Graham had the diction of a white man.[123] Graham concludes that people must be held accountable for how they conduct all aspects of their lives, not just when they are at their offices.

As people of color and women begin to slowly advance to upper organizational levels, there may be a gradual erosion of the old boy network. But with 95 percent or more of the top jobs in American corporations still being held by white males, this is likely to take a long time.

The characteristic of the old boy network to exclude minorities may be repeated in informal groups at many organizational levels. Surveys undertaken by Fernandez 10 years apart show conflicting results. In his survey of more than 4,000 minority and white managers in 1976–1978, Fernandez found that 65 percent of black respondents believed minority managers were excluded from informal workgroups; in 1988, the figure was 87 percent.[124,125] This perception was held by a growing number of white respondents, too, although significantly fewer than blacks: 29 percent in 1976–1978 versus 36 percent in 1988. Paradoxically, other minority groups perceived *less* exclusion over time. In the 1976–1978 survey, 51 percent of other minorities (Hispanic, Asian, and Native American) agreed that managers were excluded; in 1988, the share dropped to 42 percent. These results bear several interpretations.

Minorities Feel They Must Work Harder.   One black female college administrator whom we interviewed observed, "To get ahead, they expect you to walk on water." Her comment reflects the perception of many people of color. They feel they must work harder and be better performers than their white peers in order to stay even, much less advance in the workplace. Wendell Johnson, a black executive recruiter, observed, "We're always going to have to do 150 percent to match everyone else's 80 percent, and when times are bad, we have to double our efforts again."[126]

The perception of dual standards appears to be growing. White workers, too, are increasingly perceiving a dual standard for minorities. In his 1988 survey, Fernandez found that 87 percent of black, 53 percent of Hispanic, 58 percent of Asian, 57 percent of Native Americans, and 32 percent of white respondents agree that minorities must work harder.[127] These numbers represent an across-the-board increase over responses to the same question in Fernandez's 1976–1978 survey. Agreement among blacks increased 4 percentage points. Among Hispanics, the increase was 7 points; Asian Americans, 12 points; Native Americans, a stunning 49 points; and white Americans, 12 points.[128] These results suggest that either a dual performance standard is being more widely applied or people are becoming more sensitized to its existence—or both. Ironically, surveys also have shown that many whites hold a contradictory, stereotypic view that black employees do not work as hard.[129]

Other Hidden Obstacles to Minority Advancement.　Other hidden barriers block minority advancement, too. A major obstacle that is inadequately recognized in many organizations is cultural differences. In an Anglo organizational culture, minority group members are typically expected to learn to be assertive and display leadership characteristics in a manner acceptable to the dominant culture. This necessarily means that minority workers need to find some means of accommodation with the dominant culture. This requires a major application of energy and thought—an effort Anglo employees do not have to make. (All new employees, including Anglos, of course, need to spend time learning the organizational culture, but obviously this is a lesser effort for Anglos than for others.)

Lack of organizational commitment to minority advancement is a further roadblock. Organizations must be willing to change their usual practices in order to welcome diversity. They need to create new programs to ensure adequate minority advancement. One such strategy is to link progress toward advancement with pay raises. A variation on this approach was applied at *USA Today*, when founder Al Neuharth informed his staff that no one would receive raises until minorities were employed on the staff. Results followed.[130]

Strategies must also be put into place to actively advance minorities already in the workforce. These are needed not only in the private sector but also in the public sector. A 1993 report by the Merit System Protection Board found that of 35 agencies responding to Board questions, only six had established programs to address minority advancement.[131] In the federal government, whites comprised 74 percent of the white-collar workforce in the Executive Branch in 1992, but they held 88 percent of top pay grades, and 92 percent of senior management jobs. The Board indicated that federal agencies focus more on recruiting minorities than on providing them with career development plans.

Yolanda Moses cites barriers facing minority administrators at academic institutions, but her observations are more widely applicable. She numbers among them the token syndrome, which occurs when there are only a few minorities in an organization.[132] They typically receive overattention or underattention as the token minority employee. At administrative levels they are frequently expected to handle minority and diversity affairs, regardless of whether or not they have expertise to do so.

Moses also refers to the shifting-sands syndrome. Here, rules shift as a minority employee moves toward positions of increased responsibility. For example, an employee may be told he or she is being groomed for a particular position, only to find the job given to a nonminority candidate who is supposedly better qualified. Moses adds that, typically, there is no objective difference in the candidate's qualifications.

The Language Dilemma—A Special Issue. Many minority employees grapple with a language issue at work. In the past, low-level proficiency in English did not impede workers in many lower-end occupations. Their jobs usually involved repetitive functions that required little communication. But today, the situation is changing. Across occupations, work is becoming more varied, a higher level of skills is required, and teamwork is frequently an important ingredient, even in blue-collar jobs. What's more, as the manufacturing sector declines, clerical positions in the service and other sectors are growing, and these necessitate higher-level English-language skills.

These changes are occurring at a time when a large segment of the workforce consists of first-generation immigrants who have low levels of proficiency in English. The 1990 census found that nearly 32 million people in the United States speak a language other than English at home. Of them, over 40 percent say they do not speak English very well.[133] The portion may well be even greater than the statistics indicate. The National Adult Literary Survey, testing adult literacy levels as opposed to people's *perceptions* about their literacy levels, found that about half of American adults had problems reading English.[134]

Employers then face a dilemma of whether to train employees in English-language skills to enable them to perform more productively. *The Wall Street Journal* found that a growing number of employers are doing so—"at company expense and increasingly on company time."[135] On the other hand, because many organizations think the cost of teaching English outweighs the benefits, they are reluctant to hire workers without English-language literacy.

For employees, there are also dilemmas. There is wide recognition that facility with the English language is an important skill in the workplace, and in many cases it is a critical skill. A large segment of the Spanish-speaking population strongly supports bilingualism. According to a study by the Latino National Political Survey, an overwhelming majority of Spanish-origin respondents support or strongly support bilingual education.[136] Many workers who are first-generation Americans fail to attain English-language facility, not because they do not wish to but because they do not have the chance to learn. Many are isolated small businesses within their ethnic and racial communities where English is rarely spoken.

Controversy revolves around whether bilingual workers should be permitted to speak their native languages at work even in informal situations. It is natural for people to feel more comfortable conversing in their native languages. On the job many do so informally—in elevators and lunchrooms, around coffee stations, etc. This practice may create misunderstanding among peers who do not speak the language and feel excluded. A common assumption is that the group is talking about the outsider, or, if the group is laughing, the outsider may assume a joke is at his or her expense. Greater sensitivity to the needs and feelings of others is required by all. But without astute managers to handle the issue or diversity training to sensitize workers, this kind of culture clash can damage employee relations and even affect productivity.

Another consideration arises when the public is present. Clients who do not speak the language are likely to have the same reaction as the coworker who does not. In the Los Angeles area, where Spanish is widely spoken, the health maintenance organization Kaiser Permenente has a similar concern for its patients. Kaiser recognizes that patients feel especially vulnerable and are more likely than others to believe themselves the object of a conversation held in their presence in a language they do not understand. As a result, the organization encourages employees to speak English in areas where they may come in contact with patients.

In some organizations, employees who speak a foreign language are on the offensive. Angered by English-only rules, they have taken their case to the EEOC. The EEOC has determined that such rules are discriminatory unless required for business reasons.[137]

Fluency in a foreign language can also be an asset on the job. Workers with facility in a foreign language can use it with customers who have poor English skills, thereby enhancing business transactions. Some workers are requesting—and getting—bilingual incentive pay, though this practice is under scrutiny.[138]

These culture clashes in the workplace over language do not occur in a vacuum. They are part of a broader trend linked to immigration. Jean Molesky of the University of California, Berkeley, observes that the United States is in a period in which nativism is on the rise. She draws a parallel with the nativist upswing at the end of the nineteenth and early part of the twentieth centuries, when "multilingualism began to be seen as threatening to the welfare of the nation, and English supremacy was increasingly promoted."

References

1. Donna E. Thompson and Nancy DiTomaso, *Ensuring Minority Success in Corporate Management*, Plenum Studies in Work and Industry (New York: Plenum Press, 1988), p. 124.

2. Lawrence Otis Graham, *The Best Companies for Minorities* (New York: Plume, 1993).

3. Sydney and Leslie G. Shields, *Work, Sister, Work: Why Black Women Can't Get Ahead and What They Can Do About It* (New York: Birch Lane, 1993). The book can be read with profit by women of all identity groups—and men too.

4. *Ibid.*, pp. 4–5, 8.

5. *Ibid.*, p. 9.

6. Joel Glenn Brenner and Liz Spayd, "Bankers Describe Roots of Bias," *Washington Post*, June 8, 1993, p. A1. Subsequent to this and other *Washington Post* articles on bias in banking, federal banks regulators proposed federal sanctions for loan bias.

7. John P. Fernandez, *Racism and Sexism in Corporate Life* (Lexington, Mass.: Lexington Books, D. C. Heath, 1981), pp. 19, 21.

8. Jill Nelson, *Volunteer Slavery: My Authentic Negro Experience* (Chicago: Noble Press, 1993), p. 231.

9. Cited by Priscilla Painton, "The Quota Quagmire," *Time*, May 27, 1991, p. 20.

10. "Women, Minorities on TV Shown in Bad Light, Report Says," *St. Louis Post-Dispatch*, June 16, 1993, p. 21A.

11. John Dovidio, "The Subtlety of Racism," *Training and Development*, vol. 47, no. 4, April 1993, p. 52.

12. Marttila & Kiley Inc., "Highlights from an Anti-Defamation League Survey On Anti-Semitism and Prejudice in America" (New York: Anti-Defamation League, November 16, 1992), p. 2.

13. Anti-Defamation League, "1992—Audit of Anti-Semitic Incidents" (New York: Anti-Defamation League, 1993), p. 3.

14. Dovidio, *op. cit.*, pp. 52–57.

15. Lynne Duke, "Blacks and Whites Define Word `Racism' Differently," *Washington Post*, June 8, 1992, p. A1.

16. Bob Blauner, *Black Lives, White Lives: Three Decades of Race Relations in America* (Berkeley: University of California Press, 1989).

17. *Ibid.*

18. John P. Fernandez, "Racism and Sexism in Corporate America: Still not Color- or Gender-Blind in the 1980s," Thompson and DiTomaso, *op. cit.*, p. 85.

19. John Fernandez, *Racism and Sexism in Corporate Life, op. cit.* p. 315.

20. Taylor Cox, Jr. and Stella M. Nkomo, "Invisible men and women: A status report on race as a variable in organization behavior research," *Journal of Organizational Behavior*, vol. 11 (1990), pp. 419–431.

21. Thompson and DiTomaso, *op. cit.*, p. 124.

22. U.S. Department of Commerce, Bureau of the Census, *1990 Census of Population, Asians and Pacific Islanders in the United States*, 1990 CP-3-5 (Washington, D.C.: U.S. GPO, 1993), p. 145.

23. *Ibid.*

24. Peter Kwong, comments at a conference, "Breaking Down Racial Barriers in the Workplace: Successful Models for Diversity," University of Maryland School of Public Affairs, December 3, 1993, College Park, Maryland.

25. U.S. Department of Commerce, Bureau of Census, *Money Income of Households, Families and Persons in the United States: 1992*, 1990 Current Population Reports, P60-184 (Washington, D.C.: U.S. GPO, 1993), p. 10.

26. *Ibid.*

27. U.S. Department of the Interior, Bureau of Indian Affairs, *Indian Service Population and Labor Force Estimates* (N.P.: BIA, 1991).

28. Cited by Ann Moriano, "Nation's Poor Sink Deeper in Poverty," *The Washington Post*, June 26, 1993, p. F1.

29. The Black Population in the United States, *op. cit.*, p. 2.

30. Arai Chideya, *et al.*, "Endangered Family," *Newsweek*, August 30, 1993, p. 17.

31. *Ibid.*

32. *Ibid.*

33. Wilson, *The Truly Disadvantaged: The Inner City, the Underclass, and Public Policy* (Chicago: University of Chicago Press, 1987), p. 57.

34. The Black Population in the United States, *op. cit.*, p. 3.

35. *Ibid.*

36. Kathryn M. Neckerman, "What Getting Ahead Means to Employers and Inner-City Workers," paper presented at the Chicago Urban Poverty and Family Structure Conference, Chicago, 1992, p. 2.

37. William Celis, III, "Study Says Half of Adults in U.S. Can't Read or Handle Arithmetic," *The New York Times*, September 9, 1993, p. A16.

38. Irwin S. Kirsch, Ann Jungeblut, Lynn Jenkins, and Andrew Kolstad, *Adult Literacy in America: A First Look at the Results of the National Adult Literacy Survey*, National Center for Education Statistics, Department of Education (Washington, D.C.: U.S. GPO, September 1993), pp. 17, 78, 96.

39. Seymour Spilerman, "Sources of Minority Underrepresentation in Corporate Employment," Donna E. Thompson and Nancy DiTomaso, *op. cit.*, p. 27.

40. Reynolds Farley and Walter R. Allen, *The Color Line and the Quality of Life in America* (New York: Russell Sage Foundation, 1987), p. 190.

41. U.S. Bureau of the Census, Current Population Reports, p. 20-464, *The Black Population in the United States: March 1991* (Washington, D.C.: U.S. GPO, 1992), p. 28.

42. Farley and Allen, *op. cit.*, pp. 188–208.

43. A. J. Jaffee, *The First Immigrants from Asia: A Population History of the North American Indians* (New York: Plenum, 1992), p. 189.

44. Thomas Sowell, "'Affirmative Action': A Worldwide Disaster," *Commentary*, vol. 88, no. 6, December 1989, p. 24.

45. Gary Jordan, "In Cities Like Atlanta, Whites Are Passing on Public Schools," *The Washington Post*, May 24, 1993, p. A12.

46. Gary Jordan, "Segregation In Schools Increases," *The Washington Post*, December 14, 1993, pp. A1, A6.

47. Steve Twomey, "Graduates Who Lack a Passing Knowledge," *The Washington Post*, September 9, 1993, p. C5.

48. *Ibid.*, p. D3.

49. Lena H. Sun, "Chinese Swaddled, Not Coddled," *The Washington Post*, June 30, 1993, pp. A1, A14.

50. Gary Jordan, "5% Fewer Black Males Attend College," *The Washington Post*, February 28, 1994, pp. A1, A10.

51. Anthony P. Carnevale, Leila J. Gainer, Ann S. Meltzer, and Shari L. Holland, "Skills Employers Want," *Training and Development*, vol. 42, no. 10, October 1988, pp. 23–30.

52. *Ibid.*, p. 34.

53. Lawrence Mishel and Ruy A. Teixeira, *The Myth of the Coming Labor Shortage: Jobs, Skills, and Incomes of America's Workforce 2000* (Washington, D.C.: Economic Policy Institute, 1991), p. 2.

54. Donald R. Atkinson, George Morten, and Derald Wing Sue, *Counseling American Minorities: A Cross Cultural Perspective*, 2d ed., (Dubuque, Iowa: Wm. C. Brown, 1983), pp. 34–41.

55. Derald Wing Sue and David Sue, *Counseling the Culturally Different: Theory and Practice* (New York: John Wiley, 1990), p. 107.

56. *Ibid.*, p. 111.

57. Lloyd Dickens, Jr. and Jacqueline B. Dickens, *The Black Manager: Making It in the Corporate World* (New York: Amacom/American Management Associations, 1982).

58. Ella Louise Bell, "Bicultural Life Experience of Career-Oriented Black Women," *Journal of Organizational Behavior*, vol. 11, 1990, pp. 459–477.

59. Shields, *op. cit.*, p. 88.

60. *Ibid.*

61. George Davis and Glegg Watson, *Black Life in Corporate America: Swimming in the Mainstream* (New York: Anchor/Doubleday, 1982), pp. 173ff.

62. *Ibid.*

63. Thompson and DiTomaso, *op. cit.*, p. 213.

64. Yolanda T. Moses, "The Roadblocks Confronting Minority Administrators," *Chronicle of Higher Education*, January 13, 1993, B2.

65. Thompson and DiTomaso, *op. cit.*, p. 202.

66. U.S. Department of Commerce, Bureau of the Census, *1990 Census of Population, Supplementary Reports, Detailed Occupation and Other Characteristics from EEO Files for the United States,* 1990 CP-S-1-1 (Washington, D.C.: U.S. GPO, 1992).

67. Vera Cohn, "Work Force Disparity Seen Narrowing," *The Washington Post,* November 5, 1992, pp. C1, C3. Although the article says 600,000 new jobs, authors believe *net* new jobs may be more accurate.

68. Priscilla Painton, "The Quota Quagmire," *Time,* May 27, 1991.

69. Dianne Lewis, "As economy sours, work bias complaints are reported to soar," *Boston Globe,* May 27, 1991.

70. Rochelle Sharpe, "Losing Ground: In Latest Recession, Only Blacks Suffered Net Employment Loss," *The Wall Street Journal,* September 14, 1993, p. A12.

71. Sharpe, *Ibid.,* pp. A1, A12, A13.

72. Stephen Barr, "More Minority Workers Discharged than Whites," *The Washington Post,* December 15, 1993, p. A21.

73. Thompson and DiTomaso, *op. cit.*, p. 33.

74. Caroline V. Clarke, "Downsizing Trounces Diversity, 1994," *Black Enterprise,* February 1994, p. 70.

75. U.S. Department of Labor, Bureau of Labor Statistics, *Employment and Earnings,* January 1993 (Washington, D.C.: U.S. GPO, 1993), p. 222.

76. Farley and Allen, *op. cit.*, p. 209.

77. Proprietary to UPI, "Study shows racial discrimination in labor market," *Nexis,* July 4, 1992.

78. James P. Smith and Finis R. Welch, *Closing the Gap: Forty Years of Economic Progress for Blacks,* U.S. Department of Labor, R-3330-DOL/Rand (Santa Monica: Rand, 1986), p. 4.

79. U.S. Bureau of the Census, *The Black Population in the United States: March 1991,* Current Population Reports, p. 20-464 (Washington, D.C.: U.S. GPO., 1992), p. 2.

80. *Ibid.,* p. 16.

81. Smith and Welch, *op. cit.*, p. viii.

82. *Ibid.,* p. viii.

83. *Ibid.*

84. Bureau of the Census, *Money Income of Households, Families, and Persons in the United States, 1992,* Current Population Reports, Consumer Income, Series P60-184 (Washington, D.C.: U.S. GPO, 1993), p. B-7.

85. Bureau of the Census, *1990 Census of the Population: Asians and Pacific Islanders in the United States, 1990, op. cit.,* p. 141.

86. *The Black Population in the United States, March 1991, op. cit.,* p. 15.

87. U.S. Department of Commerce, Bureau of the Census, *Hispanic Americans Today, Population Characteristics,* Current Population Reports, pp. 23–183 (Washington, D.C.: U.S. GPO, 1993), p. 18.

88. Bureau of the Census, *The Asian and Pacific Islander Population in the United States, March 1991 and 1990,* Current Population Reports, Population Characteristics P20-459 (Washington, D.C.: U.S. GPO, 1992), p. 17.

89. *Ibid.,* p. 10.

90. *Ibid.*

91. *Ibid.,* p. 11.

92. *Ibid.,* p. 17.

93. *1990 Census of the Population: Asians and Pacific Islanders in the United States, loc. cit.*

94. U.S. Department of the Interior, Bureau of Indian Affairs, *Indian Service Population and Labor Force Estimates* (N.P.: BIA, 1991), p. 3.

95. *Ibid.*

96. Cited by Kirsch, *op. cit.,* p. xv.

97. See Smith and Welch, *op. cit.*

98. *The Black Population in the United States, March 1991, op. cit.,* pp. 68, 69.

99. *Asians and Pacific Islanders in the United States: March 1991 and 1990,* Current Population Reports, *op. cit.,* pp. 56–57, 59–60.

100. Bureau of the Census, *1990 Census of Population, Detailed Occupation, op. cit.,* p. 1.

101. Dr. Adrian Chan of the University of Wisconsin, Milwaukee, in a letter dated February 28, 1994.

102. Based on figures cited by Nancy DiTomaso and Donna E. Thompson, "The Advancement of Minorities into Corporate Management: An Overview," *Sociology of Organizations,* vol. 6, 1988, p. 283.

103. Barbara J. Saffir and Stephen Barr, "A Snapshot of Women and Minorities in Federal Jobs," *The Washington Post,* January 3, 1994, A17.

104. Cited by Sylvester Monroe, "Does Affirmative Action Help or Hurt?," *Time,* May 27, 1991.

105. Howard Gleckman *et al.,* "Race in the Workplace," *Business Week,* July 8, 1991, p. 52.

106. Quoted by Clarke, *op. cit.*, p. 74.

107. See the survey of corporate managers by Thompson and DiTomaso in *Ensuring Minority Success, op. cit.*, pp. 119–136.

108. Ann M. Morrison and Mary Ann von Glinow, "Women and Minorities in Management," *American Psychologist*, vol. 45, no. 2, February 1990, p. 201.

109. Davis and Watson, *op. cit.*, p. 17.

110. *Ibid.*, p. 41.

111. *Ibid.*, p. 42.

112. *Ibid.*, pp. 46–48.

113. *Ibid.*, p. 46.

114. Thompson and DiTomaso, *Ensuring Minority Success, op. cit.*, pp. 110–113.

115. See for example, Kurt Kraiger and J. Kevin Ford, "A Meta-Analysis of Rate Race Effects in Performance Ratings," *Journal of Applied Psychology*, vol. 70, pp. 56–65.

116. According to D. R. Ilgen and M. A. Yountz; cited by Jeffrey H. Greenhaus, Saroj Parasuraman, and Wayne M. Wormley, "Effects of Race On Organizational Experiences, Job Performance Evaluations, and Career Outcomes," *Academic Management Journal*, vol. 33, no. 1, 1990, p. 68.

117. *Ibid.*

118. Cited by Mary J. Winterle, *Workforce Diversity: Corporate Challenges, Corporate Response*, Report No. 1013 (New York: The Conference Board, 1992), p. 21.

119. Zandy Leibowitz, Beverly Kaye, and Caela Farren, "Multiple Career Paths: Motivating, Developing, and Retaining the Technical Workforce."

120. Kathy E. Kram, *Mentoring at Work* (Glenview, Illinois: Scott, Foresman and Company, 1985), pp. 106–108.

121. Fernandez, *Racism and Sexism, op. cit.*, p. 315.

122. Gleckman, *Business Week, op. cit.*, p. 52.

123. Comments in a seminar, "Breaking Down Racial Barriers in the Workplace: Successful Models for Diversity," sponsored by the University of Maryland, School of Public Affairs, December 3, 1993, College Park, Maryland.

124. Fernandez, *Racism and Sexism, op. cit.*, p. 54.

125. John Fernandez, *Managing a Diverse Work Force: Regaining the Competitive Edge* (Lexington: Lexington Books/D.C. Heath, 1991), p. 196.

126. Clarke, "Downsizing Trounces Diversity, 1994," *op. cit.*, p. 74.

127. *Ibid.*, p. 192.

128. Fernandez, *Racism and Sexism, op. cit.*, p. 63.

129. Comment by Dr. Nancy DiTomaso, summarizing survey results in a telephone conversation, March 16, 1994.

130. Comments by Barbara Reynolds, Editorial Board, *USA Today,* at conference, "Breaking Down Racial Barriers in the Workplace," *op. cit.*

131. Cited by Steven Barr, "Efforts Urged for Minorities, Older Workers," *The Washington Post,* December 6, 1993, p. A21.

132. Moses, *op. cit.*

133. Barbara Vobejda, *The Washington Post,* May 29, 1992, p. A1.

134. Kirsch, *Adult Literacy in America, op. cit.*

135. Jolie Solomon, "Firms Grapple with Language Barriers," *The Wall Street Journal,* November 7, 1989, p. B1.

136. Rodolfo O. de la Garza *et al., Latino Voices, Mexican, Puerto Rican & Cuban Perspectives on American Politics* (Boulder: Westview Press, 1992), p. 10.

137. Solomon, *op. cit.,* p. B5.

138. Leah Beth Ward, "When the Language Gap Alienates," *The New York Times,* December 27, 1992, p. 25.

9

Gender in the Workplace*

The number of women in the American workforce almost equals that of men; in 1990 they formed over 45 percent of the civilian labor force.[1] They have proven their worth on the job countless times. Yet women still face discrimination on the job—and sometimes even before they get there. Access discrimination exists in some industries and occupations so that women have a hard time getting entry-level positions there. And once they are in the workplace, they often face restricted career options, unequal pay, and other forms of discrimination.

One of the most challenging tasks facing employers and employees today is working through gender-related problems in the workplace to create a productive environment and benefit from the richness women can offer.

Workplace policies are often based on a conception of society—a snapshot—that is sadly outdated. The days when a significant portion of female workers derived their main support from a husband or a father are clearly long gone. Indeed, history shows this circumstance never existed for many minority working women. It does not exist today for a broader range of women. In 1991, two-thirds of all families with children depended on the mother's earnings for their well-being.[2] Yet the lingering unspoken, often unconscious, assumption that a woman is the second wage earner in a traditional family is partly to blame for the persisting pay inequity between men and women.

---

*This chapter was written with Lee Adair Lawrence. The authors are grateful for her work.

Despite the tenacity of such stereotypes, studies about women have become increasingly particularized, a trend which suggests that observers—be they sociologists, economists, business and labor analysts, demographers, feminists, or psychologists—no longer view women as a homogeneous, single-interest group. As economists Teresa L. Amott and Julie A. Matthaei state in *Race, Gender & Work,* "Women throughout the United States have not experienced a common oppression as women. The process of gender, race/ethnicity, and class—intrinsically interconnected—have been central forces determining and differentiating women's work lives in U.S. history."[3]

Recognition of women's heterogeneity, more than the growing number of women in the workplace, explains why gender-based issues have multiplied. Concerns of working women used to focus mainly on discriminatory hiring practices and unequal pay—two issues that were addressed in legislation. Title VII of the Civil Rights Act of 1964 prohibited employers, employment agencies, and unions from discriminating on the basis of sex, while the Equal Pay Act of 1963 was amended in 1972 to give women legal recourse in cases of pay discrimination.

Then came less generic complaints: Some women found themselves unemployable not because they lacked qualifications, but because they were going to be mothers. Working women sometimes faced outright sexual extortion or were forced to endure rude and upsetting remarks about their gender day after day. Again, Congress passed legislation that addressed these concerns. In 1978, it broadened the Civil Rights Act to protect specifically the rights of pregnant women seeking jobs. Two years later it amended Title VII to include a definition of sexual harassment and a prohibition against what it terms "quid pro quo" demands and a hostile environment.

As these laws were promulgated, other issues emerged. One was concern about women as a group being prevented from reaching the higher rungs of the corporate ladder. This much-written-about phenomenon was dubbed "the glass ceiling." In turn, it gave rise to concern about a "sticky floor," defined as factors that keep women as a group lodged in lower-paying jobs. Further, as the number of working mothers increased, they began to articulate the need for what might be called a "family package" that would include a variety of benefits such as flexible work schedules, some form of child-care assistance, job-sharing or part-time work, and liberal family and medical leave policies.

Such requests made it clear that not every issue had equal impact on all women. Under the spotlight of analysis, "women" as an identity group dissolved into a conglomeration of individual faces and histories: from single mothers, heads of household to working spouses; from executives in big cities to factory workers in industrial towns;

from women who had left the workforce while they raised families to those who had no choice but to give their children latchkeys. The rubric, people began to realize, had also to be broken down according to racio-ethnic variables: Women were black, white, Hispanic, Native American, and Asian and each had faced, overcome, or been beaten down by circumstances specific to their racio-ethnic group as well as their internal makeup as individuals.

This profusion of women's issues understandably has triggered confusion and not a small degree of annoyance among some men. But the more particularized look at women bodes well for men, too. The current trend highlights the fact that men have also been historically treated as a monolithic, single-interest group. They have been regarded literally as "working stiffs," devoid of many of the characteristics that a man might feel define him as an individual. There have been incidents in which men could legitimately complain about reverse discrimination based on stereotyping. As early as 1978, Congress recognized this and mandated that existing maternity leave policies also be extended to men. Nonetheless, reverse discrimination persists in subtle ways, as a female vice president in a major New York bank explains: "Assuming a good employer and a good personal reputation, a woman can scale down to part-time and still be taken seriously because she has the caretaker role in society's eyes. Conversely, a man who asks to scale down is considered to be unserious." Just as a woman may suffer from being judged by an outdated gender model, so can a man.*

The more the particular issues facing women and men in the workplace today are explored and quantified, the better the chances that employers and employees can find answers and devise solutions. "What gets measured in business gets done, what is not measured is ignored," maintains Edward W. Jones in *Harvard Business Review*.[4]

Some Cultural, Social, and Psychological Underpinnings of Today's Workplace

Before considering specific gender issues, it is useful to look beneath the conflicts and problems in today's workplace to some social and

---

*June 25, 1993, telephone conversation with a female vice president in a leading New York bank.

attitudinal underpinnings. Systems, institutions, and traditions are always slow to catch up with reality, and even though today the workplace comprises more women than men, its structure remains strikingly male. For the workplace, like most other social institutions, was molded by white men, who were superior in both number and socioeconomic status to other men, as well as to women of all races.

The Politics of an Unequal Society

Psychiatrist Jean Baker Miller, formerly a member on the Committee on Women's Employment and Related Social Issues of the National Research Council, describes the hallmarks of an unequal society in her book, *Toward a New Psychology of Women*. When it comes to assigning roles, she explains, the dominant group delegates to the subordinate groups whatever functions it deems less desirable. "It is interesting to note," she writes, "that these tasks usually involve providing bodily needs and comforts. Subordinates are expected to make pleasant, orderly, or clean those parts of the body or things to do with the body that are perceived as unpleasant, uncontrollable or dirty."*[5]

What is more insidious, perhaps, is the value system that emerges in this unequal society. In short, the dominant group deems those tasks it delegates to subordinates intrinsically less valuable than the roles it claims for itself. Elizabeth Janeway, a noted author who frequently writes on women's issues, refers to men's "valuable power to define the elements of our world and to declare how weighty, how urgent and how pressing they are."[6] It would be more accurate to add that, in the United States, this valuable power belonged to white males exclusively.

Postulating dominance, however, is only half the battle. The dominant group then needs to preserve its superior position, and it typically does so by convincing subordinates that they are incapable of performing anything but the tasks assigned to them. By the same token, members of the subordinate groups develop behavioral patterns that will ensure their survival. Women—and, to a great extent, minorities—learned the value of accommodation, adjustment, outward submission, and what Miller calls "disguised and indirect ways of acting and reacting."[7] At one level, the subordinates hope thereby to keep the peace

---

*India's caste system is perhaps the clearest illustration of this theory. The hierarchy of caste and occupation ranges from the outcasts, who clean toilets, carry away trash, and tend to the cremation grounds, to lower castes of workers, and on up through merchant and warrior castes to the pinnacle: Brahmins, who traditionally deal with spiritual and scholarly matters.

and please the dominant group. At another level, however, subordinates use these wiles to get their own way in a manner the dominant group will not notice, and therefore not punish.

Gender Roles in a Divided Society

The principles of an unequal society combine with a division of labor postulated by the political theorist Hannah Arendt and elaborated upon by journalist Anthony Astrachan in his book, *How Men Feel.* According to Arendt, women's work is defined as an occupation that unfolds in privacy and is devoted to bodily functions. In the United States, the ideology of domesticity grew from this division and reinforced job segregation. This, Astrachan argues, "testified to the strength of the desire to keep [women] away from the `public' that was male."*[8] The strict division between the public (male-work) and the private (female-home) realms helped produce rigid gender roles that have stubbornly resisted change.

Given that one's gender is an inescapable, immediately visible part of one's identity, it is not surprising that gender roles and relations affect the workplace as they do virtually every other area of our society. The problem arises not so much because a man recognizes that a woman belongs to the opposite sex or vice versa, but because the strong public/private division means that a man most strongly associates women with the private realm. There, a woman is not a colleague, supervisor, or partner, but a wife, lover, courtesan, sweetheart, daughter, mother, or caretaker. The workplace, however, demands that people relate to one another in other, more public ways, regardless of their sex: a recognized, distinct work role is essential.

According to journalist Susan Faludi, author of the 1991 book, *Backlash: The Undeclared War Against Women,* the conservatism of the last decade-and-a-half strengthened these gender roles. She argues that the 1980s witnessed a concerted effort to return women to their "rightful" place at the bottom of the totem pole. "By the early 1980s, the fundamentalist ideology had shouldered its way into the White House," she writes. "By the mid-1980s, as resistance to women's rights acquired political and social acceptability, it passed into the popular culture. [As in earlier periods of backlash,] the timing coincided with signs that women were believed to be on the verge of a breakthrough."[9]

---

*The use of `public' and `private' here does not denote the common differentiation between the public and the private sectors. The terms here are used to distinguish between the outside world and the home.

In spite of evidence that the economy might have been primarily responsible for the slippage in women's wages relative to men's in the 1980s, there is widespread agreement that cuts in social programs disproportionately affected women. There is also much agreement with the allegation that the leadership's conservative view of women encouraged complacency among employers and short-circuited the process of attitudinal change. What counts is not whether someone can prove or disprove this hypothesis. What counts is that many women believe this to be the case.

The Nineties' Man: Confusion, Anger, and Fear?

Anger at this perceived backlash perhaps explains why 71 percent of women 45 years old and younger polled by *The New York Times* in 1989 said that the country needed a strong women's movement, while 27 percent picked job-related concerns as the most important problem facing women today.[10] Similarly, a December 1989 Gallup Poll showed a drop in the number of people who felt that women had the same job opportunities as men: 48 percent said yes in 1975 compared to 42 percent in 1989.[11] On the surface, this might seem strange, given that the battle for equality of the sexes has been raging for more than 30 years and has produced protective and affirmative action legislation.

At a deeper level, however, it is clear why women believe they are still in the early stages of the battle. Now that legislation has removed the gross obstacles in their path, they are addressing the fundamental values and stereotypes that gave rise to the obstacles. While American society is no longer strictly divided between dominant, white males and their subordinates, the social structure nevertheless continues to reflect these values, sometimes subtly, sometimes overtly. By shifting their focus to the (male) values that underpin the structure of the workplace, women have taken the fight to a deeper and more disturbing level, provoking not a little fear, confusion, and anger among men. Men have been taught to function according to a set of rules, but all around them the rules are changing, and, worse, new ones have not yet been put in place.

This is one area where there need be no distinction made between white males and minority men. Though the latter, like women, have been subordinate to white males, they have nonetheless regarded themselves generally as dominant in relation to women, particularly women of their own race or ethnic background. Black or white,

Hispanic or Asian, men, in the main, have been socialized to play the game, follow and work the rules, climb the ladder. As children, boys and girls often refuse to play together because they play differently. If relationships are at stake in a rules dispute, for example, girls will more readily give up the game, whereas boys will insist on using the rules to decide the matter, no matter whose feelings might get hurt. Boys will often select a playmate on the basis of his ability to play a certain game, not according to whether they like him or not.[12] These boys grow up into men whose socialization and experience in the school system have trained them for the workplace hierarchy as established by their forefathers.[13] Challenges to the status quo in the workplace are therefore all the more unsettling and upsetting, for they affect men's primary domain.

Job Insecurity...

The changes affect men on two levels. As a practical matter, women's presence in the workplace makes the competition for jobs fiercer, especially at a time when the job market is shrinking. The competition is most direct among white-collar workers, where men increasingly compete with both other men and women for employment. In blue-collar work, where women have made relatively few inroads, the changing workplace nevertheless gives men cause for resentment and fear. With the restructuring of the manufacturing sector, many blue-collar men have either lost their jobs, taken pay cuts, or live in fear of being the next one in line for retraining.[14] Meanwhile, women have been generally sheltered by the boom in the services industry, where many of them work.

The numbers are enough to give a man pause: For the last several years, the unemployment rate for women of all races working full-time has been consistently lower than men's, as detailed in Figure 9-1. At the same time, more and more men are coping with the stresses of a dual-career marriage. At home, they shoulder more tasks than their fathers did, while at work they are given no reprieve or special consideration. In this sense, many a man believes that women have exceeded their desire for parity and secured the sweeter deal. They have the same opportunities as men in the job market, according to this view, yet the persistence of old-fashioned values allows them to take a protracted leave of absence or decide against working if they so wish.[15]

...And Plain Old Angst

At the same time, men are grappling with complex emotional and psychological reactions to the presence of women at work and the resul-

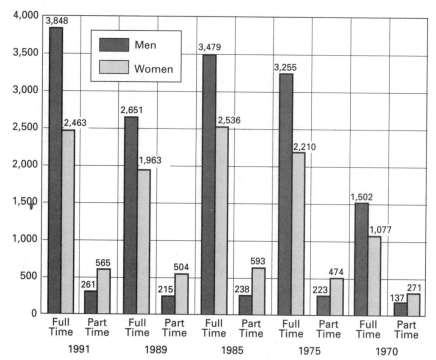

Figure 9-1. Male and female unemployment by full and part-time status (in thousands). (*Source: U.S. Department of Labor, Bureau of Labor Statistics*)

tant changes in the nature of the workplace. Not all men, of course, react the same way. Just as the demands placed upon men have changed from those of a generation ago, so has their socialization evolved. Notwithstanding the variety of their reactions, some general trends can be discerned.

In exploring men's reactions to women's advances in the workplace, Anthony Astrachan points out that "most of us (men) identify our masculinity so completely with our work and our traditional modes of dominance that we start to feel unmanned—which is to say, we start to lose our identities, our selves, our very humanity when women show that they can do the same work or exercise the same power."[16] Moreover, if tradition has defined a man's identity in terms of his dominance over women, then there is more involved than a mere loss of face when a woman challenges his authority.[17]

Women, on the other hand, have been traditionally socialized to invest their identities in the private sphere and in their relationships to others. A poll that asked executives to identify the biggest challenges they had ever faced illustrated this. Only 3 out of 100 challenges cited by male executives had to do with their private lives. Female executives, on the other hand, cited with 20 percent more frequency personal decisions or events.[18] At work, this shows up in women's greater "people skills," the importance they attach to developing and maintaining affiliations.[19] For this and other reasons which will be explored later, women reach out to their male colleagues, often triggering a negative response. What is going on? According to Anthony Astrachan, men view this as an attack: women charging the wall men have built around themselves. Men look out from the parapet of their fortress and see women as breadwinners and women performing traditionally male tasks. As though this were not enough, the women are waving and shouting and asking the men to lower the drawbridge. Reaching out, they say? "If threats to power lead to anger," Astrachan writes, "threats to dissolve boundaries lead to fear."[20] In this case and in the view of many men, women are doing both.

As a journalist covering a day-long conference devoted to the "Man of the Nineties" writes: "Men are staring down both barrels of big change, and they're understandably nervous about the new marching orders."[21] With so much emphasis on women's issues and the need to change the workplace to respond to their needs, men's plight has often been overlooked or dismissed. Under attack for everything they do wrong, they complain that nobody is giving them clear signals about what they should be doing to get it right. More disturbing yet is the accompanying sense of weakness or powerlessness, not so much vis-à-vis women, but vis-à-vis themselves. The vast majority of men have not reached the highest ranks of government or private business. Only a few are chief executive officers, admirals, and chairmen of the board. By clamoring to climb the ladder, women arouse in some men a sense of their own inadequacy. Not only does it remind them that they have not made it to the top, but it deprives them of the confidence that once came from knowing that there would always be someone beneath them in the hierarchy.[22]

But Who's Listening?

Worst of all, men feel that no one takes any notice of their plight, so intent is society on accommodating women. Few talk of the pressures a dual-career marriage puts on men. Few worry about the man who would like to take time off to be with a sick child, but dare not ask lest he be deemed unserious about his work. Few give men a forum in which to express their misgivings and concerns about the changing workplace without being labeled antifeminist or politically incorrect.

Instead, men—especially white men—find themselves tried and convicted of perpetrating all the wrongs in the workplace. They are being asked to make all the accommodations, provoking some like Michael Levin, of the City College of New York and author of *Feminism and Freedom*, to denounce women's demands as "totalitarian."[23] Men are confronting and dealing with members of the opposite sex in a relatively new situation, yet they have no guidelines, no historical precedent on which to rely, no myths which credit either the fear or the excitement they feel. For men do not uniformly regard the presence of women in the workplace as a negative development;[24] more than a few view women's presence as enriching, and many in their 20s and 30s can understand the genesis of many women's workplace complaints. They empathize with their female colleagues, for they, too, are coping with pressures to which the older, senior managers cannot relate.[25]

Perhaps the 1989 Gallup Poll, "The Gender Gap in America," most vividly illustrates the truth that men, too, have come a long way. Of the male respondents, 59 percent agreed with the statement, "men get a greater sense of satisfaction from caring for their family than from a job well done." Asked to respond to the same statement made about women, again 59 percent agreed. Perhaps even more telling, a large number of men hanker for more time with their families. In the Gallup Poll, 68 percent of the respondents stated that men with successful careers ended up sacrificing too much of their family and personal life,[26] and 72 percent of working fathers polled by *The New York Times* were torn by the conflict between the demands of their jobs and the desire to see more of their families.[27] Their answers confirm that the values that have long defined the culture of the workplace are increasingly uncongenial to the women and men who inhabit it. Given these reactions, it is no surprise that senior, mostly male, executives in companies such as Kraft-General Foods and US West, among many others, introduced liberal family leave policies before the politicians were willing to support a family leave bill.[28,29]

A New Look at Women

These enlightened—or pragmatic—CEOs may be recorded in the history of corporate America as being among the first to recognize that men and women had to join forces to build a new workplace. History will also record that they were in the minority, while the majority of their brothers either just didn't get it or got it but ignored it. Many find it difficult, at best, to understand women. The confusion is perhaps due in part to the proliferation of women's images. In order to achieve parity in the workplace, women for years emphasized their similarity to men. They debunked prevailing myths by building bridges, conducting experiments in physics, performing surgery. They donned fatigues and survived boot camp. Perhaps 2nd Lieutenant Charlene Wagner best symbolizes this image of women: The first woman to benefit from a fundamental policy change announced by then Secretary of Defense Len Aspin on April 27, 1993, she stands on the tarmac in her unisex flight suit. Behind her is the lethal-looking attack helicopter she could one day fly into combat.

But what about the women in tight skirts and broad-shouldered jackets that grace the pages of *Working Woman* and similar magazines? Everything about them consciously exudes femininity, from the mascara on their eyelashes to the jewelry that adorns them. They embody another image, the one that proclaims that a woman has her own style and that it is just as valid as a man's.

Yet a third category of images reclaims and exalts some archetypical female traits. The bestseller, *Women Who Run with the Wolves*[30] celebrates women's intuitive nature, their sensitivity, their nurturance, and, ultimately, their strength, a power beyond sexuality and outward appearance. In a similar vein, though in a more systematic manner, Miller's work extols women's ability to listen more intently and relate to others more effectively, just as the abundance of literature on parenting underscores a woman's invaluable contribution to society through the raising of her children.

All three images accurately represent the Nineties' woman and illustrate the pressures on her to shine in several, often fundamentally different, spheres. While it might prove at times confusing, the plethora of images in fact points to a trend that will in the long run help both sexes: the realization that women and men are also individuals whose needs change over time. They, and the situations they find themselves in, cannot be dealt with, let alone understood, simply by applying a convenient label and producing an all-purpose response. Director of the Center on Work and Family at Boston University, Bradley Googins, touched on one aspect of this in a discussion of men's unwillingness to take paternal leave. "This next phase of the women's movement," he said, "is as much about helping men deal with their needs beyond work as it is about helping women."[31] The particularization of gender issues also shows that the general discussion about gender has reached a new, deeper level. Thanks to attitudinal changes that allow Lieutenant Wagner to enter a previously all-male domain, women seem less afraid to explore the differences between themselves and men. Taken broadly, this shows that society has evolved enough to recognize, at least at the conscious level, that "different" does not mean "lesser."

As a result, employers and employees today are better equipped than ever to take stock of what women offer the workplace.

Higher Degree of Education

The most striking and most easily quantifiable asset of women today is their education. Since graduation day 1982, when 480,000 women stepped up alongside 473,000 men to receive their bachelor's degrees, women have been completing college in consistently greater numbers than men. On graduation day 1990, a little over one million women had completed some form of higher education, outstripping the number of male graduates by more than 14 percent. Women took 39 percent more two-year associate's degrees than men, which accounted for most of the difference. The gender gap narrowed at the B.A. level, with 13.6 percent more women than men earning degrees. At the graduate level, women took 10.6 percent more M.A. degrees, ceding the educational advantage to males only at the doctorate and professional degree levels as seen in Figure 9-2. The gap between men and women widens to a chasm among blacks: In 1990, 79 percent more black women received master's degrees than black men.[32]

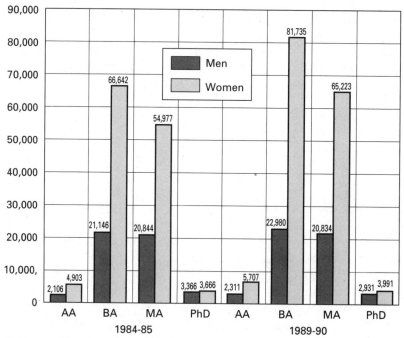

Figure 9-2(a). Education degrees conferred, 1984–1985, 1989–1990; U.S. (*Source: U.S. Department of Education, Office of Educational Research and Improvement, National Center for Educational Statistics, May 1992*)

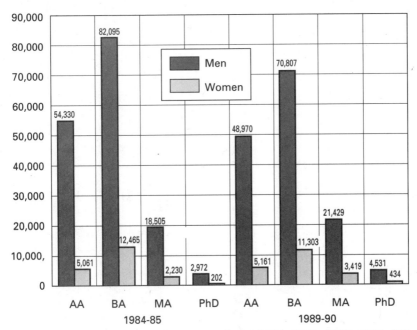

Figure 9-2(b). Engineering degrees conferred 1984–1985, 1989–1990; U.S. (*Source: U.S. Department of Education, Office of Educational Research and Improvement, National Center for Educational Statistics, May 1992*)

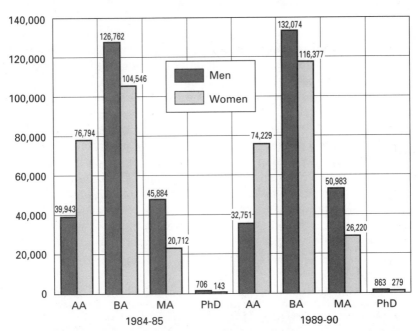

Figure 9-2(c). Business and management degrees conferred 1984–1985, 1989–1990; U.S. (*Source: U.S. Department of Education, Office of Educational Research and Improvement, National Center for Educational Statistics, May 1992*)

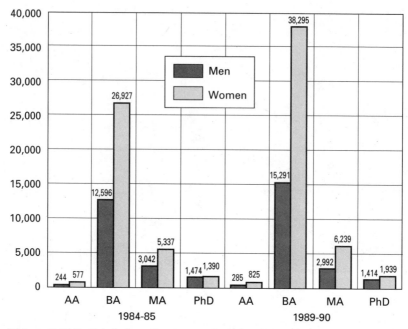

Figure 9-2(d). Psychology degrees conferred, 1984–1985, 1989–1990; U.S. (*Source: U.S. Department of Education, Office of Educational Research and Improvement, National Center for Educational Statistics, May 1992*)

In spite of the well-documented existence of a "female" curriculum* that concentrates on humanities and "soft" sciences, educated women are a valuable resource in an economic environment characterized by heightened global competition and a fundamental shift from manufacturing to high technology and information management. Additional education usually indicates a broader base of knowledge that enables employees to learn faster and perform better. Managers expect that the more educated the individual, the better this person will be at working with ideas, and, in general, women fulfill this expectation better than men.[33] Finally, any amount of higher education, even if limited to two years at a local community college, builds confidence and self-esteem. On the job, this translates into a higher chance of being motivated and making the most out of the job.[34] For all these reasons, some predict that by the year 2000 only 14 percent of jobs will be open to those who have less than a high school education.[35]

---

*Many researchers and educators argue that women are still being encouraged in overt and covert ways into either traditionally female fields, such as education and health, or into training that will prepare them for staff jobs.

An "Immigrant's" Determination and Loyalty

Given women's academic achievements over the last several years and the changing requirements of the labor market, it is safe to project their continued advancement through the halls of academia. More difficult and less certain are projections of women's future attitudes and perceptions based on what we know of the realities to this point. For example, discussions of women's behavior in the workplace provide snapshots that may be only partially valid for more recent and future entrants. An individual's attitude at work, after all, grows out of a number of variables: her socialization at home and in school, her early experience in the workplace, the expectations she is encouraged to harbor, and the attitude of employers and colleagues. Generational differences among women are already manifesting themselves in the workplace. A government political analyst in her mid-40s describes the younger women in her section as more aggressive, more willing to speak up in meetings, and more prone to dress in ways that maximize their femininity. Until these younger women joined her section, she could have generalized about gender differences among her colleagues. Not anymore. This, she says, is a different breed.[36]

This caveat, however, does not obviate the validity of current observations about women's particular strengths. If anything, it should impel employers to create the conditions under which women can best use them. A case in point: The head of personnel for a large pharmaceuticals company remarked that "women come into the workplace like immigrants, determined to succeed on the basis of what they know, not who they know."[37] The analogy is compelling. Like immigrants, women have come into the workplace in waves, in many areas they are still in the minority and they have often been resented and mistrusted. These attitudes, reinforced during lean economic times, place women in the unenviable position of being "damned if she does, damned if she doesn't." If, under the watchful eyes of her male colleagues, a woman performs less than outstandingly well, she reinforces negative stereotypes and does a disservice to her gender. If she does well, she still might lose, because her success could trigger resentment and defensiveness on the part of the male establishment.

Yet outperform men she often did and does. At work, women typically focus more closely on their tasks, devoting less time than men to the office politics that get them known in the corporation. In research, many women prefer to carve out their own niches rather than vie for high-visibility projects. Women also tend to publish one well-researched, thorough study, while male colleagues typically spin off multiple articles from one piece of research.[38] This explains at least in part why women sometimes are accused of being too narrow[39] and why they sometimes lack the support necessary from upper management to get ahead. Their work is not what falls short; it is their self-promotion. They often do not play the game.

Dedication to the job shows up in another telling way. When a woman makes a career choice, she often does not base it on purely financial considerations but on factors in a number of personal criteria that may have little or nothing to do with material rewards.[40] This could lead the male establishment to regard her as a pushover; however, if these men are perceptive they might also interpret this as commitment to the substance of the job rather than to potential financial rewards.

A Successful Management Style

Is there a female management style? Or is it a myth? Experts disagree. Summarizing the debate, author and leading pundit on workplace issues, Ann Morrison writes, "Evidence of a `female management style' is scarce and has been countered with substantial contrary evidence. Is it women's values that shape their career choices, or the options that they [seem to] have? Is the style that many women use more relevant to their sex or to the lack of power that they have had?"[41] Although the jury is still out—and the issue may never be conclusively resolved—there is a set of behaviors that have been so widely practiced as to be regarded as traditionally feminine. On the job, for whatever combination of reasons, be it nature or nurture, many women managers seem to use a leadership style that varies significantly from that generally associated with male managers. This alternate style needs to be acknowledged and valued in its own right.

The same set of values that many women apply when making choices about jobs may also make them more ready than many men to share information with colleagues, no matter where they sit in the hierarchy. This quality has an impact that goes beyond mere style. Information sharing not only helps build morale, but it can also make a crucial difference in the overall effectiveness of the workplace, whether the task at hand is to develop new product lines, formulate new marketing strategies, or administer public funds. In short, it directly affects a company's bottom line or an institution's effectiveness.[42]

The readiness to share information denotes a nonterritorial approach to work, one that contrasts sharply with the traditional, command-and-control style of leadership. It not only blurs the lines among workers, it also alters the nature of the worker-supervisor relationship. This approach gives rise to managers like Judith Rogala, one of the country's few women CEO's, who has never locked her desk drawer and encourages subordinates at Flagship Express to read the reports on her desk. In many ways, she is typical of women managers who opt to pursue their own style rather than imitating men's. "They are succeeding," as the *Harvard Business Review* pointed out, "because of—not in spite of—certain characteristics generally considered 'feminine' and inappropriate in leaders."[43] As employers around the country have discovered, women are particularly talented when it comes to motivating people. Rogala doesn't encourage her employees to rifle through her papers just to be friendly: "The more information people have," she reasons, "the more inspired they are to do good work."[44]

In the same vein, many women managers take time to "massage" employees, to understand their concerns and help work out whatever problems they might be facing. This relates directly to the so-called "constructive" scales by which some psychological tests evaluate managers, and in which women excel. Subordinates give female managers consistently higher marks for their ability to get quality results from their staffs, set and communicate goals, define realistic performance standards, and balance the need to obtain results with concern for the people involved. They also score high marks for respecting individuality and creativity.[45] This orientation toward other people tends to make women more open, receptive, and attentive to supervisors, peers, and subordinates. Whether by nature or nurture or both, women also tend to shy away from conflict, and this translates into a softer, less confrontational approach toward colleagues and subordinates.

With an increasingly heterogeneous workforce, there is much to recommend this management style, for those women and men to whom it feels right. In order to motivate employees, such managers are more willing than traditional supervisors to tailor an individual's work requirements to suit her or his needs. This is most apparent in young companies in such fields as biotech and software, which have a relative large proportion of women in management and research. These women are writing the rules of the corporate culture with their male colleagues and are creating a more open, creative atmosphere. "There are not as many stereotypes to break," says a software-testing manager in North Carolina. "We're making the stereotypes."[46] As a result, the unwritten rules are more congenial to women. Female leadership also puts its own stamp on older, "traditional" professions. When she founded a law firm in the Chicago suburbs, 38-year-old Robin Schirmer bucked the established practice of rewarding the "rainmakers" for bringing in business while downplaying the value of those who do the less high-profile work.[47]

The key lies in a woman's ability to inject her ideas and values into the workplace. In traditional, male-dominated hierarchies, as we shall see, those relatively few women who have managed to ascend the corporate ladder beyond the glass ceiling seem to have adopted many of the attitudes and characteristics of the established corporate culture as a matter of survival. The degree to which their successors will be subject to the same pressures remains a matter for speculation.

Gender-Related Issues and Conflicts in the Workplace

A Clash of Values

No matter how many surveys and studies praise women's management and work styles, the workplace has yet to reflect its appreciation in practice. In the mid-1980s, there was talk of a "forced fit" to describe women who had to conform to male styles and values in order to survive in the workplace. Less than a decade later, the situation has improved, but it still requires a great deal of courage, self-confidence, and perseverance for women to fly in the face of tradition. They continue to be seen through a perceptual filter that undervalues many of their strengths and patterns of behavior.

We have seen that when a woman makes a decision regarding a new position or career move, she will often place a great deal of value on family time, her emotional comfort level at work, and other personal, nonobjective factors. By not focusing entirely on the financial or career-enhancing aspects of a position, she risks being viewed by male superiors as unserious, uncommitted, or risk-averse. She may also reinforce the traditional assumption that her salary is not crucial to the well-being of her household—otherwise, they reason, objective factors would outweigh any personal considerations. There is ample room for misreading the cues, however. If a woman bursts into tears at the office, how many men will read her weeping as a sign that she cares deeply about her work? More likely, they will see it as proof that women are entirely too emotional to handle the thorny, uncomfortable situations that arise in the world of business. Similarly, no matter how often women are lauded for accommodating the individual needs of their subordinates, listening to, motivating, and encouraging them with praise, many men still view these attitudes as signs of weakness, naiveté, lack of authority, and as generally more appropriate for a cheerleader than a manager. And the flip side of a woman's willingness to give approval more readily than men is her own greater need for it.[48] At the office, these differences in needs and approaches can easily translate into misunderstandings and miscommunications.

Pay Inequity

A woman's paycheck speaks volumes about the assumption the establishment makes regarding her value to the workplace. Throughout their working history, women have earned less than men. While the situation has steadily improved, women still lag behind, making 72 cents for every dollar a man earns, according to the 1990 census. Women working full-time and year-round were twice as likely as men to earn between $7,500 to $9,999. By contrast, men were four-and-one-half times more likely than women to record earnings of $50,000 or more.[49] A look at what men and women in the same occupational categories earn highlights a more disturbing discrepancy: In January 1992, men's weekly median earnings exceeded those of women by a minimum of 20 percent in farming, forestry, and fishing and by as much as 45 percent in two other categories: technical, sales, and administrative support and precision production, crafts, and repair.[50]

The discrepancy permeates all levels of the workplace and results from two related, but independent, phenomena: women making less money for the same job and a heavy concentration of women in lower-paying jobs. Together, they spell poverty. In 1990, more than one-half of all families below the poverty level were maintained by women; women constituted more than 60 percent of all minimum-wage earners; and 40 percent of all working mothers earned less than $10,000 a year.[51]

Same Job, Lower Pay

If women have made gains and today earn, for the same job, close to three-quarters of what their male colleagues make, it is largely because they themselves have changed. They now bring to the job the same or better educational attainments and experience, with the latter accounting for as much as a one-quarter of the narrowing in gender pay gaps.[52] Other factors to consider are that men's wages slid by 8 percent in the 1980s and that many low-paying jobs were cut, putting some women out of work and therefore out of the calculations of median earnings. All this gave an extra boost to women's comparative earnings, but it was not enough to put an equally qualified man and woman on a par financially, as Figure 9-3 illustrates. It appears that either women do not possess the skills that the workplace most values—or, more likely, the workplace still does not truly value the skills

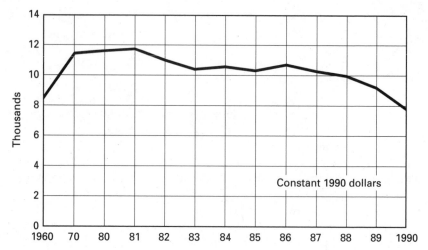

Figure 9-3. Difference between men's and women's earnings—based on the median earnings of full-time, year-round workers, 15 years and older. (*Source: Department of Commerce, Bureau of the Census*)

women possess—and they are somehow assumed to be secondary wage-earners.

Pay inequity does not seem to depend on any factor other than gender. Occupations such as registered nurse or information clerk were 10 percent and 19 percent, respectively, more lucrative for a man than for a woman in 1989. By the same token, male lawyers recorded earnings that were 26 percent greater than those of their female colleagues.[53] This pattern can be observed across the occupational spectrum. For a while, high-tech companies were considered the shining exception: They had a good record of promoting women and paid women higher wages than the national average. Yet even in high tech there are problems. A study of men and women MBAs, found that they all started off with the same salaries, but five years later the women were making only 85 cents for every dollar earned by their male colleagues. What happened? Women in this sector, too, become typed. Their skills are viewed as technologically inferior, and they are assigned jobs that exclude them from design and research and the chance to familiarize themselves with the technology. When promotions are being handed out, they get passed over because of this lack of experience.[54]

Ironically, when analyzing and evaluating women, the male establishment adopts what might be considered a more female approach. It gives more weight to relationships than to objective rules of fairness. Typically, the establishment assumes that a woman who makes a change in her work situation—e.g., she decides to change jobs or to resign—does so based solely on personal, family considerations. Asked to explain a man's decision to resign or switch jobs, the same people immediately cite job conditions: a man's professional growth, his desire for higher pay and greater responsibilities. A woman's poverty was also most often assumed to be a byproduct of divorce or other personal change, while a man's poverty was attributed, again, to job conditions.[55] Similarly, a woman's pay scale is based in part on assumptions concerning her family life. Because women are given, and accept, primary responsibility for caring for the family, they are consistently assumed to be poor investments. Employers and superiors routinely expect a woman to leave her job, never to return, after having a child, which makes her a poor investment and justifies lower pay. Yet, year after year, the data show that those women who do ask for—and receive—a protracted leave do return to work and that, in the context of an entire career, the interruptions are negligible. This attitude goes hand in hand with the assumption that a woman is a secondary, and therefore not essential, wage-earner in the family. For most minority women, this assumption has no historical validity, and today it applies to almost no one, regardless of race or ethnic background. Sixty-five percent of all women with children work outside the home, three-quarters of them at full-time jobs. For the majority, this is not a matter of choice: Some two-thirds say they would cut back their hours, but they can't afford the luxury. Twenty percent of all working women are their family's principal, sometimes sole, breadwinner, and two-thirds of black working women provide 50 percent of the family's income.[56] In fact, women today are more likely than men to spend some portion of their lives as the sole wage-earner in a family[57]—not surprising when one considers that in 1991, more than 11 million families were maintained by women, up by 29 percent over 1980.[58]

As for the evaluation of women's skills, it is significant that there appears to be a correlation between the amount of mathematics a woman has studied and her chances of achieving pay equity.[59] Although this relationship may appear odd and needs further verification, it nevertheless highlights the fact that the underlying structure of the workplace has yet to fully recognize the strengths of women when these differ from men's. A manager may receive accolades for her sensitive, inclusive, and cooperative style; she may even get promoted. But her pay lags. Female and male managers at 20 *Fortune* 500 companies across eight industries were matched up in terms of qualifications and promotions over a five-year period. The men's salary increased by 65 percent; the women's increased by only 54 percent.[60]

Other rewards also prove more elusive for women than men. Even if being paid at comparable rates, women in high management positions by and large are assigned smaller budgets and have less autonomy than their male colleagues. Over time, discrimination at all levels exacts a severe toll on women's standard of living and prospects for future advancement.

Lower-Paying Jobs

At the other end of the spectrum from managers, there is a high concentration of women in low-paying jobs. Of the women working in 1990 in state and local governments, 55 percent were in the lowest-paying employment categories.[61] As will become clear in the discussion of occupational segregation, the pattern extends to the private sector. Here, the model of an unequal society discussed earlier provides a useful tool with which to analyze why women are clustered in these jobs and industries and why these are generally remunerated less than male-dominated ones. In that model, jobs that appear as extensions of traditional female duties, for example, child care, housekeeping, and nursing, are clearly considered subordinate tasks. So are primary- and secondary-school teaching—for what is teaching if not a continuation of a mother's duties of imparting a structure of knowledge and social conventions to children and youths? Clerical jobs, too, fall into this category, because the function of these jobs is to make life easier for clients and customers. Women in these positions are not asked to design new consumer products or help build a new office complex; rather, they are asked to connect a client's phone line, cash his check, find her a residence suitable to her family and budget, or show him an array of summer wear—all functions that relate directly or indirectly to bodily comfort.

Within the context of a corporation or a government institution, a parallel distinction exists between caretaking jobs and line or outwardly oriented production jobs. Internal publications, human resources, and public relations all pertain to the inner working of the organization, and are mostly performed by women. The pay scales for these and other internal jobs—for example, finance, administrative and support services, and research—are low relative to the male-dominated jobs requiring contact with important clients to drum up new business or line jobs relating to the operations side of the company. This differentiation between line and staff jobs does not always reflect the true importance the latter has on the bottom line. True, bringing in new business is critical for future profitability and survival, but so is good administration, sound financial analysis and prompt support: all those internal—almost private, to invoke another model—functions that enable the company to perform its outward—public—activities effectively and efficiently.

The Glass Ceiling

Women often do not feel the full impact of discrimination until they have been on the job a few years. Those in low-pay, low-status jobs one day realize that they are also dead-end jobs. At the high end of the socioeconomic scale, dead-end means never rising beyond a certain point in the hierarchy. Or, in today's parlance, hitting a "glass ceiling," defined as an informal—hence, largely invisible—set of barriers that effectively blocks women as a group from climbing to the highest levels of management.* In spite of equal opportunity legislation, women's advancements in education, and hard as well as anecdotal evidence that women can manage and manage well, the top echelons of business and government continue to be staffed predominantly by white males. In 1990, the Department of Labor reviewed nine *Fortune* 500 companies and found that white males comprised more than 90 percent of their executive-level managers.†[62] By contrast, white males accounted for only 43 percent of the civilian labor force that year.[63] Of 800 newly promoted corporate chairmen in 1987, 97 percent were males.[64]

Even in the federal government, where affirmative action programs have helped raise the overall participation of women to 48 percent, women face attitudinal and institutional barriers.[65] They fill 86 percent of the federal government's 300,000 clerical jobs but only 11 percent of the senior-level managerial and policy-making positions.[66] In 1974, women held only 2 percent of the highest positions and 5 percent of the jobs at the next echelon of government. This indicates that, despite improvements, women in government start bumping their heads against the glass ceiling around the GS-12 grade level.

In private business, the ceiling is fixed in the upper reaches of middle management. Some 30 percent of employed women work as professionals and managers, yet only an estimated 2 to 4.5 percent have made it into the top executive suites of large corporations.[67] Between 1981 and 1991, the number of women managers and officials grew by 12 percent, and this vertical movement was accompanied by a horizontal spread across industry categories. A Department of Labor study found that, in 1981, close to 53 percent of all women officials and managers worked in three industries: finance/real estate, retail, and communications. This means that women accounted for one-third of management in these

---

*The term "glass ceiling" was popularized in a March 24, 1986, article in *The Wall Street Journal*, entitled "The Corporate Woman."

†Defined as assistant vice president and higher, or the equivalent thereof.

industries, as well as more than half the managers and officials in health services.* Ten years later, the concentration of women managers in these industries had intensified, even though demonstrable progress had been made in other industry groups where women had previously held under 10 percent of all management positions. By 1991, there was no major industry group in which women accounted for less than 10 percent of its officials and managers. Yet at the same time, the concentration of women in management passed the 40 percent mark in finance/real estate, communications, and the retail trade, while the proportion of female managers in health services jumped to 64 percent.[68]

These statistics paint a somewhat overly optimistic figure, however, for the titles "official" and "manager" here include low-level managers as well as chief executives. Although more women inhabit the top executive suites than ever before, their participation rate is still meager. Asked about this, many male top executives said women needed to broaden their base of experience if they wanted to rise further. This is easier said than done. In many companies, women might bump up against the ceiling in upper management, but it is while they are at far lower levels that their dead-end journey gets charted. The first corporate areas to welcome women were those divisions dealing with human resources, public relations, and communications. These still show a high concentration of women, many of whom will rise to upper managerial levels but will lack the breadth of experience to go further. Given the earlier discussion of unequal societies and the value systems they engender, it is interesting to note that these staff and support departments relate to the well-being of the company and its employees. Women in these positions are paid less, have fewer opportunities for advancement, and command smaller budgets relative to operational, line jobs, which remain male-dominated.

There is good reason, then, for the many discussions of the glass ceiling, its unfairness to women employees, and the disservice it does to corporations whom it robs of new ideas and talent. Yet for all the talk, the barrier is still there. The recession of the early 1990s and the anemic recovery put decision makers under added pressure and created conditions under which some male managers may find it more difficult to reach beyond their comfort level to groom a woman for senior management.

Their reaction can be viewed as part of a broader phenomenon and a fundamental reason for the existence—and persistence—of the glass ceiling. Although performance and other career-enhancing moves are

---

*It is interesting to note that these industries fall under the broad definition of "subordinate" categories as defined in the unequal society model.

important in the final screening for membership in the elite club of senior management, the comfort factor looms large. People tend to trust and feel comfortable with people who are most like themselves. That is the basis, whether conscious or unconscious, for top management's propensity to give white male up-and-comers more of the informal advice and formal help that they need to climb the top rungs of the career ladder. In a sense, they can be described as defending the comfortable maleness of the club[69]—sometimes by deliberately manning the ramparts against intruders, but more often by lowering the drawbridge to those to whom they relate most easily.

To be overlooked for a top executive job solely on the basis of one's gender is especially galling and frustrating, because in most cases women have had to struggle, make more sacrifices, and cope with more pressures than their male peers to reach the upper levels of management. Throughout their careers, they feel they are under intense scrutiny, knowing that, as women, assumptions are being made about their abilities and potential based not on performance, but on role expectations. They are, therefore, required to turn in a consistently outstanding performance: Mere excellence is not enough to prove that, at work, they are first and foremost managers and that their gender is incidental. Women also realize that they are being judged according to criteria that they do not necessarily share. A woman manager might value her ability to accommodate the views and needs of her subordinates as well as her superiors to accomplish her work objectives in a cooperative, collegial manner. A male manager evaluating her may well interpret this accommodation—much like crying in the office—as a weakness that indicates that she is not tough and demanding enough to make the hard decisions required at higher levels of management.

Being under constant scrutiny and not always knowing what impression she is making can place strong pressure on a person. Added to this is the pressure of having to adapt to a male, corporate culture that requires her to exhibit behaviors that do not come naturally to many women. Studies indicate that the women who broke through the glass ceiling in the 1980s displayed virtually the same personality or behavioral traits as their male peers.[70] One conclusion that can be drawn is that they were rewarded not only for solid performance, but also for internalizing the corporate culture.

Ironically, the women who do make it do not always take the time to extend a helping hand to their younger women colleagues. In many cases, it is not a matter of ill will: They simply lack the time and energy to do so. With children to raise and a demanding career to manage, many find it impossible to carve out the time to consult and nurture other women.[71] But there is also another reason. A senior woman executive walks a fine line when it comes to gender. She is expected to put her job before her family, but more important, she has to convey this to her superiors, who often make the assumption that a woman is unwilling to subordinate family needs to the job. And in the 1980s, that was often what she did. A 1984 survey by *The Wall Street Journal* revealed that 52 percent of female corporate vice presidents had no children, as opposed to only 7 percent of their male counterparts.

While proving her commitment to her career, a woman must also demonstrate that she is tough, decisive, and demanding, yet can simultaneously retain a degree of femaleness. Otherwise, she runs the risk of having men label her as too aggressive and abrasive. She is also often expected to accept without complaint lower pay and fewer perquisites than her male peers lest she be accused of wanting too much. To be accepted as one of the boys, she must repeatedly demonstrate that she is a reliable team player. Finally, she has to win the confidence and support of a mentor. Corporate insiders all agree that help from above is indispensable.

A woman who manages to walk this tightrope and break through the glass ceiling might understandably be reluctant to call attention to her gender by championing other women.[72] This places her younger female colleagues in a double bind: They have a role model, but one who cannot or will not bond with them, while senior male managers may pay them little attention, assuming that their female counterpart is taking promising younger women under her wing. In the end, many in the second generation of executives have no one to help them navigate the shoals of career advancement.

On the other hand, there are women who receive the mentoring they need from a female superior. With more attention being paid to the glass ceiling by males as well as females, support groups have mushroomed. Sometimes they are initiated by a female executive who wants to give younger women the role model and female mentor she never had. Or women may band together around a common cause: Black women who find themselves the victims of double discrimination, women forced to reenter the workforce due to divorce or widowhood, or middle-level managers who are frustrated by their employers' blindness to their needs. Whatever their genesis, these groups provide women with an embryonic old girls' network that gives them an opportunity to learn about the thinking at the top as well as to affect it. In the same vein, some companies have instituted a mentoring program which teams female managers with top male executives in an effort to build bridges between the genders.

In the short run, these forums for discussions and channels of communication will help ease the pressure on women and allay the fears of men. Since 41 percent of all managers, as of mid-1991, were women, there is reason to believe that, thanks to these support groups and other helpful policies, the glass ceiling will begin to resemble the ozone layer over the coming decades: It will be full of holes. The long-term effects could be enormous. The more women access the top echelons, the more they will be in a position gradually to erode the female stereotypes that are being unconsciously perpetuated. By the same token, closer cooperation at the top will alter the prevailing male stereotypes, which are increasingly out of touch with today's man.

The Mommy Track

In many cases, the dead-end career path has a name: the mommy track. In some cases, the term denotes a formal arrangement between an employee and employer whereby the woman opts for a less-demanding career path. Typically, she makes the choice in order to take an active role in the rearing of her children. In law firms, for example, a woman might opt to remain an associate indefinitely and not compete for a partnership in return for fewer hours, less travel, and a more flexible work schedule. By diverging from the usual career path, she can continue to work without having to take on more responsibilities than she feels she wants. This is the plus side, providing all parties are in full agreement.

Problems arise when the employee switches to the mommy track with the understanding that in a few years she can resume the fast track, only to discover later that she has been permanently shunted onto a course that precludes significant advancement.

In other cases, however, the mommy track may never be formally discussed. The employee never asks for any special treatment, but finds that her employer has simply assumed that, as a mother, she does not want to travel, work overtime, take on the stress of a large budget or a challenging division and has cut her out of career-enhancing opportunities. When women and feminists rail at the mommy track, these scenarios are usually what they have in mind. They are reminders of the propensity to treat women as a single, homogeneous group based on role assumptions rather than addressing individual situations and needs.

The results can be degrading and destructive for the individual and the organization. One corporate research scientist hid her pregnancy from her employer for $7\frac{1}{2}$ months for fear of losing her chance for a promotion and being shunted, against her will, onto the mommy track.[73] A banker waited until she made vice president before asking to switch temporarily to a part-time schedule to allow her more time with her two children. In a more extreme case, when a senior vice president in a large New York bank asked if she might scale down her activities following the birth of her second child, her supervisors stripped her of her title and gave her a year to get back on the fast track. She quit instead.[74]

The Sticky Floor

Most working women, however, do not worry about being excluded from partnership in a law firm or the top-floor executive suite. They do not agonize about being passed over for a six-figure salary and a multi-million-dollar budget. They do not even refer to their work as a "career," but as a "job."[75] Unlike those hurling themselves against the glass ceiling, the bulk of working women are intent on getting a fair crack at a $700 raise, some overtime, and a chance to move up one small notch in the low end of the hierarchy. More than 68 percent of women working full-time and year-round earn less than $25,000, including the 11.5 percent whose W-2 forms report only a four-digit salary.[76]

As Atlanta team-training specialist and communications consultant Patricia H. Dutter puts it: "Never mind the ceiling. These women have never been able to look out the window."[77] Regardless of a woman's personal ambition and proven work ethic, she finds it virtually impossible to switch to a better-paying section. Entry-level jobs no longer lead to better jobs, as they did in the old days when senior executives could boast of starting their careers in the mail room. Today, American society as a whole too often places more importance on ascribed status than on an individual's achievement. This makes upward mobility more difficult for those starting off on the lowest rungs of the ladder. Based on educational attainment and, later, job experience, workers get typed and locked into low-wage jobs. This is particularly acute for the "subordinate" classes: women and minorities. Indeed, the numbers show that men are more likely to move into better-paying positions when they leave or lose low-level jobs: 47 percent of them as opposed to 21 percent of their female counterparts, most of whom end up in other low-wage jobs, unemployed, or on welfare.[78]

For many years, the women's movement tended to focus on the well-educated, upwardly mobile, aspiring career woman and her difficulties in the workplace. (Women, too, relate better to those who are most like themselves.) The working mother, often a woman of color, who cleaned the glass ceiling every night and who had no career to advance was largely forgotten. The experience of women in these low-wage, dead-end jobs on the "sticky floor" is that they are also largely ignored by their employers, even though their work is essential to the

smooth operation of the organization. Even state and local governments consign more than half of their employees, and especially
minority women, to the lowest-paying job categories: paraprofession-
als, administrative support, and service/maintenance. There is little or
no upward mobility.[79]

The problem now has a label and is being measured and studied,
which is always the necessary first step in addressing it. For minority
women in particular, discrimination and lack of educational attainment are certainly contributing factors; however, structural impediments exist as well, and these are slow to change. Still, in state and
local governments, the representation of women in the lowest-paying
job categories dropped from 64 to 55 percent between 1980 and 1990,
chiefly because the number of these jobs has declined.[80] In the corporate sector, some employers are putting programs in place to help
these low-wage employees improve their education and skills.
Nevertheless, for some of the nation's most vulnerable women, the
floor remains perilously sticky.

Occupational Segregation

The glass ceiling and sticky floor phenomena feed into a larger trend
in the workplace: occupational segregation. This is not to be confused
with job segregation, which has been ruled illegal. Every man or
woman has the legal right to become qualified and apply for any job
that she or he desires. Unlike the days of the mill girls, no workplace is
declared single-gendered; however, many a division, department, or
industry is dominated by one or the other gender, and it is still common to hear occupations or industries referred to as being traditionally
male or traditionally female (see Figure 9-4). As noted earlier, female-
dominated occupations are lower paid—for example, staff and clerical
jobs as opposed to sales and production, or health services as opposed
to most manufacturing. This also applies to female-dominated industries as seen in Figure 9-5, which record consistently lower weekly
median earnings than male-dominated industries.

Moreover, some blue-collar industries remain virtual male strongholds. In the construction and repair industries, women hold only 3
and 4 percent, respectively, of nonsupport staff jobs. A female mechanic
or repairer makes 11 percent less than her male co-worker, while the gap
between a male construction worker and his female counterpart is as
much as 21 percent.[81] A woman carpenter/electrician attributes the
difficulties of breaking into the blue-collar world to an instinctual,
openly negative male attitude: "This kind of work is more obviously
tied to masculinity, virility," she says. "Women doing the same job

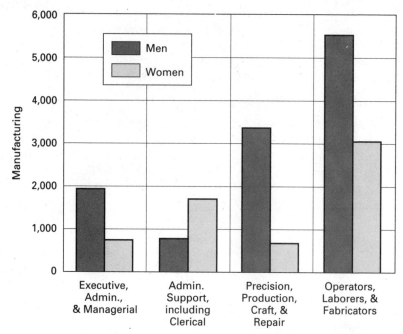

Figure 9-4(a). Employed civilians in selected sectors by occupation and sex; U.S. 1990 (in thousands).

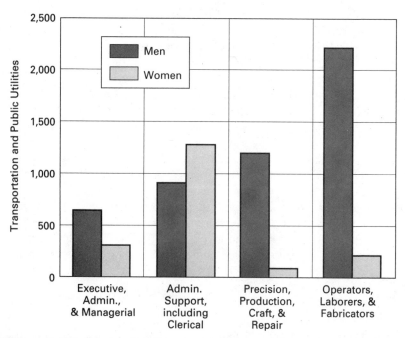

Figure 9-4(b). Employed civilians in selected sectors by occupation and sex; U.S. 1990 (in thousands).

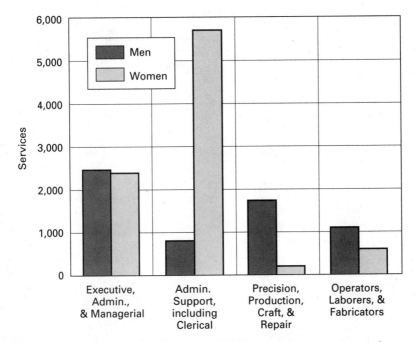

Figure 9-4(c). Employed civilians in selected sectors by occupation and sex; U.S. 1990 (in thousands)

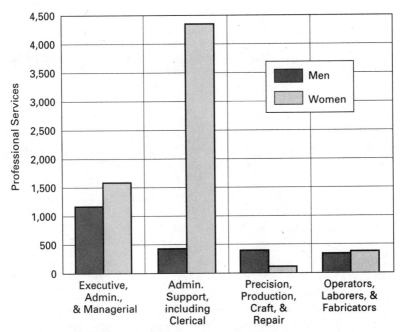

Figure 9-4(d). Employed civilians in selected sectors by occupation and sex; U.S. 1990 (in thousands).

Figure 9-5(a). Male-Dominated Industries,* 1983, 1990, and 1992 earnings

Industry	Percent of employed workers in industry who are male		1992 median weekly earnings
	1983	1990	
Agriculture	80	79	$505
Mining	83	84	632
Construction	92	91	486
Manufacturing	67	68	514
Transp., comm., & public utilities	74	71	599
Wholesale trade	73	72	492
Public admin.	60	57	615

*Male-dominated industries are those where males make up 51% or higher of the total number of workers employed in that industry.

SOURCE: U.S. Department of Labor, Bureau of Labor Statistics, unpublished tables.

Figure 9-5(b). Female-Dominated Industries,* 1983 and 1990, and 1992 earnings

Industry	Percent of employed workers in industry who are female		1992 median weekly earnings
	1983	1990	
Retail trade	52	52	$273
Finance, insurance, & real estate	58	59	404
Services	60	62	372

*Female-dominated industries are those where females make up 51% or higher of the total number of workers employed in that industry.

SOURCE: U.S. Department of Labor, Bureau of Labor Statistics, unpublished tables. Compiled by Janice Hamilton Outtz, "Changes in Employment and Earnings," 1993.

threatens men's self-identity." She makes another interesting point: Only women who truly love their work stick it out. "This is even more threatening, then, because she is more committed to doing the work well and is probably willing to bid low to get the job."[82]

More subtle is the segregation that occurs in other industries, such as transportation. When women succeed in breaking into traditionally male sectors, they tend to be hired in areas where they work alone: as bus drivers, dispatchers, postal carriers. By their very nature, these jobs minimize friction with male colleagues and certainly lessen the risk of sexual harassment on the job.[83]

Viewed against the historical background of the segregated mill girls and the subsequent near-invisibility of working women, the lonely nature of these blue-collar jobs takes on broader significance. Indeed, women have increased their representation in the blue-collar world of men, but they have been relegated to positions which virtually guarantee that their presence can be overlooked by the majority of the male workers. They may be undetected, unnoticed, and therefore unheard, which is a problem if and when the needs, styles, and values of these women fail to coincide with those of the men.

Sexual Harassment

Occupational segregation, a high concentration of women in subordinate positions, and the concomitant erosion of all-male domains—whether this takes the form of a woman operating a crane at a construction site or settling into a corner office with a view of Central Park—are all potential ingredients for incidents of sexual harassment. According to EEO guidelines, sexual harassment comes in two guises: "quid pro quo," which at its extreme could be labeled "sexual extortion"; and a hostile working environment, the definition of which ranges from the presence of offensive pictures to frequent remarks that call attention to one's gender and sexuality.

Since the EEOC first addressed the subject, it has refined its definition in an effort to lay out more precise, detailed guidelines of behavior. Since 1986, court rulings in landmark cases have also sought to get a handle on the issue, although there are still areas of disagreement and debate. Men and women agree in condemning a supervisor who makes a job or promotion contingent on the subordinate's providing sexual favors. But more often than not a man reports feeling flattered by the very same speech or behavior that upsets and offends his female co-worker.[84] This discrepancy in perceptions gave rise to the 1991 court ruling in the case of *Robinson v. Jacksonville Shipyards,* wherein the judge established that actions constituted sexual harassment if a "reasonable woman" deemed them so. Previously, the actions had to be judged against the standard of a "reasonable person." More recently, in the 1993 case *Harris v. Forklift Systems,* the court bolstered protections for women by declaring that a woman who claims sexual harassment need not prove that she was psychologically injured. In other words, she need not have a nervous breakdown before she can claim harassment. The court ruled that hostile or abusive work environments are unlawful. In *Harris v. Forklift,* the U.S. Supreme Court also concluded, though, that the "reasonable person" standard is the appropriate criterion for determining what constitutes sexual harassment.

The ruling validates a woman's point of view even when it diverges from that of man, but it by no means provides a hard and fast rule by which to judge an individual's behavior. A journalist covering a recent sexual harassment scandal at a staid New York financial institution neatly summarized the problem: "The EEOC and the corporate world have discovered that trying to prove the difference between a longing look and a look of longing can be an excruciating ordeal."[85]

Unlike most criminal proceedings, the burden of proof here lies with the victim, for it is up to the accuser to prove that she or he did not welcome the advances, comments, or other offensive behavior. This became apparent during the October 1991 Clarence Thomas Senate confirmation hearings, in which Anita Hill testified that the Supreme Court nominee had repeatedly made improper and offensive remarks. Television spectators watched as Hill became the defendant in a hearing that had been scheduled to review not her ethical and moral standards, but those of Clarence Thomas.

For many women activists, Thomas's appointment to the Supreme Court decision symbolized the establishment's continued dismissal of sexual harassment as a real and destructive problem. They found it especially galling since the appointment followed on the heels of a 208 percent rise in sexual harassment claims filed with the EEOC from 1980 to 1988.[86] Looking back, however, we can see that it was not the result of the hearings, but the public debate they triggered that has had a significant impact on the issue. Anita Hill's televised testimony forced members of the public to determine for themselves what constituted a breach of conduct as opposed to what they considered simply a display of bad taste or rudeness. Over the course of the following year, many wrestled with the question, in the process, changing their minds about the hearings: In an October 1991 poll, most people believed that Hill was lying; a year later, 53 percent of those polled by *The Washington Post* and *ABC News* believed Thomas had indeed harassed Hill.[87] As people thought about it, they seem to have broadened their definition of what constitutes sexual harassment to include the kinds of incidents Hill related. Moreover, many Americans no longer regarded Hill's tacit acceptance of the offensive language and her long silence as sure indicators that she was either lying or had forfeited her right to bring charges.

Indeed, the entire tenor of people's attitudes shifted. Before the hearings, a tiny minority of both women and men had considered sexual harassment a major problem, and less than a quarter credited it with even "minor problem" status.[88] In a 1992 poll, however, more than 80 percent of men and women said that sexual harassment was a problem for women at work.[89] Charges of sexual harassment jumped from 728 between October and December 1990 to 1,244 during the same three-month period a year later.[90] Not that the workplace had suddenly become a den of misbehavior, but the hearings and the debate they spawned empowered victims. They recognized that certain forms of behavior they found personally demeaning were also objectively wrong, and they were now emboldened to take a stand.

The new cases confirmed patterns researchers had already begun to detect. There is now general agreement that the more segregated the workplace, the higher the risk of sexual harassment. Where physical appearance plays an important role in the workplace, there is also a greater likelihood of problems developing. In most cases, victims are women, under 35, unattached, and working in nonsupervisory positions. Their harassers may be co-workers or supervisors, though not necessarily with direct responsibility for the victim, and it is likely that they habitually engage in this type of behavior. One of the few differences between male and female harassers, who account for some eight percent of cases,[91] lies in their relationship to the victim. Women harassers tend to be the victim's direct supervisor.

The reactions of victims also tend to form a pattern. Like Hill, many may wait years to speak out, and some never come forward. The reasons for this are complex. One woman might believe, usually with justification, that if she reports the incident she will in all likelihood be the one to suffer the consequences. It will be her word against his, and she fears losing her job or being pegged as a troublemaker. Many victims also agonize over having unwittingly provoked the offensive behavior and, paradoxically, worry that their accusations will damage the career of the man involved. They believe it is up to them to handle it, and, if they feel they have not done so well, they often feel anxious and depressed.

Finally, the attitude of management has a major influence on the incidence of harassment. Research has shown that where a nonprofessional atmosphere is tolerated or, worse, encouraged in the workplace—where, for example, provocative pictures are allowed to be displayed, or sexually oriented jokes and remarks are the norm—incidents of harassment rise sharply. The Navy's Tailhook scandal, which even involved sexual assaults on female officers by their male colleagues, illustrates the importance of senior-level concern. In the wake of Tailhook, the only senior Navy official to take the incident seriously and demand a genuine investigation was the Department's first female Assistant Secretary for Manpower. The first thing Barbara S. Pope did was to point an accusatory finger at her colleagues and superiors. "That lack of outrage on the part of the senior leadership at the behavior (at Tailhook)," she said, "was one of the largest abrogations of leadership in Navy history." She also sought to spell out the broader implications of condoning sexual harassment, be it in a military or a civilian work environment: "Anything that demeans people demeans the organization."[92]

A Power Issue

"Demeaning" precisely describes the effect of sexual harassment on the victim. In this respect, harassment has little to do with sex and much to do with power,[93] for it serves as a weapon to subordinate and establish dominance over another person. Sexual advances or comments strip the victim of her work identity and define her only by an attribute that has nothing to with her abilities and role in the workplace: her sexuality.

Between a manager and a lower-ranked individual, a sexual advance can be akin to extortion or bribery because the manager is presumed to wield power over the subordinate. His crime is to extend his power beyond the legitimate boundaries of their work relationship and either present her with or set up the conditions for quid pro quo. In a televised discussion on the subject, there was general agreement among female and male panelists that even an innocuous and sincere dinner invitation by a CEO to a subordinate was inappropriate because he was in a position of power relative to her. Had a co-worker issued the invitation, the panel members would not have considered the exchange to have been harassment.[94] Under current law, of course, such an invitation from a superior does not constitute harassment, but common sense suggests that the managers should avoid actions that might even appear improper. In the workplace, this is neither an alien nor a new concept, given that managers and officials routinely have to avoid the appearance of a conflict of interest.

The issue of power is also relevant to sexual harassment incidents between co-workers, where a man trivializes a female colleague by reducing her to her sexual identity. A remark here, a pat there, another remark and a wink, and the message the woman hears is: You're not really my peer, you're a woman who happens to be in my workplace. Many a man would demur, claiming that he never intended such a message. But, wittingly or unwittingly, the man's behavior has a cultural and historical resonance, and the image it conjures is that of women as subordinate creatures, unequal to men, regardless of how he may consciously view his actions and motives.

This is somewhat akin in spirit to what may transpire in a predominantly male work environment, such as a construction site, where women are 25 percent more likely to be sexually harassed.[95] Here, sexual remarks or advances can be said to provide men with a tool by which to fight what they perceive as encroachment on their domain by a female. For many a man, the sight of a woman performing his job can prove profoundly disturbing. If she does it, doesn't that make it "woman's work?"[96] Sexual remarks become, in this context, his way of reestablishing his maleness by emphasizing her femaleness. At another, less subtle level, it may also be one way to encourage her to quit and "leave men's work to the men."

A Gender Issue

It would be misleading, however, to talk about sexual harassment only in terms of power. While it may not have much to do with sex, it does have a lot to do with gender, specifically gender roles. When a male construction worker gives the female crane operator a friendly pat and a wink, he may be doing so because he does not know how else to relate to a women in that setting. Having never worked with one before, he reverts to treating her the way he treats women outside work. As in the case of the supervisor inviting his secretary out for dinner, it is not always the actual behavior that is wrong, but its setting or the relationship of those involved. On a date, at a party, or in a bar, much of what constitutes sexual harassment would be tolerated. It would perhaps not always be appreciated, but, for the most part, nonsexual touching, "looks of longing," and their verbal equivalent, would not be deemed a matter for litigation.

The issue here is which roles are appropriate for which setting. In a place of worship, adults habitually relate to one another primarily as co-believers, because the context demands that men and women turn their attention away from one another onto other matters. In the same vein, the focus in the workplace is the job at hand, not another's sexuality. It is that simple—and that complicated. This is where occupational segregation enters the picture, since it precludes women and men becoming familiar with one another in a work environment. The way in which the workplace is segregated also bears its share of the blame for sexual harassment. By and large, women are clustered in less-valued jobs, and these all too often tally with gender stereotypes of woman as nurturer, caretaker, supporter. Given these conditions, it is not surprising that many men relate to women as primarily females—as opposed to workers first, women second—and as their subordinates.

Ultimately, a Business Issue

Determining whether sexual harassment is a matter of power, sex, or gender, and to what degree, will provide fodder for sociologists, psychologists, and anthropologists for years to come. One thing, however, is already certain: It is a business issue. The time an employee spends planning and carrying out what amounts to a campaign of sexual harassment is time lost to the employer. In addition, victims of this behavior are likely to suffer depression, distress, and difficulty focusing on the job, and the cost of this to the employer can be steep. Finally, hostile work environments block channels of communication among workers to the detriment of the operation and productivity of the company. Depending on the industry, discouraging easy communication and information-sharing among male and female colleagues can have a direct and detrimental impact on decision making and, hence, on the bottom line. Companies that have already wrestled with cases of sexual harassment have learned this firsthand, losing money in downtime as well as through lawyers' fees.

The aftermath of litigation and scandal, however, can be a workplace that has been "sensitized" in all the wrong ways. Some companies have reacted by instituting strict no-dating policies (which, ironically, seems to worsen the harassment problem), as well as policies of single-sex business dinners and business trips. Ultimately, all these policies achieve is a more segregated work environment.[97] Not only does such an approach fail to prevent sexual harassment from recurring, it may also hurt the company. Management often adopts such tough measures in a punitive spirit, and employees at all levels quickly understand that they do not signal a genuine desire to create a harassment-free work environment. On the contrary, such policies penalize female employees by taking them out of the loop and thereby making the glass ceiling even more impenetrable. By entrenching occupational segregation, they also slap an extra layer of glue onto the floor. In the end, they set up a vicious circle by promoting the very conditions that lead to sexual harassment problems and the lowered morale and productivity they foster, not to mention the employer's loss of a talented, increasingly well-educated pool of workers: women.

Men are also at risk if the company does not address the issue of sexual harassment clearly and intelligently. The court's establishment of a "reasonable woman" standard robbed the issue of any predetermined context and criteria that men could rely on. Socialized to play by the rules, many men find it disturbing that there are no clear-cut rules of behavior nor any objective criteria by which charges can be judged. There is not even a statute of limitations, it seems, if women are allowed to bring charges relating to incidents that occurred years before. Not surprisingly, there has been a backlash, with charges that women are turning the workplace into a goldmine of litigation. Those closest to the cases, however, dismiss the notion that women are bringing frivolous charges for financial gain. On the contrary, women are less willing to expose themselves to the embarrassing questions and personal inquiries that such cases entail.[98]

Double Jeopardy, Double Bind, Double Whammy

The problems facing working women—and, to a lesser extent, men—are complex and deep-seated. But they are gaining the attention they deserve, and with each passing year of public discourse, legal battles, and research, the situation is improving. The discourse on gender needs to be broadened, however, to include a more in-depth look at minority and older women. They struggle with the same discrimination and problems that their white and younger sisters encounter. And then some.

Older Women: Stickier Floors, Lower Ceilings, Wider Pay Gaps

Common sense dictates that the more mature and experienced a worker is, the higher her earnings should be. Common sense also suggests that the more experience a worker gains, the higher she should climb in the hierarchy. Sadly, this is seldom the case. As shown in Figure 9-6,

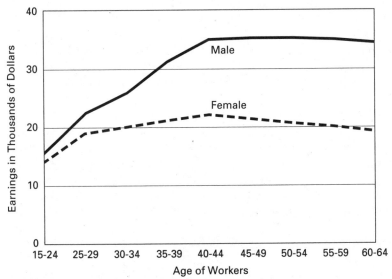

Figure 9-6. The female-male wage gap over the life cycle. 1989 median annual earnings, full-time, year-round workers, by age. (*Source: Based on unpublished data from the U.S. Bureau of the Census, Current Population Survey*)

a woman's earning power peaks when she reaches her early 40s, at which point she earns a median annual salary of $22,000. This is the same amount paid a 25- to 29-year-old man. By the time women reach their mid-50s, their wages are, on average, 45 percent lower than those of their male peers.[99]

This gap does not reflect a relative lack of education among older women. On the contrary, 1989 figures show that college-educated women between the ages of 45 and 64 earned less than their male peers who had only a high school education.[100] Nor can the higher wage disparity be traced to an older woman's propensity to be in poorer health or her reticence to change. In terms of sick leave, older women and men average 2.6 days a year, compared to 3.3 for workers under 45 years old. When asked about their willingness to receive training to hone their skills, only 9 percent of older women and men said they were not interested in any such opportunities. Even if the women constituted the entire 9 percent—which is highly unlikely—those who are recalcitrant would still be in a small minority. The figures reflect in part the fact that many older women have returned to the workforce after a hiatus during which they raised children or cared for their aging parents. Close to 8 million of the women over 45 who were working in 1989 were displaced homemakers who had been forced into the workforce because of widowhood or divorce.[101] But this still does not explain the enormity of the disparity between their wages and those of male peers, who, presumably, worked uninterruptedly.

The real culprits are not the women themselves, but the fact that upon reentering the workforce they are relegated on the basis of age and gender to low-paying jobs. As a result, there is a higher degree of occupational segregation for women in this age group, a situation aggravated by their lack of union representation. In 1990, 58 percent of women over 45 years old worked in low-paying jobs; in the 55-and-over age group, the percentage is 62.4.[102] Hired at a time when employers could legally underpay women workers, they have suffered discrimination all of their working lives. Should these women lose their jobs or decide to move on, the discrimination persists: They are three to five times less likely than a younger woman to receive any form of assistance in securing a new job. Those who manage to get hired again earn some 25 percent less than a younger woman who has undergone the same rehiring process.[103]

Minority Women

Different culturally and often physically from their white sisters and from one another, most minority women nevertheless have met with many of the same challenges, suffered similar discrimination, and fought against much the same odds. Where they have most differed from white women, however, is in their economic status: In the past, as today, minority women are more likely than white women to be the sole earners in a household that includes children, and they are more likely to live in poverty. According to the 1991 Census Bureau report on Child Support and Alimony, 25.5 percent of all children are currently born to unwed mothers, with black children in the lead with 57.5 percent.[104] Though the paths all working women have trodden can be said to parallel each other in many ways, it is important to regard them as individual groups, whose cultures, history, and present circumstances impinge on their roles and needs in today's workplace.

This is what the feminist movement forgot. In its push to establish women's rights, it glossed over differences among American women. While this may have enabled the movement to stay focused on primary issues of sexual equality, it also had the effect of setting an all-white agenda. Minority women did not relate to it, and the movement, in turn, did not address issues of racism, presuming these to come under the purview of the civil rights movement. Minority women, therefore, found themselves caught between the civil rights movement—which was most concerned with the advancement of minority men—and the predominantly white feminist movement.[105] They fell between the cracks.

Three Enemies: Racism, Sexism, and Stereotypes

Minority women can be said to be twice subordinate, and, as such, they experience more pay discrimination and occupational segregation than their white sisters.[106] For minority women, the floor tends to be stickier and the ceiling lower than for white women. This is often the case, but not always, because, as was shown earlier, minority women do not share a common experience. The only commonality among minorities today seems to be their increasing polarization and diversification. Since few studies take this heterogeneity into account, minority women find themselves fighting stereotypes that have little basis in their lives.

Asians are, for example, reputed to excel academically and climb the corporate ladder with the agility of a mountain goat. And statistics show that this is often true: The number of Asian women who received first professional degrees more than doubled between 1985 and 1990, and the rise in recipients of bachelor's and master's degrees rose, respectively, by 64 and 56 percent. The portrait is incomplete, however, until one pencils in the fact that, in 1990, 11.1 percent of Asian women worked as laborers, operators, and fabricators—about the same percentage as those recorded by Native-American (11.4 percent) and black women (12.3 percent),[107] who are generally considered not as successful as Asian women.

Another popular stereotype elevates the black woman to the status of superwoman: the matriarch, the resourceful single mother, the most likely in her community to succeed. As flattering as it may be, the myth nevertheless does the majority of black women a disservice, for it underplays the difficulties they face. It diminishes the impact of figures that show that black women are more likely than white women to work in low-paying jobs—they are overrepresented by 23 percent, compared to 15 percent for white women[108]—and that they have a more difficult time, relative to whites, breaking through the glass ceiling. In 1990, 11.9 percent of white working women held executive, administrative, and managerial positions, but the figure for black women was only 7.4 percent.[109] Moreover, the myth of the superwoman glosses over the hard conditions under which so many black women live: In 1990, 46 percent of all black families were maintained single-handedly by a woman with median annual earnings of $12,125, or 38 percent less than the median earnings recorded by white, female-headed households.[110]

For their part, Hispanics are reputed to be severely disadvantaged due primarily to their relatively lower investments in higher education. They are twice as likely as white women to work as laborers, fabricators, and operators, and only 7 percent work in executive, administrative, and managerial jobs.[111] The number of Hispanic women earning higher degrees is growing, though it remains small. In 1990, 32 percent more Hispanic women graduated from four-year programs than in 1985.[112]

When looking at problems of sexism and racism, the minority that has so far been most thoroughly researched (and even that has been minimal until recently) are African-American women. Despite the risks inherent in generalizations, it is nevertheless relatively safe to assume that some of the findings apply in principle, if not in their specifics, to other minority women.

Numbers and personal testimony underline the obvious: For black women, the road has been harder than for white women. In the private sector, special considerations based on gender have not consistently helped black (and other minority) women,[113] who have been clustered in greater proportion in low-paying occupations and sectors. The pressure felt by women working among males is intensified in the case of black women. Ella Louise Bell of the Yale School of Organization and Management documented this poignantly: "I see it as operating in a fog," one woman told her, "or swimming in a mud puddle. You know you are stroking, but you don't know how you are being perceived. You *think* stroking is the right thing to do." [Italics added] Another black women, speaking of the added demands placed on her, echoed the feelings of many white women, but with the added edge that comes from being doubly different from the predominant culture: "I am always having to stay one step ahead. I'm just tired of always trying to outsmart them. Beyond doing all the work the job requires, you must prove to others beyond a doubt that you are *not a freak,* just qualified." [Italics added][114]

Some women also have to battle the assumption that they were hired or promoted primarily because they were female, the idea being that their employers made decisions based only on a desire to comply with EEOC guidelines. Again, for black women, the fight is more intense: They feel they have to prove they were not hired as tokens, but because, in addition to being black and female, they are also capable.

Race over Gender and Juggling Cultures

Reactions to the Anita Hill testimony at Clarence Thomas's confirmation hearings illustrate another, related point. As soon as Thomas termed the hearings "an electronic lynching," he injected a powerful racial theme into the debate. Immediately, the black community rallied to defend a black man in a white man's world, effectively pushing aside the question of sexual harassment a fellow black claimed to have suffered.[115] The reaction was basically the same for both genders. Perhaps race would not have won so handily over gender had black women identified with the women's movement. But they did not. When it came to choosing sides, black women overwhelmingly supported Thomas and turned their backs on Hill.

If race won over gender, it was only partly because the women's movement has not historically embraced black women. Mostly, black women's reactions need to be viewed within the framework of black culture. Seated before a white male panel, Thomas was seen to be the vulnerable male in need of protection and support, while, for many blacks, Hill embodied the myth of the black superwoman—strong, indomitable, and requiring no protection. More important, many viewed her as wrongly placing gender before race and thereby jeopardizing the black community.

The lack of agreement between black and white women on the veracity and appropriateness of Hill's testimony indicates a deeper, more complex cultural divide that separates women of different races. Each community applies its own set of standards when judging the appropriateness of an individual's behavior. It also evaluates behavior in terms of gender roles: If in the black culture women are expected to be relatively subservient to men, then clearly Hill's accusations constituted an affront to tradition. A strong subordination of women may also explain why black women have reported far fewer cases of sexual harassment than whites.

The fact that black organizations are seldom headed by women also illustrates the existence of sexism within the black community.[116] For the individual black woman, this means she has to fight discrimination on two fronts: in the outside, predominantly white world, as well as within her own community. Moreover, most working black women find themselves daily commuting between two cultures. At home, they feel the need to maintain culturally prescribed roles that sometimes directly contradict the more assertive behavior they have to cultivate at work.

Only relatively recently have studies and workshops focused on this and other demands specific to black women in the workplace. If proof was needed that they were long overdue, it was provided by the lightning speed at which the self-help career guide for black women, *Work, Sister, Work*,[117] moved out of the bookstores. One hopes that the same attention will, in the future, be directed at other minority women, who also find themselves commuting between cultures and shouldering the double burden of sexism and racism.

Family Issues

Whatever their race or ethnic background, more and more women in the workforce have motherhood in common. By the year 2000, as many as 90 percent of all women between the ages of 25 and 40 will be working, and 86 percent of these will be mothers.[118] Already the proportion of working mothers with preschool-age children is high: 62 percent of white and 73 percent of black married women with three-year-olds are working.[119] The numbers would be even higher if more employers provided any of a variety of options for working parents. Talented, educated women are staying out of the workforce because the family cannot afford to have them work. This is not surprising, when one considers that an average family spends 10 percent of its yearly income on child care; for low income families, that service siphons off close to a quarter of their annual earnings.[120] The high cost of child care also prevents many working mothers from taking advantage of educational and training opportunities.

These numbers underline the fact that demographic and societal changes have outpaced corporate and public policy. As seen earlier, current practices are predicated on an idealized "traditional" family, in which the man works for family wages and the woman stays at home to care for children and elderly parents. The ideal was never true across the board, and today the growing number of working mothers—and the degree to which corporations and public institutions depend on them—is forcing the pace of change to accelerate. Quality of life, health, and wellness are today cited as important factors in an individual's decisions regarding work.[121] Fewer and fewer Americans believe that the promise of a slightly larger paycheck is worth the stress of worrying about a child at home alone or that of being trapped in an inflexible work schedule when a child or a parent is ill. And for more and more Americans, caring for a dependent is a real concern, as one company discovered when a 1991 survey of its employees showed that 78 percent of them faced or would face in the coming two years responsibilities for a child or elderly adult.[122]

Since working women have borne the lion's share of dependent care while also fulfilling work obligations, they have been the ones to clamor for family-friendly policies. Today, they are joined by many a working father. Some are single parents, but most are the husbands of working women whose obligations dictate that both partners must juggle the demands of their respective jobs as well as the needs of their family. What used to be solely a woman's issue is slowly becoming a worker's issue.

Already, it has become an employer's issue, as the passage of the Family and Medical Leave Bill proves. It requires employers with more than 50 workers to provide unpaid leave with job guarantees and continued benefits for the birth of a child or medical problems in the family, including care of elderly parents. The bill essentially establishes a floor to protect workers, and, although the private sector generally opposed it, the bill responds to a reality many employers had already recognized and addressed. Aside from providing legal recourse to employees, the law's most significant contribution, then, is to force the recalcitrant to take a closer look at the dynamics of their workplaces and take at least minimal steps to make them worker-friendly. They will be aided by the experience of their more farsighted colleagues who early on felt the winds of change. They understood the implications of statistics showing that few American families any longer had a mother at home full-time, caring for the children. They also recognized that a worker who is worried about a dependent cannot have her or his mind fully on the job. One effort to quantify this demonstrated that 20 percent of the women and more than 7 percent of the men surveyed spent unproductive time at work due to childcare concerns. In another survey of 1,200 employees, 53 percent of women under 35 years old reported that their concentration or judgment was affected by family concerns.[123]

Recognizing that employers had much to gain by addressing family-related issues, some 40 percent of the larger U.S. companies had by 1986 provided maternal/parental leave in addition to paid disability leave with full job guarantees.[124] The instincts of these companies proved correct: the policies yielded bottom-line results. Today, those results continue to be confirmed. Women who benefit from child-care assistance programs return to work sooner after giving birth.[125] Part-time and job-sharing arrangements often mean that employers get more work out of two part-timers combined than out of one full-timer.[126] Allowing a worker to take an unpaid year off after the birth or adoption of a child assures the worker's return and saves the company money. Aetna Life and Casualty reported savings of 93 percent of an employee's first year salary;[127] AT&T found that its leave policy saved 70 percent of the cost of recruiting and training a replacement.[128] Southern New England Telephone had a 90 percent retention rate against the national average of 72 percent.[129]

The key to a company's success seems to lie in its ability to identify what family package best suits its workforce profile and budget. For some, this might mean subsidizing child care rather than providing an onsite facility. For others, it may entail setting aside a mother's room for new mothers who wish to return to work but feel strongly that they should continue nursing their infants. Depending on the industry and the demands of the jobs, part-time work arrangements may be preferable to schemes in which workers can "bank" time—in such a scheme, they log in time with no set work-week schedule and accrue vacation time according to the hours worked. Telecommuting, job sharing, sabbaticals without change in job status, flextime—the mix of options is endless, which increases the chances of employers and employees accommodating each other's needs.

In the business of promoting mutual accommodation, Paul Rupert, the associate director of New Ways to Work, sees this as the wave of the future. "Customization will become a new watchword in the workplace," he maintains. "By customizing the work environment and its practices to meet the needs of employees, managers can develop employees' potential while strengthening their commitment to the employer. In the end, everyone wins."[130]

Conclusion

The move to customize the workplace, along with the emergence of increasingly particularized research, shows that the debate on gender has entered a new phase. Men and women are gathering the tools which will enable them to understand each other better, communicate more effectively, and, above all, collaborate as equals. The progress is already tangible. As a generation of men with working spouses moves into senior positions—along with an increasing number of women— and as the workplace digests the fact that the structure of the American family and society as a whole has dramatically changed, family and gender issues are no longer a source of concern to women only. "Women's issues are rapidly becoming workforce issues, and companies that best address them will win in the marketplace," Irene Rosenfeld, executive vice president at Kraft-General Foods, points out. A mother of two and in charge of a billion-dollar beverage division, she praises her company's family policies as helpful to her personally and as a smart business move.[131]

Nor is she the only one to think of family policies strictly in business terms. "Those employers who are learning to develop and retain women will have a great competitive edge four or five years from now," according to Felice Schwartz, author of *Breaking with Tradition* and a long-time participant in and observer of the workplace.[132] The reason for this is simple: "You can't hire the best and only hire white males," Boeing's manager of workforce diversity Aaron Hazard believes. "And once you've got them," he adds, referring to women and minorities, "you've got to be able to keep them."[133]

These comments reflect a change of attitude arising from a better understanding of the bottom-line cost of not attending intelligently to workers' concerns—be they sexual harassment on the job, shunting women onto a mommy track, occupational segregation, or other forms of discrimination. The norm was once to view antidiscriminatory policies as nonessential bonuses to be implemented only when times were good and employers flush. Workshops on sexual harassment were considered empty offerings to women and the god(esse)s of political correctness. While many still subscribe to such views, more and more employers are discovering that gender- and family-related policies are basic economic decisions that bear directly on productivity, economic growth, and, ultimately, on the well-being of society as a whole.

With the help of concerned workers, these policies are helping to reshape the workplace and its culture. This is an ongoing process which promises to be neither smooth, easy, nor rapid. It is contingent on people shedding outworn stereotypes and false expectations about others as well as about themselves. It entails open, frank discussion and a nonjudgmental recognition of differences. It demands that women and men try to understand and respect each other's perspectives. This can be as simple as taking heed of different conversation styles—as Deborah Tannen points out in her popular book, *You Just Don't Understand*, women tend to make eye contact and utter noises to signal that they are listening; a man, on the other hand, may be attentively listening while looking the other way, and frequently interprets these listening noises as attempts to interrupt or as signs of impatience. These and other gender idiosyncrasies make for fun anecdotes, but they can also lead to serious misunderstandings or sour a work atmosphere. At another, more difficult level, respect and understanding entails accepting the validity of a person's approach to such tasks as problem solving, management, or research, even when these are fundamentally different from one's own.

Developing a true collaboration based on understanding and respect takes time, for the protagonists involved are, after all, only human. Just as the male establishment finds it a struggle to change its ingrained views, so do women have difficulty abandoning old patterns. This is why it is important for the workplace to formulate behavior guidelines and policies that engender and reward changes in attitude.

In the process, these will have a positive impact on society as a whole. Policies that allow parents to take more time with their children make a difference to the children's performance in school, their self-esteem, and their values. Respect for the individual at work translates into respect for others outside the workplace. Appreciation for staff work as an integral, necessary component of the establishment's success raises people's awareness of the value of all caretaking activities. In many ways, the workplace can be viewed as an ideal laboratory for broader social change. It is heterogeneous, with almost an equal amount of men and women. And it has a unique feedback system: Red flags in the form of civil suits or sagging productivity signal mistakes, just as good morale and a motivated workforce clearly indicate that management is on the right track.

References

1. U.S. Department of Labor, Bureau of Labor Statistics, *Outlook 1990–2005*, BLS Bulletin 2402 (Washington, D.C.: U.S. GPO, May 1992), p. 123.

2. Heidi Hartmann and Roberta Spalter Roth, "Improving Employment Opportunities for Women," testimony concerning H.R. 1 Civil Rights Act of 1991 before the U.S. House of Representatives Committee on Education and Labor. Institute for Women's Policy Research, February 27, 1991, p. 1.

3. Teresa L. Amott and Julie A. Matthaei, *Race, Gender & Work* (Boston: South End Press, 1991), p. 27.

4. Ann M. Morrison, Randall P. White, and Ellen Van Velsor, *Breaking the Glass Ceiling* (Reading, Mass: Addison-Wesley Publishing, Co., 1987), p. 168.

5. Jean Baker Miller, *Toward a New Psychology of Women*, 2d ed. (Boston: Beacon Press, 1986), p. 22.

6. Anthony Astrachan, *How Men Feel* (Garden City, N.Y.: Anchor Press/Doubleday, 1986), p. 18.

7. Miller, *op. cit.*, p. 10.

8. Astrachan, *op. cit.*, pp. 24–25.

9. Susan Faludi, *Backlash: The Undeclared War Against American Women* (New York: Crown Publishers, 1991), p. xix.

10. L. J. Dionne, Jr., "Struggle for Work and Family Fueling Women's Movement," Series: Women's Lives: A Scorecard of Change, *The New York Times*, August 22, 1989, p. A1.

11. "The Gender Gap in America: Unlike 1975, Today Most Americans Think Men Have It Better," *The Gallup Poll News Service*, vol. 54, no. 37, February 5, 1990.

12. Ann-Marie Rizzo and Carmen Mendez, *The Integration of Women in Management* (New York: Quorum Books, 1990), p. 54.

13. Joe Alper, "The Pipeline Is Leaking Women All the Way Along," *Science*, vol. 260, April 16, 1993, p. 410.

14. Sylvia Nasar, "Women's Progress Stalled? Just Not So," *The New York Times*, October 18, 1992, pp. 8–10.

15. "The Gender Gap in America," *op. cit.*, p. 1.

16. Astrachan, *op. cit.*, p. 15.

17. Dr. Gary D. Cobb, "The Men's Movement—Rules for the 90's," presentation at the symposium, *Being a Man in the '90s*, held by INOVA Health System, at Tyson's Corner, Virginia, May 19, 1993.

18. Morrison, White, and Van Velsor, *op. cit.*, p. 115.

19. Miller, *op. cit.*, p. 86.

20. Astrachan, *op. cit.*, pp. 27–28.

21. Sean Piccoli, "The '90s Guy: A Work in Progress," *Washington Times*, June 8, 1993, pp. E1, E5.

22. Astrachan, *op. cit.*, p. 18.

23. Faludi, *op. cit.*, p. 297.

24. Astrachan, *op. cit.*, p. 31.

25. Anne B. Fisher, "When Will Women Get to the Top?" *Fortune*, September 21, 1992.

26. "The Gender Gap in America," *op. cit.*

27. Dionne, *op. cit.*

28. Fisher, *op cit.*

29. Robert L. Rose, *The Wall Street Journal,* June 21, 1993, p. R10.

30. Clarissa Pinkola Estés, *Women Who Run with the Wolves,* (New York: Ballantine Books, 1992).

31. Judy B. Rosener, "Ways Women Lead," *Harvard Business Review,* November-December 1990, pp. 119–125.

32. Frank B. Morgan, "Race/Ethnicity Trends in Degrees Conferred by Institutions of Higher Education: 1980–81 through 1989–90," U.S. Department of Education, National Center for Education Statistics, E.D. Tabbs, May 1992.

33. Clifford Adelman, *Women at Thirtysomething: Paradox of Attainment,* U.S. Department of Education, Office of Research and Improvement, 1991, p. 28.

34. Telephone interview with consultant Patricia H. Dutter by Lee Adair Lawrence, July 6, 1993.

35. National Commission on Working Women, *Women, Work and the Future,* Fact Sheet (Washington, D.C., National Commission on Working Women, January 1989).

36. Interview with mid-level woman government official by Lee Adair Lawrence, June 24, 1993.

37. Adelman, *op. cit.,* p. 28.

38. Marcia Baringa, "Is There a Female Style in Science?" *Science,* vol. 260, April 16, 1993, p. 390.

39. Morrison, White, and Van Velsor, *op. cit.,* p. 43.

40. Adelman, *op. cit.,* p. 29.

41. Ann M. Morrison, in an unpublished letter, February 2, 1994.

42. *Ibid.,* p. 28.

43. Judy B. Rosener, "Ways Women Lead," *Harvard Business Review,* November-December 1990, p. 120.

44. Amy Saltzman, "Trouble at the Top," *Business,* vol. 110, no. 23, June 17, 1991, p. 21.

45. Sue Mize, "Shattering the Glass Ceiling," *Training and Development Journal,* vol. 46, no. 1, January 1992, p. 61.

46. Baringa, *op cit.,* p. 400.

47. Saltzman, *op. cit.,* p. 23.

48. Miller, *op. cit.,* p. 4.

49. Department of Commerce, Bureau of the Census, table of "Earnings Distribution of Year-Round, Full-Time Workers, by Sex, 1990," reprinted in *1993 Information Please Almanac,* 46th ed. (Boston: Houghton Mifflin, 1993), p. 46.

50. U.S. Department of Labor, Bureau of Labor Statistics, table of "Median Weekly Earnings of Full-Time Workers by Occupation and Sex," *Employment and Earnings,* January 1992 (Washington, D.C.: U.S. GPO).

51. Melissa Castleman and Sandra Van Fossen, *Making Both Ends Meet: Working Mothers in America,* (Washington, D.C.: Wider Opportunities for Women, Inc., 1991), p. 6.

52. Nasar, *op. cit.,* p. 10.

53. National Commission on Working Women, *op. cit.,* p. 3.

54. Carol Kleiman, "Pay Equality Just a Myth in High Tech," *The Chicago Tribune,* February 1, 1993.

55. Heidi Hartmann and Roberta Spalter-Roth, "Improving Women's Status in the Workforce: The Family Issue of the Future," *Hearings of the Subcommittee on Employment and Productivity, Committee on Labor and Human Resources,* U.S. Senate, July 18, 1991, pp. ii–iii.

56. Castleman and Van Fossen, *op. cit.,* pp. 5–7.

57. Feminist Majority Foundation, op. cit.

58. Department of Commerce, Bureau of the Census, table of "Families Maintained by Women, with No Husband Present," reprinted in *1993 Information Please Almanac, op. cit.,* p. 833.

59. Adelman, *op. cit.,* p. 23.

60. Fisher, *op. cit.,* p. 45.

61. Barbara Presley Noble, "And Now the `Sticky Floor,'" *The New York Times,* November 22, 1992.

62. U.S. Department of Labor, "A Report on the Glass Ceiling Initiative," August 7, 1991, p. 6.

63. U.S. Department of Commerce, Economics and Statistics Administration, Bureau of the Census, *Detailed Occupation and Other Characteristics from the EEO File for the U.S.,* 1990 Census of Population, Supplementary Reports, 1990 CP-S-1-1 (Washington, D.C.: U.S. GPO, 1992).

64. Kevin R. Hopkins and William B. Johnston, "Opportunity 2000, Creative Affirmative Action Strategies for a Changing Workforce," Hudson Institute for U.S. Department of Labor, Employment Standards Administration (Washington D.C.: U.S. GPO, September 1988), p. 20.

65. Bill McAllister, "Government Women, Too, Seen Facing `Glass Ceiling,'" *The Washington Post,* October 29, 1992, pp. A1, A4.

66. U.S. Merit Systems Protection Board, "A Question of Equity: Women and the Glass Ceiling in the Federal Government," 1992, p. 9.

67. D'Vera Cohn and Barbara Vobejda, "For Women Uneven Strides in the Workplace," *The Washington Post,* December 21, 1992, pp. A1, A12.

68. U.S. Department of Labor, "Pipelines of Progress: A Status Report on the Glass Ceiling," August 1992, pp. 15–17.

69. Morrison, White, and Van Velsor, *op. cit.,* p. 125.

70. *Ibid.*, p. 52.

71. *Ibid.*, p. 162.

72. *Ibid.*, p. 164.

73. Elizabeth Culotta, "Women Struggle to Crack the Code of Corporate Culture, *Science*, vol. 260, April 16, 1993, p. 401.

74. Interview with a bank senior vice president by Lee Adair Lawrence, New York City, June 26, 1993.

75. Dionne, *op. cit.*, p. A1.

76. Hartmann and Spalter-Roth, *op. cit.*, p. 1.

77. Telephone interview with consultant Patricia H. Dutter in Atlanta by Lee Adair Lawrence, July 6, 1993.

78. Hartmann and Spalter-Roth, *op. cit.*, p. 3.

79. "Women Still `Stuck' in Low-Level Jobs," *Women in Public Service*, no. 3, Fall 1992, p. 1.

80. *Ibid.*, p. 3.

81. National Commission on Working Women, "Women and Nontraditional Work," *Wider Opportunities for Women*, November 1989, p. 1.

82. Telephone interview with independent contractor Lisa MacDonald by Lee Adair Lawrence, Washington D.C., July 1, 1993.

83. Cohn and Vobejda, "For Women, Uneven Strides," *op. cit.*, p. A12.

84. Barbara A. Gutek, *Sex and the Workplace* (San Francisco: Jossey-Bass, Inc.), 1985, p. 97.

85. Robin Pogrebin, "Allegations at Morgan Stanley Stir Sexual Harassment Debate," *The New York Observer*, May 31, 1993, p. 1.

86. Faludi, *op. cit.*, p. xvi.

87. Richard Morin, "Harassment Consensus Grows," *The Washington Post*, December 18, 1992, p. A1.

88. Gutek, *op. cit.*, p. 53.

89. Morin, *op. cit.*, p. A1.

90. Dana Priest, "Hill-Thomas Legacy May Be Challenges to Old Workplace Patterns, *The Washington Post*, March 12, 1992, p. A8.

91. *Ibid.*

92. Judy Mann, "The Woman Who Said No to the Navy," *The Washington Post*, February 5, 1993, p. E3.

93. "On the Issues: Sexual Harassment," with John Chancellor, WETA (PBS, Washington, D.C.) telecast, June 11, 1993.

94. *Ibid.*

95. American Society for Training and Development, "Sexual Harassment: What Trainers Need to Know," *Info-Line*, Issue 9202, February 1992, p. 5.

96. Miller, *op. cit.*, p. 71.

97. Segal, *op. cit.*, p. 82.

98. Pogrebin, *op. cit.*, p. 20.

99. National Commission on Working Women, *Women, Work and Age: Wider Opportunities for Women*, Fact Sheet, July 1990.

100. Older Women's League, "Paying for Prejudice: A Report on Midlife and Older Women in America's Labor Force," *1991 Mother's Day Report*, May 1991, p. 4.

101. National Commission on Working Women, *Women, Work and Age, op. cit.*

102. Older Women's League, *op. cit.*, p. 6.

103. *Ibid.*, p. 11.

104. Reprinted in *1993 Information Please Almanac, op. cit.*, p. 833.

105. George Davis and Glegg Watson, *Black Life in Corporate America: Swimming in the Mainstream* (New York: Anchor Books, 1985), p. 125.

106. Janice Outtz Hamilton, *Changes in Employment and Earnings*, Washington D.C., June 24, 1993, unpublished report for American Society for Training and Development.

107. U.S. Department of Commerce, Economics and Statistics Administration, *Detailed Occupation and Other Characteristics from the EEO File for the U.S., op cit.*, tables.

108. Women in Public Service, *op. cit.*, p. 3.

109. U.S. Department of Commerce, Economics and Statistics Administration, *Detailed Occupation and Other Characteristics from the EEO File for the U.S., op. cit.*, tables.

110. Department of Commerce, Bureau of the Census, table of "Selected Family Characteristics," compiled from data of March 1991.

111. U.S. Department of Commerce, Economics and Statistics Administration, *Detailed Occupation and Other Characteristics from the EEO File for the U.S., op. cit.*, tables.

112. Frank B. Morgan, *op. cit.*, tables.

113. Yehouda Shenhav, "Entrance of Blacks and Women into Managerial Positions in Scientific and Engineering Occupations: A Longitudinal Analysis," *Academy of Management Journal*, vol. 35, no. 4, 1992, p. 898.

114. Ella Louise Bell, "The Bicultural Life Experiences of Career-Oriented Black Women," *Journal of Organizational Behavior*, vol. 11, p. 473.

115. Katherine Tate, "The Invisible Woman," *American Prospect*, Spring 1992, p. 81.

116. Ann O'Hanlon, "Grass Roots and Glass Ceiling," *The Washington Post*, April 18, 1993, p. C5.

117. Cydney Shields and Leslie C. Shields, *Work, Sister, Work: Why Black Women Can't Get Ahead and What They Can Do About It* (New York: Birch Lane, 1993).

118. Bonnie Michaels, "Workforce Challenges of the '90s: Employees and Dependent Care," *Employee Service Management*, April 1990, p. 14.

119. A. Hacker, *New York Review of Books*, January 28, 1993, p. 15.

120. National Commission on Working Women, "Women, Work and Child Care," Fact Sheet, *Wider Opportunities for Women*, Washington D.C., May 1989.

121. Abby Livingston, "What Your Department Can Do: Special Report on Cultural Diversity in Today's Corporation," *Working Women*, January 1991, vol. 16, no. 1, p. 59.

122. The Bureau of National Affairs, Current Developments Section, "Coalition of Companies Pledges to Spend $25 Million on Elder, Child Care Programs," September 11, 1992.

123. Bonnie Michaels, "The Changing Workforce," *Managing Work & Family*, slides, 1989.

124. Hopkins and Johnston, *op. cit.*, p. 30.

125. Bonnie Michaels, "Workforce Challenges of the '90s," *op. cit.*, p. 14.

126. Beatrice Motamedi, "New Workforce Needs Different Hours, Benefits," *The San Francisco Chronicle*, September 23, 1991, p. B5.

127. Castleman and Van Fossen, *op. cit.*, p. 8.

128. Michele Galen, "Work & Family," *Business Week*, June 28, 1993, p. 82.

129. Castleman and Van Fossen, *loc. cit.*

130. Paul Rupert, "Productivity Through Flexible Management: Solving Work/Family Conflicts," No. 3247.

131. Fisher, *op. cit.*, p. 52.

132. Elizabeth Lesly, "Demand More at Work, Consultant Tells Woman," *Washington Times*, March 16, 1992, p. B4.

133. Elizabeth Rhodes, "The Work World's Next Frontier Is Gender Bias and How to Change It—Taking Gender's Measure," *The Seattle Times*, October 16, 1992, p. D1.

10

People with Disabilities in the Diverse Workplace*

Diversity in the workplace reaches far beyond race, ethnic origin, and gender. If "diverse" means those who are truly different from traditional workers, then we must include others who historically have been excluded or relegated to the lower rungs of the employment ladder: people with disabilities, older people, and gays and lesbians. This chapter focuses on workers with disabilities, beginning with an historical and social perspective. We examine the difficult issues that people with disabilities face in joining America's workforce and look at the impact of the Americans with Disabilities Act of 1990 (ADA). Our discussion leads to some practical solutions for being more responsive to people with disabilities in the workplace.

When we think of people with disabilities, our first inclination may be to use the word "handicapped." But a look at that word's history reveals why its use today is inappropriate: "Handicapped" originated in Britain after the Crimean War ended in 1856. As a result of significant medical advances, many soldiers survived injuries that would have proved fatal in previous wars. To aid the severely disabled men,

---

*This chapter was written with Mary B. Dickson. The authors are grateful for her work.

Parliament legalized begging for war veterans; they could keep a "cap handy" to accept money from people on the street.

Because the word "handicapped" suggests making beggars out of people with disabilities, it is no longer acceptable.[1] The preferred word is "disability," which refers to any long- or short-term reduction of a person's activity caused by an acute or chronic condition, a condition that can be of physical, mental, or chronic medical origin.

Although use of the word "handicapped" still exists (in "handicapped parking," for example), knowing the historical definition helps explain why people bearing such labels have faced discrimination in the workplace and elsewhere. Indeed, people who have disabilities have weathered years of discrimination based on fears, myths, and patronizing and stereotypical thinking.

The seeds of this fear and discrimination were planted centuries ago. Early nomads left people with disabilities to die, believing they had nothing to contribute to the tribe. The Greeks tried to find rational reasons for disabilities, while early Christians promoted sympathy and pity toward people with disabilities. In the Middle Ages, the prevailing view was that people with disabilities were impure and evil; so they were ridiculed and persecuted. During the Renaissance, medical treatment, research, and education focused on eliminating or curing disabilities. Afterward, those who could not benefit from treatment were institutionalized.

In the American colonies, people with disabilities were prevented from immigrating for fear they would need financial support. By the late 1880s, most states institutionalized people who were mentally ill, mentally retarded, blind, deaf, or physically disabled. On the American frontier, which encouraged rugged individualism and independence, those with disabilities were generally kept at home and viewed as burdens.[2]

The most profound example of adverse action toward people with disabilities occurred in Hitler's Germany. Medical doctors, acting as agents of death, subjected people with disabilities to horrific experiments before annihilating them. Ultimately, they became the extreme example of eradication justified on the grounds of being "different."

Following the world wars, veterans with disabilities received rehabilitation services, and eventually these services extended to civilians as well. By the 1960s, a number of movements contributed to advances for people with disabilities. Consumerism, the movement led by Ralph Nader and others, enlightened people about the shortcomings of products and services. The birth of self-help programs spawned support groups for people with common concerns, including those with various disabilities. Mental health advocates supported moving people from large institutions to independent or family-sized living arrangements in the community. And a holistic health perspective emerged as the alternative to traditional approaches to treatment.

Perhaps the most eye-opening moment in the United States was the civil rights movement, which began with African Americans and spread to other minority groups.[3] The movement awakened many to the prevalence of widespread discrimination, including discrimination toward people with disabilities.

As the twenty-first century rolled into its last decade, the United States passed the Americans with Disabilities Act of 1990. Although the ADA could be seen as part of the civil rights struggle of people with disabilities, it never had the vocal or visible trappings of other fights for civil rights—no memorable Freedom Rides or "I Have a Dream" speeches that people commonly remember. As journalist Joseph Shapiro observes, "African Americans changed the nation first by reorienting attitudes and then winning passage of civil-rights laws. For disabled Americans, the reverse was true."[4] The laws came first.

The ADA evolved from 25 years history of legislation focused on bringing people with disabilities into the mainstream of American life. The laws that served as stepping stones to the 1990 act include:

- *Architectural Barriers Act of 1968.* Prohibits architectural barriers in all federally owned or leased buildings.

- *Urban Mass Transit Act of 1970.* Requires that all new purchases of mass transit vehicles be equipped with lifts. The American Public Transit Association sought and won a court injunction barring implementation of the proposed regulations, resulting in no action until the ADA passed.

- *Rehabilitation Act of 1973.* Section 503 of this Act, which was the predecessor of the ADA's provisions on employment discrimination, provides OFCCP concurrent jurisdiction over Federal contractors and exclusive jurisdiction over employees of the Executive branch of the Federal government. Section 504 and related provision forbids discrimination on the basis of disability in programs receiving federal funds; language paralleled that of the Civil Rights Act of 1964.

- *Education of All Handicapped Children Act of 1975.* Requires a free, appropriate public education in an integrated setting for children with disabilities.

- *Voting Accessibility for the Elderly and Handicapped Act of 1984.* Improves access for elderly and handicapped individuals to registration facilities and polling places in federal elections.

- *Air Carrier Access Act of 1988.* Provides for equal access on private airlines and air carriers and prohibited discrimination in air travel on the basis of disability.

- *Civil Rights Restoration Act of 1988.* Clarifies that organizations or corporations receiving federal funds could not discriminate in any of their programs on the basis of race, ethnicity, religion, national origin, gender, age, or disability. This is the first act to include disability as a protected class.

- *Fair Housing Act Amendments of 1988.* Prohibits discrimination against people with disabilities in housing and provides for universal design (architectural accessibility) in new construction of housing units of various types and sizes.

The Americans with Disabilities Act (ADA) of 1990 is modeled after the Civil Rights Act of 1964 and Section 504 of the Rehabilitation Act of 1973. It creates broad civil rights protection for people with disabilities, intending to eliminate the discrimination that keeps them from participating fully in the economic, social, and political life of our country.

Although the ADA was passed before the Civil Rights Act of 1991, both the ADA and the Rehabilitation Act state that "the powers, remedies, and procedures of the Civil Rights Act are to be used by the Equal Employment Opportunity Commission (EEOC), the Attorney General, or by any person alleging discrimination on the basis of disability...concerning employment." The ADA allows people with disabilities who feel they have been discriminated against to request a jury trial and, in the private sector, to receive punitive damages. The Civil Rights Act of 1991 enforces the ADA and covers people with disabilities as well as other protected classes.

The ADA is a landmark law. It prohibits discrimination in employment, government services, public accommodation, and communication for America's 43 million people with disabilities. In employment, its intent is to give people with disabilities the chance to be hired because of the skills they can contribute rather than being discriminated against because of their disabilities. In other words, the ADA asks us to look at people as people—not as a disability with a person attached.

Who Are the People with Disabilities?

Just exactly what qualifies as a disability, and how many people in the United States are disabled? Those questions are not easily answered because confusion and debate continue over what specifically constitutes a disability and, therefore, how to count the people who have one. Adding to the difficulty is that different definitions prescribe who is eligible for particular government programs.

Rather than listing conditions that are considered disabilities, the ADA provides a broad, three-pronged definition of "disability":

- *A physical or mental impairment that substantially limits one or more major life activities.* Includes physiological disorders and conditions, cosmetic disfigurement, or anatomical loss affecting body systems. Also included are mental or psychological disorders such as mental retardation, organic brain syndrome, emotional or mental illness, and specific learning disabilities. Major life activities are defined as caring for oneself, performing manual tasks, walking, seeing, hearing, speaking, breathing, learning, and working.

- *A record of such impairment.* Accounts for people who may be in remission for cancer or who have a history of mental illness.

- *Being regarded as having such an impairment.* Refers either to people who look like they may have an impairment or to people who are treated as though their impairment may limit them, when in fact it does not (for example, someone who has a facial scar and wants to work as a receptionist).

The ADA does not protect individuals currently using illegal drugs; it does permit drug testing in the workplace. Excluded from coverage are the conditions of homosexuality and bisexuality; transvestism, transsexualism, pedophilia, exhibitionism, and voyeurism; sexual-behavior disorders and those gender-identity disorders not resulting from physical impairment; compulsive gambling; kleptomania; pyromania; and psychoactive substance-abuse disorders.

Additional exclusions include physical characteristics such as eye and hair color, handedness, height, weight, or "characteristic predisposition to illness or disease;" pregnancy; other conditions that are not the result of a physiological disorder; common personality traits such as poor judgment; environmental, cultural, or economic disadvantages; and advanced age.[5]

Aside from these exclusions, the ADA is very comprehensive. It covers almost everything in the life of a person who is disabled that is not covered by other laws, such as education and housing. Title I of the ADA embodies all aspects of employment: recruitment, advertising, and job application procedures; hiring, upgrading, promotion, tenure award, demotion, transfer, layoff, termination, right-of-return from layoff, and rehiring; rate of pay; job assignment and classification, organizational structure, position description, line of progression, and seniority; leave of absence, sick leave, and other leave; fringe benefits; selection and financial support for training, including apprenticeships, professional meetings, conferences, and other related activities, and selection for leaves of absence to pursue training; sponsored activities such as recreational programs, and any other term, condition, or privilege of employment. Still, with such a comprehensive definition, the gray area lies in determining at what point a "condition" becomes a "disability" in the workplace.

Types Of Disability

Given that the most frequently used symbol of disability is a wheelchair, it is not surprising that when we think "disabled," we think of obvious and visible physical conditions such as paralysis and blindness. However, even if we add people who are deaf to this group, it only accounts for 10 percent of the approximately 43 million Americans who are disabled. There are 495,000 people between ages 21 and 64 who use a wheelchair, according to census data.

"Most disabilities are the result of heart conditions, cancers, high blood pressure, and mental illness," says Walter Oi, professor of economics at the University of Rochester. "They're not the sort of poster things that you see." The same article says, "Nearly five million people in the 21-to-64 age category have a mental or emotional disability, while 860,000 are mentally retarded."[6]

Figure 10-1 shows the number of people in the United States who have some of the most common disabilities. It is interesting to note in the figure that the majority of these disabilities are invisible conditions.

Figure 10-1. Prevalence of Impairments in the United States—All Ages

Impairment	Number per 1,000 people
Hearing impairment	94.7
Visual impairment	30.6
Speech impairment	9.3
Arthritis	125.3
Epilepsy	4.8
Missing extremities (excluding toes and fingers)	5.0
Partial/complete paralysis	5.9
Diabetes	25.3
Hypertension	110.2
Heart disease	78.5
Kidney trouble	12.4
Back injury	70.3

SOURCE: Mainstream, Inc., *In the Mainstream,* November/December 1992, p. 18.

If there is confusion about working appropriately with people with physical disabilities, there is more uncertainty about working with and supervising those who have mental disabilities. The ADA defines mental impairment as "any mental or psychological disorder such as mental retardation, organic brain syndrome, emotional or mental illness, and specific learning disabilities."

Although the ADA includes learning disabilities as a mental impairment, it does not include illiteracy. Yet recent findings show that a substantial number of persons labeled functionally illiterate may actually be learning disabled, and a significant portion of these may be people of color. According to an Urban Institute report, "Adult illiteracy is an acute problem in the United States, particularly among blacks, Hispanics, and the economically disadvantaged. These groups have a higher incidence of learning disabilities because they are more likely to have suffered prenatal malnutrition, maternal substance abuse, low birth weight, premature birth, and other factors that are associated with learning disabilities."[7]

If a person's learning disability prevents them from performing job functions involving learning, reading, writing, or mathematical computations needed on a job, then the learning disability may be considered a disability requiring accommodation. But there are also other, often subtle limitations of learning disabilities such as poor attention span, inability to follow verbal instructions, or problems with spatial perception.

Learning disabilities have major implications for all aspects of employment, starting with applying for a job. Sloppy handwriting and poor spelling on an application or resume has traditionally been considered a good reason for not hiring a person. However, if the sloppy handwriting and poor spelling result from a learning disability—and if handwriting and spelling are not essential job functions—then the employer needs to look past these limitations to better assess a person's ability to perform key job functions.

Knowing that up to 15 percent of the working population is learning disabled, which may or may not affect work performance, underscores the importance of employers needing to learn more about this disability.

But an even grayer ADA area is dealing with mental disabilities such as stress and depression in the workplace. According to social services professional Jude Setian-Marston, most employers are unaware of the struggles employees with depression face, and they are less knowledgeable about how to accommodate them.[8] Disabling conditions related to mental illness vary greatly in the workplace, but can cause problems in productivity fluctuations, interpersonal communication, concentration and distractibility, and time management. Furthermore, employees with psychiatric disabilities may experience side effects of psychotropic medications that temporarily impair their work performance. For example, some antidepressants initially cause nausea, dizziness, and alter sleep patterns. Unlike people with physical disabilities, who may need a one-time specific accommodation like a mouthstick or an architectural change, workers with mental disabilities may need accommodations such as job flexibility, EAPs, communication training, or supervisory coaching.

Clearly, there is a critical need to educate employers and employees about the nature of mental disabilities. Moreover, organizations need strategies for accommodating people with mental disabilities, not only to actively implement ADA policies, but also to create a workplace that enhances job opportunities for people with psychiatric disabilities.[9]

A third type of disability is medical impairments, including all chronic or life-threatening diseases such as AIDS, asthma, arthritis, cancer, cardiovascular disease, chemical sensitivity, diabetes, epilepsy, lupus, and multiple sclerosis. According to the ADA, employees with such disabilities have the right to work if they can perform their job satisfactorily—with reasonable accommodation if necessary—and if best medical evidence indicates that continued employment does not present a direct significant health or safety threat to the employee, co-workers, or customers. Moreover, workers with chronic medical conditions have the right to work if they can resume a meaningful and productive role in the workplace following recovery. And they must be assured of complete confidentiality.[10]

Because these conditions are sometimes invisible and progress at different rates with varying impact on one's working ability, they are among the most difficult for employers to accommodate. A major issue is attendance. Absences related to the disease symptoms and medical treatment can disrupt the daily routine of a business.

Of major concern as the epidemic continues to spread is the issue of AIDS. In most cases, employers must provide continuing work opportunities to employees who are HIV-positive, even as their disease progresses and their ability to work decreases. "These issues will be resolved as the implications of the ADA continue to unfold and are tested in the workplace and in the courts."[11]

"No other aspect of supervision is as difficult as watching a formerly productive employee deal with a progressively worsening physical condition."[12] This is especially true when the employee says something like, "All I have to live for is my job." It is a supervisory challenge to maintain the productivity of a work group and keep confidentiality about the person's condition as concerned co-workers request information. Educating co-workers in general about a disease such as AIDS and their safety in being around the affected person is a sensitive issue that needs attention. And involving and including people who are disabled by life-threatening conditions will continue to be a challenge for employers.

Diversity and Disability

We tend to discuss people as though they had only one characteristic beyond their humanness—the "woman taxi driver," "teenage sports star," and so forth. But we must recognize that disability happens to people of all backgrounds and both genders, before birth and beyond age 85, and to people of all ethnic and racial backgrounds. Eventually, it may be these diverse individuals with disabilities who actually unify our society.[13]

Figure 10-2 breaks down labor force and work disability status by sex, race, and Hispanic origin. According to F. Bowe of the University of Arkansas, the overall disability rate for the working-age population is 8.1 percent. However, among all disabled working-age people, 80.2

Figure 10-2. Labor Force Status—Work Disability Status of United States Civilians, Ages 16 to 64, by Sex, Race, and Hispanic Origin, 1991

		With a work disability		No work disability	
	Total	Number	Percent in labor force	Number	Percent in labor force
Total	160,123	14,648	34.4	144,506	79.9
Female	81,511	7,380	29.3	74,052	71.1
Male	78,612	7,268	39.5	70,454	89.1
White	135,033	11,553	37.5	122,711	80.7
African American	19,130	2,661	21.5	16,305	76.5
Hispanic*	13,597	1,188	26.1	12,349	73.5
Veteran†	19,543	2,828	43.8	16,715	90.7
Vietnam	7,612	974	60.7	6,639	96.5
Korean Conflict	3,965	787	28.9	3,178	82.3
World War II	1,340	383	18.9	957	55.3
Other Service	6,626	685	51.0	5,941	94.3
Nonvet.	140,580	11,819	32.1	127,791	78.5

*Persons of Hispanic origin may be of any race.

†*Note:* Disabled Vietnam-era veterans have extremely high rates of unemployment. The Department of Labor found that 75 percent of severely disabled Vietnam veterans have dropped out of the labor force. The 300 or so disabled veterans of the Persian Gulf War may face experiences different from those of disabled Vietnam-era veterans, possibly because there was more acceptance of the Persian Gulf War as well as of people with disabilities in society.[14]

SOURCE: Compiled by Janice Hamilton Outtz from U.S. Bureau of the Census, Current Population Survey (unpublished estimates).

percent are white (compared to 85 percent of all working-age individuals), 17.7 percent are black (compared to 11.5 percent of all working-age individuals), and 7 percent are Hispanic (compared to about the same proportion of Hispanics in the working-age group). Thus, only blacks have a higher rate of disability than their overall distribution in the population, creating an additional hardship to overcome.[15] As Figure 10-2 shows, an estimated 2,661,000 African Americans have a work disability, while 1,188,000 Hispanics are so classified. The following paragraphs review how disability affects people of various cultures.

African Americans.   According to the National Institute on Disability and Rehabilitation Research,[16] working-age black Americans with disabilities typically have an average annual income not exceeding $3,000.

American Indians.   The National Congress of American Indians (1990) notes that Native Americans ages 18 to 69 report the highest levels of limitation in work due to a chronic health condition (17.4 percent, or 153,000 people.) Young American-Indian men have a seven times greater chance of becoming disabled before their 25th birthday than any other race of people in the United States. In addition, American Indians over age 45 develop disabilities from health-related problems at a 30 percent greater rate than other Americans their age. They also report that there are very few vocational rehabilitation programs in the United States designed to incorporate the cultural and linguistic needs of American Indians with disabilities.

There may be stereotypes about the American-Indian work ethic, but within various tribes, there are well-defined roles for all members. Carol Locust of the Native American Research and Training Center stresses that "being able to contribute to one's society brings dignity and self-respect. Roles for the handicapped within the tribal community provide opportunity for self-worth, dignity, and accomplishment." For example, in one tribe, a young woman with developmental disabilities became the legs for other tribal members with mobility impairments, running their errands for them. "She contributed to her society; she had worth. Her tribe, the Apache, believe that individuals like her are special in a spiritual sense, and although everyone knew she was `slow,' she was allowed to perform the work she developed for herself without harassment."[17]

Americans of Asian descent.   The 1980 census shows that 60 percent of all Americans of Asian descent reside in three states: California, Hawaii, and New York. Approximately 5.6 percent of this group, or 162,000, report having a work disability.[18] (These numbers may be higher because of the large numbers of immigrants from China in more recent years.)

Hispanics/Latinos. Hispanics' participation in the labor force will rise from 4 percent in 1976 to 20 percent by the year 2000. This represents one of the largest increases by any group and will result in 6 million more Hispanics entering the labor force for a total of 14 million. Demographic projections show that Hispanics will become the largest minority by the year 2025. Hispanic women are ethnically the fastest growing group of workers in the labor force, according to Vernice Friedlander, an official of the Women's Bureau at the Department of Labor.

Latinos share the problems of other minority groups. Disproportionate numbers are below the poverty line, have lower educational achievement, and have a high percentage of school dropouts. As Hispanics with disabilities, they are in a state of double jeopardy—discriminated against because they are Hispanics and because they are disabled.[19]

Various disabilities that are more prevalent among certain populations create the need for outreach and education in those populations. For example, the National Commission on AIDS suggests that AIDS must be viewed as a racial issue. African Americans and Hispanics accounted for 46 percent of AIDS cases last year, although they make up 21 percent of the population, according to the Centers for Disease Control.[20]

In fact, prevention programs designed for a general population are typically not helpful for groups with specific cultural or sexual habits. "For example, while half of the black and Hispanic adult males with AIDS have sex with men, HIV services in their communities are often not designed to reach them....Gay men of color frequently are left in limbo."[21]

Another aspect of the issue is the aging process among all workers from all ethnic and cultural backgrounds. Aging brings with it the potential for age-related health problems, some of which lead to work disabilities. Six in every ten disabled adults of working age are between 45 and 64 years old. Arthritis, cancer, heart disease, and decreased visual and hearing acuity are some of the causes of work-related disabilities in older employees.

The vocational rehabilitation system in the United States recognizes the importance of meeting the needs of people with disabilities from various cultural backgrounds. Until recently, vocational rehabilitation professionals had limited training in meeting the employment needs of culturally diverse individuals. But this is changing as more training programs emerge. For instance, Auburn University has a grant to provide training for rehabilitation professionals nationwide in the skills necessary to successfully meet these needs.

Workplace Perceptions

A 1991 poll conducted by Louis Harris for the National Organization on Disability sheds some light on people's current perceptions of people with disabilities. The study showed that attitudes seem to be evolving:

- 92 percent of the respondents admire people with disabilities because they must overcome so much.
- 74 percent also feel pity.
- 58 percent feel uneasy or awkward around disabled people because they don't know how to interact with them.
- 47 percent feel fear because they might become disabled themselves.
- 16 percent feel people with disabilities are an inconvenience, so they react with anger.
- 9 percent expressed resentment for what they consider special privileges, such as handicapped parking.[22]

Although the respondents admitted they knew little about people with disabilities, their comfort level increased if they knew or worked with someone with a disability. More than 8 of 10 respondents said putting people who are disabled to work would be a boost to the nation. A decisive margin said they favor increasing the number of co-workers who are disabled; they are willing to spend money to integrate this group into the mainstream, and they support setting up affirmative action programs to end employment discrimination.

The problem, according to journalist Dianne Piastro, is the "big difference between what people say about disability and how they react when actually faced with it."[23]

Although people with disabilities may be able to contribute effectively at work and in society, the perceptions of people without disabilities hold them back. Those perceptions are often based on fears and inexperience. People who visibly have no physical disabilities often revert to early learnings when confronted by those who do.[24] As children, for example, we may have been taught that it is impolite to stare at people with disabilities. Perhaps we were discouraged from playing or interacting with classmates who were disabled. In one way or another, our innate curiosity and potential acceptance of people with disabilities were stymied.[25] So, having never had successful youthful experiences with people who are disabled, many of us—employers and co-workers alike—stumble and feel awkward as adults.

As explained by psychologist Harry Levinson, we may feel "resentment over being confronted with what potentially could happen to any of us....This is not an unusual kind of feeling, but it is troublesome and can get in the way."[26]

Attitudes and Fears

One of the biggest concerns for employers is that people with a visible disability, such as a facial scar or a noticeable limp, will be unacceptable to their clients or customers in a public-contact job such as front-office receptionist or restaurant host. Rather than looking at the person as a liability, progressive companies could choose to look at hiring such a person with appropriate skills as a symbol of their acceptance of all people. And they may be seen by clients and customers as progressive in their diversity efforts.

Karin Pugh, a San Francisco attorney who is a quadriplegic, says an interviewer once patted her knee and said, "Don't worry, dear. I know plenty of handicapped people who've made a lot of themselves. You'll do just fine." Ms. Pugh, who at the time was a top law student at the University of California at Berkeley, replied, "I've already made something of my life." Then, she says, she left. "I figured the interview was pretty much over at that point."[27]

All of these attitudes can result in excluding people. Discrimination continues to be the primary problem in the workplace. People with disabilities complain that employers can easily get around the law by simply claiming a candidate is underqualified. "There is just this mindset against us," says Pat Johnson, director of the Jefferson Parish Office for Citizens with Disabilities in New Orleans. Johnson, who uses a wheelchair, adds, "They feel that if you're in a wheelchair, it not only affects your body, if affects your brain."[28]

People fear certain disabilities over others. Fears arise out of ignorance or misunderstanding. Many people struggle over accepting people living with AIDS. And although federal law prohibits employers from discriminating against HIV-infected people, many report incidences of job and insurance loss, as well as harassment.[29] This reflects the extreme fear people have about this condition and some uneasiness with the nature of its transmission.

Perhaps no other disability is as misunderstood as blindness. Employers fear that workers who are blind will have difficulty getting to work, finding their way to the bathroom, working safely, or getting along well with co-workers. These attitudes are easily disproved—people who are blind and have adequate job skills generally have the same skills as other employees. With the help of a vocational rehabilitation agency, many workers who are blind receive support onsite to get oriented quickly and achieve independence.

According to the American Foundation for the Blind (AFB), only 25 to 35 percent of those considered blind or severely visually impaired are working. However, there are thousands of blind people working successfully. The AFB keeps a database of over 250 groups of professionals with visual limitations, including electrical engineers, investment brokers, nurses, physical therapists, and graphic designers.

Another misperception is that sight is necessary for all jobs. Some employers believe they must make expensive accommodations and transcribe all material into braille for a job to be appropriate for a worker who is blind. Again, these assumptions are false, since 80 percent of those who are legally blind have some vision, and many perform their jobs with minor, if any, modifications.

Deafness also causes fear in prospective employers. Yet many deaf people work effectively as attorneys, accountants, clerks, word processors, computer personnel, factory workers, commercial artists, and other professional areas. Various accommodations, some as simple as improving acoustics and lighting to avoid interference with hearing aids and ease lipreading, can increase the person's productivity. Additional devices such as visual and tactile signaling devices, sign-language interpreters, or telecommunication devices for the deaf (TDDs) may be necessary.

Attitudes about hiring workers with disabilities are hard to change. Yet Florence Rosen, director of career counseling and job-placement services at the New York League for the Hard of Hearing, points out two advantages of hiring workers with a hearing impairment: They concentrate intensely because of minimal noise distraction and their retention rate is high. In fact, studies show that more than 85 percent of such employees remain at their jobs beyond one year, a rate better than for those with normal hearing.[30]

Impact of Other Cultures' Perceptions on the Workplace

All people in the workplace bring with them unique combinations of skills and talents. They also are unique in the basics of who they are. Their various attributes of diversity combine to present challenges for them. For example, an African-American woman faces the potential of discrimination on two facets of her personhood. Add legal blindness to her characteristics, and another set of potential challenges appear. Make her over 50, or a lesbian, and she faces additional issues. Even the most secure and self-confident person may find herself or himself wondering which characteristic is causing discriminatory behavior on the part of potential employers or co-workers!

As the American workforce becomes more diverse, more employees come from countries and cultures different from the white, Anglo-Saxon Protestant culture that established the norm for corporate behavior in this country. We have people from all countries and cultures within those countries working at all levels of public and private enterprise. They may be CEOs, technical specialists, salespeople, supervisors, maintenance people, assemblers, or service providers. We know the importance of training all employees about communicating with and valuing people from all cultures.

A look at how people with disabilities are viewed by other cultures helps in understanding the impact they have in the workplace. Examining a few countries we do business with or from which U.S. workers come may clarify these issues. One caveat: The findings presented in this section are generalizations only. We must recognize that enlightened individuals and organizations within a culture or country may view people with disabilities much differently.

Because very little on this subject appears in human resource information, most of this discussion came from anthropological literature. Anthropologist Esther Boylan provides a gloomy view on women with disabilities in developing countries, because of their poor social and economic conditions.[31]

Anthropologists define disability in any specific culture as a state of being ill or well. This definition is closely connected to each culture's perception of life, values, and the concept of personhood. A sampling of cultural perceptions of people with disabilities follows:

Latin America. The culture accepts that women with disabilities may have "good heads" but feels that their bodies can never express beauty. Women lose their sexuality to their disability.

New Zealand. The perception of a person's disability depends on whether it was caused by an accident or an illness.

Parts of Asia. Blind women have the lowest status in the community and are isolated, confined to a corner of the house, and totally dependent socially and economically. They have no chance to marry.

Singapore, Hong Kong, Thailand, and the Philippines. Some blind women find jobs as telephone operators, while in other Asian countries, they work as factory hands, packers, cane weavers, doll and paper flower makers, and dressmakers.

India and the Philippines. Well-educated blind women work as social workers, musicians, receptionists, and dictaphone typists.

Bombay. Eighty-one percent of males and 90 percent of females over age 15 with disabilities are untrained for work.

Sweden.   Attitude of support prevails for all individuals to maximize their potential. Because costs are covered by socialized medicine, workplace accommodations permit people with disabilities to work.

Germany.   Neo-Nazi skinheads have mounted attacks on people with disabilities, saying such things as "They must have forgotten you in Dachau."

We need to be aware of these differing cultural perspectives in our workplace and address them appropriately.

Impact in the United States

The impact of these diverse cultural expectations on the workplace is significant. Nondisabled workers from other cultures who hold positions of hiring authority may carry these cultural expectations into a job interview with an applicant who is disabled. If they hire that person, they may have trouble communicating or involving the person fully in the workplace. Unintentionally, they may discriminate based on their cultural expectations. And those with disabilities working in our country may not know their rights under the ADA or, if they do, they may have low expectations of the type of work they can or are expected to do.

We need to address these issues in our workplace. Because we do not want to reinforce stereotypes about any culture or country, we should know what cultural expectations our colleagues bring to their workplace. Then we need to address them on an individual basis so that all people have an equal chance to contribute their talents to their organization.

Some people are hesitant to discuss their cultural background and what they learned about people with disabilities, realizing that their attitudes may be illegal under the ADA. So in some situations, it may be more effective to educate on an individual level rather than in front of others who may pass harsh judgments.

We are all products of our upbringing, and our attitudes cannot change without assistance. Bringing them out, discussing them in a nonthreatening way, and helping people to have new and positive experiences can encourage all to accept, include, and value people with disabilities, regardless of their cultural heritage.

Many Prices to Pay

Myths such as the high cost of accommodating employees with disabilities abound. In fact, studies indicate that 51 percent of employees who are disabled require no expenditure for accommodation. Of those that require some expense, 30 percent require less than $500 and only 8 percent require over $2,000 in accommodations. The EEOC estimates that first-year costs to accommodate workers with disabilities would be $16 million, with a productivity gain worth more than $164 million resulting from that investment.[32]

Costs to People with Disabilities

Many people who are disabled must dig deep into their pockets to cover hefty expenses. Depending on the disability, there can be expenses for medical treatment, public transportation if the person does not drive, special equipment, diet, clothing, and care and maintenance of a service animal, such as a dog guide.

Employees with disabilities generally earn less than their nondisabled colleagues. A recent study by the Bureau of the Census uncovered some alarming statistics. Presented in his 1989 testimony before the House Subcommittee on Select Education, Jay Rochlin reported that the income of workers with disabilities dropped sharply compared to other workers. In 1980, men with disabilities earned 23 percent less than men with no work disability, and by 1988, this had dropped to 36 percent less than their counterparts.[33]

Disability costs are measured not only in dollars, but in time and energy. For example, a woman who uses a wheelchair and cannot drive goes to a bus stop about a block from her home, rides the bus to a subway, takes the subway, then travels up a long, winding hill and across four lanes of traffic to shop at a mall. Not all the buses have wheelchair lifts, so she must sometimes wait 35 minutes until the next bus arrives. The entire travel time can take 90 minutes. In a car, it takes about 10 minutes. She must endure the wait in all types of weather. In addition to the extra time, daily experiences like this drain energy.

On a positive note: People with disabilities and extra expenditures may, out of necessity, have a highly developed skill at planning and budgeting both time and money, a skill that employers find useful.

Costs of disability go beyond dollars. While many people with disabilities adjust well to their disability, for others there are costs related to self-concept and self-esteem. This is especially true for people with hidden disabilities, who look "normal" and are therefore expected to be and act like everyone else. If their disabilities impose limitations, they can be frustrated. Learning disabilities, which impact up to 15 percent of the working population, are a good example. The most commonly known is dyslexia, a condition that causes people to have trouble reading. They may mix up letters such as b and d or p and q. This condition may also affect ability to concentrate or to use numbers. Often, teachers who are unaware of a student's dyslexia tell the student to "try harder," and when the student tries but still cannot learn, the cycle of failure continues.

Learning disabilities are not the same as mental retardation and usually affect people with average or above-average intelligence. Many famous people have had some form of a learning disability and have overcome its effects: Leonardo da Vinci, Albert Einstein, Tom Cruise, Cher, and Henry Winkler are just a few.

In the workplace, learning disabilities may manifest themselves in an employee's inability to read technical manuals, fill out forms accurately, or deal with stock numbers. They may not perform well in noisy areas that affect their ability to concentrate. They may work better with pictured instructions rather than written or verbal instructions. They may have problems with directions and get lost easily.

Being "different" in this way may affect a person's self-concept. One woman tells of going to a special learning disabilities center when in school. It was located across the street from a psychiatric clinic, and she was terrified that someone would think she was a mental patient. She was sent to see a psychiatrist, but refused to tell him anything, fearing that he would think she was crazy. This woman finally graduated from NYU, and was hired as a news clerk for the *CBS Morning News.* She says:

> For the next four years, I watched in growing despair as all the kids I had started with were promoted from news clerk to broadcast producer to segment producer. I stayed put and earned very little money. My supervisors saw the misspellings in my phone messages and assumed I was too stupid to move up. I knew I could do what the others were doing and proved it when I put together all the guests for a show during black history month. But no one else believed in my capabilities, and I remained a news clerk until I became so depressed I quit.[34]

People with disabilities such as this face daily challenges of completing even the simplest tasks correctly without being discovered, or worse yet, being fired. They may become masters at deceiving supervisors and co-workers by getting other people to perform tasks they cannot do.

Most people react to the onset of a disability in the same way they deal with other major changes in their lives. When a person becomes disabled through accident or illness, services from a vocational rehabilitation agency may be needed during a readjustment period. And others may benefit from counseling to rediscover who and what they are.

Costs to the Government

Having a nation with 43 million citizens who are disabled is expensive for a government that assists them with services and compensation. Nearly 8 percent of our nation's gross national product is consumed by governmental and private programs and subsidies to people who are disabled.[35]

The government spends an estimated $200 billion annually on people with disabilities. Yet less than $2 billion of that budget goes toward assisting people who are disabled in becoming tax-paying citizens through vocational rehabilitation (VR). An investment worth its return, VR programs return $11 in taxes for every $1 spent on services.[36]

The irony is that many more citizens would like to work than can be served by VR programs. And if enough dollars and service providers were available to train this group of people, all government expenditures made on behalf of people with disabilities could be reduced.

Costs to Companies Employing People with Disabilities

Companies incur costs for every employee, but there may be additional expenses for an employee who is disabled. These costs—whether for specific accommodations, health insurance, disability prevention and management, or workers' compensation—vary dramatically from one worker to another.

One cost to organizations with employees with disabilities is accommodations. Employers frequently assume that the cost of accommodating workers with disabilities will be outrageous. Yet there are many examples of accommodations that cost very little. For example, National Medical Enterprises (NME) began a program in 1989 aimed at hiring people with disabilities. Spurred on by its Chairman and CEO, Richard Eamer—who has a severe hearing impairment—NME hired 105 people with disabilities over the summer of 1991. Accommodating these workers cost NME a total of $351, according to Miriam Shakter, NME's assistant vice president. "A $7.50 footstool may be all that's needed for someone with a back injury....When large sums are required, such as when NME bought a $5,500 portable braille computer for an employee, the expense is simply one of the ways that NME ensures that employees have the tools needed to do their jobs," Shakter said. Of NME's 49,848-member workforce, 3.2 percent have identified themselves as people with disabilities. They include quadriplegics and paraplegics, people with mental retardation, and people who are deaf or blind. They work at all levels of the organization.[37]

The Job Accommodation Network, a service of the President's Committee on Employment of People with Disabilities, estimates that for every dollar an employer puts into making an accommodation, the company realizes $9 in benefits, including eliminating the cost of training a new employee, reducing workers compensation or disability insurance costs, creating a greater sense of job security among co-workers, and fostering greater acceptance and support from the community.[38]

"Benefits perceived by employees with disabilities included increasing productivity, making the work more enjoyable, making it easier to do and less tiring, helping with the attitudes of coworkers, and increasing the employee's self-confidence."[39]

Health care costs are another compelling issue. Employers and workers alike claim the cost increases can't continue. According to Lisa Sprague, manager of employer benefits policy for the U.S. Chamber of Commerce, "looking at someone's health history as a reason for hiring is less common than looking at whether or not you can insure them."[40]

Employer health insurance costs have climbed dramatically over the last few years. Between 1980 and 1986, increases averaged 10 percent a year and then shot up 15 to 20 percent a year beginning in 1987. Last year, the average U.S. company spent 26 percent of its net earnings—an average of $3,161 per worker—on health care benefits.[41]

A common misperception is that all workers with disabilities consume more health care benefits than other employees, further driving up costs. Concerns about these costs and potential absenteeism can underly discrimination in the workplace. However, employers need to remember that many people have disabilities that are stable—hearing loss, for example—and do not require medical treatment any different from what an able-bodied employee requires. People who have recovered from heart disease through surgery are often healthier than they were for years prior to surgery. But even considering potential use of health benefits—which is illegal under the ADA but is a common thought in employers' minds—it is important to remember that all employees have the potential for expensive accidents or illnesses.

While the law allows employers to refuse job applicants with disabilities who would pose a "significant risk" to their own or others' health and safety, issues about health and disability become intertwined. "What is the catalyst for poor health, and how is it affecting that person? It all depends on how each illness is looked at. A person may fit the definition of being disabled even if that is manifest as poor health. Employers may be on shaky legal ground by assuming that an individual's poor health makes that person a risk," says Gary Phelan, a Connecticut lawyer.[42]

In time, the courts will clarify those distinctions between health conditions and disabilities. But for now, companies need more information about employee health in order to contain rising insurance and workers' compensation costs.[43] This is clearly a major issue needing attention by the EEOC, the insurance industry, and the nation's companies, as well as by people with disabilities themselves.

A further cost lies in the area of disabilities preventions. Because it is more cost-effective to prevent disabilities than to deal with them once they happen, organizations and their insurance companies are doing more in this area. Statistics show that employees returning to work shortly after an injury are less likely to incur long-term disabilities.[44]

What is disability prevention? It includes assessing a work site for potential accident or illness-causing factors before anything happens. Likewise, it involves identifying and acting on conditions that may lead to extended disability once an injury occurs. Return-to-work programs feature treatment designed to address the injury and return employees to the same task they performed prior to injury.

Return-to-work program costs average less than conventional therapy programs and can significantly reduce recuperation time. One hospital cites a $40,000 savings for every claim handled through its disability prevention program as compared to its average work injury claims. Another hospital credits its return-to-work program for a portion of its 50 percent savings in workers' compensation costs. These figures are testimony to the effectiveness of such programs.[45] These programs need to be implemented where none exist and expanded to meet increased needs.

Workers' compensation is another concern. Despite a company's best efforts at preventing accidents and injuries, there will always be some. In 1980, private carriers, public agencies, and employers' self-insurance policies disbursed $13.6 billion worth of workers' compensation funds nationwide. By 1988, the last year of available federal Department of Health and Human Services figures, compensation payments rose to $30.7 billion. Other sources place the figure at a slightly lower level of $22 billion annually.[46] Whatever figure is accurate, the costs are enormous.

The workers' compensation system creates a disincentive for employees. By "ignoring medical improvements and incentives for rehabilitation, the workers compensation program clings to the outdated notion that benefits should reflect damages. Paying benefits to injured workers who can work is costly and making payments available for impairments discourages rehabilitation and recovery."[47]

Companies must do their part to keep costs down. Creating a corporate culture that values all people means encouraging people with disabilities to return to work after an injury. Employers need to work closely with their insurance carriers to abandon the old concept of disability and never-ending claim payments. It makes solid business sense to evaluate injured employees and facilitate their return to work.

Disability management is a final area of costs associated with employees with disabilities. There will always be a need for extended benefits for some injured workers. But more can be done to help employees manage their disabilities and return to work.

With the high costs of maintaining disability payment programs—and shortages of trained employees—more employers are participating in return-to-work programs. Employers have a vested interest in helping their employees make speedy returns to full productivity. And some are succeeding at facilitating an employee's return to an established career built on positive worker traits. So a continuing investment in disability management at the workplace seems inevitable.[48]

Clearly, instituting such programs can positively impact both a person disabled by an injury as well as the organization. One young man working for an electronics manufacturing facility lost his dominant arm in a water-skiing accident. The company, valuing his productivity, videotaped someone doing his job and supplied the videotape to his doctor. The occupational therapists, prosthetic designer, and team members at the company—in conjunction with the young man and his supervisor—made some simple modifications in the setup of his job station and he is now back to full productivity.

Issues People with Disabilities Face in Becoming Fully Involved in the Workplace

During the early days of ADA implementation, attention focused on what organizations must do to comply with the law. But we must remember that this law is about people with disabilities, so we should be aware of the issues they face in becoming part of America's workforce.

Getting in the Door

Literally getting to and in through the door of a potential employer may be impossible. Lack of accessible transportation at many work sites hampers employment opportunities for those who don't drive.

Work sites themselves may be inaccessible to potential employees with mobility impairments.

A Harris Poll study found that 66 percent of the estimated 8.2 million people with disabilities eligible to work are unemployed. This high rate exists at a time when the workforce will be starving for inclusion of all those presently outside the economic mainstream.[49]

Opportunities for employees vary according to the size of a company. Studies reported in *Rehab Brief* indicate that people with disabilities working for small businesses with under 500 employees had much shorter mean job tenure than their counterparts who were employed by large companies. Workers with disabilities stayed with small companies for a mean of 6.7 years, compared with a mean of 11.6 years with large companies. Workers in the general labor force have a similar pattern of shorter mean tenures with small companies.[50]

But the same study verified that employees with disabilities tend to stay longer with both small and large employers than employees without disabilities. This trend may occur because employees who are disabled fear losing their employer-provided medical benefits and lack confidence about securing another job.[51]

Typically, small businesses are less reluctant to hire people with work limitations. Many employees with disabilities are employed first by a small company—usually for part-time, nonunion, low-wage, and short-tenure situations. Informality and short chains of command allow work-limited employees to "go to the top" to discuss their needs, such as accommodations. Yet, small employers may not have the resources to make accommodations and may need assistance from rehabilitation professionals or others.

On the other hand, large companies are more likely to be self-insured, making it financially advantageous to accommodate employees and avoid disability-related separations. Human resource (HR) staff may have prior experience accommodating workers with disabilities. Also, large companies have more employees who can pick up the slack when other employees are absent or make work reassignments because of the greater variety of jobs. In terms of cost-efficiency, expenses for individual workers can be spread over a larger total labor cost base.[52]

Disclosing the Presence of a Disability

Because many disabilities are invisible, those who live with them must decide when and if to let employers know about them. The ADA does not require disclosure of a disability. Many people feel that, if they can do the job without accommodation, there is no reason to tell anyone. Some have had bad experiences, such as being fired or denied a promotion, because they revealed their disability.

Lynn Watts, a Berkeley, California, word processor who is blind, says she lost an interview opportunity because she mentioned her disability on the telephone. "The man said I couldn't do the computer work," says Watts, who has been unemployed for more than a year. "When I told him I had equipment to help me, I could just feel him squirming." In response to these situations, many job seekers hide their disabilities until the last possible moment, often surprising recruiters when they show up at a job interview.[53]

Some experts estimate that the number of workers disguising a disability may be in the hundreds of thousands, but no one knows for sure. "There are many people who are still not reporting themselves," says Deborah Kaplan, director of the division on technology policy for the World Institute on Disability in Oakland.[54]

Co-worker Acceptance

Those with visible physical disabilities may fear rejection by co-workers. Fears are based on past experiences, taunting, being set up for failure, pitied, overhelped, or ignored—all experiences that people with disabilities have faced.

Financial and Insurance Dilemmas

Employers are often unaware of some of the financial and insurance dilemmas people with disabilities face in going to work. A person with a disability may be receiving support from the local or federal government, including unemployment, food stamps, Supplemental Security Income (SSI), or Social Security Disability Insurance (SSDI). Different programs provide various benefits, including health insurance under Medicare.

Especially for people with multiple disabilities needing extensive medical coverage, going to work may eliminate the security of medical care. These people face the dilemma of risking secure income and benefits for pay and benefits that may not provide the same standard of living. Added to this, frequent layoffs give little reassurance of continued employment and benefits.

A young man with severe disabilities chose to work part-time so as not to jeopardize his Medicare. His employer, who wanted him to work full-time, was frustrated and angry about this man "ripping off the system, double dipping." But, when asked if he could guarantee the employee continued employment and medical insurance, he replied, "Of course not." For this employee, that continued medical coverage was literally a matter of life and death. Recent legislation—Public Law 101-239, Section 1818A—permits SSDI beneficiaries who discontinue benefits because of work to purchase Medicare. For those who can afford to buy the health care benefits, this should remove a major disincentive to work.[55]

Another obstacle some people with disabilities encounter involves critical health plan exclusions. Because company health insurance plans often do not cover preexisting and other relevant conditions, many qualified individuals with disabilities are discouraged from entering or reentering the workforce.

The EEOC states that the ADA is not violated by blanket preexisting condition clauses that exclude from coverage the treatment of all conditions that predate the person's eligibility for benefits under the plan. However, the EEOC says a preexisting condition clause that applies only to preexisting blood disorders is a disability-related distinction and will be considered a violation of the ADA. It is also permissible to place a limit or cap on the maximum amount of benefits that will be paid.

Recently, the EEOC issued interim guidance on how the ADA applies to employer-provided health insurance. Its position is that distinctions in a health insurance plan not based on disability and applied equally to all employees do not violate the ADA. One ramification of this is that providing a lower level of benefits for treatment of mental/nervous conditions than for treatment of physical conditions is not an ADA violation. Nor is it a violation to provide fewer benefits for "eye care" than for other physical distinctions. The EEOC claims that these are not distinctions based on disability, even though they may have a greater impact on individuals with disabilities.

The EEOC promises to address the relationship between the ADA and other issues such as employer-provided pension plans, life insurance, and disability insurance in the future.[56]

Wage Rates and Promotions

People with disabilities work for all the same reasons that everyone else works, including wages. However, according to a 1988 Health Interview Survey, men with disabilities earned an average annual income of $24,000 while women with disabilities earned an average of $16,000. This is contrasted with $30,000 and $19,000, respectively, for their nondisabled counterparts.[57] Especially for people who must pay their own insurance, these rates do not justify going to work!

An analysis of job retention by people with disabilities who obtained jobs through the vocational rehabilitation program found that 48 percent of 1974 rehabilitants had earnings in each of nine successive years. They earned much larger wage increases in the first, second, and third years of employment than did other rehabilitants. Their earnings did not, however, increase at rates comparable to workers in the general labor force with similar length of employment participation. This suggests that even these relatively successful workers with disabilities may be participating in a secondary labor market with only sporadic employment and no real advancement.[58]

Job Retention

It is not enough that people with disabilities get a job, are paid equitably, and are promoted. Like other workers, there is the issue of keeping a job, especially in times of layoffs, mergers, and hiring freezes.

NME, one of the country's largest health care providers, began a program called "Overcoming Challenges." This program teaches HR personnel and company managers skills in recruiting, interviewing, hiring, and accommodating people with disabilities. Shakter, assistant vice president responsible for the Overcoming Challenges initiative, describes the HR factors that lead to retaining employees with disabilities. They include clear performance standards, effective performance coaching, open communication between worker and supervisor, training opportunities to enhance and develop skills, and an EAP to handle personal problems.

These needs are the same for disabled and nondisabled workers. The only addition for workers with disabilities is the ability to deal with reasonable accommodation issues and changes brought about by either a job change or a change in the functional limitations imposed by the disability.[59]

Once hired, employees with disabilities require appropriate training and supervision:

> Workers with disabilities need feedback on their performance just like other employees, praise when appropriate and corrective counseling or coaching when needed. Do not wait until there is a serious problem. Involve the employee in problem-solving discussions before the situation becomes job-threatening.[60]

They also should be promoted when appropriate.

Technology

While computers are wonderful productivity devices, they may cause problems for some employees with disabilities and be a boon to others. For a person who is deaf, computers can aid communication and be a work tool as well. Flashing icons can replace computer beeps. And for a person who is blind, adaptive equipment can make what appears on a screen accessible. But graphic user interface programs are more difficult to translate into braille or speech output, although that problem is being addressed. Specialized hardware and software permit access and productivity without vision.

For employees with motor impairments that affect finger dexterity, adapted keyboards or mouthsticks can provide keyboard access. Spell checkers help dyslexic users produce high-quality documents.

"The power of telecommunications is amazing," says David Clarke, a 21-year-old part-time programmer at Pacific Bell, who was born with cerebral palsy. "You can be talking and communicating with other people, and they never have to know you're disabled. There's no inbred stereotype." James Barry, an in-house consultant on disabled issues at Nynex Corporation, and a person with a visual impairment, says "The computer is a nondiscriminatory device. It doesn't care whether you are black or white, male or female, able or disabled. It's going to respond to your command, whether it's given by a mouthstick, an eye beam, a touch screen, or the spoken voice."[61]

Expanded Use of Temporary Employees

To cut costs, some companies depend heavily on temporary agencies. It is against the ADA for agencies to discriminate against people with disabilities; however, the trend toward using temporary agencies could have a negative impact on people with disabilities. Because temporaries tend to work for brief periods and rarely receive benefits, employers do not make substantial accommodations for them. And it is difficult for workers with some disabilities to constantly adjust their time and travel schedules.[62]

Implications for the Workforce

As baby boomers age, they have a greater potential for age-related disability. They also may work longer in life. These two factors will increase the need for accommodations in the home and workplace.

More People with Disabilities as a
Result of the Aging Workforce

As we discuss elsewhere, there are many issues connecting the aging workforce with systems serving people with disabilities. As older workers bring a greater potential for health problems, such as coronary disease and strokes, the demand for rehabilitation and health care services also increases.[63] These same issues become workplace concerns because more companies are retaining workers longer.

Aging people with disabilities also provide a market for goods and services, from health care to financial planning to travel services. Already, catalogues offer products for people with arthritis, mobility impairments, and visual and hearing impairments. Once relegated to stores near hospitals, now catalogues and stores offer additional products to meet workplace needs. National organizations specialize in products for people with specific disabilities, such as diabetes. General retail stores, now accessible to people with disabilities, recognize the buying power of 43 million potential customers.

Insurers will play a larger role in advising their corporate customers about essential job functions and other aspects of the ADA. Insurers can work directly with their customers' disabled employees through telephone contact, early intervention, and rehabilitation. They will also need to work closely in reviewing medical plans to remain compliant with the ADA.

> In the insurance marketplace, the ADA is likely to have resounding ramifications. The potential market for disability insurance currently is $26 billion, including $5 billion in force under traditional plans and $5 billion in self-insured plans. That $10 billion market of insurance in force could double as the law stimulates awareness of disability in the workplace.
>
> An emphasis on short-term rather than long-term disability, spurred partly by the ADA, also will change the disability insurance market. With early intervention programs, a return-to-work focus, and a more accepting workplace, most disability cases will be short-term. Although provisions for long-term disability will be the exception rather than the rule, they will continue to serve people, such as those with multiple sclerosis, who are unable to work for long periods.[64]

Economic and Technological
Changes Increasing the
Importance of Successful Human
Intervention at Work

The interaction between people with disabilities and technology is a crucial issue in productivity. While technological changes make jobs more accessible for some people, they can also cause problems for people with certain disabilities. For example, the graphic user interface computer programs are becoming more widely used. But they are difficult for a blind or visually impaired person to access.

Equipment is not designed with people with disabilities in mind, and modifications must be made for people with disabilities.

> In response to legislation and in keeping with sound business practice, equipment manufacturers are considering the needs of people with disabilities at the design stage, with a view toward making fewer modifications necessary later on. In purchasing new equipment for use in the work setting, care should be taken to assure that it will be usable by persons with disabilities and that they are trained in its operation.[65]

This may be a laudable goal; however, modifications are usually custom-designed for an individual with specific disability-imposed limitations, and design for one person may not be appropriate for another.

Also crucial for productivity and harmonious working relationships are skills such as communication, teamwork, problem solving, and flexibility. As people representing all aspects of diversity join together in the workplace, they will succeed or fail based on their ability to work well together.

Total Quality Management and People with Disabilities

Quality management principles can be used effectively throughout the process of job accommodation. Total quality management (TQM) can free organizations to be more responsive to their customers and employees. Then, reasonable accommodation in meeting the needs of employees and customers with disabilities would become a natural part of the TQM process. "People with disabilities should be seen as both internal customers (employees) and external customers whose input should be valued in product design and marketing. And, like all employees, when they are fully empowered to do their jobs, their productivity will grow."[66]

Legal Redress of the ADA

For instances when people with disabilities feel they have been discriminated against, the ADA provides for a complaint process. As of July 1993, despite the ADA's emphasis on encouraging hiring of peo-

ple with disabilities, over half of the complaints filed with the EEOC
have been from people who were fired. EEOC records show that nearly 12,000 complaints were filed by individuals alleging discrimination,
a 20 percent jump in complaints to the EEOC. In addition, the Justice
Department, which enforces accessibility provisions, is investigating
more than 1,000 complaints.

People with disabilities comprise nearly 80 percent of the employment discrimination cases filed by current employees. Generally, these
are individuals who had a prior disability and are now exercising their
right to file suit, or people who became disabled and are suing
employers for not accommodating their needs. Back injury is the most
common disability alleged, followed by mental impairments and heart
conditions.[67] Of the 2,200 resolved to date, the EEOC found discrimination in only 29 of the cases. An additional 684 were resolved in favor
of the complainant. Favorable settlements averaged $16,000.[68]

In a Chicago lawsuit, the first job-bias case to go to trial, a federal
jury awarded 59-year-old Charles H. Wessel damages of $572,000
when he was dismissed because his terminal brain cancer forced him
to miss work for treatment. "The EEOC had argued that closely held
AIC Security Investigations Ltd. fired Wessel as executive director last
July because of stereotypical fears about his cancer—and without
warning him that his treatment-related absences had harmed his performance. AIC contended that Wessel's full-time attendance was an
essential part of his job." In June of 1993, a judge reduced the March
jury award to $222,000. AIC is seeking a retrial.[69]

While the goal of the ADA is to end discrimination toward people
with disabilities, some fear that the mechanism of the Act was the
wrong instrument. "The labor market for people with disabilities may
indeed be flawed by discriminatory practices, but it also reflects the
effects of economic forces," argues Walter Oi. "A civil rights approach
worked well for race and gender, but the same tool will not do for the
task at hand," Oi wrote in an article for *The Annals of the American
Academy of Social and Political Sciences*. "Disability defies a neat dichoto-
mous classification. It is not a simple, black-and-white distinction."[70]

In the same article, Richard Burkhauser, an economist at Syracuse
University, argues that the ADA will increase the employment of people who have the least serious disabilities and the strongest education
and job skills. On the other hand, he points out that ADA will do little
for people dually disabled: those who are physically disabled and who
lack education and job skills.

Burkhauser found that in countries that mandate employment of
people with disabilities, there is still discrimination. He observes that
"in the Netherlands, for example, few employers comply with man-

dates to accommodate disabled workers, even though the government picks up the full cost of compliance. Germany requires strict quotas on hiring people with disabilities, but allows companies to pay fines if they can't or won't comply, an avenue many companies take."[71]

Where Do We Go from Here?

Attitude Adjustment

More than any other one action, we need to adjust the attitudes we may have about people with disabilities. We need to update our language, talking about "people with disabilities" rather than "the handicapped." We talk about the "person who uses a wheelchair," rather than "wheelchair bound." A man who has multiple sclerosis and uses a motorized scooter to get around said, "I wish people would meet me before they meet my disability."

Disability Prevention

Forward-looking companies are recognizing the desirability of helping prevent disabilities among present workers, retaining employees who become disabled, and hiring qualified individuals with disabilities.

Faced with a labor shortage and a skills deficiency, employers are fast recognizing the substantial investment they have in current employees, and many are beginning to nurture that investment. As a consequence, many employers are starting wellness programs to encourage employees to remain physically fit so medical costs can be better controlled. As a result, employees who participate remain physically fit, healthy, and more productive.

EAPs are becoming prevalent to assist employees in dealing with personal problems such as family, marital, financial, emotional, stress, and substance abuse problems. Return-to-work initiatives are another new concept. All of these programs have demonstrated the value of early intervention in the prevention of medical problems, in assisting employees in dealing and coping with personal problems, and in facilitating a speedy return to work after a disabling injury or illness. Light-duty work programs are being implemented to transition an injured or disabled employee back into the workplace. Gradually, employers are beginning to realize that employees are truly one of their most valuable assets—one that can no longer be looked upon as a disposable resource.[72]

Other companies require stretching and back-strengthening exercises—on paid time—to prevent common back injuries, one of the largest categories of lost-time injuries and the most common category of complaint under the ADA.

The Centers for Disease Control and Prevention has begun a new program to help businesses educate their employees about AIDS and keep those with the disease working as long as possible. Known as "Business Responds to AIDS," this program is designed to help corporate America establish workplace AIDS policies, train supervisors to deal with infected employees, educate employees and their families, and encourage community service and volunteerism.[73]

"National education programs such as the `America Responds to AIDS' campaign have been generally ineffective in reaching communities of color. The information is often vague and targeted toward an anonymous general public."[74] In order to be effective, public awareness and education campaigns about all disabilities need to be appropriately written and targeted to specific groups.

With the increase in the number of employees for whom English is their second language, materials need to be written in culture-sensitive ways in a number of languages. They also need to be in formats accessible to people with vision, hearing, and learning impairments.

Education

Education about people with disabilities is crucial to their acceptance in the workplace. ADA compliance training is insufficient. Awareness and sensitivity training is also critical.

Acceptance

Looking ahead, experts say the process of hiring and equipping workers who have disabilities will slowly continue into the next century. A consortium of major software and services vendors such as Microsoft Corporation is working with the General Services Administration, and the University of Wisconsin is researching adaptive software for the disabled. Many say they also expect interest to grow rapidly as the decade progresses and the pool of skilled workers shrinks.

"ADA created a new wave of immigrants...who are going to have to be assimilated into our society like other waves of immigrants before us," says James Barry, a consultant on disabled-related issues at Nynex Corporation, and who is visually impaired.[75]

How will we know that people with disabilities are truly included and valued in our workplace? "When I see more disabled people who are CEOs of companies and not just the March of Dimes girls," says

Kim Dudley, staffing specialist at GMAC Mortgage Corp, Elkin Park, Pennsylvania.[76]

Underemployment of people with disabilities is almost as big a problem as unemployment. There is a perception that people with disabilities may be capable of low-level, routine-type jobs, but some managers find it hard to accept that people with disabilities also function well at the higher-level jobs. "While the law has yet to open up many new jobs for disabled managers, it is improving certain managers' chances of moving ahead despite an existing disability. Others now find less employer resistance when they want to resume work after developing a disabling injury or illness. In the past, executives often found themselves fired or forced to retire."[77]

As the nature of jobs in the workforce changes, people with disabilities will need to demonstrate skills to match the available jobs. With assembly line jobs disappearing, the National Center for Disability Services in Albertson, L.E., now trains people for medical or environmental testing laboratories. It placed 300 people in 1992, 25 percent fewer than in 1991. "Still, those 300 people turned into wage-earners now earning $4.5 million instead of the government paying them $2 million in Social Security benefits," says Edwin Martin, the center's president.[78]

A few major concerns, including Southwestern Bell Corp. and Sears, Roebuck & Co., have begun to recruit disabled college graduates for entry-level management-training programs. More organizations will need to recognize the entire range of talents of people with disabilities.

Policy Development and Implementation

Organizations will need to incorporate disability issues into their workforce planning, budgeting, and human resource policies. They will have to monitor court cases related to the ADA, especially in the areas that are still uncertain, such as insurance.

The insurance industry has echoed corporate America's new outlook with changes in disability insurance. Today, managed disability products increasingly combine short- and long-term disability into one policy and offer claims organizations that support early intervention and claims management. Ideally, managed disability products should offer progressive work incentives, such as day-care allowance for parents or a benefits increase for participation in rehabilitation programs or part-time work. Insurers that relax their definitions of disability, enabling individuals to qualify for benefits more easily, can reduce costs and premiums. Allowing individuals to qualify for benefits without proving total incapacity facilitates a quicker return to work.[79]

More innovative and progressive ideas about how we view people with disabilities will accomplish several goals: getting people with disabilities back to work and off of disability benefit payments, saving everyone money, and increasing productivity. The future inclusion of people with disabilities in the workforce depends on forward thinking, flexibility, dealing with hard issues such as insurance, and being innovative. All employees, disabled or not, must work together to value all workers as they contribute to an organization's success.

References

1. From the President's Committee on Employment of People with Disabilities, reported in *OPM Message to the Senior Executive Service*, SES 93-02, October 1992, p. 5.

2. Maggie Shreve, *The ADA: Basic Training Outline*, 1990, p. 5.

3. *Ibid.*, p. 6.

4. Joseph P. Shapiro, Disabled and Free at Last, *U.S. News & World Report*, May 17, 1993, p. 52.

5. Susan R. Meisinger, "The Americans with Disabilities Act: Begin Preparing Now," *Society for Human Resource Management Legal Report*, Winter 1991, pp. 2–3.

6. Joann S. Lublin, "Law Does Help Some Managers to Move Ahead," *The Wall Street Journal*, July 19, 1993, p. B2.

7. The Urban Institute, "Improving Job Skills of the Learning Disabled," *Policy and Research Report*, vol. 22, no. 1, Winter/Spring 1992, p. 21.

8. Interview with Jude Setian-Marston, LCSW, March 21, 1994.

9. Veronica Vaccaro, Assisting Employers to Accommodate People with Mental Disabilities, *Community Support Network News*, vol. 8, no. 3, December 1991.

10. Mary B. Dickson and Michael Mobley, *The Americans with Disabilities Act: Techniques for Accommodation* (Alexandria, Va.: American Society for Training and Development, April 1992), p. 15.

11. Edward L.C. Haslam, "Disability Post-ADA: Americans with Disabilities Act Health Insurance Prescription," *Best's Review—Life-Health Insurance Edition*, vol. 93, no. 7, Nov. 1992, p. 46.

12. Mary B. Dickson, *Supervising Employees with Disabilities: Beyond ADA Compliance* (Menlo Park, CA: Crisp Publications, Inc., 1993), p. 32.

13. Marty Cushing, "Attitudes about the disabled need repair, along with buildings," *Star Tribune*, Oct. 10, 1992, p. 19A.

14. Drach, "Desert Storm's Disabled," *The Washington Times*, Oct. 13, 1991, p. B4.

15. F. Bowe, *Disabled in 1985: A portrait of American adults* (Fayetteville: University of Arkansas, Arkansas Research and Training Center in Vocational Rehabilitation, 1986).

16. National Institute on Disability and Rehabilitation Research, *Chartbook on Work Disability in the United States* (Washington, D.C.: U.S. Department of Education, 1991).

17. Carol Locust, *Handicapped American Indians: Beliefs and Behaviors* (Tucson, Ariz.: Native American Research and Training Center, undated), pp. 12–13.

18. F. Chan, C. S. Lam, D. Wong, P. Leung, and X. Fang, Counseling Chinese Americans with Disabilities, *Journal of Applied Rehabilitation Counseling*, vol. 10, no. 4, pp. 21–25.

19. Antonio Suazo, "Window of Opportunity: Disabled Hispanics in the Labor Force," *Employment and Disability: Trends and Issues for the 1990s* (Alexandria, Va.: National Rehabilitation Association, 1990), p. 66.

20. Dana Priest, "U.S. Is Urged to View AIDS as Racial Issue," *The Washington Post*, Jan. 12, 1993, p. A3.

21. *Ibid.*

22. Dianne B. Piastro, "Equal opportunity may be credo, but it's not reality for handicapped," *Minneapolis Star Tribune*, Jan. 12, 1992, p. 6E.

23. *Ibid.*

24. Dickson, *Supervising Employees with Disabilities: Beyond ADA Compliance*, *op. cit.*, p. iii.

25. *Ibid.*, p. 11.

26. Marc Hequet, "The Intricacies of Interviewing," *Training*, April 1993, p. 33.

27. Carl Quintanilla, "Disabilities Act Helps—But Not Much," *The Wall Street Journal*, July 19, 1993, p. B1.

28. *Ibid.*, p. B2.

29. "U.S. Officials Help Businesses Educate Workers About AIDS," *The Washington Post*, Dec. 2, 1992, p. 2.

30. Katie Muldoon, "Employing People with Disabilities," *DM News*, Oct. 12, 1992, p. 12.

31. Esther Boylan, *Women and Disability* (London and Atlantic Highlands, N.J.: Zed Books, 1991).

32. Drach, *op. cit.*, p. B4.

33. Tom O'Bryant, "Employment and the Worker with a Disability: A Corporate View," *Employment and Disability: Trends and Issues for the 1990s* (Alexandria, Va.: National Rehabilitation Association, 1990), p. 22.

34. Susan Brown, "My Battle with Dyslexia," *Cosmopolitan*, p. 116 (no date available).

35. O'Bryant, *op. cit.*

36. Information from Office of Management and Budget, quoted in *In the Public Interest*, p. 2.

37. Steve Taravella, "Hospitals act to accommodate Americans with Disabilities Act, *Modern Healthcare*, Special Report, Jan. 27, 1992, p. 29.

38. Meg Fletcher and Sara J. Harty, "How Doing the Right Thing is Paying Off," *Business Insurance*, July 13, 1992, p. 25.

39. *Ibid.*

40. Timothy L. O'Brien, "Disabled Get New Weapons in Battle Against Discrimination; New federal, state legislation takes aim at bias in workplace," *Newsday*, Sept. 1, 1991, p. 106.

41. *Ibid.*

42. *Ibid.*

43. *Ibid.*

44. Gregory T. Smith, Guest commentaries: disability prevention pays off, *Oregon Health Forum*, vol. 3, no. 7, July 1993, p. 11.

45. *Ibid.*

46. O'Bryant, *op. cit.*

47. E. D. Berkowitz, *Disabled Policy: America's Programs for the Handicapped* (Cambridge: Cambridge University Press, 1987), p. 40.

48. Reed Greenwood, "Employment and Disability: Emerging Issues for the 1990s," *Employment and Disability: Trends and Issues for the 1990s* (Alexandria, Va.: National Rehabilitation Association, 1990), p. 14.

49. Louis Harris and Associates, *The ICD Survey of Disabled Americans: Bringing Disabled Americans into the Mainstream,* for the International Center for the Disabled, 1986.

50. "Job Retention for People with Disabilities," *Rehab Brief,* vol. XV, no. 2, 1993, p. 4.

51. *Ibid.*

52. *Ibid.*

53. Quintanilla, *op. cit.*, p. B1.

54. Jay Mathews, "Disabilities Act Prompts More People to Come Forward," *The Houston Chronicle,* Nov. 27, 1992, p. 4.

55. Greenwood, *op. cit.*, p. 13.

56. "EEOC Issues Guidance Application of ADA to Health Insurance Plans," *The HRIN Review: Human Resource Information Network Newsletter,* June/July 1993, p. 2.

57. J. Waldrop, "From handicapped to advantage," *American Demographics*, 12, 233-35,54, 1990.

58. "Job Retention for People with Disabilities," *Rehab Brief,* vol. XV, no. 2, 1993.

59. *Ibid.*

60. Dickson, *Supervising Employees with Disabilities: Beyond ADA Compliance*, *op.cit.*, p. 61.

61. Mitch Betts and Jean S. Bozman, "Executive Report: Technology and the Disabled Worker," *Computerworld*, Nov. 25, 1992, p. 63.

62. Sara D. Watson, "Employment and Disability: Emerging Issues for the 1990s," *Employment and Disability: Trends and Issues for the 1990s, op. cit.*, p. 21.

63. Greenwood, *op. cit.*, p. 10.

64. Haslam, *op. cit.*, p. 46.

65. Lana Smart, "Employment and Disability: Emerging Issues for the 1990s," *Employment and Disability: Trends and Issues for the 1990s, loc. cit.*

66. Dale S. Brown, "Quality Through Equality, Use of Principles of Total Quality Management to Hire and Retain Workers with Disabilities," downloaded from *Series* computer network, no date specified, but approximately Dec. 1992.

67. Liz Spayd, "The Disabilities Act, One Year Later," *The Washington Post*, July 29, 1993, p. A23.

68. John Merline, "Is the Disabilities Act Working?" *Investor's Business Daily*, vol. 10, no. 76, July 28, 1993, p. 1.

69. Lublin, *op. cit.*

70. *Ibid.*

71. *Ibid.*

72. O'Bryant, *op. cit.*, p. 24.

73. "U.S. Officials Help Businesses Educate Workers About AIDS," *loc. cit.*

74. Priest, *op. cit.*

75. Betts and Bozman, *op. cit.*

76. Quintanilla, *op. cit.*, p. B1.

77. Lublin, *op. cit.*, p. B1.

78. Kathleen Teltsch, "Tearing Down the Barricades to the Disabled: New York City Is Seen as the Proving Ground for a Federal Anti-Discrimination Law," *The New York Times*, Feb. 11, 1993, Sec. B, p. 1.

79. Haslam, *op. cit.*, p. 46.

11

Gay, Lesbian, and Bisexual Workers

Gay men, lesbians, and bisexual individuals are one of the "new minorities" in the workplace and among the least understood. Gay people (meaning gay men, lesbians, and bisexuals) have long been subjected to harassment based on ignorance, fear, or religious writings and teachings, and sometimes a combination of all three. Now, however a new openness is beginning, slowly and unevenly, to develop in the workplace and elsewhere and, with it, growing public acceptance.

In the 1990s, which some have glibly designated the "gay '90s," gay and lesbian issues are gaining a place on the national agenda. A small number of openly gay people are being appointed to government posts. And scientific research is beginning to probe the origins of sexual orientation. Eventually it may shed light on questions such as whether homosexuality is a matter of nurture or nature or both. For example, a 1991 study found an anatomical difference between the brain structures of gay and straight men. More recently, a 1993 study by the National Cancer Institute suggested a genetic link for male homosexuality.[1] But scientific research on homosexuality is in its infancy, and studies that have been undertaken are controversial.* But such research is a two-edged sword: Many gay people fear that scientific findings might be abused and lead to increased homophobia rather

---

*See, for example, Ruth Hubbard, "False Genetic Markers."[2]

than lessen it. Public debate over lesbian and gay issues is anything but conclusive, and despite growing acceptance, erroneous stereotypes about gay people abound.

Because negative stereotypes are pervasive, many gay men, lesbians, and bisexual people choose to remain "invisible" in the workplace. They do not come out publicly and acknowledge their sexual orientation for fear of discrimination, limiting their professional opportunities, or outright firing from their jobs. Adding to their stress is the fact that they may be out in other areas of their life, such as with friends and family; the process of needing to switch identities continually can be confusing and painful.

Based on the steady stream of reported cases of workplace discrimination as well as anecdotal information, these fears are justified. Although to date there has been little systematic exploration of the issues, a few studies do exist, and they support the legitimacy of the fears. A survey in the summer of 1991 by Overlooked Opinions, a Chicago research firm, showed that, of 6,500 gay workers polled nationally, 14.6 percent reported employment discrimination in the preceding 12 months as a result of being lesbian or gay. Of these, over 32 percent reported more than one instance of discrimination; almost 10 percent of them indicated they had been subjected to discrimination more than five times in the 12-month period.[3] Because the surveyed population included individuals who had not identified their gay orientation at work, it can be assumed that homophobia is, in fact, more widespread than the statistics indicate.

Similar results were found in a recent survey conducted by the Gay and Lesbian Community Action Council (GLAC) in the Minneapolis–St. Paul area. The GLAC survey found that 11 percent of the gay and lesbian respondents indicated that they were threatened with job loss due to their sexual orientation; 7 percent had lost jobs; 5 percent felt they had been denied employment; and 6 percent had been denied promotions.[4]

The prevalence of homophobia probably varies region by region. A recent survey undertaken in Kansas City by a commission established by Mayor Emanuel Cleaver showed that a full third of the gay and lesbian workers surveyed experienced discrimination.[5] Further, according to a 1987 *Wall Street Journal* poll of *Fortune 500* chief executives, 66 percent of the CEOs indicated they would hesitate to give a management job to a homosexual person.[6]

The nature of discrimination seems to differ according to job category. White-collar gay, lesbian, and bisexual workers tend to face a glass ceiling. Blue-collar workers are more likely to be subjected to direct harassment from co-workers as well as finding their chances for advancement limited.

Workplace homophobia flourishes partly as a result of a lack of federal legal protection. Unlike other major identity groups in the workplace, gay workers are not covered by Title VII of the Civil Rights Act of 1964, which prohibited discrimination based on race, color, sex, religion, and national origin, or by subsequent legislation that extended protection to older and disabled workers. For years, gay activists and their supporters have lobbied without success to obtain an amendment to the 1964 Civil Rights Act based on sexual orientation. (The word "sex" in the 1964 Civil Rights Act refers to gender, not sexual orientation.) A bill to add sexual orientation has been stalled in Congress since 1978; however, it seems to be gaining support gradually, and many are hopeful that it will be passed in the next few years. In February 1994, a small but possibly significant step was taken in this direction when a federal assistance package for earthquake victims in California explicitly banned discrimination on the basis of sexual orientation. It is the first time lesbians, gay men, and bisexual people have been added to the list of protected categories. One constitutional scholar remarked that it "represents a gain for those who are trying to inject sexual orientation into mainstream civil rights law."[7]

Gay and Lesbian Strategies in the Workplace and Their Impact

Unlike members of other major identity groups, gay workers are camouflaged by gender and ethnicity. They have the option of whether or not to indicate their sexual orientation at work. Traditionally, most have opted for silence. A 51-year-old marketing executive expressed the fears of many gay workers when he said, "All the people I know at work would make fun of me, put me down at work, and that type of thing. Everybody would find out; I would be ruined completely. My family would find out....I would be left out in the cold by myself."[8] These fears are intensified by the possibility that, once they have embarked on an approach of silence and passing as a heterosexual, subsequent exposure would cost them the confidence of their co-workers.

Traditionally, most gay workers have used two strategies at work: hiding their sexual orientation by pretending to be heterosexual and adopting avoidance practices to keep from revealing their homosexuality. More specifically, these involve hiding sexual identity by actively pretending to be heterosexual. To mislead people, some lesbian and gay workers assume a dual identity, inventing fictitious events about their private lives and attending organization functions with a member of the opposite sex. Some, who are deep in the closet, may go to the extreme of openly discriminating against other gay people. Leonard Hirsch of the Smithsonian believes that many of those who keep their sexual orientation private are older workers, noting, "These are often our worst enemies because they would like to shut us up."[9] The issue is particularly serious when gay workers encounter closeted, hostile men and women in supervisory positions.

A second strategy is avoiding references to loved ones in order not to disclose sexual orientation. Less extreme and more frequently used than hiding, this strategy may be employed in degrees. At one end, a gay worker, invoking a value for privacy and a belief that discussing personal issues at work is unprofessional, will try to avoid the casual, social conversations that are a natural part of daily work life. Such a worker will appear to be all business and aloof. Others try to engage in social conversation, but are uncomfortable and evasive about the personal relationships (spouses, dates) and plans (e.g., for the weekend) that form a large part of the casual conversation among heterosexual people.

These strategies take a toll on both the worker and the organization. Gay workers face the dilemma of whether to continue to protect themselves through lying or to come out at work and face possible consequences. Continual lying undermines self-respect. It alienates gay workers from their environment, heightens stress levels, and diminishes their effectiveness on the job because a great deal of energy, which could otherwise be applied to work, is channeled into hiding or avoiding disclosure of sexual identity.

These strategies result in a sizable decrease in productivity for organizations. No one knows for sure how many gay people are in the workplace or in the general population. Until 1993, the figure commonly cited was 10 percent, based on studies by Alfred Kinsey in the late 1940s and early 1950s.[10] A 1993 study found the figure to be much lower. According to the Battelle Human Affairs Research Centers in Seattle, only 1.1 percent of the over 3,000 male participants in their survey reported being exclusively homosexual; 2.3 percent reported having ever had sex with another man.[11] (Women were not included in the survey.) Because sexual orientation is a subject many are reluctant to discuss openly, there remains much room for debate about the actual share.

Whatever their share in the workforce, gay men and lesbians are not evenly distributed throughout. Evidence suggests that gay persons are particularly highly represented in management positions and are more highly represented in certain industries. A 1991 survey of 8,031 gay men and lesbians nationally by Overlooked Opinions, Inc., shows that more gay and lesbian workers hold management positions (12.5 percent) than clerical (6.3 percent). In terms of percentages of gay workers by industry, at the high end are health (12 percent), education (10.5 percent), and sales and marketing (8.8 percent); at the low end are science (2.6 percent), food service (2.4 percent), and public safety (1.7 percent).[12]

These figures may be skewed somewhat by the existence of "invisible" gay workers overlooked by polls. The percentages in some industries are likely to be higher. The point, however, is that gay workers form an important segment of any organization. The cost of their giving anything less than their best effort is a negative impact on the bottom line. And the cost of diminished effectiveness of invisible gay workers, who do not feel free to communicate openly with co-workers, will increase as the workplace environment becomes more highly interactive and as co-worker relations become more important to the successful completion of tasks.

Fortunately for organizations and for their own well-being, gay workers are increasingly questioning their silence in the workplace on the issue of sexual orientation. There is, as Ed Mickens pointed out, a growing "awareness that secrecy perpetuates shame, thwarts the building of community, and feeds prejudice."[13] Gay workers are questioning the unfairness of the double standard by which many heterosexuals, while honestly and casually presenting personal information about their personal lives, wonder why lesbians and gay men feel a need to be open about theirs.[14]

More and more, gay men and lesbians are feeling the need to be open about their sexual orientation. These people are turning to a third strategy for operating successfully in the workplace: integration. Integration involves an effort to be as open and natural about personal information as are heterosexuals.[15]

A growing number of gay workers are reaping positive payoff for making the decision to come out at work. These include normalization, increased respect, and more comfortable relationships. "By removing the stress of the double life, and by allowing individuals to be more fully themselves, the coming out process can offer surprisingly clear advantages. Individuals profit, and the interpersonal dynamics of the workplace gain through increased trust, understanding, and acceptance."[16]

Because homophobia is still widespread, however, and the professional risks are great, the decision to be open at work about one's identity involves a level of courage that is not required of other workers. Some lesbian and gay workers opt to go into business for themselves rather than take the risk. Others, who have come out at work, find the harassment too stressful and take the same option.

Although, to our knowledge, no systematic study has been undertaken about the gender and racial identity of those who chose to come out at work and participate in support groups, informal reports suggest they are mainly white, mid-level professionals. They tend to be younger workers, and there seems to be more men than women. According to Eric Keller, a director of the federal Gay, Lesbian or Bisexual Employees (GLOBE) organization of government workers, many older workers are too deeply closeted to come out. He also notes that, because women and minorities face other barriers on the job, they may be reluctant to subject themselves to a double whammy by declaring their sexual orientation.[17]

Gay and Lesbian Activism

The growing trend toward openness at work is no accident. It is the result of years of activism by gay men, lesbians, bisexuals, and their supporters. The long, rough road of homosexual activism has been traced through oral histories recorded by Eric Marcus in *Making History: The Struggle for Gay and Lesbian Equal Rights, 1945–1990.*[18] Marcus's book points out that during the 1940s and 1950s pioneering activists faced seemingly insurmountable odds: uncertainty as to whether it was legal for them to meet, seizure of their publications, and periodic visits by the FBI. Strengthened by the civil rights movement of the 1960s, the struggle for gay rights was transformed from an educational endeavor into a political movement. After the June 1969 Stonewall riot in New York, young gay activists changed the social meaning of homosexuality by redefining "coming out" as a public declaration of identity and pride.

While the movement experienced both gains and losses during the 1970s, the extreme conservatism of the 1980s paradoxically helped the movement attain a second wind. Assaults by the political right wing and some religious organizations have galvanized activists, who now made the workplace a new frontier.* Further, the devastation caused by the AIDS epidemic gave a new, deeper meaning to activism. James Kelly,

---

*The Vatican is among the religious organizations that have opposed gay rights activists in the workplace. In June 1992, the Vatican announced support for discrimination against gay people in certain workplace hiring practices as well as in public housing and family health benefits in order to "promote the public morality of the entire civil society on the basis of fundamental moral values."[19] However, the Vatican seemed to drop the issue after prominent Catholics, including the Bishops of Seattle and Honolulu, publicly criticized the directive.[20]

professor and director of the social work program at California State Long Beach, summed up the impact of these forces when he said, "You have to stand up and be your own advocate. That's the one thing AIDS has taught us....People are more active, particularly in the workforce."[21]

Still, in many workplaces, gay, lesbian, and bisexual people are just beginning to organize into support groups. Although, as in any minority group, informal social networks of gay workers have long existed in the workplace, gay rights activism has not and, in some cases, group members face an uphill battle. Acceptance is growing, but their right to receive organizational support is still not universally accepted in the private sector.

Another problem gay support groups face is that lesbian, gay, and bisexual workers who are also members of traditional minorities often choose activism in the traditional minority support groups rather than in gay groups.[22] This is a further reason why white males seem to predominate in many gay support groups in the workplace. Lesbians face a double problem of sexism and homophobia. One lesbian comments, "Lesbians know that they have to educate gay men on issues of sexism....Because sexual orientation crosses all other group lines, many times the dynamics within a gay/lesbian group can be as tumultuous as working in any other kind of coalition."[23]

The Legislative Context

To ensure civil rights for gay men and lesbians, gay activists and their supporters have worked jurisdiction by jurisdiction to obtain passage of nondiscrimination laws. There have been many victories: Since 1982, seven states (Connecticut, Hawaii, Massachusetts, Wisconsin, Vermont, New Jersey, and Minnesota) plus the District of Columbia have passed laws protecting gays and lesbians from bias in housing and employment. An eighth state, California, bans employment discrimination. Similar protection is extended by more than 100 localities nationwide. In addition, nine states protect lesbian and gay employees in government (Iowa, Michigan, Minnesota, New Mexico, New York, Ohio, Pennsylvania, Rhode Island, and Washington). This patchwork of laws covers over 40 percent of the population and most major business centers. Further, several unions, including federal workers' union locals, have succeeded in getting antidiscrimination language incorporated into contracts.

Gay rights activists point out, however, that the goal is federal nondiscrimination legislation. Some federal legislation already has moved in this direction. The 1978 Civil Service Reform Act prohibited federal employees from being fired on the basis of conduct not adversely affecting their work, and a 1980 Office of Personnel Management memo defined "sexual orientation" as non-job-related conduct. Ultimately, however, activists state that there needs to be an amendment to Title VII of the 1964 Civil Rights Act that provides gay people with the same kind of protection that is extended to other identity groups. The bill to this effect that has been stalled in Congress since 1978 now has more than 100 signatures.

Hopes are high that federal legislation will pass in the near future. The growing number of states and cities passing laws protecting gays is "an implicit signal to Congress that a federal law is more realistic," commented William B. Rubenstein, director of the American Civil Liberties Union's National Lesbian and Gay Rights Project.[24] These hopes are further fueled by the fact that the Clinton administration is more responsive to gay rights issues than preceding administrations.

At the same time, however, the gains that have been made have created a backlash. Violence against gay people is on the increase. Fearful that protecting gay people will sanction promiscuity and foster the rise of AIDS in their communities, anti-gay groups are springing up to press their viewpoint in public forums. They are having some success. In fall 1992, Colorado passed an amendment banning antidiscrimination legislation against gays and prohibiting courts from hearing cases involving discrimination based on sexual orientation. A *Newsweek* poll in August 1992 found that 51 percent of the people surveyed thought gay rights are a threat to the American family and its values.[25]

Yet even among those who see gay rights as a threat there is support. The same *Newsweek* poll found that a full 78 percent supported equal job opportunities for homosexuals. A majority or more felt gays should be hired in a wide range of occupational categories. And far more than a majority approved of health insurance, inheritance rights, and social security for gay spouses.

In the Private Sector

The gay rights movement has taken a quantum leap by affirming the right to be natural and open about identity in the workplace. The new strategy of gay integration is predicated on equality, dignity, and the elimination of homophobia in the workplace. Suzanne Pharr, in her book *Homophobia: A Weapon of Sexism,* stated:

> Equality is more than tolerance, compassion, understanding, acceptance, benevolence, for these still come from a place of implied superiority: favors granted to those less fortunate. These attitudes suggest that there is still something wrong, something not quite right that must be overlooked or seen beyond. The elimination of

homophobia requires that homosexual identity be viewed as viable and legitimate and as normal as heterosexual identity.[26]

More specifically, gay and lesbian goals in the workplace include :

- Adopting explicit statements of policy that prevent discrimination on the basis of sexual orientation, and applying them organization-wide, regardless of local law

- Establishing safe, harassment-free work environments

- Expanding organizations' definition of diversity to embrace gay and lesbian workers

- Providing diversity education and training to help all employees better understand gay and lesbian issues and thus keep prejudice from interfering with communication and productivity

- Sanctioning gay and lesbian employee associations and supplying them with the same support provided to similar employee groups

- Acknowledging and supporting gay family relationships by including a "partner" option for "spouse" on standard forms, and including partners when inviting spouses to company activities

- Equalizing compensation through benefits for family units (including bereavement leave, relocation assistance, discounts, health insurance access, and pension and survivor benefits)

- Providing AIDS education both to reduce AIDS-inspired fear and discrimination against gay people and to help prevent the spread of AIDS

- Cultivating nongay allies in the workplace to help promote a positive work environment for gay and lesbian workers.[27]

Gay workers are promoting these goals through formal workplace support groups. Gay, lesbian, and bisexual employees have long maintained informal networks in the workplace. With the movement's heightened momentum in the late 1980s, they began organizing formal support groups in large numbers within and across organizations.[28]

The decision to form or join a gay and lesbian support group is often hard because it involves a commitment to coming out publicly. Commenting on such difficulties in the union setting, Miriam Frank and Desma Holcomb observed that ad hoc and issues committees are an important part of local union life because committee recommendations may be incorporated into union policy. Many gay union members, however, "do not feel that we can employ the regular union apparatus to announce our interest in working on lesbian and gay concerns....Many of us feel vulnerable among our co-workers and would rather not speak out when our rights are threatened or biased comments are made."[29] They point out that the cost of not forming a group is also high. "If we don't make our presence known, we'll never meet our allies. We'll have a tough time making the union understand the importance of our issues."

At present, thousands of union as well as nonunion lesbian and gay workers, recognizing the cost of nonaction, have formed groups in the workplace. The process has taken on a momentum of its own; the presence of the groups encourages other gay workers to follow suit and join, thereby coming out at work. The groups support them in their decision by providing a forum for networking with other gay workers who have gone through the same experience. The groups also help their members explore psychological aspects of coping with homophobia on the job.

Among the many issues lesbian, gay, and bisexual support groups deal with is an effort to gain membership in their organization's diversity groups. In a statement to a coalition of groups representing minorities, women, and employees with disabilities at the U.S. Department of Transportation, Tom Sachs, chair of the DOT's Gay Lesbian or Bisexual Employees (GLOBE) group, referred to gay people as the "last minority." He noted the "symbolic importance" of their inclusion in the DOT coalition and stated that, more concretely, "the absence of DOT GLOBE would hamper the ability of the Coalition to assist one of the most vulnerable constituencies within every minority community..."[30]

In the Federal Government

The experience of gay workers in the federal government parallels that of gays in the civilian sector. During the 1940s, '50s, and '60s, gay workers were routinely fired from government posts. Although acceptance of gay workers grew in the 1970s, even at present homophobia is widespread. Some government departments and agencies—such as the Departments of Defense and Justice, the FBI, and the CIA—are considered particularly inhospitable employers for gay individuals.[31,32]

Gay activists look forward to changes. Many federal agencies now have gay support groups, and in the summer of 1992 an umbrella organization, GLOBE, was established. At first linking separate gay groups in the Smithsonian Institutions and the General Accounting Office, GLOBE now has groups in a growing number of departments, including Commerce, Labor, Transportation, State, and other foreign affairs agencies. Globe is also connecting with government workers in various cities outside of Washington, D.C., such as Dallas, Los Angeles, and San Francisco.

These newly established gay support groups are pressing for changes in discriminatory practices within their departments. These include the adoption of an EEO statement specifically protecting gay workers from discrimination. Some departments like Health and Human Services and Housing and Urban Development have adopted such a statement. In 1993, the Departments of Transportation and Agriculture joined their ranks, and other departments and agencies are considering it. Also, unions representing government employees, such as the American Federation of Government Employees at the Department of Labor, include such an EEO clause in their contracts. In a further item on their agenda, gay support groups are preparing to reach out to blue-collar federal government workers, who face even more discrimination than white-collar workers.

Gay government workers face similar issues as their civilian counterparts. They also face some issues that are especially characteristic of government. Key among these is the security clearance process. Gay federal employees maintain that they are routinely asked intimate questions that heterosexual applicants are not required to answer.

Gay and Lesbian Workers and Unions

Gay activists who are union members are working for the same equal rights goals as nonunionized activists. They also face special concerns as a result of the union setting.*

Gay activists are working to get protection based on sexual orientation written into nondiscrimination clauses. A standard feature of many collective bargaining agreements, nondiscrimination clauses frequently do not cover gay workers. Such coverage is the foundation stone for a discrimination-free workplace.

Unions can be a critical resource in activists' efforts to obtain equal rights in the workplace. For example, the standard union grievance procedure provides lesbian and gay union workers with the option of an additional channel, not available to nonunionized gay activists, through which to pursue discrimination complaints. Activists urge that, even in localities where gay and lesbian workers are covered by basic legal protections, the grievance procedure may be a means to obtain results. This is especially true when the slow-moving civil authority is overloaded with complaints (as it usually is).

To successfully pursue these and other goals, however, gay activists need the backing of their unions, and particularly the support of national union policy. Within the past few years, they have become engaged in

---

*A major resource consulted in this section is Miriam Frank and Desma Holcomb, *Pride at Work*.[33]

efforts to sensitize unions to their needs. And they are meeting with success. Several international unions, as well as the AFL-CIO, have recently adopted unionwide policies supporting gay and lesbian workers' rights. Armed with such policy statements, gay workers are now in a position to quote them to their negotiators in support of their demands to have nondiscrimination language written into contracts.

Unions have been adopting other acts of support for gay and lesbian workers. For example, the Services Employees International Union (SEIU) of the AFL-CIO sponsored the March for Gay and Lesbian Rights in Washington, D.C., in 1987. The first union newsletter to focus special attention on gay and lesbian issues was the June 1989 special supplement for Gay Pride Month in the *New York Teacher*. Local unions have made financial contributions to gay and lesbian charitable causes. Some are negotiating for domestic partner rights and benefits.

A key factor in the achievement of gay rights goals is for gay workers who are invisible to come out publicly. Each individual worker must act according to his or her own best judgment on this issue. Activists, however, forcefully state the case for gay union members to come out:

> ...Silence=Death. In other words, if gays and lesbians keep on letting ourselves be unheard and invisible in the labor movement, we'll never be able to push for a stronger labor/AIDS agenda, and lives will be lost. Even though we are everywhere, we have only started to speak up. It's always risky to come out, but we won't be able to lobby our leadership to make any of these programs happen until we can feel confident that gay or straight, we are brother and sister union members with an urgent common cause.[34]

Organizational Responses to Gay and Lesbian Workplace Issues

Within the past few years, organizations have begun to become sensitive to gay and lesbian issues from two perspectives: as a market for their products and as employees within their organizations.

The Gay Market

There are at least three reasons why companies are wooing the gay market. First, is numbers and education level: Gay people constitute a sizable and educated market. Thirty percent have four-year undergraduate degrees, and 26 percent have graduate degrees—far higher than the national average. And they are careful consumers. Research shows that 80 percent of gay and lesbian people make purchases based on gay media advertising.[35] Second, gay and lesbian households tend to be better off financially than the average household. Homosexual male couples in particular have a financial advantage, earning two male incomes. According to Rick Dean of Overlooked Opinions, Inc., the average household income for gay men in $51,624; for lesbians, it is $42,755. The national average household income is $36,800. Moreover, gay households tend to have more disposable income than others earning the same amount because they have fewer children. The national average household consists of 2.6 people; the average gay male household consists of 1.7 people, and the average gay female household, 1.9 people.[36] Finally, the ethical dimension may also be a factor. This is reflected in the decision in July 1991 by the Calvert Social Investment Fund to include in its investment criteria concerns about sexual orientation. Calvert is the first and largest group of socially and environmentally responsible mutual funds in the U.S.[37]

Organizations as Employers of Gay and Lesbian Workers

In the absence of federal legislation extending comprehensive nondiscrimination protection to gay, lesbian, and bisexual workers, the workplace (and society in general) has become a forum for debate about their proper status. In the workplace, the controversy forms around the issues of whether sexual orientation is a legitimate workplace concern and whether lesbian, gay, and bisexual workers should be protected from workplace discrimination as are other minorities. An affirmative answer to one implies an affirmative answer to the other.*

As employers of gay workers, many organizations are beginning to respond in the affirmative. They are starting to extend the definition of workforce diversity to cover their gay employees. They increasingly recognize that the impact of discontented workers on the bottom line is real. Thus, the need to ensure a work environment that encourages all workers, including gay workers, to extend their best efforts is becoming clear.†

---

*How the debate is playing out in the legal profession is examined by Jana Eisinger, "Firms Step Up Hiring of Gay and Lesbian Lawyers."[38]

†In one respect, gay workers may be an exceptionally important identity group, whose talents an organization can ill afford to forfeit: Gays and lesbians tend to be better educated than their heterosexual counterparts. Overlooked Opinions, Inc., found that 62 percent of gay men over the age of 25 are college graduates compared to 24 percent of all American men over 25. And 59 percent of lesbian women over 25 are college graduates compared to the national female average of 17 percent.[39]

Recognizing gay workers as members of a workforce identity group has some concrete implications for organizations. They must deal with the issues of equal benefits for gay workers as well as diversity training.

Equal Benefits for Gay and Lesbian Workers

Forbidden by civil law from marrying, gay and lesbian couples are typically ineligible for spousal benefits at work, for these are applicable only to legally married persons.* One result is unequal pay for gay workers: While a married heterosexual person can enroll his or her spouse for medical and other benefits, a gay person must pay for such services from his or her salary.[40] Another result is that, unlike the situation for spouses, any employer contributions toward partner benefits is taxable income for the employee; any payment the employee makes toward partner benefits is not tax-deductible.

Forward-looking employers are beginning to offer some types of benefits to the domestic partners of lesbian and gay employees. These range from relocation assistance and bereavement leave to merchandise discounts and health care coverage. The movement is still small, however. In early 1993, only some 40 major U.S. organizations offered health benefits to unmarried partners of homosexual and heterosexual employees.

Beyond organizational inertia and an omnipresent bias against paying for additional benefits, there are two reasons why organizations will think extra hard about providing domestic-partner health care benefits: the recession and AIDS. The recession of the early 1990s had a hampering effect on spending. Bill Custer, director of research for the Employee Benefit Research Institute, a nonprofit group in Washington, D.C., indicated that he would "be surprised" if many employers developed domestic-partnership plans, since most firms "are holding tight or cutting back on employee benefits."[41] The AIDS issue has also warded off employers, who fear that providing benefits to a population with a high rate of AIDS would mean exorbitant expenditures.†

---

*Each state determines civil law regulating marriage. At present, all states prohibit marriage between same-sex people. A few cities, such as San Francisco, Washington, D.C., Seattle, and New York City, do offer a domestic partner registry.

†The incidence of AIDS is high among gay men. Among lesbians, it is thought to be lower than for the heterosexual population. According to a report by the Centers for Disease Control and Prevention, 56 percent of AIDS cases among males reported between April 1991 and March 1993 occurred among men who have sex with men. The report did not specify the incidence of AIDS among women who have sex with women.[42] It should be noted, however, that AIDS is not just a "gay disease." Heterosexual women are among the fastest growing populations with HIV.

Despite these concerns, more employers adopted domestic-partner health care benefits plans in 1992 than in all previous years combined.[43] The experience of organizations that provide such benefits shows AIDS-related fears to be unfounded. To date, no employer has reported an increase in health benefit expenses over what it would cost to add a spouse to the roles. Further, more heterosexual than homosexual workers tend to sign up for domestic-partner benefits. The positive effect of implementing the policies goes beyond the numbers. According to Jim Young, director of personnel at the Minnesota Communications Group, which initiated its policy in early 1992, "even employees who aren't eligible have been appreciative. They think it's the right thing to do. Gay employees have been superappreciative. They say it makes them feel included."[44]

Diversity Training

Diversity training programs typically overlook lesbian and gay issues or deal with them only in a cursory way. Nor do EEO plans and policies usually acknowledge them. Ann Quenin of Lotus believes that homosexuality is "far and away the scariest" diversity issue because it concerns sex and involves religious beliefs. She noted that even well-educated people are misinformed about the topic.[45]

For gay workers, the objective of homophobia diversity training is to create an environment in which co-workers are well-informed so that gay employees can feel comfortable to reveal as much about their personal lives as they wish. (The goal is *not* for all gay and lesbian workers to come out at work.) Only in such an environment do gay workers feel free to reach their full potential.[46] Homophobia awareness training also aims at reducing irrational fears and bias among heterosexual workers. These factors can impede communications and lower productivity. "Putting the oppression of homophobia (heterosexualism) on a par (with other forms of discrimination)...demonstrates the interconnectedness between all oppressions, and lets employees know that those kinds of behaviors and attitudes are inappropriate in the workplace," observes Bonnie J. Berger.[47]

Federal Government Responses to Gay and Lesbian Workers

As an employer of gay, lesbian, and bisexual workers, the federal government is becoming more open and responsive to their workplace needs. Beyond the discrimination issues discussed elsewhere in this chapter, federal government responses on two other topics have gained a high-profile: military service and security clearances for lesbian and gay people.

After a high-profile public debate in 1993 over gay men and lesbians in military service, a new policy took effect in March 1994. The policy allows gays and lesbians to serve in the military as long as they do not reveal their sexual orientation. Billed as "don't ask, don't tell, don't pursue," the policy ends the practice of questioning recruits about their sexual orientation and investigating unsubstantiated reports of homosexuality. It also prohibits disclosure of sexual status and all forms of homosexual conduct. Neither proponents nor opponents of gays in the military find the plan satisfactory, but the administration points out that it is an advance over the ban on gays in the military. It ensures that people are not rejected from military service on the basis of their sexual status only. At the same time, it is responsive to deeply entrenched military opposition to gays in the armed services.

The military services have long been perceived as being highly homophobic. According to a 1991 poll by Overlooked Opinions, Inc., the military ranks as the job category with the highest levels of discrimination, almost four times the national average.[48] The issue of lifting the ban on gays and lesbians in the military became front-page news during the 1992 presidential election and the early days of the Clinton administration. To that time, gays and lesbians were prohibited from uniformed military service. In effect since World War II, the ban was first explicitly stated by the Pentagon in 1982. Questions about sexual status were routine. Many gay and lesbian people joined anyway, lying about their sexual orientation. They served with honor and some were highly decorated. But all kept their identity secret for fear of harassment and dismissal. They found themselves in a dilemma, loving the military but living in fear that their identity would be discovered.

Although most of the public debate over lifting the ban on gays in the military centered mainly on men, it is generally believed that there are more lesbians in military service than gay men. The military services have prosecuted service women more harshly than men for homosexual conduct. According to *Newsweek* magazine, military investigations and discharges for homosexuality are, overall, three times more likely to be targeted to women than to men, and in the Marines, the figure is six times.[49] In response to sexual harassment complaints from both gay and straight service women, the military has often investigated the women's sexual conduct instead.[50]

The adoption of the new policy does not resolve these issues. Opponents remain uncomfortable at the prospect of serving in close quarters in combat with gays and lesbians. Some have noted irony in the situation, because it was well known that they had long been doing so anyway. As one officer, who opposed lifting the ban, pointed out, "There have been homosexuals [in armies] since before Christ."[51] Nonetheless, the discomfort remains. For their part, gay and lesbian service people still fear discovery and are dismayed that they must continue to be hypocritical with their peers and themselves.

A second major issue affecting lesbians and gays in government service is security clearances. The government has maintained that gay workers are security risks on the grounds that they are potential targets for blackmail by foreign governments. The irony of this premise is that gay workers are theoretically vulnerable because they are reluctant to disclose their sexual orientation due to discrimination. Reducing discrimination would diminish reluctance to come out and thus diminish any vulnerability to blackmail. According to one source, there have been no known cases of gay-related blackmail for espionage.[52] Both civilian and military sectors of the government are beginning to acknowledge this. A 1991 Defense Department study concluded that gay men and lesbians are no more likely to spy against the government than heterosexual men and women. Then Defense Secretary Dick Cheney asserted there is no reason to think homosexuals are a greater security risk than anyone else. In August 1991, he said that the assumption that gay employees present a security risk is "a bit of an old chestnut."[53] Nonetheless, the State Department and other foreign affairs agencies remain wary about assigning homosexuals to overseas posts, according to Eric Keller of GLOBE.[54]

References

1. Cited by Natalie Angier, "Report Suggests Homosexuality Is Linked to Genes, *The New York Times,* July 16, 1993, pp. A1, C18.

2. Ruth Hubbard, "False Genetic Markers," *The New York Times,* August 2, 1993, p. A11.

3. Overlooked Opinion, Inc., "Gay Workers Survey," unpublished survey, Chicago, Ill., 1991.

4. Cited in Glenn Howatt, "Coming Out At Work," *Star Tribune,* September 6, 1992, p. 1A.

5. Andrea Warren, "Hiding in the Corporate Closet," *Business Dateline,* March 1992.

6. Cited by Glenn Howatt, "Gay, Lesbian Workers Becoming More Outspoken in the Twin Cities," *Star Tribune,* September 6, 1992.

7. Kenneth J. Cooper, "Hill Bans Gay Bias in Quake Aid," *The Washington Post,* February 19, 1994, p. A12.

8. Jay Lucas, "Working Under Cover: The Professional Lives of Gay Men and Lesbians: Implications for Human Resource Professionals," excerpt from a forthcoming book by Jay Lucas and James D. Woods entitled *Working Under Cover*; excerpts appear in *Invisible Diversity: A Gay and Lesbian Corporate Agenda*, September 20, 1991, New York.

9. Elizabeth Kastor, "In Federal Workplace, Gays Open Doors and Step Out; From Silent Signals to Desktop Photos," *The Washington Post*, August 8, 1992, p. A1.

10. Alfred Kinsey, *Sexual Behavior in the Human Male* and *Sexual Behavior in the Human Female* (Philadelphia: Saunders, 1949/53).

11. Boyce Rensberger, "Sex Survey: What Men Want and Think They Might Get," *The Washington Post*, April 15, 1992, p. A1.

12. Overlooked Opinions, Inc., "Gay Workers Survey," *op. cit.*

13. Ed Mickens, "The Invisible Minority: Gays and Lesbians in the Workplace," *Business Ethics*, July/August 1990, p. 21.

14. Jay Lucas, "Working Under Cover," *op. cit.*

15. Jay Lucas and Mark Kaplan, "Workplace coping strategies of gay men and lesbians," *Working It Out: The Newsletter for Gay and Lesbian Employment Issues* [henceforth referred to as WIO], Spring 1992, p. 7.

16. Mickens, *op. cit.*, p. 22.

17. Telephone interview with Eric Keller, August 11, 1993.

18. Eric Marcus, *Making History: The Struggle for Gay and Lesbian Equal Rights, 1945–1990* (New York: HarperCollins, 1992).

19. Laura Sessions Stepp, "Vatican Backs Bias Against Gays," *The Washington Post*, July 17, 1992, pp. A1, A10.

20. *WIO, op. cit.*, Summer 1992, p. 6.

21. Gary Libman, "A New Acceptance: Gay Support Groups Are Beginning to Pay Off in the Workplace," *Los Angeles Times*, July 18, 1992, p. 1.

22. Telephone interview with Eric Keller, August 11, 1993.

23. Bonnie J. Berger, in an unpublished letter, August 31, 1993.

24. Barbara Presley Noble, "Legal Victories for Gay Workers," *The New York Times*, June 21, 1992, Section 3, p. 23.

25. Bill Turque, *et al.*, "Gays Under Fire," *Newsweek*, September 14, 1992, p. 36.

26. Suzanne Pharr, *Homophobia: A Weapon of Sexism* (Inverness, Calif.: Chardon Press, 1988), p. 45.

27. Based on goals compiled by Ed Mickens in an unpublished letter, January 21, 1993, and from an address by Bonnie J. Berger to the Washington, D.C., Diversity Networking Group Meeting, Federal Aviation Administration, July 15, 1993.

28. Libman, *Los Angeles Times*, July 18, 1992, p. 1.

29. Miriam Frank and Desma Holcomb, *Pride at Work: Organizing for Lesbian and Gay Rights in Unions* (New York: Lesbian and Gay Labor Network, 1990), p. 9.

30. Tom Sachs, "Statement to Coalition of DOT Minority, Disabled and Women Employee Associations," unpublished statement, July 12, 1993.

31. Elizabeth Kastor, "In Federal Workplace, Gays Open Doors and Step Out," *The Washington Post,* August 8, 1992, p. A1.

32. Interview with Eric Keller, a director of the federal GLOBE organization, August 11, 1993.

33. Frank and Holcomb, *op. cit.*

34. *Ibid.,* p. 93.

35. "Finder Facts," based on a survey by Overlooked Opinions, Inc., January 1, 1992.

36. Telephone conversation with Rick Dean, Overlooked Opinions, Inc., December 8, 1992.

37. Neenyah Ostrom, "Calvert Social Investment Fund Strengthens Sexual Orientation Screen," *New York Native,* Issue 435, August 19, 1991.

38. Jana Eisinger, "Firms Step Up Hiring of Gay and Lesbian Lawyers," *The New York Times,* February 7, 1992, p. B6.

39. Andrea Warren, "Hiding in the Corporate Closet," *Ingram's,* vol. 17, no. 3, March 1992, Sec. 1, p. 35 ff.)

40. Jayne Garrison, "Levi Strauss tailors health plan to workers' unmarried partners," *Chicago Tribune,* March 1, 1992, p. 8.

41. Chris Bull, "N.Y. Hospital OK's Partners Benefits; Others May Follow," *The Advocate,* May 28, 1991, p. 3.

42. Centers for Disease Control and Prevention, U.S. Department of Health and Human Services, *HIV/AIDS Surveillance Report,* 1993, vol. 5, no. 1, p. 6.

43. Ed Mickens, letter, January 21, 1993.

44. *WIO,, op. cit.,* Spring 1992, p. 3.

45. Thomas A. Stewart, "Gay in Corporate America," *Fortune,* December 16, 1991, p. 54.

46. Jay Lucas, "Working Under Cover: The Professional Lives of Gay Men and Lesbians: Implications for Human Resource Professionals," excerpt from a forthcoming book by Jay Lucas and James D. Woods entitled *Working Under Cover;* excerpts appear in *Invisible Diversity: A Gay and Lesbian Corporate Agenda,* September 20, 1991, New York.

47. Berger, unpublished letter, *op. cit.*

48. Overlooked Opinions, Inc., "Gay Workers Survey," *op. cit.*

49. Melinda Beck, Daniel Glick, and Peter Annin, "A (Quiet) Uprising in the Ranks," *Newsweek,* June 21, 1993, p. 60.

50. *Ibid.*

51. Charles W. Hall, "Area Servicemen Split on Lifting Ban on Gays," *The Washington Post,* November 21, 1992, p. A10.

52. Kim I. Mills, "Civil Service a Mixed Bag for Gays; Security Clearances a Problem, Associated Press, July 14, 1991.

53. General Accounting Office, "DOD's Policy on Homosexuality," GAO/NSIAD-92-98, July 1992.

54. Eric Keller, in a telephone interview, August 11, 1993.

12

Older Workers*

Millions of Americans 50 and older have seen their country mobilize to take on enemies in hot wars and cold ones; they have participated in a scientific revolution that has taken America from cars with running boards to sophisticated deep-space probes and from medicines derived from spores and bark to those based on biogenetic engineering. They have experienced fundamental shifts in American society: The civil rights movement challenged them to examine their prejudices, the women's movement insisted they reevaluate their most intimate relationships, the gay pride movement forced them to ponder time-honored values, and the counter-culture denied the validity of their lives. They have wrestled with deeply divisive issues such as pro-choice versus pro-life, prayers in public schools, and the morality of the death penalty. This generation has even had to worry about whether or not Elvis is still alive.

They have weathered it all. They have questioned, reevaluated, adopted new ways of working and new kinds of technology. Again and again, they have made the changes demanded of them by a new world they, or their peers, played a large role in shaping. Yet today they are told that, because they have crossed an arbitrary, chronological boundary, they are no longer able to adapt.

There is no question that the workplace today demands a great deal of adaptation. Its ground rules are being radically altered, its economic context is shifting dramatically, and U.S. industries are rushing to restructure in the face of internal and external pressures. In the process, industry and society are redefining the nature of work and the workplace.

---

*This chapter was written with Lee Adair Lawrence. The authors are grateful for her work.

From the older worker's perspective, one of the most far-reaching changes occurring today is the redrafting of the long-standing "psychological contract" between employers and employees. But if older workers report anxiety about the future, fear, and uncertainty about their value as productive members of society, it is not because they dread change for change's sake. Rather, they fear discrimination. They fear being excluded solely on the basis of their age from the new opportunities springing up in the workplace. They worry about being shunted aside to make room for younger workers who are presumed (again, solely on the basis of their age) to be less costly, more productive, and more needy.

Older workers looking out at the economic landscape see companies, especially in the manufacturing and service sectors, downsizing primarily at the expense of their peers. Many have seen younger men and women routinely offered retraining opportunities that were denied to them. They have watched younger colleagues receive more positive performance evaluations for equivalent work. They remained in the anteroom when younger job candidates were called in for that crucial second interview. Yet, all the while, these same older workers have heard top management extol their virtues in general meetings, company publications, and in interviews with pollsters. But these praises are not apparent where they count: in face-to-face discussions about retraining options, part-time work opportunities, reassignments, and other alternatives to early retirement or layoff. A report by the American Association for Retired Persons (AARP) shows managers praising older workers as being the ones that "come in to work on Monday morning. They don't take off because the spirit moves them, they come when it snows," says Martin Sicker, head of the AARP's Work Force Programs Department. "The managers say: `They're great employees!' Do you hire them, we ask? `No, we don't,' or words to that effect."[1]

This is not to imply that nobody hires older workers or that employed older workers are not being valued anywhere. In companies with innovative human resource management policies, employers and employees are sitting down together as individuals, not as the embodiments of a myth or stereotype. Where this occurs, the results are heartening. Management learns that older workers are not necessarily more expensive than younger workers, and that their health care costs—a primary source of concern to most—need not put older workers out of the running. Experience shows that any higher costs in wages or health care are often offset by other factors: older workers are, in the main, healthy; they may have fewer dependents who need coverage; they learn and retrain just as readily and easily as workers of other ages; and their experience and maturity can translate into high productivity and quality work. Indeed, in many instances, they are better candidates than their younger counterparts for jobs that require mastering and applying more than one skill. Those companies that have made the effort to assess the contributions of their older employees on the basis of their individual performances, rather than on attributes assumed because of their ages, have reaped significant benefits, as we shall see.

These findings are bolstered by a growing body of evidence that clearly disproves many of the myths, stereotypes, and givens about older people and their capacity to work. If science agrees on anything, it is that older people are heterogeneous. Indeed, they display the widest variety of any other age group. This may explain why "older worker" keeps getting redefined. Although many statistics refer to a 55-to-64 age range, the law defines an older worker as a person 40 years old or more. This tallies with the attitude of many corporate recruiters who consider 40 and up unacceptably old. But this is by no means uniform. In some industries, 35 can be considered over the hill. In this chapter, "elderly" is defined as 65 and over, while an "older worker" is considered to be 50 and older, unless otherwise specified.

The arbitrariness of these definitions illustrates what a slippery task it is to define what is "old," despite our myriad preconceived notions on the subject. It also gives us some inkling of how frustrating it can be for a worker to find himself labeled "too old" when he has just turned 42 and had his first child, or celebrated her 53rd birthday and her child finally declared a major at college. Being treated as though one were suddenly deficient by virtue of one's date of birth is all the more galling when hard scientific evidence gathered since the 1940s has testified to the durability of physical and mental ability well into old age.

The attitude of employers cannot be entirely explained by the well-known phenomenon of institutional lag—like generals fighting the last war, or policies that are developed to meet the needs of yesterday's society. What, then, molds the thinking that results in the dismissal or nonhiring of an older worker? In many cases, it is age discrimination. Gerontologist and author Robert N. Butler named this phenomenon *ageism* in 1968, and it persists because it is subtle, deeply rooted, and largely unconscious.[2]

Our societal values and youth-oriented culture unwittingly perpetuate the negative attitudes that underlie age discrimination. Moreover, increased specialization and a rapidly expanding base of knowledge with easy-to-access information have combined to rob the elderly of the one strength Western culture recognized: their ability to transmit accumulated knowledge and experience. Today, older Americans find that many of their young colleagues do not look to them for guidance as they themselves once looked to their elders. Rather, they are routinely consigned to the background while newer generations rely on their advanced degrees, technosense, and youthful enthusiasm. In turn, many an older worker finds himself dismissing the mere "book learning" of his younger, less-experienced colleagues. At times, an older worker may also find herself or himself envying a colleague's youth, especially when it seems to garner the social and professional rewards he used to assume were his due. Thus, those at both ends of the age spectrum may cling to simplistic generalizations and assumptions that get in the way of clear thinking. In the case of older workers, this carries a steep price tag. In the words of one observer, "American corporations are trashing an entire generation."[3]

But the same economic upheaval that has hurt so many older Americans is engendering what may prove to be their saving grace: the redefinition of the workplace and of work careers, and forward-looking, cutting-edge management. This may provide an unprecedented opportunity for employees and employers to slay the dragon of age discrimination and get on with the business of rescuing the corporate maiden.

The Roots of Ageism

Every day, older Americans are subjected to a barrage of advertising, fashion photos, and television sitcoms in which youth is defined in terms of attractiveness, strength, potency, speed, productivity, innovation, and conquest. The mistakes of youth are dismissed with a smile as the product of overenthusiasm and charming naiveté. Harder hitting still are other common but powerful images, such as gray-haired women incapacitated by "minor arthritis pain" or older men concerned that they might lose their dentures when biting into an apple. They express the unspoken flip side of the portrayal of youth: the assumption that all who are no longer young are also no longer attractive, potent, strong, productive, innovative, or aggressive enough to conquer. In other words, they can no longer contribute fully to society. And it is this unconscious association of age with imminent mortality that provides the foundation for ageism, which gerontologist Butler defines as an attitude that allows us to "avoid, for a time at least, reminders of the personal reality of our own aging and death."[4]

Death, the end of life, is the great, forbidding unknown, and men and women have, from humanity's earliest days, sought ways to come to terms with their mortality. This quest has taken a particular bent that leads Butler to conclude that "we are so preoccupied with defending ourselves from the reality of death that we ignore the fact that human beings are alive until they are actually dead."[5] Death is embarrassing to us as a society, something to be denied as long as possible, then hurriedly dealt with so that we can get on with our lives. Death is positively un-American.

America the Youthful

America's particular history is greatly responsible for turning a natural and human fear of the unknown into a bias against anyone displaying signs of aging. From the beginning, America defined itself as a young country with all the attributes of youth: It was vigorous, productive, ever on the move, enthusiastic, and aggressive in pursuit of its goals. There was a country to be won, a wilderness to be tamed and settled, and a new frontier to be explored. Later, America devoted its efforts and energies to creating an industrial base that was the wonder of the world and instrumental in winning two world wars and a Cold War and in putting Americans on the moon. America was getting the job done, spurred on and glorified by folk myths that emphasize feats of work prowess and boast of superhuman effectiveness.[6]

Nationhood was not the only thing young about America. Americans, the movers and shakers, the explorers and discoverers, were themselves young. In 1776, few could expect to live more than 35 years; a century later, on the brink of our industrial revolution, life expectancy for Americans was a mere 40 years. By the centennial, people were living longer, but the country still boasted a population whose median age was 21.[7] Our economic system, mixed but essentially market-capitalist, produced a set of attitudes that reinforced our infatuation with youth. Such an economy puts a high premium on efficiency, productivity, and the maximization of profit, all of which were achieved by the kind of energetic enthusiasm for hard work that entrepreneurs and workers of all kinds were expected to display as America industrialized. With life expectancy relatively low and ill health still largely unchecked by medical science, the workplace came to view older workers as short-termers, unproductive relative to their healthier and younger colleagues.[8]

Along with this glorification of youth, however, Americans displayed a degree of respect for elders that was similar to that of many other societies throughout the world. The elderly were seen as the repositories of knowledge: They had lived and made history, they knew life firsthand and had dealt with its problems and challenges, and this made them wise in the ways of the world, understanding, knowing. However, these positive labels failed to carry the same weight in America as in other cultures that prized reflection and knowledge over action. In this country of doers, wisdom and experience were valued, but never at the same level as action and high achievement. Horatio Alger did not stop to ponder: He got busy.

The spread of literacy and the transformation of America into an information society marginalized the elderly even further. Now, technology brings accumulated knowledge to the younger generation at the touch of a button. The information explosion made archaic the ideal of the wise elder transmitting his wisdom to his student. Nor was the older generation called upon to teach values to a baby boomer generation that believed it was capable of redefining them for itself. As for providing a conduit to the living past, someone once remarked that "Americans don't believe in history." Perhaps because we are too busy making it.

At the same time, advances in medicine were ensuring longer lives for Americans, but not necessarily peak health. In the nineteenth century, if a man or woman reached 80, in all likelihood that octogenarian had been an exceptionally strong and fit individual. By the mid-twentieth century, octogenarians were more commonplace and represented a spectrum of health and much ill health. The word "old" began to be associated with "tired," "sickly," "debilitated." Older Americans traveled "over the hill," they "faded fast," and when the 1935 Social Security Act helped make retirement feasible, the notion was that they should be "sent out to pasture."

Exacerbating this trend was the way in which our cities and life cycles developed. In the growing number of two-generation, two-wage-earner nuclear families, a new generation of Americans began to move through life relating primarily with their peers. After years spent with classmates their own age, they moved on to child-rearing and establishing careers, living in neighborhoods populated predominantly by other families in roughly the same age group. For a time, many baby boomers even banned children from their "adults only" or "singles only" apartment complexes. They were Peter Pans exulting in their unending youth. Their elders meanwhile slipped off to spend the so-called golden years in retirement communities, enjoying an unheard-of independence.

Not everyone followed this pattern, but enough did to effectively layer American society by age group, which meant that there was less of the contact with older people that would allow the young to come to terms with their own, inevitable aging. Late life took on the featurelessness of the unknown. It became forbidding territory, unexplored because one's own old age and death lurked there.[9] In the absence of positive models in their daily lives, the young have little identification with the old, who remain "other," much like any minority. Out of this lack of contact grows what Butler terms our "schizophrenic" view of older Americans: the benignly smiling Rockwellian grandmother serving Thanksgiving turkey to her adoring grandchildren versus the crotchety, rumpled old geezer or pathetic, youth-craving wannabe. Older Americans hear these contradictory attitudes echoed in everyday language through euphemisms like "golden agers" and "senior citizens" for whom a compliment is to be told they "don't look their age" or "don't act their age."[10,11] Witness television sitcoms that titillate audiences by portraying seniors who act like their libidinous grandchildren in defiance of cultural expectations.

The Golden, Anxious Years

This schizophrenic view, shared to a large degree by many older people, partly grows out of America's lack of myths or rituals to help us come to terms with and value stages of the life cycle beyond youth. In pointing out this gap, the noted historian, sociologist, and journalist Max Lerner laments that it "leaves the American without much sense of wonder at the successive phases of the individual's life history." The great transitions in a person's life are thus "conceived as burdens somehow to be borne," while American popular imagination remains "fixed upon the more abstract goals of the society. In the process, the sense of wonder is replaced by anxieties and tensions."[12]

This has never been more true than today, when economic pressures are dredging up deep-seated attitudes and older Americans find themselves fighting against outdated definitions of who they are, what they need, and what they are capable of contributing. The anxiety expressed by older workers is not a function of their age, but rather a normal reaction to being misunderstood, disregarded, and undervalued. Indeed, anxiety is a misleading term for what they are feeling, for anxiety implies that there is no concrete cause for their worry. Fear is a better word—fear of being treated according to unfounded assumptions and expectations rather than one's own strengths, experiences, and desires; fear of being overlooked in the reshuffling of the workplace and not offered the same opportunities for empowerment as younger workers.

What many older Americans need is not a spot on the golf course, but a job. Of people 65 and over, 12.2 percent—some 3.6 million people—live in poverty.[13] Pension benefits and Social Security are often insufficient to guarantee a decent lifestyle, yet older people continue to be popularly regarded as a leisured class. They are not necessarily assumed to be pulling in large sums of money, but whatever they do receive is generally regarded as disposable income. The popular belief is that older Americans have paid off their homes, educated their children, and fulfilled the expensive responsibilities that accompany middle age. The picture may differ slightly depending on the racial or ethnic group involved. Older Asians, for instance, are inaccurately perceived as uniformly being cared for by family.[14] For Asians as for whites, blacks, Hispanics and others, the myth that the golden years are serene persists even though common sense and statistics tells us that these are the very years in which Americans face the greatest stresses: the loss of a spouse or life partner, the fear that a catastrophic illness will cast them into poverty, uncertainty over whether there will be enough retirement income to last an extended lifetime.[15] How galling when these fears are not acknowledged, when one is unfailingly depicted in the popular imagination as a grandfather who starts off the day with an easy-going game of golf while his wife gathers her friends for a game of bridge in her well-appointed home. How galling to have others assume that this is all one wants or needs.

These images disregard and trivialize the profound changes that longer, healthier lifespans, postponed stages of the life cycle, and new economic times have wrought in the expectations of Americans. Many people today reject the notion of radically altering their lifestyles upon reaching "retirement" age. Most Americans 45 years old and older would prefer a certain continuity as they make the transition between their work lives and their increasingly active retirement years.[16] This could mean anything from working at a reduced level of involvement and responsibility in the company, to taking on volunteer activities, or setting up as a part-time temporary or consultant.

Americans who are indeed struggling just to get by suffer the unstated judgment that if a man reaches retirement age and cannot afford to live happily ever after, he has only himself to blame. He must have squandered his savings, planned inadequately for his old age, preferred to take fancy vacations rather than make house payments and save prudently.* Barbara Lawrence of the University of California traces this kind of intolerance to expectations that are deeply rooted in human society:

> Chronological age is one of the few universal human experiences, and as a result provides a basic structural link between individuals and social systems. People use age to classify the members of a social sys-

---

*Women are not subjected to the same assumptions. Rather than being guilty of irresponsibility, they are regarded as the victims of a man's lack of forethought or irresponsibility. Their crime is one of judgment in choosing partners.

tem into categories and to match them with roles and statuses. The matching process produces widely shared beliefs about the standard or typical ages of members holding each social position.[17]

Although Lawrence's study was set in the hierarchy of the workplace, it helps explain why we pass judgment on those individuals who somehow do not fulfill expectations—like the 55-year-old man who finds himself in need of a job because his pension is inadequate or the 60-year-old widow who suddenly discovers she cannot meet her house payment. Often, such judgments are based on an older life pattern. Today, as we continue to postpone childbearing, it is also not uncommon for those in this age group to have one or more children who depend on them for partial financial support. Some contribute to the care of parents or in-laws, while yet others have dependents both older and younger than themselves. They are the so-called sandwich generation. Whatever the emotional or financial reasons, many older Americans need and want to work, while society at large still clings to outworn notions of what is appropriate to them "at their age."

Given the pervasiveness of popular misconceptions and myths about the elderly, it is hardly surprising that many older workers come to regard age as a personal failure. When they run up against age discrimination, many feel they must suffer it in silence as punishment for what and who they have become.*[19] There are many examples of workers who have bought into the ageist belief that they had, at a certain age, suddenly become useless, so much so that the Gray Panthers worried that nobody would speak up at a January 1991 public gathering called to denounce age segregation. Happily, they were wrong. One after another, salespeople, engineers, managers, social workers, executives, and other older workers stood up to recount their personal tales of discrimination. Nevertheless, there is still evidence that the prevalence of stereotypes and myths continues to engender feelings of inadequacy among older workers. Take the statement of a former manager at Union Carbide who was laid off at the age of 52. "After 10, 12, 15 years," he told an interviewer, "you've learned 90 percent of what your knowledge and ability in the field is going to be. Somebody 10 years into the market is still in the growth curve, and is willing to work for less than someone who gets to the top of the pay scale."[20]

---

*To illustrate this point, Robert N. Butler cites the study of a psychologist who gave the Rorschach test to elderly volunteers who were resigned to aging. He found similarities between their tests and those of American G.I. prisoners who had collaborated with their captors in Korea.[18]

Transforming Gold into Lead in the Workplace

The assumptions that underlie this statement echo the ageist stereo-type that insists that a person over 40 or 50 has little if any room to grow, and cannot learn new skills or improve on existing ones. It also presupposes that an older worker would be unwilling to work at a reduced rate of pay, and that, all in all, the older worker will end up costing the employer more than a younger one. Most insidious and damaging of all, the statement implies that all older workers are alike. Perhaps the latter assumption more than any other single factor is responsible for transforming the elderly into a minority subject to derogation, discrimination, and damaging stereotyping.[21]

In the world of work and profit margins, ageism translates into the belief that older workers have fewer resources to exchange for a job. They are deemed to have less or somehow inappropriate education, too few working years left to justify training, and to be less physically and mentally capable than those more attractive younger workers.[22] Many of the assumptions about very old age have been transferred to workers in their 50s and early 60s, with the result that "retirement age," which has for years been creeping lower, has come to be viewed as a cutoff point after which people are less capable of working. Differences in individual circumstances, abilities, and preferences are simply disregarded.[23]

Older workers find themselves also battling another set of assump-tions. Just as older Americans tend to be regarded as responsible for their misfortune if their latter years are not "golden," so do older work-ers find themselves judged more harshly because they have not reached an "appropriate" point on the career path. Although this point varies from industry to industry and among companies, studies sug-gest it is a rare workplace that does not have an unspoken expectation of where in the hierarchy a worker should be at a given age.[24] A lawyer who has studied the problem closely is Anne C. Vladeck, who has rep-resented age discrimination cases in fields as varied as investment banking and the media. "The thinking is," she concludes, "that people who are not chiefs—people who are still at mid-level when they're in their 50s—must not be so good."[25] But what if that particular mid-level manager had delayed her career by taking time off to raise children? What if the performance of this mid-level worker is uniformly excel-lent? What if this worker has been asking for additional training to enhance his value to the company and been consistently refused?

The point is simple: Nobody asked; assumptions were made. An experiment conducted by Professor Bruce Avolio of New York University at Binghamton revealed just how insidious and unconscious are people's assumptions about age—and how damaging. He asked young professionals to listen to audiotapes of simulated interviews. He told them that the candidates had similar work experiences and equivalent on-the-job performances. Avolio even had the same people impersonate both the young and older candidates on the tape. When it came time to evaluate the candidates, the listeners tended to regard the older workers as dead wood while judging the younger ones as adequate performers. In spite of identical work histories, the listeners rated the young candidates higher than the older ones.[26]

In good economic times, this kind of bias may produce similar injustices on occasion, easily repaired in an expanding job market. As long as the United States was unchallenged as the preeminent economic power, most workers could expect to remain with a well-established firm for a lifetime, helping it to mass produce standardized items in return for "family wages" that allowed a gradually improving standard of living. There were, of course, differences in wages and levels of affluence, but, in the main, American workers were spread out on an economic escalator that seemed always to be moving up. While this reality held, the underlying cultural and psychological bias in favor of youth had a less visible effect on older workers. Yet, as Labor Secretary Robert Reich reminds us, the "fabled Fifties" was a narrow little world that excluded or, at best, confined minorities and women and wasted human resources by using people where machines could better do the job.[27] Managers might have unjustly assumed that their older workers were less productive, but as long as they were doing their jobs, the "contract" held.

By the mid-1970s, however, the situation was changing. Companies started to feel the pinch of global competition, government deregulation, and a sluggish economy. In what can now be viewed as a portent of things to come, the frequent large-scale layoffs in cyclical industries such as aerospace affected older workers to a disproportionate degree. In a survey at the time, respondents 55 and older were "much more likely" to report they had experienced age discrimination,[28] illustrating that a harsher economic climate had forced underlying assumptions and deeply held stereotypes—in other words, ageism—to the surface. There is little to suggest that these attitudes had changed by the mid-1980s, when once again a potent combination of perceived economic necessity and a widely held belief that older workers are at the same time more costly and less productive shaped many corporate downsizing strategies. Downsizing, which has significantly affected older workers, has continued into the 1990s.

The underlying attitudes have been carried forward as well. Corporate management continues to be ambivalent about older workers, subscribing at least tacitly to the myth that they are significantly different from younger ones. They are typically believed to be more set in their ways, unwilling and unable to learn new skills or technologies, slower, more forgetful, weaker, and sicker. They are regarded as having fewer working years in them. Thus, investing in older workers—whether by hiring them, training them, broadening their skills through varying work assignments, or retaining them—yields a poor return for company resources expended. Ironically, where any of this holds true it is largely because management or company policy has created a self-fulfilling prophecy. By devaluing its older workers, especially by denying them training, management creates a depressing work environment that encourages neither high quality nor productivity. Under these circumstances, workers' skills can indeed erode along with their morale. Any worker would be only too happy to escape from such a situation.[29] The converse is also true, as a recent Organization for Economic Cooperation and Development study indicates. It found a strong link between employment stability—how long a worker stays with a company—and the training he gets from his employer.[30]

Another related phenomenon is the fact that managers develop their own set of equations between age and the contributions of workers. An analysis of data gathered in the Louis Harris *Laborforce 2000* study identified four distinct views concerning workers and their value over the course of their careers. Of the human resource executives surveyed, 37 percent said they subscribed to the notion that a worker's value to the employer over time depends on whether or not that worker has maintained his or her skills. The researchers labeled this the *training-dependent pattern,* followed in popularity by the *upward-sloping pattern* and the *plateau pattern,* to which 28 percent of the executives subscribed. The first pattern maintains that a worker's value to the corporation increases with time, while the second holds that it plateaus sometime in mid-career and remains at that level until the end. Finally, the *inverted U pattern,* with which only 4 percent of the executives said they agreed, describes a worker's contribution during the early stages of his or her career as steadily growing, then plateauing for a period before dropping off sharply in the later stages of his or her working life.[31]

Although these four patterns are presented as distinct, mutually exclusive sets of assumptions, in practice they sometimes merge. An older worker who has not had the opportunity to gain new skills throughout his career finds that he has plummeted in value in the eyes of the manager who believes in a training-dependent pattern. In other words, this employee's contributions are considered to conform to the inverted U pattern. Unsurprisingly, an earlier study by the Conference

Board indicates that the belief in the inverted U pattern is more wide-spread than the results suggest. The study concluded that management generally believed "that aging necessarily means declining health and safety, motivation, and productivity," and that this assumption presented the greatest impediment to the retention of older workers[32] in an era of rampant downsizing.

Another seldom-articulated idea that has been around since the 1930s and continues to inform hiring and retention policies is that older workers should be encouraged to retire to free up jobs for younger, needier workers. Social Security was established in large part to achieve this goal, which continues to be seen as valid in a time of labor surpluses. The younger worker, it is felt, has a family to support and needs the job more than someone who has worked all his life and surely deserves the gold watch and a pension. This compelling scenario, however, does not take into account the radical changes in our life cycles pointed out earlier. With the postponement of childbearing and greater longevity, it is no longer a safe bet that a worker aged 50 is somehow unencumbered and has less need for a job and a steady income. Our longer life expectancy has also made a 30-year retirement increasingly likely—a long time to spend in even the lushest pasture, let alone a semibarren one.

Infinite Shades of Gray

Knowing how difficult and downright inaccurate such assumptions can be, the focus should be on the individual, recognizing that the diversity that exists among older Americans today will intensify as we enter the next century. The image of a retiree as white, male, well-educated, and comparatively well-off is commonly held to represent the majority. However, it might be distorted by the fact that studies on retirement until recently usually overlooked women. They were regarded as returning to their primary role upon retirement and, therefore, were denied the counseling offered to their male colleagues and were excluded from studies about retirees and their adjustment problems.[33]

If, among today's retirees, there are more women than reported in many statistical compilations, projections about tomorrow's older Americans are not guilty of this oversight. These tell us that America's future retirees, many of whom will continue to work in some capacity, will be increasingly female and members of minority groups. The Spanish-speaking population will be especially well represented, as their numbers are expanding at the most rapid rate.[34] The oldest baby boomers will begin to retire around the year 2005 and they still will be

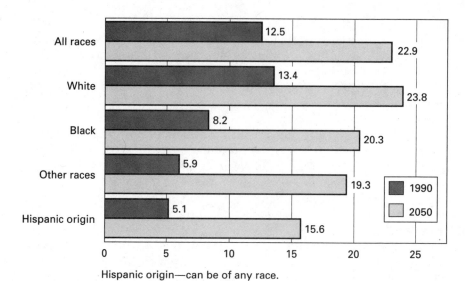

Hispanic origin—can be of any race.

Figure 12-1. Percentage of population 65 years and over by race and Hispanic origin: 1990 and 2050. (*Source:* U.S. Bureau of the Census, 1990 from 1990 Census of Population and Housing, Series CPH-L-74 *Modified and Actual Age, Sex, Race, and Hispanic Origin Data*; 2050 from Projections of the Population of the *United States, by Age, Sex, and Race; 1988 to 2080,* Current Population Reports, Series P-25, No. 1018. U.S. Government Printing Office, Washington, D.C., 1989. Hispanic from *Projections of the Hispanic Population: 1983 to 2080,* Current Population Reports, Series P-25, No. 995. U.S. Government Printing Office, Washington, D.C., 1988)

overwhelmingly white. As Figure 12-1 shows, by 2050, the lower average age of minorities will not be as great a factor. According to some projections, the total number of those 65 years and older will have jumped to 69 million from some 32 million, with blacks accounting for 10 million and Hispanics representing 8 to 12 million (up from 1.1 million in 1990).[35] Minority groups will thus account for a larger percentage of the elderly population than ever before—and each group will be pursuing its own agenda, even as they do now.

Women and minorities in the ranks of older workers and retirees are not likely to forget the political action and consciousness-raising efforts that have put their special concerns on the national agenda. Just as today's older Americans are generally more literate, conscious of issues, and more activist than their predecessors, so will future generations of baby boomer retirees and older workers across the racial, ethnic, and gender spectrum enter this important stage of their lives with a direct knowledge of the power of numbers.

With each passing year, our older worker population resembles less and less a monolithic, white male group and more and more the shifting patterns inside a kaleidoscope. Each component has particular strengths, particular weaknesses, and individual needs and desires. Attempts to deal with older workers as a homogeneous group or to dismiss their concerns altogether will undoubtedly be fiercely challenged and prove even more counterproductive than they already are.

Who, then, *is* the average older person? Increasing racial and ethnic diversity is but one reason a sociologist would be hard-pressed to draw a meaningful portrait of Mr., Mrs., or Ms. Average at, say, age 62. Medical science, too, provides few guidelines, because doctors find that chronological age is useless as an accurate predictor of an individual's physical capabilities or condition.[36] Yet 40 percent of corporate respondents to the Louis Harris *Laborforce 2000* survey shied away from employing older workers because of the physical demands of work, despite the fact that relatively few jobs today require the ability to perform hard physical labor. There are, of course, jobs where speed and stamina are important—as in some areas of the automotive and construction industries—and concern over an older worker's ability to perform safely and efficiently are entirely justified. Still, it pays even here not to assume. Some employers have found, upon closer inspection, that the judgment and caution that comes with the experienced greatly offset their slower speed.[37]

In the Harris survey, the mental demands of work were invoked by 25 percent of managers as a reason for giving older applicants a wide berth.[38] On this point, science is clear: Even more than the concern over physical ability, worrying about an older person's cognitive and related abilities is grossly misguided. As early as the 1950s, scientists studied healthy elderly people who lived independently and concluded that "psychological flexibility, resourcefulness, and optimism characterized the group rather than the stereotype of rigidity. Many of the manifestations heretofore attributed to aging *per se* clearly reflected mental illness, personality factors, and social-cultural effects." To those who preached that a certain deterioration in mental faculties was inevitable, science retorted—and has since repeated—that there is no confirmation of the "previous belief that cerebral blood flow and oxygen consumption necessarily decrease as a result of chronological aging."[39] The intervening years brought more supporting evidence to light, including an analysis of brain activity that showed that healthy people in their 80s display activity levels comparable to those of 20-year-olds.[40]

This is not to suggest that scientists claim that a woman or man is physically and psychologically the same at age 20 as at 50, 65, or 82. Age clearly leaves its mark on appearance, physical strength, speed of reflexes, and brain function, but it does so to a far lesser extent than assumed, and the losses are often compensated by gains in other areas. The results of recent laboratory tests, for example, show that cognition seems to decline slightly with age. But the degree to which this happens would not affect performance of workers in most professions until after their seventieth birthday.[41] Moreover, the brain can compensate for physical deterioration, and it can learn and remember as well—if perhaps at a different pace and using different techniques—as it could at an earlier age.[42]

The preponderance of evidence leads social gerontologist Ken Dychtwald to reiterate the assertions made close to 30 years ago by Butler. "When we look beyond the myth," Dychtwald observes, "there is no age group more varied in physical abilities, personal styles, tastes and desires, or financial capabilities than the older population."[43] Dychtwald tells of one elderly woman who put it more quaintly, telling him she believed in the "more so" philosophy that holds: "If you're a jerk when you're young, you'll be `more so' when you're older."[44] To put it more positively, if a man was enterprising and hardworking at 20, he is likely to be "more so" at 55. The thesis, admittedly the product of experience and observation rather than an academic study, is that people do not change fundamentally as the years go by; they become more of who they are. It stands to reason, then, that if the spectrum of personality, abilities, and health is broad in a given group of young people, it will broaden even more as they age. This assumes that no illness has felled or radically transformed the person in question—in which case, that person is not likely to be the one filing a job application, asking for retraining, or angling for part-time employment instead of full retirement.

This relates to an important point: Older and elderly workers represent a self-select group within the larger category of older and elderly Americans. It is perhaps not surprising, then, to discover that older and elderly workers consistently get high marks in studies that compare their rates of absenteeism and turnover, the thoroughness of their work, and their diligence and reliability with those of younger workers. Even in jobs that may demand physical stamina and quick reflexes, age does not per se influence performance. This was confirmed in a study of police, firefighters, and corrections officers by the Center for Applied Behavioral Research at Pennsylvania State University. The center concluded that public safety was in no way jeopardized by older people performing these jobs.[45]

Another study, carried out by the Conference Board, confirms that age is a poor indicator of physical or mental ability. The study also shows that older workers have a lower turnover rate than younger ones; that they learn as well as workers of other ages, as long as they are not placed under undue stress; and that retaining an older worker and updating his or her skills proves one-third less expensive than hiring a new graduate who has been schooled in the latest technologies.[46] Higher wages and health care costs were more than offset by older workers' performances and their tendency to stay on the job longer, a contention that has been amply proven by the experience of Grumman Aerospace Corporation. When the economic constraints of the mid-1970s forced the company to lay off 13,000 workers, management decided who would go on the basis of each individual's performance, regardless of age. At the end of the exercise, the average age of its labor force had risen from 37 years to 45.[47] By 1980, Grumman's age-blind policy had created an effective workforce in which 83 percent of its officials and managers, 70 percent of its professional employees, and 66 percent of its technical staff were age 40 and older.[48] Grumman and other companies who have learned to value their older employees are keenly aware that investing in a 50-year-old worker could yield performance and quality dividends for as long as another 15 to 20 years.

Black and White Policies Toward Graying Workers

Shedding Older Workers

Such good experiences with older workers support the positive views of their virtues as reported by managers in studies and polls. Yet these same managers admit that they do not make any effort to retain older workers, hire them, or retrain them. The gulf between what they say and what they do is vast. Most of the 1,000 human resource managers who responded to a survey by AARP and the Society for Human Resource Management in the fall of 1992 praised older workers for their job skills, low absenteeism, high motivation, mentoring abilities, and flexibility in scheduling. Yet 85 percent of the respondents said they had no special practices to spur recruitment of older workers, and 66 percent believed there was no reason to encourage older workers to stay on the job.[49]

It is possible that managers assessed older workers so positively in part to avoid any appearance of discrimination—especially since they were being surveyed by a group supporting the rights of older people. Other surveys have uncovered a more ambivalent assessment. In the *Laborforce 2000* survey of 406 companies, managers considered older workers more reliable, more highly skilled, and more positive in their attitudes than younger ones, but they also believed them to be less suited for training and less flexible when it came to accepting new assignments.[50] This is a common belief, and it can have a significant impact on older workers when economic conditions dictate downsizing. In this case, "ambivalent" equals "negative," because in a situation in which a mistake can negatively impact management on the company, few managers will take a new direction unless they are certain that the policy will work. Despite a growing number of positive experiences, there is still more precedent for releasing than for retaining older workers.

The often unconscious bias that has produced the tug-of-war between fact and belief accounts for much of the difficulty and discrimination older workers are suffering as their companies seek ways to become more profitable and competitive. It also accounts for the gap between what companies say and what they do when dealing with older members of their workforces.

Layoffs

At the depth of the recession, when U.S. companies were cutting costs by closing down production units and excising costly layers of middle management, workers 55 years and older lost jobs at five times the rate of workers of other ages.[51] They were concentrated in the traditional, mature industries that were hardest hit by the economic downturn, and they were heavily represented in middle management, whose functions were greatly eroded by the introduction of information technology. And the trend toward downsizing has yet to play itself out. Edward S. Hyman, Jr., of International Strategy & Investment Group, Inc., calculates that, in 1993, the number of jobs slated to be eliminated per month averaged 56,000.[52] On the heels of his prediction, Eastman Kodak announced in August 1993 that it would cut 10,000 jobs by 1996 in addition to 2,000 jobs already planned for elimination.[53] Even the most cursory glance at the financial press yields more examples daily, as represented in Figure 12-2.

There is no telling what percentage of these cuts will directly affect older workers, but the unemployment statistics to date indicate a disturbing trend. Keeping in mind that the figures exclude those workers who have given up looking for jobs, the unemployment rate for people 50 and over stood at 4.1 percent in August 1991. By August 1992, it had jumped to 5.2 percent.[54] Equally telling is the finding that between 1969 and 1989, the percentage of 60-year-olds employed in career jobs fell from 56 percent to 40.[55] The trend is more pronounced among minorities, with unemployment among elderly black males consistently twice as high as that among white males. Black women fare slightly better than black men on the employment front, but low wages and

Figure 12-2. Expected extent of downsizing over next five years

Percentage of jobs lost	Total	Revenues				Number of Employees			Industry			Company Held	
		100 million and under	101 to 500 million	501 to 1 billion	Over 1 billion	1,000 or under	1,001 to 10,000	Over 10,000	Manufacturing	Financial services	Other services	Publicly	Privately
A lot of jobs	5	2	3	2	8	3	4	8	5	7	2	6	3
Some jobs	63	53	57	53	73	43	63	82	69	64	59	70	56
No jobs at all	28	40	38	37	15	52	27	9	23	27	33	21	33
Not sure	4	5	2	7	3	3	5	2	4	2	6	3	8

other factors combine to drag 60.1 percent of them—as opposed to 44 percent of black males—below the poverty line. Among the elderly, whites are the best off financially, but their mean income is barely over $15,000, with Latinos recording 58 percent of this amount, and black Americans only 56 percent.[56]

These trends have older Americans of all races and ethnic backgrounds feeling singled out—if not by managers then by fate—and they are worried, angry, and frightened. They are frightened that they will never work again. They are angry that life is so unfair to them while it appears to smile on the young. And they are worried that, had they not had gray hair, they might still be on the job. As vociferously as managers deny the stereotypical, negative view of older workers, the evidence suggests that they may be holding on to this view as a way of making tough decisions easier to make. Few acts are more distressing than looking an employee in the eye and laying him off or sending a long-time worker her notice. In cases like this, falling back on negative stereotypes may help reduce the distress of depriving a person of a job, and a livelihood.[57]

At the moment of dismissal, older workers may be excused for feeling as though they have dissolved into a cliché. The reflection they catch of themselves in the eyes of their managers no longer bears much relation to who they are, what their circumstances are, or what particular strengths they have shown during their years of employment. The reflection they see is of someone who is considered to be dead wood, getting up there, unable to make all the adjustments demanded by the company's new way of working, someone who probably wants—hey, deserves!—to take it easy.

Biased Performance Evaluations

When an entire unit is closed down and workers both young and old are laid off, crying discrimination is just that: crying. But when managers choose to retain some workers by retraining them for the new technology, relocating them, or offering them a lateral transfer, then an older worker who is let go is not being paranoid. The older worker is basing his perception of discrimination on precedent and fact.

Many a manager's argument for laying off a particular worker depends on the evaluation of that worker's performance. Improperly done, performance evaluations can be a tricky and subjective means of measuring a person's value to the company. The father of the art of evaluating workers, Douglas McGregor, used to claim that the best performance evaluation was a piece of blank paper.[58] On a clean surface, at least, there can be no risk of biases having unconsciously crept in.

And the biases that can influence the evaluation of an older worker's performance as opposed to that of a younger co-worker are numerous. This was highlighted in a study conducted by Gerald R. Ferris, professor of labor and industrial relations at the University of Illinois at Urbana-Champaign. Rating the work of employees in a southwestern bank as well as that of a sample of nurses and supervisors in the Midwest, Ferris found that there was no significant difference between the work accomplished by older and younger workers. The only area in which they differed was in the evaluations they received from their supervisors: the older workers were consistently rated lower.[59]

Did this occur because of personality traits that had nothing to do with performance? Ferris thinks so. He believes that supervisors like younger workers "because they try harder to ingratiate themselves, whereas older workers are more confident about themselves and their work and less likely to try to curry favor."[60]

Or could it be that age norms came into play? Just as society expects its members to reach certain prescribed stages at given ages, so does the workplace evolve its own set of expectations. This is the nucleus of Barbara Lawrence's theory, whereby "unarticulated and probably unconscious use of [age-related] timetables in evaluation, in conjunction with the appearance of age-graded norms in virtually all social systems, suggests that age norms may be basic assumptions within organizational cultures."[61] This means that an organization assumes a worker should have attained a certain level by a given age. When the time comes to evaluate the identical performances of an older employee and a younger "fast-tracker" at the same level, Ms. Lawrence's theory predicts that the supervisor will be influenced by the organization's perception of where both are "supposed" to be at their respective ages.[62] Typically, the manager will inflate the evaluation of younger employees and rate the older person as less effective if his age does not meet the norm for that position. The very expressions, "he's on track" or "she's a fast-tracker," assume a degree of failure for whoever is on a "slower track," regardless of the reasons. More important, the assumption of failure disregards the quality of the older worker's actual performance, substituting an informal, unstated age-based criterion.

A study cited in *Building the Competitive Workforce* also reported that supervisors consistently gave older workers more negative ratings than the objective data supported. And still other studies found that biases were expressed in performance evaluations, feedback, and promotion decisions.[63] Determining the precise nature of the ageism at work in these experiments and studies may prove impossible, but the similarity of their conclusions leaves no doubt as to the presence of subtle, unconscious age discrimination that the perpetrators themselves may be unaware of.

Even in cases where evaluation accurately reflected their performances, it is misleading to then conclude that older workers naturally reach a plateau or even decline. When this occurs, the nature of the job may be as much to blame as the capability and work ethic of the individual. Having observed that routine jobs inevitably led to routine workers and a falloff in performance with time, some employers have taken steps to transfer more responsibility onto the worker. Such a move may entail as much as restructuring an entire unit or department, so that many a company has only paid lip service to the notion of increasing worker satisfaction. Interestingly, these are the sorts of jobs most often associated with large manufacturing companies engaged in mass production, whose human resource management policies are typically conservative and unimaginative. These are the same companies, in fact, that are most likely to have a large component of older workers—30 percent or more—and face the most severe cost and productivity problems.[64]

Early Retirement Incentive Plans

Given the average age of the labor force in those firms with the greatest need to downsize and the age bias that surfaces in evaluations and expectations, it is not surprising that luring older workers into retirement has become a popular way to trim operations and turn a lumbering, costly company into a sleek, mean, money-making machine. Or so management hopes, as it formulates the latest round of ERIPs—Early Retirement Incentive Plans—a form of "golden handshake" for the rank-and-file. These typically add a sweetener to a worker's pension—perhaps a salary bonus, or lifetime health or other benefits—to reward early retirement. Though, by definition, ERIPs target older workers, human resource managers and employers profess not to use them to rejuvenate their workforces. As Figure 12-3 illustrates, few say they see using ERIPs as a tool to eliminate the most costly or the least productive workers and managers on their payrolls. Rather, a large proportion of managers opt for ERIPs for the same reason a lemming rushes off a cliff: Others are doing it.

ERIPs have become the "conventional, predictable, and safe way to cut the size of a workforce in a short time."[65] And it is a testimonial to the power of precedent that employers continue to offer ERIPs, even though companies report that they are not always an effective cost-cutting tool. Increasing numbers of human resource managers are finding that ERIPs no longer make good business sense, though such man-

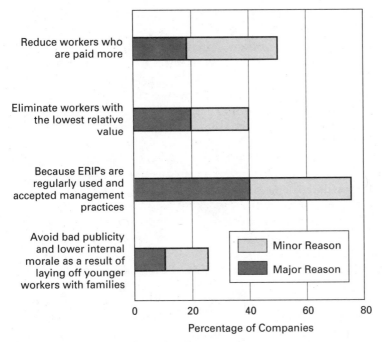

Figure 12-3. Why companies offer older workers early retirement.
(*Source: Building a Competitive Workforce—Investing in Human Capital for Corporate Success. Philip H. Mirns, editor, p. 173*)

agers remain a (growing) minority.[66] Many continue to pin their hopes on ERIPs as though they were a magic wand that enables them to shrink their largest expenditure—labor—while avoiding the unpleasantness of mass layoffs. By leaving the decision theoretically in the hands of the employee, ERIPs allow the company to fulfill its end of the employer-employee contract and avoid litigation. A golden handshake, management figures, feels better all around than the boot.

This attitude comes through clearly in a 1991 American Management Association (AMA) study of 800 companies, in which most employers said they favored hiring freezes and salary reductions to avoid laying off employees. Yet two in five had offered ERIPs to older workers.[67] In the same vein, firms with a history of full employment favor ERIPs: August 1993 news reports announced that IBM was planning to offer early retirement incentives to 35,000 employees, who would join the 50,000 others who had taken the money and walked just a few months earlier.[68] Taking its cue from business, the federal government will, under Vice President Gore's report on "reinventing government," also look at ERIPs as a way of trimming the bureaucracy and creating a government in which decision making is decentralized and workers empowered.

For a minority of older workers, ERIPs are a tool for empowerment. They give older workers a tidy sum of capital and assured benefits that translate into an effective safety net when they strike out on their own. They may start up their own companies or, as is sometimes the case, return to work for their employers on a part-time basis or as consultants. Worse for the company, those with valuable skills may walk across the street and work for the competition, as was the case when Texas Instruments retired one of its top lawyers, who had brought in more than $1 billion in licensing fees in the preceding five or six years. He moved immediately to a seat on the board of a rival chipmaker.[69]

In the experience of most older workers, however, ERIPs lead to the scaffold, different only in that the steps are now carpeted and strewn with flowers. At 50 or more, Americans can expect to remain unemployed for months and even years; if and when they get a job, they can expect to be underpaid or underemployed. Yet when presented with an ERIP, they feel they have no choice because the unstated—sometimes not so unstated—choice is between accepting early retirement or finding pink slips on their desks a few months down the road. This is what has happened to thousands like Philipe Van Itallie, an IBM manufacturing systems engineer, who at 50 took the company up on its offer to let him retire with a year's salary and lifetime medical benefits, even though he says he would have preferred to keep working.[70] Van Itallie accepted the offer because he felt it might be the best—or only—offer he could ever expect to get. Like many others, he felt the unstated threat of the pink slip. Indeed, employers have at times dangled such fat carrots that the courts now carefully study the "degree of inducement placed upon a candidate for retirement" to determine "when that inducement rises to the level of `involuntary' retirement."[71] In that case, an ERIP may be considered to be illegal discrimination on the basis of age.

This is not to say that the use of ERIPs is never justified. When part of a comprehensive, goal-oriented strategy, they can be a useful tool. ERIPs employed in the service of a reactive, short-term policy aimed primarily at cost-cutting for its own sake can, on the other hand, be harmful to the company and especially its older employees. In such cases, little thought is given to measures that would bring about real long-term efficiency: studying what services or products they may need to cut, forming strategic business units that would improve quality, speed up production, and deliver goods and services more effectively; empowering work teams for a higher-performance work system; or replacing traditional, vertical hierarchies with the flatter, more decentralized organization. In the early 1980s, at the onset of the most recent wave of downsizing, Robert P. Ewing, president of Chicago-based Bankers Life and Casualty Company, warned against this short-term approach. He stated that "experience shows that it is bad business to exclude competent people from the workforce on the basis of age alone. It is the myths about older workers that should be retired, not older workers."[72]

Negative Side Effects

The intervening years have served only to confirm Ewing's statement. A number of companies that laid off older workers or pushed them into early retirement would have, in many instances, been better off retaining them. Downsizing through ERIPs and layoffs of older, more expensive workers without a concomitant restructuring has ended up costing firms both in outlay of money and in competitiveness. They were more likely to hire temporary workers or consultants, to increase overtime, and to lose their most qualified and valued employees.[73] Fewer than half of the 1,005 companies surveyed by *Fortune* met their cost-reduction targets, in spite of much "blood-letting,"[74] and IBM recently took a $2 billion hit against its earnings in unanticipated severance pay. Eastman Kodak had to refill 2,000 jobs of the 8,300 that unexpectedly were vacated after an ERIP offer, and a Philadelphia consulting firm told *Business Week* that two-thirds of the companies offering ERIPs in recent years unintentionally lost "particularly valuable" employees.[75] The moral of the story is that there is no good way to control the number and quality of those who head for the exit.

Figure 12-4 highlights another, more insidious and difficult problem engendered by downsizing: low morale. Even companies with cutting-edge human resource policies reported this negative side effect, though in far lesser measure than companies with traditional approaches to human resource management.

There can be no comparison between the effect on morale of seeing a colleague learn of his layoff from an armed guard carrying packing boxes (an actual occurrence) and hearing a manager explain in detail why cuts must be made and where they will come from.[76] But even in companies where the downsizing is handled honestly and sensitively, there can be ill effects. Workers approaching the early retirement zone feel vulnerable and, depending on the industry, this can affect workers as young as thirtysomething. "If you're over 40," a spokesman for a Wall Street securities firm stated, "you're old. Does it worry me? You bet!"[77] The survivors often resent the heavier work loads and worry about layoffs to come.[78]

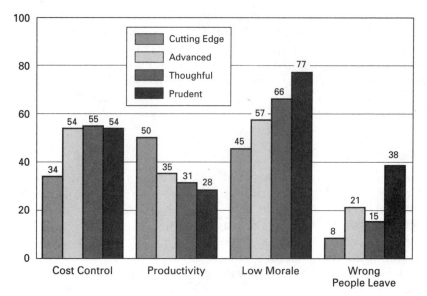

Figure 12-4. Corporate downsizing and human resource philosophy. (*Source: Philip H. Mirns, Editor, Building the Competitive Workforce—Investing in Human Capital for Corporate Success, p. 83*)

Some express worry by becoming distracted on the job, feeling depressed, or registering a sudden and fundamental disconnectedness from their company or employer. In most cases, employees do not feel they can trust the decision makers[79] not to opt for "washing out the gray," and the one thing about which they are all certain is that they will, in time, turn gray. At some point, they will cross the magic dividing line between young and "old," and it is this certainty that prompts a 37-year-old banker to confide, "I'm glad I look young." In industries that prize the enthusiasm, energy, aggression, and optimism that our culture associates with youth, the ripples from mismanaged downsizing spread to every corner of the organization.

Examples are not confined to traditional smokestack industries. A former creative director in advertising at J. Walter Thompson and DMB&B laments the effects of that industry's "insane love affair with youth." By firing all the 50-year-olds, he says advertising agencies are left without the discipline imposed by seasoned professionals and without training programs for the newcomers. What they have instead are enthusiastic youngsters "who make expensive stabs at greatness with no experience of apprenticeship." An editor who was laid off when she crossed into her forties makes a similar point about the risks the publishing industry is taking by remaining "young." She calls it a field that relies on optimism, which translates into shedding employees whose experience tells them that every manuscript that crosses their threshold is not a best-seller. "It's a real question," she says. "At what point do you sacrifice wisdom and perspective for enthusiasm?"[80]

As industries that refuse to grow up pluck out their older employees and companies in other fields latch on to ERIPs as a panacea, the number of disillusioned, unmotivated, and cynical workers increases. The damage is not confined to the suddenly unemployed older Americans who subsequently suffer higher incidents of substance abuse, family conflict, and suicide, along with a decline in health.[81] It also affects the workers of tomorrow. Dorothea Braginsky of Fairfield University, Connecticut, concludes from her own research and that of others that the rash of downsizing has already impacted on the work ethic of the children of terminated workers. "It's not just a tremendous social loss to the man or woman losing his or her job," she says, "but it has a trickle-down effect on their kids. It changes their whole attitude toward work and the company they work for. The message is, `Everything depends on the bottom line.' So there are no values to depend upon."[82]

This means that there is little if any loyalty that the employer can count on, having shifted so much of the current economic uncertainty to his workers. Employees will have little reason to care about the long-term health of the company, since its connection with their own well-being has been effectively severed. Labor surpluses will not last forever, a fact leading an editorial in *The Economist* to predict, "the fiercest competition between firms (in the near future) may not be for customers, but for the hearts and minds of employees."[83]

Employing Older Workers

It stands to reason that those employers who have implemented forward-looking human resource policies will have a head start in the competition for loyal employees. But these firms do not have to wait for future benefits. Companies that retain older workers have already gained materially, as can be seen in Figures 12-5 and 12-6. Though they constitute a minority of the human resource managers AARP surveyed—139 out of 1,000—those with programs to recruit or retain older workers say they have benefited from their skills, flexibility, low absenteeism, motivation, and their ability to mentor younger colleagues.

As noted earlier, there seems to be a consensus on the strengths of older workers; however, they encounter situations daily in which age discrimination rather than performance determines their future. Perception and policy seem to match up all too rarely, a phenomenon

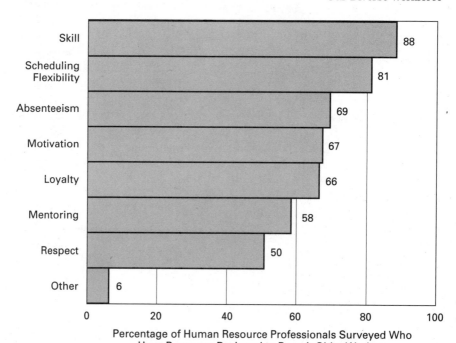

Percentage of Human Resource Professionals Surveyed Who
Have Programs Designed to Recruit Older Workers

Figure 12-5. Benefits of recruiting older workers. (*Source: "The Older Workforce: Recruitment and Retention." AARP Survey*)

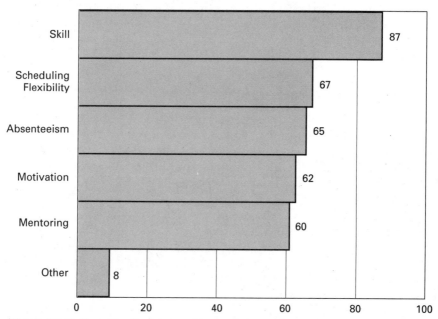

Figure 12-6. Benefits of retaining older workers.

linked in this discussion to the ambivalence engendered by other negative, shared perceptions by managers that make them reluctant to commit to their older workers.

Without management support, corporations will not be inclined to mount programs geared to the needs of older workers, and it is unlikely that such support will be forthcoming if management harbors an unfavorable notion of their ability to contribute. As shown in Figure 12-7, when the Commonwealth Fund compared management's attitudes to its actions, it found a high correlation between management support and the percentage of companies having in-place programs, such as retraining and job redesign, that focus on the needs of older workers.

Nevertheless, managerial ambivalence is highly evident in the across-the-board lag between expressed support and the actual establishment of programs. The study supports the view that, beneath all the talk, most managers believed that "employing older workers was simply too costly."[84] Significantly, this belief has not grown out of experience. In fact, among major organizations, fewer than 11 percent had even tried to evaluate the costs and benefits associated with training older workers.[85] Indeed, few respondents to the *Laborforce 2000* survey spoke about the cost of older workers—only 16 percent cited high training costs as a reason not to retain or hire older workers.

Training

Older Americans routinely run up against barriers erected by management's unjustified assumptions, particularly when it comes to competing

Figure 12-7. Management support vs. programs in place

Policy	Percent of management support*	Percent of in-place programs†
Formal assessment to identify training needs	76	38
Training and development for senior employees	58	29
Job redesign	46	20
Creation of new roles for senior employees (as mentors, consultants, entrepreneurs)	37	13
Organizational incentives for older workers who keep skills current (promotion, incentives, skill-based pay)	36	12

*Percentage of moderate to high management support for policy.
†Percentage of organizations having program in place.
SOURCE: Moloney, Thomas W., and Barbara Paul, *Enabling Older Americans to Work*, 1959 Annual Report of the Commonwealth Fund.

with younger people for training. They work in a culture that prizes those workers who have maintained and improved their skills, yet they are refused the opportunity because management pegs them as an unwise investment of educational funds. In those instances when they are given the option to retrain, older workers may be thrust back into a formal classroom situation, where they often feel uncomfortable and inadequate. Should they fail to learn quickly under these conditions, older workers may correctly feel that they are thereby helping to create a vicious circle; that is, by not excelling, they help perpetuate the myth that gray hairs on one's head mean a lack of gray cells inside, which in turn makes management wary of investing in their training. This further erodes self-confidence and the willingness to accept new challenges. It is easy to see why older Americans find themselves combating the unvoiced assumption on the part of some supervisors that, by virtue of age alone, they are disinterested and would rather just coast until retirement.

To claim that this is never true, that all older workers are eager to improve themselves, would be equally ridiculous. In the absence of any accurate generalizations, then, it is far better to let the individuals involved speak for themselves—and they have. Several surveys reveal that millions of older Americans would welcome training either to improve their employment opportunities or hone their skills.[86,87] Employers who offer training confirm that older workers are indeed interested in learning, leading researchers in the field to conclude that the stereotype about older workers' suitability for training says more about the managers' calculations of immediate return-on-investment than about the workers themselves.[88]

Past failures have reinforced negative stereotypes that undergird employers' reluctance to train older workers. A case in point is the 1973 to 1978 government project to retrain 2,500 air traffic controllers whose average age was 45. The program cost over $100 million and yielded a paltry 7 percent rate of success, as defined by the number of controllers who found employment in second careers. Examples like that seem, at first glance, to confirm the old saw that you can't teach old dogs new tricks, but a closer look reveals that the problem lies more with the nature of the program than with its participants. The air traffic controllers did not respond well, not because they were too old to learn, but because the classes were "geared to youngsters in their twenties, not to 40-year-old males with 20-year career histories."[89] On the other hand, when programs are tailored to the age, knowledge, and experience of older workers, training proves just as effective and no more expensive than for younger workers.

This is not news to companies such as General Electric, whose Aerospace Electronic Systems Department in Utica, New York, set up a program in 1977 to usher design engineers from the world of analog technology into that of digital. Dubbed a "technical renewal program," the training sessions successfully updated the skills and knowledge of older engineers, whose average age was more than 40.[90] The Russell Corporation, a large apparel company with a strong commitment to worker education, finds that small accommodations can produce large results. Russell uses computer-based learning, but finds that older workers can also learn well in classroom situations if adjustments are made. According to Becky Dunn, manager of educational services at Russell's Alex City, Alabama, plant, older workers do well if the classroom instruction is done on-site in familiar surroundings by qualified specialists in adult education.[91]

The more recent and ongoing experience of the Days Inn hotel chain also explodes many a myth about age. Unlike GE, Days Inn was not building on specific skills or knowledge. In a program designed to staff its national reservations system in Atlanta, Georgia, the firm was and is teaching computer-illiterate, older workers how to operate a sophisticated automated system. At first, employees 55 and older required three more weeks of training than their younger colleagues, costing the company a full 50 percent more. Had the firm left it at that, the Days Inn experiment would have served only to fuel prejudices about the capabilities of older workers.

But the firm did not leave it at that. Trainers analyzed the needs and backgrounds of their students and adapted their sessions accordingly. In the end, older workers unfamiliar with computers needed only half a day of familiarization with the technology, after which they learned the company's complex system as easily as trainees of other ages and backgrounds.[92] More relevant to the bottom line, training older employees cost no more than training younger ones. On the contrary, it cost less, for the expense is amortized over a period of employment that is on average three times longer for older workers than for younger ones.[93]

These case studies are not merely happy exceptions. Motorola and 3M, among others, have linked learning to its practical application through the creation of work tasks.[94] Most recently, the Russell Corporation introduced a self-paced curriculum for workers of all ages in their plants. With 11 personal computers housed in a trailer, one teacher assists workers when they come in shifts to study with the software that best suits their needs. "The older workers were fearful at first," Dunn recalls. "But we met with them on shift and explained that this was an opportunity for them to enhance their skills." Dunn also assured them that they would impose no schedule on the workers and that they would not be in direct competition with anyone. Again, a modicum of adjustment and consideration brought these older workers fully on board.

The result is a program that is exceeding even Dunn's high expectations. "We saw an acceptance of computers by the older employees, and that was very enlightening, very encouraging, and I think it meant a lot to the older employees because they were no longer intimidated by the increasing use of computers in the plant."[95]

The success of Russell's program does not surprise Alabama State Commissioner for Education Henry Hector, a long-time champion of the use of computers in adult literacy programs. "Most adult workers do not want to be taught by some young teacher anyway," he says. "Most of them are unhappy with that model of education."[96] This view is supported by experiences suggesting that perhaps the most effective form of learning for older workers takes place in real-time situations involving mentoring and other relationship-based forms of learning. ARCO is among an increasing number of companies that believe that these special efforts can play a critical role in career development. The company has been successful in using personal consultants to give older managers very focused, skill-building coaching in short, two-hour sessions.[97]

If there was a question of just how crucial it is for American business to understand what model or models best work with older Americans, the following statistics put it to rest. More than 50 million workers, according to one estimate, will need to upgrade their skills in order to perform tomorrow's jobs; and 83 percent of companies surveyed for the *Laborforce 2000* study expect to have to expand their training programs in the 1990s.[98] And the competition won't be forgiving. As Hector stresses, "what we have not yet come to terms with is that the only grade that is important to America is `A.' A gentleman's `C' is no longer good enough."[99] When choosing training methods, it is important to remember that a large number of workers in need of skills updating will be 50 and more years old, a category that will grow as the baby boomers enter their golden years. It is equally important to remember that these older workers generally will be the ones best placed to earn the required `A.' In addition to learning the task at hand, upgraded skills will make them even more likely than younger workers to prove flexible, reliable, and able to perform multiple tasks, in part because many will be building on a better educational base.

Hiring

Given all we now know about the potential benefits of hiring older workers, one would think employers would be combing the unemployment lines in search of gray hair. This is obviously not the case. In fact, if there is a single instance in which ageism in all its forms kicks in, it is at the moment the older American knocks on the door asking for a job. If the job requires training, the older applicant rarely makes it to the interview stage, but even in the contest for other jobs, older workers typically suffer longer periods of joblessness than younger workers. Current Population Survey studied the fate of workers dislocated by a plant closing and reported that 25 percent of workers aged 50 to 59 never found another job, and those who succeeded usually had to accept lower wages. If the older workers were forced to change industries, they tended to move into jobs where shorter-duration employment was the norm.[100] By contrast, the unemployment figure for younger workers was about 16 percent and the rest found jobs that paid more.[101] It is no wonder that many older workers give up trying, preferring the hardship of unemployment to the humiliation of constant rejection.

The fate of older workers is all the more tragic because the extra difficulties they face in finding employment rarely arise from an honest reading of their experience, qualifications, and desired compensation. Rather, prospective employers often seem to inject their own beliefs and assumptions about older workers into the application process. An objective evaluation, on the other hand, is not always as simple as it sounds, because to be fair and honest, it must take into account that ineffable quality that can only develop over time: maturity. Daniel Knowles, former director of personnel at Grumman, described the validity of this as early as the late 1970s. "A 40-year-old worker is mature and realistic, and will stick to a task," he told a researcher. "You need three career development analysts to steady a youngster just out of school."[102] He believes that, all things being equal, a firm is better off hiring 45-year-olds over 25-year-olds because the former "have come to terms with life: They know who they are, what they can expect in their career."[103]

Maturity and experience are the tricky unquantifiables that make it nearly impossible to calculate the relative productivity of an older worker simply by measuring raw output over a given time period. Depending on the industry, the incidence of error, quality of end product, or downtime because of accidents or absenteeism may greatly influence the value to the company of a given worker. And these are all areas in which older workers tend to shine. On average, they record lower accident rates, exhibit better judgment, and make fewer errors than younger colleagues.[104]

In most cases, these advantages more than offset the extra time older workers might require to complete a given task. This certainly was the case at the Days Inn reservation center, where workers 55 years and older averaged about 4 percent more time per phone call. As a result, they trailed their younger colleagues in the number of calls processed per day. However, these older workers boasted booking rates that were 5 percent higher, a percentage that translated directly into earnings for the company.[105] In the absence of further study, it is impossible to conclude whether or not the added time older workers spent with customers added value to their work. Did the personal touch, for instance, increase the likelihood of customers using Days Inn again? Did it then generate new business through positive word-of-mouth publicity?*

More readily quantifiable are the assets many older workers bring to a new job in the form of time-tested, experience-honed skills. According to Sally Kera, who coordinates senior job programs for the Jewish Council for the Aging of Greater Washington, this asset is especially valuable in times of economic downturn. "It's to an employer's advantage to hire a person who would not require much training," she says, adding that the employers who participate in job fairs she organizes are generally surprised at the impressive backgrounds and advanced skills of the applicants.[106] This is one of the reasons behind the consistent success employment agencies have had in placing older workers.

James E. Challenger, president of Challenger, Gray & Christmas, Inc., has also analyzed the reason for his success in placing older workers, and concludes that this trend will only strengthen as the workplace increasingly demands unprecedented versatility and quality from its workers. For some industries, that time is already here, and the race is on to find new ways to slash costs and shrink manufacturing cycles. Will Boddie, an engineer at Ford, headed up a 400-member production team that redesigned and "saved" the Mustang, getting it ready for market in 25 percent less time and at 30 percent less cost than for any comparable new car program.[107] At Boeing Co., project manager Grace Robertson defied all norms and practices by organizing 400 employees into cross-functional teams so that specialists in design, planning, manufacturing, and tooling worked for the first time as teammates. The impetus was an "impossible" commitment to

---

*What was recorded was the fact that over time, older workers shortened their phone calls; concomitantly their booking rates fell off. This suggests that speed was mistakenly being equated with productivity, either overtly or unconsciously, in the firm's culture. Perhaps with this in mind, the researchers studying Days Inn postulated that the company could find a way to keep booking rates high among its older workers, and they based the rest of their analysis on this premise.

design and build 30 aircraft nine months faster than the usual cycle time and at a reduced price for an important customer. To date, the team is on schedule and within the budget. Ironically, Boddie and Robertson are 48 and 40, respectively—in other words, too old to be hired by many firms.[108]

Their approach illustrates the kind of reorganization and streamlining with which more and more firms will meet fierce competition and contain costs. In many cases, workers will be required to handle two or more different tasks. This trend plays to the strengths of older workers. "Among the prime candidates for the two-or-more-for-one category are workers aged 50 and up," Challenger contends. "These individuals often have work experience which is likely to include the knowledge of how to perform more than one job. The employer gains the advantage of hiring someone who can provide `value added' performance as well as fitting into the new demand for versatility." He concludes, "Increasing numbers of employers are finding that the experienced worker is a strong resource in the area of quality."[109] This has already begun to occur as companies report growing difficulty in recruiting qualified, skilled workers among the younger generations of graduates. In one survey, three of every four companies said that, as a result, they are starting to think about hiring older workers.[110]

Cost vs. Benefits in Hiring Older Workers

What holds many employers back, however, is cost. Generally managers agree that older workers are more likely than younger ones to bring quality to the job, but they are not sure that they are willing to pay for it in higher wages, pension benefits, and health care costs. There are times, to be sure, that it is not worth buying the experience of an older worker. If a job really requires two years of experience, then it makes little sense to pay for 25.[111] There really can be such a thing as being overqualified. AARP's Sicker would argue, however, that older workers should not be dismissed out of hand as more expensive. This often happens because employers do not believe an older worker when he says that he is willing to take a job at less than his former salary, common as that is. Or they worry about health coverage without checking whether the applicant, a retiree, might not already have insurance.

As for older workers' performance, many corporate managers are taking a closer look and, as positive examples of older new hires make the business news, attitudes may be changing. The first to gain visibility were older workers in some service industries. Reflecting perhaps a mixture of fact and fiction (insofar as positive stereotypes concerning age can be just as fictitious as negative ones), customers tend to react more favorably to a mature salesperson or bank teller. This is especially true of older customers, perhaps because they have fewer occasions to socialize outside the home and therefore value the social contact that can accompany everyday errands. They may appreciate the clerk who takes his time with them or the reservations agent who does not rush them, and they may also trust the gray-haired lady with their bank deposits more readily than they would tellers who look too much like their teenaged grandchildren.

For those who have long since found their place in the workforce, the issue of the relative cost between retaining an old employee or replacing him or her with a young one continues to be tricky at best. As with America's attitudes toward aging, in general, there are conflicting perceptions regarding the relative costs and benefits. The predominant theme in an era of downsizing is that, by virtue of long years of service, older workers are in senior positions or at least command higher wages because of seniority. As the organization of work changes, those in the ranks of middle management are sometimes seen as superfluous, and, in other cases, it is less expensive to retire them than keep them on. One promising approach to the cost-benefit dilemma is the move toward linking pay solely to performance, disregarding seniority. Although to older workers this may violate the longstanding contract that equated seniority with cash, an objective system could work in their favor, underscoring their productivity and value.

Another tactic companies are using attempts to neutralize the age effect in pensions by moving from expensive, defined-benefit plans—the traditional pension plan—to defined-contribution plans that put the burden of retirement planning more squarely on employees. If, however, management does not objectively measure the value of older workers to the company, in the short-term this shift could give them an incentive to move older workers into retirement as quickly as possible to minimize the lifetime pension costs. Like so many policies affecting this group, such an approach would be shortsighted and not necessarily cost effective. Senior management is often too prone to recite, "Costs come on two legs," like a mantra. But it ignores the fact that, beyond the next quarterly earnings statement, value also "comes on two legs." In a machine-led productivity recovery, human capital is too often forgotten. So, older workers would quickly add, are their solid contributions to the bottom line.

It is precisely those contributions that need to be seriously considered when judging the cost of an older worker—or any worker. Perhaps the current indecision on this point will be resolved as more companies take advantage of their experience and education. One bank reported to the Mature Temps agency that the older people it had hired through the agency actually lowered its cost because of their greater productivity.[112] The well-documented study at Days Inn yielded the same conclusion. Based on data collected over a five-year period, researchers built models of two reservation centers, one staffed entirely with younger workers, the other with their seniors. In terms of operating costs, the first center won, hands down. Because of high turnover, younger workers seldom accumulated seniority, so their wages were slightly lower, on average. Since older workers spent longer on the telephone, telecommunications costs were higher and the center had to add staff to guarantee that it could process the same number of calls per day as the younger center. This entailed purchasing additional equipment and expanding the supervisory staff. Despite these added costs, the two centers cost Days Inn essentially the same, because the older workers logged more bookings, and their low turnover allowed the company to spread training costs over a longer period. Significantly, health care costs for the older workers were no higher than those of younger employees.[113]

Although the authors of the study are careful to limit their conclusions to the specific job of reservation agents in the specific market of Atlanta, Georgia, they nevertheless argue that the lessons of Days Inn have a wider applicability. "The reservations agent job has attributes usually considered favorable to younger, not older, workers, and it is fairly typical of many jobs in the growing service sector. Also, we know of no reason why the Atlanta labor market differs greatly from labor markets in other reasonably prosperous metropolitan areas."[114]

Health Care Costs: Misplaced Concern?

In the Days Inn study, health care costs do not vary significantly between younger and older age groups, as might be expected in the case of new hires. Many companies are concerned over this issue, however, and believe that health care costs will affect their ability to compete.[115] In the early 1990s, rising health care costs caused many companies to shift more of the burden of health coverage onto employees, a trend that, in turn, sparked its share of strikes and employee discontent.[116] Even in industries where workers have not called strikes, the issue of health care has become the focus of a heated, often divisive debate in which older workers have unjustifiably taken the fall. A primary concern here is the fact that the discussion has been based primarily on an outdated image of the sickly, frail older person.

Regardless of their individual medical histories, older employees are uniformly presumed to require more visits to the doctor, more medication, and longer hospitalizations than younger employees.

It is true that the risk of cancer, heart disease, and some chronic illnesses increases with age, but this actuarial fact does not necessarily boost the cost of health care to the employer relative to the health costs of younger workers. Indeed, how accurately can actuarial tables for an entire age group reflect the medical conditions of older working Americans, who are a self-selected group of individuals shown to be healthier than their peers? And, again, any analysis of health care costs must be accompanied by a study of what, if any, factors might offset them. Older employees are known to have a lower rate of absenteeism, for example. It would be interesting to know the degree to which this typically compensates for the extra sick leave they might incur relative to younger workers. In the same vein, older employees' health costs may be offset by Medicare benefits. Or they may be among the 72 percent who, in a Commonwealth Fund study, stated that they did not consider employer-provided insurance important.[117] Or some older employees may indeed want medical coverage, but only for themselves, as opposed to younger co-workers, who may need family coverage.

Some of these considerations may well be made obsolete by the new national health care plan that proposes providing more coverage at the expense of employers. As it stands now, the plan would also oblige employers to pay for a portion of health coverage for part-time employees working more than 10 hours per week. Should this survive the legislative process, it would inevitably raise the general costs for employers and possibly have a negative impact on the employment prospects for older Americans, including the increasing number seeking part-time work. Already the debate is raging, and until it is resolved, employers—even large ones with a large number of older employees, such as GM and Ford—cannot reasonably calculate the cost of health care coverage. Meanwhile, those who are concerned about the implications of an older workforce can be informed by the experience of employers who have in the past adopted a more particularized approach to the question. These firms factored in health care as one of many cost variables, zeroed in on the particular needs of individual employees, and made the adjustments necessary to ensure that work conditions allowed those with physical problems or medical conditions to continue to perform effectively.

As a case in point, the Oregon manufacturer of medical instruments, Tektronix, found that it often took little to modify an individual's work requirements or workstations to suit his particular physical needs. A carpenter who had suffered back injury was no longer able to bend, so the company reassigned some of the duties that required physical flexibility and added deliveries to his set of tasks. Similarly, an audit inspector had developed a spur under the collar bone that compressed nerves and blood vessels if she kept her arms elevated for extended periods of time. Since all the commands at her workstation were placed at shoulder level, her operation caused her a great deal of pain and might have triggered long-term damage had the company not taken action. In this case, it entailed simply lowering the controls.[118] It is not always possible to tailor a job to the limitations imposed by arthritis, cardiovascular disease, or other chronic conditions whose likelihood increase with age. But where the employer can accommodate the individual, the worker need not take as much sick leave and can therefore compensate for his or her higher health costs by turning in the quality performance often associated with mature, experienced workers. Where employers refuse to focus on the individual, workers may find themselves incapacitated and ultimately discarded because of conditions that could have easily been corrected. In the end, both employee and employer lose.

Legal Protection and Recourse

Looking at the individual as an individual is precisely what the law requires employers to do. Since the 1935 Wagner Act, the legal system has delineated ever more precise protections for workers against unfair employment practices. In the case of age, legal protections were advocated as early as the 1950s, though it was not until a 1965 report by the Secretary of Labor stated the problem that government took action. Congress directed the Secretary of Labor to submit specific legislative proposals, and upon receipt of the draft bill, President Johnson brought the issue into the limelight with his 1967 Older Americans Message. That same year the Age Discrimination in Employment Act (ADEA) was enacted, offering legal protection against age discrimination to employees 40 to 65 years old working in the private sector.

It has since been expanded, amended, and later complemented by the Older Workers Benefit Protection Act of 1990 to provide the legal framework for class-action and private suits that have benefited thousands of unfairly treated older Americans. More than 20 years later, many of the 1965 findings that gave rise to these laws continue to hold true. Among them is the observation that age discrimination is based on stereotypes unsupported by objective fact and often defended on grounds different from its actual causes. Research has also since bolstered with new empirical data the report's contention that arbitrary age limits are generally unfounded and that, overall, the performance of older workers is at least as good as that of younger workers.[119]

The great difference between then and now is the availability of legal recourse, because the ADEA specifically prohibits the refusal to hire, retrain, or transfer; employee discharge or involuntary retirement; and unfair treatment in other areas of employment on the basis of age. It also bans want ads that indicate a preference for younger workers or a prejudice against older workers. The interdictions, however, are not as straightforward as they may seem, nor, indeed, can they be. As Joseph E. Kalet rightly observes in his study of age discrimination laws, "the grayest, and thereby the most troublesome, area of employment discrimination involves employment decisions based on an individual's age. From hiring to training, to promotion, to involuntary retirement, employers are making decisions that affect individuals' lives based on a characteristic they involuntarily assume: age."[120]

Legal interdictions notwithstanding, reputable publications still occasionally carry a classified ad that indirectly specifies the preferred age of applicants,[121] and older Americans report continued widespread discrimination. Complaints that age caused a worker to be laid off, forced into early retirement, or refused employment pour into the offices of the AARP Worker Equity advocacy at the rate of 50 to 60 per week.[122] Similar complaints of age discrimination flood the Equal Employment Opportunity Commission (EEOC). In 1991, the number totaled 17,449 and, in the year ending June 1992, it jumped to 30,444.[123,124] This, however, does not give the entire picture because cases are routinely settled out of court and the EEOC sees only a fraction of complaints filed around the country.

The numbers speak in other ways as well. Of the more than 30,000 complaints registered with EEOC from 1991 to 1992, less than 12 percent led to further action and only a minute percentage—83 complaints—resulted in lawsuits. This illustrates the difficulties presented by both the sheer volume of age-discrimination cases and their complexity. Was the firing of a 55-year-old engineer rooted in a legally recognized RFOA ("Reasonable Factor Other than Age")? Does the hiring of a 25-year-old over a 40-year-old with similar qualifications reflect the younger applicant's "Bona Fide Occupational Qualification?" When does the cost of an employee constitute a Reasonable Factor Other than Age and when is it a disguise for age discrimination?

In an age of massive downsizing and economic upheavals, the task of sifting discrimination from legitimate economic decisions is a difficult one.* A lawyer in Los Angeles who handles discrimination cases acknowledges this, observing that there "is a concerted effort to get rid of older people. What I don't see," he adds, "is the evidence to prove it."[126] Moreover, each case presents its own set of challenges. In professions that affect public safety, such as airline pilots, the courts have to wade through medical and scientific evidence to determine whether or not a 60-year-old is less "safe" than a 35-year-old. In many cases of early retirement, the plaintiff has previously signed a waiver agreeing to forego any charges as a condition of accepting a lucrative retirement package. Should the employee later file charges, the court's task is complicated by the need to examine the legality of the waiver.

In most cases, the onus on the courts pales by comparison with the stress an age discrimination suit places on the plaintiff. One successful veteran called her legal battle "an intense emotional roller coaster." The stakes are high: If she lost, she'd be marked as a loser; if she won, she'd be branded a troublemaker. Like many such legal battles with deep-pocketed companies, hers dragged on for years and entailed placing her 15-year career on the line.[127] It is no wonder that many older workers think twice before pursuing a grievance. In addition to the time investment and the stress, lawyer's fees can be prohibitive unless the EEOC takes on the case.

Older Workers in the Workplace of the Future

By giving aggrieved workers legal recourse and compensation, age discrimination laws have done more than protect the rights of older workers. Insofar as they sharpen the awareness of employers and force them to look at the facts, the laws promote sound business. Sometimes this objectivity will directly benefit older workers; on other occasions, it will result in their losing jobs. In either case, if the decision is rooted in an objective assessment of the company's needs and the particular strengths and weaknesses of a given employee, then it is likely to be a just one. And there is a better chance that it will be the right one.

"Empowerment"—Just Another Buzzword?

The way the economic trends are shaping up, older workers will most probably experience more suffering before they experience some real gains. The first ripples of the baby boomers are lapping against the

---

*Mr. Kalet himself unwittingly illustrates the all-pervasiveness of age-related stereotypes by asserting in his preface that increased age "invariably brings with it diminished physical and/or mental capacity."[125]

50-year mark, with a greater swell of younger men and women right behind. This affluent, well-educated generation was raised to expect a steady upward mobility. They clamor for room to be made at the top, or at least in the middle as a temporary waystation. Where are the jobs? At the same time, top management will keep up its calls to cut costs, meaning people, so that the company can show restless shareholders that it is profitable and competitive. And the human resource manager's troubled gaze fixes on the graying older employees who occupy the career high ground. He notes that their ranks have swelled in number over the good years. In one likely scenario, the manager instinctively reacts to the pressures upon him by shedding his older employees, and ERIPs climb back up the popularity charts after a dip in the late 1990s.

In many ways, Americans who are 45 years old and more today will bear the brunt of adjusting to the new set of rights and responsibilities that characterizes the emerging workplace. As workers, they came of age at a time when employees could expect to climb steadily and spend the lion's share of their career with one employer or industry. More important, they shared an understanding with their employer over each one's respective rights and obligations.

Perhaps the most difficult aspect of today's economic climate for the older worker to digest is the dissolution of this long-standing employee-employer contract. Having paid their dues in low pay, long hours, and loyalty, 55-year-olds may now step up to claim their just rewards only to find pink slips on their desks one fine Monday morning. They are told that they are not up-to-date in skills and knowledge, that they've not had promotions in years, that they're on a dead-end track, and that they are simply too expensive. But they think of the training opportunities they were never offered and how that kept them on the career track to nowhere, of the performance evaluations that unjustifiably undervalued their performance after midcareer, and of the promotions this cost them. Is it any wonder that bitterness, cynicism, and disillusionment are the hallmark of terminated workers? Is it surprising that their daughters and sons enter the workplace with the wariness of a fox listening for the baying of hounds?

No matter how cleverly one might phrase it, the suddenly jobless older worker may have more than a little trouble embracing the new buzzword, "empowerment," which may just sound like one more fancy term sociologists and economists have devised to mask pain and pass it off as progress.

This is not to say that older workers don't want or aren't capable of becoming empowered. On the contrary, many display the necessary willingness, motivation, and energy necessary to participate in the more challenging and, ultimately, more fulfilling employer-employee contract that is developing. Moreover, opportunities to do so will mushroom in the emergent workplace of tomorrow.

Tomorrow Is No Longer a Day Away

To describe the structure of this new and improved workplace, many economists invoke the analogy of a shamrock with three interconnected but distinct leaves: core companies, contingency workers, and contractors. In this workplace, companies (now reduced to a central core) delegate a number of functions, such as auditing, legal services, or the manufacturing of components, to outside sources. In turn, contractors and companies alike rely on contingent workers to complete specific projects or to meet seasonal demand the way retailers typically boost their salesforces at Christmas time and tax preparers take on additional part- and full-timers between January 1 and April 15.

In such an arrangement, the organization and the nature of work itself is changing. More than ever before, it places the individual worker in control of his or her future. Gerontologist Robert Butler could have been writing about the new American worker when he asserted "that a continuing lifelong concern with one's identity is a sign of good health, and the right to have such a concern is one of the important rights of life. Human beings need the freedom to live with change, to invent and reinvent themselves a number of times throughout their lives. By loosening up life," he concludes, "we enlarge the value of the gift of life."[128] One might add: at all ages.

In today's parlance, this translates into a potent form of empowerment, into taking control and responsibility for one's life, into adapting to and taking advantage of the unprecedented possibility of tailoring work to one's lifestyle and needs.

Employment Options and Older Workers Programs

It would take an incorrigible Pollyanna to believe that all older Americans will be able to avail themselves of the new employment opportunities. For many, opportunities in the new workplace are ripening at a bad time, because the current labor surplus pitches them in head-on competition with younger men and women and members of minority groups to whose plight in the workplace employers have been sensitized. A crucial element in an older worker's competitiveness is his employer's willingness to live up to his end of the new bargain. Having asked employees, and especially older employees, to sacrifice job security, employers must continually update the skills that are their chief marketable asset. The record with regard to older workers does not inspire confidence, but there are developments that suggest that employers may place a higher value on this seasoned group.

Even as the labor surplus takes its job toll, there are signs of a skill shortage. Many employers deplore the low level of skills among young applicants, and many anticipate difficulties in recruiting engineers, scientists, and high-skill blue-collar workers.[129] At the same time, the shift from production-oriented tasks to service-oriented jobs shows no signs of abating. Combined, these two phenomena give older workers a leg up on the competition. In many cases, they already know the industry or company to which they are applying. Older workers more than compensate for the lack of an up-to-date degree with years of accumulated knowledge and experience and, for the service industry, older workers have a better record than other age groups in their ability to communicate effectively with customers.

Finally, the move toward less rigid work formats greatly increases opportunities for older workers, who might want to lighten their load or need to make time to take care of an elderly parent. In this regard, the experience of several forward-looking companies bodes well for the future. These are employers that have incorporated such options as job-sharing, part-time employment, flextime, telecommuting, demotion, sabbaticals, team projects, and other arrangements. Depending on the circumstances, any or all of these can be used as a way of phasing in retirement for the many American workers who do not want suddenly to break with the past and give up their work life.

One employer that has received well-deserved publicity for its innovative policies is Travelers Corporation, a Connecticut-based financial services company. In the early 1970s, the company started to rehire its own retired employees on a part-time basis to staff a new customer-service hotline. The program was an immediate success, satisfying retirees' desires and needs for some form of employment and enabling the company to offer a new service without the disruption of shifting full-time personnel or the cost of training new hires unfamiliar with the company operations.

A few years later, the company took a survey to gauge interest among older employees in an expanded rehire program. A whopping 85 percent of its full-time older employees responded positively, as long as the hours were flexible and the work part-time. It was the turn of management to respond enthusiastically, which it did by establishing the Travelers' Retiree Job Bank. The Job Bank acted as a matchmaker for retirees who registered and Travelers managers who sent in their requirements for part-time help.

The Job Bank concept took off. Requests began to outstrip the number of retirees available as department after department discovered the value of this pool of reliable and flexible workers. As needed, they came in on a temporary basis, pairing up in job-sharing arrangements or taking part in team projects. To keep up with demand, the Job Bank opened its registry in 1985 to retirees from other local insurance companies and, five years later, the company established its own in-house agency, TravTemps, that broadened the pool of available temporary workers to include younger people.[130,131] Georgia-Pacific, a leading producer of paper and wood products, took similar measures with the same success. It founded Georgia Temp, which proved so successful that it became a full-fledged business providing temporary workers to the company and other corporations.[132]

Temporary workers, or "temps," represent one leaf of the corporate organization scheme represented by the shamrock. They are contingency workers called on to work when needed, providing corporations with skills ranging from clerical to engineering to management. Their use is considered by most observers to be part of a permanent change in the workplace. The statistics support this. Such noncore jobs have accounted for some 20 percent of the 18 million created since 1983, and in the past few years, the number of workers—some 1.6 million—working for temporary agencies has risen 240 percent as corporations continue to downsize. Moreover, in a November 1993 *Fortune* magazine poll, 44 percent of the CEOs surveyed say they relied more on contingency workers now than five years ago, and the same percentage expect to employ more contingency workers five years hence. Only 13 percent say they rely less on these workers today.[133]

For older workers who have retired but who want to work, this trend could be a godsend. Their knowledge and experience, especially in jobs requiring specialized skills, should make them effective in team project work and thus highly desirable to corporations seeking the flexibility and lower labor costs that keep them competitive. For those older workers fortunate enough to have a pension or social security income, the lower wages and lack of benefits will pose no great problem. They will be able to remain involved at a lower level of commitment and enjoy the structure and collegiality that so many miss when they retire. For those who rely on the income to meet current needs and are among the estimated 6.4 million part-time workers (of whatever age) who need and want to work full time,[134] the situation can be grim. This is especially true for older workers, who may still be paying off mortgages and college tuitions and who need steady, respectable incomes to build their retirement credit with their companies and social security. As one 58-year-old professional, now on his own after

33 years with IBM, puts it, "My view of myself as economically secure is shattered. And the world is a scarier place."[135] This is the flip side of those enthusiastic stories about corporate refugees who embrace the freedom and fulfillment of entrepreneurship or the professional who abandons her law firm to become a consultant while caring for a new child rather than bear the stigma of the mommy track.

Where will this trend take us? Opinion is divided. Some look at corporate plans to continue downsizing and use more contingency workers and, on this basis, estimate that half of all American workers will be counted in this category by the year 2000. Others are doubtful, noting that U.S. government statistics usually lump together both part-timers and the self-employed—often doctors, lawyers, and other well-heeled professionals—and claim that the size of the contingency workforce has not gone up since 1983, except perhaps anecdotally.[136] It is impossible to create an accurate, linear projection to the end of the decade, but it is nevertheless instructive to note that many companies are finding that hiring contingency workers is not a panacea. On the downside, they cite high competition for skilled people which drives up hiring, problems in integrating contingency workers into core work teams, and the discovery that these workers work best when given training and careful management—which, again, adds to their cost.

High turnover and having to work with a large number of agencies, not altruism, led Georgia-Pacific to create Georgia Temp, but CEO Pete Corell says he will hire only clerical staff as contingency workers. For skilled manufacturing jobs, he says, "we want workers who will buy into our dream, which is to be the highest-quality, most competitive forest products company in the world." In Corell's mind, that is not a description of a contingency worker.[137] Corporations who cannot or will not now take the necessary steps to create a well-motivated, creative, empowered core workforce that includes older workers or whose thinking is short-term and tactical will almost certainly fail to get the hoped-for results from workers whose stake in the company is minimal, whether they are aged 20 or 50.

While contingency workers will continue to have a place in corporate strategies, it behooves companies to take a long, hard look at how they can utilize their more experienced workers effectively. As Travelers and others have discovered, employment can take many guises—369, to be precise, according to a study of variations in flexible working arrangements undertaken by the Institute of Gerontology at the University of Michigan.[138] In the 1970s, Maremont, a manufacturer of automotive components and ordinance parts for machine guns, established an arrangement called "down-placement" that proved a 50/50 success. Others sometimes call it "demotion," or, more sensitively, "shifting to a lower involvement track." Essentially, it means giving older employees the option of stepping down a rung or two on the corporate ladder as an alternative to termination or retirement. The alternative proved successful in only half of the cases, but Maremont discovered in the process how it worked best. Its success was contingent upon three conditions: mutual consent, time for the employee to explore the alternatives, and the possibility of transferring to another unit within the company.[139]

Considering the premium our culture places on promotions, even a 50 percent success rate was promising enough to encourage others to try it. By the time of the *Laborforce 2000* survey, 35 percent of the companies said they gave older workers the opportunity to transfer to jobs with reduced pay and responsibility—a form of phased retirement. Another 27 percent of the companies surveyed offered older workers a variation on this theme: an alternate career path. By the mid-1990s, the proportion of firms offering phased retirement was expected to rise to 41 percent, and to 46 percent for those using alternate career paths.[140]

Lower down on the hit parade are sabbatical leave programs, which had been instituted by 14 percent of U.S. firms in the late 1980s. By the year 2000, an estimated 20 percent of companies will offer Flexplace, whereby a worker need not even come into the office,[141] and phased retirement, an option that companies are expected to make increasingly available.[142] Many companies also offer outplacement help for terminated workers and preretirement counseling, but few, as yet, are responding adequately to the needs of older employees. Again, Travelers leads the way: Aware of the pressure that caregiving for elderly parents places on many older workers, the company has instituted a support group and informational program under the umbrella of the Employee Caregiving Initiative.

The benefits of adopting innovative policies toward older workers go beyond financial gain. "We believe that older workers have a very strong work ethic," a former manager of Travelers' Older Americans Program, Barbara Greenberg, wrote, "and that they serve as positive role models for younger people within the organization. We believe that loyalty to our old workforce contributes to good morale among employees of all ages."[143]

Intergenerational Conflict: The Problem of the Future

The experience at Travelers and other companies with similar human resource management policies will provide a powerful role model if a "workplace war between the generations" erupts. According to the well-respected analyst and author Peter F. Drucker, the great divide in the workplace will no longer be between management and labor, but between the young and old in an "age-heavy" society.[144] To the extent that it is real, his much-touted "intergenerational struggle" seems poised to play itself out on many fronts, and, indeed, there have already been reports of skirmishes.

In the face of a faltering, jobless recovery, sensitivity to who gets how big a slice of the economic pie becomes important. Employers who want to redress the wrongs done to older workers risk a backlash from the young, who, in effect, say, "If you give to older workers, you're giving less to younger workers."[145] This can apply to resources for in-house programs, but where the battle lines are most firmly drawn is over the question of retirement benefits. Many firms are retiring older workers with relatively generous benefits, increasingly leaving younger workers with defined contribution plans that require them to manage their own retirement nest eggs. Done correctly, and given steady financial markets, this can be a plus. The problem is that most people do not understand that this is all they will have from the company and, being inexperienced in the arcane ways of finance, do not invest wisely. The worry is that, if things go wrong, the country will have a generation that cannot afford to retire.[146]

What the younger cohorts do not realize is that many older Americans are already in that boat. A U.S. government–sponsored survey issued in June 1993 showed that 40 percent of people ages 51 to 61 expect to have no retirement income except Social Security. About 20 percent have no real assets.[147] This may go far to explain why so many feel a need to work that goes beyond emotional satisfaction.

That social security looms so large in the well-being of so many is also a bone of contention. The young increasingly fear that that safety net will not be there for them because a growing number of retirees will have absorbed its assets. The complaints of younger workers open a window onto a greater divide that is becoming increasingly apparent in our society. For younger workers, the future is not a foreign country. It is the terrifying dip in a roller-coaster ride they did not map and lack the power to reroute. They accuse the older generation of delegating to their children all the liabilities while they claim all the benefits and rights. They deeply resent having to foot the bill for an enormous deficit and having to support those responsible for it during their unproductive, golden years.[148] The face of the "greedy geezer" looms large in the minds of many, and a frightening image that is when one considers that, if the AARP were a country, it would boast the 30th-largest population in the world, just a shade less populous than Argentina.[149] The Chamber of Commerce estimates that by the year 2020, every retiree will be supported by 1.78 working Americans; in 1935, 40 workers shared the burden of one retiree.[150]

Since nobody can return to the past and rewrite history, part of the solution is to redirect the future by giving the nation of older workers what they happen to want: a fair chance in the fight for jobs. "If [employees'] work life is extended," Greenberg argues, based on her experience at Travelers, "older people will be contributors to pensions and social security systems and not recipients. And we will benefit from their extended, productive employment through increases in the gross national product and tax revenues and in reductions in social welfare outlays."[151]

Retaining or hiring older workers in a variety of capacities will also alleviate the source of another form of intergenerational conflict. The tendency of age groups to clump together as they move up the hierarchy has robbed young and old workers of the chance to understand each other's perspectives and approaches, and to respect and value them. The knee-jerk reaction in many cases is for the young worker to think of his gray-haired partner in the stereotypical terms already discussed in detail. Similarly, the older worker regards his young cohort as making decisions based on books and not life.[152] Pride in one's experience can rapidly become the excuse for deriding the young, whose youth, education, and opportunities the older worker may envy.

This phenomenon takes on a particular twist in the relationship between an older female employee and her younger, also female, boss. There is more to envy on the part of the older woman, for she most likely never had the opportunities later generations are beginning to expect as their due. The flip side of this can be condescension from the younger woman, who in addition to youth (which is intimately connected to beauty in our culture), is likely to have a superior education and is clearly on a faster track than her older subordinate ever was. Not that this relationship is easy between two men when the older man is in a subordinate position relative to the younger one. There is evidence to suggest that many young supervisors of either sex are embarrassed and uncomfortable wielding authority over an older person and that this makes them reluctant to hire older workers. What is called for in these cases is nothing esoteric. As AARP's Martin Sicker puts it, all it takes is "flexibility on the part of managers to recognize that older workers' experience requires that they be motivated in different ways than people without experience."[153]

Age Neutrality—Impartiality

In terms of managing intergenerational conflict, once again the leitmotif is individuation. Companies that have ignored age and taken pains to retain, retrain, or hire workers based on their potential value to the company build workforces in which men and women of different ages have the chance to communicate, collaborate, and forge a better understanding of each other's relative strengths. Advocacy groups such as AARP, the Gray Panthers, employment agencies for the over-40, and other organizations that champion the rights of older workers welcome this. "We are not suggesting that a preference be given to older workers in the competition for jobs," Mr. Sicker asserts. "What we are saying is that age should not be a factor. What we want is age neutrality in the workplace."[154]

The age neutrality that he and others advocate simply means removing a meaningless term from the workplace. It means basing decisions on a study of relevant, meaningful facts: the work experience, skills, and qualifications of individual workers and how they serve the employer's interests. The cost of their wages, health care, and pension benefits needs to be weighed against the quality of work, turnover, reliability, judgment, and other factors influencing total productivity.

This approach requires energy on the part of the hiring manager, just as the new workplace demands more of workers. As empowering as this can be, older workers nevertheless greet the change with some wariness. They fear that they will be denied the chance to work in teams, the chance to update their skills and knowledge to remain marketable, and the opportunity to compete on a level playing field. They also see more hard times ahead as companies such as GM, with many older workers, prepare to lay off another 90,000 in the next few years. This is also reflected in the recent agreement between the United Auto Workers and Ford—which will serve as the industry model—that trades more generous retirement packages for lower wages for new hires.[155] There is no clearer signal that older workers will continue to bear the brunt of corporate America's streamlining. Mixed in with the bitterness, however, is a plea for humaneness. As one veteran of the pink slip says, "If you eliminate a division, ease people out; give them a feeling of goodwill. Let them use an office. Whatever it takes to have a goodwill effect. I hope corporations begin paying attention to this." In her view, echoed by many others, there is more at stake here than the bruised feelings of scattered individuals. "For too long, the blame has been on the employee. But now people are beginning to ask, `What has happened to us as a country?'"[156]

Some contend that demographics, the aging of the American workforce, will force corporations to pay attention. Yet it would be a pity for corporate America to keep putting off until tomorrow what it can best and most effectively accomplish today. Now is the time to study the opportunities and demands the emerging workplace will bring; now is the time to earn the loyalty of tomorrow's workforce by implementing age-neutral policies following a careful study of one's workforce and its needs. Nobody can deny that the new workplace is already taking shape. Part-time, temporary, and contract-leased employees make up 25 percent of the labor force; the number of core jobs has shrunk,[157] and the project-oriented team approach is catching on rapidly. At the same time, we now know more than ever before how different individuals learn and how to train workers of different ages and backgrounds effectively and economically.

Current trends can bode well in the long run for older workers and employers alike. The new workplace is spawning countless employment options at a time when older Americans are healthier, more active, and—equally important—undergoing a fundamental shift in attitude. Less and less do they see their working life exclusively in terms of a one-track career with a leisured retirement at the end of it. Rather, today's older workers increasingly welcome the flexibility of phased-in retirement programs or the chance to structure their golden years around part-time or consultant work that allows them time to pursue other interests or take on caregiving or volunteer roles. For many, participating in a team assembled for a specific project satisfies their desire to work and contribute their knowledge and expertise to younger generations.

There also remains a large number of not-so-old older workers who need and want full-time jobs—notably those caught in the "sandwich generation" or those whose assets are insufficient for a long retirement. These workers will probably face more difficulties, but the difficulties may dissipate in time as economic pressures on companies diminish and they realize the pitfalls of early retirement as a cost-cutting device. In some positive scenarios, technology-driven growth will create literally millions of new and better jobs over the next decade.[158] The restructuring of the pension system will also help level the playing field between younger and older applicants. All in all, the new system is bringing the absolute cost of hiring a 45-year-old more in line with that of hiring of younger applicant, particularly when one factors in the reality that Americans' working life today extends beyond age 60.

For employers, these changes vastly enlarge the labor pool, injecting it with a large selection of skilled, experienced, and flexible workers. For older workers, it unfolds new avenues for a productive, constructive, and healthier second—or third, or fourth—career. And for both the call is urgent: Carpe diem!

References

1. Interview with Martin Sicker, Head of the Work Force Programs Department, American Association of Retired Persons (AARP), by William U. Lawrence, Washington, D.C., July 29, 1993.

2. Helen Axel, "Employing Older Americans: Opportunities and Constraints," Summary of a symposium held September 21–23, 1987, Wingspread Conference Center, Racine, Wisconsin, published by The Conference Board, 1988, p. 64.

3. Melinda Beck, Lydia Denworth, and Nicole Christians, "Finding Work After 50," *Newsweek*, March 16, 1992.

4. Robert N. Butler, *Why Survive? Being Old in America* (New York: Harper & Row, 1975), p. 12.

5. *Ibid.*, p. xi.

6. Max Lerner, *America As a Civilization* (New York: Henry Holt & Co., 1987), p. 547.

7. Ken Dychtwald and Joe Flower, *Age Wave* (New York: Bantam Books, 1990), p. 6.

8. Elizabeth S. Johnson and John B. Williamson, *Growing Old: The Social Problems of Aging* (New York: Holt, Rinehart and Winston, 1980).

9. Butler, *op. cit.*, p. 404.

10. *Ibid.*, p. 1.

11. Lerner, *op. cit.*, p. 548.

12. *Ibid.*, pp. 547–548.

13. U.S. Bureau of the Census, "Persons Below Poverty Level by Age, Region, Race, and Hispanic Origin, 1990," reprinted in 1993 *Information Please Almanac*, 46th ed. (Boston: Houghton and Mifflin, 1993), p. 830.

14. Butler, *op. cit.*, p. 5.

15. *Ibid.*, pp. 10–11.

16. Daniel Yankelovich Group, "Pioneers on the Frontier of Life: Aging in America," study for the Markle Foundation (New York: Markle Foundation, 1985).

17. Barbara Lawrence, "New Wrinkles in the Theory of Age: Demography, Norms, and Performance Ratings," *Academy of Management Journal*, 31, no. 2, p. 310.

18. Butler, *op. cit.*, p. 14.

19. Jean Dietz, "Fighting Age Bias on the Job," *The Boston Globe*, January 20, 1991, A25.

20. Marilyn Webb, "How Old Is Too Old?" *New York Magazine*, March 29, 1993, pp. 66–73.

21. Butler, *op. cit.*, p. 404.

22. Johnson and Williamson, *op. cit.*, p. 76.

23. *Ibid.*, p. 78.

24. Douglas T. Hall and Philip H. Mirvis, "The New Workplace and Older Workers," paper prepared for the Joint Project on U.S. Competitiveness and the Aging American Workforce of the National Planning Association/National Council on the Aging, p. 35.

25. Webb, *op. cit.*

26. *Ibid.*

27. Robert Reich, "Introduction for Symposium on U.S. Competitiveness and the Aging American Workforce," National Planning Association/National Council on the Aging, presented June 16, 1993, unpublished proceedings, p. 5.

28. Johnson and Williamson, *op. cit.*, p. 8.

29. Axel, *op. cit.*, p. 16.

30. "Musical Chairs," *The Economist,* July 17, 1993, p. 67.

31. Philip H. Mirvis, ed., *Building the Competitive Workforce—Investing in Human Capital for Corporate Success* (New York: John Wiley & Sons, Inc., 1993), p. 166.

32. David Nye, "Writing Off Older Assets," *Across the Board,* September 1988, p. 46.

33. Johnson and Williamson, *op. cit.*, pp. 68–69.

34. Chris Reidy, "'Geezer' Stereotype Begins to Fade as America Ages," *Sun-Journal* (Lewiston, Maine), May 27, 1993.

35. Cynthia M. Taeuber, *Sixty-Five Plus in America,* U.S. Department of Commerce, Economics and Statistics Administration, Bureau of the Census (Washington, D.C.: U.S. GPO, 1992).

36. Butler, *op. cit.*, p. 7.

37. Dychtwald and Flower, *op. cit.*, p. 42.

38. Mirvis, *op. cit.*, p. 180.

39. Butler, *op. cit.*, p. 370.

40. Michael J. Driver, "Workforce Personality and the New Information Age Workplace," paper prepared for the Joint Project on U.S. Competitiveness and the Aging American Workforce of the National Planning Association/National Council on the Aging, *op. cit.*, p. 16.

41. According to Timothy Salhouse, editor of *Psychology and Aging,* as quoted in Webb, *op. cit.*

42. Driver, *op. cit.*, p. 16.

43. Dychtwald and Flower, *op. cit.*, p. 47.

44. *Ibid.*, p. 29.

45. Sandy Pasqua, "Older Workers Most Vulnerable As Recession's Ripples

Broaden," *Morning Call* (Allentown, Pa.), May 31, 1993, p. B7.

46. Thomas W. Moloney and Barbara Paul, "Enabling Older Americans to Work," reprint from the 1989 *Annual Report* of the Commonwealth Fund (New York), p. 8.

47. Axel, *op. cit.*, p. 17.

48. Beverly Jacobson, *Young Programs for Older Workers* (New York: Van Nostrand Reinhold, 1980), pp. 94–96.

49. The American Association of Retired Persons and the Society for Human Resource Management, "The Older Workforce: Recruitment and Retention," Washington, D.C., 1993.

50. Mirvis, *op. cit.*, pp. 162–163.

51. Martin Sicker of AARP as quoted by Peter Vilbig, "Recession Hit Older Workers Hardest," *Sunday Journal*, May 18, 1993, p. 51.

52. Gene Knetz, "Economic Trends," *Business Week*, May 10, 1993, p. 16.

53. Steven Pearlstein, "Kodak Will Cut 10,000 Positions," *The Washington Post*, August 19, 1993, p. D9.

54. Department of Labor, as reported in *News and Observer*, January 21, 1993.

55. Barbara Keenan, "He's Over Fifty and Out of a Job," *Foster's Daily Democrat* (Dover, N.H.), March 30, 1993, p. 7.

56. The National Black Caucus and Center on Black Aged, Inc., "A Profile of Elderly Black Americans," June 1992, pp. 5, 7.

57. Mirvis, *op. cit.*, p. 176.

58. Jacobson, *op. cit.*, p. 95.

59. Webb, *op. cit.*

60. *Ibid.*

61. Lawrence, *op. cit.*, p. 333.

62. *Ibid.*, pp. 309–310, 331.

63. Mirvis, *op. cit.*, p. 175.

64. *Ibid.*, p. 161.

65. *Ibid.*, p. 173.

66. *Ibid.*, p. 179.

67. Michael Useem, "The Restructuring of American Business and the Aging Workforce," paper prepared for the Joint Project on U.S. Competitiveness and the Aging American Workforce of the National Planning Association/National Council on the Aging, *op. cit.*, p. 9.

68. Eric Schine, "Take the Money and Run—Or Take Your Chances," *Business Week*, August 23, 1993, p. 28.

69. *Ibid.*

70. *Ibid.*

71. Joseph E. Kalet, *Age Discrimination in Employment Law* (Washington, D.C.:

Bureau of National Affairs, Inc., 1990), p. 99.

72. Jacobson, *op. cit.*, p. 81.

73. Mirvis, *op. cit.*, p. 77.

74. *Ibid.*, p. 62.

75. Schine, *op. cit.*, p. 28.

76. Mirvis, *op. cit.*, p. 89.

77. Webb, *op. cit.*

78. Schine, *op. cit.*

79. Mirvis, *op. cit.*, pp. 89–90.

80. Webb, *op. cit.*, p. 68.

81. Mirvis, *op. cit.*, pp. 78–79.

82. Webb, *op. cit.*, p. 68.

83. "For Now," *The Economist,* July 17, 1993, p. 13.

84. Moloney and Paul, *op. cit.*, p. 9.

85. *Ibid.*

86. Anthony P. Carnevale, "Developing the New Competitive Workforce," paper prepared for the Joint Project on U.S. Competitiveness and the Aging American Workforce of the National Planning Association/ National Council on the Aging, *op. cit.*, p. 16.

87. Hall and Mirvis, *op. cit.*, p. 38.

88. Mirvis, *op. cit.*, p. 165.

89. Jacobson, *op. cit.*, pp. 20–23.

90. *Ibid.*, p. 103.

91. Telephone interview with Becky Dunn by William U. Lawrence, September 13, 1993.

92. Mirvis, *op. cit.*, p. 193.

93. William McNaught and Michael C. Barth, "Are Older Workers `Good Buys?'—A case study of Days Inn of America," *Sloan Management Review,* Spring 1992, vol. 33, no. 3, pp. 56–57.

94. Hall and Mirvis, *op. cit.*, p. 23.

95. Interview with Becky Dunn, *op. cit.*

96. Interview with Henry Hector III, Commissioner for Education for the State of Alabama, by William U. Lawrence, August 9, 1993.

97. Hall and Mirvis, *op. cit.*, p. 26.

98. Mirvis, *op. cit.*, pp. 102, 238.

99. Interview with Henry Hector III, *op. cit.*

100. *Ibid.*, p. 9.

101. Olivia S. Mitchell, ed., *As the Workforce Ages* (Ithaca, N.Y.: ILR Press, 1993), p. 9.

102. Jacobson, *op. cit.*, pp. 73–74.
103. Axel, *op. cit.*, p. 17.
104. Dychtwald and Flower, *op. cit.*, p. 42.
105. McNaught and Barth, *op. cit.*, p. 57.
106. Sue Anne Presley, "Re-Entering the World of Work: Maturity and Experience of Retirees Catch the Eye of Some Employers," *The Washington Post*, April 24, 1991.
107. Joseph B. White and Oscar Suris, "How a `Skunk Works' Kept Mustang Alive—On a Tight Budget," *The Wall Street Journal*, September 21, 1993, pp A-1, A12.
108. Dori Jones Yang, "Grace Robertson: Piloting a Superfast Rollout at Boeing," *Business Week*, August 30, 1993, p. 77.
109. James E. Challenger, "Two Or More for One," *Industry Week*, July 5, 1993, p. 25.
110. Mirvis, *op. cit.*, p. 231.
111. Interview with Martin Sicker by William U. Lawrence, *op. cit.*
112. Jacobson, *op. cit.*, p. 52.
113. McNaught and Barth, *op. cit.*, pp. 59–62.
114. *Ibid.*, p. 60.
115. Mirvis, *op. cit.*, p. 231.
116. *Ibid.*, p. 207.
117. "Demographics, Economy, Underscore Need for Older Workers, Officials Say," *Daily Labor Report*, March 12, 1990, p. A5.
118. Jacobson, *op. cit.*, pp. 27–28.
119. Kalet, *op. cit.*, p. 2.
120. *Ibid.*, p. 1.
121. Webb, *op. cit.*
122. Pasqua, *op. cit.*
123. Keenan, *op. cit.*
124. Linda Grant, "Fired at Fifty: Older Workers Feeling the Sting of Recession," *Los Angeles Times*, September 20, 1992.
125. Kalet, *op. cit.*, p. 1.
126. Joseph Posner as quoted by Linda Grant, "Fired at 50," *News and Observer*, January 21, 1993, p. 66.
127. Webb, *op. cit.*
128. Butler, *op. cit.*, p. 401.
129. Mirvis, *op. cit.*, p. 226.
130. *Ibid.*, pp. 196–197.

131. Axel, *op. cit.*, pp. 24–26.

132. Jaclyn Fierman, "The Contingency Work Force," *Fortune,* January 24, 1994, p. 36.

133. *Ibid.*, p. 32.

134. *Ibid.*

135. Anne Murphy, "Do-It-Yourself Job Creation," *Inc.*, January 1994, p. 40.

136. Fierman, *op. cit.*, p. 31.

137. *Ibid.*, p. 36.

138. Dychtwald and Flower, *op. cit.*, p. 184.

139. Jacobson, *op. cit.*, pp. xiii, 60.

140. Mirvis, *op. cit.*, p. 186.

141. Dychtwald and Flower, *op. cit.*, p. 198.

142. Mirvis, *op. cit.*, p. 185.

143. *Ibid.*, p. 23.

144. Rhoda Amon, "Learning New Tricks To Deal With Young Top Dogs," *Newsday,* February 8, 1992.

145. Lisa Sprague of the U.S. Chamber of Commerce, as quoted in Andrew Leigh, "Cutting Older Workers Can Be Dangerous for Firms," *Investor's Business Daily*, April 15, 1992, p. 3.

146. Leslie Eaton, "Cloudy Sunset," *Barron's*, July 12, 1993, p. 9.

147. *Ibid.*, p. 8.

148. Paul Magnusson, "Young America's Rallying Cry: `Dis the Deficit,'" *Business Week,* August 9, 1993, p. 37.

149. Dychtwald and Flowers, *op. cit.*, p. 57.

150. *Ibid.*, p. 68.

151. Axel, *op. cit.*, p. 24.

152. Amon, *op. cit.*, p. 21.

153. Interview with Martin Sicker by William U. Lawrence, *op. cit.*

154. *Ibid.*

155. Neal Tomplin and Robert L. Simison, "GM, Selected as 2nd Target by Union in Canada, Faces More Contract Woes," *The Wall Street Journal,* September 21, 1993, p. A4.

156. Webb, *op. cit.*

157. Barbara McIntosh, "Emerging Labor Markets and Productive Activity: Race and Gender as Critical Contexts," paper prepared for the Joint Project on U.S. Competitiveness and the Aging American Workforce of the National Planning Association/National Council on the Aging, p. 4.

158. Michael J. Mandel and Christopher Farrell, "Jobs, Jobs, Jobs—Eventually," *Business Week,* May 10, 1993, p. 16.

13

To the Future:

An American Advantage in the International Context

Americans, not new to the role of pioneering, are blazing trails in a new way. In this book we have maintained that the growing diversity of our workforce can provide American organizations and the economy as a whole with a competitive advantage. We also stressed that this can happen only when organizations are responsive to the many challenges of heterogeneity. Interestingly, the process of exploring constructive ways to meet diversity's challenges itself may become an advantage. This process, and its successes and failures, may offer a model for nations as they, too, more frequently cope with workforce diversity issues.

It is risky to suggest that the behavior of one group or nation can provide a model for others. It implies superiority, that the first group is doing something right and the others, something wrong. It also implies that the circumstances of the first are directly applicable in other contexts and to other cultures. Obviously, such assumptions are not valid with regard to workforce diversity. In each nation, unique historical, cultural, and economic factors shape workforce issues. Each must respond to these issues according to its needs and circumstances. Efforts to copy American approaches to diversity are likely to create problems rather than offer means of addressing issues effectively.

At the same time, however, workforce diversity is a growing international issue and it needs to be recognized. Heretofore relatively homogeneous workforces are changing, and as they do, organizational leaders need to find new ways to relate to their workers in order to maximize productivity and reduce the tensions associated with difference in the workplace. Because these are issues that many American organizations are actively confronting, their experiences may offer useful insights to others, who may want to assess them in terms of applicability to their own circumstances.

In many nations, especially in industrialized economies, workforces are quickly becoming more diverse. New workers—women, workers from other cultures, and others—are participating in growing numbers. They often encounter problems similar to those being addressed in the United States: Gender, culture, and other differences often are not highly valued. In older societies where class lines are sharp, old boy networks may be even more dominant and exclusionary than in the United States. In many countries, the new workforce is disadvantaged by access discrimination, job segregation, pay inequity, and limited advancement opportunities. Little attention is given to the special needs of workers with disabilities. Age discrimination is prevalent in employment decisions in many nations, and workers are typically expected to conform to the prevailing organizational culture.

Changes in the composition of the international labor force are being driven by the rise in the numbers of women who work outside the home. Older workers, too, are becoming a larger segment of the labor force as a result of the increase in the average life span due to medical advances. This is especially true in Western Europe and Japan, which are experiencing their own versions of a graying workforce.

Heterogeneity in the global workforce is also being driven by the mismatch between the abundant supply of human resources in third-world nations and the demand for them in the cities in the industrialized world. Discussing the new world labor market, Husdon Institute research fellow William B. Johnston foresees that "during the 1990s, the world's work force will become even more mobile, and employers will increasingly reach across borders to find the skills they need."[1] This dynamic will, among other things, stimulate massive relocation of people to the industrialized cities of the world, says Johnston.

Further adding to workforce diversity in many nations is the massive migration of populations, especially in recent years. According the United Nations High Commissioner for Refugees, war and other upheavals have forced one of every 125 persons in the world from his or her normal life. Almost 20 million are living as refugees outside their home countries, about 14 times the number in 1960.[2] This figure does not include the many millions who have migrated by choice, drawn by better economic opportunities offered elsewhere. As these people settle in new countries, a portion of their population is entering the workforce, creating a growing multicultural contingent of workers.

Samuel Huntington of Harvard University maintains that a defining feature of global politics of the near future will be conflicts between cultures occurring along civilization "fault lines."[3] In fact for many nations, the clash of civilizations is much closer to home: It is occurring within their own borders. In many countries, the influx of immigrants and refugees is generating, with depressing frequency, internal conflicts over culture—rising xenophobia, racist incidents, violence, and political instability.

The wealthy nations of Western Europe are feeling especially vulnerable. Generalizing about nations as diverse as those in the European Union (EU) is difficult, but it is clear that, since the collapse of communism in 1989, the bulk of refugees from former Soviet-bloc countries have headed their way. In 1993, about 1 million refugees fled to Western Europe.[4] This is a sharp rise since the mid-1980s, when less than 100,000 persons a year sought asylum in Western Europe.[5]

But even before the present influx of refugees, Western Europe struggled to cope with the legacy of empire. Since colonialism's demise after World War II, many people from Africa and Asia have settled in the homelands of their former colonial masters. Some, invited as temporary labor (guest workers and émigrés) during a period of labor shortage in the 1950s and 1960s, stayed on despite financial incentives offered by their host nations to return home. Many more came later. Moslems from North Africa form an especially large portion of the third-world population in Europe. With large communities in many West European countries, some Europeans fear they form a nation within a nation, a "13th nation" in the then 12-member European Union (EU), as French historian Jean Marie Domenach characterizes them.[6]

Part of Europeans' discomfort with their third-world residents flows from a fear of being swamped by people who are racially and culturally different. While third-world immigrants form only a very small portion of the population in Western Europe, their birth rate is significantly higher than that of native Europeans, among whom a declining birth rate prevails. Immigrants are often seen as a threat at the low end of the labor market. They are also resented for the benefits they receive when unemployed, as many are now when much of Western Europe is experiencing record levels of unemployment. This potent mix of factors has produced a range of reactions: Across Europe, nations have responded by restricting immigration. In some, xenophobia and racist incidents are increasing.

While some third-world residents in Western Europe are among the world's superrich—or merely rich—and influential, most are part of the underclass. They do the dirty work that many Europeans prefer not to do, such as garbage collecting and street cleaning. In these countries, immigrants have organized into associations, some of them government-supported, to help them improve their employment opportunities, fight racism, and attain other rights.[7] For many, however, advancement in the workplace is not even a pipe dream. Among third-world residents in Europe, there is also a rising middle class. Some work at lower-level jobs in large European firms. Others, recognizing that they have little chance of advancement in most large organizations, have struck out on their own as independent entrepreneurs. Many send their children to European colleges and universities where they gain qualifications for professional occupations. In short, whether or not Europeans ease their increasingly restrictive immigration policies, multiculturalism has already crossed the threshold of Europe's workplaces.

Western Europe's vision is to create "industrial dynamism through large-scale investments in technology and human resource in all the member states," as British-based author Amin Rajan observed.[8] Toward this admirable goal, Europeans already have exerted much effort. They have yielded elements of the national sovereignty that nations usually closely guard. And additional measures are on the agenda. Driven by the need to remain competitive in the global economy, they are unlikely in the long term to let their experiment falter on an unwillingness to use their human capital fully. And as they invest more in their human potential, a growing number of organizational leaders are bound to recognize that a corollary of their effort is the valuing of differences in the workplace.

Some Europeans are already concerned, though their concern does not necessarily stem from the business rationale for valuing diversity. The Netherlands, where there are sizable populations of residents from Indonesia, North Africa, Turkey, Surinam, and the Antilles, seems to be a leader in this respect. The Dutch constitution, which asserts that everyone in the country will be treated equally under the same circumstances, provides a legal foundation for valuing differences in the workplace. On the more practical level, the community of Amsterdam makes diversity part of its hiring practices, based on the premise that its employees should reflect the demographic composition of the area. Police organizations in Holland receive schooling to help them understand their colleagues from varying racial and ethnic backgrounds as well as to enable them to deal with the public more effectively. Several private companies focus on management training issues with regard to visible minorities. Synact is one of them. In its management training and coaching functions, Synact stresses the importance of diversity, emphasizing that management teams need to consist of members with diverse talents and outlooks. Further, although women are a relatively smaller component of the workforce in the Netherlands than in other European countries, a significant number hold senior management positions.

For the most part, however, Europeans do not view diversity as a resource in the workplace. In comparison with the United States, there appear to be relatively few diversity efforts initiated by business organizations. Activities such as diversity statements by top management, networking groups and diversity councils, mentoring and other programs aimed at developing minority employees are not common. Moreover, diversity is not defined as an umbrella movement that encompasses a broad range of identity groups, as it is in the United States. Though such a definition is not necessary in order for nontraditional workers to be valued, it provides a conceptual framework and gives impetus to these issues. Nor is the European workplace commonly understood as the forum in which issues concerning racial and ethnic diversity should be treated. In Europe, immigrants are usually viewed as a political matter rather than a business issue. They widely receive language and job training and other support through government programs, but business-sponsored training programs aimed at developing immigrant workers and other activities focusing on hiring and providing special support on the job are unusual.

It is not likely that a broad-based diversity movement will develop in Europe in the near term. At present, coping with recession and severe unemployment are top workplace priorities. Organizations are struggling to survive and adapt to technological changes, while workers are scrambling just to hold on to their jobs. Adopting European equivalents of workforce diversity strategies is not on the agenda of most organizational leaders. Once economic conditions improve, evolution in this direction seems natural. Based on several factors, only a small shift in outlook is necessary to produce a mindset that values diversity in the workplace.

First, Europeans already are practiced at valuing differences *across* workforces. In countries where national borders are often just a few hours away by car, cross-cultural communication is a way of life. As a result, organizational leaders have long had to understand and skillfully deal with the differing ways cultural priorities influence communication, and the need is increasing as European countries forge closer links with one another. (In this context, an organization such as the Society for Intercultural Education, Training and Research [SIETAR] in Europe, which provides cross-cultural training, seems to have a bright future.) Only a small shift in orientation is needed to recognize the value of applying such strategies *within* workforces that are culturally and ethnically diverse.

In fact, diversity is beginning to be viewed as a resource rather than a liability in other areas of life. Member nations of the Organization for

Economic Co-Operation and Development (OECD)—which include leading European nations, among others—are now trying new means to cultivate the skills of school children from cultural and linguistic minorities. Rather than routinely assigning them to special (lower) educational tracks and prohibiting them from using their native language in the class room (which was the former practice), they are emphasizing ethnicity, valuing cultural differences, and trying to provide skills to enable the children to be productive adults in a multicultural environment.[9] Can transference of this principle to the workplace be far behind?

Beyond the issue of diversity in racial and ethnic groups, examples can be found of sensitivity to other workforce differences. In some European countries, there is a legal mandate to employ workers with disabilities. Such laws are in place in the Netherlands and Germany, for example, though compliance is not enforced and many companies do not make the effort.[10]

Further impetus for valuing diversity on the job may flow from Europe's current economic downswing. West European economies are under massive pressure as employment drops, and workers are being laid off, put on flexible work schedules, and having their fringe benefits cut. In many organizations, restructuring appears inevitable. After the dust has settled, workers who remain—presumably the best workers—will likely shoulder greater responsibilities and have greater powers to carry them out. Bellwether firms such as Germany's Babcock-Borsig, a turbine and compressor manufacturer, already has undertaken restructuring, and in 1993, made its first profit in years. Hans Westphal, the firm's chairman, states, "In this country we have highly trained, highly educated people. And yet we still treat them like highly specialized idiots." At his company, Westphal asserts, "We're trying here to encourage initiative and creativity....We have to understand that everybody here has at least a couple of good ideas."[11] Where employee empowerment is an option, valuing diversity is likely to be close behind.

Another set of factors involves aging and the declining birth rate. The lengthening of the average life span has created a graying population: About 20 percent of the EU's population is over 60, and the share will increase in the future. Declining European birth rates mean there is an insufficient tax base to support the elderly. In some cases, such as Italy where population growth is zero, workforces are beginning to shrink. Europeans need a new source of younger workers to pay the pensions of the elderly, and immigration may provide an answer. Some nations are already beginning to rethink their immigration policies. For example, France recently revised its goal of zero immigration to admit 100,000 refugees annually.[12]

Finally, the economic rationale that diversity makes good business sense is being carried into Europe and other countries by American firms. For example, in Japan, with its strongly male-dominated culture, Citibank N.A., Japan, recruits and develops women for professional positions. Management and technology consulting firm Booz, Allen & Hamilton Inc. often meets with local skepticism and sometimes with legal barriers as it works to implement employee-oriented, flexible work policies in its offices in Latin America, Europe, Japan, and elsewhere. As understanding grows about how such practices enable American competitors in their countries to recruit and retain high-quality employees, non-American organizations will have incentive to follow suit.

In Japan too, some attention to workforce diversity may be in the offing—eventually. Ever since the bubble of steady economic growth burst in 1990, many Japanese organizations have been undergoing profound change. Like their counterparts in Europe and the United States, businesses in Japan are restructuring and laying off workers in the process. The cherished Japanese practice of providing "womb to tomb" security, which employees in large organizations counted on for themselves and their families, is fast fading. Once the economic overhaul is complete, will business as usual—which is to say, Japanese competitive brilliance—continue to prevail? There is no reason to think that Japanese organizations will abandon that goal. In the past, Japanese organizations were able to pursue the goal by focusing on homogeneity. But the Japanese workforce is slowly changing and so, too, are expectations. In their quest for excellence, leaders may need to begin to reckon with the competitive advantage conferred by valuing and managing diversity in the workplace.

Japan has a large Korean population and, during the labor shortages of the 1980s, workers from other countries—especially from the Middle East and other Asian nations—were encouraged to emigrate. Workforce diversity in Japan has other dimensions too: About half of the Japanese labor force are women, though a sizable percentage are part-time workers. Older workers, too, form a growing segment of the workforce.

If any diversity efforts are eventually adopted, they will undoubtedly take a very Japanese form. Such efforts would encounter formidable opposition. The tremendous force of conformity in that society undercuts any efforts to honor the varying needs of specific groups. Rooted in a strong cultural value on collectivism, group members (women, older workers, etc.) typically are unskilled in identifying, much less demanding, responsiveness to their own needs. From the context of the traditional Confucian value of harmony, diversity efforts would rupture the prescribed, hierarchical functioning of human relations. Thus, not only organizational leaders but also employees would likely resist diversity efforts.

Still, changes are occurring in tradition-bound Japanese society: A quiet women's movement is gaining momentum. A benchmark in its evolution occurred in 1993 when, for the first time, a case involving sexual harassment at work was decided in favor of the female plaintiff. The business argument for valuing diversity and the fact that U.S. competitors have such policies may also be influential. Thus, while Japanese leaders are unlikely to adopt Japanese equivalents of workforce diversity efforts in the short run, they may be more receptive over time.

Despite imperfect progress, America's efforts to value and manage diversity in the workplace are showing that difference can be a strength, not a weakness. The American experience is illustrating that, when the civilization fault lines exist internally, they can point the way to a truer humanity. An epigram runs: I saw in the distance what I took to be a beast, but when I came close, I saw it was my brother and my sister.[13] But people need to be willing to come close and open their eyes. It is a hard journey, but Americans increasingly are doing this in the workplace, and these efforts confer an advantage on the United States. The advantage may not last long, however. Other nations are bound to adapt such efforts to their own environments. Like America, they are likely to do so not mainly because they aspire to moral heights but because they need to remain competitive in the global economy.

References

1. William B. Johnston, "Global Work Force 2000: The New World Labor Market," *Harvard Business Review,* vol. 69, no. 2, March-April 1991, p. 115.

2. Cited by James Rupert, "World Welcome Strained by 20 Million Refugees," *The Washington Post,* November 10, 1993, p. A32.

3. Samuel P. Huntington, "The Clash of Civilizations?" *Foreign Affairs,* vol. 72, no. 3, Summer 1993, pp. 22–49.

4. "Germany's Open Door Closes," *U.S. News & World Report,* June 7, 1993, p. 12.

5. "Another brick in the wall," *New Statesman & Society,* June 4, 1993, p. 5.

6. Cited by Joel Kotkin, "Europe Won't Work: Sloth, Ignorance, and Xenophobia Threaten to Leave It Far Behind Asia and America," *The Washington Post,* September 15, 1991, p. C1.

7. Riva Kastoryano, "Guests, immigrants, minorities: Services for immigrants in Europe Minorities," *UNESCO Courier,* June 1993.

8. Cited by Joel Kotkin, *loc. cit.*

9. Alan Wagner, "Teaching in a multicultural environment," *OECD Observer,* no. 178, October 1992, p. 29.

10. Joann S. Lublin, "Law Does Help Some Managers to Move Ahead," *The Wall Street Journal,* July 19, 1993, p. B2.

11. Rick Atkinson, "German Workers Getting Stiff Shot of Reality," *The Washington Post,* February 22, 1994, p. A14.

12. William Drozdiak, "Europe's `Birth Dearth' Spawns Reappraisal of Immigration," *The Washington Post,* January 20, 1994, p. A19.

13. A comment by author Sam Yette, paraphrased by William Welsh at Diversity Network Meeting, Giant Food Inc. Headquarters, February 10, 1994, Landover, Maryland.

References and Suggested Readings

Abraham, Sameer, Y., and Nabeel Abraham, editors. *Arabs in the New World: Studies on Arab-American Communities*. Detroit: Wayne State University, 1983.

Adelman, Clifford. *Women at Thirtysomething: Paradox of Attainment*. Prepared for U.S. Department of Education, Washington, D.C., 1991.

Alper, Joe. "The Pipeline Is Leaking Women All the Way Along." *Science*. April 16, 1993.

Amott, Teresa L., and Julie A. Matthaei. *Race, Gender and Work*. Boston: South End Press, 1991.

Astrachan, Anthony. *How Men Feel*. Garden City, New York: Anchor Press/Doubleday, 1986.

Aufderheide, Patricia, editor. *Beyond PC: Toward a Politics of Understanding*. St. Paul, Minnesota: Graywolf Press, 1992.

Axel, Helen. "Employing Older Americans: Opportunities and Constraints." Summary of a symposium held September 21–23, 1987, Wingspread Conference Center, Racine, Wisconsin.

Baytos, Lawrence M. "Launching Successful Diversity Initiatives," *HR Magazine*. March 1992.

Bean, Frank D., Barry Edmonston, and Jeffrey S. Passel, editors. *Undocumented Migration to the United States: IRCA and the Experience of the 1980s*. Washington, D.C.: The Urban Institute Press, 1990.

Bean, Frank D., and Marta Tienda. "The Hispanic Population of the United States," *The Population of the United States in the 1980s*. A Census Monograph Series, for the National Committee for Research on the 1980 Census. New York: Russell Sage Foundation, 1987.

"Being a Man in the '90s," symposium, sponsored by INOVA Health Systems, Tyson's Corner, Virginia, May 19, 1993, proceedings, unpublished.

Bell, Ella Louise. "The Bicultural Life Experience of Career-Oriented Black Women," *Journal of Organizational Behavior*. Volume 11, 1990.

Berkowitz, E. D. *Disabled Policy: America's Programs for the Handicapped*. Cambridge, Massachusetts: Cambridge University Press, 1987.

Borjas, George, and Marta Tienda, editors. *Hispanics in the U.S. Economy*. New York: Academic Press, 1985.

Bowe, F. *Disabled in 1985: A Portrait of American Adults*. Fayetteville: University of Arkansas, Arkansas Research and Training Center in Vocational Rehabilitation, 1986.

Boylan, Esther. *Women and Disability*. Atlantic Highlands, New Jersey: Zed Books, 1991.

Brecher, Jeremy, and Tim Costello. *Building Bridges: The Emerging Grassroots Coalition of Labor and Community*. New York: Monthly Review Press, 1990.

Bronfenbrenner, Kate. *Successful Union Strategies for Winning Certification Elections and First Contracts: Report to Union Participants. Part I: Organizing Survey Results; Part II: First Contract Survey Results*. Penn State University, New Kensington Campus. No date, unpublished paper.

Browne, Robert S. "The Road to Rectification," *The American Prospect*. Number 10, Summer 1992.

Brownstein, Ronald. "Racial Politics," *The American Perspective*. Number 9, Spring 1992.

Buenker, John D., and Lorman A. Ratner. *Multiculturalism in the United States: A Comparative Guide to Acculturation and Ethnicity*. New York: Greenwood Press, 1992.

"Building on Diversity," *Labor Research Review*. Volume XII, Number 1, Spring/Summer 1993.

Butler, Robert N. *Why Survive? Being Old in America*. New York: Harper & Row, 1975.

Carnevale, Anthony P. *America and the New Economy*. San Francisco: Jossey-Bass, 1991.

Carnevale, Anthony P., Leila J. Gainer, Ann S. Meltzer, and Shari L. Holland, "Skills Employers Want," *Training and Development Journal*. Volume 42, Number 10, October 1988.

Carnevale, Anthony P., and S. Kanu Kogod. *The American Advantage, Tools for a Diverse Workforce*. Washington, D.C.: U.S. Department of Labor/American Society for Training and Development: forthcoming.

Carter, Stephen L. *Reflections of an Affirmative Action Baby*. New York: Basic Books, 1991.

Castleman, Melissa, and Sandra Van Fossen. *Making Both Ends Meet: Working Mothers in America*. Wider Opportunities for Women, Inc.: Washington, D.C.: 1991.

Clarke, Caroline V. "Downsizing Trounces Diversity, 1994," *Black Enterprise*. February 1994, pp. 69ff.

Clayton, Susan D., and Faye J. Crosby. *Justice, Gender, and Affirmative Action*. Ann Arbor: University of Michigan Press, 1992.

Cobble, Dorothy Sue, editor. *Women and Unions: Forging a Partnership*. Ithaca, New York: ILR Press, 1993.

Cordova, Teresa. *Chicana Voices: Intersections of Class, Race and Gender*. Austin, Texas: Center for Mexican American Studies, 1986.

Cox, Taylor, Jr. *Cultural Diversity in Organizations: Theory, Research & Practice*. San Francisco: Berrett-Koehler, 1993.

Cox, Taylor H., Sharon A. Lobel, and Poppy Lauretta McLeod. "Effects of Ethnic Group Cultural Differences on Cooperative and Competitive Behavior on a Group Task," *Academy of Management Journal*. Volume 34, Number 4, 1991.

Cox, Taylor, Jr., and Stella M. Nkomo. "Invisible Men and Women: A Status Report on Race as a Variable in Organization Behavior Research," *Journal of Organizational Behavior.* Volume 11, 1990.

Culotta, Elizabeth. "Women Struggle to Crack the Code of Corporate Culture," *Science.* April 16, 1993.

Cushner, Kenneth, and Gregory Trifonovitch. "Understanding Misunderstanding: Barriers to Dealing with Diversity." *Social Education.* Volume 53, Number 5, September 1989.

Daniels, Roger. *Asian America: Chinese and Japanese in the United States Since 1850.* Seattle: University of Washington Press, 1988.

Davis, George, and Glegg Watson. *Black Life in Corporate America: Swimming in the Mainstream.* New York: Anchor Books/Doubleday, 1985.

Day, Jennifer Cheeseman. *Population Projections of the United States, by Age, Sex, Race, and Hispanic Origin: 1992 to 2050.* Prepared for U.S. Department of Commerce, Economics and Statistics Administration, Bureau of the Census, Current Population Reports, P25-1092. Washington, D.C.: U.S. Government Printing Office, 1992.

DeFreitas, Gregory. *Inequality at Work: Hispanics in the U.S. Labor Force.* New York: Oxford University Press, 1991.

DeFreitas, Gregory. "Unionization Among Racial and Ethnic Minorities," *Industrial and Labor Relations Review.* Volume 46, Number 2, January 1993.

De la Garza, Rodolfo, Louis DeSipio, Chris F. Garcia, John A. Garcia, and Angelo Falcon. *Latino Voices: Mexican, Puerto Rican, and Cuban Perspectives on American Politics.* Boulder, Colorado: Westview Press, 1992.

DeLoria, Vine, Jr. *Custer Died For Your Sins: An Indian Manifesto.* New York: Avon, 1971.

Denton, Toni C. "Bonding and Supportive Relationships Among Black Professional Women: Rituals of Restoration," *Journal of Organizational Behavior 11* (1990).

Dickens, Floyd Jr., and Jacqueline B. Dickens. *The Black Manager: Making It in the Corporate World.* New York: Amacom/American Management Association, 1982.

Dickson, Mary B. *Supervising Employees with Disabilities: Beyond ADA Compliance.* Menlo Park, California: Crisp Publications, Inc., 1993.

Dickson, Mary B., and Michael Mobley. *The Americans with Disabilities Act: Techniques for Accommodation.* Alexandria, Virginia: American Society for Training and Development, April 1992.

DiTomaso, Nancy, and Donna E. Thompson, editors. *Ensuring Minority Success in Corporate Management.* New York: Plenum Press, 1988.

Dovidio, John. "The Subtlety of Racism," *Training and Development Journal.* Volume 47, Number 4, April 1993.

Dychtwald, Ken, and Joe Flower. *Age Wave.* New York: Bantam Books, 1990.

Elkholy, Abdo A. *The Arab Moslems in the United States, Religion and Assimilation.* New Haven, Connecticut: College & University Press, 1966.

Faludi, Susan. *Backlash: The Undeclared War Against Women.* New York: Crown Publishers, 1991.

Farley, Reynolds, and Walter A. Allen. *The Color Line and the Quality of Life in America*. New York: Oxford University Press, 1989.

Fernandez, John P. *Managing a Diverse Work Force: Regaining the Competitive Edge*. Lexington, Massachusetts: Lexington Books, 1991.

Fernandez, John P. *Racism and Sexism in Corporate Life*. Lexington, Massachusetts: Lexington Books, 1981.

Foreman, Anita K., and Gary Pressley. "Ethnic Culture and Corporate Culture: Using Black Styles in Organizations," *Communication Quarterly*. Volume 35, Number 4, Fall 1987.

Frank, Miriam, and Desma Holcomb. *Pride at Work: Organizing for Lesbian and Gay Rights in Unions*. New York: The Lesbian and Gay Labor Network of New York, 1990.

Fuchs, Lawrence H. *The American Kaleidoscope: Race, Ethnicity, and the Civic Culture*. London: Wesleyan University Press, 1990.

Fulmer, William E. "Anticipatory Learning: The Seventh Strategic Imperative for the Twenty-first Century," *Journal of Management Development*. Volume 12, Number 6, 1993.

Gann, L. H., and Peter J. Duignan. *The Hispanics in the United States: A History*. Boulder, Colorado: Westview Press, 1986.

Gardenswartz, Lee, and Anita Rowe. *Managing Diversity: A Complete Desk Reference and Planning Guide*. Homewood, Illinois: Business One Irwin and Pfeiffer & Co., 1993.

Garvin, David A. "Building a Learning Organization," *Harvard Business Review*. Volume 71, Number 4, July-August 1993.

Gilsdorf, J. W. "The New Generation: Older Workers," *Training & Development Journal*. Volume 46, Number 3, March 1992.

Glazer, Nathan. *Ethnic Dilemmas, 1964–1982*. Cambridge: Harvard University Press, 1983.

Gody, Cecilia, Linda Andrews, and Christina Harter. *The Thirty-Five Million: A Preliminary Report on the Status of the Young Woman*. The Young Women's Project, released in conjunction with a conference on "Common Ground: Toward a Collective Voice of Young Women," Washington, D.C.: October 1990.

Gold, Gerard G., editor. *Business and Higher Education: Toward New Alliances, No. 13, New Directions for Experiential Learning*. San Francisco: Jossey-Bass, 1981.

Graham, Lawrence Otis. *The Best Companies for Minorities*. New York: Plume, 1993.

Greenhaus, Jeffrey H., Saroj Parasuraman, and Wayne M. Wormley. "Effects of Race On Organizational Experiences, Job Performance Evaluations, and Career Outcomes," *Academic of Management Journal*. Volume 33, Number 1, 1990.

Gutek, Barbara A. *Sex and the Workplace*. San Francisco: Jossey-Bass, 1985.

Haddad, Yvonne, and Adair T. Lummis. *Islamic Values in the United States: A Comparative Study*. New York: Oxford University Press, 1987.

Hartmann, Heidi, and Roberta Spalter-Roth. *Improving Employment Opportunities for Womem*. Testimony before U.S. House of Representatives Committee on Education and Labor. Institute for Women's Policy Research: Washington, D.C., February 27, 1991.

Hartmann, Heidi, and Roberta Spalter-Roth. *Improving Women's Status in the Workplace: The Family Issue of the Future.* Testimony before the Senate Subcommittee on Employment and Productivity, Committee on Labor and Human Resources. Institute for Women's Policy Research: Washington, D.C., July 18, 1991.

Hecker, Steven, and Margaret Hallock, editors. *Labor in a Global Perspective, from the United States and Canada.* Portland, Oregon: University of Oregon Books, 1991.

Helgesen, Sally. *The Female Advantage: Women's Ways of Leadership.* New York: Doubleday, 1990.

Heywood, John S. "Race Discrimination and Union Voice," *Industrial Relations.* Volume 31, No. 3, Fall 1992.

Hill, Norman. "Forging a Partnership Between Blacks and Unions." *Monthly Labor Review.* August 1987.

Hofstede, Geert. "Cultural Constraints in Management Theory." International Scholar Lecture, 1992 Annual Meeting of the Academy of Management, Las Vegas, Nevada, August 11, 1992, unpublished paper.

Hofstede, Geert. *Cultures and Organizations: Software of the Mind.* London: McGraw-Hill, 1991.

Hofstede, Geert. "Culture's Consequences: International Differences in Work-Related Values," *Cross-Cultural Research and Methodology Series.* Beverly Hills: Sage Publications, 1980.

Hopkins, Kevin R., and William B. Johnston. *Opportunity 2000: Creating Affirmative Action Strategies for a Changing Workforce.* Prepared for Employment Standards Administration, U.S. Department of Labor. Indianapolis: The Hudson Institute, September 1988.

Hunter, James Davison. *Culture Wars: The Struggle to Define America.* New York: Basic Books/HarperCollins, 1991.

Huntington, Samuel P. "The Clash of Civilizations?" *Foreign Affairs.* Volume 72, Number 3, Summer 1993.

Immigration and Naturalization Service, U.S. Department of Justice. *Our Immigration: A Brief Account of Immigration to the United States.* Washington, D.C.: U.S. Government Printing Office, 1990.

"Improving Job Skills of the Learning-Disabled," *The Urban Institute Policy and Research Report.* Volume 22, Number 1, Winter/Spring 1992.

Inouye, Daniel K. "Indian Tribes in the 21st Century," address to the Tribal Leaders Forum on Framing a National Indian Agenda for the 1990s. Np: American Indian Resources Institute, February 9–10, 1990, unpublished report.

Jacobson, Beverly. *Young Programs for Older Workers.* New York: Van Nostrand Reinhold, 1980.

Jaffee, A. J. *The First Immigrants from Asia: A Population History of the North American Indians.* New York: Plenum Press, 1992.

Jamieson, David, and Julie O'Mara. *Managing Workforce 2000: Gaining the Diversity Advantage.* San Francisco: Jossey-Bass, 1991.

Jaynes, Gerald David, and Robin M. Williams, Jr., editors. *A Common Destiny: Blacks and American Society.* Committee on the Status of Black Americans,

Commission on Behavioral and Social Sciences and Education, Washington, D.C.: National Research Council National Academy Press, 1989.

Jiobu, Robert Masao. *Ethnicity and Inequality.* New York: State University of New York Press, 1990.

"Job Retention for People with Disabilities," *Rehab Brief.* Volume XV, Number 2, 1993.

Johnson, Elizabeth S., and John B. Williamson. *Growing Old: The Social Problems of Aging.* New York: Holt, Rinehart and Winston, 1980.

Johnston, William B. "Global Work Force 2000: The New World Labor Market," *Harvard Business Review.* Volume 69, Number 2, March-April, 1991.

Johnston, William B., and Arnold H. Packer. *Workforce 2000: Work and Workers for the 21st Century.* Prepared for the U.S. Department of Labor, Indianapolis: Hudson Institute, June 1987.

Joint Project on U.S. Competitiveness and the Aging American Workforce of the National Planing Association/The National Council on the Aging, draft of proceedings, June 13, 1993.

Jones, Augustus J. *Affirmative Talk, Affirmative Action.* New York: Praeger Publishers, 1991.

Kastoryano, Riva. "Guests, immigrants, minorities; Services for immigrants in Europe Minorities," *UNESCO Courier.* June 1993.

Keefe, Susan E., and Amado M. Padilla. *Chicano Ethnicity.* Albuquerque, New Mexico: University of New Mexico Press, 1987.

Kennedy, Randall. "Race, Liberalism, and Affirmative Action (I): Yes and No," *The American Prospect.* Number 9, Spring 1992.

Kim, Elaine. *With Silk Wings: Asian American Women at Work.* Oakland, California: Asian Women United, 1983.

Kirsch, Irwin S., Ann Jungeblut, Lynn Jenkins, and Andrew Kolstad. *Adult Literacy in America: A First Look at the Results of the National Adult Literacy Survey.* National Center for Education Statistics, Department of Education. Washington, D.C.: U.S. Government Printing Office, September 1993.

Knouse, Stephen B., Paul Rosenfeld, and Amy Culbertson, editors. *Hispanics in the Workplace.* Newbury Park: Sage Publications, 1992.

Kochman, Thomas. "Black and White Cultural Styles in Pluralistic Perspective," *Test Policy and Test Performance: Education, Language, and Culture.* Boston: Kluwer, 1985.

Kochman, Thomas. *Black and White: Styles in Conflict.* Chicago: University of Chicago Press, 1981.

La Luz, Jose. "Creating a Culture of Organizing: ACTWU's Education for Empowerment," *Labor Research Review. An Organizing Model of Unionism.* Volume X, Number 1, Spring 1991.

La Luz, Jose. "A Multicultural Framework for Workers' Education," *Labor Education. International Labor Organization, Worker Education Division.* Number 53, February 1991.

Leonard, Jonathan. "The Effect of Unions on the Employment of Blacks, Hispanics and Women," *Industrial and Labor Relations Review.* Number 39, Volume I, 1985.

Lerner, Max. *America As a Civilization.* New York: Henry Holt & Co., 1987.

Lerner, Stephen. "Let's Get Moving," *Labor Research Review.* Volume X, Number 2, Fall/Winter 1991/1992.

Levitan, Sar A., and Elizabeth I. Miller. "The Equivocal Prospects for Indian Reservations," *Occasional Paper 1992–3.* Center for Social Policy Studies. Washington, D.C.: George Washington University, May 1993.

Locust, Carol. *American Indian Beliefs Concerning Health and Unwellness.* Unpublished monograph. Native American Research and Training Center, University of Arizona, Tucson, Arizona. No date.

Locust, Carol. *Learning Difference—Handicapped American Indians: Beliefs and Behaviors.* Unpublished monograph. Native American Research and Training Center, University of Arizona, Tucson, Arizona. No date.

Loden, Marilyn, and Judy B. Rosener. *Workforce America! Managing Employee Diversity as a Vital Resource.* Homewood, Illinois: Business One Irwin, 1991.

Lyden, Fremont J., and Lyman H. Legters, editors. *Native Americans and Public Policy.* Pittsburgh: University of Pittsburgh Press for the William O. Douglas Institute, 1992.

Lynch, Frederick R. *Invisible Victims: White Males and the Crisis of Affirmative Action.* New York: Praeger, 1991.

Mann, Arthur. *The One and the Many: Reflections on the American Identity.* Chicago: University of Chicago Press, 1979.

Marcus, Eric. *Making History: The Struggle for Gay and Lesbian Equal Rights, 1945–1990.* New York: HarperCollins, 1992.

Marttila & Kiley, Inc., *Highlights from an Anti-Defamation League Survey on Anti-Semitism and Prejudice in America,* prepared for Anti-Defamation League. New York: ADL, November 16, 1992.

McKay, Sandra Lee, and Sau-ling Cynthia Wong, editors. *Language Diversity: Problem or Resource?* Cambridge: Newbury House/Harper & Row, 1988.

McNaught, William, and Michael C. Barth. "Are Older Workers `Good Buys?'—A Case Study of Days Inn of America," *Sloan Management Review.* Spring 1992.

Melendy, Howard Brett. *Asians in America: Filipinos, Koreans, and East Indians.* Boston: Twayne, 1977.

Metcalf, Ann. "The Effects of Boarding School on Navajo Self-Image and Maternal Behavior." Ph.D. dissertation. Stanford University, 1974.

Michaels, Bonnie. "Workforce Challenges of the '90s: Employees and Dependent Care," *Employee Services Management.* April 1990.

Mickens, Edward, editor/publisher. *Working It Out: The Newsletter for Gay and Lesbian Employment Issues,* quarterly, New York, New York.

Miller, Jean Baker, M.D. *Toward a New Psychology of Women.* 2d edition. Boston: Beacon Press, 1986.

Miranda, Leticia, and Julia Teresa Quiroz. *The Decade of the Hispanic: An Economic Retrospective.* Washington, D.C.: National Council of La Raza, 1990.

Mirvis, Philip H., editor. *Building the Competitive Workforce—Investing in Human Capital for Corporate Success.* New York: John Wiley, 1993.

Mishel, Lawrence, and Ruy A. Teixeira. *The Myth of the Coming Labor Shortage: Jobs, Skills, and Incomes of America's Workforce 2000.* Washington, D.C.: Economic Policy Institute, 1991.

Mitchell, Olivia S., editor. *As the Workforce Ages.* Ithaca, New York: ILR Press, 1993.

Mize, Sue. "Shattering the Glass Ceiling," *Training and Development Journal.* Volume 46, Number 2, January 1992.

Mobley, Michael, and Tamara Payne. "Backlash! The Challenge to Diversity Training." *Training and Development.* Volume 46, Number 12, December 1992.

Moore, Joan and Harry Pachon. *Hispanics in the United States.* Englewood Cliffs, New Jersey: Prentice-Hall, 1985.

Morrison, Ann M. *The New Leaders: Guidelines on Leadership Diversity in America.* San Francisco: Jossey-Bass, 1992.

Morrison, Ann M., Marian N. Ruderman, and Martha Hughes-James. *Making Diversity Happen: Controversies and Solutions.* Greensboro, North Carolina: Center for Creative Leadership.

Morrison, Ann M., and Mary Ann Von Glisow. "Women and Minorities in Management." *American Psychologist.* Volume 45, Number 2, February 1990.

Morrison, Ann M., Randall P. White, and Ellen Van Velsor. *Breaking the Glass Ceiling.* Reading, Massachusetts: Addison-Wesley Publishing Co., 1987.

Moses, Yolanda T. "The Roadblocks Confronting Minority Administrators," *Chronicle of Higher Education.* January 13, 1993.

Naff, Alixa. *Becoming American: The Early Arab Immigrant.* Carbondale, Illinois: Southern Illinois University Press, 1985.

National Center on Education and the Economy, Commission on the Skills of the American Workforce. *America's Choice: High Skills or Low Wages!* Rochester: 1990.

National Rehabilitation Association. *Employment and Disability: Trends and Issues for the 1990s.* Alexandria, Virginia: NRA, 1990.

Neckerman, Kathryn M. "What Getting Ahead Means to Employers and Inner-City Workers," paper presented at the Chicago Urban Poverty and Family Structure Conference, Chicago, 1992.

Needleman, Ruth. "Women Workers: A Force for Rebuilding Unionism," *Labor Research Review.* Volume VII, Number 1, Spring 1988.

Nelson, Jill. *Volunteer Slavery: My Authentic Negro Experience.* Chicago: Noble Press, 1993.

Nieli, Russell, editor. *Racial Preference and Racial Justice: The New Affirmative Action Controversy.* Washington, D.C.: Ethics and Public Policy Center, 1991.

Nkomo, Stella M., "The Emperor Has No Clothes: Rewriting `Race' in Organizations," *Academy of Management Review.* Volume 17, Number 3, 1992.

Ogbu, John U. *Minority Education and Caste: The American System in Cross-Cultural Perspective.* New York: Academic Press: 1978.

O'Hare, William P. "American Minorities—The Demographics of Diversity," *Population Bulletin,* Volume 47, Number 4, December 1992.

Older Women's League. *Paying for Prejudice: A Report on Midlife and Older Women in America's Labor Force.* Washington, D.C.: OWL, May 9, 1991.

"On the Issues: Sexual Harassment with John Chancellor," PBS-WETA, Washington, D.C., June 11, 1993.

Outtz, Janice Hamilton. *Washington Women in the Labor Force: The Year 2000 Is NOW.* Washington, D.C.: D.C. State Federation of Business and Professional Women's Clubs, Inc. and the D.C. Commission for Women, May 1989.

Petrini, Catherine M. "The Language of Diversity," *Training & Development Journal,* Volume 47, Number 4, April 1993.

Pharr, Suzanne. *Homophobia: A Weapon of Sexism.* Inverness, California: Chardon Press, 1988.

Portes, Alejandro, and Ruben G. Rumbaut. *Immigrant America: A Portrait.* Berkeley, California: University of California Press, 1990.

Ries, Paula, and Anne J. Stone. *The American Woman 1992–93: A Status Report.* New York: W.W. Norton & Co., 1992.

Rizzo, Ann-Marie, and Carmen Mendez. *The Integration of Women in Management.* New York: Quorum Books, 1990.

Rosener, Judy B. "Ways Women Lead," *Harvard Business Review.* Volume 68, Number 6, November-December 1990.

Schlesinger, Arthur M., Jr. *The Disuniting of America: Reflections on a Multicultural Society.* New York: W.W. Norton, 1992.

Sedmak, Nancy J., and Michael D. Levin-Epstein. *Primer on Equal Employment Opportunity.* Fifth Edition. Washington, D.C.: BNA Books, 1991.

Sharpe, Rochelle. "Losing Ground: In Latest Recession, Only Blacks Suffered Net Employment Loss," *The Wall Street Journal.* September 14, 1993.

Shenhav, Yehouda. "Entrance of Blacks and Women into Managerial Positions in Scientific and Engineering Occupations: A Longitudinal Analysis." *Academy of Management Journal 35.* Number 4, (no date).

Shields, Sydney. *Work, Sister, Work: Why Black Women Can't Get Ahead and What They Can Do About It.* New York: Birch Lane, 1993.

Sitkoff, Harvard. *The Struggle for Black Equality, 1954–1992.* New York: Hill and Wang, 1993.

Smith, Gregory T. "Guest Commentaries: Disability Prevention Pays Off," *Oregon Health Forum,* Volume 3, Number 7, July 1993.

Smith, James P., and Finis R. Welch. *Closing the Gap: Forty Years of Economic Progress for Blacks.* Rand Report to U.S. Department of Labor. Santa Monica, California: Rand, 1986.

Smith, Mary Ann, and Sandra J. Johnson, editors. *Valuing Differences in the Workplace.* Alexandria, Virginia: American Society for Training and Development, 1991.

Sowell, Thomas. "'Affirmative Action': A Worldwide Disaster," *Commentary.* Volume 88, Number 6, December 1989.

Spalter-Roth, Roberta, and Heidi Hartmann. *Increasing Working Mothers' Earnings.* Washington, D.C.: Institute for Women's Policy Research, November 1991.

Starr, Paul. "Civil Reconstruction: What to Do Without Affirmative Action," *The American Prospect.* Number 9, Winter 1992.

Stayer, Ralph. "How I Learned to Let My Workers Lead." *Harvard Business Review.* November-December 1990.

Steele, Shelby. *The Content of Our Character: A New Vision of Race in America.* New York: St. Martin's Press, 1990.

Steinberg, Stephen. *The Ethnic Myth: Race, Ethnicity, and Class in America.* New York: Atheneum, 1981.

Stolarik, M. Mark, and Murray Friedman. *Making It in America: The Role of Ethnicity in Business Enterprise, Education, and Work Choices.* Lewisburg, Pennsylvania: Bucknell University Press, 1986.

Stone, Deborah A. "Race, Gender, and the Supreme Court," *The American Prospect.* Winter 1992.

Sue, David. *Counseling the Culturally Different: Theory and Practice.* New York: John Wiley, 1990.

Taeuber, Cynthia M. *Sixty-Five Plus in America.* Prepared for U.S. Department of Commerce, Economics and Statistics Administration, Bureau of the Census, Washington, D.C.: U.S. Government Printing Office, 1992.

Takaki, Ronald. *A Different Mirror: A History of Multicultural America.* Boston: Little, Brown, 1993.

Tannen, Deborah. *You Just Don't Understand: Women and Men in Conversation.* New York: William Morrow, 1990.

Tate, Katherine. "The Invisible Woman," *American Prospect.* Spring 1992.

Thacher, Rebecca A. "Preventing Sexual Harassment in the Workplace," *Training and Development Journal.* Volume 46, Number 2, February 1992.

Thiederman, Sondra. *Bridging Cultural Barriers for Corporate Success: How to Manage the Multicultural Work Force.* Lexington, Massachusetts: Lexington Books, 1990.

Thiederman, Sondra. *Profiting in America's Multicultural Marketplace: How to Do Business across Cultural Lines.* Lexington, Massachusetts: Lexington Books, 1991.

Thomas, R. Roosevelt, Jr. *Beyond Race and Gender: Unleashing the Power of Your Total Work Force by Managing Diversity.* AMACOM/American Management Association, 1991.

Thomas, R. Roosevelt, Jr. "From Affirmative Action to Affirming Diversity," *Harvard Business Review.* Volume 68, Number 2, March-April 1990.

Tollett, Kenneth S. "Race, Liberalism, and Affirmative Action (I): The Liberals' Loss of Nerve," *The American Prospect.* Number 9, Spring 1992.

Triandis, Harry C., Judith Lisansky, Gerardo Marin, and Hector Betancourt. "Simpatia as a Cultural Script of Hispanics," *Journal of Personality and Social Psychology.* Volume 47, Number 6.

Tsai, Shih-Shan Henry. *The Chinese Experience in America.* Bloomington: Indiana University Press, 1986.

U.S. Department of Commerce, Bureau of the Census. "The Asian and Pacific Islander Population in the United States, March 1990 and 1991," *Current Population Reports.* Washington, D.C.: U.S. Government Printing Office, 1992.

U.S. Department of Commerce, Bureau of the Census. "The Black Population in the United States: March 1991." *Current Population Reports.* Washington, D.C.: U.S. Government Printing Office, 1992.

U.S. Department of Commerce, Bureau of the Census. "Hispanic Americans Today, Population Characteristics," *Current Population Reports.* Washington, D.C.: U.S. Government Printing Office, 1993.

U.S. Department of Commerce, Bureau of the Census. "Money Income of Households, Families, and Persons in the United States, 1992," *Current Population Reports, Consumer Income.* Washington, D.C.: U.S. Government Printing Office, 1993.

U.S. Department of Commerce, Bureau of the Census. "Population Characteristics: The Black Population in the United States: March 1991," *Current Population Reports.* Washington, D.C.: U.S. Government Printing Office, 1992.

U.S. Department of Commerce. *Statistical Abstracts of the United States 1986.* Washington, D.C.: U.S. Government Printing Office, 1985.

U.S. Department of Commerce, Bureau of the Census. *1990 Census of Population, Supplementary Reports: Detailed Occupation and Other Characteristics from the EEO File for the United States.* Washington, D.C.: U.S. Government Printing Office, October 1992.

U.S. Department of Commerce, Bureau of the Census. *1990 Census of Population, Supplementary Reports, Detailed Occupation and Other Characteristics from EEO Files for the United States, 1990.* Washington, D.C.: U.S. Government Printing Office, 1992.

U.S. Department of Education, National Institute on Disability and Rehabilitation Research. *Chartbook on Work Disability in the United States.* Washington, D.C.: U.S. Government Printing Office, 1991.

U.S. Department of Education, Office of Educational Research and Improvement, National Center for Education Statistics. *Race/Ethnicity Trends in Degrees Conferred by Institutions of Higher Education: 1980–81 through 1989–90,* and *Race/Ethnicity Trends in Degrees Conferred by Institutions of Higher Education: 1984–85 through 1990–91.* Washington, D.C.: U.S. Government Printing Office, May 1992; August 1992.

U.S. Department of the Interior, Bureau of Indian Affairs, *Indian Service Population and Labor Force Estimates.* Washington, D.C.: Bureau of Indian Affairs, 1991.

U.S. Department of Labor, Bureau of Labor Statistics. *Employment and Earnings, January 1993.* Washington, D.C.: U.S. Government Printing Office, 1993.

U.S. Department of Labor, Bureau of Labor Statistics. *Outlook 1990–2005.* BLS Bulletin 2402. Washington, D.C.: U.S. Government Printing Office, May 1992.

U.S. Department of Labor, Bureau of Labor Statistics. *1991 Annual Averages, Employment and Earnings, January 1992.* Washington, D.C.: U.S. Government Printing Office, 1992.

U.S. Department of Labor. *Pipelines of Progress: A Status Report on the Glass Ceiling.* Washington, D.C.: U.S. Government Printing Office, August 1992.

U.S. Department of Labor. *A Report on the Glass Ceiling Initiative.* Washington, D.C.: U.S. Government Printing Office, August 7, 1991.

U.S. Merit Systems Protection Board. *A Question of Equity: Women and the Glass Ceiling in the Federal Government.* Washington, D.C.: August 1992.

Waldrop, J. "From Handicapped to Advantaged," *American Demographics.* Number 12, 1990.

Weiss, Francine K. *Older Women and Job Discrimination.* Washington, D.C.: Older Women's League, 1984.

West, Cornel. "Equality and Identity," *The American Prospect*. Number 9, Spring 1992.

West, Cornel. *Race Matters*. Boston: Beacon Press, 1993.

Williams, Patricia J. "Racism and Justice: The Case for Affirmative Action," *The Nation*. Volume 253, Number 17, November 18, 1991.

Wilson, Robert A., and Bill Hosokawa. *East to America: A History of the Japanese in the United States*. New York: William Morrow, 1980.

Wilson, William Julius. *The Truly Disadvantaged: The Inner City, the Underclass, and Public Policy*. Chicago: The University of Chicago Press, 1987.

Winterle, Mary J. *Work Force Diversity: Corporate Challenges, Corporate Responses*. Report Number 1013. New York: The Conference Board, 1992.

Woods, J. D., and J. H. Lucas. *The Corporate Closet: The Professional Lives of Gay Men in America*. New York: The Free Press, 1993.

Zogby, John. *Arab America Today: A Demographic Profile of Arab Americans*. Washington, D.C.: Arab American Institute, 1990.

Index

About the Authors

ANTHONY PATRICK CARNEVALE is vice president and director of human resources studies at the Committee for Economic Development, the nation's oldest CEO-led think tank. Formerly chief economist with the American Society for Training and Development, he was appointed by President Clinton to chair the National Commission for Employment Policy and is on the Board of Overseers for the Malcolm Baldrige National Quality Award.

SUSAN CAROL STONE heads Stone Communications, a management consulting and training firm in Bethesda, Maryland.